COMMON GOODS

## TRANSDISCIPLINARY THEOLOGICAL COLLOQUIA

Theology has hovered for two millennia between scriptural metaphor and philosophical thinking; it takes flesh in its symbolic, communal, and ethical practices. With the gift of this history and in the spirit of its unrealized potential, the Transdisciplinary Theological Colloquia intensify movement between and beyond the fields of religion. A multivocal discourse of theology takes place in the interstices, at once self-deconstructive in its pluralism and constructive in its affirmations.

Hosted annually by Drew University's Theological School, the colloquia provide a matrix for such conversations, while Fordham University Press serves as the midwife for their publication. Committed to the slow transformation of religiocultural symbolism, the colloquia continue Drew's long history of engaging historical, biblical, and philosophical hermeneutics, practices of social justice, and experiments in theopoetics.

Catherine Keller, *Director*

# COMMON GOODS

Economy, Ecology,
and Political Theology

MELANIE JOHNSON-DeBAUFRE,
CATHERINE KELLER,
AND ELIAS ORTEGA-APONTE,
EDITORS

FORDHAM UNIVERSITY PRESS ❖ NEW YORK ❖ 2015

Copyright © 2015 Fordham University Press

All rights reserved. No part of this publication may be reproduced, stored in a retrieval system, or transmitted in any form or by any means—electronic, mechanical, photocopy, recording, or any other—except for brief quotations in printed reviews, without the prior permission of the publisher.

Fordham University Press has no responsibility for the persistence or accuracy of URLs for external or third-party Internet websites referred to in this publication and does not guarantee that any content on such websites is, or will remain, accurate or appropriate.

Fordham University Press also publishes its books in a variety of electronic formats. Some content that appears in print may not be available in electronic books.

Visit us online at www.fordhampress.com.

Library of Congress Cataloging-in-Publication Data

Common goods : economy, ecology, and political theology / edited by Melanie Johnson-DeBaufre, Catherine Keller, and Elias Ortega-Aponte. — First edition.
    pages cm. — (Transdisciplinary theological colloquia)
  Includes bibliographical references and index.
  ISBN 978-0-8232-6843-6 (cloth : alk. paper) — ISBN 978-0-8232-6844-3 (pbk. : alk. paper)  1. Political theology.  2. Common good.  3. Public goods.  I. Johnson-DeBaufre, Melanie, editor.
   BT83.59.C66 2015
   261.8—dc23

2015018250

Printed in the United States of America
17 16 15   5 4 3 2 1

First edition

CONTENTS

Introduction: Plurisingular Common Good/s | *Melanie Johnson-DeBaufre, Catherine Keller, and Elias Ortega-Aponte*     1

PLANETARY POLITICAL THEOLOGY

Process Philosophy and Planetary Politics | *William E. Connolly*     25

How Not to Be a Religion: Genealogy, Identity, Wonder | *John Thatamanil*     54

Non-Theology and Political Ecology: Postsecularism, Repetition, and Insurrection | *Clayton Crockett*     73

The Ambiguities of Transcendence: In Conversation with the Work of William E. Connolly | *Kathryn Tanner*     91

Dreaming the Common Good/s: The Kin-dom of God as a Space of Utopian Politics | *Melanie Johnson-DeBaufre*     103

A Cosmopolitical Theology: Engaging "The Political" as an Incarnational Field of Emergence | *Dhawn B. Martin*     124

ECONOMIES AND ECOLOGIES OF (UN)COMMON GOOD/S

Reconfiguring the Common Good and Religion in the Context of Capitalism: Abrahamic Alternatives | *Joerg Rieger*     149

Christian Socialism and the Future of Economic Democracy | *Gary Dorrien*     169

The Myth of the Middle: Common Sense, Good Sense, and Rethinking the "Common Good" in Contemporary U.S. Society | *Charon Hribar*     191

Elements of Tradition, Protest, and New Creation in Monetary Systems: A Political Theology of Market Miracles | *Nimi Wariboko* — 209

The Corporation and the Common Good: Biopolitics after the Death of God | *Elijah Prewitt-Davis* — 229

Breaking from Within: The Dialectic of Labor and the Death of God | *An Yountae* — 248

Thoreau Goes to Ghana: On the Wild and the Tingane | *Anatoli Ignatov* — 267

Climate Debt, White Privilege, and Christian Ethics as Political Theology | *Cynthia D. Moe-Lobeda* — 286

## COMMON FLESH, COMMON DEMOCRACIES

Between a Rock and an Empty Place: Political Theology and Democratic Legitimacy | *Paulina Ochoa Espejo* — 307

From the Theopaternal to the Theopolitical: On Barack Obama | *Vincent Lloyd* — 326

Democratic Futures in the Shadow of Mass Incarceration: Toward a Political Theology of Prison Abolition | *Elias Ortega-Aponte* — 344

Rupturing the Concorporeal Commons: On the Psychocultural Symptom of "Disability" as Life Resentment | *Sharon Betcher* — 365

The Common Good of the Flesh: An Indecent Invitation to William E. Connolly, Joerg Rieger, and Political Theology | *Karen Bray* — 386

A Socioeconomic Hermeneutics of *Chayim*: The Theo-Ethical Implications of Reading (with) Wisdom | *A. Paige Rawson* — 407

Acknowledgments — 427
List of Contributors — 429
Index — 435

# ❧ Introduction: Plurisingular Common Good/s

MELANIE JOHNSON-DEBAUFRE, CATHERINE KELLER, AND ELIAS ORTEGA-APONTE

The thought of the common might do us some good. The ordinary, the least common denominator of social calculability, the "least of these" in the ancient parable, the shared body of a people, a multitude, a planet: What effectual solidarities might yet coalesce in its midst? How can shared spaces—social, physical, and virtual, opened, staked out, and contested—shape a common good to come? Does the traditional rhetoric of hope and its collective good—so familiar among progressive Christians and liberal political thinkers—ring false or just passé? Too naïvely impractical or myopically identitarian? "Get real," says a flat, familiar voice (oh dear, it is one's own). As we tarry in this text, the remaining commons of the planet—its lands, its waters—are being captured and commodified, depleted and degraded for the future, mined and morphed into corporate goods. And the global South carries the costs. A transnational economy of multiplying enclosures shuts in the spaces, shuts down the times, of any common human becoming.

So why then stir up the sluggish hope for some vibrant and viable recollection of the human collective? Won't what William Connolly calls "the slow burn of conjunctions between capitalism and climate change"—ever less slow—betray every hope for a sustainable planetary justice as pathetic self-reassurance or virtuous propaganda?[1] By the time you read what we now write, will the advance of corporate depredation seem even more invincible, the evidence of climate destabilization more apocalyptic, and political action less effective?

Nonetheless, we collect ourselves in this textual assemblage in order to consider some uncommonly good perspectives. These are theories that practice a multiplicity of goods, for the sake of divergent multitudes on an inescapably shared planet. No pep talks for the promised future are offered. We recognize that "hope is critical and can be disappointed."[2] Perhaps, then, there is something about the present convergence of views, theological and political, religious, interreligious, and irreligious, that stirs possibility. However differently we couch the terms of its planetarity, this possibility gathers force in a spirit that feeds—and feeds upon—far-flung connections. It may be characterized as a *political theology of the earth*. For on our stressed and badly shared planet, perhaps the commons that the great activist physicist Vandana Shiva signifies as "earth democracy" remains vibrantly, wildly, desperately possible.[3]

And "theology" in its conjunction with "political" has come through democratic secularization into a new register, postsecular or merely pluralist, a polydoxy contradictory of the religious right, nettlesome to the secular left.[4] In the collective of the present volume this theology translates into such variants as "non-theology" (Clayton Crockett) or "cosmopolitical theology" (Dhawn Martin). The "death of God" is invoked—theologically—along with "the kin-dom of God" (Melanie Johnson-DeBaufre) and even an ambiguously persistent divine transcendence (Kathryn Tanner). But across this theological spectrum we would agree with the final thesis of Crockett's *Radical Political Theology* (2011): "We seek to transform the world, not to exchange it for another one that conforms to our desires. The urgency is the awareness that overpopulation, resource exploitation, and global climate change may bring an end to human civilization within the next century."[5] The gaping maw between the 1 percent and the global 99 percent is widening. How then, we all wonder differently, might we open discursive and practical spaces in which the multiplicity of the goods of divergent multitudes shape a planetary commons? We want in other words—and worlds—to mobilize the unsurpassed affective potentiality of theological-political figures, tropes, and stories to strengthen the dream of collective transformation, to stir desires and disciplines that are not cowed by the impossible. The language of the justice to come, of nonattachment to the acquisitive ego, of a renewal of the earth, of a hope against the hopes of every empire of self-interest can be, has been, radically secularized; but it cannot be purged of its religious sources. Rather, we turn the resources of wisdom, prophecy, and song against the aggressive sovereignties with which they come mixed. And now, needing language ancient and novel, we might gratefully and with greater urgency draw on select theisms, atheisms, pantheisms, panentheisms, and posttheisms, opening them to critical engagement with each other for the sake of the earth.

We are seeking language amid vast wordscapes of modern failure; language that might breathe new life into barren hopes. Every emancipatory tradition becomes toxic with abuse; every brave new word turns to cliché. So these essays forage and create within the chaos of disappointed messianisms. They hold already much in common: a disruptive democratization of the good; an economic and ecological insistence on planetary flourishing; a theologically trandisciplinary planetary politics. In this emergent discourse our networks of relation brook no separable identity, no monocausal narrative of class, race, gender, sex, ability, culture, or species. Let alone "religion." These complex systems come asymmetrically and irrevocably entangled. Their possible commons is not One. For this reason we think this emerging discourse may have a chance. Its thinkers know that to every great hope cling the vestiges of past utopian futures. These moments of vast possibility haunt us with their broken dreams, their messianic traces of unrealized futures. And in the breach—they beckon with some new kind of solidarity. Some cloud of witnesses—some crowd of alarmingly multiplying humans, dense with the nonhuman, the nonhumans, common to us all—insists itself upon us.

## CHALLENGES TO THE COMMON GOOD

Any notion of the common and its good became suspect over the past few decades—and from opposite conceptual angles. On the one hand, movements for the liberation of divergent identities, within their singular contexts, and on the other, the philosophical challenge to any substantive identity, any totalizing oneness, both pressed the question: *Whose* common? *Whose* good? The social movements intertwined academically with the deconstruction of any language of unity, community, or universality, notions that so routinely, and often with good intentions, efface difference. The suspicion of difference characterizes—differently—most traditional cultures, tribal or national, and systemically amplifies even as greater multiplicities are incorporated into imperial or totalizing political orders. So we began to forfeit any language for the common, from which all threat to difference can never be eliminated. (*Which* difference?) These salubrious suspicions did not mean to serve the fragmentation of the left, let alone individualism. They seek coalitions wrought of irreducible alterities, mutually respectful, mutually challenging. This volume belongs amid the continued experiments in such coalescence.

During the same loosely postmodern period, the common was coming undone on another front, antagonistic to both social movements and deconstruction. The new empire of capital was taking hold. The 1980 election of Ronald Reagan would politically lock it into a rightward shift—to this day—that retroactively reads, given its climate effects, as a journey of no return. Swiftly undoing state and local structures by which the multiplicity of witnesses might coalesce in democratic spaces as "the People" (Ochoa Espejo) and demand their changes, the neoliberal global economy has remade the *common* into the *corporate*. It manufactures us as a corpus alienated from the vulnerable varieties of what Sharon Betcher calls the "concorporeal commons." Capitalism promises redemption from the monotony of the merely common, from the oppressiveness of the collective. It sells variety, freedom, the new. It imposes the slick uniformities of image, production, agribusiness, intellectual properties, and of course currency. The unacknowledged homogeneities of capital are traded against the democratizing demands of a common multitude. Individualism is the sham of difference. It offers the monochrome idols of the 1 percent as everyone's impossible dream. The neoliberal good was to trickle down bountifully through "free trade" from the economic top, bringing prosperity while ushering in political orders free of "the People." In the capitalist utopia that is still managing to sell itself to a sufficient mass, the "rising tide" will float all boats. Even as the necessary sacrifice of the most common, the most vulnerable, the gospel of Matthew's "least of these," becomes routine. As Joerg Rieger demonstrates in *No Rising Tide*, capitalism offers greed as the motive force of the widest possible good. And maybe that would be no problem if it actually worked. But the rising tide has sunk many boats. The gaps are growing: in income, in how people and their work are valued, in how much control people have over their lives.

Rieger with Kwok Pui-lan proposes instead "a common good growing out of deep solidarity of the majority—indeed of the 99 percent." They argue that "the unity of the 1 percent might be described in terms of uniformity, whereas the solidarity which the 99 percent may effect can only be unity in diversity."[6] Such language springs from the prophetic and gospel texts of social justice, channeled through the twentieth-century tradition of liberation theology, and freshly inspired by the very twenty-first-century occupy movement. Though recent theology has shared the suspicion of the common, the universal, it can, no more than the secular left, afford to disregard our common planetarity. We join Gayatri Chakravorty Spivak in imagining "ourselves as planetary subjects rather than global agents, planetary creatures rather than global entities."[7] The alterity of the planet engulfs us in a spatiotemporality alien and resistant to techno-economic globalization. Effectual solidarity will now carefully distinguish between the sham difference of global capitalist currency and the networks of difference that articulate an emergent common good.

Not coincidentally, one of the earliest systemic accounts of the havoc that neoliberal globalization would wreak on human community and planetary ecology came as the joint work of a theologian and economist. In *For the Common Good: Redirecting the Economy toward Community, the Environment, and a Sustainable Future*, John Cobb and Herman Daly laid out the justifications, the mechanisms, and the practical solutions to the ideology of *homo economicus*: a worldview cashing in the commons for individual profit, but doing so with a globalizing aggression seductively concealed by its appeal to personal happiness.[8] Neoliberalism dispenses with issues of ethics and ecology as "externalities" to economic reality. The book demonstrates how the very organization of academic disciplines, among which economics remains the extreme case of insular specialization, inhibits their possible work on solving human problems.

Perhaps such prophetic warnings and careful analyses of the condition would have been better heeded had liberal thought in the Academy not developed its allergy to the common—and, it goes without saying, to any link to theology or even to the academically more neutral but nonetheless suspicious religion. Yet although Cobb is the major creator of process theology (always as a collective practice), *For the Common Good* proceeds with no God-talk. Its profound theological motivation is precisely what drives its systemic transdisciplinarity. Process thought, based originally on the cosmological relationalism of Alfred North Whitehead, for this reason plays an ineluctable if delicate webbing role in this and other volumes in this Transdisciplinary Theological Colloquium series.[9]

## COMMON GOOD/S

We propose *common good/s* as one sign of the return of the common under the ethos of its multitudes and the ecology of its multiplicity. This would be a good that is redistributed in a multiscaled manifold of political strategies, values, and needs befitting the planetary commons. Pluralizing the good, with its ancient heritage of political philosophy, collapses the hierarchy of the One that the Platonic Good delivered, without giving up on the utopian social dream of a just and flourishing city. At the same time "goods" signals the materiality of an economics that does not conceal human and ecological shalom as external to what matters. Such goods include the things we need, receive, give, and create, as well as the values, rights, and enjoyments more or less materialized in each act of creation. The singular good is good inasmuch as it remains open to the conflictual complexity of values actualized in specific goods—which themselves can only remain good to the extent that they participate in the shareable planetary weal. This volume does not perform a terminological debate on our titular trope. But the grammatically funky plurisingularity of the term *common good/s* will we hope serve to remind us all of the multiplicity—not a mere *many* of demands and desires but an interlinked manifold—that enlivens the planet itself as a collective and charges its life with value.

The *good* is not one: So it works here in *common* with innumerable other strategies to democratize the polis. "Democracy is democratization."[10] Far from a given, a possession, "democracy as we know it," writes Romand Coles, remains "a practice largely in search of itself," happening when it happens "as a generative activity in which people seek to reinvent it in challenges and contestations concerning the question of what it might become."[11] "Democracy is coming," croons Leonard Cohen hoarsely, "democracy is coming—to the U.S.A." (The song was written at the same time as Derrida's "democracy to come.")[12] When democratization happens—in outbursts and actions of abolition, feminism, populism, antiwar activism, movements for civil, First Peoples, or LGBTQ rights, ecological sanity, living wage, debt relief—possibilities concealed by established forms of democracy come to light. Their good in its particularity insists itself on the common, exposing its contradictions in the hope of social metamorphosis.

By now democratization means first of all: Do not cash democracy in to capitalism. The common good/s work in resistance to the capitalization of the good as a cosmos of consumer goods. But the plurisingular sociality of this common good breaks up any collectivist totality. Although it may lament the bitter disappointment of the communist states, even laugh at any nostalgia for their return, it may yet meditate with Derrida on the *Specters of Marx* and the indeconstructibility of justice. Although the majority of the 99 percent may seem hopelessly capitalized or else demoralized, experiments in democratization continue. The participatory dynamism of planetary publics in local actions globally entangled remains nonnegotiable. If, as Connolly puts it in his recent book, the "fragility of things has become palpable, and political activism is needed at several interinvolved sites," we underscore "the urgent need to think and act in ways that activate the subterranean links between beliefs, role performances, social movements, electoral politics, state actions, and cross-state citizen movements."[13] Such cross-state movements require more than national citizenship; the ancient Stoic imperially ambiguous dissidence of the cosmopolitan as "citizen of the world" now takes on an ecocosmological intensity, permitting no detachment from local electoral politics and yet no reliance on them. The authors in this volume would concur with Connolly's conclusion: "The overriding goal is to press international organizations, states, corporations, banks, labor unions, churches, consumers, citizens, and universities to act in concerted ways to defeat neoliberalism, to curtail climate change, to reduce inequality, and to instill a vibrant pluralist spirituality into democratic machines that have lost too much of their vitality."[14]

In the hope of fueling the vibrancy of a pluralist spirituality exceeding any theism, this collection makes explicit the *theologies* we practice. These also are not one. Some are contextually linked to those churches, all of them to universities, some to activist movements. Yet each nourishes a deep solidarity among global commoners; each stirs the hope of a convivial planetarity that may yet be possible—not just abstractly possible but possible actually to *actualize*. Such hope requires an imagination resilient and realistic enough to face down the aggressive common sense forged by economics, signed by politics, and sealed by ecological demise. This hope can be sustained, we believe, only by way of a new relationship between politics and religion. Charles Taylor's monumental *A Secular Age* questions a separative and subtractive secularism, deconstructing the "death of God" for the sake of a more meaningful life and more honest democracy.¹⁵ It is a possibility Connolly, without Taylor's theism, marked with another book's title: *Why I Am Not a Secularist*.¹⁶ Other theorists mark such a possibility as the "postsecular," in light of the failure of religion to die away as predicted by a long tradition of secularism. It is especially Jürgen Habermas, in his later work, who has emphasized the need to cultivate a postsecular approach, one that can "translate" the ethics of a religious tradition into a universally accessible language. A fertile debate as to the character of such translation and the public opportunity offered by this religious resurgence continues to develop among political philosophers—and often under the banner of "political theology."

## THE RETURN OF RELIGION AND POLITICAL THEOLOGY

Reflecting on shifts evident already in the 1980s, José Casanova seems to have been the first to capture the sociology of the new phenomenon of global religious vitality. In *Public Religions in the Modern World*, he advanced the thesis of the "deprivatization of religion." It repudiated the liberal presumption that religion eventually would be relegated to the private sphere. Far from the standard narrative of a progressive receding of the religions and their replacement by secular rationality, religion had begun a public resurgence. And this took not only the form of the new religious right, with the political enfranchisement of Protestant fundamentalism in the United States. Casanova tracks also the immense impact of the Catholicism of liberation theology in Latin American resistance to the dictatorships funded by U.S. neoimperialism, and of the Solidarność movement, just as manifestly Catholic, which in Poland initiated the downfall of the Soviet empire.

Not coincidentally, it is within the same period that what is called political theology came into its own, or rather, came into theology. It is Carl Schmitt who made the phrase (in)famous, responding to its original use by the Russian social anarchist Mikhail Bakunin. Certainly no theologian, the German political theorist and jurist advanced a critique of liberalism that, in frustration with the Weimar Republic, drove not to the left but to a religiously stimulated political right. Here is his now unavoidable thesis: "All significant concepts of the modern theory of the state are secularized theological concepts not only because of their historical development—in which they were transferred from theology to the theory of the state, whereby, for example, the omnipotent God became the omnipotent lawgiver—but also because of their systematic structure, the recognition of which is necessary for a sociological consideration of these concepts."¹⁷ Thus the notion of political sovereignty cannot be separated from its prototype, the sovereignty of God, which generated the forms of Western politics, from its ideas of power and the good, through the divine right of kings, and so on. "Sovereign is he who decides on the exception."¹⁸

That exceptionalism permits the breaking of logjams in emergencies. Specifically, it lets the sovereign unify the "friends" of the state against a "foe." Without the sovereign's mimicry of the divine omnipotence at such moments, a state falters and weakens. In the face of the paralysis to which democracy, in its "relativism" is prone, Schmitt alluringly draws an analogy between the "the exception in jurisprudence" and "the miracle in theology."[19] Note the attractive force of his compressed thesis: "The exception is more interesting than the rule. . . . In the exception the power of real life breaks through the crust of a mechanism that has become torpid by repetition." And then he cites at length "a Protestant theologian who demonstrated the vital intensity possible in theological reflection in the nineteenth century"—none other than Kierkegaard: "Endless talk about the general becomes boring; there are exceptions. If they cannot be explained, then the general also cannot be explained."[20] This is not far from Whitehead's critique of the fallacy of misplaced concreteness, an exceptionally sharp tool in the hands of progressive critiques of religious or economic orthodoxy. But Schmitt followed certain "Catholic philosophers of the counterrevolution," to argue for the transfer of a "decisionistic and personalist" notion of divine transcendence to the state.[21] (The recent U.S endowment of corporations with personhood pressures the political theology of the state in new ways.[22]) Schmitt sought to strengthen the state by reviving aspects of theocracy, that is, by desublimating the authority of the theological origins of the very idea of sovereignty.

The discourse of political theology arose again—also among German-speaking thinkers—in the late twentieth century in firm repudiation of Schmitt's version, which had entangled him in service to the Third Reich.[23] The philosopher and scholar of Judaism Jacob Taubes's enigmatic last work, *The Political Theology of Paul*, not only refutes Schmitt's politics of enmity but engages it profoundly—on the basis of a debate about the Pauline signifier of "Israel" as simultaneously "enemies of God for your sake" and "beloved . . . for the gifts and the calling of God are irrevocable (Rom. 11:28)."[24] And so Taubes can be said to have seeded the densely multiplying set of philosophers and other thinkers enamored—often with no theistic interest—with Paul's political theology (Agamben, Žižek), his universalism (Badiou), and of course with his theopolitical radicality as a Jew (Boyarin). The post-Holocaust Germany of the 1980s is also the setting—within the discipline of theology—of the reception of political theology. The Catholic theologians Johannes Metz and Dorothee Sölle, as well as the leading European Protestant theologian Jürgen Moltmann, retrieved the concept of "political theology" in solidarity with liberation theology while respectfully recognizing the radical difference of context (the lives of liberation theologians and their publics in Latin America were after all at risk). The concept also was transported to the United States by John Cobb in his *Process Theology as Political Theology*.²⁵ As a theologian, Cobb has consistently argued for the pluralist secularization of the religious traditions—or rather argued that each one of the great Ways, Western or Eastern, was at its incipience a secularizing event, turning a community's attention back to worldly practice.²⁶ Secularization here, however, is opposed to "secularism," which counts as another "religion." As John Thatamanil performs this theological problematizing of the modern category "religion" in this volume, it undoes every theological fetish of unquestionable truth and so becomes a matter of comparative theology. Recognizing the artificial delimitation of a "religion" both from religious and secular others, he insists that "the task at hand is not to *depoliticize* religions but to *dereligionize* them." But neither then does religious diversity collapse into a single truth, sacred or secular, private or public. Only emergent assemblages of entangled multiplicity can surface the common good/s of religion and politics. A democratizing political theology has long depended on the evolving forms of such theological pluralism.

In other words, those 1980s receptions of political theology among progressive theological thinkers, each working for the democratization and socialization—without totalization—of the public sphere, each presuming the need for Christianity to emancipate itself from its oppressive and supernaturalist modalities of transcendence in order to follow the prophetic path of justice for the least, for the common, predate by decades the current appropriations of political theology. Yet the language had almost disappeared for a decade or so. For all of those Christian theological thinkers, other more current and concrete social movements and concerns preempted further engagement with Schmitt and his language. Yet under other conceptualizations of sustainable social justice the impetus continued. Later theological engagements of postcolonial and cosmopolitan theory build on this legacy more or less consciously, while evolving the transformative waves of Latin American, *Minjung*, and Black liberation, and of feminist, womanist, and queer spiritual activism, of interreligious democratization. And in the meantime the discourse of political theology pursued by nontheologians has burst upon the scene. But on the whole, with exceptional moments, it has ignored these multiple waves of emergent, highly political, theology. In Schmittan tradition, Giorgio Agamben, Slavoj Žižek, Jürgen Habermas, and Simon Critchley largely debate versions of Pauline and orthodox Christianity. We do not dispute the value of radicalizing Paul, let alone of serious engagements with later waves of conservative theology and its range of politics. But the conversation also tends to reinscribe the orthodox exclusion of decades of dissident theological diversity.

In a sense then this volume comes full circle. The highly secularized thematic of the postsecular along with the often atheist engagement of political theology is brought back—or forward—into an explicitly theological force field. The political philosophers who form a crucial minority in the collective of this book do not write as theologians political or otherwise, but have always practiced a coalition-building generosity and a spirituality of plural "existential faiths" vis-à-vis the institutional religions. So in this volume a political theology certainly will not mean any wholesale return to religion (even if religious goods are now available at wholesale prices, as the old line—and sidelined—denominations sell off their properties). It does mean the uncommonly good possibility of new alliances between multiple constituencies of the planet's majority, its 99 percent, its commoners.

Religiously speaking, we do presume several points. First, a majority of those global commoners, at least the human ones, are and will be for the foreseeable future religious, and their practices will transform the meaning of religiosity in novel ways. This is inescapably clear in Africa, Latin America, parts of Asia, and the United States. Indeed, the religious left or liberal/progressive wing of the major world religions remains largely incapable of "winning" the competition with radical conservatives. This stalemate mirrors the larger political and economic situation. But this wing also will not be stilled and will continue to represent major and influential minorities among self-identified religious populations, exercising tremendous attractive power on religious moderates, younger evangelicals, and democratically or pacifically oriented communities. At the same time conservatives may be losing ground to the "spiritual but not religious" population, with whom the religious left, in its pluralism, can make common cause. In the hope of amplifying the agency of ecological and social justice impulses within and through the religious traditions, the critical-pluralist-deconstructive-liberation-decolonial-feminist-process-relational-apophatic thinkers of this volume join our intellectual energy to these pluriform and multinodal networks.

The deep solidarity of the 99 percent cannot come to fruition without its religious voices, and in particular the thinkers and leaders who can articulate our common good/s are needed. These must be voices affirmative of religious diversity. They must also be voices affirmative of irreligious diversity. The relation between the religions is no more and no less important than the relation between religion and atheism. Therefore, theologies in the venerable tradition of the death of God, represented in this volume by the postsecular "non-theology" of Crockett, serve as indispensable mediators between ethically pluralist theologies and ethically pluralist atheisms. Finally, with a rapidly widening network of thinkers, we presume the ecological context of all theology and all politics. Michael Northcott's *Political Theology of Climate Change* comes from an orthodox Christian point of view to as strong a critique of economic imperialism as, say, Bruno Latour's *Facing Gaia*. We reduce no political issues to "nature" by embedding all of them within their divergently but inescapably shared ecology. If the prediscursive resonance of the earth releases vitalities and forces of the nonhuman into our asymmetrical fragilities, we might translate its conceptual echo into a cosmopolitics with *cosmos*. It will also be readable as a political theology of the earth.

Amid our insanely asymmetrical liabilities, will collective crises of economic and environmental survival merely provoke more violent injustice? Or might they galvanize new collective actions on behalf of the planetary commons and its contentiously diverse commoners?

Amid the spirited polyglossia of this possibility, and indeed of this volume, prophetic moments may occur, but no predictive certainties. However, of this much we are confident: The common good/s of the planet will now be best served, we believe, by a manifold of motivating discourses, urgently heedful of each other. If, as William Connolly writes in this volume, "a politics of positive engagement with the fragility of things is actively pressed by a positive constellation of minorities, it may also be possible to expand the cadre whose political commitments express attachment to the planet. Besides the dangers they bring, some shocks and interruptions set conditions of possibility for positive modes of creative action."

## THE STRUCTURE OF THE VOLUME

Religions of various sorts of course have much to do with constellating these minorities that together add up to the planetary majority. If the present transdisciplinarily theological project is first of all indebted to William Connolly's contribution to the conversation and indeed to the textual conditions of its possibility, it is because his characteristic pincer movement of "presumptive generosity" and "democratic militancy" parallels or indeed patterns much of the thinking of the philosophers, theologians, and scholars of religion of this collection. Together the voices of this volume advance the growing countercultural challenge to the machine of corporate omnipotence and the theopolitical sovereignties that sacralize it. The essays are organized into three parts, beginning with a wide-angle exploration of philosophy, theology, and religion on planetary, cosmological, transcendent, and transhistorical scales, moving to engagements with contemporary economic and ecological systems, and ending with critical entanglements with democracy, the flesh, and the multitudinous potentialities of embodiment.

## PLANETARY POLITICAL THEOLOGY

In first part of the book, "Planetary Political Theology," the engagements of theology display the wide spectrum of strategies coalescing in the present experiment. Each of the essays confronts the problem posed by theorizing "the political" in isolation from "the theological" or "the religious." All the essays demonstrate how the standard secular dichotomy acquiesces in definitions of the divine as ultimate sovereign power, constructed of relations of superiority and subordination, and so continue to uproot transcendence from the materiality of life. William Connolly's "Process Philosophy and Planetary Politics" probes deep currents of that materiality. Connolly finds there a cosmos of differential degrees of creativity, arising and passing away through layered and partly indeterminate processes of self-organization. And so he creates for political theory an extraordinary conceptual rhizome of Whitehead, Nietzsche, and quantum entanglement. He is building here on a long-term occupation with "Jamesleuzian" cosmological speculation, as well as the biology of complexity theory.[27] If here the complexity-craving "primordial nature of God" is brought into struggle with purely naturalistic force fields, the becoming cosmos of the cosmopolitical only gains in creative intensity. Connolly's deepening engagement with Whitehead serves his consistent commitment to fomenting a "many-fronted social movement," acting "at multiple sites, including electoral politics, church assemblies, public protests, corporate boycotts, media interventions, and union meetings."[28] The "world of becoming" assembles itself not on the basis of already common properties but in the emergent force fields of deep pluralism.

The comparative theologian John Thatamanil turns to the "return of religion" and its threat to the kind of capacious and agonistic—not antagonistic—politics of positive engagement figured in William Connolly's decades long refusal of secularism, which does not presume that the religious and the secular political can be tightly cordoned off from each other. Marking the provinciality and modernity of the category "religion," Thatamanil argues that the modern secularization project was the context in which "religion" was invented—through textualization, literalization, creedalization, reification, and fetishization—and precisely to be marginalized and excluded from the public sphere. The task at hand, he says, is to dereligionize religions, to set traditions free from the constraints that come with being religions. Religious communities are thereby enabled to participate in public life in a capacious and generous spirit.

Clayton Crockett seeks to develop an insurrectionist non-theology "to think about the nature and stakes of political ecology as opposed to simply stretching the traditional forms of theology to incorporate nature as Go(o)d." Adopting and adapting François Laruelle's non-philosophy, Gilles Deleuze's analysis of energy and entropy, and Lacan's unattainable object of desire (*objet petit a*), Crockett presses radical political theology through nontheology to a radical political *ecology* that thinks with the earth. He challenges readers "to think of ourselves as planetary objects *a*, which we are *in common*, rather than how we are signified by capitalist *jouissance*. The idea is to construct a theological ecology of Earth as a totality in its becoming."

Kathryn Tanner engages the critique of transcendence and its links to sovereignty. In deep sympathy with Connolly's project, yet noting its resonance primarily with process theologians, she asks whether one can "pluralize the sensibility of more traditional Christian claims of divine transcendence to produce allies in the formation of a counter machine?" Answering affirmatively, Tanner describes a range of factors that pluralize the implications of a belief in a transcendent God, wholly other from the world. Proposing that a God of radically apophatic transcendence "need not amplify the (evangelical) Christian-capitalist machine" and that God's agency is noncompetitive and all-giving, Tanner opens room for assemblages across Christian doctrinal lines, animated by visions of mutual human fulfillment that push current configurations of capitalism in more eco-egalitarian directions.

Melanie Johnson-DeBaufre focuses on the persistence of the theological versus the political among the several structuring binaries that dictate interpretations of the "Kingdom of God" (*basileia theou*), the central metaphor of Jesus' teaching in the synoptic gospels. Recognizing the Janus-faced nature of religion, which both "inspires and terrifies," in public life, she explores this central Christian symbol as akin to utopian social thought and practice. Although enclosure is always a risk of the utopian, contemporary utopian studies reject the equation of utopia with social perfectionism and useless fantasy. Her essay positions the basileia of God and its interpretation as a utopian method of social dreaming, that is, as the imaginary reconstitution and materialization of the world as it simultaneously is and is not. This locates Christian social imaginaries of the common good fully within the sphere of the political without translation out of the theological, and configures the *kin-dom* as ever moving, undoing, and reconstituting itself lest it be drained of its creative and animating utopian energy.

In Dhawn Martin's essay, the cosmopolitical unfolds as a lively and plurivocal "christo-eccentric" theology, whereby incarnational confessions and political projects—as enfleshed and enmeshed in the human, extrahuman agencies of life—are not closed or inert but changing and dynamic, ever emergent. Drawing on Pheng Cheah's and William Connolly's philosophical engagements of Kantian cosmopolitanism as well as the theologies of Graham Ward, Mayra Rivera, and Laurel Schneider, she proposes a cosmopolitical theology characterized by eccentric connections that disrupt concentric enclosures. Such configurations of "the political" reframe the good of life as a robust if always contestable common good that "strives toward the fullness of life, not as a universal precept, but as an ever-emerging possibility."

## ECONOMIES AND ECOLOGIES OF (UN)COMMON GOOD/S

Moving from the broad-scale categories of political theology, the second part, "Economies and Ecologies of (Un)Common Good/s," focuses analysis, critique, and creativity on the problems of economy and ecology that threaten planetary commons and common life itself. There are multiple diagnoses and equally multiple proposals for ways to reclaim, restore, revise, and redeploy the traditions and symbols of religion, most often Christianity, toward enlivening the solidarities for life-giving planetary common good/s.

To begin, Joerg Rieger analyzes the links forged by the invisible hand of the marketplace between the common good and the de facto ideals of capitalism: selfishness and greed. These ideals have been increasingly called into question, he suggests, owing in part to the experience of sustained economic hardship and downturn. Rather than developing alternatives by juxtaposing one set of ideals with other sets of ideals, Rieger identifies robust notions of the common good growing out of the lived experiences and the emerging deep solidarity of the majority of people who no longer benefit from the structures of capitalism. In this process, alternative experiences of religion develop that resonate with core Abrahamic religious traditions, which have their roots in situations marked by power differentials and struggles for liberation.

The essay by the Christian social ethicist Gary Dorrien performs the role of theologian in the public square with characteristic precision and insight. He reconsiders the social gospel movement and its calls for a cooperative commonwealth of worker and community ownership. The essay proposes that lessons from the social gospel are important for today as capitalism prevails in more global and predatory forms than ever. Because there is such a thing as social structure, salvation has to be reconceived to account for it. Salvation has to be personal and social to be saving. Resonating with Rieger's deep solidarity, Dorrien encourages decentralized experiments in economic democratization to be "built from the ground up, piece by piece, opening new choices, creating more democracy, building an economic order that does not rest on selfishness, consumerism, and the prerogatives of shareholders."

For Charon Hribar, the persistence of the myth of the American Dream and the politics of aspiration threaten to mask perpetually the contradictions of global capitalism. Drawing on Antonio Gramsci, Johannes Baptist Metz, and H. Richard Niebuhr, she explores how a revolutionary Christian tradition can help challenge the fundamental social relationships that promise opportunity but produce poverty in the midst of plenty. Hribar proposes cultivating a critical consciousness on the ground—responding to the call from the grassroots to "Put People First"—that can begin to disrupt a worldview of American exceptionalism. For Hribar, "It is the unsettling force emerging from worsening conditions that encourages us to construct a new vision for the common good that centers not on providing 'opportunities' that benefit the few, but rather on ensuring our *right to not be poor* and a radical Christian belief that everyone's needs can and must be met."

Nimi Wariboko provides a religious theory of the tripartite (tradition, protest, and new creation) articulation of economic life in order to craft a *weak-messianic* conception of market miracles that "reveal a form of weak or contestable sovereignty, one that is dependent on the openness and fallible decisions of millions of dispersed market agents." Recognizing that "markets are suffused with state interventions in favor of exceptionally nimble and fiercely free finance capital," Wariboko asks, "What kind of freedom do we need to forge today to enable citizens squeezed between these two forces to resist the market?" The answer lies, he suggests, in the praxis of human freedom, both the potentiality to do and the potentiality, with Agamben, to *not-do*. Such a freedom "will strive to *de-complete* finance capital's order, the logic of pure and complete actualization, in the name of impotential freedom without destination or determination," unleashing improvisational practices within the market but outside of alienation and surplus extraction.

Elijah Prewitt-Davis engages the all too immanent biopolitical power of corporations as grounding subjectivity after the death of God. Drawing on Philip Goodchild's argument that it is capital itself that has murdered God and Hegel's proposal that corporations are the second dialectical universal that opened human subjectivity to a fuller realization of the common good, Prewitt-Davis argues that the legal notion that corporations are persons, coupled with the way they produce values biopolitically, signifies the corporation's consummation as the Universal. Exposing the place of the corporate apparatus in providing the recognition that subjects desire, Prewitt-Davis concludes by attempting to "mistrust" or rethink the death of God with Deleuze, who had asserted that the fallout of Hegelian dialectics was resentment. "Perhaps we can turn this resentment into an active force that embraces the ambiguity, flipping the tables of corporate power like Jesus *did*, not dialectically, but literally and dramatically. Or, to put it another way, perhaps we do not yet know what a corporate body working for the common good can do."

An Yountae examines an unresolved tension framing the meaning of labor—as creative force and a forced activity—in the Hegelian master-slave dialectic, which shadows Antonio Negri's dialectical reading of Job as a figure of revolutionary resistance and Marx's notion of class struggle. In order to clarify and bridge this tension between the two contradictory meanings of labor, he borrows critical insights from Frantz Fanon and Enrique Dussel. This creative conversation signals the paradox conditioning the Hegelian dialectic in which "living labor" (Dussel) signifies both the site of oppression or suffering and the inappropriable alterity emerging from *within*. "If recognition and freedom are denied by the master or the capitalist system of production," An writes, "perhaps we could suggest that there exists another kind of common good for the dispossessed that lies beyond the measures of appropriation: the shared experience of suffering out of which a renewed and self-determined consciousness or subject might emerge." Hope ignites in solidarities of loss and grief: "The revolutionary labor of proclaiming the death of the ontotheological deity and the totalitarian system of domination begins from the grief born out of this suffering."

At this point in the volume, Anatoli Ignatov's essay interrupts any emphasis on the marketplace as the only space from which to rethink political economy. His essay stages a dialogue between Henry David Thoreau and the Gurensi people of Ghana, reworking key concepts of the anthropocentric repertoire of mainstream political economy—property, production, labor, and wealth—as a web of socioecological relations between humans and the land. The dialogue revises property as poetic/spiritual enclosures that highlight ways of apprehending the land without possessing it as enclosed commons. It also outlines a practice of political theory that is less concept-centric. Shifting back and forth between theory and ethnography, economy can be perceived as a practice with an ecological and political cast: a process enacted by various assemblages of natural bodies and forces.

The second part ends on a note of urgency and a call to responsibility because the "Earth's atmospheric ability to maintain a climate amenable to life may be the most fundamental of all goods needed in common by all humans and by otherkind." In her essay, Cynthia Moe-Lobeda discusses the links between climate change and the economic and racial privilege evident in its devastating impact on impoverished people who also are disproportionately people of color. Many voices of the Global South figure this as a "climate debt" (or climate colonialism) and situate it as a continuation of the colonialism that enabled the Global North to enrich itself for five centuries at the expense of Africa, Latin America, Indigenous North America, and parts of Asia. Moe-Lobeda thus posits climate change as a moral matter of white privilege and class privilege. She draws on tools of Christian ethics as political theology to frame key aspects of a moral response, including uncovering historical and structural roots and long-term consequences of power imbalances and accepting commensurate responsibility, as well as pursuing change on the levels of behavior, social structures, and worldviews, guided by values of environmental and economic equity and economic democracy.

## COMMON FLESH, COMMON DEMOCRACIES

As discussed above, political theorists have been revisiting the debate about the theological origins of the concept of sovereignty. At stake are both the legitimacy of contemporary democracy and the power of the state to form subjects and regulate bodies. This third part, "Common Flesh, Common Democracies," turns attention to the theory and practice of democracy as well as to its vast array of constitutive agents, whether collectively figured as "the People" or materializing in and as flesh the myriad differences and commonalities of life itself.

We begin with the political philosopher Paulina Ochoa Espejo's exploration of popular sovereignty and the problem of the "empty place" or negative trace of the divine required, according to the political theorist Claude Lefort, to keep a democratic order from collapsing into totalitarianism. Arguing that Lefort's view cannot provide the positive political morality that democracy requires because it retains certain hang-ups of early modern sovereignty, such as its decisionistic conception of divine and earthly power, Ochoa Espejo suggests that democracy could profit from acknowledging the inherent indeterminacy of the people. "Rather than thinking of the people as a radically disembodied and purely symbolic reference standing for ideal justice and right, a positive conception of the people can challenge actual injustices and create alternatives for action that had not been possible before." "The people as process," she says, is not unified or complete, but it does exist and it can be a site where the political morality and the "energy and power of symbolic and religious thinking can play a creative and change-oriented role in politics." Ochoa Espejo powerfully illustrates this idea by looking at the border of the United States and Mexico, where the "Security Fence" symbolizes sovereignty, and the people as process creatively works around it: "Society changes when immigrants cross the border, and 'The People' is constituted as a conversation in different voices."

Pressing into the depths of difference that constitute "the People," gender and race come explicitly to the fore in Vincent Lloyd's exploration of the theopaternal, that is, the analogy between divine and human fatherhood, and its implications for politics. Lloyd argues that there is a common but problematic concept of authoritarian divine and human fatherhood, rightly criticized by feminists, which continues to reinscribe the status quo. Yet Lloyd sees an opportunity in the theopaternal. Examining racialized experiences of fatherhood, he says, can challenge the standard account of the theopaternal, and thus of the theopolitical. The essay proceeds through a close reading of Barack

Obama's writings, showing that his first book, *Dreams from My Father* (1995), "is an example of the theopaternal: Father and God are effectively interchangeable, and the young Obama is on a dialectical quest for both." The missed alternative is under erasure: the black father, whose eligibility as a legitimate father is "systematically undermined by a state apparatus that treats black men as incapable of fatherhood." *The Audacity of Hope* (2006) then demonstrates the theopolitical implications of this problematic account of the theopaternal, refusing deep ideological critique in favor of a committed moderation and pragmatism that favor the wealthy and powerful and that stymie collective efforts to further the common good.

Critical race analysis also fuels Elias Ortega-Aponte's essay on the crisis of mass incarceration in the United States. Political theology's radical democratic discourse, as it outlines the shape of possible democratic futures, he argues, has remained silent around the question of mass incarceration and the threat it represents to the social and political inclusion necessary for democratic existence. For communities of color this silence reveals the democratic hopes that political theology seeks to offer as yet another deferred democratic moment, an outwork of the economics of white supremacy that fuels the growth of the prison-industrial complex and the constant punishment of communities of color. Building on the works of Frederick Douglass, W. E. B. Du Bois, James Baldwin, Angela Davis, and David Goldberg, Ortega-Aponte proposes that political theology, in order to chart a way forward to possible democratic futures, should give way to an "abolitionist political theology of prison."

Difference, that is, particularly of class, race, and gender, have figured prominently in the volume so far. Yet, as Sharon Betcher argues, even critical analyses of these categories of diversity often overlook the unspoken role of "disability" in making distinctions between valuable difference and that which is "invalid." In a world of becoming, she notes, of Darwin's "endless forms most beautiful and wonderful," "disability" would seemingly be but variation. However, disability has been affectively greeted with disgust, which "creates" disability as unpalatable otherness. Existential *ressentiment* (in Connolly's Nietzschean sense) against life itself thereby comes into political, economic, and theological formation, rupturing "social flesh." Betcher draws on Simone Weil to "put disgust to work," spiritually speaking, so as "to free it from its history of mediocre moral and religious conditioning." Betcher proposes that religious practice can further—by training one to still one's judgments amid aversion—a "loving attention to the real," a forbearance necessary to live and love life amid evolutionary becoming.

Karen Bray's essay remains with the flesh. It addresses a lacuna within political theology, that of erotic desire. Employing a "methodology of the obscene," formulated out of the work of Marcella Althaus-Reid, she argues that although the works of Connolly and Rieger already fruitfully "undress" American capitalism, revealing its theological undergarments, these authors along with political theology as a whole may need to disrobe capitalism further, acknowledging the implications for sex, gender, and sexuality within the theologies by which it is formed and those which it proposes. Bray moves from acts of theological deconstruction to the construction of a political theology that draws potency from quotidian moments of erotic desire. Crucial for this construction are the work of Connolly on pluripotentiality, resonance-machines, and the microtactics of the self; queer readings of the sexual politics encased within everyday practices; and Gilles Deleuze and Félix Guattari's conception of the body-without-organs. Ultimately, Bray asserts that how people relate to erotic desire at the most intimate levels has an infinite impact on how people desire God, receive God's desire, and become political and theological actors.

Apropos of the theological spirit of our open-ended and plurisingular *common good/s*, the third part concludes in pursuit of the biblical figure of wisdom. A. Paige Rawson's essay on Proverbs 8–9 where, in the (re)appropriation and reconfiguration of wealth and creation-production, the feminine personification of Wisdom contends that s/he is always already accessible to any and every *body* in search of her. This despite socioeconomic systems structured to sustain the division of labor by privileging certain "recognizable" normative bodies over others. Taking Gabriela, a Filipina NGO, as an intertext, Rawson articulates the text's complex relationship between wisdom, wealth, and (wo/men's) bodies. In light of the unfettered availability of Wisdom and her fluid and fractured representation as (the indispensable substitution for) wealth, Rawson proposes that we reinterpret Wisdom as a "locus for life," who is always already creating the spaces necessary for the boundless incarnations of a way of being and becoming accessible to *all* life.

It is time to yield the floor to the essayists themselves. These uncommonly good contributions from scholars who coalesced under the sign *common good/s* at the Drew Theological School Transdisciplinary Colloquium (amid record-breaking, flight-canceling weather) and again in collaboration for this volume embody a bit of the boundless coalition we would assemble. Just a few words more: Given the urgency of the climatic times, the systematic mayhem of global capital's drive, the fears and hopes of the return of religion to politics, and the vibrant, if fragile, irruptions of solidarities and assemblages on behalf of all the earth, we are all the more persuaded of our starting point. Thinking the common together might do us some good.

### NOTES

1. William E. Connolly, *The Fragility of Things: Self-Organizing Processes, Neoliberal Fantasies, and Democratic Activism* (Durham, N.C.: Duke University Press, 2013), 177.

2. Ernst Bloch and Theodor Adorno, "Something's Missing: A Discussion between Ernst Bloch and Theodor W. Adorno on the Contradictions of Utopian Longing," in Ernst Bloch, *The Utopian Function of Art and Literature: Selected Essays*, by Ernst Bloch, trans. Jack Zipes and Frank Mecklenburg (Cambridge, Mass.: MIT Press, 1988), 16–17.
3. Vandana Shiva, *Earth Democracy: Justice, Sustainability, and Peace* (Cambridge, Mass.: South End Press, 2005).
4. We understand "polydoxy" as relational rather than relativist pluralism, an affirmation of plurality insistent on just relations between the interlinked diversity it assembles. See Catherine Keller and Laurel C. Schneider, eds., *Polydoxy: Theology of Multiplicity and Relation* (New York: Routledge, 2011).
5. Clayton Crockett, *Radical Political Theology* (New York: Columbia University Press, 2011), 165.
6. Joerg Rieger and Kwok Pui-lan, *Occupy Religion* (Lanham, Md.: Rowman and Littlefield, 2012), 27.
7. See Stephen Moore, "Situating Spivak," in *Planetary Loves: Spivak, Postcoloniality, and Theology*, edited by Stephen D. Moore and Mayra Rivera (New York: Fordham University Press, 2011), 27.
8. John B. Cobb Jr. and Herman E. Daly, *For the Common Good: Redirecting the Economy toward Community, the Environment, and a Sustainable Future* (Boston: Beacon Press, 1989; 2nd updated and expanded edition, 1994).
9. See Catherine Keller, Michael Nausner, and Mayra Rivera, eds., *Postcolonial Theologies: Divinity and Empire* (St. Louis: Chalice Press, 2004); Laurel Kearns and Catherine Keller, eds., *Ecospirit: Religions and Philosophies for the Earth* (New York: Fordham University Press, 2007); Keller and Schneider, *Polydoxy*.
10. Romand Coles, *Beyond Gated Politics: Reflections on the Possibility of Democracy* (Minneapolis: University of Minnesota Press, 2005), xi.
11. Ibid.
12. Jacques Derrida, *Specters of Marx* (New York: Routledge, 2004). Originally published in French as *Spectres de Marx* (Paris: Editions Galileé, 1993).
13. Connolly, *Fragility of Things*, 19.
14. Ibid., 195.
15. Charles Taylor, *A Secular Age* (Cambridge, Mass.: Belknap Press of Harvard University, 2007).
16. William Connolly, *Why I Am Not a Secularist* (Minneapolis: University of Minnesota Press, 2000).
17. Carl Schmitt, *Political Theology: Four Chapters on the Concept of Sovereignty*, trans. G. Schwab (1922; Chicago: University of Chicago, 1985), 36.
18. Ibid., 5.
19. Ibid., 36.
20. Ibid., 15.
21. Ibid., 37–49.
22. See Michael S. Northcott, *Political Theology of Climate Change* (Grand Rapids, Mich.: Eerdmans, 2013), 201–36, where he relates Schmitt's defense of state and the political to his postwar analysis of U.S. economic power.

23. He had joined the National Socialist German Worker's Party (the Nazi party) in 1933, the same year as Heidegger (ibid., vii).
24. For the interactions of Schmitt and Taubes, see Christoph Schmidt, "Review Essay of Jacob Taubes' *The Political Theology of Paul*," *Hebraic Political Studies* 2, no. 2 (2007): 232–41.
25. John B. Cobb Jr., *Process Theology as Political Theology* (Philadelphia: Westminster, 1982). The Common Good came soon thereafter, but in its focus on economics and ecology, and in the ensuing outpouring of his activist texts, Cobb does not carry forward the semantics of "political theology."
26. John B. Cobb Jr., *Spiritual Bankruptcy: A Prophetic Call to Action* (Nashville: Abingdon, 2010).
27. In *Capitalism and Christianity, American Style* (Durham, N.C.: Duke University Press, 2008), Connolly synthesizes the work of William James and Gilles Deleuze to support his concept of a pluralist universe and its "tragic possibility with meliorist potential" (133).
28. Connolly, *Fragility of Things*, 196.

Planetary Political Theology

# Process Philosophy and Planetary Politics

WILLIAM E. CONNOLLY

The future's not what it used to be. What's more, it never was. I steal this saying from the Weavers, a radical folk band of the 1950s and beyond, because it fits my thesis to a T. It means to me that dangers to the human estate itself press on the horizon during an era when capitalism has intensified and when encounters between it and a variety of nonhuman force fields with independent powers of metamorphosis have once again become dicey. It also means that we need to recraft the long debate between secular, linear, and deterministic images of the world on the one hand and divinely touched, voluntarist, providential, and/or punitive images on the other. Doing so to come to terms more closely with a world composed of interacting force fields set on different scales of chronotime that compose an evolving universe open to an uncertain degree. As we approach concepts of the common and its goods, such an image may better allow us to sense, feel, and engage both the fragility of things and our modest participation in modes of creativity that extend beyond the human estate.[1]

## GREEK AND QUANTUM SOURCES OF THE VISION

Friedrich Nietzsche, if you bracket his statements about eternal return as the return of long cycles and attend to almost everything else he says, is one modern source of such a vision. Alfred North Whitehead, if perhaps you *qualify* his discussions of "eternal objects," is another. What is interesting is that each thinker approached such a vision through a different set of engagements. Whitehead, writing during the advent of quantum mechanics, extrapolated from those ideas in ways that other leading practitioners did not. Nietzsche, writing before quantum theory was in the air, drew inspiration from Hesiod, Heraclitus, and Greek tragedians. In each case obdurate features of both Christian monotheism and Newtonianism had to be challenged.

The different materials of inspiration for each make a difference to the position articulated. Nietzsche engaged both Hesiod and Heraclitus as a young man. Hesiod's multiple, interacting, and contending gods introduce modes of causality into the world that exceed the conception of efficient cause, that trouble a notion of fixed "laws" of nature, and that disturb in advance the Humean idea that laws and causes are mere projections of human habit onto external processes. When Zeus lay with a human, Semele, and gave birth to Dionysus—the god of joy and the element of wildness in the world who entranced Nietzsche for his entire adult life—each event engendered a future that was not what it used to be projected to be. What's more, these "events" were marked by modes of sensuality, deceit, digestion, strange attractions, and uncertainties that make early modern ideas of mechanical cause and eternal laws of nature decreed by a distant god look sterile. How could the formation of life from nonlife or species change or a variety of complex civilizations emerge from such dry, bleached processes?

It was not that difficult, soon enough, to translate those gods from beings into natural forces of different sorts. Heraclitus starts the process, and the young Nietzsche is touched by him. He loves this formulation: "This universe which is the same for all, has not been made by any God or man, but it always has been, is, and will be, an ever living fire, kindling itself by regular measures and going out by regular measures."[2] Consider a few statements from an early course by the young teacher on the ancient sage, replete with the exaggerations Nietzsche admired in the Greeks and poured into his own work so as to fix its effects on our "entrails" as well as our refined conceptual capacities:

> Nowhere does an absolute persistence exist, because we always come in the final analysis to forces, whose effects simultaneously include a desire for power [*krafterlust*]. Rather, whenever a human being believes he recognizes any sort of persistence in living nature, it is due to our small standards.
>
> Yet at the greatest level nothing absolutely unalterable exists. Our earthly world must eventually perish for inexorable reasons.
>
> Well, this is the intuitive perception of Heraclitus: there is no thing of which we may say, "It is." He rejects Being. He knows only becoming, the flowing. He considers belief in something persistent as error and foolishness.[3]

The themes of cosmic innocence and becoming persist in Nietzsche, too, so that as late as the *Twilight of the Idols* he complains about the lack of a historical sense among philosophers who continue to search for a stable resting place from which explanation can proceed, in which morality can be anchored, and through which the outlines of the future can be discerned. Such philosophers express "the hatred of even the idea of becoming.... All that philosophers have handled for millennia has been conceptual mummies; nothing actual has escaped from their hands alive."

> Death, change, age, as well as procreation and growth, are to them objections—refutations even. What is does not *become*; what becomes is not.... Now they all believe, even to the point of despair, in that which is. But since they cannot get hold of it, they look for reasons why it is being withheld from them.... We've got it they cry in delight, it is the senses! These senses, *which are immoral as well*, it is they which deceive us about the *real* world.[4]

In resisting the "Egyptianism" of philosophers who give too much priority to being over becoming, Nietzsche, like William James and Whitehead after him, suggests that the protraction, connectedness, and liveliness of our experience illuminates much about the course of the world beyond the human estate too.

What about the source of somewhat similar themes in Whitehead? He does pay attention to early Greek thought, in this case to the *Timaeus* of the later Plato. But the main impetus of his exploration comes from the shock he received when the Newtonian science he had accepted as apodictic was shattered by the advent of quantum mechanics at a key moment in his intellectual development.

It (almost) goes without saying that I am not really competent to give an account of quantum theory and only partly because it has been subjected to many, contradictory accounts. I will say just enough to allow us to sense how it moved Whitehead to make adventurous cosmological extrapolations from it.

The Newtonian world was deterministic and linear, with space functioning as a container of things and the arrow of time potentially reversible by inverting the direction of causality. This universe was also created by a God who defined its fundamental laws and then left it to unwind. That explains why Whitehead rejects the Newtonian conception of laws as "impositional" in favor of an "immanent" conception. This is an important move, for it enables a conception of lawlike relations that include noise, messiness, and disturbances within them, some of which might form part of an impetus to creative change at key conjunctions. The impositional ideal of Newton also explains why he was committed—secretly, but in letters and texts that survive—to the Arian heresy in which a single God created the world and its eternal laws from scratch rather than to the trinitarian image that makes Jesus divine from birth. All these Newtonian assumptions are contested by Whitehead.

Although multiple interpretations persist of the Heisenberg and Bohr approaches to quantum theory, we must remain "content" for now with this version. Bohr at first tended to treat the problem of not being able to discriminate in the same test procedure between the location of an electron and its momentum—what he calls the problem of complementarity—as an epistemological issue. It is due to the effect of our instruments on the phenomenon itself. He himself, however, also developed suspicions about what this inability indicates about the real character of "quantum entanglement."[5]

Heisenberg, on the Epperson account I am following, moves robustly beyond the confines of an epistemological reading of the entangled relation between the subject of experimentation and the object of experimentation. He gives an ontological rendering of quantum process. Here is a formulation by him about the complex relation between "potentia" and "actuality":

> The question is no longer, "What is the mechanism by which a unique actuality physically evolves from a matrix of co-existent actualities?" but, rather, "What is the mechanism by which a unique actuality evolves from a matrix of coexistent potentia?"[6]

"Coexistent potentia." These potentia are real but inactual in the sense that when they are most active and on the way they have not themselves "decohered" into a fixed actuality or object. They are real but not actual unless and until decoherence occurs. And decoherence is apparently as dicey to understand as is the "coherence" of multiple potentia. Here is quotation from Epperson, who accepts Heisenberg's rendering, that may help provide a context for Whitehead's adventure:

> For Heisenberg, again, potentia are ontologically significant constituents of nature that provide the means by which the facts comprising the system measured (and environment) are interrelated in quantum mechanics.[7]

For Whitehead such potentia never disappear, and they are more or less active in real entities from time to time, depending on the circumstances. They help drive real novelty into the universe. As Epperson says, "For Whitehead, the potentia driving novelty constituted a different species of reality, as they did for Heisenberg—realities that do not derive entirely from some particular antecedent actual datum but rather from a spatiotemporally generic, and therefore primordial, actuality."[8]

At this point we merely state three points that Whitehead draws from quantum mechanics. They are not "derived" either from the theory or from quantum reality, as the case may be. Whitehead contends that each cosmology carries a *speculative* dimension with it that is unlikely to be subtracted from it entirely. These are, then, themes that make sense as speculations if you take quantum mechanics seriously as a real phenomenon.

The first, perhaps the closest to the phenomenon itself, is Whitehead's articulation of the "fallacy of misplaced concreteness," a "fallacy" still committed in parts of philosophy, economics, political theory, and science. If Whitehead were writing today, he would doubtless say that misplaced concreteness refers in the first instance to those who still ignore that mysterious process by which two "particles," separated after having been adjacent, now shift together simultaneously, even when at a great distance from one another.[9] Nobody seems even now to have a deep account of this simultaneity. For him misplaced concreteness means more broadly the tendency to overlook entanglements between energized, real entities that exceed any atomistic reduction of them, as when a climate pattern and ocean current system intersect and enter into a new spiral of mutual amplification or a cultural disposition to spiritual life befuddles the academic separation between an economic system and religion by flowing into the very fiber of work motivation, consumption profiles, investment priorities, and electoral politics. Such an image of multiple entanglements does not, however, devolve into a kind of organic holism, for that move would in its turn subtract the element of real creativity from the universe. The entanglements are close enough to exceed a philosophy of atomism consisting of either autonomous particles or larger entities, but they are too messy, incomplete, and on the way to fit an image of holism. I call this, in honor of William James, protean connectionism.

The second, related upshot is that space is not a mere container of things to Whitehead; it consists of relations of spatialization, engendered by formations as they unfold. This leads Whitehead to reduce the emphasis in European grammar on substantives and predicates—"the rock is solid; the ocean is blue"—and to underline the importance of prepositions and conjunctions. The metaphysical suggestions of the preposition "in" are particularly misleading. Either the preposition should be dropped, which is very difficult to do, or its meaning should be extended beyond the sense of a container. So, you move closer to Whitehead's thinking if you read the sentence "In the beginning" in the King James Bible so that the "in" involves the protraction of a moment interwoven with what came before and arrives next.

The interesting thing is that the style of writing actually adopted by Nietzsche heeds such injunctions more than that adopted by Whitehead. Nietzsche, you might say, writes cinematically, allowing scenes to flow, bump, or meld—as the case may be—into each other so that things emerge during the protraction and dissonance of a "moment" related to the past but not always "implicit in" it. And he uses ellipses often, allowing the three dots at the end of a sentence to suggest entanglements that exceed his articulation of them, inviting you to pursue a line of thinking the thought suggests to you.

Whitehead also emphasizes not only entanglement but the persistence of "actual entities" before they perish under pressure and evolve into something new.[10] So it might be best to say that the ideal Whiteheadian style would be to shift back and forth between a grammar of things and that of process, expressing in its mode the fluctuations between periods of slow and rapid movement that mark the lives of things.

Another difference of style between Nietzsche and Whitehead is pertinent. Whitehead, writing in the Cambridge-Harvard mode of the day, adopted a magisterial style that projects the presumption that the leading intellectual ideas of his day will eventually filter into the operative assumptions of the wider, democratic culture. Nietzsche, writing in a different context and challenging the dominant images of science and monotheism of his day more bluntly, often conveys a mood of trying to ward off a barbarism that repeatedly threatens to overwhelm modern culture. I will return to this difference in the last section.

Back to Whitehead. The third theme, more speculative yet but still entangled with the quantum theory under scrutiny, is the idea that real creativity is distributed differentially across the universe and "over" time. A world of becoming expresses the "agency" of real creativity lodged in the sometimes bumpy spatiotemporal relations between real entities. It is this issue that I explore further in Whitehead before Nietzsche reenters the fray.

## ACTUAL ENTITIES, VIBRATIONS, AND REAL CREATIVITY

Creativity is an "ultimate term" in Whitehead's philosophy, meaning, I take it, that you can show when it occurs and point rather roughly to how it happens but not delineate the process in complete explanatory terms.[11] It happens within preconditions and constraints, so there is never creation ex nihilo. The constraints are explained in large part by the fact that at any moment in chronotime the universe is composed of "actual entities" of innumerable types that help set preconditions for new events. An actual entity is any formation that has some tendency toward self-maintenance such as, differentially, a rock, a cell, a tornado, a system of ocean currents, a continent, an organism, a civilization, or a mist. Creativity is not the simple product of an agent or subject. Rather, it is embedded in processes that to varying degrees go through periods of what might be called "teleodynamic" searches. My intent here is to allow some recent work in complexity theory to fold into Whitehead's themes, wherever the former seems to support and coalesce with his general agenda. The creative process occurs, in its most active modes, in teleodynamic searches within and between entities whose relative equilibrium has been disturbed, and it draws on the noise within and entanglements between entities. So insofar as Henri Bergson thought of time as an independent force separate from space—and it is not perfectly clear that he did—Whitehead is at odds with him, even though his debt to Bergson is important in other respects.[12]

It is through the periodic acceleration of "vibrations" within and between entities that novel formations emerge. As he says, "Newton would have been surprised at the modern quantum theory and at the dissolution of quanta into vibrations."[13] And, as we began to see earlier, Whitehead would have been surprised to see how entanglement exceeds his own theme of vibrations, though it too applies to many of the processes we are exploring. When elements from one entity press toward another, there is the issue of whether they will "ingress" into it, and if so in what ways. The receiving entity "prehends" some of its dimensions positively and others negatively, depending in part on its prior organization and in part on the creative responses it engenders. As the interinvolvement occurs, there is "feeling" on the part of the receiving entity, even if it is only "vector feeling" in the simplest cases.[14] And periodically a new "concrescence"—or searching self-organization by the entity—of the prehended elements alters it in an important way. In this period of accentuated movement back and forth, the present creatively draws on the past without simply replicating it.

We might draw on Whitehead to make a distinction between two ideas that are sometimes equated. Unpredictability and creativity are related but not identical processes. You can have unpredictability when there is an epistemic screen separating you from the real determinants. But creativity involves a mode of self-organization that operates within constraints to bring something new into being. Whitehead challenges the speculative ontology that asserts that every inability to predict is due to a screen that hides full determination. Often this common ontology is not articulated because it *is* so common and seems so obvious to its defenders. But it has never been proven. His counterontology of differing degrees of real, conditioned creativity is speculative, defensible, and grounded in some aspects of experience. The first chimp to filter chaff out of grain by floating the mess in water participated in a creative process, and that routine was then passed on to other chimps.

Whitehead, unfortunately, is surprisingly short on examples of creative change in nonhuman processes. So let's try out a contemporary and controversial one merely to allow some of his key concepts to be placed in operation. According to biologists, a bacterium needs phosphorus to survive. But in one experiment, with bacteria that had lived in the vicinity of arsenic, infusions of arsenic encouraged the bacteria to evolve so that arsenic replaced phosphorus to a great degree as the life-giving source.[15] From a Whiteheadian perspective this creative development, if true, is complex: It involves a process of ingression, a "feeling" by the bacteria of some degree of affinity to the arsenic, and creative self-organization on the part of the bacteria as the "concrescence" by which it evolves into a mode of life—an actual entity—previously indiscernible on the face of the earth.

Other elements might have been ingested, each resulting in decline or death. And bacteria that had not previously been surrounded by arsenic might fail in such an evolutionary process of creative self-organization. So there has to be a potential affinity between the bacterium and the newly intruded element. But the potential, neither felt by it before ingression nor knowable by us prior to the experiment, becomes discernible after the creative work has been accomplished. Who knows, such a new form of life might provide a base from which other novel species are launched.

It must be emphasized that this example remains at the center of experimental controversy. If it stands, it gives an operational sense of what Whitehead means by real creativity in the production of novelty. If it does not, it might still count if, as all the contestants seem to agree, self-organization by the bacteria has rendered the proportion of arsenic to phosphorus much higher than it had been heretofore.

It seems to me that the phrase "real creativity" fits Whitehead's image whenever a reductionist explanation of change fails, when something new is added to a preexisting environment, when the newness involves a degree of self-organization on the part of at least one of the entities involved, and when that self-organization invokes a searching process in which the end pursued is cloudy at first and becomes consolidated later. It is true that I have added the phrase "self-organization" to the reading of Whitehead. But it does seem to fit with what he says about "ingression" and "concrescence," and it speaks to recent work on the character of self-organization. My approach, again, is to work modestly on Whitehead as I draw sustenance from him.[16]

Does Whitehead think that creativity reaches all the way down, to electrons, stones, lava flows as well as to species evolution and simple organic life? Today there are roughly two positions on this—among those who take creativity seriously. There are those who study the emergence of life from nonlife, even if life reaches below organisms to a degree, and those who speak of a kind of panexperientialism that to sharply varying degrees, reaches into all aspects of the world. If Terrence Deacon and Stuart Kauffman represent variants of the first view, Whitehead seems to represent a variant of the second. The theorists of emergence have difficulty explaining how these transitions could have occurred. The theorists of panexperientialism have difficulty in showing that life of some sort reaches all the way down. I am trying to leave that question open at the moment.[17] The creative relation, to Whitehead, operates by *attraction* and *repulsion* within and between interacting entities; otherwise there would be little power of an entity to maintain itself. That involves a process of teleo-searching, in a way that parallels more complex versions of self-organization in nonhuman processes.[18] It also means, and Whitehead is explicit about this, that an *aesthetic* element is in play within relations of ingression, prehension, and concrescence. This aesthetic element is not merely operative in human relations or in the human relation to things. It is involved in several thing/thing relations too. That is why he insists on extending the word "feeling" to involve relations between entities beyond the human and organic estates.

Creativity for Whitehead, again, is not total, complete or ever ex nihilo. It is always a conditioned creativity in which that which is created involves enabling and constraining relations of ingression and concrescence between actual entities. That is one reason why, at least on my reading, he construes the creative process as one that may slow down in a domain for a time as the forces of self-maintenance prevail and then accelerate when an ingression poses a more severe shock. Whitehead is not a philosopher of things in perpetual flux, as some critics of a philosophy of becoming project on it so that they do not need to think about it further. His notion of "actual entities" works against that.

His claim is that the play of attractions and repulsions becomes more sophisticated as entities become more complex, that is, as they become able to transfigure more incompatible or antagonistic elements into *contrasts* that do not dissolve into simple unity but are brought into complex harmony in the same entity. He is drawn to an evolving aesthetic of beauty more than to one of the sublime. But it may be well to recall that one aspect of beauty is its fragility, so that it may be possible to think of creativity as sublime when it is on the way.

Before we move to criticisms and further possible adjustments, it might be wise to ask whether anything more can be said on behalf of Whitehead's thesis about conditioned creativity. Well, it curtails the need to adopt a Kantian rendering of the world in which it must *appear to us* to be governed by mechanical laws while we must also *postulate* a human power of freedom that escapes those determinations as it also possesses almost magical power to act back on bodily processes to guide behavior. It also makes more sense than what Kant was able to do with those organic modes of self-organization in which the whole acts on the parts and the parts on the whole. Indeed, it employs them to make sense of creative evolution, a process Kant eschewed. Finally, it relieves the postulate of the "anthropic exception" adopted by some physicists who project an entirely deterministic world, punctuated only by the capacities of those humans who conceive and experiment on it. By adopting an axiom of real creativity distributed differentially through the world, neither of these strategies is required.

I will now crystallize a pincer movement discernible in Whitehead's texts. The idea is to move back and forth between human experiences of apparent creativity and reasoned assumptions about nonhuman processes that may best redeem those experiences. Pointing to putative human experiences of creativity in the plastic, poetic, and musical arts, Whitehead might say, "Isn't it probable that creativity in those domains expresses something real? If so, aren't such modes of creativity also apt to find *some* expression in ethics, politics, religion, and economic life? For why would such a process stop arbitrarily before infiltrating the latter activities? If you concede this much, is it not also likely—at least for those theists and nontheists who embrace a theory of species evolution and doubt that human beings are *unique* agents made in the image of a personal, omnipotent god—that there are degrees of creativity at lower levels of sophistication in force fields outside the human estate? If so, might there also be surprising intersections between some of the latter fields, out of which something new is created?"

A pincer movement is thus put into play by which you pursue the theme of differential creativity by moving through quantum theory to protean experiences of the human estate and then back again from protean human experiences to novel formations in nonhuman force fields. One pincer clamps up, the other clamps down. It may take both pincers to render the argument most plausible, for, *if* there is real creativity anywhere, it is apt to operate to some degree in both human and nonhuman venues. And it does seem difficult to participate in thinking without projecting creativity into that enterprise. This is a site at which we echo Kant without replicating Kant.

Such a pincer's movement, then, does not produce a knockdown argument of the sort Kant attempted. There are counterspeculations available to cut it off. But these have not been proven either, and that awareness in conjunction with distinctive experiences of the time we inhabit may open more people to modes of experimental exploration as they bracket the most familiar alternatives. Whitehead's speculations, it should be acknowledged again, might be disproven someday by deterministic accounts that profit from new sophistications of conceptualization and experimentation. But this has not happened to date. And if his speculations continue to accumulate persuasive power in several domains, as a growing number of humanists and scientists think they are doing, the thesis of a cosmos of *differential degrees of creativity* may inform the ways we engage artistic activity, sports innovation, entrepreneurial invention, the activation of new social movements, scientific productions, species evolution, ocean current shifts, climate change, and civilizational evolution.

The idea, again, is that the complexity of human feeling, agency, and creativity would probably not have evolved unless traces and aspects of such powers precede, infiltrate, and surround the human species. This is another aspect of conditioned creativity, one that functions to save cultural theory from the closures pushed on it by the most reductive versions of biology, neuroscience, and social science.

The more complex, according to Whitehead, arises from the less complex, even as its evolution means that some powers, skills, and sensitivities are lost along the way. Those are the "scars" of creative evolution. Nonetheless, terms such as "higher" and "lower" must be used with caution, partly because of the element of perceptual and ethical provinciality inside our species perspective. With respect to humanity the goal is neither to deny a degree of species provincialism nor to allow its boundaries to be frozen by transcendental arguments nor to assume that the objects of our apprehension and prehension are entirely constituted by us: The objective is to *stretch* human subjective capacities by artistic and experimental means so as to *respond more sensitively* to other force fields. To extrapolate, the objective is to replace both the Kantian idea of a universal constitution of the world by the human subject and simple realist images of it with an image of evolving codependence in which our *responses* to what is outside us can be stretched and amplified as we experiment on ourselves and the world. The idea of real creativity challenges classical idealist and realist models alike with a notion of speculative and experimental realism.

### ETERNAL OBJECTS AND AN IMPERSONAL GOD

What, more closely, holds things (and systems) together before they evolve into something new? One of Whitehead's most controversial ideas is that of "eternal objects." An eternal object is a potential on the way, not consolidated until it has been successfully absorbed and "realized" in a specific way by an entity. An eternal object is relational, emerging as an actual mode "only when there is a potential ingression into an actuality."[19]

But what makes this potential an *eternal* object? There are strong and weak readings of the idea of eternity in Whitehead. Perhaps he himself fluctuated in this respect. On my reading of him a "complex" eternal object is a potential pattern that could become instantiated. The repetition with variation of certain patterns in leaves, wings, and mammal limbs, the similarities in shape of a tornado and hurricane—these are patterns that subsist as potentials during "this cosmic epoch." As the new comes into being, these patterns help hold the new formation together. They are realized, as it were, after the fact rather than before. The new bacterium subsisted as cloudy pluripotentialities on the way rather than either operating as a fixed potential implicit in actuality or being the sole effect of antecedent, blind causes.

The emphasis by Whitehead on eternal objects may throw a conundrum into his philosophy. If he postulates many that are too definite, the element of real creativity in process philosophy becomes cramped. If he dissolves eternality into pure potential—intense, diffused energies sometimes entering into creative vibrations with each other—his philosophy may lose the sense of cosmic optimism that seems to permeate it. Whitehead agrees that this or that tragedy can confront a human civilization in its interactions with itself, with nonhuman forces, and with other civilizations. But he also seems to think that the universe is progressing—creatively, as it were—from one period of complexity to futures of greater complexity. In this respect you can sense the melding of eternal objects into the developing nature of God in Whitehead, a God conceived by him as an impersonal entity within the evolutionary process that absorbs and collects creative impulses as they emerge. Here are a few things he says:

> But we have to ask whether nature does not contain within itself a tendency to be in tune, an Eros urging towards perfection.[20]

> This final phase of passage in God's nature is ever enlarging itself.

> It belongs to the goodness of the world that its settled order should deal tenderly with the faint discordant light of the dawn of another age.[21]

Whitehead may not emphasize the fragility of things enough. Immortality, for Whitehead, is embedded in the process by which aspects of the past are preserved in the formation and persistence of new entities. God is the impersonal agent of that preservation. The idea, *if* I understand him, is that the combination of creativity, evolving entities, eternal objects, and an impersonal God as spur and collector of creative "advance" ensures the progressive complexity of the universe, even though particular human civilizations will bite the dust and the human estate (my term) will itself eventually go under.

It might seem that Whitehead's sense of growing cosmic complexity denies the second "law" of thermodynamics, the drive over the long term for entropy to increase. I suspect he does deny it as an iron law, and I wonder to what extent he accepts it as a strong tendency. Perhaps it makes sense to say, to qualify Whitehead, that there are some systems in the cosmos that delay and defer tendencies to entropy, and that they are involved periodically in processes of real creativity. Organisms, organic evolution, and ecosystems would be good candidates. Nietzsche, I suspect, would be inclined to accept some version of the idea that entropy tends to increase and to focus more actively on a subset of systems and processes that work against this tendency.

To what extent does the march of real creativity in human and nonhuman processes require eternal objects? It seems to me, now at least, that a universe of real creativity could be marked by flexible *tendencies* toward patterns that persist and evolve as the world changes.[22] These tendencies, for instance, could be embodied in what Stuart Kauffman calls "preadaptations," a pattern that has evolved in one system that is redundant or serves one function now and, under new circumstances, sets a preliminary condition from which creative change occurs. Thus the wings of primitive birds set preadaptations from which the limbs of animals and humans eventually evolved, as Brian Goodwin contends.[23] And the amygdala—the primitive brain node in reptiles—acquires new functions and abilities as it joins others in the human body/brain/culture network. Such preadaptations were not implicitly designed to become human limbs or brain nodes—though the name Kauffman gives to these uncertain preconditions may inadvertently suggest that—nor were they simply determined to do so by genetic mutations that were automatically "replicated."[24] They set flexible enabling conditions and limits from which creative evolution proceeded.

So I suspect that Whitehead, though he has a hand to play, overplays it. It may be that his doctrine of eternal objects both reduces the scope of possible creativity in the world and obscures some dimensions of real danger to the human estate in a cosmos composed of multiple, interacting force fields. That "may be" is pertinent, since I concur with Whitehead that a philosophy of becoming, as well as those with which it competes, contains a "speculative" element that can be defended comparatively by reference to evidence and argument but is unlikely to be susceptible to definitive proof.

On this latter point, the great logician and mathematician concurs in an uncanny way with the philologist Nietzsche, though he apparently had not read Nietzsche. The powers of logic are inflated by those who ignore the unconscious, creative work that must be done by entities to absorb into themselves outside energies. And that smoothing is doubled if the mobility and entanglements of thinking are then flattened out into identities from which definitive logical arguments proceed. A credible philosophy, Whitehead thinks, can seek rough coherence, but, given the interentanglements of things, thought, and language, it is unlikely to be demonstrable. Classical logic and process do not mesh neatly, just as time and closed transcendental arguments do not. There are, apparently, modes of logic and mathematics through which such complexity and openness can be better expressed.[25]

## WILL TO POWER AND CONSTRAINED POSSIBILITY

If you read some of Nietzsche's experimental formulations, particularly those collected in the *Will to Power*, through the lens provided by Whitehead some interesting things happen. For, first, the latter's concepts help illuminate some things that Nietzsche, writing before the advent of quantum mechanics, was trying to say. And, second, we soon reach a point at which persisting differences between them can be seen more clearly, thus opening up issues that we—the "we" is invitational—can seek to resolve.

In several notes Nietzsche focuses on creative condensations in the rush of action-oriented perception forward and the process of thinking.[26] These condensations occur *before* a tight logical argument starts to do its work. His formulations touch those made by Whitehead when the latter presents human consciousness as the afterglow of a complex organization that precedes it and when he also contends that the light consciousness can shine on itself is weak. But Nietzsche moves further. He suggests that modes of creative self-organization of simple organisms, and even of some nonorganic processes, display traces that find complex expression in human feeling, perception, thinking, and judgment. In Whitehead's terms Nietzsche injects an aesthetic element of attraction and repulsion into the nonhuman world, that is, into nonhuman expressions of the "will to power" from which the impetus to creative evolution proceeds. Here are a few formulations:

> "Thinking" in primitive conditions (pre-organic) is the crystallization of forms, as in the case of crystal.

> All thought, judgment, perception, considered as comparison, has as its precondition a "positing of equality," and earlier still a "making equal." The process of making equal is the process of incorporation of appropriated material in the amoeba.

> The fundamental inclination to posit as equal . . . is modified, held in check, by considerations of usefulness and harmfulness. . . . This whole process corresponds exactly to that external mechanical process (which is its symbol) by which protoplasm makes what it appropriates equal to itself and fits it into its own forms and files.[27]

It is wise not to move *too* quickly from the preorganic and organic instances Nietzsche cites to his critique of the philosopher's excessive trust in logic, though that upshot is pertinent too. Nietzsche's basic point parallels that made by Whitehead in pointing to modes of attraction and repulsion in some preorganic and simple organic processes that enable negative and positive prehensions. Moreover, creative processes of self-organization in the receiving entities enable them not merely, say, to *represent* similarity as identity but to work on the digested elements until they *become* more "equal," until they are actually "incorporated" or fit "into its own forms and files."

The "absorbing and fitting" activity means both that the ingested elements change as they are metabolized and that the receiving, organizing entity changes too. The aesthetic and creative elements in a world of becoming are expressed together in these passages. Representational thinking, you might say, comes into play after the organic processes of absorption and equalization have occurred.

The most fundamental dimension of "will to power" is expressed in activities of creative relation and becoming, though the most habitual Euro-American reception of that phrase obscures this dimension in favor of others also there, such as drives to domination and expansion. The phrase Nietzsche adopts too readily suppresses other pregnant dimensions rolling around in it so that a post-Nietzschean with Whiteheadian affinities may find it wise to replace "will to power" with other expressions. Once these preliminary moves are made, a potential debate is now opened up between Whitehead and Nietzsche about the proportionate roles played by creative reception and creative expansion in the universe.

But before dropping the phrase, let's listen to a subtext operating *within* the Nietzschean theme of domination in relational processes, as we note again how for him, too, such creativity includes and extends beyond the human estate:

> Physicists believe in a "true world" in their own fashion, a firm systematization of atoms in necessary motion, the same for all beings. . . . But they are in error. The atom they posit is inferred according to the logic of perspectivism of consciousness and is therefore a subjective fiction. This world picture that they sketch differs in no essential way from the subjective world picture: it is only construed with more extended senses [with microscopes, etc.] but with *our* senses nonetheless—And in any case they left something out of the constellation without knowing it: *precisely this necessary perspectivism by virtue of which every center of force—and not only man—construes all the rest of the world from its own viewpoint, i.e., measures, feels, forms, according to its own force.* . . . (Emphasis added.)
>
> My idea is that every specific body strives to become master over all space and to extend its force (its will to power) and to thrust back all that resists its extension. But it continually encounters similar efforts on the part of other bodies and ends by coming to an arrangement (a "union") with those of them that are sufficiently related to it: thus they then conspire together for power. And the process goes on.[28]

The resonances between Whitehead and Nietzsche are intense here. First, subjectivity is not a ground of being. It is a formation. Second, subjectivity and intersubjectivity are not only ineliminable, they find differential degrees of expression in numerous processes outside the human estate that are entangled with it. Every "center of force" or "actual entity" expresses a "perspective" through which it receives and repels potential relations. It "measures, feels, forms, according to its own force." Third, that is why it is often wise for us to extend our capacities of sensitivity to other force fields, to the extent it is possible to do so. Fourth, Nietzsche, before the advent of quantum theory, joins Whitehead in advance in resisting the sufficiency of efficient causality and impositional laws of nature.

Doing these things, Nietzsche also becomes suspicious of the typical replies critical philosophers make to mechanistic theories, in which they merely point to an element of "chance" in change. Chance, you might say, is the only counter to invoke if you yourself both think that much of the universe is mechanistic and lack a philosophy of creative process. So Nietzsche, who rejects the sufficiency of *both* the organic and mechanical images, projects relations that exceed mechanical cause without reducing the excess entirely to chance. He says that we need "to recognize the active force, the creative force in the chance event—chance itself is only the clash of creative impulses."[29] He thus moves in advance toward the Whitehead idea that creative change is irreducible to chance, mere unpredictability, or efficient cause. Or when chance is in play, it is often the result of intense interactions between two exploratory processes. The intense *vibrations* back and forth between two entities that enter into relations of accelerated disequilibrium sometimes set new possibilities of being into play that exceeds the efficient causality of either or both in aggregate. This makes creativity an ultimate property of the universe, not entirely reducible to classic categories of explanation, not entirely assimilable to bits of chance within mechanical processes, and incompatible with finalist conceptions of being. It is probably the bogeyman of finalism that has discouraged many from exploring teleodynamic processes periodically involved in real creativity.

You might say that Nietzsche embraces the idea of transcendence as that which is going beyond what has been, but he does not accept it as a *being* beyond, a divinity whose commands or love are separate from humanity and reach down into it to a problematic degree. The terms of connection and dissonance between Whitehead and Nietzsche at this point become delicate.[30]

Out of such periodic encounters between entities of different types a new "union" or "arrangement" is sometimes forged, bringing something new into the world—a new bacterium-arsenic bond, a new bird/human flu jump, a new weather pattern, a new climate system, a new social movement, a new religious practice, a new economic system. Finally, as the previous formulations by Nietzsche suggest, he and Whitehead concur that no entity beyond the most simple *merely* seeks to preserve itself. Both contend that such entities, though to varying degrees, exude excess energies, loose ends, and unsettled remainders, which, when a new situation arises, may excite novel vibrations. Even protoplasm, Nietzsche says, does not just aim at self-preservation, "for it takes into itself absurdly more than would be required to preserve it."[31] This is the most fecund meaning of will to power, the aspect that I have elsewhere tried to adumbrate under the "powers of the false."[32]

So the affinities between these two thinkers are real, and each helps us highlight elements in the other that might otherwise slip away. The differences, however, are also notable. Nietzsche may not focus enough on the degree of responsiveness we must cultivate to allow something new to become creatively consolidated in our thought or lives, although there are places in *Thus Spoke Zarathustra* that move in this direction. Nietzsche also gives no sense of accepting something like Whitehead's notion of eternal objects that, first, help mediate creative relations between mobile entities, second, help explain what holds things together, and, third, set limits to creativity in concrete situations

Finally, Nietzsche not only challenges an omnipotent God as a personal, moraline Being who monopolizes creativity and commands us to be moral, he would also be wary of the Whiteheadian impersonal God who provides an impetus to creative unions and collects the complexities that emerge as the universe advances from lower to higher levels of complexity. He hesitates, perhaps out of concern for the history of uses to which the name has been put, to give the name God to such an impetus. Nietzsche is more attracted to the contending gods of Hesiod, translating them into a world of multiple, interacting force fields ungoverned by an overriding center, moving at different speeds and degrees of complexity. He, again, responds to them by including the idea of transcendence as a reaching and going beyond that is purely naturalistic.

## NEGOTIATING THE DIFFERENCES

I take Nietzsche to concur in advance with my attempt to qualify eternal objects with conditional processes of preadaptation that periodically set the platform for a new creative "union." He criticizes Darwinism, I think, because the version he received diminished or eliminated the creative element in species evolution.

Let's briefly compare him to Whitehead on aesthetic relations. In a discussion of the "Gift Giving Virtue" in *Thus Spoke Zarathustra*, Zarathustra speaks of an aesthetic drive to expand the "inflow" of experience and to allow that influx to become organized unconsciously by the human sensorium until a new sensitivity and excess of energy become available to bestow "gifts" of generosity upon others and the earth. The "others" he has in mind are particularly those whose professions of faith, identity, self-interest, and moral imperative differ from yours in important respects. For example, nobility cannot be unless several nobilities, expressing different existential creeds, contend with and against each other in noble ways. Thus, to Zarathustra and Nietzsche, the ground of morality is not found in a transcendent command or a set of universal principles from which concrete imperatives are "derived." Such conceptions are too lazy and crude for a world marked by twists and turns that periodically challenge congealed habits. We need to cultivate presumptions of care and agonistic generosity to draw on as we respond to new, unexpected situations. We need to pursue a "spiritualization of enmity" with others, to the extent they allow it, in which each accepts the agony of challenge to its heartfelt beliefs, and each also challenges the other. We also need to stretch our sensory, perceptual, experimental, and conceptual powers so that the species and cultural provincialisms with which we start can be extended. This, at least, is one side of Nietzsche, though it is periodically compromised by other moods.

Whitehead would pursue such adventures more consistently. He expresses a debt to Wordsworth's nature poetry in which our sensitivity is enhanced by visiting protean scenes twice, the first time to receive the inflow of experience and the second to amplify its effect on memory and future powers of perception. From this perspective Nietzsche, despite his alter ego's love of the earth, still may not do enough to cultivate heightened sensitivity to various aspects of the nonhuman world. The domination element in will to power sings too loudly. In a world composed of multiple attractions and repulsions that exceed our everyday practices of action-oriented perception, we need to work on ourselves to become more *responsive* to the artistry of whales who compose music as they travel, to the quantum complexity of bird powers of sonar navigation, to the self-organizing powers of ocean currents, to the complexity of lava flows that issue in unpredictable patterns of granite, to the simple, unconscious intentionality of a bacterium as it adjusts its movement up a glucose gradient, and to yeast as the intense sounds it emits express feelings of pain when alcohol is poured on it. The aesthetic element of becoming finds expression in Nietzsche, but the human/nonhuman dimension of aesthetic relations is pursued even more sensitively by Whitehead.

Jane Bennett, Timothy Morton, Davide Panagia, Brian Massumi, and Anatoli Ignatov make valuable contributions to this dimension of being.[33] Today, new scientific instruments and artistic endeavors—and often both together—can alert and extend our perceptual and relational capacities. They can sensitize us to some aspects of processes that were previously opaque to us, as when, for instance, biologists amplify the sounds of yeast when it is at rest and when alcohol has been poured on it and the intensity of its perturbations increases. Nietzsche, let us say, was *not enough* of a romantic in this respect, even if his Dionsysianism carried him to the edge of that movement and even if he had reasons to question *other* aspects of romanticism.

What are those "other aspects"? Nietzsche, much more than Whitehead, measured in advance cultural resistance to signs in favor of a world of becoming on the part of many who had imbibed Judaism, Islam, and Christianity for centuries and, in some cases, then unconsciously absorbed "the remains" of those theologies into Enlightenment/secular notions of linear, progressive time, a deterministic model of science, a moral image of the world, or the promise of human mastery. Moreover, Nietzsche also detected resistance to an ungoverned cosmos of becoming in romantic drives. The romantic drive, he thinks, was to find a world predisposed in its largest compass to the human estate as such. Whether he is right about those judgments is an interesting issue. Perhaps it fits some cases and not others.

But, regardless, Nietzsche, the modern philosopher of an ungoverned cosmos, was highly sensitized to subterranean currents of existential resentment that proliferate when many harbor suspicions that disrupt two familiar and contending images of cosmic reassurance: the idea of secular mastery and the idea of divine providence. The issue of ressentiment now enters the scene, with the embattled Nietzsche more alert to its modes of expression and danger than the magisterial Whitehead.

## THE COSMOPOLITICAL DIMENSION

It is serious enough to resent, first, human mortality and, second, time's "it was" in which you cannot reverse past events or actions you regret the most. A third, related, dimension is activated when people who have imbibed traditional monotheisms and/or secular/humanist notions of human uniqueness encounter living evidence on behalf of a bumpy, multitiered world of becoming. Today such encounters can be resisted but perhaps not easily ignored. They are lodged in the accelerated pace of some dimensions of cultural life in dissonant relation to other slow processes, in the rapid, global, media communication of earthshaking natural events, in scientific speculations about the evolution of the cosmos as well as solid evidence of species evolution, in renewed intensities of conflict between regionally anchored religions with contending claims to universality in a world of rapid communication, in recent research in neuroscience that makes the human body-brain-culture system look closer to a teleodynamic system oscillating between decoherence and coherence than to either a carrier of free will floating above earthly life or a system of mechanical causes, in impressive evidence of previously unexpected conjunctions between late capitalism and the acceleration of climate change that upsets the idea of an autonomous nature, in action-oriented films required to inflate human powers of heroism grotesquely to retain an image of mastery, and in widespread experiments in film that complicate action-oriented modes of perception with the uncanny complexity of duration. Such experiences can accumulate to jolt previous assumptions about the place of humanity in the cosmos. They can, therefore, amplify intensities of existential resentment in many, as those intensities surge *through* the issue of mortality and teeth gnashing over the "it was" *into* anxieties about the shaky place of the human estate in the cosmos.

Such cosmic issues have never been absent, as several religious traditions testify. But the issue does wax and wane in its political expressions, and we are living through a global time when it waxes, a period when every creedal minority in a world of minorities is acutely aware of how several others define and respond to the issues.

When such existential issues are inflamed, they do not remain confined to the late-night anxieties of isolated individuals. They become burned into institutional practices and political conflicts, infusing media news reporting, church assemblies, consumption practices, investment routines, electoral campaigns, state priorities, military elites, action films, global conflicts, and the resonances back and forth between these venues. Such anxieties are not always *confessed*, for such confessions too readily challenge official *professions* of secular or religious confidence. They are *expressed* indirectly in the exacerbation of religious struggles, in the avoidance of certain issues, in hyper-confidence in the impersonal rationality of economic markets, and in the demonization of constituencies who address the fragility of things. For today we need to slow down and divert human intrusions into various planetary force fields, even as we speed up efforts to reconstitute the identities, spiritualities, consumption practices, market faiths, and state policies entangled with them. This tension helps constitute the contemporary fragility of things.

Today we encounter not just the issue of mortality, or the precariousness of a state, or the severe challenges to this or that civilization. Those, as it were, continue, and they can be agonizing. Today we encounter intensely again the fragility of a human estate entangled by a thousand threads and resonances to a cosmos of multiple force fields, most of which are not first and foremost predisposed to our welfare. Our world has moved closer to that of Hesiod and Sophocles. When you link the fatefulness of these imbrications to the acceleration, intensification, and globalization of neoliberal capitalism, the situation becomes yet more highly inflamed. For these planetary force fields set on different tiers of chronotime—such as climate patterns, glacier flows, viral evolution across species, bacteria in our guts, tectonic plate movements, water-filtering processes, the ocean conveyor belt, and processes of soil self-renewal—pose challenges to both received conceptions of time and to the anticipated trajectory of capitalism. Since both of these latter traditions are wound deeply into the ethos of modern life itself, the tension we have posed easily slides into a cul-de-sac: The planetary fragility of things is increasingly sensed; and many protest against admission of that very sense to remain loyal to traditions of belonging woven into their bodies, role performances, and institutions. Festering there, such anxieties *could* morph into concerted experiments to modify established patterns of attachment and belonging. But they can also become transposed into bellicose political movements of denial and deferral, movements joined to virulent attacks on any constituency that challenges the complementary modes of cosmic and civilizational assurance already in place. Witness the media attacks on scientists of climate change and proponents of sustainable energy. Or think about the dogmatism with which many impugn any notion of species evolution, because it might open the possibility that neither a creator God nor military might nor benign capitalism really rules the world. Or think about those new atheists who dismiss with disdain every theological faith or concern for spiritual vitality. Or, again, think about the dismissiveness with which a subset of scientists, secularists, and religious leaders treats the hypothesis that we inhabit a cosmos of becoming. Or, finally, consider how carriers of the evangelical/neoliberal machine in the United States reject the legitimacy of every exploratory effort to rethink either the terms of capitalism or the creeds with which capitalism is closely entangled. These examples could easily be extended to other places and domains. But we have perhaps cited enough to indicate how many "signs" available today cut against the reassuring set Kant identified at a high point during the Christian Enlightenment.

Nietzsche was prescient about the contemporary escalation of ressentiment as cosmic uncertainty rumbles again beneath cultural refusals to articulate it. He sensed the potential cul de sac in advance, as a seer traces one tendency in play among others to sense where it might go if it is inflated. He also composed one alternative *response* to the existential suffering that comes with being alive and self-conscious. He calls it "my theodicy," with the word "my" bringing out both its contestable character and his identification with it. Here is one way he put it:

> This type of *artist's pessimism* is precisely the *opposite* of that religio-moral pessimism that suffers from the "corruption" of man and the riddle of existence—and that by all means craves a solution. . . . The profundity of the tragic *artist* lies in this, that his aesthetic instinct surveys the remote consequences . . . , that he affirms *the large scale economy* which justifies the terrible, the evil, the questionable—and more than merely justifies them.[34]

Before we appraise the *double-entry* approach Nietzsche sometimes embraces in his own *theodicy*, we need to be clear about the entry he embraces in his own voice in pursuit of a positive "spiritualization of enmity" with other voices. Nietzsche himself affirms "the large scale economy" of an ungoverned cosmos of becoming that includes and surpasses us. That is, he "more than justifies" it in the sense that we can affirm or resent this world but are unable to change its most fundamental parameters. He does not take delight in human suffering and evil, though some love to deflect his challenge by pretending so. Nor does he merely *believe* in an ungoverned cosmos with fluctuating periods of relative quiescence and unruliness in its entanglements with the human estate. Rather, he first acknowledges the experience of existential suffering that involvement in such a cosmos engenders; second, he calls on us to subdue and sublimate that suffering by tactical means; third, additionally he appreciates *that* mode of suffering as a possible condition of creative thinking and action; and, fourth, he works to *affirm* the sweetness and vitality of life in such a cosmos. He treats the cosmos as a precarious condition of possibility for the sweetness of human life and attachment to the world. He seeks to drain existential resentment from existential experience to overcome or divert destructive and self-destructive human drives.

He admits on several occasions that his is only one positive "conjecture" through which to acknowledge and address the human predicament. The hope is that many who adopt other cosmic creeds will also affirm the gift-giving virtue in their worldly relations with diverse creeds, even though he came to doubt that a majority could or would do so. Given the more rapid minoritization of the world and the globalization of fragility since the time of Nietzsche, it is now even more urgent to forge a positive ethos of engagement between diverse and contending creeds.

Nietzsche, as I dramatize tendencies discernible in his work, adopts a double-entry relation to other perspectives. He first evangelizes an ungoverned cosmos that exceeds the assumptions of providence, human uniqueness, and mastery. In doing so, he works on us to *affirm* simultaneously (a) the sweetness and miracle of life in which mortality is unavoidable and extreme misfortune very possible, (b) the irreversibility of time and "it was," and (c) modest human participation in creative powers that extend into an ungoverned cosmos composed of multiple force fields. We belong to that world, amid the temporary enclosures we construct and maintain to provide sustenance in it. It too comes with pleasures, disruptions, and periods of creativity. As Nietzsche says in defense of a tragic *vision* of *possibility* and a critique of tragic *resignation*, "the faith that a good meaning lies in evil means to abandon the struggle against it."[35]

In a second gesture, however, Nietzsche affirms, when he is at his best, that the theodicy he embraces is not the only affirmative way to engage things. There are others. They become "noble" when practitioners of this or that *creed* of immanence or transcendence mix into it a spirituality of cosmic gratitude and draw on it to pursue positive assemblages with carriers of other creeds. So, when he is not mesmerized by the judgment that only a very few noble ones in any faith will ever entertain relations of agonistic respect across difference, he offers his *theodicy* as *one* minority faith to press into comparative exchanges with others. Who knows, a potent pluralist assemblage could eventually emerge from such crossings and contestations, though Nietzsche's double, Zarathustra, himself shied away eventually from investing hope in politics.[36]

Dropping the phrase "will to power" and playing up more than he did the fragility of things, I otherwise embrace much in Nietzsche's vision of the cosmos and the human relation to it. I admire the double-entry approach he sometimes pursued in relations with other visions, and I seek to press it more consistently. And Whitehead? My double-entry stance in its first gesture pulls me a little distance from Whitehead's cosmic image of ever-growing complexity, but it then expresses a welcome indebtedness in a second move to the way he pursues the question of creativity and the affirmative *spirituality* he brings to an open cosmos. My sense is that periods of real creativity in the evolution of worldly objects and systems may be even more robust at key junctures, for good or ill, than Whitehead imagined. This sense distances me from his notions of eternal objects, automatic tendencies toward greater complexity, and an impersonal God who conveys new levels of complexity into the future, even as I accept the idea that a previous mode of complexity sets a condition of possibility from which new ones may evolve. So Whitehead has a hand to play here, but he may push it too far.[37] To accept it unrevised may be to underplay the human risks of hubris, complacency, and ressentiment in late-modern capitalism.

It must be emphasized that the positive spirituality Whitehead pours into his speculative philosophy is at least as affirmative as that of Nietzsche, and more consistently so. These two process philosophers are thus worthy protagonists from whom others can draw sustenance: They advance contending, overlapping cosmic creeds that speak to today; they address the spiritual quality through which a creed is lived in relation to others; and they throw up for grabs a set of established, complementary assumptions during a period when many constituencies both feel and suppress doubts about those assurances. Each, at his best, argues with the carriers of other creeds while inviting their proponents to fold positive spiritualities into their creedal relations.

When you fold intercoded concepts such as "the human estate," "a cosmos of becoming," "heterogeneous, intersecting planetary force fields," "a tragic vision of possibility," "existential resentment," "existential affirmation," "the fragility of things," and "the spiritualization of enmity" into interpretations and interventions that are also pitched at the levels of local, state, interstate and global politics, political thought may approach the layered, exploratory engagements appropriate to the contemporary condition. Now interpretation becomes more multilayered so that dicey intersections between late capitalism, regional religious practices, and nonhuman, planetary forces with their own powers of metamorphosis become more closely defined *objects* of inquiry. Not by striving to encompass everything about all of them in one totalizing system, for a philosophy of becoming engages multiple scales without enacting closure. You proceed, rather, by tracing a significant problem complex up and down its scales of intercalation and imbrication wherever such a slippery adventure takes it. You become a problem-oriented pragmatist while expanding the potential scope of fields relevant to those problems. This means, for instance, that sometimes you attend to how existential issues and anxieties infiltrate into specific political formations and at others you sink into how a glacier amplification process and capitalism impinge on one another. You engage the planetary dimension of politics when you explore how ocean current flows, climate patterns, regional patterns of drought and flood, water self-purification processes, hurricane patterns, and so on impinge on us and cultural processes impinge on them. You touch the cosmic dimension when you consider how tacit and articulated images of the cosmos itself fold into established patterns of response to local, global, and planetary processes. Each must be engaged in relation to the others.

The existential tempers of ressentiment, hubris, and studied complacency, discernible as contending spiritual forces invested in politics today, may not simply be distributed as diverse responses by different constituencies to larger world processes. It may be, as Sophocles showed in another era, that each temper often subsists as a minor chord in the others, so that today some evangelical and secular carriers of ressentiment are also activated by a degree of hubris, so that neoliberal and military purveyors of hubris often convey subtones of existential resentment, and so that many "moderate" carriers of studied complacency contain enough traces of the first two spiritualities to be more susceptible to contagion from them than otherwise would be the case.

To speak of a cultural constellation composed of multiple existential tones and subtonalities is to point to a generic feature of contemporary life. It secretes a shifting politics of surge and flow across diverse constituencies. The complex that emerges is not entirely reducible either to traits of individual character or to fixed cultural blocks. The entanglements and movements are too variable and invested in the vicissitudes of political life to succumb entirely to either mode of analysis. In something like the way the tones, themes, and refrains of a piece of music performed in a concert hall with excellent acoustics saturate the room as the music waxes and wanes, so too do the shifting tones of hubris, ressentiment, and studied complacency inflect constituency and interconstituency relations. That is the danger. In the United States, at least, one strategic constituency singularly susceptible to allowing the first two tones to pour into its complacency calls itself the cadre of "moderates" and "independents."

Some of the dangerous combinations erupt during protean periods when interruptions shock established modes of identity and reassurance, as with the Lisbon quake during one moment, the introduction of Darwin's theory of evolution at another, the shock of the European holocaust, the dropping of nuclear bombs on Japan, and the slow burn of conjunctions between capitalism and climate change today. Such examples could be multiplied. Nonetheless, if and as extreme demands for the cosmic entitlement of the human estate are subdued, suitable spiritual arts are more widely adopted by more constituencies, and a politics of positive engagement with the fragility of things is actively pressed by a positive constellation of minorities, it may also be possible to expand the cadre whose political commitments express attachment to the planet. Besides the dangers they bring, some shocks and interruptions set conditions of possibility for positive modes of creative action. We can take the examples listed in chapter 2 of *The Fragility of Things* as instances of the latter. At some level, many already exude differential degrees of gratitude for the vitality of human existence, the modes of attachment it makes available, and the creative adventures it opens.

This, then, is a *cosmic* dimension folded into contemporary politics, in part because it speaks to a time when several planetary force fields become entangled densely with several aspects of daily life, in part because our capacities to explore and respond politically to such imbrications with affirmative intelligence are severely challenged, in part because dangerous existential dispositions surge and flow again into defining institutions of late modern life, and in part because these very intersections convey the need to rethink the contemporary condition.

Nietzsche and Whitehead articulate the planetary and cosmic dimensions in diverse concepts and affective tones that also touch, though neither may have anticipated how densely planetary processes with differing degrees of self-organizing power are entangled today with local, regional, and global issues. Each expresses, in his inimical way, a spirit of deep attachment to a cosmos of dispersed, conditioned processes; each, if he were to confront the contemporary condition, might appreciate the potential contribution an ethos of existential gratitude forged across territories, constituencies, and existential creeds could make to addressing the fragility of things. Or so I project into the magisterial Whitehead and the volatile, agonistic Nietzsche. The task, merely launched here, is to draw selective sustenance from each to think our place in the cosmos, to come to terms with the fragility of things at local, regional, global, and planetary sites, and to fend off the existential resentment that threatens to become severe under late-modern conditions.

NOTES

1. This chapter is a revised version of chapter 4 of the author's *The Fragility of Things: Self-Organizing Processes, Neoliberal Fantasies, and Democratic Activisms* (Durham, N.C.: Duke University Press, 2013).
2. Friedrich Nietzsche, *The Pre-Platonic Philosophers* (Urbana: University of Illinois Press, 2001), 64.
3. Ibid., 60, 62, 62, 63.
4. Friedrich Nietzsche, *Twilight of the Idols* (Harmondsworth, Eng.: Penguin, 1968), 35. How, it is surely to be asked, does this formulation, and innumerable others like it in several Nietzschean texts, square with the idea of the eternal return as the return of long cycles, in which everything that becomes during one cosmic cycle returns in exactly that mode in future cycles? There is no tension if this idea is merely posed as an existential test: "Would you choose life again if everything in it repeats?" But Nietzsche, besides treating it as only a test sometimes also experiments with long cycles as a metaphysical theme. To me, that theme is incompatible with a real philosophy of becoming. So to the extent that Nietzsche supports a philosophy of long cycles, I oppose that philosophy. I am drawing on the numerous other elements in his exploratory thinking.
5. See Karen Barad, *Meeting the Universe Halfway: Quantum Physics and the Entanglement of Matter and Meaning* (Durham, N.C.: Duke University Press, 2007). Barad contends that Heisenberg's rendering of the "uncertainty principle" is corrected by Bohr in a way that the former eventually accepts and that Bohr replaces his own early account with a reading that becomes increasingly ontological, in which the "complementarity issue" becomes more central, i.e., the inability to detect both position and momentum in the same test procedure. The entanglement of test and object, Barad says, signifies the entangled character of becoming itself rather than merely expressing an effect of limited human instruments of detection on a world otherwise following classical laws.
6. Michael Epperson, *Quantum Mechanics and the Philosophy of Alfred North Whitehead* (New York: Fordham University Press, 2004), 56.
7. Ibid., 51.
8. Ibid., 102.
9. As Stuart Kauffman summarizes the claim, "After the particles are entangled they can separate to arbitrary distances at speeds up to the speed of light and remain entangled, and if one of the particles 'is measured' as having a given property the other particle instantaneously has a corresponding property. This deeply puzzling feature of quantum mechanics gave Einstein the gravest concern. . . . The

implied instantaneous correspondence has now been confirmed experimentally, and is called nonlocality." Stuart Kauffman, *Reinventing the Sacred* (New York: Basic Books, 2008), 221.
10. Whitehead can be called both a process philosopher and a speculative realist. The latter term speaks to the speculative element explicitly invested in his philosophy and the important role that the persistence of "actual entities" plays in it. These terms speak not only to Whitehead but to an interesting group of philosophers who until recently had called themselves "object oriented" philosophers. Some now call themselves speculative realists. One leader is Graham Harman, whose book *Prince of Networks: Bruno Latour and Metaphysics* (Prahran, Vic., Aus.: Re.Press, 2009) is very rich. It distinguishes itself from thinkers such as Gilles Deleuze by labeling them "lump ontologists" and radical "relationists." Bruno Latour and Whitehead come out a bit better in this text, though they too are criticized for being too relationist. My sense is that Whitehead has it about right on this score. He focuses on the *entangled* stability of "actual entities," as they periodically morph. For a recent discussion of the issues with which I largely agree see Jane Bennett's response to the interesting essays by Harman and Morton in "Systems and Things: A Response to Harman and Morton," *New Literary History* 43, no. 2 (2012): 205–24.
11. Alfred North Whitehead, *Process and Reality: Corrected Edition* (New York: Free Press, 1978), 7.
12. Whitehead is not shy about using the terms "metaphysical" and "cosmological" because he thinks such modes of reflection are essential to thought about science, ethics, human culture, and nonhuman forces that impinge on all of these. He presents his distinctive ontocosmology as speculative in a way that presses others to come to terms more reflectively with the ontocosmologies they hold. His can be coherently developed in relation to recent scientific findings and cultural experience, but it is unlikely to be proven. It is, in my terms, *defensible* in that it brings arguments and evidence forward to support it and *contestable* in that some other readings could credibly make sense of the processes under review.
13. Whitehead, *Process and Reality: Corrected Edition*, 94.
14. The question arises, how deep into organic and nonorganic process do traces of creativity sink? The quotation about vector feeling suggests that they sink far indeed for Whitehead. In *Incomplete Nature*, Terence Deacon distinguishes between thermodynamic, morphodynamic and teleodynamic processes. He would probably reserve the word "creative" for organic processes with teleodynamic capacities. He defines "autogens" as intermediate, autocatalytic processes of an unusual complexity that most probably allowed life to emerge from nonlife (New York: W. W. Norton, 2012). I want to keep the issue of creativity relatively open for now, once we proceed beyond systems that clearly express a teleodynamic dynamic.
15. Paul Richards, "Scientists Discover a Bacteria That Can Grow in Arsenic," http://www.discountvouchers.co.uk/news/scientists-discover-a-bacteria-that-can-grow-in-arsenic-8963.html (accessed July 5, 2014).
16. Isabelle Stengers, in *Thinking wth Whitehead*, admirably works on the texts as she charts changes that emerge as his work proceeds and as he does not go back to

identify that a change has been made (Cambridge, Mass.: Harvard University Press, 2012). A thinker in process.

17. For two recent books that explore these issues, with both favoring what I am calling panexperientialism, see Galen Strawson et al., *Consciousness and Its Place in Nature* (Charlottesville, Va.: Imprint Academy, 2006), and David Skribna, *Panpsychism in the West* (Boston: MIT Press, 2007).
18. Connolly, *Fragility of Things*, Second Interlude, 349, 339.
19. Whitehead, *Process and Reality*, 291.
20. Whitehead, *Adventures of Ideas* (New York: Macmillan, 1933), 251.
21. Whitehead, *Process and Reality*, 349, 339.
22. Philip Ball, in *The Self-Made Tapestry*, explores a whole host of patterns that recur in different domains of nature and culture, as they also evolve into new forms. This quote may give a sense of his project and the way in which it could open a promising conversation with Whitehead on eternal objects. "Competition lies at the heart of beauty and complexity in pattern formation. If the competition is too one-sided all form disappears. . . . Patterns live on the edge, in a fertile borderland between these extremes (randomness and featureless homogeneity), where small changes can have large effects. . . . Pattern occurs when competing forces banish uniformity but cannot quite induce chaos. It sounds like a dangerous place to be, but it is where we have always lived" (New York: Oxford University Press, 1999), 253.
23. Brian Goodwin, *How the Leopard Changed Its Spots* (Princeton: Princeton University Press, 1994). Here is a sample of what Goodwin says: "The first is a hind limb that belonged to a fossil fish *Ichthyostega*, from the Devonian period. The second is the hind limb of a salamander. Then there are the wings of a bird and a bat, the front leg of a horse and a human arm" (142). His point is that, when you observe these similarities and differences of pattern you detect how the later could have evolved from the former. Some may have set preliminary conditions from which others evolved.
24. Evan Thompson, in *Mind in Life*, provides an excellent review of critiques of the "genocentric" model in recent biological work (Cambridge, Mass.: Harvard University Press, 2007). I came across this book as my study was nearing completion. The more I sink into it, the more it seems to complement and enrich the thinking pursued here. I agree, for example, that neuroscience and phenomenology need each other. I pursue that issue in an essay, "Experience and Experiment," *Daedalus* 135, no. 3 (2006): 67–76, and in chapter 2 of *A World of Becoming* (Durham, N.C.: Duke University Press, 2011).
25. In *Reinventing the Sacred* Stuart Kauffman charts several processes that are not susceptible to algorithmic treatment now and, he suspects, will not be in the future (New York: Basic Books, 2008).
26. Friedrich Nietzsche, *The Will to Power*, trans. Walter Kaufmann (New York: Vintage Books, 1968) ##501, 512, 514, 515, 516, 517.
27. Ibid., ##499, 501, 510.
28. Ibid., #636.
29. Ibid., #673.

30. My thinking on this point is sharpened by an email from Catherine Keller in 2012. She suggested that transcendence does not have to be merely a being beyond; it can also be a going beyond. I concur, noting only how the pair immanence and transcendence now become a very tricky pair, with each maintaining some distance on some renderings of transcendence—*being* beyond, the outside as *divine*—while at least partially flipping into the other on a couple of other readings—the *outside* and *going* beyond. Whitehead and Nietzsche have more affinities with each other across distance than either does with strong finalism or determinism.
31. Nietzsche, *Will to Power*, #651.
32. Connolly, *World of Becoming*, chap. 4.
33. Jane Bennett, *Vibrant Matter* (Durham, N.C.: Duke University Press, 2010); Timothy Morton, *The Ecological Thought* (Cambridge, Mass.: Harvard University Press, 2010); Davide Panagia, *The Political Life of Sensation* (Durham, N.C.: Duke University Press, 2009); Brian Massumi, *Semblance and Event* (Cambridge, Mass.: MIT Press, 2011); Anatoli Ignatov, "Practices of Eco-Sensation," *Theory and Event* 14, no. 2 (2011): 1–22.
34. Nietzsche, *Will to Power*, #852, pp. 449–53.
35. Ibid., #1019, pp. 526–27.
36. In *Identity/Difference* (Minneapolis: University of Minnesota Press, 2002), I examine the metaphors Zarathustra uses to justify a world in which "passing by" those who seek to pull down a spiritual nobility is possible and politics is avoidable. My argument is that those spatial metaphors of relative isolation no longer carry the same weight in a world in which distance has become compressed, the pace of many processes has accelerated, and the interinvolvement of everyone with everything has intensified. This chapter presupposes those arguments.
37. In a 2010 exploratory seminar I taught on Whitehead and Nietzsche, some students argued that Whitehead had, at least by the time of *Adventures of Ideas*, softened the presentation of eternal ideas so that they assumed a character close to pure potential. I merely say that *insofar* as Whitehead retains a strong reading of eternal objects and an impersonal God, I contest that reading while also respecting it. However, those (like me) who support a more open rendering of the cosmos still have to cope more closely with the question, "What, then, holds evolving things together?" I would like to express my appreciation to the students in the 2010 seminar for the contributions they made to our collective understanding of issues posed by the conjunctions and disjunctions between Nietzsche and Whitehead. This essay is indebted to those debates and discussions.

# How Not to Be a Religion: Genealogy, Identity, Wonder

JOHN THATAMANIL

## ON THE CURIOUS TALK OF RELIGION'S RETURN OR RESURGENCE

Sociologists, political theorists, and theologians now not only recognize that the long forecasted death of religion has failed to materialize but observe instead that religion has returned, with teeth: *Diehard with a Vengeance*, starring not Bruce Willis but Jerry Falwell and the Moral Majority in the United States, Narendra Modi and the BJP in India, and Mohamed Morsi and the Muslim Brotherhood in Cairo. But just what is this "religion" that has returned? Where was it in the offing?

What if secularization is itself responsible for the invention of "religion"? Or put more precisely, what if "the secular" and "the religious" both coemerge from the process of modernization? What if modernity invented religion precisely in order to marginalize it?[1] On such an account, "resurgent religion" may be best understood as a politicized version of a *relatively recent* creation. What returns is not what was once dismissed. But if religion is in fact a late development, then religion cannot be imagined as always already there waiting to be distilled out from adventitious accretions and then confined to the private sphere.

The constitution, marginalization, and resurgence of a phenomenon that is anything but ancient suggest that we must interrogate the very configuration of religion qua religion (and the secular qua secular—with the political securely residing within the latter) before venturing projects that attempt to stipulate the proper relationship between the religious and the political. Too often, conversation proceeds under the assumption that we know what the religious and the political essentially and even transhistorically are but just don't yet know how these provinces of culture ought properly to be related. Such assumptions are unwarranted if the very meaning of these notions is subject to historical reconfiguration. Particularly problematic is the assumption that contemporary politicized religion constitutes a return to the proper and antique form of religions prior to modernity. This anachronism fails to consider what has become of traditions when they became religions. True, ancient traditions were privatized and depoliticized at the birth of modernity, but politicizing their contemporary offspring does not constitute a return to the status quo ante.

This chapter contests these assumptions under the influence of William Connolly's decades-long refusal of secularism.[2] Connolly felicitously leaves open the relationship between the political/secular and the religious in a salutary posture that does not presume to know what we mean by these categories. By appeal to a variety of historical and genealogical projects that have alerted us to the provinciality of the category "religion," I will suggest that politicized *religions*—the noun rather than the adjective is the problem—pose special challenges to a robust and healthy civic life. The alternative to politicized religions, however, is not a thinned-out secularism of the sort that Connolly rightly rejects. The task at hand is not to *depoliticize* religions but to *dereligionize* them. To depoliticize is to domesticate traditions and to impoverish public life; to dereligionize, by contrast, is to set religious traditions free from the constraints that come with being religions. Religious communities are thereby enabled to participate in public life in a capacious and generous spirit.

The work of dereligionizing traditions must be distinguished from the work of deprivatizing them because far more than privatization took place when traditions became (configured as) religions. No comprehensive list of features of religion making can be enumerated herein, but I suggest that when traditions became religions—or presented themselves as religions on the global stage—they acquired the following features: textualization, literalization, creedalization, reification, and fetishization. When a tradition so configured becomes politicized, the result is politically mobilized actors who lack the capacities and sensibilities that make for what Connolly calls a generous "ethos of engagement."[3] Religionization has served to coarsen and harden constructions of identity. Or more accurately still, a new category of identity arose alongside the invention of religion, namely religious identities. I am thinking here by analogy to the invention of the category of race. Just as the invention of the category "race" makes possible the invention of racial identities, so the invention of religion gives rise to religious identities. An example: The Jewish people have existed for millennia, but Jews have not always understood themselves to be members of a religion and hence as having religious identities.[4] Many still do not.

"Religious identities" have become sites of acrid contestation because of the factors enumerated above. Hence the task at hand must be to mitigate, if not reverse, the features that risk rendering religious identities toxic. We must detextualize, deliteralize, decreedalize, dereify, and defetishize our traditions. This "we" refers first to theologians and their analogs in the respective traditions, but this labor of dereligionization can and must be supplemented by the work of religious studies scholars, genealogists, and political philosophers such as William Connolly.

An especially problematic feature of the process of religionization is that it seems to marginalize critical therapeutic regimens installed within all of our religious traditions, practices of self-cultivation, *pratiques de soi*, that function to transform and mobilize identity otherwise.[5] That is, all of our traditions contain within them programs for self-cultivation that serve to contest and render malleable conventional configurations of identity. Hence, to engage in Buddhist forms of meditation is to undergo a process whereby one comes to see that there is no enduring substantial self and eventually, in Mahayana traditions, to dismiss the idea that any-thing exists apart from its relationship to all other "things." Hence, Buddhist practices go so far as to contest attachment even to the idea of being Buddhist and, in the most radical of Buddhist teachings, one's attachment to the Buddha and his dharma.

The most rigorous forms of such self-cultivation were available often only to religious elites like monastics, but they enjoyed a prestige and centrality in the life and work of the tradition nonetheless. But as traditions became creedalized—as traditions were reconstructed as centered more on belief than practice—the work of transforming the body-mind complex by means of therapeutic regimens has become marginalized.[6] Might one hypothesize that diminished attention to practice has something to do with the fact that traditions relinquished and ceded the authority to discipline bodies to the state? Whatever the causal factors may be, the ritual and contemplative work of self-cultivation has steadily receded as traditions became religionized. It may be the case that contemporary SBNR ("spiritual but not religious") discourse reflects a felt impoverishment that follows from a dissipation of attention to the body and to practice. We have come now to such an impasse that we cannot, by and large, look to theologians to talk about the role of spirituality and self-cultivation on political life and the promise of such discipline for robustly pluralist civic space. Rather, we must look to a Nietzschean-Deleuzian atheist to teach us once more about the recursive labor of self-cultivation.

## THE INVENTION OF RELIGION, OR THE WORK OF "RELIGION-MAKING"

Beginning with the work of Wilfred Cantwell Smith and Talal Asad, there has been a growing appreciation in religious studies that the category "religion" is an elusive category, not least because although it has about it an antique aura, its usages and meanings, upon closer inspection, show themselves to be of recent vintage.[7] The suspicion grows that regnant notions about religion are provincial, not only because they are relatively new but also because of their Western provenance. Persons must be tutored to think of some aspects of life as "nonreligious" or secular in order to conceive of other aspects of life as properly "religious" and vice versa. This work of imagination is anything but universal, and its origins can be traced, albeit with great patience and persistent historical excavation. We must ask when, where, how, and why the West first learned to make this distinction between the religious and the secular.

To raise these questions is to set about learning to see at work in history the process of what Arvind-Pal Mandair and Markus Dressler call "religion-making." Mandair and Dressler describe what they mean by "religion-making" as follows:

> We conceived of "religion-making" broadly as the way in which certain social phenomena are configured and reconfigured within the matrix of a world-religion(s) discourse. In other words, the notion refers to the reification and institutionalization of certain ideas, social formations, and practices as "religious" in the conventional Western meaning of the term, thereby subordinating them to a particular knowledge regime of religion and its political, cultural, philosophical, and historical interventions.[8]

Time does not permit us to generate a rich picture of what Mandair, Dressler, and their colleagues mean by religion-making, but it suffices for now simply to name that such a process has in fact taken place and taken place globally but differentially and with varying tempos. Such a process, although it has earlier roots, reaches its culmination in and with modernity. Indeed, a case can be made that a, perhaps *the*, constitutive feature of modernity is precisely *the invention* of religion through this work of religion-making, a process that generates as its correlate the space of the secular as the nonreligious.

The phrase "religion-making" serves to dispel the notion that religion has always already been there waiting for moderns to discover and distill out from its adventitious accretions, such as economics and politics. The latter domains can subsequently be rationalized and governed by the state, thereby freeing religion to go about its proper business, often configured as the work of making transcendental/transempirical claims and saving souls. A failure to appreciate the point that "religions" have to be made can give rise to slippery discourse of the following sort: (1) Religion once existed but was politicized; (2) then modernity came along, and religion was privatized and hence purified to be what it truly is; (3) and now post- and antimoderns have come to appreciate that religion was always intrinsically political and so seek to include it once more as a political actor in the public sphere. Such talk can fall prey to the errant conviction that religion remains a steady and stable configuration throughout these transformations with politics as the only variable. One catches a possible hint of this anachronistic error in the work of the otherwise fine recent book by Clayton Crockett and Jeffrey Robbins, when they write that in "the shift from the secular to the postsecular,"

> ... we indicated how the privatization of religion, which conformed to the modern secular norm, was in effect a depoliticization of religion, and correlatively, that the postsecular might thereby be understood as a repoliticization of religion by its recognition of the inherently political nature of all forms of religion.[9]

Taken at face value—likely a bad idea when dealing with scholars of the caliber of Crockett and Robbins—this claim suggests that there exists a stable reality, a certain something called religion, that stays constant save for modernist interruption. The genealogists say otherwise. As Talal Asad, Richard King, Timothy Fitzgerald, Tomoko Masuzawa, and many others have shown, religion is not a transhistorically constant reality.[10] Religion is made/invented and not out there to be found.[11] If the genealogists of religion are right, and I believe they are, it follows also that Crockett's and Robbins's inspirations—Feuerbach, Marx, and Freud—are mistaken to think that there is a transhistorical reality called religion, the nature of which is misconstrued by religious people, but nonetheless genuinely real and properly to be explained by some mode of reductionism.

Close attention to the processes of religion-making, in concrete historical detail, has served to dispel the taken-for-granted Western sense that the category religion has always enjoyed universal recognition and meaningfulness. On the contrary, in some cases, scholars can date with striking precision just when a people had to learn to use the category. Jason Ananda Josephson's recent and impressive work, *The Invention of Religion in Japan*, is an especially telling entry into the scholarly literature on the genealogy of religion.[12] Josephson can date the moment when it became necessary for Japanese translators to first figure out the meaning of the word "religion": the arrival of American warships off the coast of Japan on July 8, 1853.[13] On that date, Josephson notes, the Americans insisted that they would not leave until two letters were presented to the Japanese emperor, letters that twice contained the word "religion." After this arrival and over the course of subsequent decades, the Japanese had not only to make sense of the foreign word "religion" but were then, as Josephson shows, compelled to reconfigure Japanese life in such fashion that some dimensions of culture could be demarcated as religious and others as not. As Josephson shows, this work was not one of distilling out a discretely religious sphere already there waiting to be discovered and named when the right category arrived on the historical stage.[14]

What do such histories and genealogies mean for statecraft and for political life broadly construed? What can the Japanese instance teach Western political theorists and culture workers about the ways in which the category "religion" structures our imaginations and, by way of our imaginations, the organization of our political lives? The invention of religion qua religion—a complex, multidirectional global process—was a process of privatization and transcendentalization.[15] Around these processes is retrospectively projected a sense of threatening danger—the sense that religion can be a kind of potent, virulent force that, unless defanged and depoliticized, will ineluctably usher in violence. Thankfully, so it goes, for the sake of the religions and religious people themselves, the violent propensities of religion are not intrinsic and native to religion. Religion, "properly understood," can be severed from its putatively reactionary impulses and function richly in the private lives of a nation's citizens so long as religion does not seek to reemerge into the public square and make claims thereupon.[16]

Ironically, though we are not yet historically in a position to fully appreciate the dynamics at play, I have begun to suspect that the invention of religion on these terms may have created the very conditions for the peculiarly dangerous and virulent forms that religion now takes. When our traditions become religionized, they give rise to rigid and inflexible configurations of identity that threaten to interrupt pluralist possibilities. I refer to the following taken-for-granted notions of what it means to be a religion:

> Religion is taken to be defined by singular and exclusive claims to allegiance. You can be a part of only one religion at a time.
> The various religions are innately incommensurable.
> Religious identity is one kind of identity among others, but different from all others because it is marked by a necessary and final nonnegotiability.
> Most peculiar, as W. C. Smith noted quite some time ago, are the processes by which the loyalty of religious persons has been shifted away from the "object" of devotion—namely God or ultimate reality—to one's religion as such.[17]

If W. C. Smith is right that "religion" itself has now become an object of devotion, then it has also become configured in modern imagination as a fragile, imperiled, and contested mode of identity—one that must be protected perhaps at any cost. We can well imagine that religion so configured might become a threatening reality when politicized.[18]

## THE MARKS OF RELIGIONIZATION

Early in this chapter, I listed a number of marks of religionization, namely textualization, literalization, creedalization, reification, and fetishization. These marks are characteristic features that religious traditions take on when they become religionized. This list is not meant to be exhaustive, but these factors do nonetheless play a determinative role in the work of transforming rich, variegated, porous traditions into religions. Not all of these markers are equally prevalent in the various religions, but I am hard-pressed to think of religions that have altogether escaped these processes.

The global production of religion through colonial encounter largely takes place after the category of religion was formulated in the wake of the Protestant Reformation and European conflict occasioned by the Reformation. The quest to define religion and identify its essence was prompted by the desire to overcome such conflict by identifying what all religions putatively have in common. A variety of voices conspired in that conversation, including prominent Deists such as Lord Herbert of Cherbury.[19] Nonetheless, although this claim cannot be defended herein, what has come most decisively to shape regnant understandings of religion is no generic or Deist version of the same but rather a specifically Protestant understanding thereof. The Deists themselves were operating within a Protestant ethos, one, for example, that constantly criticized so-called superstition and the prevalence of "priestcraft." This Protestant specificity accounts for and is evident in the marks of religionization I will now consider.

The modern process of religionization, it is well understood, seems to require *textualization*. To be a proper candidate for the status of a world religion, one must have a scripture, a sacred text, which is taken to be the authoritative deposit of a tradition's primordial revelation.[20] Traditions lacking such a text are unlikely to win for themselves membership in the family of world religions. Traditions in which a single text or canon of texts have heretofore played only a marginal role must be reconfigured to foreground their importance and thereby also the importance of elite textualists who claim custodianship over those texts. Once such texts and textual traditions are identified, constructions of authentic religious identity itself are closely linked to such texts; internal diversity is diminished as textual strands come to stand in as normative for traditions as a whole. The Sanskritization and Brahminization of Hinduism make up but one marked example of the wholesale reconfiguration of a tradition in which many Hindus remain illiterate and so necessarily marginalized when their tradition is textualized.

Once texts are identified that can serve as central scriptures—the Bhagavad Gita for Hinduism, for example—they have become subject in modernity, increasingly, to literalistic readings. Mythic Hindu deities are now said to have specific sites of birth, and the quest commences to find a historical Krishna and a historical Rama. Those who remember the destruction of the Ayodhya mosque by the Hindu Right and the violent shock waves that resulted therefrom will not find it difficult to discern the toxic consequences of literalization: This violence is, at least in part, a consequence of the claim that the Babri Masjid rests on just that patch of ground that happens to be the literal birthplace of Rama.[21]

What precisely do we mean by *literalization*? Here, I am indebted to oral conversations with the Boston University philosopher Harold Oliver.[22] Oliver argued that modernity's notion of literal truth is the remainder of a double negation. The process begins when Enlightenment critics of religion assert the proposition "The myths of religious traditions are not literally true." Persons who then take themselves to be defenders of these traditions retort, "It is not true that our myths are not literally true." The precipitate of this double negation is a peculiarly modern conception of literal truth. Readers of ancient and premodern Christian writers know that the fathers had ready to hand a variety of conceptions of truth; even what premoderns meant by "literal truth" is far removed from any modernist construal of the same. In and through the process of literalization, these expansive and variegated conceptions of truth are lost to view, and a constricted conception of literal truth wins out. This process takes place first in the Enlightenment critique of the Christian tradition but is then exported through colonial encounters, and literal conceptions of truth gain global currency.[23]

When traditions become religions, they also become *creedalized*. Through colonial contact, Christianity, configured as a religion, serves as prototype for other would-be religions. Thereafter, one finds, for example, the creation of Buddhist catechisms.[24] Under the influence of creeds and catechisms, religions are constituted as centered on beliefs, and faith is often understood as cognitive assent to these aforementioned lists of propositions. The primary question to be posed to persons in other traditions is, "What do you believe?" on the assumption that belief trumps practice. Orthodoxy comes to shape if not define even orthopraxic traditions.

*Reification*, about which W. C. Smith has written a great deal, refers to the processes by which historically malleable and porous traditions come to be constructed as fixed, transhistorically static, tightly integrated and bounded conceptual systems (possessed of a single dominant metanarrative or an internally consistent transtemporal deep grammar). Under the influence of such notions, religious belonging is construed to be an exclusive matter, and multiple religious participation is marginalized. If religions are tightly bounded and characterized by incommensurable deep grammars that lead to necessarily incompatible doctrines of salvation, then it is a mark of incoherent and misguided syncretism for persons and communities to be deeply shaped by more than one religion. That is just not the sort of thing a religion is. This reification of traditions, however, runs counter to fluid patterns of belonging that characterized much of East Asia and even South Asia prior to modernity.

By *fetishization*, I refer to the processes by which the religions—configured as described above—become the objects of religious devotion. Wilfred Cantwell Smith makes this point with inimitable flair:

> The notion that a religion is a nice thing to have, even that it is useful, has arisen, as it could arise only, in a secular and desperate society. Such a notion is a kind of blasphemy, to those whose faith is sensitive. One has even reached a point today where some Christians can speak of believing in Christianity (instead of believing in God and in Christ); of preaching Christianity (instead of preaching good news, salvation, redemption); of practicing Christianity (instead of practicing love). Some even talk of being saved by Christianity, instead of by the only thing that could possibly save us, the anguish and the love of God. . . . A Christian who takes God seriously must surely recognize that God does not give a fig for Christianity.[25]

Fetishizing is this transference of religious energies from objects of devotion—God, the Buddha, or the Torah—to the religion itself. If what saves is not God but assent to a certain set of propositions about God, then the religion that alone offers those propositions can become the object of such devotion.

Time does not permit a detailed explication of the toxic potentialities of these features of religionization. For now, I suggest only that religions as so constituted serve to generate brittle and rigid conceptions of exclusive identity and allegiance. When such religions become themselves the object of devotion and then politicized, they can unleash disruptive and antipluralistic energies into public space that are difficult to call back and to constrain.

### DERELIGIONIZING TRADITIONS

If we are to enter into a robust postsecular moment, one that might give rise to a new postsecular politics marked not only by tolerance but also by a rich ethos of engagement between religious traditions and between nontheists and the religious, then we must do more than generate new conceptions of public life in which religious voices can once again be political actors. That task is necessary but insufficient. We must also forthrightly ask, "What risks obtain when religions, as configured during modernity, are now politicized?" Can persons who belong to these often rigid and brittle configurations bring into the public sphere capacities for engaging in political life with charity and generosity? I fear that politicization without dereligionization is a risky proposition.

So dereligionize we must, because the markers described above serve to introduce toxic elements into political life. Theologians and their analogs within the religions—and here I speak of "religions" because virtually all our are traditions have become religionized to some extent just as our bodies have become raced as the fiction of race has been inscribed upon our skins—must take up the labor of dereligionizing our traditions in order to open up pluralist possibilities and to deepen spiritual life. Again, W. C. Smith puts the matter with compelling power: "A task of the modern religious reformer is to help men [sic] not to let their religion stand between them and God."[26] In addition to Smith's task, we might add that modern religious reformers also have an obligation not to let religions stand between adherents and their neighbors who are not coreligionists.

The work of detextualization begins by recalling that the relative importance of texts to religious life has been exaggerated during modernity. Texts have, of necessity, always mattered more to literate elites than to the vast nonliterate majority of any tradition's adherents. Even when texts enjoy reverence and prominence within traditions, for most, access to those texts has come by way of artistic depiction and dramatic performance. Of course, the text as depicted and performed is recognizable as text interpreted: The motile character of the text is more readily apparent when it is danced and sung than when it remains fixed on the printed page. Those who seek to detextualize a tradition must work to bring attention to ritual, aesthetics, contemplation, and ethical action, which have all been overshadowed by the bright and singular light cast on scripture. Any tradition's capacity to shape the affective and practical orientation of human beings rests precisely on these now neglected dimensions of religious traditions.

A second component of that labor is the work of deliteralization. Theologians within traditions must work to show that religious texts have not always been read literally. Our traditions contain vast treasuries of reading practices that have become marginalized in modernity. The recovery of these ancient modalities of reading religious texts can offer a corrective to conceptions of literal truth and inerrancy that impoverish the creative multiplicity inherent within any religious tradition.[27] The attenuation of the polydox character of traditions makes it far easier to generate facile oppositions between religions. By marginalizing or even removing from collective consciousness features of one's own traditions that richly overlap with features of other traditions, we become increasingly incapable of recognizing ourselves in the other and the other in ourselves. Literal readings that remove from vision mystical interpretations of Christian scriptures, for example, can serve to undergird dichotomies between the rational and historical West and the mystical and ahistorical East. So many elements within traditions must be rendered marginal or even invisible before such fictive oppositions can seem plausible.

To dereify a tradition is to situate it within a larger social and historical matrix that would permit us to see it as constituted by its interactions—with other traditions, with critics and opponents, and with larger political and economic flows. To dereify a tradition is also to attend to persons who inherit and in turn transform traditions and thereby to recognize their intrinsic mutability. Also, attention to persons will demonstrate that they are almost always shaped by more than one tradition at a time and have been so for most of human history and in most geographical locations. To recognize traditions as porous, ever-changing, and internally multiple is to give up on fictitious representations of religious traditions as immutable or possessed of essential features always and everywhere the same. Such recognition also frees persons to recognize their own indebtedness to more than one tradition. To remove from vision our own and our community's internal multiplicity is to generate the conditions under which antagonisms can flourish.

To defetishize a tradition is to remove the conditions under which traditions themselves become the objects of religious devotion. Human beings are historical creatures, creatures of context and culture; appreciation of this truth has become commonplace thanks to the work of Herder, Troeltsch, and others. If knowledge of ultimate reality or the real as such is to be had, it will be had only by means of thick instrumentalities made possible by religious traditions. Even traditions that hold to the possibility of unmediated encounter with ultimate reality understand themselves to be custodians of just those practices that make such encounter possible. Hence, reverence for tradition is indispensable to religious life.

But such reverence need not amount to fetishization. Religious traditions must be understood as complex sign systems and networks of practices that enable persons to rightly engage the relevant features of ultimate reality.[28] They are not themselves that ultimate reality and so are unworthy of idolatrous attachment. They are means to an end and not that end itself. Making that truth plain to adherents is a central task for theologians and religious teachers if adherents are to participate in the public square as articulate and passionate but also generous, self-critical, and humble advocates of the traditions to which they belong.

The marks of religionization are problematic and even potentially toxic because, taken collectively, they tend to generate inflexible identity configurations. First, what it means to be part of any tradition is impoverished when that tradition is homogenized and its internal diversity domesticated by creedalization and literalization. Second, reification obscures from view the extent to which all our traditions are fluid and porous, thereby preventing an appreciation of the truth of our multiplicity, that all of us have been and continue to be shaped by resources from more than religion narrowly construed. Finally, fetishization binds persons to traditions in such a fashion that no critical distance from one's tradition seems possible; belonging to a religion makes an exhaustive and final claim to one's loyalty and allegiance. It no longer seems possible to entertain the notion that all our traditions are provisional, contestable, and subject to constant transformation. The notion that we have much to learn from other religions seems hardly intelligible. How can persons and communities bearing such constricted identities be generous participants in pluralistic public life?

Even religious life itself is impoverished when traditions are reduced to religions. Central to the various religious traditions are projects that call into question virtually every conventional mode of identity, including religious identity, in the face of mystery. Dare we say that authentic religious life is imperiled by traditions when they become religions? Hence, the project of dereligionization, which seeks to undo these markers, is an urgent matter for both public life and for the intrinsic aims of religious life itself.

## UNBINDING IDENTITY: ONTOLOGICAL WONDER AND THE LABOR OF SELF-CULTIVATION

A core component in the labor of dereligionizing traditions is the recovery of practice, broadly construed. By practice, I mean to include what now falls under the headings of ritual and spiritual discipline. In my own idiom, I prefer to speak of therapeutic regimens, which serve to comport bodies—personal and social—to the world as rightly interpreted. On my account, to be religious is to seek comprehensive qualitative orientation. Here, I make a transhistorical claim that human beings seek orientation *to the whole of things or reality as such* rightly understood.[29] They seek that orientation by means of *interpretive schemes* by which some conception of the real is derived.

But orientation is not accomplished by generating interpretive schemes alone. Qualitative orientation requires proper comportment to reality as understood by means of interpretive schemes. What dispositions should we cultivate in ourselves given what we take reality to be? Therapeutic regimens are the means by which persons and communities are rightly comported to reality rightly understood. To speak of qualitative orientation is to specify that the labor of orientation and comportment is richly affective in character and not merely a matter of propositional knowing. Qualitative orientation is not accomplished merely by having in mind a set of propositions to which one gives cognitive assent. Qualitative orientation is erotic labor, a work of determining what is worthy of desire and then tutoring the heart so that unworthy desires are relinquished and authentic ones embraced. Therapeutic regimens are how traditions seek to accomplish this work of right orientation through comportment.

The religionization of our traditions has led to the relative marginalization of therapeutic regimens that were once a robust and integral part of traditions before they became religions. I would venture to assert that we have nonetheless given ourselves over to other therapeutic regimens by means of which our bodies are comported to the real as understood within modernity, broadly speaking. Thus, the state commends and even compels bodies to adopt a host of rituals (devotion to a flag, for example) and spiritual disciplines by which bodies learn to defer to state power and become bearers of patriotic dispositions. Likewise, therapeutic regimens of production and consumption serve to discipline bodies and comport them to the demands of the market. The cumulative force of these therapeutic regimens inscribes in our mind-body complexes prescribed identities that teach us how to be citizens and consumers within particular kinds of local and global configurations.

Other possibilities, that is to say other therapeutic regimens, are offered by religious traditions—regimens that are meant to evoke and sustain modes of ontological wonder without which human beings fail to be properly oriented to reality as rightly understood by the traditions in question. To evoke and be imbued by these varieties of ontological wonder is to be properly oriented to deep features of reality as such. But in order to be so oriented, conventional configurations of selfhood and identity must be contested and transformed. That is, configurations of selfhood as ordinarily understood must be deconstructed and reconfigured if human beings are to be awakened to and rooted in the kinds of ontological wonder that traditions seek to cultivate in their adherents.

In other writing, I have spoken of three kinds of ontological wonder that I correlate with a certain trinitarian configuration.[30] I then proceed to show that various religious traditions also show themselves to be open to and even claimed by these modes of ontological wonder. Although no set of terms is adequate to capture precisely what I mean, I nonetheless speak of the wonder that anything is at all, wonder that anything that is is contingent, and that anything whatsoever is what it is by virtue of being related to all other things. I then correlate these three kinds of ontological wonder to dimensions in the divine life, namely, ground, contingency, and relation.

No extended explication of this double threefold is possible herein. I will give only the briefest hints about what I have in mind because my primary purpose is not to sketch out a theological ontology but to suggest that religious orientation at this ontological level serves to challenge, disrupt, and reconfigure conventional investment in reified identities. Even or perhaps especially "religious identities" are challenged by these ontological awakenings as each, in its own way, serves to unearth an apophatic dimension that undoes every conventional identity configuration by means of which we navigate mundane life.

The first sort of ontological wonder is the wonder that there is anything at all. The sheer mystery of being, that there is something rather than nothing, the mystery that to any given in experience we can say it *is*, rather than it is not. The various religious traditions give a host of explanations for this primary ontological given. Not all traditions or strands of traditions are equally open to and committed to cultivating in adherents a sense of the mystery of the sheer being of things. Advaita Vedanta, in particular, is committed to cultivating an awareness of being as such (*sat*) and then proceeds to claim that this sheer being is Brahman. Moreover, to say that we just are being understood as Brahman is not to be able to say *what being is*. We can say only that it is that without which nothing would be, but it is not itself a discrete and knowable something. That which grounds and just is our very being is nameless mystery (*nirguna brahman*). The ontological wonder about the sheer being of things is taken to point to ultimate reality itself, Brahman, which is the ground and substance of all things.

A second kind of ontological wonder is aroused not by the sheer being of things but by awareness that each given, each experienced "thing," is contingent and singular. Any thing considered as a discrete particular is colored by its "might/need not have been and will not be but now is" character. Still more, each given in experience is marked by utter singularity: No leaf is identical to another, and no arch of an eyebrow traces out the same arc as any other. I believe that this is in part what Connolly means when he speaks about the fecundity of being.[31] When religious traditions speak to, account for, and sustain in devotees a sense of contingency, some variety of the doctrine of creation customarily comes into play. Theists appeal to God as the creator of every contingent thing, the whence of the wondrous world of exuberant diversity. A nontheist may speak instead of immanent creativity that gives rise to a contingent world without positing a noncontingent creator, but both can recognize and share a sense of ontological wonder at the sheer fact of contingency.

A third and final sense of ontological wonder is evoked by the intuition that not one of the aforementioned contingent realities is what it is apart from its relationships. To be is to be related. Any thing deeply considered shows itself to be intimately related to every other thing. Indeed, some religious traditions suggest that the very idea that reality is made up things at all is a mistake inasmuch as that intuition artificially separates a notional object of reflection, identified for some conventional purpose, into an object as such. This claim is the most rigorous refusal of reification imaginable. There are no things anywhere to be found but only nodes in a network of inexhaustible relationality. Here, I have in mind in Madhyamaka tradition as well as the Hua-Yen tradition, both part of the larger canopy of Mahayana Buddhism.

I cannot here narrate how I move, as a Christian trinitarian, from sheer being, contingent being, and relationality to three dimensions of the divine life, namely God as ground/abyss (*grund* and *ungrund*), God as (source of) contingency, and God as relation. I leave it to readers to note that my double threefold correlates well with certain conceptions of God as Father, Son/Logos, and Spirit. The point of this highly compressed theological ontology is to suggest that religious traditions seek to draw persons into right orientation to reality as such by awakening and sustaining in persons these ontological intuitions by way of therapeutic regimens that open persons onto these vistas. Although persons may unbidden trip and fall into such ontological intuitions and be awakened briefly to these modes of wonder, commitment to therapeutic regimens is necessary if one is to abide in and be guided by these intuitions. The Advaita Vedantin practitioner must undertake practices that diminish attachment to caste identity in order to awaken to his or her true identity as unknowable Brahman. That *ascesis* may be rigorous, initially disorienting, and even painful, but the result is a nondual compassion that grows from the knowledge that you and I are not-two. As ordinary identity is disrupted and another identity takes its place, one's ethical disposition is transformed and the exclusiveness of caste identity is called into question.

To be awakened in Christian experience to the contingency and singularity of each being is to know every other as a site of value. Awakening to the singularity of each thing is the ground of an authentic *eros*, for recognition of the desirability of each particular in its nonsubstitutability. This kind of desire is different from the Advaitin's compassion rooted in the sense that you and I are not-two, that ultimately, we are both Brahman. Hence, Advaita compassion and Christian eros/agape (eros without the desire to possess the particular for one's own is agape—hence, eros and agape should not be dichotomized) are not the same.

To awaken to and be rooted in an appreciation for the truth that I am not I without you, that nothing at all exists apart from relation—that too awakens in me a mode of compassion that is both like but different in texture to the Advaita understanding of compassion. On Buddhist accounts, you and I are not the same by virtue of both being Brahman, but I am not I without you, and hence, I would labor under profound ignorance if I sought my private welfare at your expense. I must, therefore, undertake a therapeutic regimen that diminishes my egoism in order to replace egoism with nonduality and compassion.

These three sites of ontological wonder, and the strands of the religious traditions that I have hastily sketched, suggest that our identities are never securely knowable because they open up into the mystery of being-itself, because they are marked by contingency and singularity, and because they are through and through constituted by an open-ended network of relationality. Moreover, I suspect that naturalists and theists can also recognize these sites of ontological wonder as sacred. Attending to these ontological mysteries that elicit wonder can open up ways of being together that honor difference. Connolly is right to suggest that only such recursive labor—the labor of working on ourselves so that we come to see what we could not otherwise—can help us appreciate that there is more to human beings than our conventional identities.[32] These conventional identities, including religious identities, must not be reified and fetishized because our traditions are meant precisely to contest impoverished convictions about who and what we are.

When we understand these dimensions of religious traditions and commit to therapeutic regimens that are other than and even opposed to the therapeutic regimens of state formations and market forces, we inhabit our traditions otherwise than as "religions" narrowly understood. To so inhabit our traditions holds both promise and peril for state and market. Insofar as the therapeutic regimens of religious traditions challenge attachment to conventional identities as absolutized, as idolatrous objects of devotion, therapeutic regimens that awaken us to capacious understandings of selfhood open up pluralist possibilities in public life. These pluralistic sensibilities can help sustain polities that can withstand the shearing pressures behind the impulse to demonize those whom we take to be other, those whom we exclude from status and voice in the body politic. But insofar as these therapeutic regimens challenge and interrupt what the state and the market have to offer, religious traditions counter and threaten the hegemonic claims of these institutions to shape our lives without remainder. Dereligionized traditions are anything but domesticated traditions.

## NOTES

1. This very claim is, in a rough and ready way, the thesis of John Milbank's magisterial *Theology and Social Theory: Beyond Secular Reason* (Cambridge, Mass.: Blackwell, 1990).
2. See most especially his book, William Connolly, *Why I Am Not a Secularist* (Minneapolis: University of Minnesota Press, 2000).
3. On the work of cultivating a generous ethos of engagement in pluralist polities, see ibid., 137–61.

4. For a careful study of how one particular ancient and living tradition became a religion, see Leora Batnitzky's important book, *How Judaism Became a Religion: An Introduction to Modern Jewish Thought* (Princeton: Princeton University Press, 2011).
5. On care of the self, see Michel Foucault, *The Hermeneutics of the Subject: Lectures at the College de France, 1981–1982* (New York: Palgrave Macmillan, 2001), 86–89. See also the work of Pierre Hadot, *Philosophy as a Way of Life* (Malden, Mass.: Blackwell, 1995). Hadot mobilizes the expression "spiritual exercises" for the recursive work of self-cultivation. See 81–109.
6. An alternative claim might be that such practices have only become more popular as they have been made more broadly available beyond monastic communities during modernity. See Richard Gombrich's and Gananath Obeyesekere's important discussion of the modern laicization of meditation in Sri Lanka in their book, *Buddhism Transformed: Religious Change in Sri Lanka* (Princeton: Princeton University Press, 1988), 237–40. What is striking about their claim is that the laicization of contemplative practices seems to have severed these practices from the core soteriological purposes to which they were formerly tied. The practices may be more popular, but their purpose is no longer the same.

    The popularization of meditation on the American scene might also challenge the claim I make about the marginalization of therapeutic regimen, and yet might not the same case be made here as with Sri Lanka? Is it not the case that here too meditation and other disciplines like yoga are routinely severed from the soteriological purposes at the heart of religious traditions? Perhaps that is why such practices seem more popular among those who claim not to be religious but spiritual. Indeed, the very intelligibility of the distinction rests on the notion that spiritual disciplines are external to and other than what stands at the heart of the religious.
7. See Wilfred Cantwell Smith, *The Meaning and End of Religion* (Minneapolis: Fortress Press, 1991; originally published by Macmillan, 1962); Talal Asad, *Genealogies of Religion: Discipline and Reasons of Power in Christianity and Islam* (Baltimore: Johns Hopkins University Press, 1993); and Talal Asad, *Formations of the Secular: Christianity, Islam, Modernity* (Stanford: Stanford University Press, 2003).
8. Arvind-Pal S. Mandair and Markus Dressler, "Introduction: Modernity, Religion-Making, and the Post-Secular," in *Secularism and Religion-Making*, ed. Dressler and Mandair (New York: Oxford University Press, 2011), 3.
9. Clayton Crockett and Jeffrey W. Robbins, *Religion, Politics, and the Earth: The New Materialism* (New York: Palgrave Macmillan, 2012), 44.
10. See Richard King, *Orientalism and Religion: Postcolonial Theory, India and "The Mystic East"* (New York: Routledge, 1999); Timothy Fitzgerald, *Discourse on Civility and Barbarity: A Critical History of Religion and Related Categories* (New York: Oxford University Press, 2007); Tomoko Masuzawa, *The Invention of World Religions; Or, How European Universalism Was Preserved in the Language of Pluralism* (Chicago: University of Chicago Press, 2005).
11. A note of clarification: I myself am prepared, like W. C. Smith, to talk about a religious dimension to human experience. I am even willing to run the risk of stipulating that this dimension is universally present. However, I insist that what I

am designating as "the religious" is broadly dispersed throughout a whole range of cultural activities. I read Western modernity—speaking simplistically here as though there is but a single modernity—as an unsuccessful attempt to distill and confine the "religious" into a discrete sphere or province of life as opposed to the secular and then to organize the traditions so confined into "religions." See more on my conception of the religious in the final section of this chapter.

12. Jason Ananda Josephson, *The Invention of Religion in Japan* (Chicago: University of Chicago Press, 2012).
13. Ibid., 1.
14. Josephson writes, "For more than thirty years after Perry's arrival, Japanese intellectuals grappled with the concept of religion. . . . They produced different translation terms, each of which seemed to imply a different object: a type of education, something unknowable, a set of practices, a description of foreign customs, a form of politics, a kind of Shinto, a near synonym for Christianity, a basic human impulse. That other terms with very different meaning were equally in play suggests it was far from clear what analogs existed for the Western concept. Not only did Japanese intellectuals and translators produce different terms for religion, they also debated which indigenous traditions and practices fit into the category. If religion was the genus, there was no native species on which taxonomists could agree. This is clear evidence that it is glib to talk about Japanese religion projected back through the centuries" (ibid., 8).
15. I will add further specifications below.
16. On the liberal depiction of religion as constantly threatening violence, see William T. Cavanaugh, *The Myth of Religious Violence* (New York: Oxford University Press, 2009).
17. On this matter, see the discussion of Smith on reification below.
18. That the modern invention of religion brings with it new problems that make religions especially vulnerable to violence when politicized does not require making the claim that prior to modernity the traditions were innocent. One does not have to make such claims in order to discern new dangers.
19. On Herbert's role in shaping and defining the category of religion, see Peter Harrison, *"Religion" and the Religions in the English Enlightenment* (New York: Cambridge University Press, 1990), 61–73. The story I am telling here about the formation of religion is, to a considerable extent, a simplification. Increasingly, genealogical and historical work demonstrate that the category was formulated in global processes of contact and exchange between colonizers and the colonized. Still, it is impossible to ignore the truth that the origins of the category are solidly rooted in Europe and America.
20. For a helpful and extended discussion of textualization, see chapter 3, "Sacred Texts, Hermeneutics and World Religions" in King, *Orientalism and Religion*, 62–81.
21. On the wide-ranging influence of Protestant literalism in the Indian context, see the new and invaluable book by Robert A. Yelle, *The Language of Disenchantment: Protestant Literalism and Colonial Discourse in British India* (New York: Oxford University Press, 2013).

22. For an essay that begins to treat of Oliver's worries about inadequate engagements with and translations of the multivalent iconic images of mythic discourse, see his chapter, "Myth and Metaphysics: Perils of the Metaphysical Translation of Mythic Images," in Harold Oliver, *Metaphysics, Theology, and Self: Relational Essays* (Macon, Ga.: Mercer University Press, 2006), 33–38.
23. For a fascinating conversation, which demonstrates just how constricted conceptions of truth—in this case a certain kind of Christian claim that a statement is true only if it describes a historical occurrence—function in cross-cultural encounter, see King, *Orientalism and Religion*, 39–41. King narrates an exchange between a Western anthropologist and a "young Balinese," who makes an important distinction concerning the story of Prince Rama: "'What is it that you want to know?' he asked. 'Do you want to know whether the story is true, or merely whether it occurred?'" (39). In this particular case, Western conceptions of truth are resisted; in others, they are all too readily embraced.
24. See, for example, Stephen Prothero's fine work on Henry Steel Olcott, America's first convert to Buddhism and his role in the creation of a Protestant Buddhism including a Buddhist catechism, *The White Buddhist: The Asian Odyssey of Henry Steel Olcott* (Bloomington: Indiana University Press, 2010). For a copy of that catechism itself, see Olcott, "The Buddhist Catechism [1908]," *Internet Sacred Text Archive* (2010), http://www.sacred-texts.com/bud//tbc/index.htm.
25. Wilfred Cantwell Smith, *The Meaning and End of Religion* (1962; Minneapolis: Fortress Press, 1991), 127.
26. Ibid.
27. For an argument about the loss and the needed recovery of allegory in Christian theology, see, for example, Andrew Louth's fine work in *Discerning the Mystery: An Essay on the Nature of Theology* (Wichita, Kans.: Eighth Day Books, 2007), 96–131.
28. For just such an account of religious traditions, see Robert Neville's *On the Scope and Truth of Theology: Theology as Symbolic Engagement* (New York: T&T Clark International, 2006).
29. To be clear, "religion" is a historically variable and provisional configuration; the religious impulse is not. Moreover, the attempt to corral the religious into the religions has never and can never succeed. Religiousness is a pervasive and fugitive impulse that resists attempts at containment.
30. See John Thatamanil, "God as Ground, Contingency, and Relation: Trinitarian Polydoxy and Religious Diversity," in *Polydoxy: Theology of Multiplicity and Relation*, ed. Catherine Keller and Laurel Schneider (New York: Routledge, 2011), 238–57.
31. For Connolly on fecundity, see *A World of Becoming* (Durham, N.C.: Duke University Press, 2011), 72.
32. For Connolly on the need for self-cultivation and even "spirituality," see *World of Becoming*, 68–92.

# ∽ Non-Theology and Political Ecology: Postsecularism, Repetition, and Insurrection

CLAYTON CROCKETT

What do we share in common? I suggest that we all have an implicit or explicit ecology insofar as we are all related to the earth as a common planet. Ecology names a theoretical orientation toward the planetary situation we have in common. Theology has not always been ecological, but it needs to become much more so, if it wants to have a future.[1] In this essay, I explore some of the ideas of François Laruelle, and apply his notion of non-philosophy to theology. From the standpoint of non-theology, we acquire a better perspective on contemporary political economy and political ecology by viewing it in terms of energy. I survey some of our recent political history, using ideas from Gilles Deleuze and Jacques Lacan along with those from Laruelle to elaborate a political theology of insurrection.

## RADICAL POLITICAL THEOLOGY

My theological tradition is not a traditional form of theology, but rather a kind of radical theology going back to the "death of God" theologies of the 1960s. This radical theology, furthermore, has recently become more explicitly self-conscious of political issues and problems. "Radical Political Theology" here names the coincidence and even conflation of two distinct discourses.[2] First, it indicates the tradition of radical theology as it emerges out of the "death of God" theologies of the 1960s, although I also see it as a radicalized response to the theology of Paul Tillich. The phrase "death of God" has a variety of meanings, and although predominantly associated with Thomas J. J. Altizer's work, it is also represented by Gabriel Vahanian, William Hamilton, Richard Rubenstein, and Paul van Buren. These death-of-God theologies mutated, partly in response to European philosophies of hermeneutics and deconstruction, into a distinctive American postmodern theology in the 1980s. Mark C. Taylor is the most well-known representative of this tradition, although Charles Winquist and Carl Raschke are also affiliated with it. As Raschke puts it in an essay titled "The Deconstruction of God," deconstruction is "in the final analysis *the death of God put into writing*."[3] This tradition of American radical theology is important, but it is more academic, more unorthodox, and more distant from the church than other forms of progressive theology such as liberation theology and process theology.

The second reference of the phrase "radical political theology" is political theology, which traces its origin to the famous and controversial work of Carl Schmitt in the 1920s and 1930s. Political theology has become an important contemporary philosophical perspective on biopolitics and questions about sovereignty, especially in the recent work of Giorgio Agamben. Political theology is also the locus of the resurgence of philosophical interest in St. Paul, in the work of Jacob Taubes, Alain Badiou, Agamben, Ward Blanton, and others.[4] Political theology today means that religion "returns" in thought and culture in important political ways. Although Carl Schmitt's political theology is a conservative critique of modern liberalism, the perspective of radical political theology allows one to appreciate the importance of Schmitt's critique without simply endorsing Schmitt's position.

For me political theology implies a form of postsecularism. Postsecularism means that the religious and the secular cannot be simply or completely opposed to each other. This opposition deconstructs. Modern secularism is premised on a neat division between public and private where political discourse and decisions take place in a neutral or secular public sphere while religion is relegated to the realm of private belief. This separation was never fully or consistently maintained, but scholars are now recognizing the impossibility of making this opposition, and we can perceive the limits of secularism as an ideology.

This important and necessary critique of secularism does not mean, however, the triumph of religion as it is sometimes celebrated with the term postsecular, as if we used to be secular but now are not anymore. Here I follow and endorse William Connolly's arguments in *Why I Am Not a Secularist* and his attempts to refashion secularism "to pursue an ethos of engagement in public life among a plurality of controversial metaphysical perspectives, including, for starters, Christian and other monotheistic perspectives, secular thought, and asecular, nontheistic perspectives."[5] We need to think about and study both the religious and the secular, in philosophical, cultural, and theological terms, without the temptation that we could simply eliminate one or the other. As Talal Asad concludes in his important study *Formations of the Secular*, "The categories of 'politics' and 'religion' turn out to implicate each other more profoundly than we thought, a discovery that has accompanied our growing understanding of the powers of the modern nation-state."[6]

Radical theology is not primarily confessional theology; radical theology, including theological insights into the death of God, involves the freedom to question doctrines and dogmas without necessarily submitting these questions to any overarching authority, any predetermined answers, or having to subscribe to their truth. For me, the phrase "death of God" indicates the very questionability of faith. Radical theology is a kind of theology without church, or what John D. Caputo calls, following Derrida, a "religion without religion." Of course, radical theology can be pursued in the church as well as in the academy. And "religion without religion" does not mean that there cannot also be a determinate religious commitment or faith; the idea is that religion also harbors something excessive in relation to these particular institutions.

## NON-PHILOSOPHY

There is a structural similarity between how I am treating theology and how the contemporary French philosophy François Laruelle understands philosophy. Laruelle has been a significant writer in France for a few decades, but his work is just now being translated and read by English readers, beginning with the 2010 publication of *Future Christ: A Lesson in Heresy*, translated by Anthony Paul Smith.[7] For Laruelle, philosophy is too magisterial, too caught up in its own authoritative discourse because it subscribes to the principle of sufficient philosophy, the idea that philosophy's discourse is or can be sufficient to describing and theorizing reality. For this reason, Laruelle calls his project non-philosophy, where the prefix "non-" indicates that philosophy is always already infected by what it is not, including science and religion. Non-philosophy is a rigorous attempt to understand and express otherwise than in philosophical terms what philosophy is doing, or what philosophy is capable of achieving. In order to do this, Laruelle is forced to adopt some idiosyncratic terminological distinctions, and his vocabulary is awkward and forbidding at first glance. Furthermore, I do not intend to summarize Laruelle's thought here; instead, I am mining it for some of his terminology and concepts, to apply them to theology. The reason that Laruelle's thought is useful for radical theology is that what the "non-" does to philosophy for Laruelle is similar to how I understand and use the designation "radical" to apply to theology.

So what is non-philosophy? For Laruelle, non-philosophy begins with the traditional philosophical problem of the One. Poststructuralist French philosophy abandons the One for the sake of thinking the Other, but Laruelle claims that this is not radical enough. He proposes to think *from* the One, rather than *to* the One, which produces a kind of "vision-in-One" of identity. Thinking from the One acknowledges that we cannot simply think the One or identify it with the Real, but we can think from it. This sort of thinking challenges the presumption of philosophy that is "regulated in accordance with a principle higher than that of reason: the *principle of sufficient philosophy*."[8] Ultimately this principle allows philosophy to maintain a status of surveillance over the other disciplines and over the world, but Laruelle attempts to theorize beyond or without this self-sufficiency.

For Laruelle, non-philosophy is both theorematic and axiomatic, and this brings it close to science. Laruelle's thought can appear as a reinstantiation of modernist scientism, but I don't think that's ultimately what he's doing. He's trying to develop tools for conceptual analysis that are not dependent on preestablished notions of what philosophy is and does, but the difficulty of forging such tools means that his work is difficult to read, especially without understanding what these terms mean. Laruelle is not trying to think the One, which is unthinkable, but to think from the One, which is a "vision-in-One" of a nonrelation, or a "unilateral duality."[9] Unilateral duality means that non-philosophy is not a unitary system, but it is "radically heterogeneous" because it posits a vision of identity that does not really exist but gets "determined-in-the-last-instance."[10] Unilaterality emerges out of duality, but there are not two sides or two things because one "side" is the perspective of the real, which is unthinkable in itself, just as the One is unthinkable. The real-One is foreclosed, but it is still a force for thinking, for thinking nonphilosophically.

Non-philosophy is based on an assumption of radical immanence, and it dispenses with any transcendent referent, even if non-philosophy is technically a kind of transcendental generic science. If we think theologically about God as a name for the One, then non-theology would dispense with thinking to the One, or with any attempt to adequately conceive God in transcendent terms. Non-theology is radically immanent; it is concerned with theological thinking and its effects in the world. Non-theology produces a kind of identity, but that identity does not precede theological reflection. According to Anthony Paul Smith, who has been instrumental in bringing Laruelle's thought to English readers, "Non-philosophy appears to mimic theology in its thinking from the Real and not of it. Simply replace the Real with the name of God. Theology thinks from God and not of God."[11] Smith claims not only that non-theology functions analogously to non-philosophy, but that non-philosophy requires a discourse of non-theology to complement it. Smith argues that "a unified non-theology and non-philosophy constitutes a real secularity (of) thought," or a generic field in which to do philosophy of religion.[12]

Non-theology, like non-philosophy, is an operation that transforms the very nature of theology (and philosophy). Laruelle says that non-philosophy "cannot 'transform' . . . the objects of philosophy or the entities in the world. But it can *transform* . . . philosophy as a whole which is a self-presenting hybrid of identity and difference."[13] In an analogous way, non-theology cannot change the objects of theology or the things in the world, but it has the capacity to radically transform theology itself, which then has important insights and implications for what we think and do. Non-theology is not antitheology, and it is not not-theology, as if we can simply dispense with theological thinking. That was the secularist dream, which is what we are waking up from.

So a radical theology, or even more provocatively, a non-theology, provides a critical distance from the logic and presumptions of most forms of critical theology, even reformist modes of progressive theology. Non-theology also offers a critical perspective to reflect on the urgent issues concerning political theology and the breakdown of secularism. The breakdown of secularism and the public return of religion are connected to the breakdown of modern liberalism and a desperate crisis of global capitalism, which is ultimately an ecological crisis. Capitalism as a modernist ideology takes both political and economic forms. In political terms, it refers to the practice of representative democracies who act to preserve and promote "free" trade. As an economic practice, it is predicated on freeing up more and more capital to use for growth, which involves the transformation of natural resources into capital reserves for the production of goods and the creation of wealth. Capitalism is based on the presumption of growth, even as it hides the fact that growth is uneven, unfair, and sporadic. The history of liberal capitalism is not based on a linear upward slope of production, but better understood as a series of cycles of boom and bust, and the need to create ever-larger speculative bubbles.

The financial or speculative economy is linked to a material and an energy economy, even if this is a complex relationship. We cannot grow without exploiting enormous reserves of energy in the form of stored fossil fuels, and we cannot have money and other financial derivatives unless they are based on something material or physical, however tenuously. We need to find a new way to think about earth that is material but not reductionistic or atomistic, and certainly not consumeristic. The problem with some contemporary modes of ecological reflection, including some ecotheologies, is that they are based on some of the same illusions that our financial and economic system is based on. Insofar as ecotheology names a traditional form of theology that simply expands God's stewardship to include the planet or substitutes nature for God as the source of order and goodness, ecotheology is insufficiently radical, although of course there are important exceptions.[14] The idea that a new and better form of spirituality would enable us to live in harmony with the planet is a kind of wishful thinking. Many of our reflections and prescriptions about economic growth, resources, recycling, spirituality, and sustainability fail, despite their best intentions, to break out of the cycle of global capitalism. In many ways, this is because it is impossible to break out of global capitalism, but at the same time, global capitalism itself is breaking down. Here I am provocatively suggesting a form of theology that becomes non-theology to think about the nature and stakes of political ecology as opposed to simply stretching the traditional forms of theology to incorporate nature as Go(o)d.

## THINKING ENERGY

In order to really grapple with the fundamental questions about the earth, we need to think more deeply about energy, in philosophical, theological, and ecological terms. Being is energy transformation and energy itself, not simply matter or spirit, but we can conceive it nondualistically as both. Energy is infinite in the sense that it is always conserved. This is the first law of thermodynamics. The second law, however, formulates the difficulty, which is the law of increasing entropy. The second law of thermodynamics means that any closed system will tend to equilibrium, and that more energy is needed to maintain a system than can be profitably derived from it. According to Gilles Deleuze, thermodynamics names "a strange alliance at the end of the nineteenth century between science, good sense, and philosophy."[15] The result is that thermodynamics is viewed as the inevitable progression from order to disorder, "from more to less differenciated, from a productive to a reduced difference, and ultimately to a cancelled difference."[16] Our understanding of thermodynamics as the inevitable entropic progress from order to disorder is a legacy of this nineteenth-century model.

In his book *Difference and Repetition*, published in French in 1968 and translated into English in 1994, Deleuze helps us think differently about energy and entropy. He rehabilitates difference over against identity, and he is rightly seen as a philosopher of difference. However, readers of Deleuze have sometimes neglected the second term, repetition, and its significance for this book and for philosophy more generally. Repetition is repetition of difference, but difference does not drive or produce repetition; it is rather the reverse. Repetition produces differences. Repetition is a kind of force, which Deleuze calls intensity, and it is intensity that generates difference. The problem with entropy for Deleuze is that it appears to cancel out difference or intensity, which is a kind of force or energy in extensity, which is the form of what appears. "Intensity is difference, but this difference tends to deny or to cancel itself out in extensity and underneath quality."[17] Intensity is the name for the energy that produces novelty and creativity. Differences are generated by intensity, and they appear to us in the form of extensive or actual differences. The problem that Deleuze is wrestling with in his book is that the intensive energy seems to cancel itself out in the production of extensive difference. Differences occur, but when they result, the net energy dissipates in entropy and there is less productive energy or work to generate new differences. Energy appears to be irretrievably lost.

But this is not the last word, because it is intensity that produces this extensity that cancels it out in appearance. "Difference of intensity is cancelled or tends to be cancelled in the system, but it creates this system by explicating itself," according to Deleuze.[18] There is an affirmation of difference in intensity that produces differences that then get canceled out in extensity, or what we call entropy. At the same time, intensity drives the process of production of differences, and there is always a remainder of intensity hidden underneath the cancellation of differences, that contributes to further differences. This is a very technical discussion, but the point is that when we associate intensity with productive energy and extensity with the entropic result of energy dissipation, we fall into the stereotypical viewpoint of classical thermodynamics. Entropy generally manifests itself as heat, which is why it is sometimes called "heat death." Heat death means that productive or intensive energy is ultimately lost in the generation of extensive or actual difference. Deleuze is suggesting that that is not the best way to view this process. Entropy is not just the passage from an ordered to a disordered state.

By viewing thermodynamics in a nineteenth-century manner, we commit ourselves to what Deleuze calls a "transcendental illusion" that is "essentially tied to the *qualitas*, Heat, and to the extension, Entropy."[19] The transcendental illusion of thermodynamics leads to the apparent paradox of one river of increasing complexity, associated with the evolution of life, that is diametrically opposed to the other river or the arrow of time, which is associated with the production of entropy and the dissolution of order.

What Deleuze is suggesting philosophically is something that some scientists in the late twentieth century have been suggesting, which is that there is only one river or arrow. It's not that somehow there's this miracle of negative entropy that demands a deus ex machina to explain. Energy is intensity; it is the production of differences by means of repetition. Repetition is not just psychological, dependent on a consciousness to observe it; repetition is physical, tied to the nature of things themselves. We are a process and a result of individuating and individuated repetition.

What does this mean? Being is energy transformation, and nontheology considered in itself is energy. There is no God beyond or outside this process, who excepts himself and reserves his power to intervene or not into it. Energy is intensity, which is a kind of repetition of difference in Deleuzian terms. This is not just philosophical speculation. Ilya Prigogine, a Nobel prize–winning scientist and collaborator with the philosopher of science Isabelle Stengers, spent most of his theoretical work on open or dissipative systems that take place far from equilibrium. Stengers, Prigogine's collaborator and coauthor, is strongly influenced philosophically by Deleuze, as well as by Alfred North Whitehead. According to Prigogine and Stengers, dissipative systems, which include organic systems, are not closed systems that work according to the law of entropy increase but continually take in and emit energy in different forms so that they are dynamic and nonlinear systems. In *Order Out of Chaos*, they write that "the interaction of a system with the outside world, its embedding in nonequilibrium conditions, may become . . . the starting point for the formation of new dynamic states of matter—dissipative structures."[20]

## GRADIENT REDUCTION

Prigogine's work is connected to a new science of nonequilibrium thermodynamics. In their book *Into the Cool*, Eric D. Schneider and Dorion Sagan redefine entropy in terms of gradient reduction. A gradient is a differential that is established by two forces, like a pressure differential between high and low pressure. Nature works to reduce the gradient as efficiently as possible, and this produces what we call entropy. Citing the work of Don Mikulecky on mathematical electrical networks, Schneider and Sagan claim that this gradient reduction is "as much a fundamental property of thermodynamics as the change in entropy itself."[21] Entropy measures this reduction of gradients, and "focusing on gradient destruction, not just entropy production, provides a more complete analysis of these systems."[22] Schneider and Sagan conclude that "nature abhors a gradient."[23]

A gradient is a differential between two forces, for example, temperature. Given a temperature differential, like a mass of warm air colliding with a mass of cold air, the system works to reduce that gradient as quickly and efficiently as possible, which can generate a storm. There are also pressure gradients as well as chemical or redox gradients. The point is that whenever a gradient is established, there is a force that works to reduce it, and this is what we call entropy. Most of the time, the reduction of gradients leads to a loss of organization, but sometimes, in special circumstances, this process of gradient reduction actually produces order and sustains it as long as energy flows through the system. These are open systems, and they are not at equilibrium; they occur along the edges of a chaotically complex system.

Life is an extraordinary case of a nonequilibrium system, but it is not an exception to the processes of entropy production and gradient reduction. Physical systems organize into patterns when gradients are set up and maintained with a continuous flow of energy. What are called Taylor vortex flow patterns are produced when cylinders filled with fluids rotate within other cylinders. These patterns produce distinctive flow patterns and vortices: "In addition to the vortices spawned simply by spinning were the waves that varied dramatically in number and size."[24] Precisely which vortices and wave patterns are produced varies: In their search for equilibrium, they cycle through various states, and "in their cyclicity they embody past modes of reaching equilibrium."[25] That is, nonliving physical systems exhibit a kind of memory, or hysteresis.

This science of nonequilibrium thermodynamics is very similar to what Deleuze theorized in 1968. Deleuze writes, "Constructed on at least two series, one superior and one inferior, with each series referring in turn to other implicated series, intensity affirms even the *lowest*; it makes the lowest an object of affirmation."[26] Superior and inferior, high and low, are metaphoric here; Deleuze indicates the intensive gradient differential set up between two or more series. Energy flows from high to low, from the differential to the reduction of difference in the reduction of a gradient. Entropy proceeds from the hot *into the cool*. But this process does not completely cancel out or destroy intensive difference, which preserves itself underneath the gradient reduction. The system remembers, which is why existence takes the form of a complex repetition in Deleuzian terms. And it is energy or intensity that drives the system and sustains its structure as long as it flows.

Where does energy come from? We do not know. But in our universe, what is called dark energy, which was "discovered" in 1998, is thought to constitute over three-quarters of everything that exists. On earth, repetition has generated living organisms as incredibly efficient machines of gradient reduction, and this efficiency allows us to survive. Our civilization is also the result of energy flows, but the resources needed to sustain our postindustrial, postmodern civilization may be running low. It's not that energy will run out, but the kinds of gradients we need for so many of us to thrive may run short, because we've been living off of stored energy from the past, what Thom Hartmann calls "the last hours of ancient sunlight."[27]

The point is that we cannot have electronics, technology, airplanes, media, and money without energy, and this energy is physical and material, even if it is not inert stuff. Theology risks irrelevance to the extent that it ignores this material aspect of our existence, which is where non-theology comes in. Non-theology works with and against the image of thought that is conventional theology, to reduce, refocus, and redeploy it. Theology as such struggles to make sense of what's going on, although various progressive and radical forms of liberation and process theology are among the most vital areas of theory and practice today. How can non-theology help map out a political ecology and contribute to an insurrectionist thinking and practice? In my analysis to follow, it's not that non-theology is doing something that theology cannot do, but in breaking with the principle of sufficient theology, perhaps what I am calling non-theology can offer another perspective on our situation.

## BREAKING WITH SUFFICIENT CAPITALISM

Returning to a more historical political-economic analysis, we can speculate that 1967 is the high-water mark of hope for global revolution, and 1968 is a kind of tipping point. The events of May 1968 still carry enormous charge for

French theory, but in some ways this insurrection is the result of defeat and despair, as the psychoanalyst Jacques Lacan understood at the time. According to Slavoj Žižek, "What effectively happened in the aftermath of '68 was the rise of a new 'spirit of capitalism': the hierarchical Fordist structure of the production process was gradually abandoned and replaced with a network-based form of organization founded on employee initiative and autonomy in the workplace."[28] This shift toward a new spirit of capitalism coincided with the abandonment of Lyndon Johnson's ambitious War on Poverty as well as intensification of U.S. military engagement in Vietnam, the murders of Martin Luther King Jr. and Robert F. Kennedy, the betrayal of the Chinese Cultural Revolution, and the rise of what Naomi Klein calls "disaster capitalism."[29]

In 1968, I think that we began to experience an energy inflection point, when for the first time in global terms humans start to come up against physical ecological limits as a planet. In 1970, domestic oil production peaked in the lower forty-eight United States, not counting Alaska. In 1971, President Nixon was forced to abandon the Bretton Woods accord that established the post–World War II economic framework with a dollar that was pegged to $35 for an ounce of gold. After this gold standard disappeared, the U.S. currency became a fiat currency. Soon afterward, the OPEC oil embargo, which was a response to the U.S. support of Israel in the Yom Kippur War of 1973, shocked the American economy. As a result, the United States reaffirmed its special alliance with Saudi Arabia, and the Saudis pledged to ramp up supply to fuel the U.S. economy and to sell oil in dollars. In the early 1970s, the financial economy delinked from the real economy, which is why the stock market continued to grow tremendously over the next four decades, while inflation increased dramatically and real wages stagnated. The early 1970s also saw the initial awareness of a global ecology, including the famous Club of Rome's book *The Limits to Growth*, published in 1972. That year was also the date of the first truly ecological work of theology to address these global limits, John B. Cobb's *Is It Too Late? A Theology of Ecology*.

This is a broad sketch, but the point is that from about 1945 until 1969, the world saw unprecedented levels of increasing production, based on the widespread utilization of an almost unbelievable source of energy in the form of hydrocarbon petroleum. The so-called Green Revolution in the 1960s was actually the application of petroleum products and methods to agriculture, which produced incredible yields. But beginning in the early 1970s, real productive growth began to slow in per capita terms, and the dreams of utopia in first world nations as well as the hopes for development in third world countries, not to mention the drive for communist revolution in the second—all ground slowly to a halt. Capitalism is based on indefinite growth, but population levels, industrialization across the globe, and overutilization of finite natural resources have combined to make it impossible to grow anymore in overall terms. We are running up against real limits, as Michael T. Klare shows in his book *The Race for What's Left: The Global Scramble for the World's Last Resources*.[30] If corporate capitalism cannot grow in absolute terms, then the only way that it can grow is in relative terms. That is why the rich are getting richer and the poor, poorer. This is happening both within the United States and other countries, and between rich and poor countries. It's a physical process, and we need to come to terms with it if we want our thinking and our actions to be efficacious.

It's not simply that corporate capitalists want to crush the poor and steal their money, although that desire is partly intrinsic to the system; it's that they have no choice if they want to survive. Capitalism has mutated into a more savage form even as it presents a more seductive facade, because it is consuming its own means of production in a desperate attempt to stave off collapse. At the same time, most of our contemporary economic theories ignore their ecological situatedness and simply externalize environmental costs. The economy is struggling to grow, which demands energy inputs, but we are running low on these inputs, which are getting scarcer and more expensive. That's why we cannot fully recover from the global recession of 2008. And that's why the United States has to spend so much money on its military, which is essentially a police force for global oil and gas pipelines, to ensure that this country, which has less than 5 percent of the world's population, continues to consume nearly a quarter of the world's energy.

I mentioned Lacan earlier, and I want to look briefly at what Lacan analyzes about this whole process as it was happening in 1969–70, in his Seminar XVII, *The Other Side of Psychoanalysis*. This is a crucial theoretical insight, although it is somewhat dense, as most of Lacan's work is. In Seminar XVII, Lacan talks about four distinct types of discourse, which are the master's discourse, the university discourse, the hysteric's discourse, and the analyst's discourse. Lacan is drawing on Hegel's famous master-slave dialectic from the *Phenomenology of Spirit*, and the master's discourse is the point of view of the Hegelian master who dictates law and order to an other, a slave. The slave is in the position of subservience to the master, because he does not want to lose his life, but this situation of servitude generates a kind of knowledge of his situation specifically and the world more generally. Lacan says that the discourse of the modern university proceeds from the point of view of Hegel's slave because the slave wants to understand the world, not control it, at least initially. The analyst's discourse is the discourse of psychoanalysis, the perspective of analytic insight that Lacan is developing and promoting. The hysteric's discourse is one that simply cuts off the master and avoids both the understanding of the slave/university as well as the analytic awareness.

As Žižek explains in *Living in the End Times*, in this seminar Lacan is analyzing a "the crisis of a certain form of the University discourse" that took place around the events of May 1968.[31] The university discourse represents a kind of scientific discourse, which is derived from the slave's perspective. The master does not care how things work, only that things work; it is the slave who is forced to try to understand things.

So what is happening? Well, what Lacan is analyzing right after the events of May '68 is connected with a theoretical shift that takes place in the 1960s from what Lacan calls the big Other, which represents the symbolic order, to the little other, or the *objet petit a*, which is a specific imaginary object that substitutes for the entire symbolic order. The big Other is the guarantee of the entire social system, and what the people in the streets thought was that if you didn't believe in the big Other anymore, then the entire system would collapse. This represents a hope for liberation and revolution that flourished across the world in the 1960s. And it is connected with the theological movement of the death of God, also in the 1960s. There is no big Other.

But here's the problem: Capitalism doesn't collapse when the big Other is called into question. In some ways, it works better, even more efficiently, and this is the transformation to post-Fordism that Žižek discusses. You don't have to believe in capitalism for it to work; you just have to practice it: that is, buy and consume. And it all turns on the objet a. The objet a is the object of desire; for Freud it is the mother's breast, but this object of desire that encapsulates or stands for all of a person's desires later gets associated with other things, including objects of consumption. Desire is what Lacan calls *jouissance*, which is desire taken to an extreme. The Other's jouissance is what maintains the symbolic order, but what happens when this jouissance gets repeated in a certain way such that it becomes more attached to and generated by the object, the object *a*?

Lacan raises the question of capitalism in this seminar, because he is talking about the relationship between surplus value, in the Marxist sense, and surplus jouissance. Capitalism only works based on this surplus. Lacan praises Marx as well as Freud, by the way, because "they don't bullshit."[32] They help us see what's really going on, rather than reflect back to us our own fantasies. At a certain point in the history of early European modernity, Lacan says, "surplus jouissance became calculable, could be counted, totalized. This is where what is called the accumulation of capital begins."[33] Value is a form of jouissance, and the surplus value or surplus jouissance becomes quantifiable, which allows for what we call capitalism. This surplus value works entirely on the side of the master, however, whose discourse and practice is solidly entrenched. The master is the capitalist who benefits from putting a price on everything, and putting everything in circulation. It's on the side of the slave, or what becomes the university discourse, that things get interesting.

The university discourse is a kind of scientific discourse in a broad sense, because it tries to comprehend what's going on. At the same time, it is marked by a fundamental naïveté, because it cannot strictly account for jouissance. With the shift from the Other to the other, the big A to the little *a*, there is a splitting that takes place in jouissance. "Surplus value combines with capital," Lacan says, which means that "the master signifier only appears even more unassailable."[34] The objet a works even better without reference to an external big Other, and capitalism becomes surplus jouissance, *tout court*. We all know something about how are desires are manipulated in and through objects of consumption even when they hurt us, even when the system crushes us because we cannot afford to buy what we most need and when it marginalizes and destroys what cannot be bought or sold.

Lacan understands the hopelessness of the rebellion that took place in May '68. He perceives that this process only ends up reinforcing the power of capitalism and the efficacy of the master's discourse. The university comes to a point of crisis, but the university cannot really understand what's going on, because it is structurally and intrinsically stupid about jouissance. Furthermore, the university is fracturing and corporatizing, into a schizophrenic split between a relatively impotent theoretical discourse about ethics and values, on the one hand, and a powerful but uncritical application of technology and the hard sciences, on the other.

Nevertheless, despite his pessimism, Lacan asks a provocative question: "don't you think some ground is being won here?"[35] What is being won and on what ground? Well, the ground is repetition, and the question is the *repetition* of the objet a. Objet a is tied to an object, and fastened to a body, so it becomes a kind of fetish. And in a weird way this splits signification itself, because the signifier is supposed to function as a unitary or unary trait.

How does repetition split open the signifier into master signifier on one hand, and objet a on the other? Even if they are consolidated for the sake of postindustrial global capitalism, repetition introduces a fault line that is crucial. Lacan says that "inaugural repetition is directed at jouissance," which means that jouissance is inaugurated by repetition. Repetition constitutes jouissance, and it is the intensity of repetition that produces jouissance as difference, to put it in Deleuze's terms. And keep in mind that there is always a remainder.

The remainder *appears* as a loss of jouissance. According to Lacan, there is a loss of jouissance, and "it is in place of this loss introduced by repetition that we see the function of the lost object emerge, that I am calling the *a*. What does this impose on us? If not this formula that at the most elementary level, that of the imposition of the unary trait, knowledge at work produces, let's say, an entropy."[36] The work of knowledge produces an entropy at the elementary level of the signifier, the unary trait. This entropy effect is also a kind of transcendental illusion from the standpoint of the real, because Lacan says that "entropy is defined precisely once one has started to lay this apparatus of signifiers over the physical world."[37]

The play of signifiers over the world appears entropic, because repetition cancels out the intensity of signification in the extensity of the object, to apply some of the insights and language from Deleuze. At the same time, there is always a remainder, which is why the object is not a simple object, but an object *a*. The object has a little bit of jouissance stuck in it, and this "stuckness" is what allows for the flow of energy to be organized. Lacan writes mostly from the point of view of symbolic signification, but he is grasping something similar to Deleuze here in his discussion of repetition and entropy. Everything becomes surplus jouissance, or object *a*, which entirely coincides with global capitalism and the discourse of the master. Capitalism abandons the big Other, whether in the form of God or Truth or the gold standard and works free. But it does not thereby cease to repeat.

What was more minute in 1969 is clearer now, and writ large, although many of us still refuse to see the realities of peak oil, global warming, and the acceleration of poverty. The global recession of 2008 was just the beginning, and it was touched off by the bursting of the real estate bubble, which is also related to the fact that the rate of world oil extraction has reached a limit either in 2005 or 2006. What has been achieved is manifestly not a recovery, but rather a precarious stabilization, even as sovereign debt eats away at the Eurozone and rising fuel prices shut down any starts of increased economic production. Here is a curious calm before the next wave, the next storm erupts. Object *a* is turning and grinding in its repetition underneath it all the time.

Everything hinges on the object *a*, which is also intrinsically theological in its essence, even if it requires a non-theological perspective to fully appreciate it. All things circulate, become exchangeable with each other for money, and capital works only through the surplus jouissance of things, the desire for investment and consumption. But how does it stand with the Real? In the real, repetition concerns the repetition of the object *a* itself, not simply its signification. Lacan says that despite the stupidity of the university discourse, "nowhere else can there be the possibility that things should move a bit," because "at the level of the university discourse the *object a* comes to occupy a place that is in play each time it moves, the place of more or less tolerable exploitation."[38] The repetition of object *a* introduces "a little bit of air into the function of surplus jouissance" precisely by means of this repetition. Capitalism works more efficiently than any other system to reduce gradients so long as it can maintain its energy flow, and this is entropic in thermodynamic terms. According to Lacan, "there is in every case a level at which things don't work out," even if their not working out concerns their hyper-efficient working.[39]

Everything turns on a little *a*, a little object that sustains jouissance because it becomes the primary vehicle for jouissance and thereby the maintenance of capitalism and the master's discourse. We struggle to imagine a future without capitalism because it has become universal and unbeatable, as well as increasingly unbearable. You cannot defeat it: It is too little; it is everywhere and nowhere. Even if you refuse, protest, boycott, or shut down one thing, there is always an other (*a*). Capitalism also feeds off of the religious gradients between Christianity and secularism, Christianity and Islam, and so on. It stages these religious and cultural conflicts partly as spectacles for its own financial and militaristic ends. But capitalism is consuming itself, because the object *a* does not simply circulate. It repeats. It turns. It grinds. Away.

> If it's one's wish that something turn—of course, ultimately, no one can ever turn, as I have emphasized enough—it is certainly not by being progressive, it is simply because it can't prevent itself from turning. If it doesn't turn, it will grind away, there where things raise questions, that is, at the level of putting something into place that can be written as *a*.[40]

Lacan asks, What can it (*a*) hope for? What can it do? We need an insurrection of *a*, which is also the little *a* that makes a *différance*.

## INSURRECTION

While traditional theology remains more focused on personal resurrection, non-theology thinks the insurrection. In some of his recent work, Laruelle suggests that there is a radically immanent messianicity of thinking the "Christ-in-person" of human beings.[41] Christ is not the transcendent model of belief, but the life of faith, and resurrection depends on and repeats insurrection. For Laruelle, Christ is less a referent to a supernatural being within a Christian religious framework and more the name for a generic human being, the Human-in-Human freed from all religions and all philosophical characterizations, including humanism. The human-in-human is the subject of non-philosophy, and Laruelle's version of "science fiction" concerns the future of humanity as such, "which tears it away from its traditional foundational tasks in the World and consecrates it to utopia."[42] This human-in-human is named Future Christ and given a messianic status to-come, rather than the divine or resurrected Christ who is the subject of Christianity.

In his book *General Theory of Victims*, Laruelle claims that the victim, like Christ, exposes what is purely and solely human about humanity, or the human-in-human. The resurrection is not the revival of a corpse, but the coming to life of a human by means of an insurrection. Humanity is insurrectionary; it revolts against its relegated ontological status, and this is a political and non-philosophical insurrection. Laruelle says that "resurrection is a specifically generic and human operation" that brings the victim to the condition of the "future-in-person."[43] This operation is not a bestowal of immortality but occurs by means of an insurrection, which is the heart of resurrection. Insurrection results from the superposition of the two waves of life and death in such a way that it produces a resurrection of the victim as future person, or future "Christ." Insurrectionist theology, following Laruelle, dispenses with the principle of sufficient theology in order to make theology more vital, faithful, and powerful as an intervention into the order of things.

Insurrection is not simply a political movement, although we also desperately need those. It's just that, as Lacan says, "if there is any chance of grasping something called the real, it is nowhere other than on the blackboard."[44] Non-theology dissolves the familiar categories and concepts of theology and deploys them with and against theology, with and against capitalism, for the purposes of an insurrectionist thinking. Non-theology takes elements of poststructuralism, postcolonialism, process theology, and liberation theology and welds them not into an eclectic stew but an intensive project. Non-theology is insurrectionary with objects *a*. It repeats them differently, which is a kind of forcing, but only insofar as it works with the energetic intensity that reduces gradients.

We need to think with the earth, to think of ourselves as planetary objects *a*, which we are *in common*, rather than how we are signified by capitalist jouissance. The idea is to construct a theological ecology of Earth as a totality in its becoming. This is what Deleuze and Guattari calls a mechanosphere in their book *A Thousand Plateaus*. They sketch a geology of morals that asks, "Who does the Earth think it is?" Earth is a complex self-organized system or mechanosphere, sustained by flows of energy including nuclear, electric, and magnetic reactions that generate an atmosphere that is hospitable to life. In our hubris we think we can destroy or save the earth itself, but we do not have this divine power. We may, however, possess the ability to save or destroy ourselves and many other large species.

We are using up all the cheap and easily available energy to sustain our current technological way of life, so we will need all our resources of creative imagination and empathetic resistance to re-create our species in cultural, biological, social, and technological terms. Is it possible to have less in physical, material terms but not be impoverished in our metaphysical imaginations? We will use up everything we can until we can't anymore, and then we will die or we will learn how to do something else. The insurrection is coming, and it is also here and now. This is an apocalyptic insight, even if we want to ward off apocalyptic catastrophe. However, the religious task is one of unveiling, which is the literal meaning of the word apocalypse, so let's have eyes to see and ears to hear.

NOTES

1. See John B. Cobb, *Is It Too Late? A Theology of Ecology*, 2nd ed. (1972; Denton, Tex.: Environmental Ethics Books, 1995).
2. See my book *Radical Political Theology: Religion and Politics after Liberalism* (New York: Columbia University Press, 2011).
3. Carl A. Raschke, "The Deconstruction of God," in *Deconstruction and Theology*, by Thomas J. J. Altizer et al. (New York: Crossroad, 1982), 3.
4. See Ward Blanton and Hent de Vries, eds., *Paul and the Philosophers* (New York: Fordham University Press, 2013).
5. William E. Connolly, *Why I Am Not a Secularist* (Minneapolis: University of Minnesota Press, 1999), 39.
6. Talal Asad, *Formations of the Secular: Christianity, Islam, Modernity* (Stanford: Stanford University Press, 2003), 200.
7. See François Laruelle, *Future Christ: A Lesson in Heresy*, trans. Anthony Paul Smith (London: Continuum, 2010); as well as Anthony Paul Smith's book on Laruelle's nonphilosophy and ecology that situates them in relation to theology, *A Non-Philosophical Theory of Nature: Ecologies of Thought* (New York: Palgrave Macmillan, 2013).
8. François Laruelle, *The Non-Philosophy Project: Essays by François Laruelle*, ed. Gabriel Alkon and Boris Gunjević (New York: Telos Press, 2012), 25.
9. Ibid., 28.
10. Ibid., 32.
11. Anthony Paul Smith, "What Can Be Done with Religion? Non-Philosophy and the Future of Philosophy of Religion," in *After the Postsecular and the Postmodern: New Essays in Continental Philosophy of Religion*, ed. Anthony Paul Smith and Daniel Whistler (Newcastle upon Tyne: Cambridge Scholars Press, 2010), 296.
12. Ibid., 297.
13. Laruelle, *Non-Philosophy Project*, 38.
14. For example, see Mark I. Wallace, *Finding God in the Singing River: Christianity, Spirit, Nature* (Minneapolis: Fortress Press, 2005). Wallace does a great job of reenvisioning Christianity in environmental terms, but he also argues that the solution to the environmental problems that Christianity has created is a better, greener Christianity (in the same way that many people argue that the solution to the problems raised by technology are better technology). Here Christianity for Wallace is the *pharmakon*, both poison and cure. In practical terms, too, he locates the solution at the level of intentional consciousness: "The problem is a matter of the heart, not the head," which suggests that if we really want to change our relationship with nature we can (27). The idea is that if we transform our spiritual consciousness. then we can alter our behavior and bring about a better, more harmonious accord

between humans and other beings and biospheres on the planet. I think this perspective is largely an illusion, funded by a theological imaginary that is beautiful but not real.
15. Gilles Deleuze, *Difference and Repetition*, trans. Paul Patton (New York: Columbia University Press, 1994), 223.
16. Ibid.
17. Ibid.
18. Ibid., 228.
19. Ibid., 229.
20. Ilya Prigogine and Isabelle Stengers, *Order Out of Chaos: Man's New Dialogue with Nature* (New York: Bantam Books, 1984), 143.
21. Eric D. Schneider and Dorion Sagan, *Into the Cool: Energy Flow, Thermodynamics, and Life* (Chicago: University of Chicago Press, 2005), 77.
22. Ibid.
23. Ibid., 72.
24. Ibid., 128.
25. Ibid., 129.
26. Deleuze, *Difference and Repetition*, 234.
27. See Thom Hartmann, *The Last Hours of Ancient Sunlight: The Fate of the World and What We Can Do Before It's Too Late* (New York: Three Rivers Press, 2004).
28. Slavoj Žižek, *Living in the End Times* (New York: Verso, 2010), 355–56.
29. See Naomi Klein, *The Shock Doctrine: The Rise of Disaster Capitalism* (New York: Metropolitan Books, 2007).
30. Michael T. Klare, *The Race for What's Left: The Global Scramble for the World's Last Resources* (New York: Metropolitan Books, 2012).
31. Žižek, *Living in the End Times*, 355.
32. Jacques Lacan, *The Other Side of Psychoanalysis*, ed. Jacques-Alain Miller, trans. Russell Grigg (New York: W. W. Norton, 2007), 71.
33. Ibid., 177.
34. Ibid., 178.
35. Ibid., 177.
36. Ibid., 48.
37. Ibid., 49.
38. Ibid., 178.
39. Ibid.
40. Ibid., 179.
41. See François Laruelle, *Christo-fiction: The Ruins of Athens and Jerusalem*, trans. Robin Mackay (New York: Columbia University Press, 2015).
42. François Laruelle, *Struggle and Utopia at the End Times of Philosophy*, trans. Drew S. Burk and Anthony Paul Smith (Minneapolis: Univocal, 2012), 4.
43. François Laruelle, *Théorie générale des victimes* (Paris: Mille et une nuits, 2012), 158.
44. Lacan, *Other Side of Psychoanalysis*, 151.

# ❧ The Ambiguities of Transcendence: In Conversation with the Work of William E. Connolly

KATHRYN TANNER

Can sociopolitical alliances be formed between upholders of transcendence and immanence, between those, on the one hand, who believe in a transcendence over the world, a world open to a God external to it, and those, on the other hand, who believe in an immanence of the world, a world in which externality and openness reside only within it? The development of a genuinely pluralistic ethos would seem to be at stake according to William Connolly:

> Cultural antagonisms between transcendence and immanence [must be transmuted] into debates marked by agonistic respect between partisans, with each set acknowledging that its highest and most entrenched faith is legitimately contestable by the others.... The pursuit of such an ethos is grounded in the assumption that ... *between* a fundamental image of the world as either created or uncreated and a specific ethico-political stance resides a *sensibility* that colors how that creed is expressed and portrayed to others. The sensibility mixes into the creed, rotating its ethico-political compass in this way or that.... The most urgent need today is to mix presumptively generous sensibilities into a variety of theistic and nontheistic creeds, sensibilities attuned to the contemporary need to transfigure antagonisms between faiths into relations of agonistic respect.[1]

Equally at stake would seem to be effective mobilization of opposition to what Connolly terms the (evangelical) Christian-capitalist resonance machine, in which religiously funded resentments against the human condition of mortality and diversity are complemented and amplified by "exclusionary drives and claims to special entitlements running through the cowboy sector of American capitalism" to form a culturally and politically influential whole greater than the sum of its parts.[2] If capitalism is to be stretched into more egalitarian and ecologically responsible configurations, a counterresonance machine will need to be created, informed by multiple constituencies, across different creeds, all of whom nonetheless share similar sensibilities of care for the earth, acceptance of the hard facts of a world beyond human mastery, and a willingness to embrace the challenge, disturbance, and disruption posed by others to their own claims to rectitude and truth.

Connolly maintains that such a sensibility can be shared by any creed, because creeds (or beliefs) and sensibilities, though infusing one another and not entirely separable, remain loosely bound with one another: "It is therefore possible that you might confess the Trinity and fold either a punitive or generous disposition into that confession."[3] Indeed, if none of that were true, one would be hard-pressed to hope for any resonance machine with sufficiently wide inclusivity, particularly across the crucial creedal divide distinguishing transcendent from immanent faiths, to counter the current Christian-capitalist machine. Yet, to date, Connolly has been most successful aligning the sensibility of his own immanent faith with those upholding theological beliefs of a very specific sort. For the theologians of transcendence (William James, Catherine Keller, and John Thatamanil) whom Connolly most fruitfully engages, divinity is itself characterized in terms of a world of becoming. God is, for example, finite, conditioned, open to indeterminacy, emergent, or active and changing in ways that bring human and divine closer together in the world as we know it. More traditional affirmations of divine transcendence, associated with the evangelical Christian pole of the current resonance machine, seem a much harder nut to crack, perhaps suggesting (once again) a surprisingly tight link of creed to (in their case) hopes in an overly simplistic, unidirectional, providential arrangement of the world and sentiments of revenge against the world of becoming. In deep sympathy with Connolly's project and in step with his sense of a loose connection between creed and sensibility, I would like to ask: Can one pluralize the sensibility of more traditional Christian claims of divine transcendence to produce allies in the formation of a countermachine? And I would like to answer affirmatively.

Such an effort would clearly be futile if a one-to-one correspondence held between beliefs in divine transcendence and that particular set of dispositions to judgment and action toward others—that spirituality in Connolly's terms—typical of the Christian-capitalist resonance machine. But as I have argued elsewhere (in *The Politics of God*), it is generally the case that, while beliefs, on the one hand, and attitudes and actions, on the other, are logically interrelated, logical gaps exist between them as well.[4] Thus, beliefs about what is the case—beliefs about the character of the world and God, for example—can help make certain courses of action appear reasonable and motivated, and certain attitudes appropriate. The belief that society has been organized inequitably by misguided human agents helps render dispositions to rebel intelligible.

The belief that good deeds bring God's blessings can motivate efforts to lead a moral life. The belief that God is the source of everything good in one's life makes gratitude a suitable attitude toward God. But the logical connections here are tighter on the score of exclusion than positive promotion. Particular beliefs can rule out certain forms of attitude and action rather definitively. For example, a happy-go-lucky optimism about one's future prospects is rendered unintelligible by belief in a hostile, perpetually threatening world that takes no account of human wants or needs. But no one particular belief is required to show the propriety of a particular course of action and attitude. Any number might do. Thus, both the belief that God elects no one and the belief that it is impossible to discern whom God elects suggest the appropriateness of egalitarian attitudes and actions toward others. This is one sort of logical gap. And, crucial for our considerations here, there is another: One cannot deduce the propriety of a single, specific course of action or attitude from a particular belief about the way things are. The same, at least general, belief can fund a whole range of forms of attitude and action. Thus, belief in God's predestinating will—the belief that God has decided one's fate from all eternity apart from merit—has historically prompted both terror and comfort, rage against and love for God.

Pluralizing the sensibilities (or spiritualities as Connolly usually terms them) of the same general belief are a variety of factors, whose specification bridges the latter sort of logical gap and works to bind more tightly a particular belief with a particular form of attitude and action: how the belief in question is more exactly defined, the other beliefs with which it is combined, and situational factors of its application (*Politics of God*, 19–22). Thus, belief in God's predestinating will pushes attitude and action in a particular direction—say, toward comfort and love for God—once belief in God's predestinating will is defined more precisely as a single will for salvation, is combined with strong affirmations of God's mercy in Christ, and addressed to someone who previously felt unable to merit God's favor and yet now believes herself to be among the elect. Rage and terror are prompted to the contrary when God's predestinating will is defined as double (to include both salvation and damnation), where the fear of God's arbitrary will is not seriously tempered by the love and mercy of God's revealed will in Christ, and one therefore has serious doubts about one's salvation despite having lived in one's own case, one believes, a good and pious life.

I suggest that a similar pluralizing set of factors affects the import of fairly classical understandings of divine transcendence, in which God is different from the world and works in some significant sense from outside rather than within it. Certain specifications of those factors have the potential to draw that sort of belief in divine transcendence away from its capacities otherwise to align with authoritarian repudiations of pluralism and revenge against a world of becoming. What more exactly would divine transcendence mean, how might it be employed, and combined with other (for example, Christian) beliefs, in that case, so as to enable belief in divine transcendence to resonate with the sensibilities of a countermachine?

To affirm divine transcendence in a classical vein is to affirm an ultimate, unconditioned, and absolute standard of truth, reality, and goodness beyond the world. Considered simply as such, without further ado, an affirmation of this sort can easily be aligned with opposed sensibilities of either openness or exclusiveness. On the one hand, the transcendent locus of such a standard might serve to undercut human tendencies to pretend an ultimate, absolute, and unconditioned status for human beliefs and values. There exists some absolute standard of reality, truth, and goodness, but it is to be identified with a transcendent God and is for that reason different from any such standards espoused by humans (68). Functioning, therefore, as a protest against all human claims to absolute and unconditioned status, the transcendence of God helps propel recognition of the limited and finite nature of human ideas, proposals, and norms, their historically and socially circumscribed bases, and their essentially fallible and defeasible character (69).

Far from being reducible to a simple agnosticism about the reliability of all human claims, this understanding of divine transcendence is the assertion of their imperfection and susceptibility to critique vis-à-vis a realm of ultimate truth and goodness that exists beyond them (73). Appeals to a transcendent God become in this way a means of criticizing rather than reinforcing human opinions about right belief and action. The transcendence of divinity suggests any and all human notions and norms can be found wanting, inadequate, and in need of change (68).

Human understandings of the real, the true, and the good become suspect, therefore, the more they presume an ultimate validity for themselves. The final truth of any human understanding is to be undermined by directing attention to a divine standard that human beings, because of God's transcendence, fail to achieve (200). All human claimants to truth and goodness are relativized over and against a divine standard, thereby preventing authoritarian, dogmatic pronouncements. The absolute certainty about the truth of one's own opinions that fuels exclusivist rejections of opposing views is condemned as a form of pretension to a divine status (200). Overweaning conviction and an inflated sense of the probity or rectitude of one's own judgments are no longer permitted to exempt one's opinions from the possibility of error while discounting any element of truth in the positions with which one disagrees (199). Like everyone else's convictions about proper belief and action, one's own are susceptible to criticism and correction (199).

On the other hand, the simple purported existence of such an ideal locus of reality, goodness, and truth serves as a constant temptation for the very same human inclinations to maintain the ultimacy and finality of one's own beliefs (71). The belief in a more than human divine goodness and truth makes possible a human claim for their instantiation (122). Seduced by the confident presumption that those standards at least exist, one is tempted, despite God's transcendence, to identify one's own account of truth and goodness with the standards for them that God represents (76). Specifically religious forms of fanaticism and dogmatism are the result. One dares to speak for or as divinity (71). One makes one's own views sacrosanct by equating them with a divine vantage point, whose absolute and unconditioned character renders it immune from challenge. The simple truth of one's own position then begins to be matched by the simple falsity of the positions one opposes, with such absolute distinctions between truth and falsity at best promoting patronizing dismissals of opposing views or at worst demands for conformity from the holders of such opinions, whatever their reservations of conscience, and ugly reprisals for any failure on their part to do so (199).

Such a slide into an authoritarian deployment of divine transcendence often comes simply from the effort to make use of divine standards for critical purposes. Divine standards have no obvious critical purchase of a concrete sort apart from some effort to specify what those standards are. Religious believers feel authorized to offer their own accounts of divine standards, and they then use them to criticize understandings of truth and goodness different from their own. In the process their own religious viewpoints tend to fall out from under the awning of those human views subject to critique in light of transcendent divine standards (69). The critical potential of a belief in divine transcendence is no longer self-referential; that is, it no longer has the capacity to turn back against the views of these religious believers themselves.

The major way for accounts of divine transcendence to avoid authoritarian deployments is to radicalize that divine transcendence and thereby prevent identifications of human views with divine ones. Divine transcendence poses problems for the production of a counterresonance machine, in other words, when it is not taken with sufficient seriousness. Apophatic trends in Christian theology deepen the claim of divine transcendence, for instance; God is not just different from the world, but the ontological divide between them is so steep as to invalidate all efforts at human comprehension or adequate linguistic expression (66, 76). The critical force of divine transcendence in this way falls first and foremost on religious efforts to describe divine standards, rendering the critical force of the claim of divine transcendence fully self-referential and blocking any simple distinctions between truth and falsity as the dividing line between religious adherents and their opponents (69).

Apophatic accounts of divine transcendence can repel attempts to specify divine standards altogether for critical purposes, thereby promoting (what I have called in *The Politics of God*) a purely regulative (rather than constitutive or immanent) use of divine transcendence (55–57, 68–69). Eschewing the adequacy of any proposed account of what such standards are, an apophatic understanding of divine transcendence turns God into a mere nonsemantic placeholder for standards of truth, reality, and goodness beyond our conceptions of them. Because they are given no content, such standards cannot be implemented in the process of evaluating particular beliefs or norms. The simple assertion of them without further specification works instead to ground a general ethic of cognition or normative judgment in which *all* proffered accounts of truth and goodness are viewed as correctible and subject to revision in a give-and-take with others (56).

Religious believers may enter the fray in such give-and-take with descriptions of divine standards and thereby use them (in my terms) immanently and constitutively to criticize other proposals of truth and goodness. But an apophatic qualification of the adequacy of such descriptive efforts brings this constitutive and immanent use back under the critical umbrella of the regulative one: Such religious proposals cannot be identified, any more than any other proposals can, with divine truth and goodness, and therefore they cannot be privileged in any dogmatic, absolute, or final fashion. Apophasis, in short, while it need not preclude conviction, prevents the positions one holds from being immunized against criticism; one has to maintain them in ways that permit their challenge and enlargement (73–74, 199, 201–2).

Of course, classical Christian theology does not merely maintain that God is outside and different from the world; God is also involved with it as its creator, providential guide, and redeemer. And therefore one might expect divine standards of truth and goodness to be manifest in the world the more God is actively engaged, as Christians affirm, with it. God is acting on the basis of those divine standards in relating to the world, in other words, and therefore those standards should find expression there. Because God's agency lies behind its existence and what happens within it, God's own nature should somehow be reflected in the world.

Consequently, beliefs concerning God's relations with the world have the potential, depending on how they are more particularly understood, to bring back into the picture the close association of certain human views with divine ones (77–78, 80–97). God, for example, may be thought to be more directly, even exclusively, working God's will for the world through certain human agents, and therefore their views are considered indicative of divine standards in ways that other views cannot claim to be.[5]

Countering a return of dogmatism by way of such claims is the Christian understanding that God is working God's will in an all-encompassing fashion and indefinitely into the future (*Politics of God*, 98–107). Because God's working is universal in scope, one cannot rule out divine direction of one's opponent's views (105). And if God's direction of the whole continues into the future, what God intends cannot be identified with fixed and finished views but, at best, with only what will come of them as they are subject to contestation by others over the course of time (105). In neither case can there be a direct or easy identification of God's intentions with the views of one of the parties in a dispute. If every one of the parties is under the sway of God's influence, none of them is God's agent straightforwardly in conformity with his or her own limited intentions and goals. Similarly, the indefinite temporal extent of divine direction means that, in possible contradistinction to anyone's immediate view, an ongoing argument will eventually come around to conform to God's ultimate intentions for it in ways unforeseeable by any of the parties now.

The same sort of indirection in the discernment of what God is up to, which prevents God's will from being read directly off the intentions and self-understandings of human agents, follows from the Christian claim that God works God's will for the world in and through the fully finite character of human acts (102–3). When God works through them, God does not evacuate their essentially human character by making the acts of human beings absolute and unconditioned as God is. The taking on of divine qualities in that way is simply impossible for any creature, as the claim of divine transcendence attests. Fragile and fallible—not to mention sinful—human intentions and acts refract and filter the character of God's own will so that it is never directly evident or obviously manifest in them.

It is this belief in the ability of God to make do with the finite, the limited, and the conditioned that clarifies how Christian belief can avoid a spirituality that refuses either to recognize or positively affirm a world of becoming. In order to bring about in an absolute and unconditioned fashion what God wants for the world, God need not exercise a top-down control that overrides or bypasses the messy realities of a world of becoming. Christian theologians have often recognized the existence of chance, contingency, and unpredictability in the world—the sort of characteristics affirmed and highlighted in more modern terms for the world of becoming. They have felt no need to dispute the reality of such a world in the interest of maintaining a God whose will is absolute and unconditioned in its efficacy. Why?

The fundamental reason is that they believed God's creative agency lies behind the whole of the world and is equally immediate at every point. God is, therefore, not, strictly speaking, bringing about one thing by way of other things; God is not acting on the latter directly in order to bring about the former indirectly—through the latter's own agency. If that were to be the case, God's agency for one thing would be conditioned by the character of what gives rise to it in the world. For example, God's will for something could not be infallibly efficacious of anything unless the causes for it within the world were. Instead, God wills in an equally direct fashion at every point the whole of what is happening in the manner in which it happens. God wills a world in which certain things happen contingently, even unpredictably in light of their causal antecedents; and in happening that way everything falls out in the way God wants it to.

Crucial to the intelligibility of this sort of position is God's transcendence. God is not part of the world and therefore not acting within it, as, say, some special sort of causal force or agency. God is instead outside the whole world, working on some other plane of causality, so to speak, to hold it all into existence in the entirety of its internal complexity over the course of time. This difference between planes of causality—the one within the world and the one by which God suspends the whole of it into existence—helps make clear that what characterizes the one order of causality need not characterize the other: God's own agency is transcendent, not just in being outside the world, but in being of a different character from happenings within the world. For example, it is possible for God to bring the world into existence immediately, without the help of other causes or any intervening process, while happenings within the world are always densely interwoven within a whole complex of multidimensional factors.

The use of the language of intention—for example, language of rational volition—when talking of divine agency is designed to convey the same point: The character of the world corresponds to *what* God wills but need not correspond to the character of God's own willing of it. A changeless God can bring into existence a world full of change; God's single intention may be for a complex universe; God's timeless will can be for things that begin to be; God's agency may be infallibly efficacious of a world in which no causes exist with the capacity to necessitate or constrain outcomes. No particular conclusions about the world in fact follow, a priori, simply from the absolute, unconditioned, and eternal character of God's willing. Christians can therefore remain open to the world as it displays itself.

If the world appears to be a world of becoming (which I have no doubt it does), Christians have, moreover, reason to rejoice in that fact. This is evidently the sort of world that God brings about, and as such, it should be deemed good (for all its tragic potential and despite all the human malfeasance that mars it). A good God is behind it and is executing God's own will for the world in and through complex systems that are themselves open-ended and without inherent purpose as a whole in and of themselves. Christians have no reason to resent the world because of its failure to match God's own character, demanding of the world what it cannot provide. This failure to match, preventing as it does easy discernment of God's own plans and purposes, is just what they should expect from a God of apophatic transcendence.

Open to a world of becoming, confidence in this sort of transcendent God need not amplify the (evangelical) Christian-capitalist machine. Because God's transcendence breaks any direct correspondence between the ways of God and the ways of the world, confidence in God's providence need not translate into confidence in a beneficent capitalism with its own internal mechanisms for self-regulation independent of human efforts to push capitalism in more eco-egalitarian directions. Confident in God's providence, Christians have no reason, in short, to be confident in the providential character of capitalism itself in a world of becoming. Given, moreover, the all-encompassing character of the created causes through which God works, human efforts to counter capitalism's own inherent tendencies might very well be one of the only real bases for hope in a capitalism that neither wrecks the earth nor immiserates the many.

However, chastened by the complexities of the world of becoming through which a transcendent God works, hopes that are pinned on human abilities to make a difference are kept from feeding into the illusion of human mastery that is the other side of the (evangelical) Christian-capitalist machine. Because they believe in a God who lies both behind and beyond the open, unpredictable weave of capitalist fortunes, Christians gain, in principle, the capacity to see in a clear-sighted way the unpredictability of those fortunes on the world's own terms. Placing their confidence in a God beyond the world, they need not, for example, have any inflated hope of securing themselves—protecting against loss and assuring gain—by way of the precise calculation of the risks they run in our current, quite volatile economic circumstances. The sort of hope that financial derivatives offer—the misplaced hope of substituting statistical probabilities for what turn out to be simple uncertainties—need not lure them into capitalist ventures with the expectation of being able to work the system reliably for their own benefit by their own efforts.

Finally, a God different from the world allows Christians to imagine possibilities for economic life not obviously instantiated in the current configuration of capitalism (or in any other of its configurations for that matter). A transcendent God sets loose the Christian imagination, in other words, to range beyond the given in its discussion of possibilities for economic life. In keeping with the pluralistic sensibility discussed earlier, those possibilities can be thrown into the mix of provisional hypotheses to be considered when attempting to push capitalism in more eco-egalitarian directions as part of a counterresonance machine. Let me provide an example.

A transcendent God's relations with a world of becoming have a noncompetitive shape in that (as we have seen) God is working through, rather than replacing or evacuating of significance, the complex forces and agencies of the very world God brings about. God's absolute or unconditioned power, in short, is not one of jealously guarded exclusive possession but one of universal, all-comprehensive giving; everything in the world with any causal efficacy or agency has that power by virtue of God's own power to give it. Such an idea of noncompetitiveness can be generalized (as I have argued in *Economy of Grace* by looking more closely at a variety of theological cases in which God works for the benefit of the world) to produce a vision of a human community of mutual fulfillment, which is in a broad sense economic: All parties are to benefit at the same time from the same processes by which goods are produced and exchanged.[6]

Although radically different in its noncompetitive thrust from the fundamentally competitive principles underlying capitalism (and this is the strongly oppositional or prophetic character it gains from drawing on divine transcendence), such an economic vision nonetheless enables a very practically oriented discrimination among different forms of capitalism. For instance, such an economic vision would caution in particular against the zero-sum profit mechanisms typical of finance-dominated capitalism. Wealth generation in other forms of capitalism is ultimately dependent on increasing demand for goods and services; and therefore, for all their tendencies to exploit the workforce, those forms of capitalism have an interest (ideally) in promoting widespread employment at wage levels sufficient to prop up such demand. Finance-dominated capitalism (by which I mean capitalism in which finance separates from the production process and is a preferred means of profit generation in its own right) is unusual—and therefore unusually suspect from the standpoint of an economic vision of mutual fulfillment—in that it allows profit to be generated in economic circumstances that are generally quite dire for everyone except a small minority at the top. If one is simply betting on the ups and downs of asset values, it really doesn't matter what is going on in the "real" economy; there is as much money to be made in finance as ever. If the economy is tanking and the stock market plunging as a result, one can turn a profit by short selling and in that way do one's own little bit to drive stock prices lower, while encouraging the business contraction to be even steeper.[7]

It is not just that enormous amounts of money *can* be made by the very few while everyone else is left behind; it is quite possible to make money *off* their dire straits, in what appears to be a directly competitive scenario. For example, financial derivatives are typically ways of making money off volatility in asset prices—because derivatives often involve betting on the ups and downs of those values within or across markets—but that same volatility can be directly correlated with myriad forms of economic distress borne by others. Companies find it hard to remain profitable when commodity prices and currency values across all the markets in which they do business are swinging wildly from day to day. No one with a private retirement plan needs to be reminded about the hardships that stock market swings can portend. And the difficulties that fluctuations in oil and food prices represent for whole populations are equally obvious. But without volatility of those sorts—in the value of currencies, commodities, and stocks—the money to be made in financial derivatives dries up. Indeed, the bigger the swings, the better, since derivatives, as I said before, often simply amount to betting on those swings.

One might argue to the contrary that derivatives are designed to help people cope with those sorts of swings. Derivatives provide companies, for example, with ways of hedging against the hardships that volatility can bring. If an airline is afraid that the price of jet fuel will go up, that airline can contract for the option of buying jet fuel at a certain price in future. If that target price proves wrong and the price of jet fuel when the time rolls around is lower, one can simply not exercise the option and one will have lost only what one paid for the contract. Or one might argue that derivatives help bring volatility down, for example by signaling to market participants what those investing in derivatives think an asset will be worth in future.

But there is plenty of evidence to suggest that derivatives, rather than deflating the costs of volatility or bringing volatility down, serve instead to foment the very volatility from which they promise to protect market participants, and eventually in so doing produce some of the wildest swings, from boom to complete bust. The derivatives that repackaged mortgages worked in that way, with that result. The market for those derivatives helped propel the mortgage market for risky loans; and the resulting easy credit to even high-risk borrowers helped inflate housing prices. Anyone could get a house, and demand soared, which prompted more people to build houses and more people to refinance and take out bigger second mortgages and get further into debt. And then the whole thing collapsed when the rising price of housing became more than people could afford and the glut of new houses on the market eventually surpassed demand. A bust ensued.

Or consider a simpler scenario. Betting on the decline (or upswing) in value of some asset when a lot of people follow your lead and do the very same thing, as typically happens in financial markets, produces the very decline (or upswing) predicted and much more of one than would otherwise be justified by the underlying problem with the asset (or favorable news about it) that got anyone to bet that way to begin with. Bigger swings are the result, with greater fallout for others.

The belief in divine transcendence that I have specified allows for an honest recognition of the kind I just outlined concerning the failings of finance-dominated capitalism in general and unregulated derivative markets in particular. One has no reason to presume, in some a priori fashion, the current system's providential arrangement for the common good; it is neither self-equilibrating, nor designed, through some guaranteed telos, to produce widespread benefit. Hopes of mastering the downside potentials of a volatile world through financial instruments such as derivatives can readily be seen for what they are—a pipe dream for the many. Efforts to generate divine standards for human community help, indeed, to make sense of and motivate the active search for alternatives to such a zero-sum economic order. Belief in divine transcendence thereby aligns with a counterresonance machine to spur the emergence of new economic forms in, as I argued earlier, genuinely open debate with others about the proper shape of our economic lives.

## NOTES

1. William E. Connolly, *Pluralism* (Durham, N.C.: Duke University Press, 2005), 47–48.
2. William E. Connolly, *Capitalism and Christianity, American Style* (Durham, N.C.: Duke University Press, 2008), 7.
3. Ibid., 2.
4. Kathryn Tanner, *The Politics of God: Christian Theologies and Social Justice* (Minneapolis: Fortress Press, 1992), 11–18. Subsequent references to this work will be by page number(s) within parentheses in the text.
5. Christians often make assertions like this about Christ, of course, but in any argument with others about him, standing in for Christ himself are a variety of human views about him; and those are the views I am specifically concerned with here—how those views might be rendered sacrosanct by claims that God is working through the people who hold them.
6. Kathryn Tanner, *Economy of Grace* (Minneapolis: Fortress Press, 2005).
7. In this and the next several paragraphs I follow closely my argument in "Why Support the Occupy Movement?" *Union Theological Quarterly Review* 64, no. 1 (2013): 32–34.

# Dreaming the Common Good/s: The Kin-dom of God as a Space of Utopian Politics

MELANIE JOHNSON-DeBAUFRE

*Where there is hope there is religion, but where there is religion there is not always hope.*
—ERNST BLOCH, *Atheism and Christianity*

*We should read the Bible one more time. To interpret it, of course, but also to let it carve out a space for our own fantasies and interpretative delirium.*
—JULIA KRISTEVA, *New Maladies of the Soul*

Alongside the image of God as Creator, the metaphor of God as king predominates the biblical language for speaking of God's relation to the earth as a whole. The image of God as covenantal king of the people of Israel might suggest a limited, even parochial provenance. However, the Jewish and later Christian metaphor of God's kingship and its relative the "kingdom of God" (*basileia tou theou*) was generated and generative in the context of translocal social, political, and economic relations, that is, in the context of the history of empires.[1] As the history of Christian political thought and activity shows, the basileia of God is also a double-edged sword. Its vision of an all-encompassing kingdom of God can inspire and authorize imperialism and its antithesis. It trades on absolutist and hierarchical notions of sovereignty and yet also relativizes and subordinates all human sovereignties. Like Janus-faced "religion," which has returned—never having left—to the West's postsecular public stage, now a worldwide stage, it too "inspires and terrifies."[2]

The question of the meaning and value of the kin-dom of God crosses academic disciplines. Christian talk of the kingship of God or Jesus persists in contemporary public discourse, weirdly out of place mixed with the modern and/or the Western political discourse of democracy and rights or disturbingly resonating with unbridled and globalized cowboy capitalism.[3] Some theologians and biblical scholars have tried to address this discursive mismatch or resonance through translation, shifting kingdom, reign, or empire to commonwealth, kin-dom, or revolution.[4] In fact, the divergent Christian appeals to the basileia of God to understand, evaluate, and even shape government policies, social values, and individual and collective political agency do not miss the mark of appropriate political discourse so much as they represent the persistence of the religious imagination in the public, political sphere. The kingdom of God fuses the political with the theological, making assertions, posing questions about their interrelation, refusing to distinguish them. Although debating the precise historical or biblical genealogy of the expression is not often of interest beyond biblical studies, the concepts of divine sovereignty and *oikonomia* are prominent in philosophical discussions of political theology.[5] And because the basileia of God can plausibly be understood as the political theology of Jesus of Nazareth, it has played a role in a range of prospective theological politics such as liberation theology, feminist theology, process theology, and the emerging church movement.[6]

As a biblical scholar teaching in and writing from a progressive-leaning Christian seminary in the United States, I have an interest in both the history of the basileia of God as a central trope in the Jewish and then Christian political imagination and a hope that I might somehow support grounded yet capacious experiments that disrupt, challenge, and change lives shaped by local and planetary inequalities, environmental devastation and injustice, and the culture of war. For biblical scholars, a common way to go about this work is researching the historical contexts, textual and intellectual genealogies, and ethical effects of particular understandings of the basileia of God in order to identify trends, articulate problems, and propose an alternative, whether retrieving a past meaning or creating a new one. This process can be persuasive because either scholarly or theological authority, sometimes indistinguishable from each other, can be leveraged on behalf of the revitalized interpretation.[7] Such interpretations carry weight because they have the legitimacy of an academic discipline, or can claim a plausible connection to Jesus and/or Christian origins, or cohere to a particular strain of Christian doctrines or practices, be they orthodox, evangelical, or liberationist. In this essay, I take a different approach: I am asking not whether the basileia of God is political theology, or which political-theological meaning it should have, but what kind of political theology it is.[8] Here I approach the notion of the basileia of God historically, literarily, and theologically as *utopian social dreaming*, or what Lyman Tower Sargent calls "the dreams and nightmares that concern the ways in which groups of people arrange their lives and which usually envision a radically different society from the one in which the dreamers live."[9]

I have found that thinking the basileia of God as utopian political discourse helps make sense of the binaries that often characterize the broad shifts in

Table 1. Binaries

| Present | Future | Wisdom | Apocalyptic |
|---|---|---|---|
| Physical/material | Spiritual | Hellenistic | Judaic |
| Spatial | Temporal | Egalitarian | Hierarchical |
| Political | Religious | Immanent | Transcendent |
| Violent | Nonviolent | Earthly | Heavenly |
| Human agency | Divine agency | Anti-imperial | Imperial |
| Communal | Individual | National | Universal |
| Jewish | Christian | Ethical | Doctrinal |
| Prophetic | Apocalyptic | Jewish | Roman |
| Jesus | Paul | Christology | Theology |

kingdom scholarship. Of course, the deeper one goes in to the literature, the more nuance there is among and between these categories, but broadly speaking, it is easy to see the persistence of a long list of binaries shaping the discussion. See Table 1.

In a utopian framework, these binaries might shift from either-or choices to productive paradoxes. Other curious (and sometimes frustrating) features of the basileia of God talk in the synoptics become legible as traits of utopian discourse. Embracing this aspect of the Christian imaginary as utopian political thought may also serve as a bridge over certain deep chasms—real or perceived—of our academic and political landscape: between theology and biblical studies, between theology and religious studies, between Christianity and other religions, and between the religious and the secular (or the nontheistic). In this essay, I explore how utopian social dreaming may be useful both as a frame within which to parse a particular vision such as the basileia of God and as a broad *method* for assembling a multiplicity of desires "for a better way of being and living."[10]

### AN INTERLUDE FROM EDUARDO GALEANO

La utopía está en el horizonte.
Camino dos pasos, ella se aleja dos pasos
y el horizonte se corre diez pasos más allá.
¿Entonces para que sirve la utopía?
Para eso, sirve para caminar.[11]

### REHABILITATING UTOPIA

Scholars have revived the concept of utopia after the disasters of the twentieth century. This work has coalesced through the 1990s in a transdisciplinary field called "Utopian Studies," an area of inquiry running across a notably wide range of disciplines, such as history, literature, art, sociology, political theory, theology, psychology, architecture, business, and engineering. The word *utopia* came into the English lexicon with Thomas More's 1516 work by that name about an ideal society (or "best republic") located on an island (the "new Utopia").[12] Like the basileia, it has since been widely abstracted from that specific context, appearing in discussions of literary genre, philosophy, politics, and popular culture. In its everyday English usage, it often carries a negative evaluation, evoking a range of emotions from disgust to disdain and from bemusement to bafflement.[13] The adjective *utopian* marks a sociopolitical idea or plan as overly idealistic or impractical. To have one's proposal for social change called "just utopian" is to be dismissed from the grown-ups' table of political debate.

The more forceful critique has come from an anti-utopian intellectual tradition. Both the rejection of "utopian socialism" and the slaughterhouses of Hitler's fascism and Stalin's communism led to a significant if diverse intellectual recoiling from utopianism as it became equated with totalitarianism and fascism. It seemed that history had proven that utopian social engineering seeks perfection and completion, and thus demands authoritarian rule and the obliteration of dissent.[14] One person's dream of happiness is another person's nightmare, especially when it is enacted as a blueprint for society with no possibility of real difference or dissent.[15] The career of the kingdom of God as complicit with Christian empire as well as the global capitalist gospel of prosperity can similarly hamstring efforts to reenergize the metaphor. In many ways, neither utopia nor the basileia of God registers as a "good" place in light of their histories in Western social and political practices at home and abroad.

Together these mundane and monstrous detractions demand that any proponents of utopia make a case for its political usefulness in both a utilitarian and theoretical sense. As Fredric Jameson notes, utopian politics are either "not political enough or too political."[16] However, the utopian imagination neither chooses a side nor aims for a Goldilocks middle way. Its paradoxes and contradictions are central to its usefulness and vibrancy. It is always not enough and too much. The play of Thomas More's title, a neologism that plays on three Greek words—good (*eu*), no (*ou*), and place (*topos*)—builds in tension between desire and its realization. Equating utopianism with perfectionism and completeness misses the fundamental ambiguity and creativity of utopian social theory, texts, and practices.[17] Thus twentieth-century fascism and communism are not utopianisms; they are totalitarianism and absolutism. And evacuating utopia entirely means giving up on the possibilities of hope. Or so argue the "anti-anti-utopian" thinkers who have found utopia an important concept. When unhinged from a literary genre and specific political positions, this idea of social dreaming or hope for a better world can be identified and critically analyzed in and across "social and political theory, lived experiments, works of art, music, medicine, architecture, technology, and popular culture."[18] And in religion too.[19]

## AN INTERLUDE ON HOPE

> Hope is not confidence. If it could not be disappointed it would not be hope. . . . Hope is critical and can be disappointed. However, hope still nails a flag to the mast, even in decline, in that the decline is not accepted, even when this decline is still very strong. Hope is not confidence.[20]

## DREAMING BIG DREAMS (AGAIN)

As discussed in the introduction to this volume, large-scale and universal Western political concepts have lost their appeal for many in the left-progressive regions of both religion and politics. For a few decades fragmentation has characterized many academic conversations addressing inequality, injustice, and access to power in society and religion. With a multiplying of contested goods, a singular common dissipates.

In the midst of this, however, in Christian Testament studies, the basileia of God has been a central topos—one could say in both senses, as a common locus and as a literary commonplace—variously "used for walking" (*para caminar*) that is, to energize utopian dreams of a different world. A range of historical Jesus portraits counter the overly *futurist* and *individualist* kingdom that renders Christians as immobile social actors, awaiting the interventions of God to remedy the world. Troubled by the ways the basileia is often figured as specifically *religious*, scholars have configured the political basileia as countercultural secular wisdom, a nationalist renewal (or revolt), or an anti-imperial social movement.[21] Some include gender-egalitarian impulses in the basileia movement.[22] Those doing "history from below" emphasize the economic implications of the kingdom on behalf of the poor.[23]

Critiques of these politically progressive interpretations of the basileia of God can come from several directions. Two types of arguments, often conspiring, work to close off the utopian political space of the kingdom by limiting the scope of its authoritative interpreters. The first invokes the importance of historical or academic neutrality—often configured in terms of the place of religious studies in the secular university or the insistence that scholarly historical writing must not project contemporary desires onto the past. The second demands orthodoxy, whereby diverse and contesting religious ideas within a tradition are subordinated as not relevant because not representative. This preference applies not only to Christian orthodoxy, but extends across religions. Maintaining clear borders around each religion ensures clear borders among religions. A third type interrupts politically progressive or emancipatory interpretations by exposing their failures, their own enclosures: when economic interpretations do not account for gender, when gender interpretations do not account for race/ethnicity, when particular religious interpretations do not account for other religions, when scholarly interpretations do not account for everyday or nonelite readers and realities.

All of these shifts and tensions in the history of interpretation of Jesus and the basileia have been analyzed in terms of method, ideological stakes, social location and climate, and results. Here I am interested in thinking about the process by which enclosed or foreclosed utopian spaces are reopened and energized as a ground for the possible. Biblical scholars are readers and writers of the Bible: saying and unsaying around the scriptures, creating narratives that variously organize and mobilize the text and the past to confirm, disrupt, and texture the present, and open the future for both continuity and change. If we want to engage the substantial political, economic, and ecological challenges facing the planetary commons today, biblical scholars must write through the disenchantment, the disconnection, and the fragmentation, join up enough commonality to mobilize collective energy without pressing down so hard on the pen that the connecting lines harden into ties that bind or exclude.

I am thinking about utopia as method. Rather than examine how a biblical scholar "writes through" to energize, and of course be energized by, the possibilities of the basileia, I will look briefly here at how a theologian has done it; largely because, given their disciplinary history, theologians do not (always) have to make the case for doing constructive theopolitical work with the biblical text, as biblical scholars (sometimes) must. To some extent, this removes the layer of methodological posturing or disciplined throat-clearing so often performed by biblical scholars who want to address contemporary needs and concerns. Thus I briefly take up John Cobb's essay "Commonwealth and Empire" and his work of reconfiguring the kingdom of God for the common good.[24]

The utopian begins (again and again) with *disconnection*. Ernst Bloch characterized the utopian impulse with a two-word statement: "Something's missing."[25] It is this diagnosis and desire that drives the utopian process: "There would not be any process at all if there were not *something that should not be so*."[26] For Cobb, there has been a broad twentieth-century severing of the kingdom of God from the political work of social justice, equality, and peace. This is based on several factors: the influence of biblical scholars' interpretation of the basileia as the future apocalyptic action of God alone, Bultmann's existentialist emphasis on the transformation of the individual, and the idea that Jesus inaugurated the kin-dom of God among believers only. Kingdom gets located outside nature, history, and human agency; it is limited to the individual rather than society; or it is confined to the church. The basileia has been disconnected and misplaced from the spheres of the social and thus the political (not unlike religion being defined as Other and expelled from the secular; see Thatamanil in this volume).

In the space of disconnection emerges (again and again) an alternative good place. Cobb nails his flag to the mast: "It's time to recognize that the social gospel writers were closer to the truth than these alternatives." But there is more work to be done to get into motion. The enclosures of the reclaimed alternative space must be opened. Cobb engages in another round of "something's missing." The social gospel movement underestimated the power of human sinfulness to derail progress toward a world where God's purposes are realized and forgot that human action is completely a part of God's action. Social gospel did not have sufficient analysis of racism and colonialism, and "could have done much better on gender." Liberation theology had these problems too, and both needed analysis of ecological destruction and militarized nationalism.

Recognizing the truths and failures of the social gospel and liberation theology opens basileia and makes movement possible; there is now prospective work to be done. The reader is drawn forward into the (textual) past. If the ideology of empire "expresses the desires to add to one's wealth and to dominate over others," and imperial success translates military domination into claims of cultural and moral superiority, then Jesus' reversal of these values of empire is apparent in Jesus' actions and the community that developed around him. Healing the sick, release of captives, feeding the hungry, clothing the naked, sharing wealth—none of these features exploitation or domination. The basileia is also contra–religious establishment, not only in its specific address to the Jewish establishment—which cannot easily be figured as "religious" apart from the political—but in its radical challenge, as embodied in later movements, to Christian (and thus any) religious establishment. The "something is missing" in the basileia cannot be figured, therefore, simply as the religious countering the political or as the political criticizing the religious. It is a space of contested political theologies.

Both contestation and paradox are characteristic of the utopian. A productive paradox runs through Cobb's discussion of the kingdom: It is most often submerged, forgotten, lost, ignored, embodied by the persecuted, by non-Christians, by small groups protesting the Church, and yet the radically anti-imperial message and practice of Jesus and his group are also *clear and obvious*. "The centrality of the *basileia theou* in the ministry of Jesus requires no scholarship to discover. It is apparent to any casual reader of the Synoptic Gospels."[27] The basileia of God shimmers in and out of the text, in and out of space-time, ever present and not present. Plain as day and difficult to see, the substance of the basileia cannot be dismissed, and routinely has been.

Indeed, Cobb acknowledges that despite the plain sense of the gospels, imagining and materializing the "kind of order a person moved by this reversal of values should seek in the world, or even in the church" proves difficult. Some try. Most compromise. What clarity people have often comes through disgust with the imperial realities of our own day. This affective revulsion resonates with a prophetic stance: "We stand in the prophetic tradition, which is much clearer on its denunciations than in its positive proposals." Echoing Bloch's "it should not be," the Christian's "task is primarily, perhaps exclusively, criticism. Whatever society we encounter, we will measure it in relation to the commonwealth of God and find it wanting."[28] Thus the content of the utopian basileia materializes primarily in its negations: no empire, no war, no hunger, no exploitation of the planet nor its many inhabitants.

Another paradox emerges. A basileia of God with too much content overreaches, often striving for perfection of society's institutions and relations. Institutions create hierarchies; revolutionaries win and turn into oppressors. Completeness is neither possible, nor desired. Identifying a society too closely with the kin-dom diminishes the gospel's power and credibility. And yet, paradoxically, negation alone cannot suffice. "To limit the Christian role to the prophetic is a counsel of despair."[29] Cobb looks to Whitehead, who suggests a routine process of criticism, evaluative question posing, and good-faith decision making at local, national, and global levels. "In what kind of society could people live in communities in which service to one another counted more than wealth and power?"[30] The basileia hovers in a space of unsaying and saying. The negations generate the questions. The answers generate negations.

Throughout Cobb's text a sense emerges that although disconnection and misplacement characterize the diagnosis of the kin-dom's problem, overconnection and firm placement drain it of energy and motion. Christian spaces have no unique claim to the utopian impulses of the kingdom. Jesus and his group stand in the text alongside other leaders and movements both theistic and nontheistic. All kinds of non-Christians working for change struggle with similar challenges. Christians can learn from other societies. "Jesus' teaching of the commonwealth of God keeps breaking through, sometimes in the church, sometimes elsewhere."[31] The kingdom's movement also cannot be characterized as linear temporal progress. Improvements may not always be improvements, and they are not realized evenly throughout or across societies. Nonetheless, there can be evaluation and motion: Improvements are possible, and "a society in which it is more possible to live according to Jesus' values is better," even if not perfect (which would be worse).[32]

I have worked through Cobb's text in this way in order to tease out the method by which utopian space is energized and put into motion. By such a process the commonwealth of God becomes a space of possibility for the theologian and the reader. This is Christian social dreaming. The utopian basileia is reconstructed and gotten into motion in the diagnosis of something missing, in the recounting of failures, in the articulation and embrace of its paradoxes and contradictions, and in the diverse and open-ended nature of its possibilities.

## THE BASILEIA AS UTOPIAN

How might the main features of utopian social dreaming be useful for thinking about basileia in biblical studies?

*Disjuncture and Definition*
The "something missing" is diagnostic dissatisfaction with the here and now. Disjunction can be figured as negation, estrangement, neutralization, or distantiation. Thus John Lennon's "Imagine (there's no heaven . . .)," Ursula Le Guin's Gethenians, whose sex and gender are not fixed, and More's island of Utopia, physically cut from its continent by a vast trench, all emerge from disjuncture. It is easy to see such disjuncture in the kingdom of God. Peppered through the Hebrew Bible, the literature between the testaments, and in early Christian texts, there is the idea that in God's reign, in God's world, with God's sovereignty, among God's people certain things would or should not be: no injustice, no hunger, no perpetual indebtedness, no bodily, spiritual, and social brokenness, no pointless or unfair suffering, and no unjust death.

Ironically, the scholarly habit is to draw on the broad context of Jewish and Christian tradition to remedy the curious fact that although Jesus speaks of the basileia many times in the synoptic gospels, he does not directly define it.[33] Do we thereby fill up the image with *so much content* that its particular disjunctures (throughout the literature) become less distinct from each other? Utopian negation is not simply replacing the negated thing with its opposite, but opening a space through disjuncture. "Possibility is not hoary-patriotism. The opposite is also in the possible. The hindering element is also in the possible."[34] There are quite a few ways that basileia could perform productive disjunctures: It might be a kingdom that is a different kind of kingdom, or no kind of kingdom at all. Or perhaps the disjunctures are in the *of God* and thus *not* of Herod, or of Caesar, or of other gods, or on earth, or any one place. Figuring the basileia as utopian presses us to consider its unsaying, its apophasis: *not so much of what is being said positively as what is being negated.*[35]

*Conjunction and Location*
Although the utopian begins in dissatisfaction, and can even be largely iconoclastic, it cannot be completely divorced or alien to its context. As Roland Boer describes, utopia requires a "radical disjunction with this dismal world as a

condition of its possibility, yet in order to be possible in the first place, it must find another way to re-open the connection."[36] A utopia has spatial, temporal, or conceptual anchors to the present and therefore "maps the place of an imminent and concrete future, forming *within* the horizons of its present this emerging history."[37] Thus More's Utopia is not sixteenth-century England and yet is clearly sixteenth-century England in the details of its geography and in its interest in land enclosure. The basic need for conjunction, for connection and legibility, explains the use of the imperial word *basileia* in the context of the Roman Empire, as well as, not in contrast to, it local use in the province of Judea with its client kings. The need for conjunction also explains why interpreters must constantly wrestle with its translation. As it loses connections to the world as it is, it must be relocated to reconnect it to the world.

To lodge the basileia only in its displacements from the here-and-now—future, heavenly, religious, spiritual, universal, and transcendent—misses its simultaneous and necessary connections with the present, earthly, political, material, local, and immanent. Much of the wrangling over the meaning of the kingdom of God in the synoptic gospels has been generated by interpreters' efforts to resolve the tension of the basileia being simultaneously connected and disconnected from the world. If we figure the basileia as utopian, then resolving that tension drains it of its utopian energy.

This also applies to the question of the basileia being spatial. It is common, since Gustav Dalman, for "kingdom" of the King James Bible to be rejected in favor of "reign," because basileia is not primarily territorial.[38] However, thinking with the topos of utopia suggests that translating basileia as "reign" or "sovereignty" or "rule" masks its spatial imaginary and shifts the focus onto the power of God. It is actually difficult to muster basileia texts that show much interest in the nature of the power of God. It is also interesting to note that Dalman's own proposal was a sorting of political space built on negation—in this case western European from the authoritarian "Oriental," present from past, and constitutional monarchy from religion: "Today as in antiquity an Oriental 'kingdom' is not a body politic in our sense, a people or land under some form of constitution, but merely a 'sovereignty,' which embraces a territory."[39] The great deal of energy expended placing the basileia of God—over Israel, over the kings of the Earth, in the heavens, in spirit, in hearts, near, among you, in the future, in Heaven, on Earth, on a throne, not from this world—*points to its spatiality, not a lack of it.* Perhaps spatiality is precisely one of the problems being explored through social dreaming: Where is the kindom of God? This is supported by the fact that the predominant syntactical feature of the basileia in the synoptics is as *object*. "What 'happens' most to the kingdom of God is that it is 'entered.'"[40]

*Paradox, Pedagogy, Praxis*

In its concoction of disjunction and conjunction, utopia opens a paradoxical and open-ended space for imagining alternatives, for thinking what is possible in light of the negation. As with its eponymous island, utopian space can be a narration of a detailed and recognizable place. It may be a positive, negative, or mixed image.[41] But it is always also somehow not existing—a no-place. Jesus' basileia message has more content than it might seem from the lack of definition in the gospels. The stories fill out the negations: healing the sick, release of prisoners, forgiveness of debt, caring for the poor, rich sharing wealth, serving others. In various forms of Christian utopian social dreaming—constructive theology, preaching, liturgy—the gospel stories materialize in the present moment as a vision, with content, of possible futures in the elsewhere past.

And yet the space of the possible is also a space of question posing. This resonates with the Marxist theory of the utopian as providing an education of desire. The prevalence of parables in the synoptics, as well as the development of stories about Jesus posing questions, points to practices of utopian social dreaming in the teaching of Jesus and his group. Although interpreters wrangle over Jesus' tax policy, the presentation of a coin marked with Caesar's face and the statement "Give to Caesar what is Caesar's and God what is God's" poses a rather pointed question for deliberation: What, in the world, is Caesar's and what is God's? In our present reality, how do you tell what belongs to whom? Ensuing arguments about the coin produce possible alternatives to the whole world as Caesar's (or God's) through the simultaneity of the world as Caesar's and God's. Thus *both* the possibility of secular political space and the possibility that no political space exists outside the divine might be generated from posing the question of the extent of Caesar's or God's realm or territory.[42]

Biblical scholars often seek to nail down the answers to the questions posed in the teachings of Jesus. However, as William Herzog has proposed, parables might best be understood as a kind of basileia school with Jesus as a pedagogue of the oppressed. In this frame, we might consider the way parables encode the way things are and pose questions about how they should be. To read some parables in this utopian way, it is necessary to displace them, that is, to unlink them from the gospel writer's interpretation of them. For example, without the opening and concluding verses, the parable of the widow and the unjust judge poses a question to the audience: Who in the world is like the judge? Who in the world is like the widow? Has justice been served? Disconnecting the basileia of God from the landowner/master characters in the parable of the laborers raises questions to the audience about who owns everything and whether generosity is the same as justice. Unlinking God from the master in the parable of the talents suggests that the master who reaps where he does not sow is being exposed by the parable rather than celebrated. In both cases, the question "What is the basileía of God like?" should not come at the beginning of the parable (as the gospel writers have it), but at the end, launching conversation about the way the world is and what alternatives might be possible.[43] This suggests also that for the pedagogical purpose of parables to be reenergized as utopian pedagogy, or as social dreaming, they have to be continually recontextualized in the world as it is, not only as it was in antiquity. In this sense, they may be productively recoded, or the questions posed should connect to contemporary problems of economy, sovereignty, power, inequality, justice, and so on.[44] Historical research serves as a strong reminder and resource for the fact that Jewish and Christian religious imaginary was (and is) simultaneously a social-political imaginary, but it cannot alone get utopia moving.

The pedagogical function connects utopian social dreaming to the transformation of the everyday in the past and in the present. It is focused not only on the ruler/s of society or on the integrity of law or the purity or legitimacy of this or that social institution. "Utopia entails not just the fictional depiction of a better society, but the assertion of a radically different set of values; these values are communicated indirectly through their implications for a whole way of life."[45] It is social dreaming because it is joined-up thinking. "Utopianism confronts the fact that lives are whole, that children, families, marriage, education, economics, politics, death, and so on are all connected."[46]

However, this transformation of the everyday does not limit the horizon of the utopian to micropolitics or the basileia of God to small scales of action and influence. In fact, it materializes out of the tension and interconnection between the universal (or translocal or whole) and the particular (or local or part).[47] As Anna Peterson discusses at the beginning of her study of utopian communities of the Old Order Amish and progressive Catholicism in Central America, "People are most effectively moved to act on the basis of things close to home. . . . These can be connected by organizers and activists to larger questions about structures and distributions of power."[48] Thinking with this multiscaled horizon of utopian social dreaming, we might now reverse the familiar slogan to say: Think locally, act globally.

This utopian linking of the particular to the universal is what animated my discussion with my colleague, Ada María Isasi-Díaz, concerning her proposal to translate what she considered an irrelevant and problematic basileia as "kin-dom of God."[49] Her powerful alternative lays claim to the second primary semantic field of Jesus' God-talk, that is, family.[50] To what extent, though, does kin-dom (taken alone) downsize and overly localize the basileia from a social and world-spanning horizon? The basileia of God is certainly mixed with family talk, but the talk of family in both the gospels and the imperial cult is also wrapped up with empire. There is a similar problem with the translation "empire of God" as it does not communicate a sense of the worldwide and the local together. Although a good case can be made to translate basileia in large-scale terms, the local horizon is built in.[51]

*Open-Endedness and Closure*
I emphasize the issue of scale because of the strong connection of utopia to a sense of the totality or a closed whole system, which robustly persists in the Marxist strain of utopian thought, despite its rejection in the late twentieth century. The utopian dream is a big dream, imagining the impossible possibility of radical systemic change and inspiring revolution. When Cobb speaks of liberation theology's being better than the social gospel, he says it is "revolutionary not reformist." To speak of revolution or the totality is to conjure again the nightmare of twentieth-century state violence. For many, utopianism and totalitarianism and authoritarianism are synonymous or dangerous bedfellows. A fantasy of a detailed closed whole system can lead to the imposition of a closed whole system as if the fantasy were a blueprint.

However, the basileia is not a detailed plan and should not be mistaken for the world as such. A realized and closed system dismantles the disjuncture and is not utopian. Indeed, "the political function of Utopia is not its own realization" in the future, but the bringing forth of the possible in the present.[52] The combination, interplay, and reformulation of disjuctures and connections are its very generative energy. Thus the diverse intellectual, political, and artistic work of identity-based utopianisms have injected both the necessity and the possibility of multiplicity into the discussion.[53]

Open-endedness and multiplicity enable a self-reflexivity in utopian figuration. Identifying failure—regarding race, empire, gender, nation, ecology—and recognizing compromise and uneven change typify the self-reflexivity of the utopian by which we are continually educated in our desires. It is crucial that people continue to look for the "something is missing" to reenergize dreams of the worldwide kin-dom. Identity-informed critiques and disruptions have and must figure prominently in this process of opening and undoing utopian closure and completeness, because history and experience show how multiplicative structures of domination so easily remain, return, or retool. This is true of all social movements or communal dreaming projects regardless of their particular ideals. Someone or something goes missing. Even when communities think with potent utopian basileia ethics and models, they often complexly replicate the privileged view of the male, and/or the racial or class-privileged, and/or the heteronormal, and/or the abled. Articulations, embodiments, and analysis of the dystopian, alternative dreams, or iconoclastic nonparticipation are also constitutive of the vibrancy and viability of utopian social dreaming.

This constant evaluation and opening does not preclude alliance, solidarity, and loosely connected or temporary assemblages. Both flash or networked political movements and longer-term intentional communities embody or enact social dreaming and thus expand the range of practices that are conceptually and concretely possible. But these need not wholly or permanently succeed to be valuable. Failures can also be productive. Anna Peterson again: "Every movement learns from its predecessors but also that knowledge, commitments, relationships, capacities, and 'powers' all build slowly and can lead to unexpected results. There is no unilinear accumulation of forces, because every movement is subject to countless frustrations and losses. However, the mere fact of historical failure, according to instrumental criteria, should not condemn a group or its goals"[54] In this frame, we should let Jesus followers and the early Christians who obviously had social dreams and wrote about them, a bit off the hook for the ways that the biblical text shows their failures. Failures are openings too.

### AN INTERLUDE FOR THE DISCIPLES' PRAYER

> Pray then in this way:
> Our Father in heaven,
> hallowed be your name.
> Your kin-dom come.
> Your will be done,
> on earth as it is in heaven.
> Give us this day our daily bread.
> And forgive us our debts,
> as we also have forgiven our debtors.
> And do not bring us to the time of trial
> but rescue us from the evil one.
> —MATT. 6:9–13

### SEEDS OF THE POSSIBLE

Utopianists are interested in the seeds of the possible both in the past and in the present. Thus the imaginary reconstitution of society "has both an *archaeological* or analytical mode, and an *architectural* or constructive mode."[55] To think in these terms, then, a biblical scholar might take an archaeological/analytical interest in the Bible as part of the history of utopian literature. Or one can constructively look for the seeds of our present or possible futures in the past. Take for example, the disciples' prayer. In many ways it could be seen as utopian literature. The bodies of the prayers (with their needy stomachs) are plotted on a map as wide as the heavenly cosmos, with the Father as Lord of Heaven and the society spanning systems of piety, sovereignty, and exchange predictably taking up the mediating the space between. And yet the world is a little strange. One feature of utopian writing is "world reduction" in which impossible geographies are contained within limited boundaries. Here the vast distance between heaven and earth is collapsed into the distance between the Father and child (note the infants in Luke/Q 10:21, the son in 10:22, and the children who demand bread in Luke/Q 11:10).

To read the spatial reductions of the cosmos as simply ancient metaphors is to miss the way that conceived or imagined geographies always project onto the empirical world to define and order reality. Through the repetitions of such world reductions in ritual and scripturalization, the relations of the heavens and the earth are reimagined in an idealized space between a father who, of course, gives not a stone but bread to the child who demands it.[56] This ideal space is a good place, and yet this good place is also no place. Where exactly is the divine? When is basiliea coming? How does it materialize? The petitions of the prayer are unfulfilled and are endlessly deferred in the repetitions of the prayer as petition. And yet whenever the prayer is prayed, the good place is reiterated as an ideal that can be experimented with as lived space. But these space-time anomalies also resist completion and closure, figuring the utopian propensity or politics of basileia as process and bounded open space. In any context it might fail, but it is always open to the future. There is an opening for possibility in the text's unexpected connections and strange geography. One could argue that the ancient prayer was a seed of the future in the past, a future where, thinking differently about food, or debt, or fathers, or God is possible. This is the architectural/constructive mode of the reconstitution of the world. Both modes—the archaeological and the architectural—are working on hope.[57]

## A UTOPIAN COMMONS

Understanding the basileia as open-ended and always multiply located social dreaming of the common good makes it possible to build connections across familiar discursive and social divides without insisting that the same vision must occupy every space. This connects Christians with the struggles for social change among non-Christians. Recently, a utopian scholar suggested that utopianists need to develop a much more nuanced understanding of religion.[58] And Roland Boer has suggested an alliance between the nontheist and theist Left that embraces the intertwining of the secular and religious, reads the Bible with theological suspicion, denounces the abuse of the Bible, and fosters liberating readings and uses.[59] The separations of the secular and religious in public discourse persist and most biblical scholars in the public square (that is, marketplace) configure their authority either as religious or secular. The result is often a nailing down of the basileia to this or that background or meaning.[60] We still trade in most of the binaries listed above rather than open up the productive paradoxes of the basileia to critical reimagination of the world. It is possible that Stephen Colbert more effectively activates the utopian in the Christian story than I do or any of my colleagues when he plays with the dystopian image—for antigovernment conservatives—of Jesus of Nazareth as King of the Heavens:

> What frightens me *really*, is now we know that we got a liberal Jesus sitting at the right hand of the Father. . . . Anything happens to the Big Guy, we could end up with a socialist deity redistributing my loaves and fishes![61]

This utopian game locates the Christian social imaginary of a right *not to be poor* fully within the sphere of the political without translation out of the theological.

Embracing progress and failure, encompassing the whole without completion, undoing excessive saying and denying unsaying alone, materializing in places and eluding any enclosure, utopian social dreaming is widely legible across cultures and always particular to its contexts. Figuring the basileia as utopian social dreaming keeps it ever moving, undoing, and reconstituting itself, lest it be drained of the animating and creative energy that makes another world possible.

## NOTES

1. For the multivalence of the metaphor in ancient Jewish texts and its different scales in relation to nation/people and cosmos, see Anne Moore, "The Search for the Common Judaic Understanding of God's Kingship," in *Common Judaism: Explorations in Second-Temple Judaism*, ed. Wayne O. McCready and Adele Reinhartz (Minneapolis: Fortress, 2008), 131–44. For an approach that places the *basileia* in the context of the language of Hellenistic kingship, thus bringing out a contrast to Roman rule within imperial discourse, see Giovanni Bazzanna, "*Basileia*–The Q Concept of Kingship in Light of Documentary Papyri," in *Light from the East: Papyrologische Kommentare zum Neuen Testament*, ed. P. Artz-Grabner and C. M. Kreinecker; Philippika–Marburger altertumskundliche Abhandlungen 39 (Wiesbaden: Harrassowitz 2010), 153–68.
2. Hent de Vries and Lawrence E. Sullivan, eds., *Political Theologies: Public Religions in a Post-Secular World* (New York: Fordham University Press, 2006), 2.
3. During the 2012 U.S. elections, the meme "Whoever Is President, Jesus Is King" appeared again and again on my facebook page, shared by Christians from various theological positions. This may be an example of Ernst Bloch's idea of a nonsynchronous contradiction in which utopian desires of a past social order maintain

ideological value in the present. See Ernst Bloch, *The Principle of Hope*, 3 vols. (1938; Cambridge, Mass.: MIT Press, 1959). For a discussion of the resonance between right-wing evangelical Christianity and capitalism, see William E. Connolly, *Capitalism and Christianity, American Style* (Durham, N.C.: Duke University Press, 2008).
4. The bibliography for the translation of the kingdom of God is as vast as the kingdom of God. In this essay, I use the dominant translation (kingdom), the Greek word (basileia), and Isasi-Diaz's neologism (kin-dom; see note 49 below) interchangeably to signal that the term is simultaneously kyriarchal, undecidable, and utopian.
5. The classic work on sovereignty is Carl Schmitt, *Political Theology: Four Chapters on the Concept of Sovereignty*, trans. G. Schwab (1922; University of Chicago Press, 1985). Recently, Giorgio Agamben has addressed kingdom and *oikonomia*, but with no discussion of the basileia of God in the gospels (*The Kingdom and the Glory: For a Theological Genealogy of Economy and Government*, trans. Lorenzo Chisa [Stanford, Calif.: Stanford University Press, 2011]).
6. E.g., Gustavo Gutiérrez, *A Theology of Liberation: History, Politics, and Salvation* (1971; Maryknoll, N.Y.: Orbis Books, 1988); Jon Sobrino, *Jesus the Liberator: A Historical-Theological Reading of Jesus of Nazareth* (1991; Maryknoll, N.Y.: Orbis Books, 1993); Johann Baptist Metz, *Faith in History and Society: Toward a Fundamental Practical Theology* (New York: Seabury, 1980); Elisabeth Schüssler Fiorenza *In Memory of Her: A Feminist Theological Reconstruction of Christian Origins* (1983; New York: Crossroad, 2005); John B. Cobb Jr., *Process Theology as Political Theology* (Philadelphia: Westminster Press, 1982); Brian D. McClaren, *Everything Must Change: Jesus, Global Crisis, and a Revolution of Hope* (Nashville, Tenn.: Thomas Nelson, 2007).
7. For a discussion of the scholarly interest in reframing Christian identity by rewriting Christian origins, see my *Jesus among Her Children: Q, Eschatology, and the Construction of Christian Origins* (Cambridge, Mass.: Harvard University Press, 2006).
8. Gutiérrez makes links between the basileia of God and Marxist utopian thought (*Theology of Liberation*, 216–20). Mary Ann Beavis locates Jesus' basileia vision within the context of ancient utopian thought in *Jesus and Utopia: Looking for the Kingdom of God in the Roman World* (Minneapolis: Augsburg Fortress, 2006).
9. Lyman Tower Sargent, "Three Faces of Utopianism Revisited," *Utopian Studies* 5, no. 1 (1994): 3.
10. Ruth Levitas, *The Concept of Utopia* (Syracuse, N.Y.: Syracuse University Press, 1990), 7–8.
11. Utopia lies at the horizon / When I draw nearer by two steps, it retreats two steps / If I proceed ten steps forward, it swiftly slips ten steps ahead / What purpose, then, does utopia serve? / It serves this one: It gets us moving.
12. The title in Latin is *De optimo rei publicae statu deque nova insula Utopia*.
13. Some of my students from South Korea and from different African countries have told me that they are emotionally neutral about the term *utopia*, many saying that they have never heard it before.
14. Lucy Sargisson, "The Curious Relationship between Politics and Utopia," in *Utopia Method Vision*, ed. Tom Moylan and Raffaella Baccolini (Bern: Peter Lang, 2007), 25.

15. More's original meaning and notions of idealism and perfection are mixed together in the *Oxford English Dictionary* definition of utopia: "(a) An imaginary or hypothetical place or state of things considered to be perfect; a condition of ideal (esp. social) perfection. (b) An imaginary or distant country. (2) An impossibly ideal scheme, esp. for social improvement."
16. Fredric Jameson, "The Politics of Utopia," *New Left Review* 25 (January/February 2004): 42.
17. According to Sargent, these are the "the three faces of utopianism": the literary utopia, utopian practice, and utopian social theory.
18. Sargisson, "Curious Relationship between Politics and Utopia," 25. According to Ruth Levitas, utopian desire cannot be posited as a universal human propensity or essence, but is articulated or performed unevenly and differently—in terms of form, content, and function—throughout time and across contexts (see *Concept of Utopia*).
19. More than any other thinker, Ernst Bloch explored the utopian in religion, particularly Christianity. His work influenced Christian utopians like Metz and Gutiérrez as well as Tillich.
20. Ernst Bloch and Theodor Adorno, "Something's Missing: A Discussion between Ernst Bloch and Theodor W. Adorno on the Contradictions of Utopian Longing," in Ernst Bloch, *The Utopian Function of Art and Literature: Selected Essays*, trans. Jack Zipes and Frank Mecklenburg (Cambridge, Mass.: MIT Press, 1988), 16–17.
21. See John Dominic Crossan, *God and Empire: Jesus against Rome, Then and Now* (San Francisco: HarperSanFrancisco, 2007); Richard A. Horsley, *Jesus and Empire: The Kingdom of God and the New World Disorder* (Minneapolis: Fortress Press, 2003); Reza Aslan, *Zealot: The Life and Times of Jesus of Nazareth* (New York: Random House, 2013).
22. A reconstruction of gender egalitarianism in the basileia, although present in ancient utopian political thought, often draws the most virulent critique (bordering on excessive disdain). See John H. Elliot, "Jesus Was Not an Egalitarian: A Critique of an Anachronistic and Idealist Theory," *Biblical Theology Bulletin* 32, no. 2 (2002): 75–91; idem, "The Jesus Movement Was Not Egalitarian but Family-Oriented," *Biblical Interpretation* 11, no. 2 (2003): 173–210; and Mary Ann Beavis, "Christian Origins, Egalitarianism, and Utopia," *Journal of Feminist Studies in Religion* 23, no. 2 (2007): 27–49.
23. See Richard A. Horsley, ed., *A People's History of Christianity*, vol. 1: *Christian Origins* (Minneapolis: Fortress, 2005).
24. John C. Cobb Jr., "Commonwealth and Empire," in David Ray Griffin, John C. Cobb Jr., Richard A. Falk, and Catherine Keller, *The American Empire and the Commonwealth of God: A Political, Economic, Religious Statement* (Louisville: Westminster John Knox, 2006), 137–50.
25. Bloch and Adorno, "Something's Missing," 1–17.
26. Ibid., 17.
27. Cobb, "Commonwealth and Empire," 143.
28. Ibid., 147–48.
29. Ibid., 148.
30. Ibid., 149.

31. Ibid., 150.
32. Ibid., 148.
33. I suspect it is no accident that the two places in the New Testament that offer some definition are built on negations (see John 18:36 and Romans 14:17).
34. Bloch and Adorno, "Something's Missing," 17.
35. I thank Mayra Rivera Rivera for suggesting this connection between utopian negation and apophasis in her response to my paper for the transdisciplinary conference.
36. Roland Boer, "Utopian Politics in 2 Chronicles 10–13," in *The Chronicler as Author*, ed. M. Patrick Graham and Steven L. McKenzie (Sheffield: Sheffield Academic Press, 1999), 381.
37. A concept from Louis Marin (*Utopiques: Jeux d'espace*) discussed in Phillip E. Wegner, "Here or Nowhere: Utopia, Modernity, and Totality," in *Utopia Method Vision*, ed. Moylan and Boccalini, 115.
38. See Gustav Dalman, *The Words of Jesus: Considered in the Light of Post-Biblical Jewish Writings and the Aramaic Language*, trans. David Miller Kay (Edinburgh: T. & T. Clark, 1902). In fact, Dalman uses "sovereignty of God" rather than "reign."
39. Ibid., 94.
40. Roy A. Harrisville, "In Search of the Meaning of the 'Reign of God,'" *Interpretation* 47, no. 2 (1993): 143. In the second edition of *The Complete Gospels*, the Jesus Seminar recognized this issue, noting that they use "dominion" to translate basileia when "a spatial term is required by the context" (*The Complete Gospels*, rev. and expanded edition, ed. Robert Miller [San Francisco: HarperSanFrancisco, 1994], 12). In his lengthy study of the language of the basiliea, Jacobus Liebenberg argues that the notion of the basileia as an object (in this case, a possession) is distinctive to the Jesus tradition (*The Language of the Kingdom and Jesus* [Berlin: Walter de Gruyter, 2000], 528).
41. Dystopias are not the opposite of utopia but failed utopias, that is, a projection of what happens if the utopia goes wrong or only functions for a segment of society (Michael D. Gordon, Helen Tilley, and Gyan Prakash, eds.,*Utopia/Dystopia: The Conditions of Historical Possibility* [Princeton: Princeton University Press, 2012], 1). Since the 1970s, a mixing of utopia and dystopia in one work is common. Some notable thinkers have set aside the idea that the utopian is largely a depiction of an ideal society. Karl Mannheim, for example, framed utopianism as a socially located critical stance (in contrast to ideology). Bloch developed notions of a "utopian impulse" surfacing in glimpses and image-traces. Jameson's analysis touches on manifestos and constitutions to slogans and commercials; from architecture to technology to television shows, including recently *The Wire*.
42. For Cobb, the reconnection of a disconnected basileia happens early on regarding human agency in a similarly paradoxical way: "Social Gospel forgot that human action is completely a part of God's action." It is not either this or that; it is this and that. Human agency and divine agency occupy the same space-time. That produces both the possibility of human agency and the impossibility of its complete success. Thinking materially and ecologically, we have to go even further today to

reconnect the imaginary of the basileia of God to include agencies of matter (see Connolly in this volume).

43. Taken as open-ended speech-pictures, the primary function of parables is question posing. See William Herzog, "Why Peasants Responded to Jesus," in Horsley, *Christian Origins*, 47–70.

44. Liebenberg concludes that the original context and meaning of the parables and aphorisms cannot be fixed because their meaning is dependent on context. This suggests their generative rather than propositional pedagogy (*Language of the Kingdom*, 529).

45. Levitas, *Concept of Utopia*, 124.

46. Lyman Tower Sargent, *Utopianism: A Very Short Introduction* (Kindle Locations 944–946) (Oxford University Press, Kindle Edition, 2010).

47. Deleuze and Guattari's de- and reterritorialization and rhizomatic figuring comes to mind. I found Phillip Wegner's discussion of this point very helpful ("Here and Nowhere").

48. Anna Peterson, *Seeds of the Kingdom: Utopian Communities in the Americas* (Oxford: Oxford University Press, 2005), 4.

49. Working out of Catholic social ethics and building a mujerista liberation theology, Ada María Isasi-Díaz proposed "kin-dom" as an analogical appropriation of basileia, not as a translation. "My contention is that the analogical thinking that guides the use of the Gospels in our daily life is impeded or made less rich by the use of "kingdom of God," a metaphor that, at best, has little relevancy in our 21st century lives" ("Kingdom of God: A Mujerista Proposal," in *In Our Own Voices: Latino/a Renditions of Theology*, ed. Benjamín Valentín [Maryknoll, N.Y.: Orbis Books, 2010], 171–90).

50. Isasi-Díaz uses her own understanding of the meaning of family in Latino/a communities to fill out this metaphor. While she recognizes that it can reiterate structures of domination, she articulates the ways that it counterposes closed and hierarchical notions of family. For a similar focus on a counter- or queer family for rethinking *basileia*, see Schüssler Fiorenza, *In Memory of Her*, and Halvor Moxnes, *Putting Jesus in His Place: A Radical Vision of Household and Kingdom* (Louisville, Ky.: Westminster John Knox Press, 2003). In each case, there is a disjuncture between dominant views of family and the reconstruction of family in the Jesus movement. In this sense, they all surface a utopian impulse.

51. For example, the term *basileus* was commonly used in the Greek east for regional kings and their domains, such as the Pergamese kings as well as for the Herodians in Judea (see Matt. 2:1–16). The gospels themselves imagine a world of many basileiai (e.g., "kingdoms of the world" in Matt. 4:8 and "kings of the earth" in Matt. 17:25). And, of course, Jesus is accused of claiming to be king of the Jews (e.g., Matt. 27:11). The point is that the term *basileia* has local resonances as well as imperial ones. The translation "empire" masks this fact. Thus I disagree with the change in the Scholars' Translation of the Jesus Seminar, which has changed its translation to "empire of God" (*The Complete Gospels*. 4th ed., ed. Robert Miller [Salem, Ore.: Polebridge Press, 2010], 22).

52. Sargisson, "Curious Relationship between Politics and Utopia," 31.
53. See, for example, José Esteban Muñoz, *Cruising Utopia: The Then and There of Queer Futurity* (New York: New York University Press, 2009).
54. Peterson, *Seeds of the Kingdom*, 143. See also Judith Halberstam, *The Queer Art of Failure* (Durham, N.C.: Duke University Press, 2011).
55. Ruth Levitas, "Imaginary Reconstitution of Society," in *Utopia Method Vision*, 47.
56. I have benefited greatly from conversations with Jacqueline Hidalgo about the utopian imaginary as well as scripturalization as utopian practice. See her manuscript, "Reconquest of the Sacred: Scriptures, Utopias, and the Legacies of Revelation in Chican@ Aztlán."
57. The architectural/constructive mode is not the opposite of biblical scholarship. Susan Lochrie Graham (*The Flesh Was Made Word: A Metahistorical Critique of the Contemporary Quest of the Historical Jesus* [Sheffield: Sheffield Phoenix Press, 2010]), has analyzed the products of historical Jesus scholarship as narrative rather than as scientific research. She groups Crossan and Schüssler Fiorenza together within the genre of utopian tragicomedy and in comparison to other scholars whose stories cohere to the conventions of the politically conservative romance. See also Elizabeth Castelli, "The *Ekklēsia* of Wo/men and/as Utopian Space," in *On the Cutting Edge: The Study of Women in the Biblical World: Essays in Honor of Elisabeth Schüssler Fiorenza*, ed. Jane Schaberg, Alice Bach, and Esther Fuchs (New York: Continuum, 2004), 36–52.
58. Vincent Geoghegan, "Political Theory, Utopia, and Post-Secularism," in *Utopia Method Vision*, 69–86. One of the most common and influential compendiums of utopian literature strongly frames Judeo-Christianity as the source and fountain of the "paradise fantasy," utopia's irrational other, as driving violent desire without reason. See Frank E. Manuel and Fritzie P. Manuel, *Utopian Thought in the Western World* (Cambridge, Mass.: Harvard University Press, 1979), 33. This gross overstatement is indicative of disciplines not in conversation with religious studies.
59. Roland Boer, *Rescuing the Bible* (Oxford: Wiley-Blackwell, 2007). For a discussion of the divide between religious studies and theology and its problematic shaping of doctoral education in biblical studies, see Melanie Johnson-DeBaufre, "Mapping the Field, Shaping the Discipline: Graduate Biblical Education as Rhetorical Formation," in *Transforming Graduate Biblical Education: Ethos and Discipline*, ed. Elisabeth Schüssler Fiorenza and Kent Richards (Atlanta: SBL Press, 2010). For a discussion using the cyborg figure to bridge the secular and religious divide in politically engaged scholarship around the historical Jesus, see Denise Buell, "Cyborg Memories: An Impure History of Jesus," *Biblical Interpretation* 18, no. 4 (2010): 313–41.
60. Perhaps the most totalizing and closed Christian system is the one that locates the basileia of God as the center of the Christian creeds as well as the entire arc of biblical theology and the climax of human history. See N. T. Wright, *How God Became King: The Forgotten Story of the Gospels* (New York: Harper Collins, 2011).
61. http://www.colbertnation.com/the-colbert-report-videos/368914/december-16-2010/jesus-is-a-liberal-democrat.

# ❧ A Cosmopolitical Theology: Engaging "The Political" as an Incarnational Field of Emergence

DHAWN B. MARTIN

A cosmopolitical theology is a somewhat risky venture. The venture wagers that cosmopolitan imaginaries, which chart our cosmic interconnectedness, together with theological confessions, which affirm material existence as fields in and across which divine mysteries emerge, might just disrupt politics and theologies of marginalization and control. The risk concerns the effort to reconfigure well-entrenched strands of political theories and theologies that, by the manner in which they cast the relationship between "the political" and "the theological," foster practices of exclusion. Theories of secularization that, for example, attempt to banish religious impulses to private realms, reinscribe exclusionary or us/them models of engagement. Doctrines of faith that proclaim God above, beyond, and untouched by creation deify relations of hierarchic control. Theory and praxis necessarily inflect one another. In an effort, then, to construct a political theology that strives to embody practices of liberation and hospitality, practices contributory to the common good, I chart "the political" as an incarnational field of emergence.

Construction of "the political" as an incarnational field of emergence will develop across my exploration of the discourses of cosmopolitanism together with the Christian doctrine of incarnation. I trace how incarnation, as a political project and theological confession, attends simultaneously to embodied existence and to those affects, forces, and agencies that both shape and transcend the flesh of our daily encounters. Transcendence in this construct, however, neither serves as antithesis of nor stands in definitive distinction to immanence. Rather, in a sociopolitical frame, transcendence speaks to that which infuses yet surpasses static categorizations, to that which is immanently tangible yet eludes conclusive deductions. Through my theological lens, that which transcends expresses the love and goodness of God incarnate in the midst of our daily encounters. The cosmopolitical work of William Connolly, Pheng Cheah, and, to a degree, Immanuel Kant, together with the theological work of Graham Ward, Mayra Rivera, and Laurel Schneider, contributes to my proposal of an incarnational politics.

My effort to track the dynamics of an incarnational politics starts with a theopolitical trilemma. This trilemma consists of: (1) politics practiced along us/them divides, (2) sovereignty (divine or human) defined as unlimited authority, and (3) agency cast as either unencumbered by or detached from the relations, communities, and organic systems of material existence. At the heart of each problematic in the trilemma is the underexamination of exclusionary drives shaping our sociopolitical and theopolitical interactions. The trilemma, in short, presses toward what the political philosopher William Connolly has described as "concentric enclosures," or absolutist stances impervious to diversities of thought, belief, or being.[1] A first step to resist such drives is to name the mechanics of exclusion that are present in political and theological discourses. Subsequent steps entail constructing alternative frames of interpretation and models of engagement.

The constructive sections of my essay commence with a preliminary definition of "the political," building on the work of Graham Ward. Next, I turn to the "ambiguous Kantian legacy"[2] as explored by Connolly and Cheah, who each draw the cosmopolitical into immanent planes of human and extra-human agencies, thus challenging elements of Kant's work. As I detail, Connolly's and Cheah's cosmopolitical frames not only open up exclusionary systems generated by the theopolitical trilemma but also provide resources to formulate strategies that challenge traditional models or exercises of sovereignty. These strategies work internally to theopolitical models to disrupt expressions of oppressive authority. My constructive work with the doctrine of incarnation occurs throughout the essay and discovers in this confession models of hospitality, fullness of life, and eucharistic expansiveness. Building on Ward's concept of "transcorporeality," Schneider's "theology of multiplicity," and Rivera's emphasis on incarnational relationality, I approach incarnation as brimming with alternative modes of engagement, as a confession that calls individuals and faith communities to embody what I name practices of the *christo-eccentric* that challenge various theopolitical concentricities. I conclude with an examination of how incarnation theologies and the cosmopolitical might collude to create new ways of being and doing in political and theological systems.

## NAMING THE PROBLEM

Examination of the drives shaping how we name persons, groups, faiths, and phenomena proves critical if we are to create communities attentive to the exclusions lurking in our encounters with our neighbors. Everyday terms might appear neutral or even benign. "The political," for instance, like "the religious" or "the good," seeks to convey meaning in distilled form. The pithiness of such terms, however, betrays the complexities of their genealogies and trajectories. Any attempt to define "the political," for instance, need acknowledge if not contend with the various distinctions developed to refine its scope. Take, as an example, the secular/sacred divide. The vehemence with which groups seek to draw boundaries and vet adherents to their respective causes continues to inflect political debates. The September 2013 adoption of an amended Non-Discrimination Ordinance (NDO) by the city council of San Antonio, Texas, highlights the combative nature of this divide. Written to expand "the City's current non-discrimination policy to prohibit discrimination on the basis of sexual orientation, gender identity and veteran status,"[3] the ordinance provoked reactive responses. Various politicians and groups asserted that the ordinance ends up "stifling speech, repressing religious liberty, and imposing burdens on those who hold a traditional view on human relations."[4] The attempt to bind "religious liberty" to a single "traditional view" illustrates the tendency of definitive distinctions to foster Connolly's earlier noted "concentric enclosures."

Concentric enclosures establish sociopolitical cosmoses that contract toward an absolute center. For certain groups opposed to San Antonio's NDO, the "traditional view" functions as the center of a cosmos that names other views burdensome, perhaps even dangerous. Cosmoses so enclosed cast identity, ethics, "the political," or "the theological" as bounded and readily knowable. In concentric models, the center determines the "image of how political culture does and must function," while "the automatic connotation of isolation, perversity, and marginalization" stigmatizes those deemed outliers.[5] The prescribed norm and the perversion of it thus serve as founding principles of political concentricities. As will become evident, "the political" conceived and enacted as an incarnational field of emergence disrupts the us/them divides of concentric models, and challenges categorizations that marginalize. It does so through committed resistance to that which would concentrically enclose the good that is material existence.

An incarnational politics thus affirms that the life of bodies is not only good, but a good that continues to emerge, a good that continues to reveal itself in and through our cosmos. Our material existence is the substance of life lived in communion with all of creation. In other words, it is a shared or common good. The material world, however, is neither a solitary nor a static good; for the ways we name, relate to, and embody this matter determine the character and trajectories of other goods. As a "political project," incarnation speaks, as suggested by Pheng Cheah, to the embodiment of human rights or "normative" ideals.[6] In a theological vein, it is the very matter of the cosmos, as confessed in doctrines of revelation and of the Christ event, which bear witness to the love of God. The Christ confession, in which the union of the divine with the fleshy matter of existence redeems and transforms, speaks to a liberative model of encounter with others. This model of engagement offers a picture of hospitality that strives toward fullness of life. We will dive more fully into the dynamisms of an incarnational politics shortly. For now it is important to emphasize that an incarnational politics points to the revelatory or emergent character of our encounters with one another. There is no single model of engagement, no one way to name, embody, or relate to the good that is material existence, for the life of bodies is a shared, common, and emergent good.

The cosmopolitanisms that I examine in this essay situate "the political," along with its ideals, relations, and structures of meaning amid "the plurovocity of existence."[7] Attentive to the plurovocal, I therefore seek to challenge analyses that align "the theological" to a monolithic (divine) power and transcendence dissociated from the vitalities and vulnerabilities of materiality. The political progeny of such alignments include sovereignty conceived as "unlimited authority, which means the suspension of the entire existing order" (Carl Schmitt),[8] and us/them modes of political encounter, which contribute to and draw from ideologies of unencumbered agency.

## THE THEOPOLITICAL TRILEMMA

Two problematics that an incarnational politics endeavors to circumvent are the "unlimited authority" prescribed by Carl Schmitt's political theology and the contra-carnational worldview of unencumbered agency that severs connections. The unlimited and the unencumbered tend to peddle in negations with potentially catastrophic disregard for material orders. Schmitt, for a case in point, supplements his notion of sovereignty as "unlimited authority" with an "antithesis." This antithetical declares that "the political must . . . rest on its own ultimate distinctions," namely, that "of friend and enemy."[9] Ultimate distinctions leave little room for emergent possibilities. What's more, "the political" defined as antithetical tends to develop from and reinforce concentric enclosures—that name not only what is and is not the norm but also mark which bodies are and are not one of us. Now, the friend/enemy distinction functions, for Schmitt, as a boundary-marking concept that resists drives to turn the political enemy into "a monster that must not only be defeated but also utterly destroyed."[10] Schmitt's antithetical thus serves, in theory, as a brake upon politics of utter destruction. Yet once the antithetical is introduced, once others are named "the enemy," what prevents this designation from metastasizing into the monstrous? The notion that a single group can unilaterally declare which bodies matter engenders a contra-carnational worldview that would enclose or try to control the emergent goods of material existence.

As an alternative to a theopolitics of unlimited authority and us/them distinctions, I draw on the theologian Graham Ward's expansive definition of "the political" as "an act that entails power."[11] The breadth of this definition provides several structural elements to an incarnational politics. First, Ward's work points to the relational dynamic intrinsic to exercises of the political: "Political power is a social operation." In other words, power affects the body politic and corporeal. Second, it potentially opens concepts and practices of power to the polyvalent. For Ward, power is not conceived as a monolithic "entity," but rather as a relational event with multiple, or at the least three, effects. Ward's "political," as power act, entails "an act the effect of which is (a) subjection . . . (b) liberation . . . or (c) maintenance of the status quo."[12] This threefold opening proves of import to the political theology I construct, for it prepares the way for a theorization not only of power, and, therefore, political sovereignty, as polyvalent but also of the dispersion of powers across multiple agencies, relations, and bodies. Power so conceived serves, I suggest, as an alternative to contemporary conceptions and exercises of power.

Strategies that challenge traditional conceptions of sovereignty, as I develop them, express neither the antisovereign nor call for powerlessness as a political stance; rather, they potentially generate momenta to upend the power consolidations of concentric closures. These strategies build on the eccentric connections explored by Cheah and Connolly. Connolly's "eccentric" signifies that which confounds the concentrically enclosed. The concentric thus finds itself "complicated and compromised by numerous crosscutting allegiances, connections, and modes of collaboration."[13] That which lies outside the enclosed, the "eccentric," thus troubles bounded knowledges. This troubling of epistemological horizons proves critical, for "the incarnation of rational ideals," argues Cheah, "is the ontological paradigm of any normative political project."[14] Political schema thus necessarily contour the flesh and affects of bodies. Stated more broadly, systems of knowledge—their prescribed truths and targeted heresies—delimit the ontological and incarnational possibilities of projects both democratic and cosmopolitan.

At the intersection of the ontological and normative, then, we find the political potentially "complicated and compromised" by projects of incarnation. Drawing together projects both theological and political, I propose incarnation as an eccentric spacing in and across which the theopolitical might be alternatively configured, a spacing that is profoundly political and multivalent. Next we turn to Cheah and Connolly to discover the eccentric possibilities and relationalities of cosmopolitics reconceived.

## CENTER-PERIPHERY DIVIDES AND COSMOPOLITICAL ECCENTRICITIES

Political concentricities that create definitive centers require peripheries. Schmitt's antithetical politics, for example, charts the theopolitical along an ultimate center-periphery that, as a definitive divide, prescribes a "reading of the fundamental character of things."[15] Such readings, structured by the center-peripheral, instantiate dualistic economies; they tend to concretize abstraction into us/them, even friend/enemy, fields of encounter. Challenge to economies of the center-peripheral thus requires the creation of alternative axes of engagement. Across cosmopolitan imaginaries, with their emphases on interconnectedness as an indelible mark of the human condition, I chart hospitality as a rather eccentric axis of engagement.

The cosmopolitical, I submit, is unrepentantly eccentric and incarnational. It dares to acknowledge and theorize the intimate connections that weave together the polis in its local and global dimensions. We discover in Kant a foundational model of the cosmopolitical that accentuates, to a degree, global solidarities. As Kant observes, "Because a (narrower and wider) community widely prevails among the Earth's peoples, a transgression of rights in *one* place in the world is felt *everywhere*; consequently, the idea of cosmopolitan right is not fantastic and exaggerated, but . . . necessary to the public rights of men in general."[16] "Cosmopolitan right," in Kant's thought names "the right of an alien not to be treated as an enemy upon his arrival in another's country . . . the *right to visit*, to associate."[17] Law, for Kant, be it moral, cosmopolitan, or civil, is profoundly pragmatic and relational. The right to associate is not some lofty goal, but fundamental to human being and to being human in social and political communities. Ultimate distinctions and illusions of unencumbered agency thus falter before just relations in Kant's theorized cosmopolitics. Human rights—those rights intrinsic to humans as cogent beings—serve as a living matrix that connects all of "Earth's peoples." These connections might be strained, tested, or transgressed, but never severed.

Kant's cosmopolitan vision continues to inspire diverse projects. Yet postcolonial and poststructuralist critiques have identified oppressive binaries at the core of Kant's system, the most notorious evident in Kant's distinction between civilized and barbarous cultures coupled with his privileging of "the Western" perspective.[18] Post- and decolonial thinkers, in their continuing exposure of center–periphery modes of engagement, thus encourage practices of cosmopolitanism that are "entirely open, and not pregiven or foreclosed by the definition of any particular society or discourse."[19] Open cosmopolitanisms thus resist the tidy delineations of center–periphery politics.

Cheah and Connolly, through respective moves to reconfigure the cosmopolitical, challenge models of transcendence within political theory, in particular the moorings and trajectories of Kant's system. Cheah disavows cosmopolitanism as a normative political model and contests the Kantian ideal of a globe-spanning sense of common humanity. Nevertheless, he deploys "cosmopolitical" as a technical term to describe "a nontranscendable moving ground extending across the globe in which political, cultural, and economic forces are brought into relation."[20] The cosmopolitical for Cheah is not a universal right or global sentiment, but a tool to name the existent networks and forces that shape political, economic, and social transactions. Although Connolly challenges a "Kantian cosmopolitanism [that] cannot tolerate plural sources of morality," he readily endorses "possibilities of affirmative negotiation" across "a plural matrix of cosmopolitanisms." These negotiations, Connolly notes, "depend upon several parties relinquishing the provincial demand that all others subscribe to the transcendental, universal, immanent, or deliberative source of ethics they themselves confess."[21] Negotiation rather than normativity serves as the primary mode of engagement within Connolly's plural matrix of cosmopolitanisms.

As will become evident through my engagement with the two theorists, the manner by which each tackles the "ambiguous Kantian legacy" illustrates the tension between secularist segregations of and postsecular overtures toward "the theological." In their engagements with concentric cosmopolitan models, both Cheah and Connolly locate a theopolitical dualism within these models that perpetuates center–periphery systems: an immanence/transcendence divide, where transcendence occupies the center, immanence the periphery. Cheah endeavors to corral political impulses toward transcendence, which he broadly equates to "the theological."[22] In contrast, Connolly remains sensitive to multiple spiritualities and "*mundane* transcendence[s]" pulsing across political groupings.[23] Connolly's work thus proves more hospitable to the theopolitical than does Cheah's.

Connolly's political cosmos both makes space for "radical immanence replete with multiple, often fugitive encounters with *mundane* transcendence . . . an outside of immanence . . . [that] does not translate into a divinity," and issues a call "to cultivate a presumption of receptive generosity to other faiths."[24] Cheah's cosmopolitical speaks to an immanent "field of instrumentality," in which calls for openness to other faiths are somewhat muted by the necessity of "learn[ing] to track" the strategies "of bio-power." Biopower refers to systems, technologies, and sociopolitical frames that shape human and extrahuman interrelations. Power structures and indeterminate forces are the immanent fields on which Cheah focuses his cosmopolitical lens, demythologizing the transcendences of other faiths as "actually a myriad of material technologies."[25] In what follows, I develop the "eccentric" as the interpretive axis of my proposed incarnational politics by adopting, adapting, and rejecting certain elements of Connolly's and Cheah's theoretical frames.

The political practices developed by Connolly are ones "of generous negotiation/coalition/contestation with friends and strangers."[26] We see in Connolly's friend/stranger paradigm a distinction that aerates the concentric enclosures of ultimate categorizations. Counter to imaginaries of strictly bounded identities, Connolly points to a twisting or tension that marks human negotiations of the cosmos: "There must be a *torsion* between principle and innovation . . . to overcome resentment of the world of becoming."[27] The world innovates. It becomes and emerges, thus exceeding categorization. Attention to and care of, rather than erasure of, those agencies and bodies that transgress rigid boundaries necessitate practices that negotiate the tension between ideals and innovation. Torsion, as an interpretive frame for political engagement, affirms flexibility and negotiation, thus subverting the calcifications of ultimacy. In other words, the stranger may well be an enemy, yet generous engagement with the stranger refrains from practices or politics that cast agencies as ultimately bounded and knowable. "Complicated and compromised," tidy delineations falter before the lived realities and innovations of collective existence.[28] Connolly's friend/stranger cosmos, distinct from Schmitt's cosmic sovereignty, seeks neither to suspend the created order nor subscribe to fatal antitheticals. Rather, it fosters "fugitive enchantment with being and becoming from which joy emanates and care for the plurovocity of existence might grow."[29]

Cheah's interventions amplify the complications traced by Connolly. Cheah's cosmos is one contaminated, "haunted by . . . finitude," a haunting that sociopolitical designs can neither escape nor manipulate.[30] Concentric enclosures, be they universal pronouncements or ultimate distinctions, dissolve amid an "inhuman substrate absolutely other to our cognitive faculties."[31] The inhuman refers to dynamisms that exceed yet affect human constructs, without transcending the materiality of finitude. Cheah offers the inhuman as an alternative mode of engagement to political models that "presuppose[e] that we can use ideal forms to shape the external world according to human values and norms."[32] The inhuman thus compromises pretensions to cosmic mastery and dominion. In Cheah's cosmos, the absolute alterity of the inhuman shatters friend/enemy distinctions through amplification of a divide that defies categorization. This divide of alterity teems with agencies, forces, problems, and possibilities. Thus for Cheah, the incarnation of political ideals, such as freedom, entails "an interminable negotiation with and responsibility to the [inhuman] forces that give us ourselves instead of the transcendence of the given."[33] The inhuman, resonant with Connolly's generous cosmos, exercises profound mindfulness with regard to the forces and agencies that permeate material existence.

Cheah's paradigm draws the cosmopolitical into an abyssal alterity, bidding normative projects to incarnate responsibility toward others, human and inhuman. Connolly's model envisions cosmopolitical matrices that nurture "a presumption of receptive generosity" toward friends and strangers. If we return to Kant, through Cheah and Conolly's interventions and mindful of the concentricities marking his work, we discover that the cosmopolitan right to associate and "not to be treated as an enemy" extends to all policies and acts of human engagement. A composite of fugitive forces and incarnate ideals, a cosmopolitan interpretive axis thus appears to call for practices of presumptive hospitality. Jacques Derrida, in his exposition on Kant's cosmopolitanism, boldly declares that "ethics is *hospitality*."[34] The question remains, however, as to how to embody this ethic.

For the Derridean philosopher John Caputo, the answer centers on an "unconditional hospitality [which] requires a politics without sovereignty." A politics of the unconditional "would mean that *we* [sovereign nations] are the ones who are 'extradited,' driven out from our safe refuges, forced to answer the knock at our door, in order to welcome and make room for the stranger."[35] Caputo's theopolitics of the unconditional readily skews antithetical constructs, yet potentially mirrors concentric politics. The unconditional, kin to systems of the unlimited (recall Schmitt), is rather unidirectional in aim. The tables of us/them divides are overturned in Caputo's model, but then potentially reestablished in reverse. A refuge-obliterating force remains the order of the day. The unconditional thus appears ill adaptive to innovative or collaborative relations among friends and strangers. Connolly's generous ethos, alternatively, seeks to cultivate "noble relations of agonistic respect." Agonistic respect acknowledges the "contestability" of its own ideals and ways of being. The way of respect is wrought with negotiations that challenge the sacrality but not the integrity of individual beliefs in efforts to nobly engage the stranger. Connolly's *polites agonistes* points to multiple, rather than unidirectional, modes of cosmopolitical hospitality, a hospitality complicated but not rendered powerless by the contestable.[36]

In a spirit of generous and eccentric collaborations, I propose incarnation as a possible supplement to Connolly's charted relations of the agonistic. This supplement finds robust articulation in christological creedal form: Jesus the Christ incarnates the fully human and fully divine. This confession, hammered out among the clashing heresies and orthodoxies of the Nicaea (325 C.E.) and Chalcedon (451 C.E.) councils, attests to embodied relations that are full, that potentially exceed identitarian politics. For even the most ardent champions of definitive orthodoxies in early conciliar movements found themselves silenced before the mysteries of human/divine abidings. Mystery, here, stands not as code for mystifications that shut down conversation or suppress emergent knowledges. Rather, mystery attests to that which exceeds, which transcends ultimate distinctions. The mysteries of incarnation upend politics of the willing suspension of existing orders and theologies of the willing suspension of human experience. An incarnational politics thus challenges practices of unlimited authority, the ultimate distinctions of dogmatism, and myths of unencumbered agency.

Confessions of incarnation as fully human and fully divine speak of relationships and modes of hospitality abounding in the fullness of life. This fullness does not deny the agonistic aspects of existence, confine relations to that of unconditional power exchanges, or dismiss the vulnerabilities of material embodiment. All flesh can be nailed to crosses of injustice. Rather, this fullness attests to eccentric connections, unexpected collaborations, and emergent identities that strive toward reciprocity and mutuality. "Fullness," as a political aim or common good, is not a static measure; it changes as our narrower and wider communities change. So, too, "life" envisioned as a political good, what life entails and means, exceeds pronouncements of the unilateral or universal. Determinations of "fullness of life," therefore, entail ongoing processes of open and generous engagement within and across diverse communities.

An eccentric incarnational politics, then, engages friends, strangers, and even enemies as bearers of the fullness of life, as bearers of the fully human, fully divine, as bearers of that which transcends concentric consolidations. It neither practices unconditional surrender to the other nor exercises unlimited authority over the other. Instead, it practices an eccentric hospitality that negotiates the tension between the status quo and innovation, that upholds the right of all bodies and agencies to not automatically be consigned to the role of enemy, and that finds itself immersed in the mysteries of relationships with the human, extrahuman, and divine.

## STRATEGIES TO CHALLENGE TRADITIONAL MODELS OF SOVEREIGNTY

In a cosmos of concentric enclosures, politics—specific policies, interpretive frames, and social structurings—radiate from the center. If, as earlier defined, politics consist of power acts, then concentric politics tend to ground policies and relationship in systems of control. We already encountered such grounding in the "unlimited authority" espoused by Schmitt, an exercised authority that, in theory, arises only in "a case of extreme peril."[37] In practice, however, such exercises of the unlimited can lead to the indiscriminate suspension and realignment of existing orders. Stated differently, all orders other than the order of sovereignty stand in tenuous relation to sovereign power. "The political" approached as an incarnational field of emergence, however, prescribes strategies counter to models that bind "the political" and "the theological" to sovereignty-centered modes of engagement. These strategies include negotiation, the formation of eccentric coalitions, and critical openness to emergent possibilities, powers, and agencies.

As alluded to earlier, the concentric powers generated by the theopolitical trilemma are difficult to challenge, as the elements of the trilemma are mutually reinforcing. Us/them divides tend to develop out of and bolster illusions of unencumbered agency. The 2013 government shutdown exposed the devastating consequences that occur when negotiation is trounced by us/them politics. Ultimatums practiced as offensive stances or first responses sever connections and thwart possibilities for innovative political engagements. Ultimatums seldom entertain alternatives; they establish a primary mode of us/them relationship. And the *us* rarely, if ever, consider themselves necessarily encumbered by the needs, desires, or hopes of the *them*.

Schmittian models of sovereign power not only generate and are generated by us/them divides but also wield the authority to create new orders at will. The theopolitics mobilizing such political creeds stand apparent: The divine center holds all power and transcends the finite orders it creates, while the human periphery remains ever threatened by "suspension." Efforts by the 2001 UN Report of the International Commission on Intervention and State Sovereignty to reconfigure sovereignty, for instance, allude to the histories of order destroying sovereignties: "There is a necessary re-characterization involved: from *sovereignty as control* to *sovereignty as responsibility* in both internal functions and external duties."[38] Ideologies of control, whether expressed in international politics or theories of unlimited authority, rehearse creeds that exalt omnipotence, impassibility, and existential divides. In short, power exercised as control casts itself as power unencumbered by internal, external, or material responsibilities.

If sovereign political power extols control, the strategies explored here endeavor to discover and nurture the polyvalence of sovereignties. These strategies, as suggested earlier, refrain from practices of ultimate distinctions while seeking to open concentric enclosures. They potentially upend political power conceived as unencumbered by and transcendent to materiality. I locate such strategic movements within the politics of immanence constructed by both Cheah and Connolly, politics that discover powers and potencies pulsing in and across the fields of material existence.

A first strategy is the immersion of the political, of acts of power, in the finite conditions of existence. Cheah and Connolly each counter political practices that extol the "power of transcending the particular and contingent,"[39] thereby, contesting discourses that render immanence and materiality peripheral to political activism. Transcendent power paradigms tend to exercise political power as control, manipulation, and suspension of the "created order." The power politics traced by Connolly, to the contrary, are immersed in and emergent from "an immanent field that mixes nature and culture," a field of unexpected becomings.[40] Cheah, in a similar vein, maps biopower and the biopolitical as planes shaped "by forces that precede and exceed the *anthropos*." Cheah names these forces the "inhuman dynamism," which serves as "substrate of ethics and politics."[41] A politics of immanence fleshes out the pragmatic and ethical dimensions of engagement with our (in)human neighbors.

Cheah and Connolly call for broad coalitions of individuals, groups, nations, and corporations to shift their interpretive axes from power conceived as transcendent to, and therefore independent of, the material world, to power acknowledged as relational and brimming across materiality. Such shifts encounter the world and its forces not as resources to be tapped, but as agencies and dynamisms that cocreate our shared or common goods. This theopolitical worldview counters positions such as those of the agricultural corporation, Monsanto. Monsanto's worldview not only claims to know "what is best for society as a whole" but also revels in the control of and "'intervention'" in material processes to "creat[e] something of much higher value."[42] If such interventions were the result of democratic debate, or if the "higher value" claim did not reinscribe hierarchic chains of being, perhaps these practices might be opened to alternate modes of engagement. As they stand, such practices are unilateral expressions of control, intervention, and modification that transcend the integrities of material existence.

A second strategy consists in debunking philosophies and politics of the unencumbered self. Cheah and Connolly each grapples with Kant's *cosmopolis*, along with its emphasis on the freedom of human rational and moral development from the vicissitudes of finitude. "Any contemporary revival of cosmopolitanism," declares Cheah, "must take a critical distance from the ancestor cosmopolitanism of philosophical modernity best represented by Kant's project for perpetual peace."[43] The necessity for critical distance stands on one theopolitical and two geopolitical problematics. The two geopolitical elements—"the history of colonialism" and the phenomenon of global capitalism—have, for Cheah, "disproved Kant's benign view of the unifying power of international commerce and discredited the moral-civilizing claims of cosmopolitan culture."[44] The theopolitical problematic Cheah addresses entails an almighty transcendent driving political theories and praxes.

Cheah identifies "humanist onto-theologies," or the persistent correlation of liberation discourses with philosophies of transcendence, as *the* theopolitical residue with which social theorists need to contend.[45] In tracing the genealogy of the ontotheological, Cheah credits Kant with "the first modern formulation of the organismic metaphor of the political body," a formulation still theorized and practiced.[46] This metaphor envisions "organic life as a dynamic process of self-formation and self-generation, a spontaneous, rational-purposive and autocausal becoming." The political agent who is cast as autocausal equates autonomy with transcendence of "the given."[47] In Cheah's lexicon, which is indebted to Derrida, "the given" signifies the complex of human experience, including, but not limited to, capitalism, liberation, joy, tyranny. This "given" cannot be transcended or miraculously transformed; it is thoroughly "contaminated" by finitude.[48] Organismic models, however, view the given as ultimately transcendable. In fact, these models dictate that to truly be is to transcend; in short, true political agents create themselves apart from and independent of materiality. Organismic power in life, then, is that which transcends.

The theopolitical problematic of transcendent and autocausal power together with the geopolitics of global capitalism and colonialization necessitates, for Cheah, a reconfiguration of cosmopolitanism. Convinced that "the globality of the everyday does not necessarily engender an existing popular global political consciousness," Cheah embeds the cosmopolitical in and below globality.[49] The cosmopolitical, that "nontranscendable moving ground," shapes human interactions, relations, and conceptions of laws and rights.[50] Cheah's cosmopolitical is thoroughly immanent.

One aim of Cheah's project is to unhinge the "philosophical understanding of freedom as the transcendence of finitude through rational purposive endeavor," a rationale inextricably bound to (theopolitical) conceptions of life and power as unencumbered by "the given."[51] Though Cheah refrains from categorizing it as such, the unencumbered self constitutes a myth concerning the (divine) nature and shape of human (power) interactions. In contradistinction to organismic models, Cheah binds freedom to immanent planes that are resplendent with an "incalculable randomness." The potencies of randomness reside in its capacity to "mak[e] any given hegemonic state inherently unstable and susceptible to reversal, disruption, and transformation." The possibilities for disruption, and not transcendental ideals, facilitate an "inexhaustible opening of freedom."[52] The incarnation of freedom thus calls for "interminable negotiation with and responsibility to the [inhuman] forces that give us ourselves."[53] Freedom, then, is not a freedom detached. Rather, it is freedom in the mix, freedom to negotiate with and be responsible to the inhuman, and freedom to participate in the creative disruptions of an immanent plane marked by the unexpected. Where the inhuman and incalculable pulse throughout Cheah's cosmopolitical, the "infrasensible" and affective mobilize Connolly's plurovocal cosmopolitanism.

In Connolly's call to cultivate "a public ethos of deep pluralism," he offers an alternative to both a Kantian "command model of morality" and to the "teleological image of ethics set in a divine order of things."[54] The imperatives of Kant, derived from a "supersensible" beyond and bound by reason, find themselves displaced by Connolly's "immanent naturalism."[55] Parallel to Cheah's accent on the dynamisms of the given, immanent naturalism forgoes "divine or supernatural force" to focus instead on "corporeal agents *engaged in culturally mediated, practical activities.*"⁵⁶ The engaged do not seize power to lord it over the subordinate. Rather, those engaged in friend/stranger relations partake in "a politics of generous negotiation/coalition/contestation." What's more, the engaged attend to the flesh and matter of a cosmos "that simultaneously responds to . . . and exceeds" human activities and designs.⁵⁷ That which exceeds, however, dwells not in the supersensible, the Kantian noumenal, but in our material environs, which are intimately connected to what Connolly identifies as the "infrasensible."

"A layered, immanent field," the infrasensible functions as a theoretical placeholder by which Connolly not only situates philosophical and political inquiry in the given existential mix but also complicates the "image of ethics" by countering "command model(s)" with a model that is imbricated, flexible, and unpredictable.⁵⁸ Resonant with Kant's supersensible, the infrasensible speaks to that which exceeds human knowledge; the cosmos abounds in dynamisms that reach beyond "the limits of [human] argument."⁵⁹ Dissonant to the transcendental, the infrasensible speaks to

> how differential degrees of *affective intensity* in thought propel it in some directions rather than others, how such intensities render thinking too layered and wayward to be captured either by a calculative model or a juridical model in the Kantian tradition, and how these intensities sometimes open up lines of flight through which new concepts are ushered into being.⁶⁰

Connolly thus shifts ethicopolitical attention, together with cosmopolitan matrices, from a reason untouched by fleshy sentiments to a thinking inclined toward the open-ended and affective.

As Cheah dispels the myth of the unencumbered self, so, too, Connolly, demythologizes political narratives of unencumbered agency. Agencies entangled in fields of immanence dislocate the primacy of closed moral systems, and relocate them amid cosmo-plural interrelations. Connolly's "plural matrix of cosmopolitanism" thus resists the temptation to name one "cultural particularism" the power center that renders all others peripheral.⁶¹ Neither ethics nor power radiates from a solitary universal source. Power, in this model, is not exercised by divine "forces" or through sovereign agencies detached from immanent fields. Rather, power for the good emerges through coalitional tactics and negotiations directed toward a "gratitude for the abundance of being already there" in the mix, becomings, and emergences marking the existential condition.⁶²

The strategies that I locate in the works of Cheah and Connolly are intricately woven throughout their reconfigurations of the cosmopolitical. Cheah rejects the universal, humanist claims of cosmopolitanism, yet constructs the cosmopolitical as a relational substrate that marks the human and inhuman. The power dynamics coursing throughout this substrate are not those of the transcendent, but of the random. Such dynamisms defy control but call for practices of negotiation and responsibility. Connolly's plural matrix of cosmopolitanisms rebuffs unilateral moral systems in favor of innovative and generous models. Generosity, as a political act of power, attends to the layered complexities and tensions that shape human and extrahuman encounters. This attending to negotiates with and engages friends and strangers, not from a locality of transcendent authority but from one of immanent relation and affective intensity. Cosmopolitical strategies that challenge sovereignty thus appear to enact rather curious powers that (1) negotiate perceived divides; (2) challenge paradigms that command submission to universals unilaterally imposed; and (3) embrace a politics of emergent agencies and random forces, rather than entrenched identities and sovereignties of control. In other words, such strategies discover in the fugitive forces and tender fleshes of materiality multiple expressions of power. I propose that incarnation, as a reading of the fullness of life and polyvalence of power, bears its own strategies to challenge monolithic sovereignties.

## AN INCARNATIONAL THEOLOGY

Incarnation. This single word evokes, in Christian-inflected imaginaries, a vibrant matrix of doctrinal confessions and material phenomena: revelation, birth, divine/human abiding, kenosis, resurrection. Each of these confessional loci marks incarnation as an eccentric space disruptive of the status quo. This space or plane continues to reveal itself as capacious enough to entertain myriad encounters of the human and divine, adaptive enough to elude the strangleholds of dogmatism, and eccentric enough to cut across center–periphery division—in particular, transcendence/immanence divides. For the theologian Laurel Schneider, "Incarnation, divine becoming which is becoming-flesh, is a material event of distinction, a temporal and so temporary assemblage that *matters*."[63] In other words, incarnation is not restricted to one becoming-flesh but is open to multiple revelations and embodiments of the divine. Incarnation matters, therefore, not as a solitary event of antiquity untouched by experience, but "in its attention to the mutability of bodies," an attentiveness that "undo[es] . . . imperial pretensions to totality." The incarnate fractures the totalities of unlimited authority, "shatter[ing] . . . static categories."[64] Schneider's incarnational assemblages develop across her broader project to deconstruct "the logic of the One," monolithic God through proposals for a theology and ethic of multiplicity.[65]

Schneider's work, resonant with my own, seeks to challenge theopolitics grounded on the transcendent and unlimited. Schneider's location of the mutable and multiple at the material heart of incarnation leads us, once again, to the topic of hospitality. As multiply embodied and mutable events, incarnation necessarily involves encounters among friends and strangers. These encounters are attentive to and enmeshed in the needs, desires, randomness, and potencies of one another. A matrix rich in confessional densities and complicated relationalities, incarnation calls for eccentric practices in search of and directed toward fullness of life for human, extrahuman, and emergent agencies. In other words, practices of incarnation inevitably give rise to political acts, to acts of power inexpressible outside the materiality of creation, yet elusive of categorization. Incarnation, as either political project or confessional locus, thus tends toward neither the impassible nor the immutable. To the contrary, incarnation is dynamic and revelatory—or emergent.

Graham Ward offers the concept of "transcorporeality" to express the disruptive dynamisms intrinsic to incarnation. Ward's transcorporeality situates the life of Christ's body, historical and ecclesial, in the Eucharist.[66] New life in Christ renders the human body eucharistic, as "continually being given, continually moving out and being enacted elsewhere, and so it continually transcends strict identifications that it imposes on itself or are imposed on it."[67] Bodies of transcendence, multiply enacted and moving out, resist accretions of unlimited authority and ultimate distinction. The transcorporeal also marks life as profoundly communal, entangled in communities that break and share bread together. Yet the transcorporeality Ward develops is rooted in a christocentric and theocentric theology of submission: "Every act, every intuition, every emotional response, every thought is to be submitted to God, to be ruled by God. . . . So, as a people of God, we are theocratic."[68] It thus remains vulnerable to consolidations of meaning and power that inevitably establish their own peripheries.

If, however, we take Ward at his confessional word, then the transcorporeal potentially transcends and eludes "strict identifications." A transcorporeality moving out toward the eccentric might cut across strictly bounded identities and participate in eucharistic expansiveness: wherein, broken bread testifies to the pierced body on Golgotha and to all bodies broken by regimes of control; wherein, shared bread speaks to acts that subvert unilateral power exchanges and economies of commodification. Communal events of eucharistic solidarity bear witness, I suggest, against center–periphery politics while calling for practices of an eccentric christology.

What might practices of the christo-eccentric look like? As we've seen, Schneider situates incarnation amid the multiplicities of material existence.

Divine becoming matters; it "make[s] a difference"; it troubles the concentric by means of the mutable.[69] The theologian Mayra Rivera, in her "account of transcendence in the flesh," positions "open[ness] . . . to new incarnations" amid our "encounter[s] with" and our "relation[s] to multiple Others."[70] Ward's transcorporeality locates incarnation in the sharing of bread. This sharing, or distribution of goods, disrupts economies that attempt to "lay claim to or possess" the "fluidity of identity" through consolidated divides.[71] Building on Schneider, Rivera, and Ward, I construct incarnation as divine becomings, revelations, and emergences that take place in our daily communions—with one another, our communities, our environments, God—while simultaneously displacing accretions of and pretensions to unlimited authority, exploitative economies, and ultimate distinctions. "And the Word became flesh and dwelt among us, full of grace and truth" (John 1:14, RSV). So, too, our words, our daily commitments, momentary whims, and theopolitical strategies take on matter and dwell among the materialities of our communal existence.

To incarnate, then, is to matter, to "make a difference." It is to recognize your power and the power of others to act politically: to liberate, oppress, or do nothing; to welcome, exile, or ignore; to engage, categorize, or shut down; to love, dominate, or tolerate; to be responsive to, reactive to, or controlling of the other. To incarnate is to abide in the flesh with a spirit of grace and truth. It is to strive toward fullness of life, not as a universal precept, but as an ever-emerging possibility. To incarnate is to collaborate with others, and to encourage collaboration across communities, nation-states, and global systems. It is to engage in friendly contestations and to negotiate interpretive axes of the concentric and eccentric. The history of the incarnate one named Jesus attests to the tensions implicit in such negotiations: Politics of the ultimate and unlimited name perverse those bodies that disturb meaning structures, nailing them to symbols of hegemonic power. Grace, however, dares to cross boundaries, rendering the ultimate not so terribly definitive. Grace dares to say this is good, this is what it means to live and to love, yet stands willing to concede the contestability of the nominative and normative. Such concessions express awareness of the possibility that the glories of incarnation exceed human cognitions: "While they were talking and discussing together, Jesus himself drew near and went with them. But their eyes were kept from recognizing him" (Luke 24:15–16, RSV). Their eyes, or the interpretive frames through which they read the world, were kept from perceiving, perhaps by fear, distress, or by entrenched divides separating the dead and resurrected, the corporeal and spiritual, the immanent and transcendent. Incarnation blurs center–periphery divides and welcomes alliances, even intimacies, between friends and strangers: "When he was at table with them, he took the bread and blessed, and broke it, and gave it to them. And their eyes were opened." Their interpretive lenses were expanded, rendered porous by a grace that expresses gratitude for the elements of life: bread, water, and unexpected communions that inspire emergent communities (Luke 24:30–31, RSV). In short, an incarnational theology attends to material revelations, human, divine, and extrahuman, which draw and lure toward communal acts of hospitality.

## A COSMOPOLITICAL THEOLOGY

A cosmopolitical theology, as mentioned earlier, is a risky venture. This is particularly true considering that the political theorists I draw on either quarantine transcendence (Cheah) or embrace a mundane transcendence that "does not translate into a divinity" (Connolly). Cheah's corralling of the transcendent, which he equates with the (onto-) theological, fails, however, to account for theologies that trouble theopolitical doctrines of unencumbered agency and unlimited authority. This oversight consigns Cheah's cosmopolitical to the perpetuation of the concentricities fostered by theories of separatist secularization. Nevertheless, Cheah's link of the incarnational to political projects creates an opening through which to explore alternative configurations of the relation between "the political" and "the theological."

Where Cheah rebuffs the theological, Connolly's work crisscrosses secular/sacred divides. Attentive to the plurality of faiths inspiring human mobilizations, Connolly readily concedes "the profound contestability of" his and every ethos. He does so in an effort not only to "open lines of communication to theists and secularists prepared to make similar acknowledgments" but also to foster "noble relations of agonistic respect between the carriers of . . . alternative faiths."[72] A generous politics thus strives toward noble relations across multiple registers of agency and activism, negotiating the tensions between principles and innovations, concentricities and eccentricities, and (mundane) transcendences and immanence.

Praxes of negotiation, construed as those which upend ultimate distinctions and unlimited sovereignty, create, I offer, possibilities for collusion between Connolly's politics of becoming and theologies of the incarnational. In faiths both naturalist and theological, the incarnational constitutes neither isolated nor unencumbered events. Incarnation is, as Rivera describes it, "irreducibly relational." Incarnation conceived as works of the flesh that are inescapably intertwined presents an understanding of bodily phenomena with which, I conjecture, Connolly might find resonances. Rivera presses further, maintaining that this irreducible relationality "is never without limits. It is always transcendence-within, becoming within the constraints and promises of embodied existence—never dislodged from it."[73] Connolly's "*mundane* transcendence" and Rivera's divine "transcendence within," while not equivalent, speak concordantly to the uncertain processes and promises of emergence, and to the embodied and entangled character of human encounters with that which exceeds the limits of cognition. The negotiation of such entanglements disrupts center–periphery divides through practices that remain "open to mystery and unpredictable possibilities: to the ineffable, unnameable, and unutterable."[74] Connolly's politics of immanence and the incarnational theology that I seek to construct both locate power within relation, power within and emergent from the predicaments and possibilities of fleshy materiality. When theological and political projects cease to correlate God with immutable omnipotence, theopolitical configurations open to the sort of radical reconfigurations that the doctrine of incarnation suggests, but which has yet to be politically actualized.

A cosmopolitical theology, influenced by Connolly and, to a lesser degree, Cheah, works toward strategic alliances between friends and strangers, while it remains ever attentive to embodiments of the fugitive and random. It seeks to justly negotiate cosmopolitical mutations. It confesses the provinciality of its meaning structures, while striving to incarnate ideals in responsive relations to and negotiations with other provincial positionalities. It resists sacralized power drives armed to suspend created and emergent orders at will, as it locates power within and across incarnational events, which are "irreducibly relational . . . [and] never without limits."[75] It practices an eccentric hospitality that actively and in coalition with others seeks to embody the good that is fullness of life—that is material existence.

## NOTES

1. William E. Connolly, *Neuropolitics: Thinking, Culture, Speed*, Theory Out of Bounds 23 (Minneapolis: University of Minnesota Press, 2002), 186.
2. Seyla Benhabib, *The Rights of Others: Aliens, Residents, and Citizens* (Cambridge: Cambridge University Press, 2009), 39.
3. City of San Antonio, "City of San Antonio Non-Discrimination Ordinance Facts," accessed July 5, 2014, http://www.sanantonio.gov/portals/0/Files/clerk/NDOfactSheet.pdf.
4. Greg Abbott, "Statement by Greg Abbott on the Proposed San Antonio Ordinance," August 26, 2013, http://www.gregabbott.com/statement-by-greg-abbott-on-proposed-san-antonio-ordinance/.
5. Connolly, *Neuropolitics*, 186.
6. Pheng Cheah, *Spectral Nationality: Passages of Freedom from Kant to Postcolonial Literatures of Liberation* (New York: Columbia University Press, 2003), 113.
7. William E. Connolly, *Why I Am Not a Secularist* (Minneapolis: University of Minnesota Press, 2000), 15.
8. Carl Schmitt, *Political Theology: Four Chapters on the Concept of Sovereignty*, trans. George Schwab (Chicago: University of Chicago Press, 2005), 12.

9. Carl Schmitt, *The Concept of the Political*, trans. George Schwab (1996; Chicago: University of Chicago Press, 2007), 26.
10. Ibid., 36.
11. Graham Ward, *The Politics of Discipleship: Becoming Postmaterial Citizens*, The Church and Postmodern Culture (Grand Rapids, Mich.: Baker Academic, 2009), 27.
12. Ibid.
13. Connolly, *Neuropolitics*, 186.
14. Cheah, *Spectral Nationality*, 113.
15. Connolly, *Why I Am Not a Secularist*, 52.
16. Immanuel Kant, "To Perpetual Peace: A Philosophical Sketch," in *Immanuel Kant: Perpetual Peace and Other Essays on Politics, History, and Morals*, trans. Ted Humphrey (Indianapolis: Hackett, 1983), 119 (sec. 360).
17. Ibid., 118 (sec.358), also see 112, the second note continued from 111.
18. For the spurious anthropology funding Kant's geography, see David Harvey, *Cosmopolitanism and the Geographies of Freedom* (New York: Columbia University Press, 2009). For an example of Kant's distinction between civilized and "barbarous" freedom, see "Idea for a Universal History with a Cosmopolitan Intent," in *Immanuel Kant: Perpetual Peace and Other Essays on Politics, History, and Morals*, 35–36 (secs. 25–26).
19. Sheldon Pollock, Homi K. Bhabha, Carol A. Breckenridge, and Dipesh Chakrabarty, "Cosmopolitanisms," *Public Culture* 12, no. 3 (2000): 577–78.
20. Pheng Cheah, *Inhuman Conditions: On Cosmopolitanism and Human Rights* (Cambridge, Mass.: Harvard University Press, 2006), 118.
21. Connolly, *Neuropolitics*, 182, 200.
22. More specifically, Cheah discusses "humanist onto-theologies" (Cheah, *Inhuman Conditions*, 98–119). Elsewhere, Cheah does concede that praxes of transcendence need not be eliminated from the political: "For the point is not . . . that one should therefore dismiss efforts toward transcendence. . . . The ideal projects of humanism need to be persistently regrounded on a thinking of . . . the human as a product-effect of the inhuman" (Pheng Cheah, "Human Freedom and the Technic of Nature: Culture and Organic Life in Kant's Third Critique," *Differences: A Journal of Feminist Cultural Studies* 14, no. 2 [2003]: 23).
23. See William E. Connolly, *A World of Becoming* (Durham, N.C.: Duke University Press, 2011), 74–77.
24. Ibid., 74–75 (emphasis mine); for "receptive generosity," see Connolly, *Neuropolitics*, 129.
25. Cheah, *Inhuman Conditions*, 8, 266, 231, 199–202, and 246.
26. William E. Connolly, *The Augustinian Imperative: A Reflection on the Politics of Morality*, Modernity and Political Thought 1 (Newbury Park, Calif.: Sage Publications, 1993), 28.
27. Connolly, *World of Becoming*, 119–20.
28. Connolly, *Neuropolitics*, 186.
29. Connolly, *Not a Secularist*, 15.

30. Cheah, *Spectral Nationality*, 381.
31. Ibid., 110.
32. Cheah, *Inhuman Conditions*, 99.
33. Ibid., 79.
34. Jacques Derrida, *On Cosmopolitanism and Forgiveness*, trans. Mark Dooley and Michael Hughes, Thinking in Action (New York: Routledge, 2005), 17.
35. John D. Caputo, *The Weakness of God: A Theology of the Event* (Bloomington: Indiana University Press, 2006), 276.
36. Connolly, *Neuropolitics*, 171, 112, 87. Connolly's agonstic nobility draws significantly on Nietzsche's "'spiritualization of enmity'" (ibid., 164–74).
37. Schmitt, *Political Theology*, 6.
38. The International Commission on Intervention and State Sovereignty (ICISS), Report on "The Responsibility to Protect" (Ottawa, Ont.: International Development Research Centre, December 2001), 13 (Art. 2.14).
39. Cheah, *Inhuman Conditions*, 21.
40. Connolly, *Neuropolitics*, 86.
41. Cheah, *Inhuman Conditions*, 10.
42. The referenced material includes quotes from Scott Baucum, identified as "Monsanto trait stewardship lead," in an article on Monsanto's corporate website by E. Freeman, "Why Does Monsanto Patent Seeds? Part 1," Monsanto Company, 9/30/2008, http://www.monsanto.com/newsviews/Pages/Why-Does-Monsanto-Patent-Seeds.aspx.
43. Cheah, *Inhuman Conditions*, 81.
44. Ibid.
45. Ibid., 98.
46. Cheah, *Inhuman Conditions*, 98–99, for "onto-theological;" and Cheah, *Spectral Nationality*, 64, for "organismic."
47. Cheah, *Spectral Nationality*, 25.
48. Cheah, *Inhuman Conditions*, 12, 10.
49. Ibid., 30.
50. Ibid., 118.
51. Cheah, *Spectral Nationality*, 2.
52. Cheah, *Inhuman Conditions*, 265.
53. Ibid., 79.
54. Connolly, *Neuropolitics*, 138, 86.
55. Ibid., 84–85, 86.
56. Ibid., 85, 92.
57. Ibid., 92.
58. Ibid., 85, 86. The infrasensible is tied to the work of the amygdala, for Connolly; see ibid., 104–13.
59. Ibid., 200.
60. Ibid., 93–94.
61. Ibid., 200, 185.
62. Ibid., 106.

63. Laurel C. Schneider, *Beyond Monotheism: A Theology of Multiplicity* (New York: Routledge, 2008), 167.
64. Ibid., 5, 205.
65. Ibid., 1.
66. Ward, *Politics of Discipleship*, 225, 248–49.
67. Ibid., 255.
68. Ibid., 299.
69. Schneider, *Multiplicity*, 167.
70. Mayra Rivera, *The Touch of Transcendence: A Postcolonial Theology of God* (Louisville, Ky.: Westminster John Knox Press, 2007), 97, 117.
71. Graham Ward, *Cities of God* (New York: Routledge, 2000), 91.
72. Connolly, *Neuropolitics*, 87, 112, 171.
73. Rivera, *Touch*, 93.
74. Ibid., 136, for "unpredictable possibilities." Rivera is discussing key elements of panentheism as opposed to pantheism. She is, then, speaking to a transcendence that is not identical to Connolly's mundane transcendence. I am not seeking to suggest definitive correlations, but resonances for collaboration.
75. Rivera, *Touch*, 93.

◆ Economies and Ecologies
of (Un)Common Good/s

# Reconfiguring the Common Good and Religion in the Context of Capitalism: Abrahamic Alternatives

JOERG RIEGER

It is quite common to hear accusations of selfishness and greed when people talk about what is wrong with the world. Often, these accusations are leveled against people of privilege such as CEOs of large corporations, whose salaries are hundreds of times higher than the salaries of their workers. Sometimes these accusations are also leveled against members of the middle class whose lives appear to be largely self-centered, without much concern for the wider community. What these accusations overlook, however, is that what is perceived as selfishness and greed in these cases is part of a broader vision of how the common good—i.e., that which is most beneficial for all—is to be achieved. Moreover, this widely embraced vision does not understand itself as one way toward the common good among others; it understands itself as the only way.

Capitalism, the economic system in which we find ourselves, is built on the assumption that when people pursue their own interests, they automatically pursue what is in the common interest, the common good. Adam Smith, often considered the father of capitalist economics, was quite clear about this assumption.[1] Businesses will provide better products and services, it is believed, if they are focused strictly on profits and not on how they might benefit their workers or the community.

Smith also noted that the common good is curtailed when people act in altruistic fashion and seek to pursue the interests of others. Those who refuse to follow their self-interest in order to pursue the common good are seen as doing more harm than good: "I have never known much good done by those who affected to trade for the public good," states Smith. Fortunately, he continues, "it is an affectation . . . not very common among merchants, and very few words need be employed in dissuading them from it."[2] In other words, according to the logic of capitalism that is accepted even today, caring for one's workers, the community, or the environment is detrimental not only for business interests but also for the common good. And, like in the days of Smith, I see little danger that capitalists would feel tempted to waste much effort caring for what Smith called "the public good."

Today, Smith's arguments that were developed in the context of small businesses marked by personal relationships in towns and villages of eighteenth-century England are applied to giant corporations whose revenues exceed those of small countries, as well as to large-scale structural adjustments that affect the economies of whole nations. Tax cuts and subsidies for corporations and the wealthy, for instance, are justified because it is assumed that the economy as a whole will benefit from them. The self-interest of corporations and the wealthy, it is assumed, will automatically translate into the common good. Vice versa, it is assumed according to this logic that forcing corporations and the wealthy to contribute to the common good via taxes and other social commitments will damage the economy as a whole.

Despite its popularity, however, there is little solid evidence that this economic system has worked as advertised. Even the bipartisan Congressional Research Service has pointed out the flaws of its assumptions: "There is little evidence over the past 65 years that tax cuts for the highest earners are associated with savings, investment or productivity growth."[3] As some economists have argued, economics resembles religion when it promotes big ideas that are not backed up by empirical evidence. This is the way economics now functions at the top levels of the field, according to the economist Robert Nelson, and the dominant logic of capitalism appears to prove him right.[4] Religion, according to this position, is defined as the promotion of big ideas or as a kind of idealism, in opposition to other approaches that are based on observation and analysis. Nevertheless, this is not the only way to define religion. There are other definitions of religion that are more promising, with the potential to reshape how we understand economics and how we understand the common good.

In the following argument, the goal is to develop robust notions of the common good that are able to address the tremendous suffering and the power differentials that mark our age, together with robust notions of religion that grow out of communal struggles against oppression and exploitation.

## COMMON CONCEPTIONS OF THE COMMON GOOD AND OF RELIGION THAT DO NOT WORK

It is important to grasp what we are up against. As noted, the dominant logic of capitalism intends to promote the common good, that which is most beneficial for all, rather than selfishness and greed as ends in themselves. Capitalism perceives selfishness and greed as contributing to the common good via the "invisible hand of the market," which supposedly balances the selfishness of the various parties involved in the market without fail. Capitalism's logic is built on the confidence that this invisible hand consistently serves the common good. This confidence, as I have argued elsewhere in greater detail, resembles religious idealism since it is promoted despite mounting evidence that capitalism destroys the common good. Many indicators point to the fact that this confidence in the workings of the invisible hand of the market is harmful, as it was one of the key factors that have pushed us into the current erosion of the economic and political common good that we are experiencing, where the wealthiest few benefit at the expense of the many.[5]

Without dealing with the basic logic of capitalism and its quasi-religious confidence that "a rising tide will lift all boats," which is endorsed to some degree by the two large political parties in the United States, alternative visions of the common good will not only be shallow but ultimately fail to be effective.

Perhaps the shallowest affirmations of the common good are the ones that propose to fight individualism and selfishness, taken at face value, in the name of the common good. What is missing here is an engagement with the logic of capitalism and an analysis of the relationships of power that are at work in the current situation. Here, the big ideas of capitalism (for instance, that self-interest is good) are merely swapped for what are supposedly the big ideas of religion (for instance, that self-interest is bad). This approach is frequently taken by people of various religious traditions, who talk about the common good or about community without looking at the deeper causes of their distortion. Eastern religious traditions, in particular, are often used by Westerners when they want to affirm harmonious communities or a romantic notion of the common good. Others invoke Jewish and Christian traditions in similar idealizing fashion.

Two examples help clarify what the problem is: Blaming the individualism and selfishness of the powerful and wealthy in the name of the common good, my first example, not only fails to take into consideration that greedy individuals may not be the primary problem; this position assumes that individualism is real and that the powerful and wealthy are indeed the kinds of individuals that have built their success with their own hands by being selfish. As a result, this approach covers up the fact that the wealth and power of some is built not in isolation but in a relationship, on the backs of others. Furthermore, this approach covers up the relations of power that produce what has been called "structural greed," a phenomenon that is largely independent of the disposition of individuals.[6]

Moreover, the common good that is affirmed in this approach is a rather idealist category that is amorphous and ill-defined, as people can supposedly contribute to it at will, as individuals who can act independently of larger networks of power. This overlooks the fact that not everyone is in a position to support the common good and that some are explicitly charged by the system with working against it, whether they like it or not: Even CEOs, often seen as powerful individuals who can do whatever they want, have little choice in the matter because if they choose not to support structural greed, they are likely to be replaced by others who do. After all, the mission of a corporation, according to a classical legal case against the Ford Motor Company, is not to work for the common good, that which is most beneficial to all, but to work for the benefit of their stockholders and against the benefit of their workers.[7]

Another example, also very current, would be the sort of affirmation of the common good or of common interest over against what is perceived as special interests, which is how the interests of minorities are often defined. The discourse of race as it has shaped up in the United States in the aftermath of the civil rights movement comes to mind: Even when racial minorities are accepted and affirmed, they are often expected to fit in with the racial majority that understands itself as white. This discourse overlooks the fact that common interest might not always be represented best by an idealized majority (white people only exist as such an idealized group)—a deep insight found in many religious traditions but often neglected by their mainline representatives.

More important, this discourse overlooks the fact that not even the majority of those who consider themselves to be white in our example are necessarily benefiting a great deal from their racial status in a capitalist economy where privilege is tied not only to race but also to class power. This is the famous mistake of the proverbial Joe the Plumber, a Caucasian plumber who supported Republican John McCain's presidential bid in 2008. In his view of the world, shaped by the ideal of whiteness, Joe obviously failed to realize that he would have had a lot more in common with fellow African American and Latino plumbers than with a white multimillionaire.

Shallow affirmations of the common good—or of what is supposedly common interest over against self-interest—fail to be effective in part because they overlook the flow of power, which is a perennial problem with idealizing positions. Affirming an idealized notion of the common good in a situation of structural injustice is bound to fail because those who violate the community most effectively do so not necessarily by choice, and often they are not even aware of what they are doing. The wealthy, for instance, might think of themselves as staunch supporters of the common good because of substantial contributions to charity, without realizing how their collective interests contribute to the destruction of the common good. The popular image of Microsoft's Bill Gates, which notes his substantial contributions to charity but not his efforts of creating monopolies and promoting low-wage production overseas, reflects similar views. What is lacking here is a robust notion of the common good built on more than just a conglomerate of isolated individuals and held together by the innocent-sounding question of why we all cannot just get along, which implies that there is no reason why we could not.

This naïve affirmation of the common good cannot think of any sense for reasons why we all cannot just get along. Among these reasons are the vast differentials of power that separate the various players, such as, for instance, buyers and sellers, in the capitalist marketplace. Adam Smith, the intellectual father of capitalism, assumed a rather level playing field between small merchants such as butchers and their customers, which served as the basis for his confidence that the invisible hand of the market would balance out any differences. Today, such confidence in the invisible hand is less warranted, as there are few level playing fields where sellers and buyers can interact without grave power differentials. Consider, for example, the case of a seller like the small butcher shop at the corner, which is forced to compete with other sellers like the Walmart corporation, and where there are various types of buyers, from individuals with limited resources to large corporations. In this scenario, the interests of little sellers and buyers with limited resources are unable to compete with the powerful interests of corporations and thus are forced out of business (the butcher shop) or determined by these interests (the consumers, via advertising and the need to save money).

In a context of grave power differentials, shallow and naïve notions of the common good are harmful, especially when they overlook the question of power and promote big ideas instead (like simple replacements of self-interest with common interest) that are not in touch with the shape that everyday reality takes. Religion in a context of grave power differentials will not make a difference unless it helps us in providing alternatives to these shallow notions of the common good. This means that religion has to amount to more than the promotion of competing idealisms.

On second thought, one might suspect that shallow affirmations of the common good are not failures at all but are very effective, if they are seen as working for the privileged rather than for the community. Here lies the deepest problem with such affirmations of the common good: They cover up the reality of structures and powers that benefit the few rather than the many, creating the illusion that the solution is simple ("reject selfishness"). This is what may be behind God's frustrated exclamation as rendered by the prophet Jeremiah: "They have treated the wound of my people carelessly, saying, 'Peace, peace,' when there is no peace" (Jeremiah 6:14).

## ALTERNATIVE CONCEPTIONS OF THE COMMON GOOD AND OF RELIGION

Alternative conceptions of the common good and of religion are needed that take a fresh look at that which is most beneficial to all. Such notions of the common good and of religion will have to take into account the following issues in order to address the problems noted above: First, they need to develop an understanding of what the common good means in light of the flows of power in capitalism. What is common cannot be defined by the lowest common denominator of isolated individuals or by some universal "one-size-fits-all" definition. Second, alternative conceptions of the common good need to take into account those who are currently repressed or even excluded by the dominant community, not in order to include or integrate them into the dominant status quo, but in order to create room for a new reality of the common. Third, alternative conceptions of the common good need to rethink agency, as agency can no longer be perceived in terms of the agency of the dominant system that has failed to benefit the community; agency needs to be seen in terms of the people.

As I address these three points in greater detail, I take into account two moments that are often neglected in idealized discussions of the common good. The reality of people whose lives are being destroyed by the current system can instruct us about the often invisible problems and challenges that need to be addressed. Elsewhere, I have called this the "logic of downturn."[8]

Moreover, the notion of religion is broadened here, as religious traditions gain new meaning in light of these struggles. The Abrahamic religious traditions in particular originate in complex situations marked by struggle and power differentials. In these traditions, faith and liberative action are frequently linked,[9] counteracting the kinds of religious idealisms that are so typical of the religions of the status quo, which include domesticated forms of Christianity, Judaism, and Islam. To be sure, this domestication is a constant companion of religion and can be found in struggles of the earliest traditions and has at times shaped the sacred texts themselves. The complexified definition of religion that emerges here pushes beyond the dominant definitions of religion in modernity.[10] Religion is no longer the promotion of big ideas in idealist fashion or the maintenance of seemingly universal doctrines; religion develops in relation to that which makes a difference in the midst of the struggles of life.

## THE COMMON GOOD AND RELIGION COMPLEXIFIED

The common good has often been defined in terms of a generic and universal understanding of humanity. Yet since generic and universal human beings do not exist, these definitions are necessarily based on particular interpretations of what it means to be human. More specifically, such interpretations are in part based on the images of dominant humanity, since the wealthy and the powerful get to determine what is normative if power is taken for granted or covered up. If dominant humanity defines what is human, the interests of the wealthy and the powerful also define what is considered the common good, although it may be proclaimed in the name of universal humanity or a seemingly universal divinity like Smith's invisible hand of the market or ideas of a "higher power."

What would happen, however, if the common good were defined not from positions of dominance but from positions of struggle and suffering? A closer look at some key Abrahamic religious traditions reminds us of the fact that we do not have to invent such alternative approaches because they already exist, although they are often overlooked. One example for defining the common good from a position of struggle and suffering is provided by the apostle Paul, whose Jewish-Christian theology contests the dominant theology of the Roman Empire.[11]

In his letter to the Christians in Corinth, Paul notes regarding the body of Christ and its common good that "if one member of the body suffers, all suffer together with it" (1 Cor. 12:26). This statement is developed in conscious resistance to a status quo, which endorses hierarchical structures and considers the lower classes less significant for the common good than the ruling classes.[12] Paul develops a counterargument that proclaims the less prominent to be "indispensable" (1 Cor. 12:22), noting that "God has so arranged the body giving the greater honor to the inferior member" (1 Cor. 12:24). As a result, contrary to common practice in the Roman Empire, the head cannot say to the feet, "I have no need of you" (1 Cor. 12:21).

This reversal of social relations has implication for religion and images of the divine. In many of the Abrahamic traditions God is found not on the side of the dominant powers but on the side of the people: Islamic, Jewish, and Christian traditions preserve the dangerous memories of the Exodus and Moses' transformation from being as an Egyptian prince to becoming the leader of the Hebrew slaves. Paul brings the common good and religion together when he explicitly relates his metaphor of the body of the community to the body of Christ.

Although it is not clear whether Paul is completely consistent with his reversal of dominant hierarchies,[13] his vision of the body clashes with the Roman Empire's vision of the body in important ways, as it questions established hierarchies. His reminder that the "head" cannot dismiss the "feet" stands in opposition to the jobless recovery strategy of contemporary capitalism as well, which slashes salaries and benefits of workers or eliminates jobs altogether in order to create more profit for the shareholders. To be sure, we would miss the point if our focus were on Paul as an individual hero; the point is that there are reversals of dominant hierarchies at work in ancient communities as well as in modern ones and that religion can play liberative roles.[14]

The common good, in this example, is reconfigured in profound ways. The role of the weaker members is decisive for the common good; their struggles and their suffering set the agenda. This is not a matter of welfare as the special interest of a few. The lower classes determine the common good, and their suffering affects the community as a whole; that is, it is a matter of common interest. If this is to be more than pious idealism, we need to address the question of what those who suffer contribute to the common good.

One contribution that those who suffer make to the common good has to do with an understanding of the sources of suffering. Paul seems to understand that suffering is not some mysterious fate but that it is created, for instance in situations where the head dismisses the feet or the eyes dismiss the hand, that is, where the powerful and the wealthy dismiss or oppress those who work for them. This is a reality not just in the Roman Empire but also in the world of contemporary capitalism, and it takes various forms.[15] The complex sources of suffering demand a more complex sense of the common good.

As the common good is shaped by the active contributions—the work—of those who are pushed to the margins, it is complexified. After all, the active contributions of the marginalized are as diverse as their marginalizations. Paul notes that "the members of the body that seem to be weaker are indispensable" (1 Cor. 12:22). The power of the complexified common good is rooted not merely in people's identity, whether they belong to the dominant group or minority groups; the power is based in their work, which includes not only their productive agency but also their struggles and, ultimately, their suffering as well.[16]

Consider the work of construction workers, for example, who produce much of the infrastructure that we take for granted. Without their labor and expertise no architect could build a house and no city council could plan the construction of building projects and roads. In fact, architects who do not take into account what workers are able to build will fail. CEOs, too, are more dependent on labor than they might ever be willing to acknowledge, for even if they work at their desks around the clock, they are rarely producing any tangible products. No matter how skilled the CEOs, no products will be produced and no service rendered without workers. Nevertheless, dominant conceptions of the common good in economics generally fail to respect labor, as they demand that revenue for those who "lead" be constantly increased, while the salaries and benefits of workers are cut everywhere, and the wages of many construction workers—many of them undocumented immigrants—are frequently withheld.

The complexified notion of the common good that I am proposing here starts with labor and observations of how working people (as well as the unemployed) are treated in a capitalist economy. This forces us not only to reconsider the value of work but also the many things that detract from the value of work, like the exploitation of labor and the unfounded assumption that centralized top-down leadership is necessary for success and, thus, for the kind of common good that is beneficial for all. The fact that many construction workers at present are immigrants, often undocumented, or minorities adds to the complexity of the common good, as we can no longer treat matters of race and ethnicity as accidental. In addition, the world of labor is also one of the prime contexts for observing exploitation along the lines of gender, as women are still not equal to men when it comes to power in the workplace and wages, although their productive capacities are no longer in question.

What is at stake here is an understanding of the common good that moves from the common concern for distribution to a concern for production; what matters is not merely how wealth is distributed but how and under which conditions it is produced.[17] I will come back to this topic at the end.

## THE COMMON GOOD AND RELIGION "OUT OF THE DEPTHS"

The most significant distortions of the common good are rarely accidents. The common good is distorted for particular reasons, which are best seen from the perspectives of those who are forced to bear the brunt of the burden of these distortions. This matches an insight of the Psalms, according to which theology is often at its most profound when it is done "out of the depths" (Psalm 130:1; *de profundis*).

Although those who represent the status quo often seek to include the "less fortunate" back into the status quo, assuming that the common good is best served in this way, I suggest proceeding the other way around. Instead of integrating those on the margins into some idealized notion of the common good, let us take a closer look at the distortions of the common good in order to find out how they are produced by the status quo. The reason why labor is exploited in capitalism, for instance, is not primarily because of greedy or meanspirited individuals but because of systemic power differentials between those who own large quantities of capital and control the means of production and between those who do not. Owing to this arrangement, a substantial power differential is built into the economic process, as the latter group is able to survive only by selling its labor power to the former group. Note also that this latter group—people who do not own large quantities of capital and who do not control the means of production—includes the middle class as well.[18]

Who benefits from these arrangements? Supporters of capitalism often point out that an increasing number of people are benefiting today, as some shares of the means of production, for instance, are owned by more and more people through the ownership of stocks of publicly traded companies. The truth, however, is that the differences between major shareholders and small shareholders are huge, not only in terms of how many shares are owned but also in terms of power and influence. After all, the shareholders' right to vote in matters that affect the company depends on the number of shares owned. One of the most important insights of the Occupy Wall Street movement is that there is a significant distinction between the 1 percent and the rest of the 99 percent of the population, as the latter are benefiting less and less from the economic (and therefore the political and even the religious) status quo.[19] It is no longer a secret that the conditions of the middle class and of working people are worsening while the members of the top 1 percent are doing better; members of the top 0.1 percent are doing even better yet.[20]

These observations throw new light on how we think about the common good and, ultimately, about religion as well. Rethinking the common good in terms of the 99 percent rather than the 1 percent suggests a very different concept of solidarity. Whereas solidarity, even for progressives, has often meant a commitment to the less fortunate by those who considered themselves to be more fortunate, solidarity now turns into what Kwok Pui-lan and I are calling "deep solidarity." Deep solidarity is formed where it is realized that more and more of us are in the same boat, that even the members of the middle class who consider themselves better off are constantly losing power and status in a capitalist world where the rich grow richer at surprising speed. As the nonpartisan Congressional Budget Office recently reported, the income of the richest 1 percent of American households rose 275 percent between 1979 and 2007, while the income of the poorest 20 percent grew only 18 percent during the same time.[21] Although these numbers report income, they have implications for power as well—not only political power but also cultural and religious power—as the wealthy are calling most of the shots.[22]

In this climate, top-down notions of solidarity and the common good can be exposed for what they often amount to: efforts of the elites, no matter how well-meaning, to shape the rest of the world in their own image.[23] Deep solidarity, by contrast, is not about shaping others in one's image, as it does not depend on the denial of diversity: While working together in addressing the problems that benefit the few and harm the many, deep solidarity is about realizing how the system harms the community as a whole and what everyone can contribute to change this. Whereas traditional models of solidarity often play down diversity, deep solidarity thrives on it. Ideals like integration and even inclusiveness cannot be the goals any more, if they imply integration and inclusion into the common good determined by the dominant status quo. What emerges is a new reality of the common good that takes diversity seriously.

Similar insights can be found in many of our religious traditions. The reason why children play important roles in some well-known Jewish and Christian traditions, for instance, is not because of romanticizing ideas of children and their supposed "innocence" or "purity," but because they are representatives of the "least of these." Stories of Jesus and children are instructive for rethinking the common good from the margins. When he finds that his disciples prevent little children from being brought to him, Jesus famously rebukes them: "Let the little children come to me; do not stop them; for it is to such as these that the kingdom of God belongs" (Mark 10:14).

Modern readers who tend to romanticize children often assume that this close relation to the kingdom of God is somehow linked to the special qualities of children, like their innocent naïvety or their ability to trust blindly without doubt. Yet none of these qualities are found in children who are forced to grow up in poverty or on the streets, and these qualities would not have necessarily been assumed in the ancient world. In Jesus' context, children were part of the marginalized and the excluded, as they were considered to be not yet fully human and as valuable as adults, and many of them were put to menial labor at an early age. No wonder Jesus' disciples miss the point rather frequently.

If the kingdom of God thus belongs to children, this means that it belongs to the least of these, and it is on this basis that it is established for everybody else. As the Matthean Jesus says (echoed in Mark 9:36–37), putting a child before the disciples: "Whoever becomes humble like this child is the greatest in the kingdom of heaven. Whoever welcomes one such child in my name welcomes me" (Matt. 18:4–5). "Out of the mouths of babes and infants you have founded a bulwark because of your foes," says the Psalmist (Psalm 8:2), and Jesus picks up this saying in an interesting passage in Matthew 21:14–16, which reverses how we understand agency. As Jesus cures the blind and the lame in the temple, the children cry out, "Hosanna to the Son of David." It is this agency of the children that upsets the religious elites, as those who witness the power of Jesus at work now start to claim their own power. This leads to my third point.

## THE COMMON GOOD, RELIGION, SELF-INTEREST, AND AGENCY

As indicated above, alternative conceptions of the common good lead us to rethink agency, as agency can no longer be perceived in terms of the agency of the dominant system, which has failed to benefit the community. Leaving agency and control in the hands of the powerful, no matter how much they assure us of their noble intentions to serve the common good, will not change the system that keeps destroying the common good. Some might argue that there is some enlightened self-interest, which might lead the ruling class to act in more humane ways, for instance when the head of a body finally realizes that it may not be able to survive without the feet, to reference once more the apostle Paul's imagery, or when the head of a corporation develops some understanding of the contributions that workers make. But as the ongoing economic polarization shows, enlightened self-interest of the powerful and the wealthy is not enough to produce the common good, and it certainly does not represent the common interest.

At worst, the relationships of exploitation persist with more or less moderation, as the differences between workers in the United States and in Europe shows: In Europe, workers enjoy decent social security benefits, are represented on the corporations' boards, get six weeks of vacation on average, and work less than forty hours a week, yet the rich keep getting richer, and the power of working people is constantly under attack. At best, the powerful and the wealthy attempt to improve conditions by shaping others in their own image, eliminating their diversity and promoting a more self-centered way of life, a more competitive attitude, and increased personal consumption. In both cases, the dominance of the capitalist logic and its quasi-religious nature is perpetuated rather than challenged.

When agency is located at the bottom rather than at the top, a new place for self-interest is created. In addition, another kind of religion is produced. Jesus' commandment to love God and to love one's neighbor as oneself (Mark 12: 28–31) is not primarily a moral imperative but redefines self-interest in relation to others, related to a different vision of the divine. The point of loving one's neighbor as oneself is not that self-love is important, too, as liberal interpreters never tire of pointing out. The point is that self-love is inextricably related to love of neighbor because self and neighbor are always related, whether the dominant self realizes this or not. The neighbors are more likely to be aware of this fact, especially if they are living in relations of dependence on the dominant self. In capitalism, the relationship of dominant self and subordinate neighbor is at the basis of the system's success but is covered up at all cost, creating the illusion of the "self-made man" (the noninclusive language may be appropriate here), who pulls himself up by his own bootstraps.

Yet there is no "self-made man," neither at the top nor at the bottom. It is not hard to see that there can be no self without others, both in the positive sense that we owe the people who raised us and made us who we are, such as parents and teachers, and in the negative sense that we owe those on whose shoulders or backs our success is often built. This latter group includes, for instance, the people who have to endure harsh working conditions in manufacturing or the service industry at little pay, thus benefiting the fortunes of those who reap the profits of this work and, to a lesser degree, the rest of us who thus have access to inexpensive products and services.

When the illusions of dominant self-interest are thus deconstructed, self-interest can then be reconstructed from below, in relation to those who are exploited by the current system. What needs to be taken into account, in this context, is not only the self-interest of the dominant self but also the self-interest of the subordinate neighbors, particularly as this latter self-interest does not function in the dominant definitions of the common good, and as it might have the power to challenge and reshape the self-interest of everyone else. If the ruling class were to see that its own self-interest may not be well served in the long run if it is built on the backs of everyone else, things might begin to change. Of course, the ruling class would not be able to continue to rule in top-down fashion as it does now, but it might be able to sleep at night without being haunted by the ghosts of all those whose lives are ruined because their work grinds them down without mercy or because their work does not allow for a decent life.[24] If part of being human is being in relationship, the refusal to acknowledge one's relationships to others and to value them amounts to a serious loss of humanity of the members of the ruling class. It is no wonder that "rich people have problems, too"; but now we are beginning to understand that these problems cannot be solved in the privacy of their psychiatrists' offices or the confidential relations with their life coaches or pastors. The problems of the 1 percent cannot be solved without dealing with their relationships to the 99 percent.

At this point the sort of "enlightened self-interest" of the elites that maintains the status quo gives way to another form of self-interest that truly understands the self in community, from the bottom up. Life that is not lived in community is not worth living, as Charles Dickens's character Ebenezer Scrooge[25] would find out, and today we are beginning to realize that even life that is lived in communities that are too narrow (whether the self-centeredness of the family or of the gated community) may not be worth living either. If the neighbor is indeed a part of the self, the self comes to life in relationships where others are fully human and agents in their own right. Here, both the common good and religion find new life.

This brings us back to the move from distribution to production. The common good is as much about production as it is about distribution, although the factor of production is often overlooked. One of the arguments often heard in support of capitalism is that many people are better off today than they were in the past, the point being that even though goods may not be equally distributed, people on average have more than they had in the past. Truth be told, more people have color televisions and refrigerators than ever before. This argument does, of course, not address the fact that the gap between the rich and poor is also greater than ever before (greater than even in the Roman Empire),[26] and it does not address that we are dealing with suffering at a grand scale as tens of thousands of people die of hunger and preventable causes every year.[27]

Yet even if we address the problem of unequal distribution, we still have not addressed the underlying question of production. Wealth is distributed so unequally because the productive contributions of the majority of people are not valued: Either they are forced to work for very little pay, or they are pushed out of employment altogether. The middle class increasingly experiences these problems as well, as the better jobs and benefits are increasingly cut and as unemployment affects more and more college graduates.[28]

In this situation, production may be better for measuring the common good than distribution. Even if more people have more stuff, and even if we were able to reduce some of the gross inequalities in distribution, the common good is best measured in terms of how the productive capacities and contributions of people are employed and how they are valued. The common good, that which is of greatest benefit to all, has to do not only with the question of what people own (although distribution is not unimportant) but also with the question of whether people are able to live constructive lives and are free to be agents who are contributing to the good for everyone and whose contributions are valued accordingly. As we change how we value the productive contributions of people to the community, the inequalities in distribution will change as well. Of course, part of the argument will be to show that workers contribute a lot more to the community than is currently recognized.

It is not hard to envision different scenarios where work is valued differently, even under the conditions of capitalism. The Mondragon Corporation in Spain is frequently referenced as an example for this, as the salaries of executives are on average not more than five times the salaries of the workers, whereas the salaries of executives elsewhere are now hundreds of times the salaries of the workers. In addition, at Mondragon the workers receive decent benefits and own parts of the company.[29] Today, there is also a substantial list of worker-owned companies and worker cooperative companies in the United States, and it includes companies with as many as 150,000 employees.[30] It is also worth noting that labor is valued differently in other places; in European countries, for instance, the inequalities of the salaries of workers and executives are much lower than in the United States, and we should not forget that these inequalities were much lower in the United States in past decades as well.[31]

In other words, valuing labor differently is not a utopian dream that is impossible to achieve. Workers themselves have often been able to get a hearing when they were organized, and labor unions have a long history of creating conditions where work is valued differently. Labor is valued more, for instance, when it is compensated by decent wages and benefits (such as jobs with forty-hour workweeks, weekends off from work, health care, and pension plans) and when it is protected from arbitrary decisions of management. These efforts to value labor, all of which are today under attack around the globe, were not promoted by enlightened employers or politicians but by the initiative of the workers themselves, who had to fight for recognition at every turn.

Valuing work differently also implies a different understanding of agency. Not only is the agency of workers important in terms of the products they create or the services they render. The agency of workers is also important in steering and guiding the economic process and the future of the corporations. European labor movements, for instance, fought for and won seats for labor representatives on corporate boards of trustees. This is not just a matter of control; it is also a matter of leadership, as workers make much more important contributions than is often realized. It should go without saying that the agency of workers can be conceived only as a collective one: Collective action does not allow for the illusion that agency resides mostly with the genius of powerful individuals. Any agency based on collective production will have to be organized, from the bottom up, in a democratic process.

The divine itself can be rethought from this perspective. According to the Jewish traditions, in the second creation story in Genesis 2:4b–25 Godself is envisioned as a worker, who forms the human being out of clay and plants a garden, getting the divine hands dirty in the process. In the Christian traditions, the divine is envisioned as born with Jesus into a family of day laborers in construction who once again get their hands dirty as they work with various building materials. The apostle Paul, too, is presented as being proud of his work as a tentmaker, which he maintained parallel to his work as an apostle, according to the narrative of Luke (Acts 18:3, 20:33–35). In Islam, God engages in productive labor as well, creating both Adam and Jesus from dust.[32] These images of God not only enrich our theologies but challenge common images of God's agency as top-down, hierarchical, and independent of the community that produces the common good.

• • •

In sum, the common good, defined as that which is most beneficial for all, remains an important concept, but it looks different from below than from above. Gone are the dominant efforts to establish seemingly abstract universals and to do away with diversity. Gone are the benevolent efforts to shape others in one's own image. When established from below, the common good is profoundly shaped by the work of the 99 percent in all its diversity. The contributions of the members who are considered "weaker" and less "honorable" may ultimately prove to be more important, as the apostle Paul suspected in a different situation that was nevertheless also plagued by hierarchies (1 Cor. 22–23). To be sure, the 1 percent are not categorically excluded from this common good; they exclude themselves by trying to control the world economically, politically, and religiously, yet they can choose to put themselves on the side of the 99 percent as well, as has happened in some cases in the Occupy Wall Street movement.[33]

In this context our understanding of religion undergoes a transformation whose pattern can be found, for instance, in the sacred writings of the Bible. Rather than speaking with one voice and in universal and idealistic terms, the biblical writings grow out of the lives of diverse people and groups and are authored by them over periods of time, often containing a multiplicity of voices in the same book. As Ernst Käsemann has famously pointed out for the New Testament, the canon does not establish the unity of the early church but its plurality.[34] Common interest is not found in the uniformity of the Bible or in a handful of big ideas; common interest develops as groups of common people find new life in solidarity with each other and with God, mostly on the margins of the great powers of the ancient world. Of course, these and other sacred writings also contain efforts to temper the most radical traditions, and thus it is not surprising that there are conflicts in the writings themselves. In the body of work attributed to the apostle Paul, for instance, we can see both efforts of later groups to turn back the clock as well as a certain conflict embodied by Paul himself.[35]

All this has consequences for the common good in economic terms as well, which no longer has to be based on idealistic beliefs that may never become reality. Like the Abrahamic religious traditions, economics can be tied to everyday relationships, built from the bottom up by a multiplicity of agents who all contribute their share to the common good. Such economics and such religion ultimately value and encourage true productivity, doing God's work "on earth as it is in heaven" (Matt. 6:10).

## NOTES

1. Adam Smith, *An Inquiry into the Nature and Causes of the Wealth of Nations*, 5th ed., (1789; London: Methuen, 1904), bk. 4, chap. 2, para. 4. According to Smith, a merchant who only intends his own advantage is "led by an invisible hand to promote an end which was no part of his intention." Moreover, "by pursuing his own interest he frequently promotes that of the society more effectually than when he really intends to promote it."
2. Ibid., 4.2.4.
3. The Congressional Research Service, quoted in Robert Frank, "Study: Tax Cuts for the Rich Don't Spur Growth," *CNBC* report, September 17, 2012, http://finance.yahoo.com/news/tax-cuts-rich-dont-spur-151649273.html (accessed June 3, 2013).
4. See, for instance, Robert H. Nelson, *Economics as Religion: From Samuelson to Chicago and Beyond* (University Park: Pennsylvania State University Press, 2001).
5. I analyze this phenomenon in my book *No Rising Tide: Theology, Economics, and the Future* (Minneapolis: Fortress Press, 2009), chap. 3.
6. The World Council of Churches has developed several statements on the topic of structural greed. See, for instance, "A Buddhist-Christian Common Word on Struc-

tural Greed," September 17, 2010, http://www.oikoumene.org/en/resources/documents/wcc-programmes/interreligious-dialogue-and-cooperation/interreligious-trust-and-respect/buddhist-christian-common-word-on-structural-greed.html (accessed January 7, 2013).

7. In a court ruling of the Michigan Supreme Court in 1919 (*Dodge v. Ford Motor Company*), the brothers John Francis Dodge and Horace Elgin Dodge, owners of 10 percent of Ford stock, challenged Ford's decision to cut dividends in order to invest in new plants and grow production and numbers of workers, while cutting prices. Henry Ford stated: "My ambition is to employ still more men, to spread the benefits of this industrial system to the greatest possible number, to help them build up their lives and their homes. To do this we are putting the greatest share of our profits back in the business." The court ruled in favor of the Dodge brothers, arguing that a corporation is organized primarily for the profit of its stockholders, rather than for the benefit of its employees or for the community. See also the brief entry in Wikipedia, "Dodge v. Ford Motor Company," http://en.wikipedia.org/wiki/Dodge_v._Ford_Motor_Company (accessed January 14, 2013).

8. See *No Rising Tide*, chap. 2. This logic is not based on a pessimistic approach but on the insight that the truth is seen better from below. In economics, for instance, times of economic growth have often produced false optimisms that proved to be destructive, whereas tough times have produced clearer visions and programs that tended to be more beneficial for the common good.

9. This relation of faith and action has been emphasized by various liberation theologies. It is deeply rooted in the Jewish, Islamic, and Christian traditions. See, for instance, Isaiah 58:6: "Is not this the fast that I choose: to loose the bonds of injustice, to undo the thongs of the yoke, to let the oppressed go free, and to break every yoke?" In the New Testament, James 2:17 states that "faith by itself, if it has not works, is dead." Qur'an, 29:69, reads: "And those who strive in Our (cause),—We will certainly guide them to our Paths: For verily Allah is with those who do right" (Yusuf Ali translation); "As for those who strive in Us, We surely guide them to Our paths, and lo! Allah is with the good" (Pickthall translation); "And (as for) those who strive hard for Us, We will most certainly guide them in Our ways; and Allah is most surely with the doers of good" (Shakir translation). These three translations are compiled on the following website: Center for Muslim-Jewish Engagement, University of Southern California, http://www.usc.edu/org/cmje/religious-texts/quran/verses/029-qmt.php (accessed January 8, 2013).

10. For an account of the history of the modern notion of religion and the role of dominant religion in modernity see, for instance, Tomoko Masuzawa, *The Invention of World Religions; or, How European Universalism was Preserved in the Language of Pluralism* (Chicago: University of Chicago Press, 2005).

11. That Paul cannot be understood without his opposition to the Roman Empire is argued by a growing range of New Testament scholars as different as John Dominic Crossan, Neil Elliott, Richard Horsley, and N. T. Wright.

12. See, for instance, Dale Martin, *The Corinthian Body* (New Haven, Conn.: Yale University Press, 1995), 94–96.

13. The "more respectable members" of the body "do not need" the more respectful treatment of the other members, says Paul (1 Cor. 12:24). Nevertheless, he also talks about the "members of the body that seem to be weaker" (1 Cor. 12:22), not saying that they actually are weaker.
14. For a helpful critique of heroic images of Paul see Melanie Johnson-DeBaufre and Laura S. Nasrallah, "Beyond the Heroic Paul: Toward a Feminist and Decolonizing Approach to the Letters of Paul," in *The Colonized Apostle: Paul through Postcolonial Eyes*, ed. Christopher D. Stanley (Minneapolis: Fortress Press, 2011), 161–74. The authors argue that Paul's letters need to be read in the context of Paul's communities (and later communities that read Paul) as "sites of vision *and* debate" (173) in order to gain a sense of the complex and messy political struggles. This, rather than an idealized image of an individual, will allow us to draw the lessons for our own contemporary struggles.
15. Today, some of the most fundamental insights into how suffering is created by capitalism are produced where religious communities and labor meet. Wage theft is one the clearest and least ambiguous examples. See, for instance, the Interfaith Worker Justice director Kimberly A. Bobo's book *Wage Theft in America: Why Millions of Americans Are Not Getting Paid and What We Can Do About It* (New York: New Press, 2009). Wage theft is, of course, only the tip of the iceberg. Wage depression, often perfectly legal, is another problem that is increasingly addressed by religion and labor people. See, for instance, the current Our Walmart campaign, on the web: Organization United for Respect at Walmart, http://forrespect.org, (accessed January 8, 2013).
16. It is interesting to note that in Christianity there is a tradition of the active suffering of Christ, in addition to the more common emphasis on Christ's passive suffering.
17. This shift of emphasis from distribution to production is one of the key concerns of *No Rising Tide*; see, for instance, 119–20, 137–38, and 157.
18. That the middle class is not as privileged and powerful as it tends to assume is developed in *No Rising Tide*, chap. 2.
19. For further details on this phenomenon and the consequences for religion see Joerg Rieger and Kwok Pui-lan, *Occupy Religion: Theology of the Multitude* (Lanham, Md.: Rowman and Littlefield, 2012).
20. In 1973, the top 0.1 percent's share of the national income was 2 percent, by 2008 it was 8 percent. Timothy Noah, "The United States of Inequality: Why We Can't Ignore Growing Income Inequality," *Slate*, September 3, 2010. http://www.slate.com/articles/news_and_politics/the_great_divergence/features/2010/the_united_states_of_inequality/introducing_the_great_divergence.html (accessed January 8, 2013). The statistic quoted comes from slide 4 of Catherine Mulbrandon and Timothy Noah's slideshow "The Great Divergence in Pictures," which is embedded in this article.
21. See Nathaniel Popper, "U.S. Is Among Developed Economies with Highest Income Inequality," *Los Angeles Times*, December 6, 2011. http://articles.latimes.com/2011/dec/06/business/la-fi-1206-oecd-income-20111206 (accessed January 8, 2013).

22. Campaign financing and donations for which credit is given are only the tip of the iceberg, as the power of money permeates virtually everything, beginning with personal relationships, the visions and dreams of community projects (what is fundable), and the lived realities of religion (whom are we trying to please and whose feathers are we not allowed to ruffle).
23. Latin American liberation theologians noted similar problems decades ago when they opposed the development efforts of the so-called First World.
24. Workers for the Walmart corporation might provide an example here, which is significant because Walmart is the largest private employer in the Unted States and because its model of employment is more and more copied by others: Michael Duke, Walmart's CEO, earns 785 times of what a full-time Walmart worker who earns $12.67 an hour would be able earn in a year, without any time off. Caroline Fairchild, "Walmart's Average Employee Would have to Work 785 Years to Earn CEO's Annual Salary," *Huffington Post*, April 24, 2013, http://www.huffingtonpost.com/2013/04/23/walmart-wages-to-ceo-annual-salary_n_3140618.html (accessed March 30, 2015). Duke makes sure that gap is considerably wider in real life, as Walmart workers are commonly prevented from working full time so that the company will not have to pay benefits. As a result, the salaries of most Walmart workers are below the poverty line. Note also that these numbers do not take into account income from shares and investments, which are substantial for CEOs. The announcement of February 15, 2015, that Walmart will be increasing wages to $9 per hour has no impact on this calculation, as this wage is below the one used to calculate the difference.
25. Charles Dickens, *A Christmas Carol. In Prose. Being a Ghost Story of Christmas* (London: Chapman and Hall, 1843).
26. See Jillian Berman, "U.S. Income Inequality Higher than Roman Empire's Levels: Study," *Huffington Post*, December 19, 2011, http://www.huffingtonpost.com/2011/12/19/us-income-inequality-ancient-rome-levels_n_1158926.html (accessed January 8, 2013).
27. Every day about 25,000 people die of hunger or hunger-related causes. See www.poverty.com (accessed June 4, 2013).
28. Although it has been noted that the unemployment rates for college graduates are beginning to look up since 2010, job growth for this sector is slower than expected, which means, according to the Economic Policy Institute, that "the class of 2013 will likely earn less over the next 10–15 years than they would have before the recession hit and jobs were more plentiful." Mark Korba, "Job Picture Looks Bleak for 2013 College Grads," *CNBC*, April 26, 2013, http://www.cnbc.com/id/100673848 (accessed June 4, 2013).
29. For basic information on the Mondragon Corporation, see "Mondragon Corporation," *Wikipedia*, http://en.wikipedia.org/wiki/Mondragon_Corporation (accessed January 8, 2013).
30. For a list of the 100 largest majority employee-owned companies, see the National Center for Employee Ownership, "The Employee Ownership 100: America's Larg-

est Majority Employee-Owned Companies," August 2013 http://www.nceo.org/articles/employee-ownership-100.

31. A useful graph of differentials between CEO and worker pay in the United States shows that in 1965, CEOs earned twenty times more than the average worker. This ratio began to increase in the 1980s, reaching peaks of over four hundred times more in the 2000s. See http://www.stateofworkingamerica.org/chart/swa-wages-figure-4-ceo-worker-compensation/ (accessed March 29, 2015).

32. Qur'an 3:59: "The similitude of Jesus before Allah is as that of Adam; He created him from dust, then said to him: 'Be.' And he was" (Yusuf Ali translation); " Lo! the likeness of Jesus with Allah is as the likeness of Adam. He created him of dust, then He said unto him: Be! and he is" (Pickthall translation); "Surely the likeness of Isa is with Allah as the likeness of Adam; He created him from dust, then said to him, Be, and he was" (Shakir translation).

33. See, for instance: Prashanth Kamalakanthan, "We Are the 1 Percent, We Stand with the 99 Percent," Tumblr site, http://westandwiththe99percent.tumblr.com/ (accessed June 4, 2013).

34. Ernst Käsemann, "The Canon of the New Testament and the Unity of the Church," in Käsemann, *Essays on New Testament Themes* (London: SCM Press, 1964), 103.

35. There is widespread agreement among biblical scholars that the Deutero-Pauline literature is an example of later attempts to tone down Paul, but there are tensions between progressive and conservative stances even in the undisputed writings of Paul.

# Christian Socialism and the Future of Economic Democracy

GARY DORRIEN

Theologians and social ethicists have long dreamed of a transformed economic order based on democracy and the common good. A century ago the social gospel movement reverberated with calls for a cooperative commonwealth of worker and community ownership. In the 1930s Reinhold Niebuhr called for a blend of neo-Reformation theology and revolutionary socialism in repudiating social gospel idealism. In the 1970s liberation theologians revived the language of socialist criticism and the dream of moving beyond capitalism. But the dream failed, and today capitalism prevails in more global and predatory forms than ever.

Today megabyte monies zip across the planet at the speed of light, de-linked from real production, rendering quaint the dream of democratizing economic power. There is no significant movement or strategy to replace the predatory logic of capitalism. There is only the necessity of creating one through the struggles of thousands of disparate organizations and communities. For the injustices that gave rise to socialist movements still exist, still matter, and exist among new crises threatening the survival of the planet. Even the hope of merely restraining the destructive impulses of corporate capitalism has been left to stubborn types who refuse to accept that there is no alternative.

My field, social ethics, began as a response to this very problem. In the 1880s the founders of the social gospel invented social ethics and the ecumenical movement. It was not a coincidence that the social gospel, social ethics, sociology, socialism, and the very ideas of social structure, social salvation, and social justice arose at the same time; also corporate capitalism and the trade unions. The defining idea of the social gospel was novel—that Christian communities have a mission to transform the structures of society in the direction of social justice. If there was such a thing as social structure, salvation had to be reconceived to account for it. Salvation had to be personal and social to be saving. In England and Germany this idea was called Christian socialism. In the United States it had to be called something else.[1]

The social gospel happened for a confluence of reasons that influenced each other. It had a back story in nineteenth-century Anglican socialism and German social democracy. It took root in the United States as a response to the corruption of the Gilded Age and the rise of industrial society. It arose in black church communities as a response to Jim Crow tyranny and an upsurge of lynching. It rode on the back of a rising sociological consciousness and literature. But above all, modern social Christianity was a response to a burgeoning labor movement. Trade unionists blasted the churches for doing nothing for poor and working-class people. The social gospel founders realized it was pointless to defend Christianity if the churches remained guilty as charged. If people suffered because of politics and economics, the church had to deal with politics and economics.

There were seventeen things wrong with the social gospel, beginning with the fact that most of it was optimistic, idealistic, middle-class, and not very brave about racial justice. Reinhold Niebuhr got to be famous by ridiculing the social gospel on these points. But for all its faults, the social gospel movement recovered the centrality of the Kingdom of God in the teaching of Jesus; it recovered the social justice emphasis of Hebrew and Christian scripture; it created the ecumenical movement; it had a radical economic justice flank led by George Herron and Walter Rauschenbusch; it was the wellspring of the civil rights movement through the black social gospel ministries of Reverdy Ransom, Alexander Walters, Mordecai Johnson, Benjamin Mays, Pauli Murray, and Martin Luther King Jr.; and it yielded forms of social Christianity that left behind the progressive idealism of the social gospel.[2]

Catholic social theology, ecumenical theology, dialectical theology, and liberation theology kept alive the idea of a humane economic order. Leo XIII, in *Rerum Novarum* (1891), launched the modern Catholic tradition of social teaching, introducing the idea of a "solidarist" third way between capitalism and socialism, which Pius XI amplified in *Quadragesimo Anno* (1941) as a system of worker syndicates. In 1908 the newly founded Federal Council of Churches of the USA, comprising thirty-one Protestant and Eastern Orthodox denominations, issued a Social Creed calling for "equal rights and complete justice" for all, the abolition of child labor, a "living wage as a minimum in every industry," social security, an equitable distribution of income and wealth, and the abatement of poverty. The three leading theologians of the succeeding generation—Karl Barth, Reinhold Niebuhr, and Paul Tillich—were socialists on the way up, although Barth strove to keep theology and politics in different compartments, and Niebuhr eventually settled for Keynesian welfare state liberalism.[3]

These figures and traditions differed significantly on theology while agreeing that capitalist selfishness and inequality had to be replaced with something better. To the major theologians of the Progressive and Depression eras, the capitalist devotion to individual self-interest was plainly hostile to Christian teaching. Some who were far from being Marxists were unsparing about the predatory immorality of capitalism. Christian Socialists usually acknowledged, like Marx, that capitalism marked a great leap forward by facilitating crucial breakthroughs in capital accumulation and industrialization. To the Barthian theologian Emil Brunner, however, capitalism was not a prelude to anything except moral and social catastrophe. In *The Divine Imperative* he pronounced that capitalism "is that system in which all that we can see to be the meaning of the economic order from the point of view of faith is being denied: in which, therefore, it is made almost impossible for the individual to realize, in any way through his economic activity, the service of God and his neighbor. This system is contrary to the spirit of service; it is debased and irresponsible; indeed we may go further and say it is irresponsibility developed into a system."[4]

The Anglican bishop William Temple had a similar critique of capitalism and a constructive alternative to it, in his case a guild socialist model. In 1941, shortly before he was named archbishop of Canterbury, Temple called for an excess-profits tax to create worker- and community-controlled enterprises. The following year his book *Christianity and the Social Order* enlisted natural law against the spirit and logic of capitalism. Production naturally exists for consumption, Temple argued, but capitalism reverses the natural order of things by making consumption depend on production, while production depends on finance. Temple's alternative put a higher value on fellowship than profits, calling for withering capital investment, mutual export trade, economic democracy, a socialized monetary system, and the social use of land: "It is important to remember that the class-war was not first proclaimed as a crusade by Marx and Engels; it was first announced as a fact by Adam Smith. Nothing can securely end it except the acquisition by Labour of a share in the control of industry. Capital gets its dividends; Labour gets its wages; there is no reason why Capital should also get control and Labour have no share in it."[5]

In the 1950s theologians trimmed their sails, conforming to a conformist time. In the 1960s and 1970s socialist criticism made a comeback through the rise of German political theology, Third World liberation theology, Black theology, and feminism. The German theologian Jürgen Moltmann described democratic socialism as the historical form that Christian hope had to take, "given the present poverty of capitalism and its democracies as well as socialism and its dictatorial governments."[6] The Peruvian liberationist Gustavo Gutiérrez proclaimed that Christian theology needed to speak "of social revolution, not reform; of liberation, not development; of socialism, not modernization of the prevailing system."⁷ The Argentine liberationist José Míguez Bonino declared that the struggle for socialist transformation "concretely defines my Christian obedience in the world."⁸ The African American philosopher Cornel West identified liberation theology and himself with revolutionary neo-Marxist councilism, and the feminist theologian Rosemary Radford Ruether advocated "a democratic socialist society that dismantles sexist and class hierarchies, that restores ownership and management of work to the base communities of workers themselves, who then create networks of economic and political relationships."⁹

Similar visions were commonplace in the theologies of the 1970s and 1980s. Many theologians explicitly advocated democratic socialism, notably Gregory Baum, Harvey Cox, Leonardo Boff, Robert McAfee Brown, Beverly W. Harrison, Kenneth Leech, Johannes Metz, Arthur McGovern, Ronald Preston, Dorothee Soelle, Franklin Gamwell, Phillip Wogaman, Gibson Winter, Daniel Maguire, and Joe Holland.¹⁰ Usually they cautioned against equating socialism with nationalization and centralized authority, in line with previous socialist theologians such as Tillich, Temple, and Walter Muelder. Tillich warned against the "bureaucratization of the economy" and took for granted that only the market knows how to get prices right.¹¹

The debate that advocates of decentralized economic democracy always wanted was the one between themselves and state socialists. Communism was a perversion of anything deserving to be called socialism, because Communism obliterated democracy and individual rights. But after the Soviet Union imploded, decentralized socialists did not get the debate they wanted. The family arguments within democratic socialism seemed irrelevant in a world seized by the manic logic of capitalism. Economic globalization pushed aside socialist concerns about equality and humane community. Nations crawling out from decades of Communist rule in the former Soviet bloc did not aspire to democratic versions of anything smacking of socialism, which raised the question whether anything was left of Christian socialism. How much of the vision of a democratized social order could be saved or reconstructed when "socialism" mostly conjured up repulsive images of state authoritarianism? How was it possible to reclaim the social Christian vision of democratized economic power when corporate capitalism turned the planet into a single economic market?

For some Christian ethicists, the dream of economic democracy was exhausted and refuted. The Lutheran neoconservative Robert Benne urged Christian ethicists to repudiate their democratic socialist heritage. The neoliberal realists Max Stackhouse and Dennis McCann said the death of Communism refuted the defining biases of Christian social ethics: "The Protestant

Social Gospel, early Christian realism, much neo-orthodoxy, many forms of Catholic modernism, the modern ecumenical drive for racial and social inclusiveness, and contemporary liberation theories all held that democracy, human rights and socialism were the marks of the coming kingdom." But all were wrong: "The future will not bring what contemporary theology said it would and should." According to Stackhouse and McCann, history had refuted every form of socialist ideology, including forms that militantly opposed Communism. The death of socialism marked the belated end of theology's attempt to give it a human face.[12]

For neoconservatives and some Niebuhrian realists, the project that remained for Christian social ethics was to apply the chastening lessons of Niebuhrian realism to the economic order. The neoconservative social critic Michael Novak disavowed the social Christian project of breaking down existing concentrations of economic power. Noting that Niebuhr failed to press his realism into a critique of social democratic economics, Novak said that neoconservatives like himself completed this essential Niebuhrian task by repudiating the Christian tradition of economic democracy: "Niebuhr did not give much attention to economic issues. Precisely in Niebuhr's neglect, I found my own vocation. Surely, I thought, the next generation of Niebuhrians ought to push some of Niebuhr's deeper insights into the one major area he neglected."[13]

Novak's pursuit of this neglected project drew him deeply into the political Right, where, in the 1980s, he became a Reagan supporter and a chief mythologist of U.S. American capitalism. To apply Niebuhr's realism to the economic realm, Novak argued, is to relinquish the progressive Christian dream of democratizing economic power. The values and legitimizing principles of democracy are pertinent only to the political sphere. "Democratic capitalism" excludes democratic tests of legitimacy, equality, and accountability from the economic realm. It emphasizes wealth creation and allows the market to take care of distribution. It opposes government regulation of the financial sector and assures that wealth creation at the top will eventually trickle down to middle-class and working-class communities. It accepts and celebrates the triumph of corporate capitalism.[14]

Many have taken that option, supporting the upsurge of global capitalist ideology. The debates we are having today about busting public unions, cutting Medicaid, and privatizing Medicare are by-products of thirty years of economic globalization and of massive, structural, politically engineered inequality that exacerbate the worst aspects of globalization. Wages have been flat for thirty-five years, and inequality has worsened dramatically. The share of the nation's income held by the top 1 percent has more than doubled since 1982. Today the top 1 percent of the U.S. population holds 39 percent of the nation's wealth and takes in 25 percent of its annual income. The top 10 percent hold

70 percent of the wealth. The bottom 50 percent hold 2 percent. And the big banks and oil companies are more powerful than ever.[15]

Global capitalism commodifies everything it touches, including labor and nature, putting everything up for sale. Neoliberal theory says the integration of national economies into the global economy through trade, direct foreign investment, short-term capital flows, and flows of labor and technology has "flattened" the world, so deal with it. In a flat world you either compete successfully or are run over; there is no political remedy. Any nation that wants a growing economy has to wear a one-size-fits-all golden straitjacket that unleashes the private sector, minimizes government, eliminates tariffs, deregulates capital markets, and allows direct foreign ownership and investment.[16]

But neoliberals exaggerate the futility of attempts to channel economic forces. Contrary to the story they tell, the United States did not ensure its prosperity by donning the golden straitjacket and relinquishing its manufacturing base. From the late 1940s to 1975, productivity and wages soared together in the United States, creating a middle-class society; meanwhile, there were no bank crises, as New Deal reforms kept commercial banks out of the investment business. Then wages flattened while productivity kept soaring. The rich got richer in the 1980s and 1990s while everyone else fell behind, taking on debt to keep from drowning. During this period nearly every manufacturing-oriented society outperformed the United States in income growth and did so with more equitable distributions of income. In the 1980s the United States cut the marginal tax rate from 70 percent to 28 percent and cut the capital gains rate from 45 percent to 20 percent. That was a revolution, a blowout for politically engineered inequality. Then the global integration of two radically different models of growth—debt-financed consumption and production-oriented export and saving—created a wildly unstable world economy featuring asset bubbles and huge trade imbalances.[17]

First the United States hollowed out its industrial base that paid decent wages, providing incentives to firms that made things to make them elsewhere. Then it rang up enormous trade deficits that left the United States dependent on China and Japan to finance its debt. Then the economy cratered after the debt resort reached its outer limit in the housing market and the mortgage bubble burst. For twenty years we were told that governments are passé in this area. But when the housing market crashed, these supposedly obsolete governments coughed up $12 trillion in two months to save the system from itself.

## RETHINKING AND RENEWING ECONOMIC DEMOCRACY

Economic democracy, in my conception, is not a nicer-sounding stand-in for state socialism, though the phrase was sometimes used that way by twentieth-century socialists. Neither is it compatible with blueprint dogmatism, though some theorists of economic democracy are devoted to their blueprints. In my conception it is decentralized, communitarian, radically democratic, pluralistic, ecological, and a compound of realism and idealism.

The roots of economic democracy theory go back to the cooperative and guild socialist movements of the nineteenth and early twentieth centuries, notably the French section of the First Socialist International, which stressed cooperative networks of production and consumption, and the guild socialist section of the British Labour Party, which advocated a decentralized third way between syndicalism and state socialism. The usual starting point, however, is Oscar Lange.

A Polish economist and diplomat who taught at the University of Chicago in the late 1930s, Lange served as the Polish delegate to the United Nations Security Council in the mid-1940s and published his major work, *On the Economic Theory of Socialism*, in 1936. He rejected the Marxian labor theory of value, contending that socialists needed to accommodate neoclassical price theory. Essentially, he showed that market mechanisms and incentives could be integrated into socialist theory.

In Lange's proposal, a large state sector coexisted with, and benefited from, the pricing and market discipline of a private sector of small enterprises. State planners simulated and were instructed by the private sector's pricing system, and central planning boards set prices by adjusting to shortages and surpluses. When shortages occurred, prices would be raised to encourage businesses to increase production; when surpluses occurred, prices would be lowered to encourage businesses to prevent losses by curtailing production.[18]

But that was still a form of state socialism. Lange showed that market mechanisms and social ownership were compatible, and he granted a larger role for the market than state socialists. But he had centralized planners trying to replicate the innumerable and enormously complex pricing decisions of markets—a task exceeding the competence, time constraints, and knowledge of any conceivable planning board. Lange-style blueprints for "market socialism" invariably founder on this problem and the authoritarian politics that inevitably go with it.

Economic democracy has to break from the unitary logic of state socialism, featuring mixed forms of worker, community, and mutual funds or public bank enterprises. It is about democratizing economic power, abolishing poverty, and creating environmentally sustainable economies. I do not believe that factors of production trump everything else. Democratizing power applies to the point of production (as in Marxism), and electoral politics (as in liberalism), and the postindustrial community or "living place" where people seek healthy neighborhoods, a clean environment, and decent housing and health care. It requires a feminist, interracial, multicultural, ecological, and antiimperial consciousness that privileges liberationist and environmental issues.

But any serious challenge to existing relations of power has to deal with factors of production. Those who control the terms, amounts, and direction of credit play the predominant role in creating the kind of society the rest of us inhabit. Gains toward social and economic democracy are needed today for the same reason that political democracy is necessary, to restrain the abuse of unequal power.

Today seven banks control 73 percent of the nation's assets. The big banks have become giant hedge funds trading on their own accounts. The ostensible purpose of Wall Street is to raise money to finance making things in the real economy, but Wall Street has fallen in love with derivatives, which are inherently dangerous, and Collateralized Debt Obligations, which are not investments of any kind. CDO deals do not create any actual bonds or mortgages, or add anything of value to society. They are pure gambling on whether somebody else's bonds will succeed. They are like side bets at a casino, except the Federal Reserve implicitly protects these bets.

According to the SEC, Goldman Sachs, Citigroup, and other firms have looted their own customers by creating derivatives that are designed to fail, and then betting against them. The Volcker Rule was supposed to stop that, by reinstating a wall between commercial and investment banking. But to pass the Dodd-Frank financial reform bill, the Volcker Rule was gutted with exemptions for trading in treasury bonds and bond issues by government-backed entities. As always, these exemptions led to others, and today the Volcker Rule is riddled with them. Former Treasury Secretary Paul Volcker's original proposal was three pages. In the Dodd-Frank bill it was ten pages. Today it is five hundred pages of exemptions and loopholes, and the banks are wheedling for more—exemptions for bank investments in venture capital and private-equity funds, and a loophole for companies that want to trade derivatives with themselves.

The financial crash of 2008 started with people who were just trying to buy a house of their own—people who had no concept of predatory lending and who had no say in the securitization boondoggle that spliced up various components of risk to trade them separately. It seemed a blessing to get a low-rate mortgage. It was a mystery how the banks did it, but this was their business. You trusted that they knew what they were doing. Your bank resold the mortgage to an aggregator who bunched it up with thousands of other subprime mortgages, chopped the package into pieces, and sold them as corporate bonds.

Securitizations and derivatives are great at concocting extra yield and allowing the banks to hide their debt. Broadly speaking, a derivative is any contract that derives its value from another underlying asset. More narrowly and pertinently, it's an instrument that allows investors to speculate on the future price of something without having to buy it. Derivatives were developed to allow investors to hedge their risks in financial markets—in essence, to buy insurance against market movements. In each case they quickly became major investment options in their own right.

Option trading soared in the 1970s, paying for the right to exercise an option in the event that prices move in a set direction. Currency swaps came next, followed by interest rate swaps. From there it was a short step to the credit-default swaps pioneered in the late 1990s, in which parties bet on, or insure against, defaults. Credit-default swaps are private contracts that allow investors to bet on whether a borrower will default. In 1999 that market was $150 billion. By 2008 it was $65 trillion, and at the heart of the meltdown. AIG's derivatives unit was a huge casino selling phantom insurance with hardly any backing, and eventually taxpayers were forced to bail them out.[19]

Derivatives offer dangerous incentives for false accounting and make it extremely difficult to ascertain a firm's true exposure. They generate huge amounts of leverage and were developed with no consideration of the broad economic consequences. Securitization ensures unaccountability by creating new types of information asymmetries. Mortgage bundlers know more than buyers about what is in the bundles, but nobody knows very much, which leaves nobody responsible when they blow up. The big investment banks have complex mathematical models for measuring risk. The leading model, VaR (Value at Risk), was developed at JPMorgan in the early 1990s. It uses statistical ideas and probability theories to quantify portfolio risks as a single number. Traders love its ability to picture short-term trends by measuring normal probabilities. The big firms measure VaR every day.

But VaR, for all its mathematical complexity, is only as good the information fed into it, which has a very limited scope. The risk models work until they don't, and they don't measure risk because they cannot detect unexpected calamities. Their chief function is to create a false sense of security. The benchmarks for VaR modeling are a few days or weeks; even the "historical" variations measure risks only for a year or two. After the housing crash of 2007 yielded the financial meltdown of 2008, the former Federal Reserve chair Alan Greenspan told Congress that if the models had been fitted to normal historical periods, Wall Street might have known better than to keep piling on debt. He was "shocked" to learn that the big banks could not be trusted to protect shareholder equity. This discovery contradicted his "fundamental worldview," he said.[20]

Meanwhile, in the real world, all financial meltdowns are basically alike. The same thing happened in South Korea and Indonesia in 1997, Malaysia in

1998, Argentina and Russia more than once, Japan for a "lost decade" now exceeding twenty years, and the crash of 2008: A financial oligarchy rigged the game in its favor, built an empire on debt, overreached in good times, and brought the house down on everybody. When the house explodes, elites do what they always do: They take care of their own. To get a different result, a nation has to take control of the problem and break the grip of the oligarchy. Otherwise you muddle along in a lost decade of your own, which further entrenches the oligarchy.

The MIT economist Simon Johnson, who was formerly chief economist of the International Monetary Fund, says the finance industry has captured the U.S. government. In his early career Johnson tried to be skeptical about this, but then he went to the IMF and got a close look at the symbiotic relationships between the world's economic elites and its governments. In the United States it goes far beyond mere access or even collusion, he says. Here the two career tracks of government and high finance are melded together. Johnson emphasizes that when the IMF enters the scene of a crash, the economic part is usually straightforward: Nations in crisis are told to live within their means by increasing exports, cutting imports, and breaking up bankrupt enterprises and banks. Every country that is not the United States would get this prescription. But the United States controls the IMF, it has a powerful and well-connected oligarchy, and it pays its foreign debts in its own currency. So our recovery began by paying off Wall Street.

Johnson's analysis of the problem is compelling, but his answer is straight out of the IMF playbook: Find a bottom, clear out the clutter, get the fiscal and monetary houses in order, and shake up crony capitalism. There is always going to be an economic oligarchy, he says, so the best we can do is shake it up from time to time. To this end he recommends new antitrust laws that he does not specify, and he says it's pointless to cap executive compensation, since they always find a way. In his book, *Thirteen Bankers*, co-authored with James Kwak, Johnson makes a good case for shrinking the big banks.[21]

If we take the existing system for granted, Johnson's prescription is about the best we can do. But we need to talk about something bolder: creating public banks, turning the big banks into public utilities, and making massive investments in a healthy, educated, productive workforce and a clean energy economy. Today the economy is sluggish because of weak consumer demand caused by stagnant wages, job uncertainty, and the ongoing ravages of the mortgage disaster. The United States has underinvested in infrastructure, education, and technology for decades. The costs of labor, equipment, and capital will never be lower than they are today. There are many high-return opportunities, but we have absurd politics in which both political parties are beholden to Wall Street and one party doesn't believe in investing to benefit society. Though the Treasury Department has no trouble selling debt, the Beltway fixates on the hypothetical wrath of the bond market and the judgments of rating agencies that were wrong about everything for twenty years. Both political parties are so deeply tied to Wall Street that they routinely cater to the anxieties of bond traders. Somehow the imaginary threat of inflation is more real to them than the human crisis of unemployment. We need to make massive investments in things that create good jobs and make a better society.

And for that we need to talk about banks that are geared to serve the common good. It is hard to talk about this. We are easily intimidated by financial jargon; this topic has the S-word all over it; and even if we are comfortable talking about fiscal policy, it's usually another story with monetary policy. Fiscal policy deals with the management of a nation's income and spending. Monetary policy deals with the forms and supply of money. These two subjects interact in many ways, but most of our public discourse about government finance focuses on fiscal policy. All of us have experience managing income and spending. We readily grasp what this subject is about; we have debates about it constantly; and all of that gives ballast to the feeling that we have some political agency in this area.

Monetary policy has none of that going for it. The economist John Kenneth Galbraith, in his book *Money: Whence It Came, Where It Went*, aptly remarked: "The study of money, above all other fields in economics is the one in which complexity is used to disguise truth, not to reveal it." This branch of economics keeps track of interest rates, bond sales, reserve ratios, credit card rates, money supply, and public and private debt, all in technical language. But it rests on a system of debt money created by private banks that Econ 101 tends to obscure.[22]

In Econ 101 we were told that banks are intermediaries between savers and borrowers. A saver makes a deposit and the bank lends that money to a borrower. But banks are more godly than that, for when a bank issues a loan, the accountant enters two numbers. The promise to repay the loan is recorded as an asset, and the money put into the borrower's account is recorded as a liability. With these entries, the bank has created new money from nothing in the amount of the loan principal, and the borrower has taken on a legal obligation to repay the principal with interest. Nearly all the money in existence, except for coins and special notes, is created in this way.

Private banks have created nearly all the money that exists, for private gain. This simple fact is far-reaching, and too daunting for comfort. A few economists and financial professionals have persisted with it anyway, notably William Hixson, Michael Rowbotham, William Henry Pope, and Herman Daly.

They urge us to pay attention to monetary policy, because we have a debt money system controlled by huge commercial banks that are way too powerful for anybody's good but their own.[23]

Commercial banks create money out of nothing whenever they make a loan. Interest has to be paid on these loans. Banks create the principal for the loans they make, but they do not create the interest that has to be paid, except for the sliver of interest they pay on savings accounts. The party that benefits from the first use of newly created money gets the value of the money for nothing, while borrowers and society collectively are legally obligated to pay off debt with money that does not exist. This arrangement allows banks to become rich and politically powerful by controlling something that everyone needs.

The federal government has been in debt to the banks since Andrew Jackson's presidency. The rule of the banks came into question during the Civil War, when President Lincoln refused to pay up to 36 percent for loans. Lincoln issued $400 million of greenbacks to get the Union through the war with little debt, which stimulated industrial production. After the war the federal government ran huge surpluses, but even then the government did not pay off its debt, for had it done so there would have been no bonds to back the national bank notes. Retiring the government's securities would have destroyed the money supply.

The National Banking Act of 1863 authorized private banks to issue their own banknotes backed by government bonds deposited with the U.S. Treasury. This was a historic victory for Wall Street bankers and their European affiliates, delivering, to them, monopoly power to create the nation's money supply. The federal debt has been the basis of the U.S. money supply since that time. Wall Street sealed this victory in 1913 by establishing the Federal Reserve, which is owned and controlled by twelve American commercial banks. The Federal Reserve banks benefit from the appearance of being government institutions, but in fact they are private credit monopolies that have usurped democratic self-governance.

There is a wing-nut strain of the Left that wants to link arms with the populist Right to smash the Fed. Populism is notorious for bringing extremes together, usually with a conspiracy theory. I do not believe that the debt money system is the key to everything that's wrong with capitalism, and I am wary of Lefties who are eager to hook up with the Tea Party. But debt money is part of the problem, as progressives once knew. The social gospel movement was part of the Left-progressive opposition to the rule of the banks. It called for public banks and government-created money. It wanted the government to provide interest-free loans to build a good society, not borrow money from banks charging interest. That social gospel was still alive in 1932, when the Federal

Council of Churches issued a revised Social Creed calling for "social planning and control of the credit and monetary systems for the common good," a Reconstruction Finance Corporation, social security, public works employment, selective nationalization, and the curtailment of speculation.[24]

There are versions of economic democracy that centralize power, and/or make heroic demands on the political system, and/or impose somebody's blueprint of a perfect system. But economic democracy at its best does none of these things. It is undeniably visionary, challenging the borders of possibility and imagining new forms of social and economic organization. But it is fundamentally about creating viable new democratic choices, not imposing somebody's blueprint. Economic democracy is about extending the values and rights of democracy into the economic sphere, building up enterprises that do not belong wholly to the capitalist market or the state. It expands the sector of producer and consumer cooperatives, community land trusts, and community finance corporations. It creates mixed forms of worker, community, and mutual fund or public bank enterprises.

People work harder and more efficiently when they have a stake in the company, when it's their company. In Spain, the Mondragon network is spectacularly successful. Mondagron employs more than 100,000 workers in an integrated network of more than 125 financial, industrial, and service companies in virtually every economic sector, including robots and mass transit. It contains more than 75 thriving industrial firms, an agricultural cooperative, 5 schools, a technical college, and a central bank. Each Mondragon worker/owner holds one share of voting stock, and profits are distributed in the form of additions to a capital account on which 6 percent interest is paid annually. In the United States we have 14,000 firms with worker-ownership plans, and approximately 1,000 are fully worker-controlled. These are building blocks for a movement. Credit unions play a key role. Credit unions are growing; one of the best things the Occupy movement did was to encourage people to join them.[25]

But merely expanding the cooperative sector is not enough. Cooperatives usually prohibit nonworking shareholders, so they attract less outside financing than capitalist firms. They are committed to keeping low-return firms in operation, so they stay in business even when they can't pay competitive wages. They are committed to particular communities, so they are less mobile than corporate capital and labor. They smack of anticapitalist bias, so they have trouble getting financing and advice from banks. They maximize net income per worker rather than profits, so they tend to favor capital-intensive investments over job creation.

Most of these problems are virtues, and the problematic aspects can be mitigated with tax incentives. But we also need something bolder and more visionary. We need forms of social ownership that facilitate democratic capital formation, have a greater capacity for scaling up, and are more entrepreneurial. Specifically, we need public banks and mutual-funded holding companies in which ownership of productive capital is vested. The companies lend capital to enterprises at market rates of interest and otherwise control the process of investment. Equity shareholders, the state, and/or other cooperatives own the holding companies or public banks.

The central bank at Mondragon, Caja Laboral Populaire, is a prototype of this idea—a "second-degree" cooperative half-owned by other Mondragon cooperatives. The bank lends financial capital, monitors the performances of Mondragon's vast network of cooperatives, and finds outlets for their funds. The leading alternative model of mutual-funded social banking is the Meidner Plan, named after the German economist Rudolf Meidner, which was enacted in Sweden in 1982 by the Social Democratic government.

The Meidner Plan calls for an annual 20 percent tax on major company profits to be paid in the form of stock to eight regional mutual funds. Worker, consumer, and government representatives control the funds, and as their proportion of stock ownership grows, these groups are collectively entitled to representation on company boards. Locals and branch funds jointly hold voting rights of the employee shares. In the compromised form of the plan that was enacted by the Swedish government, a 40 percent ceiling was placed on the amount of stock that the eight funds in total could own of any single firm, and the funds were managed conventionally. True believers considered these compromises a defeat, but even with a 40 percent ceiling, the Meidner Plan, if carried out, would have rendered effective control over profitable firms in Sweden to the worker and public organizations.[26]

Since the funds represent part of workers' compensation, the plan contains a built-in system of wage restraints and facilitates a new form of capital formation. It requires no program of nationalization, and investors still seek the highest rate of return. Like other mutual-fund or public-bank models, the Meidner Plan separates risk in production from entrepreneurial risk, assigning production risks to worker-managed enterprises and entrepreneurial risks to the holding companies. Most important, it offers a way beyond the welfare state, by expanding the base of economic power, while saving the social and political gains of social democratic liberalism.

The fate of the Meidner Plan in Sweden is a symbol of our time. Its original backer was the Confederation of Swedish Trade Unions (Landsorganisationen I Sverige, or LO), which stressed in the mid-1970s that benefits from the capital fund should accrue to all wage earners and that the plan traded wage restraint for greater control over investment capital. Business groups howled against it, using the issue to defeat the Social Democrats in the 1976 election, even though

Social Democrats had not yet embraced it. In 1982, when the Social Democrats regained power, they enacted a version of the Meidner Plan, but made little effort to educate the public about it or to win popular support for it.

For eight years Sweden's corporate elites railed against the worker funds constantly, inveighing against their loss of control over finance. Stock markets are the home turf of financiers, a privilege that Sweden's capitalist class was not shy in defending. Managers of the worker funds, trying to legitimize themselves to the financial class, managed like ordinary fund managers, but that made the enterprise abstract to the general population. To stir popular support, the Social Democrats needed to back up the Meidner Plan with industrial policies targeting specific needs—things that ordinary people could see at work in their communities during the period that Sweden's shipbuilding industry collapsed, the steel industry specialized, wood pulp was integrated into modernized paper production, and other pillars of the manufacturing base were restructured. Instead, the charter for the Meidner Plan expired in 1990 and Social Democrats lost the 1991 election. Sweden had a banking crisis in 1992, which it resolved by nationalizing the banks, and in 1994 the Social Democrats regained power as the party best suited to manage the turbulence of economic globalization and nationalized banks. They stabilized the currency, got the government's fiscal house in order, dropped the Meidner Plan, and scaled back their historic achievement, the Swedish welfare state.[27]

That option made political sense in Sweden at the outset of second wave globalization. It may prove to be the death knell for national-scale experiments in full-orbed economic democracy. But less ambitious forms of economic democracy have succeeded in many places, and the scale question rests on politics and culture more than economic viability. Economic democracy theorists such as Gar Alperovitz, David C. Korten, Robert Dahl, Saul Estrin, David Miller, Raymond Plant, Alex Nove, Joanne Barkan, and David Winter take seriously the failures of state socialism, the limitations of worker ownership, and the necessity of building up highly capitalized forms of economic democracy. The distinct advantage of the mutual-fund approach is that it diversifies forms of risk sharing and promotes greater efficiency by forcing firms to be financially accountable to a broad range of investors. Essentially, it is a solution to the entrepreneurial deficiencies of worker-owned firms, addressing conflicts of interest between cooperative owners and profitability that often cause cooperatives to miss market signals.[28]

This approach does not rest on idealistic notions about human nature. Economic democracy is a brake on human greed and domination; the whole point of it is to fight the universal propensity of dominant groups to hoard social goods and abuse disenfranchised people. Neither should progressives absolutize any particular model of economic democracy, for the blueprint mentality is inherently problematic. Socialists were wrong to equate socialization with nationalization. They were wrong to reject production for profit. They were wrong to think that state planners could replicate the complex pricing decisions of markets. They were wrong in believing that worker-owned cooperatives could organize an economy not linked by markets. Not all Socialist traditions made these mistakes, but the blueprint mentality was deeply ingrained in virtually all of them.

From a democratic perspective, the chief problem with the mutual-fund idea is that it trades some democratic control for market efficiency. It empowers designated experts to invest collectively owned social capital by weakening the power of workers at the firm level. To the extent that the holding companies are granted supervisory control over their client enterprises, worker control is diminished. To the extent that the holding companies are kept in a weak position, the advantages of the mutual-fund model are traded off as the client enterprises essentially become cooperatives. Economic democracy theorists are usually radical democrats politically, so we place as much control as possible in human-scale organizations in which the distance between management and workers is minimized. But that can be deadly in competing with huge, aggressive, integrated corporations that focus ruthlessly on the bottom line. Any experiment in full-orbed economic democracy has to grapple with difficult trade-offs between the responsibilities of the holding companies and the rights of worker-managed enterprises. Moreover, democratic management is hard to pull off in any sector with large financing requirements.

There is no unitary answer to these problems; there is only the variable and challenging work of making gains toward democratizing the factors of investment and production in particular contexts. On the control problem, I favor a circular model that is biased toward upholding the authority of the public banks or holding companies. To minimize trade-offs between democratic control and efficiency, cooperative firms become shareholders in the holding companies or public banks. Mondragon would have crashed decades ago lacking a strong bank. Its second-degree cooperatives offer a useful model of circular ownership and control, one that diversifies risk and builds up new sources of investment capital.

More important than any model or theory is the willingness to expand the social market in different ways and find out which models work best in particular circumstances. The father of the social gospel, Washington Gladden, believed that profit-sharing industrial partnerships would put an end to the class struggle, until he lived long enough to see otherwise. Many social gospelers shared Francis G. Peabody's conviction that cooperatives were obviously the progressive Christian solution. Walter Rauschenbusch believed that a combination of state and cooperative ownership would create a good society.

William Temple, whose guild-socialist scheme prefigured the Meidner plan, was incredulous that modern democracies tolerated private banks. Reinhold Niebuhr stood for radical state socialism before opting for the welfare state. Many liberationists and social ethicists have promoted "socialism" without describing what it is.

Social theorists and religious ethicists have long operated with unitary ideas of capitalism and socialism, as though each were only one thing. Decentralized, economic democracy must be a project built from the ground up, piece by piece, opening new choices, creating more democracy, building an economic order that does not rest on selfishness, consumerism, and the prerogatives of shareholders. It allows for social contracts, common goods, and ecological flourishing. It nurtures and sustains social trust, the form of social capital that no healthy society can do without. It is a project that breaks from the universalizing logic of state socialism, taking seriously that there are different kinds of capitalism. The social theorist Roberto Mangabeira Unger aptly calls for "alternative pluralisms," step-by-step constructions of alternative political and economic institutions. Abstract concepts of a monolithic "capitalism" or "market" obscure the variety of possibilities within really existing capitalism and markets. "Capitalism" has no necessary content, but is always the product of particular historical configurations, contingencies, and struggles.[29]

There is also a role for old-fashioned, large-scale publicly controlled companies in certain areas. Most of the world's economic powers have them. Publicly controlled corporations produce 75 percent of the world's oil. In France, Spain, Belgium, Germany, Italy, the Netherlands, Turkey, and South Korea governments run high-speed rail systems that make U.S. American systems look pathetic. Japan has the world's largest public bank, Post Bank. Brazil has more than one hundred publicly owned or controlled enterprises, including major banks and utilities. The U.S. American animus against public ownership is going to look increasingly strange as the rest of the world selectively uses it as one powerful tool among others.

The earth's ecosystem cannot sustain a U.S. American–level lifestyle for more than one-sixth of the world's population. The economy is physical. There are limits to economic growth. Global warming is melting the Arctic ice cap at a shocking pace, as well as large areas of permafrost in Alaska, Canada, and Siberia, and destroying wetlands and forests around the world. The manic logic of corporate capitalism pays little heed to communities and the environment, and none to equality, reenacting the tragedy of the commons. Corporate giants like ExxonMobil succeed as businesses and investments while treating the destructive aspects of their behavior as someone else's problem. There is no legitimate argument against a government-sanctioned Green GDP account that reflects the depletion of our natural resources and the degradation of our environment. But after thirty years of talking about it the federal government still doesn't have metrics for sustainability, because the coal and oil companies don't want to be charged for the costs they impose on the environment.

The tests of any experiment in economic democracy are pragmatic. To impose something like a universal Mondragon on a capitalist society would require coercion over workers who don't want to belong to cooperatives. Today in the U.S. Pacific Northwest, some plywood workers choose employment in conventional firms over membership in the plywood cooperatives. No political economy worth building would force them into a different choice.

The issue of choice, however, is the key to the better alternative. A politics that expanded the cooperative and mutual-fund sectors would give workers important new choices. The central conceit of neoclassical economics could be turned into a reality if meaningful choices were created. The neoclassical conceit is that capitalism doesn't exploit anyone, because labor employs capital as much as capital employs labor. But in the real world the owners of capital nearly always organize the factors of production. To expand the cooperative, mutual-fund and other social market sectors would give choices to workers that neoclassical theory promises, but does not deliver. It would begin to create a culture that is more democratic, egalitarian, cooperative, and ecologically conscious than the one we have now.

To hang in there in struggles for common goods, one has to have a certain stubbornness and moral outrage. And it helps to have a spiritual wellspring. The quintessential social gospel theologian, Walter Rauschenbusch, whose work is unusable on some things, actually got the balance right in his supposed overemphasis on idealistic expectation. Rauschenbusch had a powerful awareness of personal, structural, and collective evil that he conceptualized as "the kingdom of evil." He stressed that "capitalism has overdeveloped the selfish instincts in all of us and left the devotion to larger ends shrunken and atrophied." He recognized that "idealists alone have never carried through any great social change." He warned that the possessing classes had the law on their side, "for they have made it." And he understood that all social justice movements need an energizing vision of a better world. We shall never have a just society, he wrote, yet we must seek it with faith: "At best there is always but an approximation to a perfect social order. The Kingdom of God is always but coming. But every approximation to it is worthwhile."[30]

## NOTES

1. This chapter adapts material from Gary Dorrien, *Economy, Difference, Empire: Social Ethics for Social Justice* (New York: Columbia University Press, 2010), 133–37, 168–75.
2. See Gary Dorrien, *The New Abolition: W. E. B. Du Bois and the Black Social Gospel* (New Haven, Conn.: Yale University Press, 2015); George Herron, *The New Redemp-*

tion: *A Call to the Church to Reconstruct Society according to the Gospel of Christ* (New York: T. Y. Crowell, 1893); George Herron, *The Christian State: A Political Vision of Christ* (New York: T. Y. Crowell, 1895); Walter Rauschenbusch, *Christianity and the Social Crisis* (New York: Hodder and Stoughton/Macmillan, 1907).

3. *Rerum Novarum: The Condition of Labor* (Leo XIII, 1891), and *Quadragesimo Anno: After Forty Years* (Pius XI, 1931), in *Catholic Social Thought: The Documentary Heritage*, ed. David J. O'Brien and Thomas A. Shannon (Maryknoll, N.Y.: Orbis Books, 2004), 14–39, 42–79; Federal Council of the Churches of Christ in America, "The Social Creed of the Churches," *Report of the First Meeting of the Federal Council*, Philadelphia, 1908 (New York: Revell, 1909), 238–39; Harry F. Ward, ed., *The Social Creed of the Churches* (New York: Eaton and Mains, 1912).

4. Emil Brunner, *The Divine Imperative*, trans. Olive Wyon (1932; Philadelphia: Westminster Press, 1947), 423.

5. William Temple, *The Hope of a New World* (New York: Macmillan, 1941), 54–59; William Temple, *Christianity and the Social Order* (Middlesex, Eng.: Penguin Books, 1942), 77–96, quotes 96.

6. Jürgen Moltmann, *On Human Dignity: Political Theology and Ethics*, trans. M. Douglas Meeks (Philadelphia: Fortress Press, 1984), 174.

7. Gustavo Gutiérrez, *The Power of the Poor in History: Selected Writings*, trans. Robert R. Barr (Maryknoll, N.Y.: Orbis Books, 1983), 45.

8. José Míguez Bonino, "For Life and Against Death: A Theology That Takes Sides," in *Theologians in Transition*, ed. James M. Wall (New York: Crossroad, 1981), 176.

9. Cornel West, "Harrington's Socialist Vision," *Christianity and Crisis* (12 December 1983): 484–85; Cornel West, *Prophetic Fragments* (Grand Rapids, Mich.: Eerdmans, 1988), 134–35; Rosemary R. Ruether, *Sexism and God-Talk: Toward a Feminist Theology* (Boston: Beacon Press, 1983), 232–33.

10. See Gregory Baum, *The Social Imperative: Essays on the Critical Issues That Confront the Christian Churches* (New York: Paulist Press, 1979); Harvey Cox, *Religion in the Secular City: Toward a Postmodern Theology* (New York: Simon and Schuster, 1984); Robert McAfee Brown, *Theology in a New Key: Responding to Liberation Themes* (Philadelphia: Westminster Press, 1978); Beverly W. Harrison, *Making the Connections: Essays in Feminist Social Ethics* (Boston: Beacon Press, 1985); Arthur McGovern, *Marxism: An American Christian Perspective* (Maryknoll, N.Y.: Orbis Books, 1980); Dorothee Sölle, *Beyond Mere Dialogue: On Being Christian and Socialist* (Detroit: Christians for Socialism in the United States, 1978).

11. Paul Tillich, *The Socialist Decision* (New York: Harper and Row, 1977), 160; Paul Tillich, "Basic Principles of Religious Socialism," reprinted in Tillich, *Political Expectation*, ed. James Luther Adams, Victor Nuovo, and Hannah Tillich (New York: Harper and Row, 1971), 78–82.

12. Robert Benne, review of Gary Dorrien, *Reconstructing the Common Good*, in *The Christian Century* 108 (February 27, 1991): 239–40; Max L. Stackhouse and Dennis P. McCann, "Public Theology after the Collapse of Socialism: A Postcommunist Manifesto," *Christian Century* 108 (January 16, 1991): 1, 44–47.

13. Michael Novak, "Father of Neoconservatives: Reinhold Niebuhr," *National Review*, May 11, 1992, 39–42.
14. See Michael Novak, *The Spirit of Democratic Capitalism* (New York: American Enterprise Institute / Simon and Schuster, 1982); Peter L. Berger, *The Capitalist Revolution: Fifty Propositions about Prosperity, Equality and Liberty* (New York: Basic Books, 1986); Richard J. Neuhaus, *Doing Well and Doing Good: The Challenge to the Christian Capitalist* (New York: Doubleday, 1992).
15. Joseph E. Stiglitz, "Of the 1%, by the 1%, for the 1%," *Vanity Fair*, May 2011; Joseph E. Stiglitz, *The Price of Inequality* (New York: W. W. Norton, 2012), 1–27.
16. Jagdish Bhagwati, *In Defense of Globalization* (New York: Oxford University Press, 2004); Thomas L. Friedman, *The Lexus and the Olive Tree: Understanding Globalization* (New York: Farrar, Straus and Giroux, 1999); Thomas L. Friedman, *The World Is Flat* (New York: Farrar, Straus and Giroux, 2007); Milton Friedman, *Capitalism and Freedom* (Chicago: University of Chicago Press, 1962).
17. See Eamonn Fingleton, *Unsustainable: How Economic Dogma Is Destroying American Prosperity* (New York: Nation Books, 2003); Doug Henwood, *After the New Economy* (New York: New Press, 2005); Barry Bluestone and Bennett Harrison, *The Deindustrialization of America: Plant Closings, Community Abandonment, and the Dismantling of Basic Industry* (New York: Basic Books, 1982); Michael J. Piore and Charles F. Sabel, *The Second Industrial Divide: Possibilities for Prosperity* (New York: Basic Books, 1984); Shoshana Zuboff, *In the Age of the Smart Machine: The Future of Work and Power* (New York: Basic Books, 1988).
18. Oskar Lange and F. M. Taylor, *On the Economic Theory of Socialism* (1931; New York: McGraw Hill, 1964).
19. Gary Dorrien, *The Obama Question: A Progressive Perspective* (Lanham, Md.: Rowman and Littlefield, 2012), 87–89.
20. Alan Greenspan, "Testimony of Dr. Alan Greenspan," Committee of Government Oversight and Reform (October 23, 2008), oversight.house.gov/documents; Edmund L. Andrews, "Greenspan Concedes Error on Regulation," *New York Times*, October 23, 2008, B1; Joe Nocera, "Risk Mismanagement: Were the Measures Used to Evaluate Wall Street Trades Flawed?" *New York Times Magazine*, January 4, 2009, 26–33, 46, 50–51; Nassim Nicholas Taleb, *The Black Swan: The Impact of the Highly Improbable* (New York: Barnes and Noble, 2007).
21. Simon Johnson and James Kwak, *13 Bankers: The Wall Street Takeover and the Next Financial Meltdown* (New York: Vantage Books, 2011), 39–87, 189–222.
22. John Kenneth Galbraith, *Money: Whence It Came, Where It Went* (Boston: Houghton Mifflin, 1975), 5.
23. William F. Hixson, *A Matter of Interest: Reexamining Money, Debt, and Real Economic Growth* (New York: Praeger, 1991); Michael Rowbotham, *The Grip of Death: A Study of Modern Money, Debt Slavery and Destructive Economics* (Oxfordshire, UK: Carpenter Publishing, 1998); William Henry Pope, *All You Must Know about Economics* (Toronto: Bergendal, 1997); George H. Crowell, "The Power of Monetary Policy," *Journal of the Society of Christian Ethics* 22 (Fall 2002): 49–65; Ellen H. Brown, *The Web of Debt* (Baton Rouge, La.: Third Millennium Press, 2010).

24. Federal Council of the Churches of Christ in America, *Quadrennial Report*, 1932; see Gary Dorrien, *Social Ethics in the Making: Interpreting an American Tradition* (Oxford: Wiley-Blackwell, 2009), 120–22.
25. See H. Thomas and Chris Logan, *Mondragon: An Economic Analysis* (London: Allen and Unwin, 1982); William Foote Whyte and Kathleen King Whyte, *Making Mondragon: The Growth and Dynamics of the Worker Cooperative Complex* (Ithaca, N.Y.: ILR Press, 1988); K. Bradley and A. Gelb, *Co-operation at Work: The Mondragon Experience* (London: Heinemann Educational Books, 1983); R. Oakeshott, *The Case for Workers' Co-ops* (London: Routledge and Kegan Paul, 1978); Terry Mollner, *Mondragon: A Third Way* (Shutesbury, Mass: Trusteeship Institute, 1984); Fred Fruendlich, "The Mondragon Cooperative Corporation," Conference on Shared Capitalism: Mapping the Research Agenda, National Board of Economic Research, Washington, D.C., May 22, 1998; Karen Thomas and John Logue, *Mondragon Today: What Can We Learn?* (Kent, Ohio: Ohio Employee Ownership Center Pamphlet, 2002).
26. Rudolf Meidner, "A Swedish Union Proposal for Collective Capital Sharing," *Eurosocialism and America: Political Economy for the 1980s*, ed. Nancy Lieber (Philadelphia: Temple University Press, 1982); Rudolf Meidner, *Employee Investment Funds: An Approach to Collective Capital Formation* (London: George Allen and Unwin, 1978); Jonas Pontusson, "Radicalization and Retreat in Swedish Social Democracy," *New Left Review* 165 (September/October 1987): 5–33.
27. Jonas Pontusson, *The Limits of Social Democracy: Investment Politics in Sweden* (Ithaca, N.Y.: Cornell University Press, 1992), 237; see Jonas Pontusson, *Public Pension Funds and the Politics of Capital Formation in Sweden* (Stockholm: Swedish Center for Working Life, 1984); Jonas Pontusson, *Swedish Social Democracy and British Labour: Essays on the Nature and Conditions of Social Democratic Hegemony* (Ithaca, N.Y.: Cornell University Press, 1988); Gosta Esping-Andersen, *Politics against Markets: The Social Democratic Road to Power* (Princeton: Princeton University Press, 1985).
28. Gar Alperovitz, *America beyond Capitalism* (Hoboken, N.J.: Wiley, 2005); Gar Alperovitz, *What Then Must We Do?* (White River Junction, Vt.: Chelsea Green, 2013); David C. Korten, *Agenda for a New Economy* (San Francisco: Berrett-Koehler, 2010); Robert Dahl, *A Preface to Economic Democracy* (Berkeley: University of California Press, 1985); Saul Estrin and P. Holmes, *French Planning in Theory and Practice* (London: George Allen and Unwin, 1983); Saul Estrin and David Winter, "Planning in a Market Socialist Economy," in *Market Socialism*, ed. Julian Le Grand and Saul Estrin (Oxford: Oxford University Press, 1989), 100–138; Saul Estrin and Julian Le Grand, "Market Socialism," in *Market Socialism*, 1–24; David Miller, *Market, State and Community: Theoretical Foundations of Market Socialism* (Oxford: Clarendon Press, 1990); David Miller and Saul Estrin, "A Case for Market Socialism: What Does It Mean? Why Should We Favor It?" in *Why Market Socialism?*, ed. Frank Roosevelt and David Belkin (Armonk, N.Y.: M. E. Sharpe, 1994), 225–40; Alec Nove, *Socialism, Economics, and Development* (London: Allen and Unwin, 1986); John Roemer, "Market Socialism: A Blueprint: How Such an Economy Might Work," in *Why Market Socialism?*, 269–81; Radoslav Selucky, *Marxism, Socialism and Freedom* (Oxford: Oxford Univer-

sity Press, 1989); Frank Cunningham, *Democratic Theory and Socialism* (Cambridge: Cambridge University Press, 1987).

29. Roberto M. Unger, *Democracy Realized: The Progressive Alternative* (New York: Verso, 1998), 22–27; see Roberto M. Unger, *Politics: A Work in Constructive Social Theory* (Cambridge: Cambridge University Press, 1987), 87–120; Roberto M. Unger and Cornel West, *The Future of American Progressivism* (Boston: Beacon Press, 1998).

30. Walter Rauschenbusch, *A Theology for the Social Gospel* (New York: Macmillan, 1917), see chap. 9, "Kingdom of Evil," 77–94; Walter Rauschenbusch, *Christianizing the Social Order* (New York: Macmillan, 1912), 369; Rauschenbusch, *Christianity and the Social Crisis*, 400, 421.

# The Myth of the Middle: Common Sense, Good Sense, and Rethinking the "Common Good" in Contemporary U.S. Society

CHARON HRIBAR

Economic inequality in the United States continues to grow as more people experience falling wages, increased debt, and joblessness. Yet the myth of the American Dream, an ethos rooted in an *opportunity* for prosperity, persists. As austerity measures and budget cuts are promoted by local and national governments, with one in two Americans currently documented by the U.S. Census Bureau as poor or low income, a fight to preserve the "middle class" continues to be waged by rich and poor, Republican and Democrat, urban centers and Middle America alike.[1] In this essay, I argue that the common good promoted in U.S. society is an unexamined aspiration for a strong middle class and an unsubstantiated principle of social mobility. The American infatuation with upward mobility, however, poses a problem from a Christian liberationist perspective. The vision for change tied to this ideology is not grounded in a common desire to ensure that the needs of all are met but in a fight to preserve the opportunity for each individual to achieve a "better" life. Current controversy over the North Carolina legislature's bipartisan push for House Bill 944, "Opportunity Scholarships Grant," is but one recent example of the way the principle of opportunity attempts to conceal the severe consequences that austerity measures and policies promoting this ideology will have on providing all children in the United States with quality education. Although the bill purports to offer families better educational choice, such legislation ignores the barriers a voucher program will create for poor and low-income families.[2]

A principle of opportunity, steeped in the American values of freedom and choice, masks our ability to fully recognize one of the inherent contradictions of advanced global capitalism—that wealth is created through growing impoverishment. Our economic system is failing to ensure people's basic economic human rights, namely the rights to food, housing, education, jobs with dignity, health care, water, and other basic economic necessities. This principle of opportunity has trickled into the very organizing mechanisms that were formed to protect these basic rights, turning revolutionary movements for change into transactional vehicles of social reform.³ If we are to take up the challenge to redefine the common good in the midst of our current global economic reality, we must start as Joerg Rieger suggests, not with a statistical middle ground, but with the dispossessed members of our society.⁴ In a society that has the capacity to eliminate poverty, the existence of poverty becomes a litmus test for its success.

In order to redefine the common good, we must first deconstruct the dominant ideology of American exceptionalism, or what W. E. B. Du Bois names the *American Assumption* in a time when the economic security of the so-called middle class (the newly poor) is being dismantled.⁵ I will draw on Antonio Gramsci's concept of *common sense* to analyze the concept of "middle class" as a hegemonic apparatus used to align a majority of people in the United States with a "politics of aspiration"—a belief that if provided the opportunity we can "move up in the world."⁶ I will then turn to Johannes Baptist Metz's criticism of middle-class religion and H. Richard Niebuhr's critique of capitalism to examine the particular role religion plays in shaping the social psychology of U.S. society and how a revolutionary Christian tradition can help challenge the fundamental social relationships that produce poverty in the midst of plenty. Finally, I will conclude by engaging the transformative thinking and practices that are emerging from grassroots movement building and a call among grassroots leaders to *Put People First*. This call to develop the critical consciousness to put people first is not merely a popular slogan to rally the masses, but an attempt to disrupt a worldview of American exceptionalism that masks the contradictions of capitalism and helps preserve the hegemonic power of the ruling elites. This disruptive step is necessary to begin to develop a class consciousness that can construct a new vision for a common good that centers not on providing "opportunities" that benefit the few, but on ensuring that the needs of *all* people are met.

## THE COMMON GOOD AND THE AMERICAN ASSUMPTION

> The electorate . . . [was] impregnated with the idea that individual wealth spelled national prosperity and particularly with the American assumption of equal economic opportunity for all, which persisted in the face of facts.
>
> —W. E. B. DU BOIS, *Black Reconstruction*

Like W. E. B. Du Bois, William Greider, in his book *Come Home, America: The Rise and Fall (and Redeeming Promise) of Our Country*, suggests that the dominant story line of "onward-and-upward" has always been an essential part of the American ideology. The notion that economic independence is open to all who strive for it penetrates the American consciousness. John F. Kennedy's aphorism "A rising tide lifts all boats" builds on this assumption and depicts the tremendous growth of the American middle class that followed World War II and the second industrial revolution. This unique period of middle-class growth, used to champion the success of U.S. democracy and economic prosperity around the globe, was followed by a downward trajectory beginning in the mid 1970s. This erosion of the middle class is revealed by a growing polarity of the "rich and the rest," and a reality where "one million households in the uppermost tier—the top 1 percent—now collectively earn the same amount as the 60 million families who make up the lower two-thirds of the economic ladder."[7] More than 49 million Americans live below the poverty line, and an additional 97.3 million are low-income. Out of necessity, everyday people in the United States are forced to respond to this reality, however, fear to admit that the promise of the American exceptionalism is failing remains.[8]

The ruling elites are paying close attention to the potential threat that exists if and when the promise of the American assumption fails.

> The greatest danger is one that will not be faced for decades but that is lurking out there. The United States was built on the assumption that a rising tide lifts all ships. That has not been the case for the past generation, and there is no indication that this socio-economic reality will change any time soon. That means that a core assumption is at risk. The problem is that social stability has been built around this assumption—not on the assumption that everyone is owed a living, but the assumption that on the whole, all benefit from growing productivity and efficiency.[9]

The economist Henry Wallich explains that as long as you have economic growth, you can continue to produce hope in the midst of large income disparities.[10] Those in power work to assure the "middle class" that the economic pressures they are experiencing are temporary and refuse to discuss the deeper, fundamental shifts that have taken place in the global economy over the last fifty years, which threaten the core assumption of American life. The urgency to address such economic shifts lies in the reality that conditions are going to get worse. When asked in an interview on MSNBC what the tipping point would be to launch U.S. society into civil unrest, the political scientist and security adviser Zbigniew Brzezinski suggested that if the United States continues to enable severe economic inequality in the midst of economic stagnation or decline, intensified social conflict will result. As more and more people are forced to face the reality that the tide has not risen for everyone, and in fact has lifted very few, what is morally acceptable in a "fair society" will come into question.[11] Greider further notes the inevitability of social conflict, stating that although he hopes for "a nonviolent uprising of citizens that breaks through the political barriers and forces insiders to incorporate their views in decisions," another plausible response "is an era of even uglier politics in which confused people are drawn into irrational conflicts or futile nostalgia for the 'good times.'"[12] As conditions worsen, history proves that people will out of necessity respond. The question that remains is: How will they respond? What visions for the common good will be projected and taken up as the masses are thrust into the ranks of the poor and dispossessed? Will people, in times of desperation, be pitted against one another and manipulated by the rhetoric of the ruling elites who uphold a principle of opportunity and project a solution of scarcity? Or can an alternative consciousness that recognizes the abundance that exists in our society emerge from those who have nothing to lose by maintaining the current structure? Can people be moved to overcome the American assumption and develop a new vision of the common good that is grounded in a *right to not be poor* and a belief that everyone's needs can and must be met?

## COMMON SENSE, GOOD SENSE, AND REDEFINING THE COMMON GOOD

Antonio Gramsci is often referenced in academic circles as a preeminent Marxist theoretician and a political activist. Yet to fully understand the questions Gramsci was grappling with in his writing of the *Prison Notebooks*, I want to emphasize that Gramsci was a leader in a social movement. His long struggle to build a socialist movement was shaped by the need to understand the fundamental relationships (economic, political, and social) in society and to wrestle with how to unite the peasants of southern Italy with the industrial workers of the north in order to change the power structure. It was through this effort that Gramsci reminds us that power is maintained not only through coercion but also consent. In his attempt to understand why a socialist revolution in Western Europe failed to take root among the masses and how fascism triumphed, Gramsci took great care to examine how hegemony is formed and fostered by those in power. Gramsci argues that our conception of the world is often uncritically lived and accepted. Such constructed conceptions of the world, left unexamined and accepted as *common sense*, lead to people's acceptance of oppression as natural and unchangeable.

Unpacking the belief that the current conditions produced by advanced global capitalism are natural and unchangeable is key to understanding how a ruling-class ideology is maintained. Gary Dorrien, in a 2012 article on the economic crisis, explains that "many Americans are ideologically opposed to any politics that tries to rectify severe discrepancies in wealth, and the race to the bottom unleashed by economic globalization has convinced many people that nothing can be done about it."[13] Incomes for the bottom 90 percent of Americans grew by only $59 on average between 1966 and 2011 (when you adjust those incomes for inflation), while during the same period the top 1 percent of the 1 percent gained $18,363,740. Nonetheless, we continue to overlook the relationship of forces that make such disparity possible. Americans adopt positions put forth by academics and Wall Street economists who argue that current unemployment rates are simply the "new normal."[14] As long as the economy (or rather the GDP) can rebound, the principle of opportunity perceivers. In turn, it is our consent to an ahistorical politics of aspiration that Gramsci's work can help uproot as we work to redefine the common good.

It is here that I draw a connection between Gramsci's notion of common sense and a U.S. middle-class ideology that is adopted as common good. In constructing and affirming a vision of the American assumption, we fail to recognize that the very system that produces the possibility for social mobility does so only through the creation and perpetuation of poverty. The "fluidity" of middle-class identity deters us from questioning a structure that normalizes the existence of extreme wealth in the midst of growing poverty.[15]

> Between 1973 and 2003, real GDP per capita in the United States increased 73 percent, while real median hourly compensation rose only 13 percent. Prosperity has neither trickled down nor rippled outward. In blunt terms, family incomes have stagnated or lost ground, while capital and corporate returns have soared. This disparity threatens the future of the trading system . . . maybe even the stability of capitalist, democratic society.[16]

This 2006 report made by the economic policy advisers and strategists for the Hamilton Project, a center-right think tank of the Brookings Institution, was an admission that the forces and consequences of advanced global capital are not natural states of existence. This report was not, however, a position put forth to the American public. It was an analysis offered to a small segment of the ruling elites to preempt the popular backlash that surfaced during the economic crisis beginning in 2007. The question that arises for those who have been left behind by the tide of economic practices implemented since 1973 is: How will we come to interpret the root causes of this polarity of wealth and poverty? Will we come to recognize that something can and must be done?

Identifying the danger that an ahistorical perspective of common sense has on maintaining the subordination of the populace, Gramsci takes up Antonio Labriola's concept of a *philosophy of praxis*.[17] Moving away from a passive acceptance of thought to a philosophy of praxis establishes an important nexus between theoretical and practical activity and emphasizes a unity of philosophy and history. It is through this unity of theory and practice that Gramsci argues that a revolutionary consciousness can emerge to reveal the contradictions in the ruling-class hegemony. For a philosophy of praxis to be effective, it must not only offer a critique of common sense, but it must also base itself in common sense. A philosophy of praxis must start from within the existing mode of thought, within the popular consciousness of the masses and develop critical thinking from within. Gramsci writes, "It is not a question of introducing from scratch a scientific form of thought into everyone's individual life, but of renovating and making 'critical' an already existing activity."[18] Developing this critical consciousness, or *good sense*, is for Gramsci a necessary step to deconstructing structures of domination and moving toward social transformation. A philosophy of praxis that moves from common sense to good sense engages both the theory of these contradictions and people's practical awareness of them. Gramsci argues that everyone is a philosopher, having some conception of the world. There is a second step that must then be taken to move toward a critical consciousness, a second level where our beliefs are met with awareness and criticism. Through good sense, we recognize the contradictions of the dominant worldview and can begin instead to develop a counterhegemony necessary to transform the relationships of our economic, political, social, and cultural lives.

In moving from *common sense* to *good sense*, a critical consciousness where our understanding of the world is met with awareness and criticism, Gramsci recognizes the importance of developing an intellectual-moral bloc that can foster the collective agency of a social group by expanding knowledge and political power to the masses of people and creating new social relationships. Gramsci saw the development of a revolutionary consciousness, the development of organic intellectuals, as the means through which the contradictions of our current class alliances could be revealed. It is the possibility of forming an intellectual-moral bloc that can redefine the common good. The next two sections of this essay address the attempt to place the *right to not be poor* at the center of a new vision of the common good.

## THE ROLE OF THE CHRISTIAN TRADITION IN SHAPING COMMON SENSE AND REENVISIONING THE COMMON GOOD

Gramsci's belief that we must not only provide a critique of common sense but also develop an analysis from within common sense reminds us of the need to explore the critical role that religion and politics play in shaping the popular consciousness of poor, low-income, and "middle-class" people in the U.S. context. Willie Baptist, a movement elder and poverty scholar who has been organizing among the poor and dispossessed for close to fifty years, notes in his reflection on Gramsci's theory of hegemony that in studying American history, "So much of what influences how people understand things comes from values that have national-historical origins, and the American people are very religious—Judeo-Christian, largely. What you find is that religion is a common language of the most dispossessed, regardless of their color."[19] In order to reenvision the common good in U.S. society and overcome the American assumption, we must unpack the influence that Christian beliefs and values have on the consciousness of the people. Before engaging the function of religion in the consciousness of the American people, I will begin by investigating the significant role that Gramsci saw religion having in shaping social consciousness and forming hegemony.

The socioeconomic development of capitalism in industrialized countries presented the potential for the organization of masses of people, who for the first time in history, through this shift in social relations, had the potential for self-government; however, the ruling class, according to Gramsci, recognized this potential and was able to reconfigure a new structure of governance that included not only political force but also developed a system of cultural and moral hegemony. Through the civil institutions of the courts, schools, associations, and the church, the ruling class constructed a means of maintaining control of the social relations in society.[20] In his Gramscian analysis of the role that religion plays in class conflicts, Dwight Billings explains that "Gramsci belonged to a generation of Marxists, including Lenin and Luxemburg, who believed . . . that social revolution would be the culmination of political and, for Gramsci especially, cultural struggles."[21] As the ideological cement that bound the masses of the peasantry to the political and economic authority of the Vatican, Gramsci notes that it was the practice of the Catholic Church to maintain a primitive philosophy among the masses and, in doing so, to achieve social unity by maintaining a low level of consciousness. With Gramsci's philosophy of praxis and his desire to develop the highest level of consciousness among the masses as an essential step in reordering social relationships in society, the practice of the Catholic Church stood as a major obstacle to building a socialist revolution.

Although Gramsci's analysis of religion, in his early twentieth-century Italian context, maintains a largely critical view of the role the church played in blocking the formation of consciousness among the masses, his analysis acknowledges the powerful influence religion has on shaping people's consciousness. Contemporaries of Gramsci's, like Dwight Billings, help to further illuminate religion's double function: (1) the legitimation of the status quo or (2) a means of protest and liberation. The theologians Johannes Baptist Metz and H. Richard Niebuhr investigate this dual function of religion. Acknowledging the significant role Christianity plays in influencing the core values of the American people, it is important to explore this double function of religious ideology.

I begin by exploring how the Christian tradition, as a social institution, has been used to maintain the status quo. Johannes Baptist Metz, in his critique of middle-class religion, believes that the first step we must take to counter religious beliefs that help perpetuate economic and social exploitation is to confront the ahistorical character that has dominated modern Christianity and its lack of political consciousness. He explains that the dominant principle that undergirds the existence of middle-class religion is the principle of exchange.[22] Taking up a Marxian critical method, Metz suggests that under a principle of exchange that emerged during the Enlightenment, working people came to define value in transactional terms guided by the interests of the market. The middle-class citizen no longer places value in traditional principles "such as friendliness, thankfulness, attention to the dead . . . [as there is] no corresponding counter-value."[23] The common good under this middle-class ideology relegates our social struggle and religious beliefs to a sphere of private, individual freedom/salvation. It further fails to recognize that such values are not inherent in the Christian tradition, but rather developed with the emergence of capitalism. In illuminating the historical shifts that take place in modern Western Christianity, Metz believes we can confront the exploitative social relations that are inevitable contradictions of this capitalist system of exchange.

Like Metz, H. Richard Niebuhr criticizes the institutional church for being held captive to the bonds of capitalism. Niebuhr argues pointedly that "capitalism . . . is a faith and a way of life. It is faith in wealth as the source of all life's blessings and as the savior of man from his deepest misery. It is the doctrine that man's most important activity is the production of economic goods and that all other things are dependent on this."[24] A problem arises when religion becomes beholden to the common sense of capitalism and what Metz names a principle of exchange. Niebuhr argues that the church neglects to develop a historical consciousness and to acknowledge that the Christian faith, from its beginning, has professed that it is impossible to serve both God and Mammon.

It is here that H. Richard Niebuhr argues that religion can act not only as a function of dominant culture but that religion can and has developed its own initiative that can move us toward good sense. For Niebuhr, the process for developing good sense and for transforming the worldview of American Christianity is to begin with the process of historically locating the Christian tradition and unearthing its roots in a revolutionary tradition.[25] Niebuhr believes that Christianity as a movement, rather than an institution, ought to be seen as a regenerating force, which, through God's sovereignty, seeks to transform society. It is a continual reformation of the church, connected to a larger struggle for social transformation that Niebuhr sees as the task of the Christian movement.

Believing that Christianity is a "permanent revolution," Niebuhr joins Gramsci in criticizing religious institutions for aligning with structures of domination. In his essay titled "The Ethical Failure of the Divided Church," Niebuhr argues that Christianity has become a tool of national, racial, and economic caste systems and has intersected so deeply with the ruling parties that the church has "become a mere appendage of the state."[26] He goes on to suggest, however, that this is neither the mission of the Christian movement nor the message that lies at the heart of the gospel. In his later work, *The Church against the World*, Niebuhr continues to criticize the institutional church for becoming an obstruction to the goal of social change. Niebuhr argues that "only a new withdrawal [from its participation in a system of domination] by a new aggression can then save the church and restore to it the salt with which to savor society."[27] If the church can liberate itself from its bondage to a corrupt civilization and draw on its heritage of liberation, Niebuhr argues that the church can be a source for developing an alternative worldview, a counterhegemony. What Niebuhr draws on in his reimagination of the Christian tradition is not the doctrinal heritage that Gramsci both admired and criticized within the Catholic tradition in Italy, but rather a historical and dynamic faith of protest present in the inception of Christian culture. Niebuhr argues that religion, historically, has not been a mere function of culture, but that it can also develop its own initiatives. For Niebuhr, Christianity as a movement, although it can fall into the temptations of social domination, can also provide a "third way," which through God's sovereignty can transform the world.

Niebuhr and Metz's scholarship help us take seriously the reality that American common sense is steeped in a Christian consciousness. In turn, it becomes essential to critically engage this religious tradition, to access the social, political, and economic implications of religious thought, and to reexamine Christianity as a tradition founded in a prophetic revolutionary history that opposed the domination and oppression of the Roman Empire. Their critical engagement of the Christian tradition helps us disrupt a common good that is grounded in the middle-class principle of exchange and instead enables us to move toward reenvisioning the role of Christianity as a dynamic faith that can respond to the crises of the world around us.

## "PUT PEOPLE FIRST": DEBUNKING THE MYTH OF THE MIDDLE AND REENVISIONING THE COMMON GOOD

I am convinced that if we are to get on the right side of the world revolution, we as a nation must undergo a radical revolution of values. We must rapidly begin the shift from a "thing-oriented" society to a "person-oriented" society. When machines and computers, profit motives and property rights are considered more important than people, the giant triplets of racism, materialism, and militarism are incapable of being conquered.

—THE REV. DR. MARTIN LUTHER KING JR.,
"A TIME TO BREAK THE SILENCE"

In 2010, the word *austerity* was the most searched word in the Merriam-Webster online dictionary, echoing the eruption of news stories documenting the growing worldwide economic crises and government responses, particularly those in Europe, that drastically cut government programs and social safety nets. The year 2011 followed with millions of people around the globe taking to the streets from Tunisia to Madison, Algiers to Mexico City, Egypt to Montreal, London to New Delhi, and Athens to New York City. The conditions of rising food prices, home foreclosures and increased housing costs, and unprecedented unemployment rates (particularly among the global youth population) drove people around the world into the streets. It is the effects of advanced global capitalism on the everyday lives of people around the globe that spurred the uprisings of 2011. History has taught us that as conditions continue to get worse, people will continue, out of necessity, to respond. As I illuminated earlier in this essay, the ruling elites are anticipating and assessing the threat of such outbreaks. Within the U.S. context, George Friedman argues, "The threat to the United States is [not unemployment as it is in Europe, but] the persistent decline in the middle class' standard of living, a problem that is reshaping the social order that has been in place since World War II and that, if it continues, poses a threat to American power."[28] It is the ability to preserve the expectation of upward mobility that Friedman suggests maintains global capitalism's hegemony in the United States. Yet millions of "middle-class" Americans may begin to question this assumption if they continue to feel the effects of a jobless recovery. According to a report by the National Employment Law Project, during the great recession, low-wage industries constituted only 23 percent of job loss while constituting 49 percent of recent job growth. In contrast, high-wage industries constituted 40 percent of job loss yet comprise only 14 percent of job growth. These statistics suggest that the Great Recession was (1) a job destroying recession, (2) that the jobs destroyed were higher-wage jobs, and (3) that the jobs being created since the crisis began in 2007 are lower-paying jobs. This reality, paired with rising debt, the privatization of public goods (from local schools to water plants), and government austerity measures present an opportunity for movement leaders to illuminate the contradictions of the current economic system that ruling elites are scrambling to keep concealed. The question that emerges from this reality is: What forces will align to shape the people's response?

Baptist acknowledges the need for movement leaders to move beyond the surface of the effects, to analytically understand the root causes of the problems at hand. In an article titled "It's Not Enough to Be Angry, Part 2," Baptist explains that neither spontaneous rebellion nor concession-based organizing are enough to overcome the growing disparities of wealth and poverty. He notes that the Rev. Dr. King, in the last years of his life, recognized these contradictions in our economic system and emphasized that while we have the wealth and productive capacity to end poverty, we lack the political and social will to do so. Baptist explains, "The problem today is one of a 'cruelly unjust society,' a social edifice of unheard-of abundance that continuously produces unheard-of abandonment."[29] In the midst of government appeals for austerity, Baptist, like King, recognizes that the problem we face today is not a problem of scarcity, but a problem of who controls the abundance. The challenge moving forward becomes our ability to move beyond the common sense constructed by the ruling elites that hides such contradictions toward a good sense that recognizes something can and must be done to change the unjust structure that continues to produce beggars as well as billionaires. Gramsci, Metz, and Niebuhr push us to distinguish the relationship between conditions and consciousness. Gramsci's social theory and Metz and Niebuhr's politically grounded theologies illuminate the opposition of forces at play in history. They incite us to critically examine how those forces influence our response to the world around us. As we attempt to think about what it means to redefine the common good in the midst of a global economic crisis today, we must move from a common sense rooted in the principle of opportunity to a common good that guarantees that the needs of every human being are met.

In order to fully recognize the necessity for redefining the common good in the twenty-first century, we must ground our strategy in the experience and analysis of those who have little or no stake in preserving the current system. It is this segment of society, because of their social position, that has the potential to reveal the contradictions of the current system and move the masses of the American people who are being dislocated and excluded economically and socially by recent economic events. As millions of Americans struggle to meet their basic needs, there are emerging segments of dispossessed people in this country who are striving to overcome the paralysis induced by the American assumption. They are beginning to challenge the existence of poverty in the midst of plenty and are demanding that our society "Put People First." Put People First (PPF) is an organizing strategy/vision developing among a base of people across the United States who are working to illuminate the contradictions of the current system. Seeking to develop and unite leaders in rural areas, small towns, and urban centers alike, movement organizers taking up the mission to Put People First recognize the need to demonstrate that the problems many Americans are facing today are not individual problems, but are emerging from a system that is failing to meet our most basic needs.

For the purpose of this essay I focus on two key aspects of the PPF organizing strategy and vision in an attempt to reimagine a common good that ensures that all people's basic needs are met: (1) the importance of leadership development (the development of organic intellectuals) and (2) the need to build unity across lines of division (to build a Jacobian force).[30] Returning to Gramsci's discussion of a philosophy of praxis and thinking about the strategic necessity of leadership development, PPF lifts up the leadership potential of every human being. A philosophy of praxis recognizes that everyone has some conception of the world, values the necessity of starting with people's common sense, and points to the need for developing a practice of critical reflection that moves us toward good sense. Reminded that the charge to put people first is not merely a popular slogan to rally the masses, but an attempt to disrupt our faith in the American assumption, it becomes essential to recognize the relationship between conditions and consciousness. The Occupy Movement was an important example of how conditions propelled everyday people in U.S. society to respond to the conjunctural conflicts that arise in the midst of growing disparities of wealth and poverty. But here I must emphasize that in Gramscian terms, conjunctural conflicts (specific moments of crisis) are only one necessary part in the formation of a revolutionary force. Although the objective conditions everyday people are currently experiencing are essential to reveal the contradictions of the existing system, Gramsci's experience reminds us that consciousness does not automatically emerge from the conditions of crisis. Critical consciousness must be intentionally pursued by revolutionary leaders, or what Gramsci calls organic intellectuals.[31] The development of organic analysis (a prolonged analysis of structural contradictions) is a necessary provision. What I mean to suggest is that a social movement does not emerge spontaneously; rather it is built through strategic organization and analysis that can respond to conditions of crisis. Gramsci challenges us to continuously see the connection between organic and conjunctural moments and to be ready with a developed critique when moments of crisis arise. It is this task that confronts the work of grassroots leaders and organizations such as the Vermont Workers Center, Put People First Pennsylvania, the Media Mobilizing Project, the Poverty Initiative, and the United Workers, who are helping to initiate this effort.[32] They are moving community by community, state by state, and working with people around the globe to identify and develop a core of leaders who, as the conditions intensify, can become the intellectual-moral bloc that Gramsci suggests is necessary to bring about true social transformation. Through leadership development, political education, independent media projects, and community building, these leaders are working to foster an unsettling unity of the dispossessed across race, geography, religion, and all the lines that divide us. In doing so, they seek to redefine the common good from the perspective of those who have nothing to lose. PPF affirms a vision for the common good that takes up the social welfare of every member of our society rather than the opportunity for social mobility. In a society that has continuously placed profit over people, PPF strives to reorient our social relationships in order to ensure that our human rights, particularly our economic and social rights, are guaranteed. It insists on the vantage point of poor and working people to develop a consciousness that seeks not for poor people to become "middle class" but for poverty to be abolished.

Gramsci realized that a major obstacle of organizing in post–World War I Italy had been the lack of a Jacobin[33] force, a unified popular alliance of the masses from both the city and the country. The social bloc capable of truly transforming the social relationships that maintain the current system and mask its contradictions must, according to Gramsci, move beyond syndicalism and spontaneism. The work of grassroots leaders taking up the vision to put people first draws on Gramsci's analysis in their attempt to build a social movement that is not driven by any one issue or one community, but strives to construct an offensive movement made up of clear, competent, committed, and connected leaders ready to ensure that the human rights of all are guaranteed. The work of Gramsci, Metz, and Niebuhr moves us to recognize that the masses cannot simply take over old formations that the ruling elites have used to maintain power. Niebuhr, Metz, and Gramsci propose that norms and meanings of the dominant hegemony must be deconstructed and that we must pursue the creation of new ideas and values. Gramsci suggests, "In the formation of leaders, one premise is fundamental: is it the intention that there should always be rulers and ruled, or is the objective to create the conditions in which this division is no longer necessary? In other words, is the initial premise the perpetual division of the human race, or the belief that this division is only a historical fact, corresponding to certain conditions?"[34] In working to develop a counterhegemony and not merely replace one existing hegemony with another, I conclude by exploring what potential alternatives might emerge from a critical engagement of revolutionary religious traditions.

Here I turn to H. Richard Niebuhr's examination of a revolutionary Christian tradition that emerged from a people's struggle against the oppression and exploitation of the Roman Empire. It is this revolutionary Christian tradition that a twenty-first-century social movement can draw strength from to develop a vision for social change that does not simply replace one form of hegemony with another. The womanist ethicist emilie townes reminds us that "we live in many communities—often simultaneously. This makes us a deeply historical people although the mood of our times pushes us toward ahistoricism."[35] The U.S. context is bountiful in its social, cultural, ethnic, political, and religious diversity. Within our current capitalist society, such diversity has historically been used by the ruling elites to maintain divisions among the masses. In an attempt to transform the current social order of domination, the desire to build social solidarity need not erase the diversity of our human experiences and the reality that we are a deeply historical people but, as Niebuhr and townes suggest, must utilize and analyze that history.

Acknowledging that American Christianity has stood on both sides of every divisive issue, Niebuhr argues that we must challenge the way the gospel has been used in America for the preservation of systems of privilege and power. A faith that promotes domination is not the prophetic tradition of Christianity. Emphasizing social solidarity, Niebuhr draws on the faith of Jonathan Edwards and the revival movement of the Great Awakening to make the case that the mission of Christianity was not to build religious institutions, but to continue the revolutionary movement of a Christian tradition that could unite people to respond to the crises of the time. Niebuhr's work reminds us that building social solidarity must not erase our social diversity. Rather, Niebuhr contends, "Where common memory is lacking, where [human beings] do not share in the same past there can be no real community, and where community is to be formed, common memory must be created; hence the insistence on the teaching of history in modern national communities."[36] It is this critical engagement of a revolutionary Christian tradition that calls for a deep and diverse social solidarity that an effort to Put People First can draw on in placing human needs and dignity at the center of a new vision for the common good.

Grassroots efforts to Put People First must be linked with other critical initiatives to develop a theoretical understanding and strategic practice that can respond to the urgency of the growing dispossession taking place in the United States and around the globe as a result of advanced global capitalism. Drawing on King's vision of a Beloved Community, we must bring together low-wage workers in Baltimore with people fighting for universal health care in Vermont, domestic workers in New York City, and firefighters, students, and teachers organizing in Philadelphia. A massive social movement is necessary to disrupt the massive social problems that emanate from the ever-increasing disparity of wealth and poverty in the twenty-first century. This vision to Put People First reminds us that the solution to the growing dislocation and exclusion of masses of people in this country must come from the dispossessed, those who have little or nothing to lose, who are experiencing most acutely the contradictions of the current system. The problem of poverty today is not due to a lack of productivity, a shortage of material resources, or a scarcity of wealth creation. Instead, the expansion of globalized poverty is produced by a social edifice that is constituted on unheard-of abundance. It is in this moment of unprecedented productive capacity, that a revolution of values must drive our capacity to reimagine the common good and recognize our ability to abolish poverty. Acknowledging that the economic crisis is a result of poverty in the midst of plenty, we must challenge the common sense of the American assumption and instead construct a common good that guarantees that everyone has what they need not only to live but also to flourish. It is the unsettling force emerging from worsening conditions that encourages us to construct a new vision for the common good that centers not on providing "opportunities" that benefit the few, but rather on ensuring our *right to not be poor* and a radical Christian belief that everyone's needs can and must be met.

### NOTES

1. Who makes up the so-called middle class? According to a recent Stratfor report, the median household income in America during 2011 was $49,103, $4,000 less than it was in 2000. Once social security, state, and federal taxes are taken out, that leaves the median American household with $3,300 a month. (It should be noted that most households earn less than this.) Those making a median monthly income of $3,300 must likely account for college loans, two car payments, food, clothing, utilities, a mortgage, real estate taxes, and insurance, and potentially child care or health care costs. George Friedman, "The Crisis of the Middle Class and American Power," *Geopolitcal Weekly*, January 8, 2013, http://www.stratfor.com/weekly/crisis-middle-class-and-american-power.

    This reality and the growing destabilization of the statistical middle is further exasperated by the reality that 49 million people in the United States are living below the poverty line. (Stratfor Forecasting, Inc. is a global intelligence think tank recognized as an authority on strategic and tactical intelligence issues.)

2. "Editorial: Carefully Consider Education 'Reform' Measures," *McClatchy-Tribune Business News*, April 23, 2013.

3. The Communist Party's integration into the concessions-based strategies of the trade union movement in the Cold War Era, as well as the black left's adoption of what Mary Dudziak has called "Cold War civil rights," which focused on racial reform, are but two examples of a shift from unified struggles for radical transformation to sectarian efforts for liberal reform.

4. Joerg Rieger, *No Rising Tide: Theology, Economics, and the Future* (Minneapolis: Fortress Press, 2009), 156.

5. The American Assumption, according to W. E. B. Du Bois, is a belief that every individual, as a result of one's efforts, can by thrift become a capitalist. Du Bois argues that the existence of slavery and poverty reveal contradictions that prove the American Assumption "was not and could not be universally true" (W. E. B.

Du Bois, *Black Reconstruction in America, 1860–1880* [New York: Free Press, 1998], 183–84). Further, Friedman of Strafor suggests, "American history has always been filled with the assumption that upward mobility was possible. The Midwest and West opened land that could be exploited, and the massive industrialization in the late 19th and early 20th centuries opened opportunities. There was a systematic expectation of upward mobility built into American culture and reality" (Friedman, "The Crisis of the Middle Class and American Power").

6. See Steve Thorngate, "Defining the Middle: The Rhetoric and Reality of Class," *Christian Century*, October 16, 2012, http://www.christiancentury.org/article/2012-10/defining-middle.

7. William Greider, *Come Home, America: The Rise and Fall (and Redeeming Promise) of Our Country* (New York: Rodale, 2009), 19–20.

8. According to the 2013 U.S. Census Bureau statistics, the federal poverty line for a family of four in the United States is $23,836. Incomes below twice the federal poverty line, or $47,700 for a family of four are low-income.

9. Friedman, "The Crisis of the Middle Class and American Power."

10. Greider, *Come Home, America*, 202.

11. Zbigniew Brzezinski, "Middle Class Civil Unrest to Flare Up in USA," *Morning Joe*, July 6, 2011, http://www.youtube.com/watch?v=OpTH2B99jE0.

12. Greider, *Come Home, America*, 202.

13. Gary J. Dorrien, "What Kind of Country? Economic Crisis, the Obama Presidency, the Politics of Loathing, and the Common Good," *Cross Currents* 62, no. 1 (2012), 115.

14. David Cay Johnston, "Income Inequality: 1 Inch to 5 Miles," *Tax Analysts*, February 25, 2013, http://www.taxanalysts.com/www/features.nsf/Articles/C529565725466 24F85257B1D004DE3FC?OpenDocument.

15. I use the concept of the "fluidity" of middle-class identity in two ways: (1) To denote how this category of middle class is used to identify a broad sector of people whose income ranges from $25,000 to $250,000. Further, it includes additional indicators such as educational status, home ownership, and professional affiliation. (2) To emphasis the instability of this category that has been exacerbated by the collapse of the housing market, the elimination of mid-wage jobs and job stability, and the rising reality of student loan debt (a debt that threatens to become the next major cliff in our fledgling economy).

16. Roger C. Altman, Jason E. Bordoff, Peter R. Orszag, and Robert E. Rubin, *The Hamilton Project: An Economic Strategy to Advance Opportunity, Prosperity, and Growth*, Washington, D.C.: Brookings Institution, April 2006, http://www.hamiltonproject.org/files/downloads_and_links/An_Economic_Strategy_to_Advance_Opportunity_Prosperity_and_Growth.pdf.

17. The term *philosophy of praxis* was also used in Gramsci's prison notebooks in place of the term *Marxism*. (As Labriola did, too, because using the term *Marxism* could be politically suicidal in those days in Italy.).

18. Antonio Gramsci, "The Study of Philosophy," *Selections from the Prison Notebooks*, ed. and trans. Quintin Hoare and Geoffrey Nowell Smith (New York: International Publishers, 2010), 330–31.

19. Willie Baptist, *Pedagogy of the Poor* (New York: Teachers College Press, 2011), 132.
20. The church, for Gramsci and his context in early twentieth-century Italy, refers to the Roman Catholic Church. Gramsci recognized the particular role the Catholic Church played in maintaining the hegemony of the ruling class in Italy. Further, Gramsci was fascinated by the ideological unity that the Roman church and the care taken by the church to "prevent an excessive gap from developing between the religion of the learned and that of the simple folk." Gramsci's recognition of the influence the Catholic Church had on everyday people in Italy made him realize that to build a new hegemonic consciousness, there must exist a relationship between, on the one hand, the economic and political front, to, on the other hand, an intellectual and spiritual renewal. Joseph V. Femia, *Gramsci's Political Thought: Hegemony, Consciousness, and the Revolutionary Process* (New York: Oxford University Press, 1981), 138.
21. Dwight B. Billings, "Religion as Opposition: A Gramscian Analysis," *American Journal of Sociology* 96, no. 1 (1990): 5.
22. Johannes Baptist Metz, "Political Theology as Criticism of Middle-Class Religion," in *Faith in History and Society* (New York: Seabury Press, 1979), 35.
23. Ibid., 38.
24. H. Richard Niebuhr, "Toward the Independence of the Church," in *The Church against the World*, ed. H. Richard Niebuhr, Wilhelm Pauck, and Francis P. Miller (Chicago: Willett, Clark, 1935), 128.
25. It is important to acknowledge that Gramsci's main context for speaking about the role of religion in society is the Catholic Church in Italy. Niebuhr, in contrast, is speaking largely from within the American Protestant tradition but describes this tradition as a protest movement with roots in Early Christian protest against the Roman Empire. These two particular traditions in Christianity have their own historical situatedness in relation to structures of domination, but to explore the possibility that Billings puts forth of religion as a means of protest, I will here engage this comparison.
26. H. Richard Niebuhr, "The Ethical Failure of the Divided Church," in *The Responsibility of the Church for Society, and Other Essays by H. Richard Niebuhr*, ed. Kristine A. Culp (Louisville, Ky.: Westminster John Knox Press, 2008), 7.
27. Niebuhr, "Toward the Independence of the Church," in *The Church against the World*, eds. Richard H. Niebuhr, Wilhelm Pauck, and Francis P. Miller (Chicago: Willett, Clark, 1935), 124.
28. Friedman, "Crisis of the Middle Class and American Power."
29. Willie Baptist, "Not Enough to Be Angry, Part 2" (strategy paper, Poverty Initiative, 2013), 4.
30. Gramsci uses the term *Jacobinism* to describe the emergence of a national-popular alliance. It is the coming together of the peasant masses and the leading class, a bonding of city and country.
31. Organic intellectuals, for Gramsci, are leaders who are able to develop a critical consciousness and are "organically" connected to the dispossessed class. They function as leaders, educators, and organizers for the movement to build a revolu-

tionary consciousness that can reveal the contradictions of the ruling class's hegemony and unite the discontent of the masses.
32. See Vermont Workers Center, www.workerscenter.org; Put People First Pennsylvania, www.facebook.com/PutPeopleFirstPA; Media Mobilizing Project, www.mediamobilizing.org; The Poverty Initiative, www.povertyinitiative.org; and The United Workers, www.unitedworkers.org. The Poverty Initiative is now part of The Kairos Center for Religions, Rights, and Social Justice, http://kairoscenter.org, and is also in coalition with the Southern Maine Workers Center, http://www.maineworkers.org/.
33. Jacobin is a reference to the revolutionary class of the French Revolution. Although in Gramsci's early writings he is critical of the term *Jacobinism* for its sectarian and abstract associations, his prison notebooks revalue this term to speak of the leadership of a national-popular alliance.
34. Antonio Gramsci, "The Modern Prince," *Selections from the Prison Notebooks*, 144.
35. Emilie Townes, *Womanist Ethics and the Cultural Production of Evil* (New York: Palgrave Macmillan, 2006), 6.
36. H. Richard Niebuhr, *The Meaning of Revelation* (New York: Macmillan, 1941), 84.

# Elements of Tradition, Protest, and New Creation in Monetary Systems: A Political Theology of Market Miracles

NIMI WARIBOKO

This chapter intertwines Pentecostal theology, economics, and continental philosophy to construct a political theology of market miracles. The miracle of the market is defined as shifts in the production possibilities frontier (PPF) of an economy.[1] What changes in the shifts of PPF (tiny displacements) are not the factors of production themselves but their limits. If the current state of PPF represents the *perfect* combination of extant factors of production, then a shift of the PPF is a supplement added to perfection. Everything is as it is, just a little different.[2] The shift of the PPF is about how an economy initiates something new amid ongoing social reality by way of "small things" or "weak force."[3] A shift in PPF recognizes the slight performance or emergence of the miracle of natality (in the Arendtian sense), the new birth, the new creation of technical and managerial expertise that expands the capabilities of a people or a nation.[4]

The argument and elaboration of the preceding paragraph unfolds in this way. The first section is my conceptualization of miracle. In this chapter, I work with various notions of miracles as I engage with the thoughts of different philosophers, so it is germane for me to offer the reader some initial conceptualization of miracle as it is relevant to the task of this chapter.

Second, I engage with a description and explanation of the three elements of religion. This is a framework that combines Paul Tillich's notion of Catholic substance (tradition and its reinvention) and Protestant principle (critique, protest, and reformation) with what I have elsewhere called the Pentecostal principle (initiating something new, *novum*).[5] It is my understanding (hypothesis) that every expression of the Christian religion is a mixture of the Catholic substance, Protestant principle, and the Pentecostal principle, and Christian religion will be better understood if these three parts, their interactions, changes, and dynamics, are studied. The three-part movement (Catholic, Protestant principle, and Pentecostal principle) is circular, meaning that the later phases depend on their earlier antecedents, while also deepening their performance.

Third, I apply this tripartite framework to generate a theory of money and its becoming, to explain the logic and dynamics of monetary systems, which both underlie and strategically define the market system in capitalist economies. I attempt to identify similar tripartite structures in the monetary system as a heuristic device, as a method for socioeconomic analysis. Money is both a commodity and a medium of exchange for commodities in the market. It is the general equivalent of all commodities that has itself been generally produced as a commodity and remains a commodity. How do we, as theologians, theorize the character and dynamics of a monetary system, in terms of what we already know about the dynamics of a religious system? I want to show how a theological theory can help us further discern how money and the monetary system work. I employ the religious-theological theory of the three elements of the Christian religion for the study of money as a gateway to understanding market miracles.

Of the three elements, I focus most on the Pentecostal principle. The Pentecostal principle is represented by the production possibilities frontier, or rather the PPF shows the workings of the Pentecostal principle as a method for socioeconomic analysis. The analogous equivalent of the Pentecostal principle in the economic system marks the force, the tension between the actual and virtual PPF.

The second aspect of our chapter is the analysis of the political theology of market miracles. This analysis shows how and why I interpret shifts in PPF as miracles. I engage with the philosophies of Carl Schmitt and Franz Rosenzweig to describe and explain market miracles. The findings of this engagement help develop a political theology of market miracles based on Saint Paul's and Walter Benjamin's notion of "weak messianic force."

The power of the market is not a strong force. It is only invocative and provocative, luring and alluring, but without sovereign power. It is about a promise, the attraction of what is "to come." The market lays its claims on economic agents not in the manner of an efficient cause or the way of a sovereign power but by a motivating call, which is really a weak force. It is in this sense that we will use the Benjaminian metaphor of weak messianic power to describe the market's operations. In his "The Concept of History," Walter Benjamin writes about the claim the dead or the past lays on the living or the present. As he puts it:

> The past carries with it a secret index by which it is referred to redemption. . . . There is a secret agreement between past generations and the present one. Our coming was expected on earth. Like every generation

that preceded us, we have been endowed with a *weak* messianic power, a power to which the past has a claim. That claim cannot be settled cheaply.⁶

The dead, the past, are the weak, those without sovereign power, omnipotent power of intervention, are making a claim on the powerful, and yet their appeal cannot be taken lightly. This is so because the present and the living are in a messianic position, which requires them to save or redeem the dead. The living and the present are the portal, the now-time through which the messiah may come through at any moment. Besides, the past generations waited for and expected the present generation to come and redeem the past, and to do so even as it moves forward into the future. The living save and redeem by remembrance and mindfulness and not by resurrection or by awakening the being of the ruins of history. Indeed, in this Benjaminian sense the power the living generation incarnates and actualizes as an agent of history is a weak one. Its power, as John Caputo puts it, is not that of a real messiah who will show up later on and make a real difference.⁷ Like Benjamin, Saint Paul had earlier portrayed the power of God as weakness, the weak force of God that is irresistible (1 Cor. 1:25, 27–28). It is in this sense of the weakness of power, the power of powerlessness that can initiate something new or transform lives, that we will ultimately craft our political theology of market miracles.

Finally, I conclude with an exploration of how human freedom should engage with market miracles in late capitalism by drawing from Giorgio Agamben's theory of potentiality.

## A WORKING DEFINITION OF MIRACLE

I offer a simple definition of miracle to get us started. In the course of this chapter we will become familiar with a more nuanced understanding of miracle as we encounter key thinkers and their comprehension of it. Miracle represents an impossibility (excluded, prohibited, or deferred possibility) that has been anticipated or has emerged, but is transcended such that new possibilities are revealed, and this critical transformation is endowed with a sense of the momentous or produces a feeling of wonder.⁸

Religion does not have a monopoly of miracles. The miraculous is part of mundane, everyday life; it is not necessarily transcendent. Miracles are events, occurrences, and manifestations that induce wonder and awe in a given context. In this sense, the market's ability to coordinate myriad activities of millions of economic agents or its capacity to shift the production possibility frontier is as miraculous and awe-inspiring as the unexplained (nonunderstood) healing after prayers by a group of believers. The market's capacity to transform the impossible into the possible, to turn the possible into the actual, and to translate the unthinkable into the thinkable is to many economists an everyday form of kairos. In Hannah Arendt's sense of natality and miracle, market-natality is connected to the miracles of surpassing the limits of the production possibility frontier. Any shift in PPF brings something new to the world, at least to the world of the economy. Although we may never know the exact potentiality at play here, we can say that the economy as a form of social existence has the capacity (potentiality) to begin, to enact new beginnings. This is not too dissimilar to natality in political action, which is ultimately rooted in the human capacity to begin, to act, and to start something new.

The miraculous is in the ordinary or extraordinary, regular or irregular, explained or unexplained, utilitarian or sacred, personal or social, and even in the quotidian practices of rationally relating means to ends. Each of these is an embodiment of surplus possibilities. If there were no surplus possibilities in any process or system, the novel and unpredictable would rarely arise, there would seldom be a manifestation of unauthorized, unexpected, precalculated, or prewarranted possibility or production-possibility.

*The Three Elements of Christian Religion*
There are three elements of the Christian religion: the Catholic substance, the Protestant principle, and the Pentecostal principle. The Catholic substance represents the orthodoxy, institutionalism, and inherited norms and practices that every religion or sociality requires to function properly or at least organize itself on a day-to-day basis so as to put absolute chaos at bay. Put differently, the Catholic substance is the set of the institutions, past human experiences and their memories, "deposits" of previous *kairoi*, sacraments, objects, and spaces and times of divine-human encounter of a religion. These are considered as trustworthy and always powerful, relevant and adequate to mediate the presence of God afresh. The mediation could be problematic at times. Tradition both conveys and betrays a community's heritage.

A careful study of the etymology of the word *tradition* reveals nuances that Tillich does not highlight. Tradition (*traditio*) does not only mean "handing down," "delivery," or "passing on" but also "betrayal" or "handing over" or "delivering up treacherously." For instance, Luke 22:6 uses the Greek verbal form of the word in this second sense to describe the betrayal of Jesus by Judas. Also Jesus is often portrayed in the Gospels as berating the Pharisees for their tradition that negates or betrays the crucial meanings of the Word of God. So tradition or the Catholic substance not only conveys the presence of God; it can also betray what it is meant to mediate.[9]

The Protestant principle is the moving and self-critical principle of the church and even generally of all human sociality. It opposes the absolutizing of any particular form of sociality, human arrangement, and ethos. In its lights, every cultural form, the relative, can become a vehicle for the absolute, the unconditional, but nothing can ever become absolute, unconditional itself. The Protestant principle arises in reaction to the Catholic substance.

The Catholic substance requires not merely emancipatory protest but also transformation and natality, not just an event of critique and protestation but also a long and sustained process of initiating something new, creating new socialities, liberating humanity. The Pentecostal principle is the capacity to begin, the capacity of social existence to begin something new. The principle encapsulates the notion that no finite or conditioned reality can claim to have reached its destiny. The movement of every existent to its destiny (full realization of potentialities) remains ever incompletable. Every end has only one option: to be a new beginning.

In the next section I use this three-part format to describe and analyze the monetary system. The section serves as a special heuristic device designed to get a quick but accurate understanding of how the monetary system works and in the process facilitate a path for a political theology of money. It uses theological terminology to provide a creative explanation of the workings of monetary systems.

*The Three Elements of the Monetary System: A Theo-economic Inquiry*
CATHOLIC SUBSTANCE EQUIVALENT IN THE MARKET
In the monetary system we see the Catholic substance in the form of institutions, leadership structure, practices, models and equations, core economic message, and the tradition, the history, and memories that sustain it. This is the "ground" that supports it. The Catholic sustenance mediates the immanent presence of the invisible hand (the market deity?) through social practices and material means.

PROTESTANT PRINCIPLE EQUIVALENT IN THE MARKET
The Protestant principle is the rate of return or the profit rate. It represents the split from within value in the modern economy that causes its perpetual imbalance or reformation. The value of all assets (as capital stocks or factors of production) in the capitalist market system depends, broadly speaking, on two items: exchange and the speculation on the rate of return. The two might be reduced to one: desire[10]—desire for goods and desire for profits.[11] The exchange value of a product (good or service) is a function of desire. The price a buyer is willing to pay for a product depends on the degree of her desire for it, and her desire is represented publicly by the sum of money she is willing to part with in order to acquire the product. Money represents the degree of her subjective desire for the product.[12]

The value of an asset not only depends on the degree of subjective desire of customers, but also on the desire for profit, which is quantified by its underlying rate of return. In valuation of assets in the market, the most important consideration appears to be the rate of return or profit, the changes of which destabilize all their values. The rate of return for valuation is always speculatively determined. Take, for instance, the popular *discounted cash flow* valuation model (DCF). A determinant of value in the model is the discount rate, the rate of return, which is always a projected or predicted number. And in the construction of the cash flows which have to be discounted by the rate of return to have a knowledge of the present value, past earnings are essentially excluded and the future minimized (to usually five to ten years) in favor of some kind of an "imagined eschaton" known as *steady state* (value in infinity), which usually produces the bulk of the value of the assets. In typical valuation methods, prices of assets are only a reflection of the underlying rates of return. "The value of an asset is no longer given by exchange alone, but by speculation on the rate of return of profit. Value no longer measures an accumulated stock in relation to desire, but a differential rate of profit. Fixed quantities are destabilized by underlying rates of return; asset values fluctuate wildly and become subject to speculation."[13] It is well known that, even as Karl Marx has taught us, reforms (that is economic collapse and reorganization of capital or location and relocation of capital, investment, and disinvestment of treasures) are conditioned or determined by the rates of profits. The rate of return is the bugle of protest and reform. The repetitive differential movements in the rate of returns are the signal that reorders resource allocation and revaluation of all values.

So far deployment of the second element of religion (the Protestant principle) has been limited to the explanation of how the market functions. Can it also show us ways of resisting or protesting against the market? One way to turn the second element of religion from an explanatory device of the market system into a tool of resistance against finance capital is to think of the Protestant principle as a critique of the tradition of the market system (a wholly owned subsidiary of human coexistence and nature) that has betrayed the goals of human flourishing and social harmony. As Cynthia Moe-Lobeda puts it: "If the market system is meant to mediate the economy—that is, the *oikonomia*, the operating rules that serve the well-being of the cosmic or planetary household—then the Protestant principle's equivalent in the market might just be the critique of where the market betrays the widespread economic good."[14] Let me illustrate a critique of the tradition of the market based on the role of interest rates, which are integral to the logic and dynamics of the market-Protestant principle. What is the connection between interest rate and environmental pollution?

The expansion or growth of the national economy not only promotes the public good but also threatens it, especially as it poses a threat to the global environment. In keeping with our primary focus on money and its becoming, we focus on the vexing connection between the monetary system and environmental pollution.

The foundation of the monetary system in the United States is debt. In order to create money, "high-power money," to put money into circulation the Federal Reserve Board (FRB) has to buy government securities from the commercial banks, except it wants to literally print money. If the FRB wants to pump $20 billion into the United States economy, it has to buy that amount of government securities from the banks (creating new bank reserves for them) and pay appropriate interest to them or their investors. The Fed cannot just create money as the Treasury Department does with its issuance of metal coins, which is debt- and interest-free. The reader who is not familiar with monetary economics may rightly ask: Where do the government securities come from in the first place? The Treasury Department sells bonds to borrow from the public in order to supplement tax revenues. The banks buy the debt instruments for their use or for their clients, and the government pays periodic interest to the investors. From this you can see that the foundation of the money supply in the United States is on debt, not commodity standard. Running an efficient system for generating market-clearing interest rates and payments of interest due on debts is key for the functioning of the whole monetary system.

The interest-based monetary system is one of the contributing factors to the ecological nonsustainability of economic growth. In the market economy, every producer who intends to stay in business has to cover, at the minimum, his or her cost of capital. Let us say that the risk-free, before-tax interest rate on bonds (only a part of the weighted average cost of capital as cost of equity is ignored in this example) is only 4 percent; it means the profit rate has to be higher than this level for private production to go on. This also means at the minimum the economy has to grow at 4 percent to yield this kind of profit irrespective of concern for the environment. Now this is where the argument hits home. If the economy of the United States is growing at 4 percent per year, it will double approximately every eighteen years. (This 4 percent rate does not include allowance for return on equity, a margin for national population growth rate, and the compounding of interest, which is boundless. And if it does, the years will be dramatically less.) Now imagine the huge impact on the environment if Europe and Japan are also growing at the same rate—yet we know the average cost of capital in these societies is more than 4 percent per annum. The monetary system and the whole mechanics of the capitalist production system have this built-in power to grow and grow just to make zero return on invested capital.

#### PENTECOSTAL PRINCIPLE EQUIVALENT IN THE MARKET

The Pentecostal principle is represented by the *production possibilities frontier*. More precisely the Pentecostal principle is the force, the tension between the actual and virtual production possibilities frontier. In order for us to understand what I mean by this statement I need to explain three economic phenomena or terms: (a) production possibilities frontier; (b) the actual ("what is") and virtual ("not-yet") forms of the production possibilities frontier, and (c) the tension between zero and one (0 and 1), which is not only constitutive of the tension between the actual and virtual forms of the production possibilities frontier, but is also a constituent part of it. These three discussions will enable us to grasp how an economy initiates something new amid ongoing regularity.

What economists call the production possibilities frontier (hereafter PPF) is a graph (with a bow-out curvature) that shows the optimal allocation of resources in an economy given the effects of diminishing returns on production.[15] The graph shows how the total number of output will change as different allocations of land, labor, and capital are made. It plots out the output combinations at different allocation regimes of an economy's resources or factors of production. All points on and under the curve are attainable levels of production; those above it are not reachable given the limited supply of resources (capital, labor, technical know-how, management expertise, and so on).

Production levels that correspond to points on the PPF are theoretically considered efficient.[16] At those levels an economy is considered to be producing at levels where there is no waste of resources. At such levels producers can only increase the output of a product at the expense of another one, that is, by decreasing its production. Any attempt to increase the output of a product involves trade-offs. But when the PPF of an economy shifts outward, it can increase not only the production of all items, but it might also produce new ones. The PPF shifts outward when there are technical improvements in the economy.

In our application of the Protestant principle to the market, we extended the discussion from application to the provenance of resistance to the market. Let us make a similar move here before we proceed further. It is quite conceivable from a critical, activist perspective to interpret the market corollary of the Pentecostal principle as citizens, *actors* (in Arendt's sense) coming together to create power through collective effort, cooperation, and collaboration to transform their national economies and societies, to shift to a "new economy." Actors initiate something new amid ongoing social automatism, change the direction of their countries for good, moving their nations to build more democratic, ecologically sustainable and equitable economies. Such are the bearers of the Pentecostal principle. "The Pentecostal principle of 'creating the new, the non-existent space into which an economy expands' would then be the principle of fundamental economic reordering along the lines of equity, sustainability, and democratic accountability."[17] Indeed, the three elements of religion I have crafted to illumine the unfamiliar working of money and monetary system provide vital resources to think about or exercise the freedom to resist the demands and mandates of finance capital or the concentrated powers of the market system.

Now that we have laid out the basic concept of the PPF, we need to deepen our knowledge of it at three related registers: (a) a technical explanation of the expansionary process of an economy, (b) a monetary interpretation of the underlying dynamics of PPF, and (c) a philosophical recasting of its meaning.

*Technical Interpretation of PPF*

If the PPF defines the boundary of a set of possibilities available for an economy to produce and manage its total output, then what is beyond this limit? Beyond the frontier (PPF) is a *void*. It is not a space; it is not conducive for "economic habitation" (for production and exchange). It is a nonplace, a nonexistent economic space. But as an economy expands and its constraints are loosened, it creates its own space. A cutting-edge economy creates the space into which it expands. With what "forces" does an expanding galaxy of economic activities unfurl the subsequent space it will inhabit? Technological breakthroughs and human capital improvements are some of the factors that usually shift the line (curve) outward.

I want to accent one of the features of PPF's expansions: An economy creates the space into which it expands. Take, for instance, decades ago there was no computer industry in the United States. There was no "there" of the computer industry into which the United States could move into and occupy in order to expand its economy, to increase its gross domestic product. It had to create this new space into which it would then go. The creation and movement into the new space is simultaneous, in the same way the universe expands by creating its own space and expanding into it.

The expanding economy—represented by shifts in the PPF—is in the grip of the Pentecostal principle, bending the arc of survival and sustenance toward the not-yet. For the purposes of this chapter I consider the PPF as the visible stand-in and the *name* of the Pentecostal principle in an economy. The shifts in the production possibilities frontier that mark the concrete expansion of an economy, that reveal an economy's self-revolutionizing force, and point to the ongoing partial realization of the Pentecostal principle are not only the path toward the truth of the Pentecostal principle but are also part of the truth.

*Monetary Interpretation of PPF*
Financial instruments exist in paired zeros and ones. Financial products and transactions are created, recorded, interpreted, and retired by accounting methods, a system of binary opposition, debit and credit that net to zero. Records of financial dealings are kept and reported to internal and external publics in the form of asset and liability or credit and debit. Money is both 0 and 1. Financial product is a coupling of what is known in the established symbolic order and what is missing, an object of desire, inspiration, or to use Badiou's language, an *event*. The zero is the active principle immanent in the combined static and dynamic dimensions of 0 and 1 in all monetary existence. The zero (the nothing, the *void*, the null set in Alain Badiou's thought) is the fount of possibilities. The one is conditioned, limited, and originated from the *multiplicity* that is zero, that zero that is infinite.

*Philosophical Interpretation of PPF*
The production possibilities frontier captures the notion of two forces working for the progress of every economy. It shows the vector of possibility running toward actuality and that of actuality striving toward potentiality. The PPF is about what an economy could become, but is not yet there, designating an economy that is in itself open. The Pentecostal principle is thus the very gap that separates the economy from itself. This gap is the site of the new, which always comes as a miraculous surprise. The emergence of the new is neither a matter of necessity nor that of pure contingency. It is a dialectical mixture of contingency of necessity and necessity of contingency.

In every economy there are laws and economic activities that necessarily occur according to them.[18] How these laws emerged was utterly contingent, as the famous economist and Nobel Prize winner Friedrich Hayek has taught us.[19] This is the contingency of necessity in the economy. On the other side of the coin is the freedom of human actions, which stands for the necessity of contingency. This freedom is not just sheer contingency, rather it is a free act, which retroactively presupposes its own immanent necessity, its own reason, creating its own objective condition. The subject's contingent decision is simultaneously the contingent constitution of its necessity.

Thus the miraculous new (the shifts in PPF, creation of hitherto nonexisting economic space) is neither an exception to the economic laws nor is the economy merely becoming what it was in potentia. The new is the retroactive result of the dialectical process between possibility running toward actuality and actuality striving toward potentiality, of contingency of necessity and necessity of contingency. How can political theology help us make sense of this market miracle? Political theology as developed by Schmitt accents miracles in its theorization of sovereignty, and I want to draw insights from it for my theological theorizing of money.

At the beginning of this chapter I stated that the Pentecostal principle is the force, the tension between the actual and virtual production possibilities frontier. I need to deepen our philosophical understanding of this assertion. The work of the PPF or the Pentecostal principle is always by the force of human actions, something Arendt likened to a miracle.[20] Actors undo or resist the inexorability of fate by initiating something new. Without beginnings and rebeginnings systems will get caught in a compulsion to repeat, which can become a dead drive toward nonexistence. Without activities that can open up blocked possibilities and ignite the unachieved not-yet and transform accomplishments to events, repetition cannot become a source of difference and novelty. How this happens is related to the actual and virtual forms of the PPF. The actual is the repetition-form of becoming, and the virtual is the transforming form of repetition.

On the two sides of the PPF coin, the virtual is the (fantasmatic) support of the actual. The virtual is the reference point of the economy or the productive forces in their actuality. It exists only in its effects. When changes happen only within the actual PPF, they do not lead to the emergence of the new. The actuality is only reproducing itself through the movement and struggles of its constitutive parts. The frontier of production possibilities does not shift outward. The emergence of something really new occurs when the virtual which supports the actual changes.[21] In the repetition of the same, the actuality, the actual properties of the economy remain the same, but things all of a sudden appear (or are perceived) differently. A difference appears as the same agents and processes repeat themselves. It is the minimal difference that is the source of radical change. It is a cut that interrupts the functioning and articulations of the parts of the economy, moving them away from where the economy is "stuck." The forward movement, the deportment toward the not-yet is simultaneously what the struggles and articulations are all about, expressed in the repetition and the very structuring principle of the repetition, "the impersonal compulsion to engage in the endless circular movement of expanded self-reproduction."[22] As the repetition goes on, minimal differences will always emerge, and the desire to traverse the gap between the actual and the virtual goes on endlessly. The gap (or rather the virtual) that sets the repetition in motion at the same time prevents its success in the sense of erasing the gap or capturing the virtual. Indeed, the gap is the *Real* of the economy.

## POLITICAL THEOLOGY OF MARKET MIRACLES

The production possibilities frontier (PPF) presents an economy or rather the vision of any economy as one of incompletion and openness to the surprises of productive forces. The shifts in PPF are the miracles that move, reposition, or propel an economy forward. There is no power to guarantee the truth or the desirable outcome of these shifts or even to pronounce and guarantee the reality of the manifestation of the shifts.

Here we arrive at the terrain of political theology, or at least its application to markets. How do we interpret a shift in PPF—the miracle of creating the new, the nonexistent new space into which an economy expands? Is the market miracle an exception? Schmitt develops a concept of miracle as akin to the irruption of sovereign power in everydayness as an exception to natural (political) law. Rosenzweig, "a contemporary of Schmitt's, developed a conception of miracle that points not to singular ruptural power but rather to popular receptivity and immanence."[23] Which of the famous scholars, Schmitt or Rosenzweig, holds the interpretive key to market miracles?[24]

If we follow the Schmittian concept of miracles, then the shifts in the PPF will be interpreted as an irruptive sovereign decision in the economy. At any time that indecision on the part of capitalists and consumers appears to threaten economic growth or the very existence of the economy, sovereign power can be introduced into the market as a contravention of its "natural" order. Are we not dealing with Schmitt's decisionism and the miracle's analogous function when we have state capitalism with visible hands or when the government of President George Bush intervened in the post-2008 market crash?[25] The usual "dispersed sovereignty" of the market became "decisionistic and embodied" as the distinction between the market and state (executive) was elided or as the "divine sovereignty" of the market is incarnated, to resort to Schmittian language.

The theory of the miracles put forward by Rosenzweig does not rely on the irruptive sovereign power. For him, miracles are not "exceptional" and thus are more in line with our explanation of how the Pentecostal principle works to engender shifts in PPF. Rosenzweig articulates miracles as a realization of a prediction, working out of the possibilities in an incomplete and indeterminate trajectory. Miracles are not divergence from the course of nature (market) predetermined by laws; they derive their miraculous power from the fact that their occurrence was predicted.[26] Miracles are events that happen according to predictions, thus serving as an undecidable sign and invitation to look beyond regnant explanations. His, compared to Schmitt's, is a semiotic structure of miracles, as Eric Santner puts it.[27]

Both the Schmittian and Rosenzweigian concepts of miracle do not allow us to effectively engage with the invisible-hand character of market or some elements of the efficient market hypothesis, which claims that the market is essentially unpredictable. They also do not give us enough room to incorporate our findings about the slight adjustments to PPF that result from repetitions, which initiate something new amid ongoing social reality. Schmitt's or Rosenzweig's concepts of miracle convey a strong force (irruptive sovereignty, directing Providence, future-seeing personalities) behind miracles. The market fabricates its miracles with a weak force.

*The Weak Force of Market Miracles: Moving beyond Schmitt and Rosenzweig*
I now turn to a different political theology to find a way to rethink Schmitt's and Rosenzweig's concepts of miracles and their applicability to markets as interpreted through the lens of the Pentecostal principle. This will require that we pass through the combined terrain of Schmitt and Rosenzweig to reach a new place. Whereas for Schmitt miracle is an interruption of everyday patterns of existence, for Rosenzweig it is an intensification of the everyday. In the words of Bonnie Honig, Rosenzweig understands miracles as calling us to "experience the apparently steadfast as contingent [*contingency of necessity*] . . . the apparently contingent as steadfast [*necessity of contingency*]."[28]

Arendt enables us to suture Schmitt's and Rosenzweig's theories to our PPF. She thinks of sovereignty as related more to economy—the "what" of productive and reproductive labor and work in society, which sovereignty aspires to regulate. Miracles are transformative human actions that happen in concert, not on the friend-enemy distinction. Although the "what" is predictive, the "who" of miracles, which inaugurates political power or order and thus can even elude the grasp of extant sovereignty, is unpredictable. This simple schema does not fully reveal the subtleties involved in applying Arendt's insights to bridge the thoughts of Schmitt and Rosenzweig in order to explain shifts in PPF as miracles.

There are aspects of the PPF that are predictive insofar as we are dealing with the "what" of economic and social management of society, and thus Rosenzweig's understanding of semiotic structure of miracles (with ambiguous signs, which are to be interpreted) as predictive is illuminative. But to the extent that we are dealing with human beings, who are acting as if they are in concert in the marketplace to transform and inaugurate new regimes of PPF, we have to associate sovereignty with ruptural power. Arendt associates miracles with rupture, "but specifically with the ruptural power of a form of political action that is immanent not transcendent. Hers is a nonsovereign rupture that inaugurates a new limitedly sovereign order rather than suspending an existing order in a way that delineates or exhibits decisive sovereign power."[29] So the miracle of PPF is neither purely ruptural nor exceptional nor purely predictive. This is where passing through Schmitt and Rosenzweig brings us. The notions of exception (contravention of laws) and prediction (of an event which can be recognized only *post eventum*)[30] dog the notion of PPF as market miracle.

I have to part ways with both scholars and now attempt to develop another "political theology" that can best elucidate market miracles. I will develop such a political theology around the Jewish mystical idea that when the messiah comes, he will not change the world by force but will merely make a slight adjustment to it.[31] With this turn to the coming messiah who changes the world without a strong force, I let go of Schmitt's concept of miracle; it is inapplicable to a market with invisible hands. Schmitt's notion of transgression of laws to explain PPF ultimately has less of an appeal to economic thinking, although the ruptural character of the emergence of the new is appropriate for understanding the sudden shifts of PPF.

I part ways with Rosenzweig because his notion of prediction as the key predicate of miracle is too strong to be useful in understanding economic miracles. His notion of miracle as a realization of prophecy or prediction goes against the grain of accepted thinking in the economic science theorization of efficient markets. (The new PPF, which arises out of a myriad of human actions, though foreseeable in its general movement, cannot be considered as a realization of a prediction.) His idea of prediction is too tied to Providence, always seeing miracles as an unfolding of the arc of promise and fulfillment.[32] This notwithstanding, I retrieve something of predictability as applicable to the concept of market miracles through what I develop below—a concept that will start from the "margin."

Economics since the "Marginalist Revolution" of the 1870s is about thinking at the margin. The revolution is about conceptualizing constraints to economic activities as *margin, frontier,* or *border*. The predominant concern: What is the border use of a particular resource or endowment? In this revolutionary way of thinking, the value of any product or factor of production depends on its *marginal value*—that is the value it can command given a particular configuration of constraints in the economy. Marginal changes happen when the configuration is altered, meaning constraints relax or tighten incrementally. Marginal changes are very small steps in a series that approaches some limit of a sequence.

The production possibility frontier, the line of marginality between what is attainable and what is not yet attainable, is pushed outward by the myriad repetitive marginal activities of economic agents (by and large) assessing the value of the allocation of their assets by each of their abilities to earn the marginal rate of return currently obtainable. Deciding the optimal way to allocate a society's capital, for instance, depends on figuring out the next best alternative use to which the capital currently employed in one area should be redeployed.

Miracles (innovations) occur here as in evolution (nature) because of variation and its changing patterns, which all arise from marginal actions. Minor variation is where miracle is. Changes in rules or local environment cause either expansion or contraction of variation, which in turn triggers novelty, emergence of new sectors, and complex series of branching in the economy. Variation is the spatial-temporal moment where the accumulated past of a system experiences the potentiality (im-potentiality) of livingness without teleology or determination.

Miracle is the *next small thing* that does not change an economy by force but merely makes a slight adjustment. This slight difference is a decisive one: the small door through which shifts in the PPF occur. Some of my readers will recognize in these statements the allusions to Paul (1 Cor. 1:25, 27–28; 2 Cor. 12:9–10) and Walter Benjamin ("weak messianic force").

There is a typological relation between the next small thing and shifts in PPF. The next small thing is recognized as the *typos* of the shift in PPF. Working off of the Rosenzweigian semiotic structure of miracle, indeed the very instance of the next small thing and "instant of recognition is what constitutes" the next small thing *as* messianic, the weak force of continuous everyday actions of economic agents that slightly transform the frontier of possibilities of an economy.[33] The next small thing that accompanies the accumulated past with the possibilities of being otherwise is the miracle of the market. This weak, vocative force that can only slightly adjust the order of things has no sovereign or strong power to enforce what it solicits.

Rosenzweig argues that predictability is a predicate of miracle. This is almost true for my notion of market miracles. There is an element of predictability to this weak force of the next small thing that shifts the production possibilities frontier and thus renders it amenable to the "semiotic structure of miracles." I noted earlier that there is variation in human activities that is eventually behind the shifts in PPF. Variations in most natural and social systems have left and right "walls," meaning they can lead to deterioration or improvement in system performance. But variations in the economy do generally spread only in one direction; they are right-skewed toward the not-yet.

We can then think of shifts in the PPF as either realized or not-yet realized. Since the human race as a whole cannot totally forget all its (Lamarckian) cultural inheritance from the past, all of its realized PPF—that is, return to zero or less-than-zero heritage—the distribution of variation in a human system (knowledge base, for instance) will be right-skewed, much freer to expand in the direction of not-yet realized PPF. There is a "left wall" without a "right wall." There is an unlimited potential spread in the right direction toward the not-yet. But this tendency toward the right tail is not an inevitable ladder-climbing exercise (not a linearity), but multiple branching events out of which some persons may interpret a particular pathway as an epitome of current human glory.[34] At one level I might agree with Rosenzweig that predictability is a predicate of miracle; and here I can always predict the rightward expansion of PPF. But there is no providential impulse to it; I cannot say that shifts in PPF are moving somewhere or realizing some essence or plan.

On this note of limits let me summarize Schmitt's, Rosenzweig's, and my concept of miracle. The signature of miracle in all three conceptualizations is the indetermination of a limit. Schmitt's sovereign is both included and excluded from the law, and the analogy of miracle that founds sovereign exception strives on exceeding the limits of natural laws. Rosenzweig's concept of miracle as based on prediction operates on exceeding the limits of the seeable in the here and now to celebrate the "provided-for" foreseeable in the future, which is beyond the limits of the present. Shifts in PPF are also an unraveling of limits.

## THE PRAXIS OF HUMAN FREEDOM AND MARKET MIRACLES

My analysis of the market dynamics and the framing of the PPF miracles reveal a form of weak or contestable sovereignty, which is dependent on the openness and fallible decisions of millions of dispersed market agents. Yet we also know that markets are suffused with state interventions in favor of exceptionally nimble and fiercely free finance capital. What kind of freedom do we need to forge today to enable citizens squeezed between these two forces to resist the market?

Human freedom is best positioned to resist finance capital when it fervently maintains its twofold character, which is the capacity to do, to be (potentiality), and the capacity to not-do, to not-be (impotentiality).[35] In the exercise of freedom when potentiality is disconnected from impotentiality, it becomes subservient to the actuality of finance capital. Human freedom is fast losing its impotentiality, being able to abstain from doing what finance capital demands. Freedom, as Agamben sees it, is primarily in the domain of impotentiality, not in actualization. "To be free is not simply to have the power to do this or that thing, nor is it simply to have the power to refuse to do this or that thing. To be free is, in the sense we have seen, *to be capable to one's own impotentiality*, to be in relation to one's privation."[36]

Modern democracies and late capitalism not only separate citizens from what they can do but also, and more important, from the power to not do, from what they cannot do. Everyone is seduced, cajoled, and driven to offer the flexibility that the market demands. Today's citizens believe that they are capable of everything and that every sphere of life can be commingled for the benefit of the market. The market environment is impinging on the core of every other social practice. One result of all this is that human beings seem to have severed themselves from the ability to not do what the market wants.

Another result is that the exercise of freedom by citizens seems to have lost its capacity for, the real possibility of, changing the system from below. Citizens only appear capable of doing what the market system demands from them and are separated from the experience of what they cannot do, from the alternative that they are not doing now, from the freedom to resist and reshape the apparent freedom to consume and abide by the operating rules as provided by the current market system, or are separated from the freedom to organize in collective efforts to betray the market system that does not serve "the well-being of the cosmic or planetary household."

More important, democratic citizens have become incapable of contributing to the collective, improvisatory process of defining the common good of their societies. What is often taken as the common good are sectional goods or only those public goods that fit into the calculus of the market system. The market has become transcendent to the practical definition and determination of the common good of democratic societies. The common good of any society is truly common only when it is in immanent relation with all goods in that society. The existence of a common good in a society means that for each and every one in that community the cause and effect of all goods belong to the same plane.[37] The distinction between goods (such as relations of cause and effect, prior and consequent) is precluded insofar as the common good at the collective level refuses two or multiple categories of goods, two uncommon planes of goods or priority.[38] No groups, classes, or persons stand in relation of transcendence to another even as their positions or preferences are distinguishable. All positions, preferences, and distinctions therefore are preserved in immanent relation. The common good is that good the realization of which demands that every good (of a class, group, race, person) affects others as much as others are affected by it.[39]

What form should the praxis of freedom take in order to properly engage and transform the microdynamics of national economies for the common good? Given the weak force of the market, which subjects everything to its type of freedom, its form of becoming, ethics needs to rethink human freedom under the hammer of potential and impotentiality of freedom. We need the type of freedom that will strive to de-complete finance capital's order, the logic of pure and complete actualization, in the name of impotential freedom without destination or determination.

This will be a form of freedom that is not in dialectical negation to finance capital or the market. It will only aim to create a world outside of alienation and surplus extraction, yet at the same time not be outside the market, effecting in this manner that "small adjustment" in which, we are told, the weak messianic power consists in every generation. This form of human freedom does not seek to destroy, negate, or annihilate the market, but to deactivate it in order for human action to always remain in potential.

• • •

This chapter offers a religious theory of the tripartite articulation of economic life to show how to craft a weak-messianic-force conception of market miracles as a basis for interpreting the microphysics of the expansion of a national economy and its "common good." What is at stake in the relation between market miracles and the common good is the caesura in the praxis of human freedom: the potentiality to do and the potentiality to not-do. The potentiality to not-do has been corrupted by modern democracy-capitalism and has become foreign to most citizens who need to redeem it for the (re)construction of the common good or the good commons. The center of the discourse, the threshold at which economics and theology pass into each other, the point of contact through which political philosophy and economics reflect into one another to offer a doctrine of freedom as the democratic citizen's impotence in the face of threats to the commons and its good, is an original political theology of market miracles.

## NOTES

1. What economists call the production possibilities frontier (hereafter PPF) is a graph (with a bow-out curvature) that shows the optimal allocation of resources in an economy given the effects of diminishing returns on production.
2. This explanation of PPF is indebted to Giorgio Agamben's description of the weak messianic force. See his *The Coming Community*, trans. Michael Hardt (Minneapolis: University of Minnesota Press, 1993), 52–54.
3. A "weak force" is the powerless power of the god, thing, person, group, or institution to effect a change or determine form. The power that it enacts to bring form to elements or a situation is not deemed omnipotent; it does not operate as a cause but as a call. For more discussion of this concept, please go to the sixth paragraph below.
4. Hannah Arendt, *The Human Condition* (Chicago: University of Chicago Press, 1958), 247.
5. Nimi Wariboko, *The Pentecostal Principle: Ethical Methodology in New Spirit* (Grand Rapids, Mich.: Eerdmans, 2012).
6. Walter Benjamin, "Theses on the Philosophy of History," in *Illuminations: Essays and Reflections* (New York: Schoken, 1969), 253–54, quoted in Jacques Derrida, *Specters of Marx: The State of the Debt, the Work of Mourning, and the New International*, trans. Peggy Kamuf (New York: Routledge, 1994), 181n2.

7. John D. Caputo, *The Weakness of God: A Theology of the Event* (Bloomington: Indiana University Press, 2006), 95.
8. Richard Fenn, *Key Thinkers in the Sociology of Religion* (London: Continuum, 2009), 1–4. This understanding of miracle is an adaptation of Fenn's concept of the sacred.
9. Cynthia Moe-Lobeda, "Response to Paper by Nimi Wariboko," presented at Twelfth Transdisciplinary Theological Colloquium: "Common Good(s): Economy, Ecology, Political Theology," Drew Theological School, Madison, N.J., February 10, 2013, 1–2. She made this remark as the respondent to my presentation of an earlier draft of this chapter at the same conference.
10. Please note that *desire* is used here in the sense of both rational and affective orientations, passions and interests, toward an object. It will take us too far afield to analyze the differences between—or the transition from—passion to interest in the manner of Albert Hirschman.
11. Philip Goodchild, *Theology of Money* (London: SCM Press, 2007), 66.
12. Ibid., 64–65.
13. Ibid., 67.
14. Moe-Lobeda, "Response to Paper by Nimi Wariboko," 2.
15. Sean Masaki Flynn, *Economics for Dummies* (Hoboken, N.J.: Wiley, 2005), 38–44.
16. It is important to add that points on the curve that are considered efficient by economists may not always be ethical, moral, or good for workers.
17. Moe-Lobeda, "Response to Paper by Nimi Wariboko," 2.
18. There are "underlying law[s] which regulate what appears [as] a chaotic contingent interaction." Slavoj Žižek, *Less Than Nothing: Hegel and the Shadow of Dialectical Materialism* (London: Verso, 2012), 460.
19. Friedrich A. Hayek, *Law, Legislation and Liberty: Volume 1: Rules and Order* (Chicago: University of Chicago Press, 1973).
20. Arendt, *Human Condition*.
21. Žižek, *Less Than Nothing*, 483.
22. Ibid., 497.
23. Bonnie Honig, *Emergency Politics: Paradox, Law, Democracy* (Princeton, N.J.: Princeton University Press, 2009), 88.
24. Carl Schmitt, *Political Theology: Four Chapters on the Concept of Sovereignty*, ed. George Schwab and Tracy Strong (Chicago: University of Chicago Press, 2005); Carl Schmitt, *The Concept of the Political*, trans. George Schwab (Chicago: University of Chicago Press, 1996); Franz Rosenzweig, *The Star of Redemption*, trans. Barbara Galli (Madison: University of Wisconsin Press, 2005).
25. Schmitt's theory of the sovereign intrinsically rejects Adam Smith's theory of the invisible hand of the market. The notion of the invisible hand rejects not only the transgression of the law of the market through an exception brought about by the direct intervention, as is found in the idea of miracle, but also the sovereign's direct intervention in a valid market order. Construction of this statement is an adaptation of Schmitt, *Political Theology*, 36–37.
26. For Rosenzweig on the idea of prediction as the predicate of miracle, see his *Star of Redemption*, 104.

27. Eric L. Santner, "Miracles Happen: Benjamin, Rosenzweig, Freud, and the Matter of the Neighbor," in Slavoj Žižek, Eric Santner, and Kenneth Reinhard, *The Neighbor: Three Inquiries in Political Theology* (Chicago: University of Chicago Press, 2006), 76–133.
28. Honig, *Emergency Politics*, 97.
29. Ibid., 92.
30. The PPF can be explained only as *post eventum*. But our ability to explain it after the fact does not mean it is not a miracle. Here Rosenzweig's point about explanation and miracle is instructive. Post hoc explanation of shifts in PPF is possible "not because miracle is no miracle, but rather because explanation is explanation." Franz Rosenzweig, "On Miracles," in *Franz Rosenzweig: His Life and Thought*, ed. Nahum N. Glatzer (Indianapolis: Hackett, 1998), 290. The point here is that though we can still pass off PPF as a miracle under Rosenzweig's and Arendt's concept of miracle, it is still possible to say that PPF is predictable.
31. Walter Benjamin popularized this idea.
32. Rosenzweig, *Star of Redemption*, 105.
33. Santner, "Miracles Happen," 126.
34. For the ideas about variation and "right and left walls," see Stephen Jay Gould, *Full House: The Spread of Excellence from Plato to Darwin* (New York: Three Rivers Press, 1996).
35. Giorgio Agamben, *Nudities* (Stanford: Stanford University Press, 2010), 43–44; Giorgio Agamben, *Potentialities: Collected Essays in Philosophy*, ed. and trans. Daniel Heller-Roazen (Stanford: Stanford University Press, 1999), 182.
36. Agamben, *Potentialities*, 182–83.
37. The concept of the common good as developed in this chapter is indebted to Daniel Barber's interpretation of immanence. I have followed his interpretation to creatively fashion a fresh conceptuality of the common good on the pivot of immanence. See Daniel Coluccielo Barber, *On Diaspora: Christianity, Religion, and Secularity* (Eugene, Ore.: Cascade, 2011).
38. Collective here means a sharing and not a fusion or communion.
39. I consider the common good as the ordered arrangement (*oikonomian*) of goods in the house (*oikos*) of the people. Elsewhere I have provided a rigorous philosophical understanding of this conceptualization. See Nimi Wariboko, *Methods of Ethical Analysis: Between Theology, History, and Literature* (Eugene, Ore.: Wipf and Stock, 2013), 143–51.

# ❧ The Corporation and the Common Good: Biopolitics and the Death of God

ELIJAH PREWITT-DAVIS

*The member of a corporation has no need to demonstrate his competence and his regular income and means of support—i.e., the fact that he is somebody.*
—G. W. F. HEGEL, *Philosophy of Right*

*This newly ascendant God, visible nowhere, emergent from the future, executes the murder of God.*
—PHILIP GOODCHILD, *Capitalism and Religion*

What is political theology if not a secularized political world discovering that it is still haunted by God? If only it were merely a specter, then we would not be writing now, or would be writing in another vein—not about sovereignty, sovereign power, the state of exception, the decision, and so on. The dead God for so long announced is back and perhaps more powerful than before. He decides on drone strikes, he decides on torture victims, he decides the law and when to break it.... This power, at once material and mystical, transcendent through the immanent world it shapes and destroys, both inside and outside of the law, creates what Hardt and Negri call "an apocalyptic tone recently developed in politics."[1] Minding that tone might be key to developing any working notion of the common good; it might also be key in not sliding into a passive and reactive nihilism that would forsake the future promised by every apocalypse. But Hardt and Negri's point is not that a mystified sovereign power is plunging the world toward the end but that quotidian immanent forces operate within and on our lives: "The primary form of power that really confronts us today, however, is not so dramatic or demonic but rather earthly and mundane. We need to stop confusing politics with theology."[2] I wish to follow their assertion that power today is entirely immanent, earthly, and mundane, or, in other words, that power today is always biopower.

This position may take me out of the realm of "political theology." I admit a little fear. It is so easy to compare the "bad" theology of a transcendent God with the power of the state and the abuses of the sovereign. Better to construct an immanent God, who is with us, of this world, mundane, weak, and immune to the structures of political abuse. Or better yet, let's kill God, eradicate any notion of transcendence, make all the force of God's spirit spill out into the immanent world. No matter, Hardt and Negri tell us following Foucault, power is immanent now, and your new God or dead one is just as implicated.

But there may be some theological implications roaming around even within the immanent structures of biopower. This essay seeks to uncover the theological structure of the political that Hardt and Negri assert "is not an autonomous domain but one completely immersed in economic and legal structures."[3] The techniques of control and the mundane aspects of power seem obvious enough—advertising, consumerism, communication, image culture, and so on—but why are they, today, so effective? It is precisely this question that necessitates a theological intervention. The death of God creates a lacuna in postsecular subjectivation, and it is because we are still resentful over this empty space that various biopolitical entities are allowed to affectively fill it.

This essay concerns itself with the entities that have come to be known as corporations. If we take as a starting point Foucault's definition of government in the broad sense—what he calls governmentality—as the "techniques and procedures for directing human behavior," we can see that corporations, much more than the state, or "the government," are the ones regulating our "personal" lives.[4] On the one hand, there is the corporate advertising machine—our new masters who tell us what to feel, what to desire, what to be, and what to buy in order satisfy the lack they create. On the other hand, I am not sure what "sovereign decision" today could be made without taking the pressures and forces of Wall Street and the global market into consideration. Why is it that we no longer trust the state and yet acknowledge that corporate recognition is as important as the law? Is this not precisely what was happening in the summer of 2012 when the recognition and representation of the fast food corporation Chick-fil-A became the guiding light by which marriage equality was discussed?

My primary concern is in this essay is to begin to uncover how corporations function to actively produce subjectivities and lives. Thus my thoughts here about corporations must leave out important nuances concerning types of corporate entities, what the law says and continues to say about corporations, and so on. Rather then examining the Supreme Court decisions that have made corporations persons and given privately held for-profit corporations religious rights, I instead turn to Hegel's *Philosophy of Right*, and to the 2012 Chick-fil-A debacle for my investigation. According to Hegel, *Korporationon* (corporations) function as the second synthesis of the individual and the common, with the state being the primary consummation of the individual and the common good (and subsequently the consummation of a person's dialectical journey to selfhood). When read in light of Hegel's *Philosophy of Religion*, where the second synthesis is Christ and the primary consummation God, we begin to see how God and the state perform the same dialectical function for subjectivity.

Returning to Hardt and Negri's thesis, however, we can thus argue that corporations have superseded the state and thereby become the new place that subjects can find the recognition they desire. Thus what we might call the death/decline of the sovereign power previously held by the state is coterminous with the death/decline of the sovereign God. In other words, now that the universal Other as conceived in the *Philosophy of Religion* is increasingly put into question, the subject seeking legitimacy turns to the corporation to ground its subjectivity. In this way, the "return of religion," especially religiously based fundamentalisms in the past decades can be seen as a reaction to the death of God—a struggle based in what William Connolly has called ressentiment—as an attempt to retain a vague sense of subjective recognition. However, it is not only religious people who experience ressentiment, but everyone. This essay thus seeks to add a theological component to Hardt and Negri's purely immanent political analysis, as well as to challenge the impure immanence that radical death of God theology most often profligates.

## THE DEATH OF GOD

Although I take the death of God as the a priori condition from which postsecular theology begins, I can nevertheless hear my theological colleagues ask: Which God are you talking about? What precisely has died? Such questions remain ever pertinent given the proliferation of the liberating Gods and goddesses that flourished in the '70s and '80s. Let us not forget the question, but let us also not forget the context from which these Gods spring. Radical death of god and liberation theology may have from the outset diminished the importance of the other, but they nonetheless attend to a similar crisis within theology itself. As James Cone wrote in 1972, "If God is not for us and against white people, then he is a murderer, and we had better kill him."[5] If the theocide of liberation theology never "went so far as to put the established theology into question," as radical theologian Jeffrey Robbins has said, he also makes clear that radical theology itself has been insufficiently political. Along with Clayton Crocket, Robbins has called for a "truly radical political theology . . . that puts both the political and theological order in question."[6] Perhaps we should avoid this sort of radical one-upmanship by minding the complexities of each theological endeavor in favor of forming a coalition between liberation theology and radical theology. Indeed, if each has been "not radical enough" in one area or another, such a coalition seems necessary for developing forces that are able to resist late global corporate capitalism.

For the purpose of this essay, I would like to propose thinking the death of God as a Deleuzian concept. What I mean by this is that the death of God happens when God no longer affects our lives in any immediate sense. We must, however, take this one step further, for God can only die in this affective way when the said God is replaced by something more immediate, something more immanently tangible. Thinking the death of God as a concept also allows us to trace its varied pronouncements without thereby foreclosing the death of God into a singular event with a singular meaning, as has often been the case in radical death of God theology, especially those bound to Hegel. Although I do not accept wholeheartedly the Deleuzian Nietzsche versus Hegel dichotomy, I do see in Nietzsche (and Deleuze) the potential for a radically different conception of the Death of God, one free from its essentialism and desire for a representation of a grounded subject.

In the *Phenomenology of Spirit*, Hegel relates the Unhappy Consciousness to the universal notion of God. A person with Unhappy Self-Consciousness is conscious of the "loss of itself and the alienation of its knowledge about itself" because it has no conscious relation with the absolute.[7] Hegel is referring to the splitting of the essentially grounded, or substantial subject inaugurated by Kant. In premodern apophatic theology, the Universal God was considered utterly incomprehensible in God's infinite transcendence. Kant reversed this line of thinking. It was not something in God's nature that made God incomprehensible, but rather, the function of our intuitive faculties, which are always filtered through the categories. By placing a form of time into the subject, Kant, against himself, splintered the subjective dream of sovereign autonomous subjectivity. It is here that Deleuze locates the death of God: "If the greatest initiative of transcendental philosophy was to introduce the form of time into thought as such, this pure and empty form in turn signifies the death of God, the fractured I and the passive self."[8] Hegel would not necessarily disagree. As Hegel explains, the unhappy consciousness seeks to be absolute itself, but this aim is never reached because it has no recourse to an absolute outside of itself. Hegel writes: "It is the consciousness of the loss of all *essential* being in this *certainty of itself*, and of the loss even of this knowledge about itself—the loss of substance as well as the Self, it is the grief which expresses itself in the hard saying that 'God is Dead.'"[9] Here, it is necessary to note the radicality of Hegel's thinking, for he conceives the death of God, as if lamenting, in a way that is not simply reducible to the crucifixion and which prefigures both Deleuze and Nietzsche's understandings.

The key difference between Deleuze/Nietzsche and Hegel is the latter's inability to affirm the vacuity created by God's death. Hegel thus rethinks the death of God in and through the event of the crucifixion. For Hegel, the grief and anguish of this utter paradox creates the need for sublation, the reconciliation between the antithesis of "what *seems* incompatible—the infinite and the inner ego [on the one hand], and pure essentiality, or God [on the other]." Christ resolves the contradiction by revealing himself as "divine and human nature enter into a unity wherein both have set aside their abstractness vis-à-vis each other."[10] Thus Hegel reformulates the Death of God in his *Philosophy of Religion* as God's affirmative desire to disclose godself to humanity in and through a negative synthesis. Yet Hegel is clear, this is not merely the death of the individual, Jesus. This is the very negation of the absolute, of God—"What it means is rather that *God* has died: this is negation, which is accordingly a moment of the divine nature, of God godself." This death is necessary for God's own satisfaction through reconciliation with humanity—"death is what reconciles."[11] For Hegel, Jesus comes as the incarnate God that unites the infinite with the finite, and the death of Christ as the death of God repairs the rupture and the loss of self expressed in the hard saying that God is dead.

For Nietzsche, the death of God is equally the loss of immanent progress that Hegel announced: "Are we not plunging continually? Backward, sideward, forward, in all directions? Is there still any up or down? Are we not straying as through an infinite nothing?"[12] Far from announcing progress, Nietzsche at times laments the loss, even if his hope is that the death of God might become "the meaning of our cheerfulness," the breaking through of "a new and scarcely discernible kind of light, happiness, relief, exhilaration, encouragement, dawn."[13] Nevertheless, Nietzsche is unclear as to how this might happen. We cannot forget that the madman's listeners are already atheists; in other words, have already taken the death of God for granted but are nonetheless incapable of understanding the enormity of what their atheism implies. For the death of God also announces a "monstrous logic of terror . . . an eclipse of the sun whose like has probably never yet occurred on earth."[14] We should not read these dual aspects of the death of God dialectically, as if the negative moment of error were necessary for the new dawn. Instead, these dual aspects show Nietzsche's ambivalence toward the death of God—what we will later call his "mistrust"—for he sees clearly that God was humanity's most creative stroke of genius, and he harbors not a little doubt that we can repeat such a work of art, even admitting that the "best in us has perhaps been inherited from the sensibilities of earlier ages to which we hardly any longer have access by direct paths."[15] For Nietzsche, the first step toward cheerfulness is to overcome the resentment that this loss inspired, in other words, to overcome the need for absolute essentiality. This is precisely why Deleuze opposed Nietzsche to Hegel so vigorously, for he saw that the representation that Hegel sought arose out of a spirit of resentment in reaction to Kant's fracturing of the subject. Nietzsche and Deleuze, we might say, accept Hegel's diagnosis, but find his cure—mediation—poisonous.

## THE MURDER OF GOD

What force was so great as to enact such a spectacular theocide? Nietzsche takes this event for granted; thus, as I noted, his madman reports not the death of God, but the murder of God: "We have killed him—you and I. We are all his murderers. But how have we done this? How were we able to drink up the sea? Who gave us the sponge to wipe away the entire horizon?"[16] As Philip Goodchild explains, multiple factors come together to bring about God's death: the Reformation, the Copernican Revolution, the new understanding of Nature not compatible with an omniscient deity, the experimental method of natural science, the emergence of a wealthy and powerful merchant class that displaced monarchy, and subsequently the monarchical model of God. Although all of these are factors, Goodchild holds that these explanations fail to capture the complications of what has occurred. "Nietzsche's depiction of this emergence of atheism as the 'murder of God' is at once more materialist and more spiritual."[17] These explanations fail to explain how God has dropped out of everyday consciousness and ceased to be an organizing principle in life. In other words, God ceases to have any effect on the daily operation of life. The death of God is only possible if a new source of meaning and value is first available. God dies when god is replaceable: "The murder of God therefore reflects a shift in pieties. God has stopped paying us our ordered existence; or rather, there is another god who pays us, who responds more immediately, directly, and tangibly to our prayers: Mammon."[18] The murder weapon itself takes the place of that which was murdered, a sad and reactive atheism being the unfortunate fallout.[19]

The key point for Goodchild is that the death of God takes place in and through the reorganization of daily life. The common and the community—which in Europe was mostly centered on God—gets foreclosed as previously communal resources shift to the realm of private property. One now works only for oneself. This sort of market rationality takes hold and provides an "access to truth no longer limited by moral and religious sentiments." Operating within the market means making calculable choices rather than personal and affective considerations. Whether or not such considerations have taken hold in all milieus is of course debatable. But the spread of empire seems to make the equation "if not yet . . . then soon" all the more probable. Although this calculation "gives access to economic truth," this sort of economic rationality is "unable to produce meaning, it can not define the limits of its own applicability, or even if it is applicable at all."[20] Economic rationality thus morphs into an act of faith, and this faith gets perpetuated inasmuch as the market has the potential to guarantee freedom and peace. Trade and commerce become the solution to the Hobbesian war of all against all.[21]

This type of market logic allows the market itself to supersede both the state and God as the primary way to organize daily life. "The deed of the murder of God was effected by the emergence of the self-regulating market as the organizing principle of the social order."[22] For Goodchild, the final death stroke is the state backing of the bank of England, an act that allows for banknotes to have a secure value while simultaneously creating the possibility of an infinite accumulation of capital. Although based in a sovereign decision, this move begins to shift power from the state to the market. "Self-regulating markets, however, bring into effect forces beyond the reach of sovereign powers, forces of pure exteriority, lacking an identity or nature in themselves, beyond even the reach of God."[23] The backing of banknotes by the state, coupled with the dissolution of the gold standard, secures capital's domination over nature and life. For Goodchild, this is capital's transcendence. Capital exerts its force by superseding the state, nature, history, and even time. One always invests in a future with the hope of infinite growth. "The transcendence of capital is its appeal to the future."[24] Capitalists, too, are still pious.

Is the reign of global capitalism the great error that Nietzsche prophesied? A "monstrous logic of terror" that will enact an all too literal "eclipse of the sun whose like has probably never yet occurred on earth" as the very desolation of the earth itself? This is precisely why Nietzsche remains ambivalent, even sorrowful, and mistrustful over God's death. He has little faith in the human capacity to live into the ambiguity experienced when humanity's greatest creation ceases to induce the "enhancement of feeling" it once did.[25] In the spirit of resentment, the unhappy conscious strives for a new absolute. Zarathustra—prophesying the history of the twentieth century—saw the most threatening and menacing idol as the State: "'On earth there is greater than I: the ordaining finger of God am I'—thus roars the monster [state]. . . . Yes, it also detects you, you vanquishers of the old God! You grew weary in battle and now your weariness still serves the new Idol."[26] That prophecy not only eerily captures the death-dealing nationalisms that mark the twentieth century, it also makes an important observation that extends beyond that particular context: Rather than creating, the unhappy conscious goes searching for "new Idols" to ground its sovereignty. The new Idol not only kills the old God but actively takes its place. Goodchild holds that this new ground is capital, or

Mammon, and has helped elucidate a novel concept of the death of God—or rather, the murder of God—free of its Hegelian triumphalism. It remains to be seen, however, how the corporation functions in this scheme.

## THE CORPORATE COMMON GOOD

As Clayton Crockett explains, the modern liberal state finds its bearings in Hobbes, who sought to supplant religious sovereignty and replace it with national sovereignty. Therefore, liberalism emerges out of a "bitter struggle against Christianity, and particularly the Catholic church."[27] By distinctly claiming that the "Kingdom of God is not of this world," Hobbes is able to supplant religious claims of sovereignty with the natural law of nature, which finds representation and unity in a single individual who can represent, and thereby shape, the community into one will. This is, in essence, a sovereign monarchy. Crockett argues that Hobbes "fashions a concept of medieval sovereignty by limiting ecclesiastical power and reproducing theological power in the civil sphere."[28] Locke and Rousseau would relocate sovereignty within democracy, thus creating a notion of popular sovereignty. This popular sovereignty is "derived from absolute, monarchial sovereignty because it is the unitary will of the people that is sovereign, not the individual whims of the multitude."[29] This is the basis for the ideal of sovereignty today, though, as Crocket warns, the complexity of modern nation-state politics is such that the will of the people is "rendered impotent and irrelevant in contrast to the will of corporations."[30]

It is no surprise then that in his *Philosophy of Right*, Hegel viewed corporations and the state as the very places people turn to for purpose and security, with the state being the primary source of (ethical) meaning, that place where the notion of the "common good" reaches its full consummation. His *Philosophy of Right* is structured similarly to his *Philosophy of Religion*, and in each case, Hegel outlines the ways in which the universal principle is consummated in the particular, bringing together the individual and the universal. In *Philosophy of Right*, the individual comes to understand itself through its relation to the family, the civic community, and the state. I will be focusing on the latter two, arguing that corporations have taken the place of the state within what Hardt and Negri call "Empire." The civic community represents the relation of the individual to its own culture, its dependence on others and the common good. For Hegel, there is a system of "mutual dependence" that allows for the rights of the individual to be molded into a conception of "rights for all."[31] Hegel does not discount the problems of class disparity and the ways income disparity can create differing needs and therefore interests, but he believes that such differences can be overcome through education and reason. For him, the common good comes to full fruition when individuals understand through reason that their particular flourishing is intrinsic to what is common for all.

Under the civic community lies the corporation. The corporation is a special characteristic of particular interests because it brings the individual out of the particularities of the family and opens it up to a larger sense of what is common. It is the sight where "a conscious and reflective ethical reality is first reached."[32] Hegel's concept of *Korporationen* (corporations) is of course different from our current understanding of corporations, but this does not disavow important connections.[33] For Hegel, corporations are associations of people such as guilds, religious societies, educational clubs, townships, and so on. Yet Hegel is quite clear that corporations are primarily "estates of trade and industry," and it is in this way that we can understand the modern corporation—defined by law as a person—as nothing less than the consummation of corporate universality. As Hegel makes clear, corporations possess the right—"under the conditions of public authority—to safeguard and promote their own interests."[34] The corporation grounds both individuals and the family; in fact, Hegel even says that corporations become a "second family" to its members, thus prefiguring the contemporary balance between work and family, where sacrificing one for the other is essential to climbing the corporate chain of being.[35] The family becomes secure in resources in and through its relation to corporations, just as the individual finds its subjectivity grounded in the recognition of the work it performs for the corporate collective. As Hegel writes, "The member of a *corporation* has no need to demonstrate his competence and his regular income and means of support—i.e., the fact that he is *somebody*." To be sure, Hegel affirms that the association with the corporation is supposed to open the individual to a broader sense of the common good. Certainly, we cannot gloss over the sheer importance of Hegel's analysis and its at times nuanced understanding of structured sociality and the common good it has the potential to produce. Indeed, who made these arguments before him? The problem is that for Hegel the full consummation of the corporation and the common good it is meant to engender is based on a desire for a universally recognized subjectivity.

The corporation is derivative of the state, which is the primary absolute other, and it is through the state that the individual attains the full actuality of subjective freedom, where the full knowledge of the common good is attained. He writes: "The state as a completed reality is the ethical whole and the actualization of freedom. It is the absolute purpose of reason that freedom should be actualized. The state is the spirit, which abides in the world and there realizes itself consciously; while in nature it is realized only as the other of itself or the sleeping spirit."[36] The state is thus the universal reality that grounds human freedom and subjectivity. "Since the state is objective spirit, it is only through being a member of the state that the individual himself has objectivity, truth and ethical life."[37] The state grounds subjectivity, and just as Nietzsche feared, Hegel's dialectical movement allows the state to replace God, becoming the new idol. Whereas Hegel's understanding of the state is, of course, nuanced—allowing for periods of decline and negativity brought about by the collective and indeed corporate action of the people when the state fails to fully represent itself to themselves—Hegel is clear when discussing corporations that in these moments of decline, the individual can and will fall back on the security of the corporation: "This universal, which the modern state does not always offer him, can be found in the *corporation*."[38] Let us not amputate the liberative potential that Hegel's concept of the corporation provides for the common good and common action. Hegel's notion of the corporation could equally be applied to any collective mass, to a union, or to activist organizations or uprisings such as Occupy Wall Street. Hegel is always clear that opposition to the state in this form is necessary for the creation of freedom. Such revolutionary moments maintain the continual negative movement of the spirit, as Left Hegelians have sufficiently shown, the most recent representatives of this liberative reading being Catherine Malabou and Slavoj Žižek.[39] The point that I wish to make is that the way corporate personhood functions today reveals the consummation of corporate universality. That is, the corporation—as person—has superseded the state and works today as the primary force of biopolitical subjectivation. The question is how to draw this link between the corporate, the corporation (as person), and the common good, without thereby collapsing the potential for corporate-collective action? The manipulation of the corporation—or cooperation—by economic forces is at the moment inevitable, but the resistance will be corporate or else impotent.

At Occupy Wall Street, for instance, the number of police was almost unbelievable. On large strike days, when the objective was to block entrance to Wall Street itself, I found myself in awe of the power a corporate badge yielded. The flash of an ID badge with the expressed concern of getting to work instantly mobilized police: Occupiers were snatched up, arrested, or violently displaced in order to make way for corporate workers. The oft-repeated question of occupiers to the more violent police officers: "Who do you *really* work for, who are you *really* protecting?" gets answered by Hegel succinctly. "The police . . . [are] *an external order and arrangement* for the protection and security of the masses of particular ends and interests which have their subsistence in this universal." Those masses that it meant to protect, it seems, in this historical moment get washed over by the particular ends and interests of the immortal corporate person. They are, after all, too big too fail. The police knew more than anyone else what that badge represented—that they were *somebody*. Thus Hegel concludes his section on police by saying how the actions and goals of the police "constitute the determination of the corporation."[40]

As Hardt and Negri have shown, the decline of the sovereignty of nation-states has given rise to a new form of sovereignty "composed of a series of national and supernational organisms" regulating social, economic, and political production.[41] This is not a far stretch since the economic crash of 2008, which brought into sharp relief the close tie between national and corporate interests—what is good for corporations is good for America.[42] Moreover, where the conditions of the functioning of the democratic nation-state have declined, "the unity of single governments has been dis-articulated and invested in a series of separate bodies (banks, international organisms of planning, and so forth, in addition to the traditional separate bodies, which all increasingly refer for legitimacy to the transnational level of power."[43] In this way, Hardt and Negri argue that "transnational corporations have surpassed the jurisdiction and authority of nation-states."[44] This is not to say that the power of capital has finally defeated the state after its long battle. The state still functions in its constitutional role as a means of galvanizing a sense of collective interest or, we might say, the common good. What the decline of nation-state sovereignty names is the curious intermingling of the economic and the political where "consensus is determined not through the traditional political mechanisms but by other means."[45] Transnational corporate interests shape and form political decisions. There is no longer a "he who decides the state of exception" but rather a larger, amorphous, market force that has a profound influence on any decision that can be made. Where the state once represented universality, a network of corporations has stepped in to fill this role. In this sense, we might say that what Hegel calls objectivity, truth, and ethical life now appear in a "new order that envelops the entire space . . . a notion of right that encompasses all time within its ethical foundation."[46]

For instance, Hegel argues: The state, which is "but spirit, involving a reference to itself, which is negative and infinitely free, becomes an independent existence, which has incorporated the subsistent differences, and hence is exclusive. So constituted, the state has an individuality, which exists essentially as an individual, and in the sovereign is a real, direct individual."[47] This description of the state as a real, direct individual sounds more like our contemporary understanding of corporations, considered by the law to be persons. In this way, corporations can fill the place of universality once occupied by God and the state as they seek recognition in a fragmented postsecular world. In an essay on the theological genealogy of corporate personhood George Schmitt makes a similar point, albeit with a different metaphor. He writes, "Working beneath the 'too-big-to-fail' doctrine is a religiously nauseating ideology, which locates the corporation itself as, in the language of Paul Tillich, 'the ground-of-being.'"[48]

I do not mean to suggest that the universality of corporate sovereignty congeals into a new form of centralized power. New forms of sovereign power are decentralized and horizontal, expanding out in a network with no fixed center. Yet it is also important to see that this expansion is precipitated in and through empire's positive espousal of "justice" and "peace." Empire always acts in their name, in this appeal to a universal right. Through this appeal, empire creates an aporia around those very universal concepts by throwing "our ideas and practices of justice and our means of hope . . . into question." In this way, saying that the corporations are a new "universal" might be to misconstrue the nuances of empire. The point is not that a new Hegelian universal is created but rather that after the death of God and the rise of empire "the domesticicity of values, the shelters behind which they presented their moral substance, the limits that protect against the invading territory—all that disappears."[49] In other words, we might say that the loss of both the sovereignty of God and the sovereignty of the state entails the loss of sovereignty of the Kantian moral subject. For Hegel, the sovereignty of the nation-state—sovereignty as supremacy—dialectically grounded the sovereignty of the subject—sovereignty as autonomy. "Sovereignty, which is initially only the universal thought of this ideality, can *exist* only as a subjectivity which is certain of itself and as the will's abstract—and to that extent ungrounded—self-determination in which the ultimate decision is vested."[50] Sovereignty, in all three of its senses—as decision, as autonomy, and popular sovereignty—is only legitimate in and through a relation to a universal that has now vanished. After the death of God, corporations can come to replace the universal that has now vanished by answering the questions that empire creates, especially in its subjective and autonomous sense. In the spirit of resentment over a lost security, the new universal is sought and desired precisely in the absence of a given.

The problem is, of course, that corporations produce both the questions and the answers and, in extension, the very identities needed for their own recognition. As we have seen, Hegel asserts that God's death was a necessity for God's own fulfillment, and this is what required the very negation of God's self. Similarly, in *The Philosophy of World History*, Hegel correlates the moment of negation with the downfall of the state, which we have already shown shares a conceptual relationship to God. Hegel writes that the spirit "must and will succeed in its task; but this very success is also its downfall, and this in turn heralds the emergence of a new phase of a new spirit."[51] The negation of God and the state are necessary components for the universal's concrete and particular recognition by the other. If corporations are today functioning as a universal, they too will require recognition. The difference is that the need for negation has vanished. If the corporation requires recognition, it simply produces the subjects it needs for its own survival and sustenance through the mass cultural industry that produces subjects for every product through advertisements, communication networks, the production of language, the integration of power into modes of daily life, and various other means of biopolitical subjectivation. Hardt and Negri make the point succinctly: "It is a subject that produces its own image of authority. This is a form of legitimation that rests on nothing outside itself and is repurposed ceaselessly by developing its own language of self-validation."[52] Even if the corporation does point beyond itself—to ideals of beauty, freedom, whiteness, femininity, the family, etc.—it is producing those values in the same gesture.

## RESENTMENT

It is this interplay between pointing beyond and producing in the same gesture that is at the heart of Deleuze's critique of Hegelian dialectics, for such a structured mirroring can only lead to resentment. For William Connolly, subjective resentment is a predicament shared by everyone who seeks recognition, security, or certainty, after the death of God. Connolly saw early the way God continued to haunt the "secular" world, noting how "contemporary social theory contains within it the a set of secular reassurances that compensate for those lost through the death of God."[53] As Connolly notes, one of the primary reasons for resentment in the contemporary world is the "failure to confront the *globalization of contingency* that haunts late modernity."[54] This contingency—the loss of universal recognition—is brought about by a multiplicity of factors, though Connolly is clear that one of the main reasons for this contingency today is the decline of "modern conceptions of the state as [a] sovereign . . . self-sufficient, democratically accountable political entity with the efficacy to control collective destiny."[55] When reassurances—whether God or the state—become increasingly difficult to believe in, we cease to treat the future with an ethic of care, thus allowing a spirit of resentment to set in.

Resentment thus works back and forth on itself. On the one hand, there is a generalized sense of resentment that takes shape in culture, while the person within this culture experiences existential resentment that then bleeds out into the commons. "When people devalue the legacy the present bestows upon the future, they divest selectively from common life in the present."[56] The resentment created by the death of God and decline of state sovereignty work together to expand empire's reach. "Existential resentment, profound political humiliation, and persistent exploitation can work back and forth upon each other, generating powerful resonance machines of destruction."[57] This is precisely why the rise of global capitalism is coterminous with the return of religion, and especially why, in the United States, religion has been used to spread global capitalism. As Connolly explains, there is an "affinity of spirituality" between capitalist elites and evangelical Christians based on a "drive for revenge against differences and the weight the future imposes on the present."[58] The lack of care for the future and the existential pressures created by the daily interactions with people of different creeds, beliefs, and ethnicities work together "generating powerful resonance machines of destruction."[59] Once these allegiances are formed and the resonance machines take hold, they takes on an autonomous life of their own, creating a "spiritual disposition" that finds expressions in a variety of economic and consumptive practices. The actions and the alliances they form are necessary because the spiritual disposition of existential resentment is not normally confessed.

It is ease to point to the resentment experienced by market-driven capitalists and conservative religious practitioners. For Connolly they are examples that are meant to reveal the resentment that each and every one of us experiences today—even healthy atheists and good liberals. An example of this was the "Chick-fil-A same-sex marriage controversy" of the summer of 2012, brought about when the CFO of this corporation expressed Chick-fil-A's commitment to "family values." As the controversy unfolded, those on both sides of the debate expressed a vested subjective interest in the ethical stance of this corporation—and this besides the fact that many who protested the corporate anti-LBGTQ agenda are also likely to contest corporate personhood. The offense seemed to be the lack of recognition of an LBGTQ identity by the corporate apparatus. One piece of propaganda that circulated on Facebook is particularly telling. It is a picture of a heterosexual couple eating at Chick-fil-A in support of their "anti-gay" agenda. Under the picture there is a list of pro-gay marriage corporations that the couple likely frequents, such as Target, Best Buy, and Google. The punch line: A pro-gay marriage corporation produces the Coca-Cola they are drinking in the picture. The punch line grounds the ethical stance of the pro-LGBTQ activists in the absolute otherness of corporate entities.

The same game was played on the right. Indeed, the picture was taken on Chick-fil-A appreciation day. Organized by the Christian right pundit Mike Huckabee, this appreciation day set record sales for Chick-fil-A across the country. People waited in incredibly long lines in order to show their support for a corporation that represented their own values. One supporter put together a caravan that drove for more than two hours and waited in a "very, very long line" in order to "demonstrate their support for what they believe are very important values in our society."[60] Could it be that the religious underpinnings of "appreciation day" inadvertently expose the death of God?

Supporters might say that those values come from God, but after God's death, they find it necessary to have those values mirrored back to them by a chicken sandwich. (They *are* really good chicken sandwiches though.)

## WHAT TO DO?

> Specters of the common appear throughout capitalist society, even if in veiled and mystified forms.
>
> —HARDT AND NEGRI, *Commonwealth*

Nietzsche's battle with the state as the new idol, as a poisonous theological residue that fulfills our desire of God, has now become a battle with the corporation. His point, however, was never about a particular entity; the point was always that the death of God does not enact any real change. Humanity remains what it is—a reactive force that desires essentiality in and through some universal; God remains just what it is—the machine that produces these desires. By putting God to death, we dialectically reinscribe the new universal of Christ—"a God who is universal 'for all' and truly cosmopolitan."[61] The parallels between this universal "Christ" and the corporations of empire are almost terrifying. Christ: the second movement of the (religious) synthetic universal, placed on the throne when God the father dies as the consummation of God's world-saving promise. The corporation: the second movement of the (civic) synthetic universal, the guarantor of peace through trade and the promiser of stability and identity. In each case, there is a promise of a future reward, dictated by an incarnate God who regulates just what sort of reward you should desire, what sort of subject you are, and so on. The death of God offers us a cheap immanence, a dialectical immanence—the transcendent God who offered eternal salvation is now represented immanently, and salvation becomes tangible; it represents what Simon Critchley calls "metamorphosis of sacrilization," what Goodchild calls "a shift in piety," and what Sheldon Wolin calls "inverted totalitarianism."[62] Or as Deleuze put it: "The father dies, the son creates another god for us."[63]

So long as the death of God is conceptualized through Hegelian dialectics, it contains within its framework the potentiality for something ever more dangerous than the absolute Other that it proclaims to overcome. God may be dead, but God has found bodily resurrection in the corporate empire. We no longer gaze toward the sky and hope to find our reflection in the clouds. The top of the skyscraper is as far as we can look, and we see ourselves mirrored back in the glistening glass facade of the corporate edifice. Mammon might be the murderer of God, but today it is corporations who wield the power to make us—*somebody*.

For Deleuze, when we remain within the dialectic and the labor of the negative, the active question gets replaced by a reactive ontological one. Instead of asking, "What can I do with my own affirmation of power on the plane of immanence," one asks, "What am I in relation to this representation of power before me? Who can make me *somebody*?" The ontological question thus eradicates the possibility of true novelty inasmuch as political struggle becomes the struggle for recognition. The struggle itself affirms the validity of the big Other instead of seeing the virtual potency of the plane of immanence and the possibilities always present within any given political situation. Instead of making one's own difference an object of affirmation, the dialectic leads to a diminishment of the force of one's own difference through its desire to be recognized by the other. The dialectic "makes the existence of God depend on a synthesis; it synthesizes the idea of God with time, becoming, history, and man."[64] But why? Deleuze's answer is clear: It does this out of resentment, out of a desire to be something that it is not and the inability to affirm its own difference. Humans kill God so that they might become God without ever asking if the God they had projected was worth becoming like.[65]

Unlike Hegel and most death-of-God theologians who posit that God is dead in a purely speculative sense, Deleuze asserts that the death of God is "the dramatic proposition *par excellence*."[66] Because of this, Deleuze asks us to "mistrust" the death of God. As Nietzsche pointed out, "When Gods die, they always die many kinds of deaths." For Deleuze, the death of God offers us an impure immanence, a dialectical immanence that relies on transcendence of a singular event for its power. Deleuze thus contrasts Nietzsche with Hegel: "Nietzsche . . . does not make this death an event possessing meaning in-itself. The death of God has as many meanings as there are forces capable of seizing Christ and making him die."[67] By "mistrusting" the death of God, might we then be able to uncover the forces that made Christ die?

This is precisely why Deleuze prefers Jesus to Christ. For it is Jesus who forces us to ask the essential question: What can I do? Deleuze quotes Nietzsche to make his point. "This bearer of glad tidings died the way he lived, the way he *taught*—*not* 'to redeem humanity,' but instead to demonstrate how people need to live. His bequest to humanity was a *practice* . . . his conduct on the cross."[68] The point is not to uncover the singular meaning of God's death but to uncover the forces that made him die, forces that are historical and contemporary inasmuch as they repeat cycles of domination. In this light, we begin to see the death of Jesus not as a unique event with a meaning in itself. These same forces were active in the crucifixion of thousands upon thousands of people, all of whom, in some way or another, posed the same sort of threat to empire that Jesus may have and were used not so much to silence the dissenting voice as to assert the power of empire. Crucifixion will always be a dramatic display of power. Such events of oppression relate to the cross by being absolutely unrelated to it; far from announcing any meaning in itself, they announce the pluralism of the cross and the death of God. Resentment seems a natural affect within this contingency of oppression inasmuch as we realize that nothing can set it right. This resentment can be turned into an active force that embraces the flipping of the tables of corporate power like Jesus *did*, not dialectically, but literally and dramatically. Perhaps we do not yet know what a corporate body working for the common good can do.

## NOTES

1. Michael Hardt and Antonio Negri, *Commonwealth* (Cambridge, Mass.: Harvard University Press, 2009), 3.
2. Ibid., 5.
3. Ibid.
4. Michele Foucault, "Security, Territory, Population," in *Ethics: Subjectivity and Truth*, ed. Paul Rabinow (New York: Free Press, 1997), 81.
5. James Cone, *A Black Theology of Liberation: Twentieth Anniversary Edition* (Maryknoll, N.Y.: Orbis Books, 1986), 68.
6. Jeff Robbins, "Terror and the Postmodern Condition: Toward a Radical Political Theology," in *Religion and Violence in a New Political Theology*, ed. Clayton Crockett (Charlottesville: University of Virginia Press, 2006), 196.
7. G. W. F. Hegel, *Phenomenology of Spirit*, trans. A. V. Miller (Oxford: Oxford University Press, 1977), 752.
8. Gilles Deleuze, *Difference and Repetition*, trans. Paul Patton (New York: Columbia University Press, 1994), 133.
9. Hegel, *Phenomenology of Spirit*, 752.
10. G. W. F. Hegel, "Lectures on the Philosophy of Religion (1824)," in *G. W. F. Hegel: Theologian of the Spirit*, ed. Peter Hodgson (Minneapolis: Fortress Press, 2007), 236
11. Ibid., 242.
12. Friedrich Nietzsche, *The Gay Science*, trans. Walter Kaufmann (New York: Vintage Books, 1974), sec. 125.
13. Ibid., sec. 343.
14. Ibid.
15. Friedrich Nietzsche, *Human, All Too Human: A Book for Free Spirits*, trans. R. J. Hollingdale (Cambridge: Cambridge University Press, 1986), 106.
16. Nietzsche, *Gay Science*, sec. 125.
17. Phillip Goodchild, *Capitalism and Religion: The Price of Piety* (New York: Routledge, 2002), 27.
18. Ibid.
19. The flaw I see in Goodchild's argument is that he never pauses and asks: "for whom?" For what population? What is its race, ethnic, or class inflection? I nonetheless think his notion of God ceasing to be essential to our everyday lives—what I would call a lack of affect—is pertinent.

20. Goodchild, *Capitalism and Religion*, 29.
21. Ibid., 29
22. Ibid., 29
23. Ibid., 30
24. Ibid., 37.
25. Nietzsche, *Human, All Too Human*, 222.
26. Nietzsche, *Thus Spoke Zarathustra: A Book for All and None*, trans. Adrian Del Caro (Cambridge: Cambridge University Press, 2006), 34
27. Clayton Crockett, *Radical Political Theology: Religion and Politics after Liberalism* (New York: Columbia University Press, 2012), 45.
28. Ibid., 46.
29. Ibid.
30. Ibid.
31. G. W. F. Hegel, *Elements of the Philosophy of Right*, trans. H. B. Nisbet (Cambridge: Cambridge University Press, 1991), sec. 253.
32. Ibid., sec. 255.
33. Notwithstanding that what we know as a corporation today would not be recognizable by Hegel, Hegel helps me think about how corporations function *today*.
34. Hegel, *Philosophy of Right*, sec. 252.
35. A similar point is made by Michael Hardt and Antonio Negri in *Empire* (Cambridge, Mass.: Harvard University Press, 2000).
36. Hegel, *Philosophy of Right*, sec. 258.
37. Ibid.
38. Ibid., sec. 255.
39. For more on my critique of Žižek's death of God theology and his reading of Hegel, please see my essay "Admitting a Certain Fear of Žižek's Theology: A Modest Plea for a Deleuzian Reading of the Death of God" (unpublished paper). The paper can be accessed online at https://www.academia.edu/5793178/Admitting_a_Certain_Fear_of_Zizeks_Theology_A_Modest_Plea_for_a_Deluzian_Reading_of_the_Death_of_God.
40. Hegel, *Philosophy of Right*, 270.
41. Hardt and Negri, *Empire*, xii.
42. Michael Hardt and Antonio Negri, *Multitude* (New York: Penguin, 2007), 270.
43. Hardt and Negri, *Empire*, 308.
44. Ibid., 306.
45. Ibid., 307.
46. Ibid., 306.
47. Hegel, *Philosophy of Right*, sec. 191.
48. George Schmitt, "Climbing the *Scala Naturae*: The Theological Dimensions of Corporate Personhood," presented at "Personhood, Practice, and Transformation: Classical and Contemporary Perspectives," at McGill University Center for Research on Religion, October 2012.
49. Hardt and Negri, *Empire*, 279.
50. Hegel, *Philosophy of Right*, sec. 279.

51. G. W. F. Hegel, *Lectures on the Philosophy of World History*, trans. H. B. Nisbett (Cambridge: Cambridge University Press, 1975), 52.
52. Hardt and Negri, *Empire*, 33.
53. William E. Connolly, *Identity/Difference: Democratic Negotiations of Political Paradox* (Minneapolis: University of Minnesota Press, 1991), 16.
54. Ibid. 23.
55. Ibid., 24.
56. Ibid., 23.
57. Ibid., 121.
58. Ibid., 87.
59. Ibid., 121.
60. Amy Bingham, "Chick-fil-A Has Record Sales on Appreciation Day," *ABC News*, August 2, 2012, http://abcnews.go.com/Politics/OTUS/chick-fil-record-setting-sales-appreciation-day/story?id=16912978.
61. Gilles Deleuze, *Nietzsche and Philosophy*, trans. Hugh Tomlinson (New York: Columbia University Press, 2006), 153.
62. Simon Critchley, *Faith of the Faithless: Experiments in Political Theology* (New York: Verso, 2012); Sheldon S. Wolin, *Democracy Inc.: Managed Democracy and the Specter of Inverted Totalitarianism* (Princeton, N.J.: Princeton University Press, 2008); and Goodchild, *Price of Piety*.
63. Deleuze, *Nietzsche and Philosophy*, 153.
64. Ibid., 152.
65. We should say that this specific critique is directed more toward Feuerbach and the young Marx.
66. Deleuze, *Nietzsche and Philosophy*, 152.
67. Ibid., 156.
68. Friedrich Nietzsche, *The Anti-Christ*, trans. Judith Norman (Cambridge: Cambridge University Press, 2005), 33.

## Breaking from Within: The Dialectic of Labor and the Death of God

AN YOUNTAE

*Dialectics is the self-consciousness of the objective context of delusion; it does not mean to have escaped from that context. Its objective goal is to break out of the context from within. The strength required from the break grows in dialectics from the context of immanence.*
—THEODOR ADORNO, Negative Dialectics

The ancient Christian idea of labor is derived from the theopolitical imagery involving the first human being's break from the divine realm and his descent into the abyss of his own freedom. The ambiguous meaning of labor, however, rests in its double-sided nature. Although, on the one hand, the biblical account locates the first man's labor as punishment from God, it also views labor, as the inception of human beings' work of creation, the beginning of a new life, just as the first woman's punishment resulted in the birth of new lives. In this sense, the burden of labor in human life can also be viewed as the gift of creativity (creation). However, as the classic Marxist formulation claims, labor suffers deprivation of creativity under the current mode of capitalist production since capitalism creates value through an unequal system of measure, thus alienating human labor. It is Marx and Engels's famous charge that under the structure of capitalist production, the worker's labor is subjected to the control and appropriation of wage labor that is the basic condition of capital.[1] Wage labor bases itself on minimum wage, the basic requirement "to keep the labourer in bare existence as a labourer," and the capitalist division of labor, Marx and Engels argue, deprives "all individual character" in the labor of the proletarian worker.[2]

The global expansion of transnational capital is grounded in this unequal exchange of value in which the appropriation of labor enhances the global division of labor on the basis of race, gender, and class. What the global world, or better, the global South is witnessing today as the result is the reproduction of the colonial history of appropriation, injustice, and violence.[3] The question that arises, then, is: How can the emerging philosophical discourse of religion and political theology address the problem of injustice structuring the conditions of labor underlying the neocolonial expansion of capitalist globalization? If, as Joerg Rieger argues in this volume, the dominant conception of the common good fails to attend to the unjust conditions of labor in contemporary modes of production, how do we, as the explorers of religious, philosophical, and political thought, reconfigure the notion of the common good so that labor becomes the creative agent of the just articulation of material resources rather than the object of appropriation?

Perhaps Antonio Negri's reading of Job fleshes out the creative tension and potential lurking in the notion of labor. In *The Labor of Job*, Negri offers a creative reading of Job by drawing an analogy between the injustice of Job's suffering and the place of labor in contemporary capitalism.[4] Negri suggests that Job's suffering signifies the violation of measure, that no equation can justify his suffering. This parallels, for Negri, the failure of measure in the capitalist system of labor, as "surplus value" creates a gap between the value of commodity and the quantity of labor. He reads Job's confession of "seeing God" as Job's proclamation of the death of God, a revolutionary labor of standing indignant and rebellious before God. Labor then is redefined as the source of creative power that makes transformation possible. The dialectical framework structuring Negri's Marxist reading of Job, particularly his endeavor to reconsider labor as a creative potential for a revolutionary political theology, finds its roots in Hegel.

In the section "Lordship and Bondage" of *The Phenomenology of Spirit*, Hegel also calls labor a creative source, the medium through which the slave comes to self-definition. The dynamic between the lord and the bondsman, better known as Hegel's master-slave dialectic, is framed by the structure of a mutual recognition in which labor serves as a channel of transformation. It is through labor that the slave acquires his own self-consciousness and finally negates the object of his fear, namely, the master. Both Hegel and Negri's formulations of labor as the creative force become complicated, however, when we consider the global reality of labor as both a forced option and the symptom of appropriation. Marx denounces the "alienating" nature of labor, that is, how the capitalist mode of production alienates human lives and their labor since it is based on minimum wage and sustained by surplus value; most important, human labor itself is commodified and appropriated.[5] From this, the primary complication rests on the seemingly irremediable gap between the two poles that labor indicates, namely, forced labor and labor as creative power. More concretely, the ambiguity that both Hegel's and Negri's formulations posit points to the difficulty of locating the source of creative power and opposition within the all-pervading system of capitalism.

With the end of engaging these questions further, in the first part of this essay I seek to bring to light what I see as the ambiguous meaning of labor as forced option and creativity presented in the works of both Negri and Hegel. Having brought this tension to the surface, in the second part, my aim is to clarify and bridge the tension by engaging critical questions that both Marx and Frantz Fanon raise about the Hegelian dialectic. However, in spite of the multiply converging conversations and clarifications, I argue that a further step is necessary. Thus, in the third part of this essay, I turn to the Argentinian philosopher Enrique Dussel, whose reading of Hegel and Marx, and proposal of "living labor" sheds lights on the critique of labor that I am pursuing here as a move forward from Hegel's and Negri's work. It is not my intention, however, to provide the answer missing in both Hegel's and Negri's work. Rather, by engaging Dussel's notion of the "living labor," I attempt to locate or clarify the somewhat unclear philosophical link between the two different notions of labor in the Hegelian dialectic, which are, nonetheless, implicitly present in the work of both Hegel and Negri.

Certainly, Dussel also suggests labor as a creative source of life with his innovative identification of "living labor" in the Marxist system. For Dussel, living labor lies beyond the totalitarian system of capital because it is derived from "surplus value," that is, the labor that creates value without being founded in capital. By taking Dussel's proposal, I read labor in both Negri's and Hegel's works as an absolute alterity immanent (inherently imprinted) in the system. Whereas for Hegel, labor's exteriority parallels the place of "the other" as a rupture, an exteriority inherent in the structure of the self (and of the Absolute Spirit), for Negri, the exteriority of labor finds its ground in the exteriority of suffering that lies beyond the system of measure and equivalence. The political theology of labor proposed by Negri, Hegel, and Dussel suggests labor as the creative source of power for a revolutionary politics of transformation and liberation. As a reflected image of the absolute exteriority of "life" before the totalitarian system of capital, labor never ceases to transform itself by *creating* a new life, a new force out of its immanent alterity.

## LABOR, SUFFERING, AND THE FAILURE OF MEASURE

In his recently translated book, *The Labor of Job*, the Italian Marxist philosopher Antonio Negri proposes a radical political theology with the end of addressing the issue of labor from a Marxist-revolutionary standpoint. As Michael Hardt helpfully outlines in the foreword, the starting point of Negri's argument is the theory of measure and equivalence. The two poles—justice and economic value that sustain Negri's main analogy in the book are supported by the idea of measure and equivalence.⁶ Against the stream of mainline Marxism, Negri has been arguing for decades that the theory of measure, or the "labor theory of value," is in crisis. For Negri, Job is a figure who epitomizes the failure of measure since while his friends defend divine justice and its system of measure, Job argues that "the theory of measure has been violated: no equation can justify his suffering in terms of his actions."⁷

According to the Marxist labor theory of value, the value of commodity is proportional to the quantity of labor invested in the process of production. For Marx, the problem of capitalist production lies in the unjust fact that "labor is not paid the equivalent of the value it produces."⁸ The labor theory of value demonstrates how capitalism is based in a system of unequal exchange. Negri's sharp analysis cuts through the structural absurdities of capitalism, but his unique place among his contemporary Marxists rests on his resistance to the traditional socialist narrative, which aims at restoring the theories of measure and equivalence. Negri shows that not only the capitalist system of unequal exchange but also the socialist ideal of equivalence are perpetuated by the system of measure. The socialist ideal of equivalence, in which the socialist goal is translated into the perfect system of equal distribution, is for Negri a form of a rationalized capitalism. From this perspective, Job's suffering is not a violation of a certain system of measure that can be restored. Rather, it represents the experience of absolute pain, which finds no translation in rationalized language: The very idea of measure fails in the face of absolute suffering and injustice. Negri's analogy between Job's suffering and labor in contemporary capitalism rests on the absurdity of this unbearable pain that breaks the legitimized symmetry of measure. Thus Negri concludes that the incommensurability of suffering that both Job and the workers experience exceeds the terms of equivalence.

Negri reads the drama of Job's despair, frustration, and protest in chapters 9–13 of the book of Job as the prelude to Job's confrontation with God. In Negri's reading, Job's indignation against God is evidently defiant. Job's frustration does not remain as a merely passive form of despair, agony, or self-loathing. Rather, Job's distress is elevated to the level of a strong charge against the omnipotent One. God is accused of mocking and laughing at the tragic ordeal of the innocent. With this charge, Negri argues, Job reduces the divine judge to a mere adversary while raising himself up "as power standing before divine power."⁹ It is this powerful act of confronting and rebelling against the absolute power to which Negri urges his readers to turn. Negri contends further that Job knows no resignation. He persists in seeking a justice that cannot be accorded to him. If the indefinite intensity of Job's undeserved suffering parallels what the classic Marxist analysis calls the "forced labor" of capitalist production, standing rebellious before the absolute power amounts to the creative side of labor, that is, labor as *creation*. Negri then brings a unique and interesting perspective in his reading of chapter 42, namely the story of Job's epiphany. He refuses the conventional interpretation, which reads the story of epiphany as Job's finally seeing the image of the divine reflected in his own wretchedness. Instead, Negri reads Job's act of "seeing God" as his proclamation of the death of God. This reading parallels Negri's longtime analysis that the new mode of capitalist production—in which the center of gravity of production is moved to the outside of the factory—renders capital, or more specifically surplus value, an empty form of domination.[10] In other words, as labor becomes more autonomous in contemporary modes of production and, consequently, as the productive role of the capitalist declines, "The rule of capital becomes merely matter of power," that is, an empty power, an empty signifier.[11] Similarly, Job's labor of standing indignant before God and seeing God reveals the empty edifice of the divinized transcendent power. Job has now actually "seen" God: "Thus God is torn from the absolute transcendence that constitutes the idea of him. God justifies himself, thus God is dead."[12]

The double-sided nature of labor that Negri brings to our attention through the ancient biblical drama of Job is this: while forced labor or labor detached from creative power subjects human lives into a senseless instrumentality, the key to transformation and liberation lies, nonetheless, in the creative nature of labor, in the passion of *creating* and *constructing* a new world. Theologically, the human proclamation of the death of God not only brings an end to the idea of a transcendent deity and onto-theology, but also gives birth to a new conception of divinity: the divine in history, the divine within, the immanent-transcendent which acts in the power that opposes the domineering power.

### LABOR IN HEGEL'S "LORDSHIP AND BONDAGE"

The significance of labor also occupies a central role in the system of Hegel's dialectic, particularly as it is reflected in the *Phenomenology of Spirit*. The reason that Hegel's understanding of labor is not only relevant but also crucial for the current conversation is because Marx, from whom Negri derives his revolutionary account of Job's labor, formulates his dialectical materialism on the basis of the Hegelian dialectic.

One of the central characteristics that undergirds the Hegelian dialectic is the tension between the two opposites, particularly between the positive (or progress) and the negative. If, on the one hand, progress represents the commonly (mis)represented idea of a totalitarian and closed absolute in the Hegelian system, the negative, on the other hand, plunges the Hegelian subject or consciousness into loss, uncertainty, despair, and dispossession.

One of the most symbolic and the most widely discussed sections of the entire *Phenomenology* is perhaps "Lordship and Bondage." Commonly known as the master-slave dialectic, it is also well known for being the source of inspiration that sparked Marx's idea of class struggle. The master-slave dialectic illustrates the relation between the subject and its object, or rather, between the two subjects who are marked with a strong tension instigated by the dual desire to affirm one's self while negating the other. However, what holds this tension together is not the desire to erect an all-independent subjectivity but the desire for recognition. This is because self-consciousness, that is, the Hegelian subject who partakes in the dialectical journey of self-becoming, can become itself only by being acknowledged by the other.

The relation between the master and the slave illustrates well the basic dynamics running through the dialectic in which the self-consciousness is faced by another self-consciousness. This moment of encounter is characterized first by the loss of the self. Alexandre Kojève, one of the most important interpreters of Hegel in twentieth-century France, writes, "The man who contemplates is absorbed by what he contemplates."[13] Consequently, the subject who loses itself, "finds itself in an *other* being."[14] Thus, adds Kojève, "the knowing subject loses himself in the object that is known."[15] This action of self-consciousness, of suffering the rupture and seeing itself in the other, is not exclusively owned by the subject. Rather, it also belongs to the other. That is, the other who was an object turns out to be also a subject: a self-consciousness. However recognition conditions the tension between the two individual consciousnesses, achieving self-consciousness or self-becoming is a confrontational process, a life-and-death struggle in which "each seeks the death of the other."[16]

However, the confrontational dynamic between the master and the slave also shows that each consciousness is mediated with itself through another consciousness, something that lies outside of one's self, namely, recognition. The dual meaning behind the Hegelian recognition is, first, that the subject or consciousness loses itself in the other. The subject is dissolved in its encounter with both the outside world and "the other" as they reflect the inscrutable exteriority of the subject. As Judith Butler remarks, instead of consuming "the other," self-consciousness "is instead consumed by the other."[17] Second, the outside world or the other gains meaning and reality only in the subject. As Jean Hyppolite, another major Hegel interpreter of early twentieth-century France, comments, "The truth of that world now lies in me and not in it. . . . The world no longer subsists in-itself; it subsists only in relation to self-consciousness, which is its truth."[18] After losing itself in the other, consciousness discovers itself in the other. The only way you become yourself, what Hegel calls a self-consciousness, is by gaining recognition from the other.

From this, it follows that the master's certainty of being is only established through recognition from the slave. But what binds the slave's freedom to the master is labor. The master owns the labor of the slave and enjoys the fruits of the slave's labor without being involved in labor himself. However, there are two major predicaments that make the master's superior position worthless. First, in order to be satisfied, in order to be himself, the master needs to be recognized "from one whom he recognizes as worthy of recognizing him." But, the master is only master, only himself because he is recognized by the slave, someone whom he does not recognize as worthy of recognizing him. Therefore, the master's position, Kojève writes, is "an existential impasse."[19] Second, since the master does not engage in labor, he does not benefit from the creative and educative aspects of the labor. Throughout the *Phenomenology*, Hegel holds on to a positive view of labor. For Hegel, labor is the very catalyst and the medium through which the bondsman becomes conscious of himself. Therefore, it follows that while the master is fixed in his mastery without being able to change or make any progress beyond himself, the slave "has nothing fixed in him. He is ready for change; in his very being, he is change, transformation, education; he does not bind himself to what he is; he wants to transcend himself by negation of his given state."[20] What results from this is the inversion of the subject-object dynamic or master-slave relationship. Just as mastery turns into an impotent, fixed, and slavish identity, slavery rises up to an autonomous and transformative agent of history. All of this is possible because of labor, through which the slave transforms both himself and other material objects.[21]

In the meantime, however, the negative side of labor is also caught and addressed in the *Phenomenology*. In his early work written during the Jena period, *Realphilosophie*, a manuscript which, according to Sholomo Avineri, sets the scene for the *Phenomenology*, Hegel approaches labor from the perspective of an alienation created as a result of the instrumentalization of work. As has been pointed out by Georg Lukács and reasserted by Avineri, it is evident that Hegel was aware of the dehumanizing condition of the workers of his time.[22] In *Realphilosophie*, Hegel observes the process through which labor is abstracted by taking control and creative consciousness away from the worker.[23]

Certainly, there are moments in the master-slave dialectic where Hegel draws the distinction between the positive aspect and the negative side of labor even though such a distinction is ambiguous in its nature since these two seemingly opposing poles are intricately related to each other. Yet as Marx criticized, the *Phenomenology* illustrates only the positive side of labor. When the power asymmetry between the two subjects is presented, the command of power coming from the master and the following situation of forced labor serve as a critical catalyst that spurs the slave into the revolutionary journey toward self-consciousness. Hegel claims that the slave can come to self-consciousness only by the work that he performs in the service and fear of the master. This is because in forced labor, the worker labors in the service of the other, by which "he rids himself of his attachment to natural existence."[24] Without this fear and the threat of death, the slave would remain in his slavish consciousness, fixed to the natural, given world. He would seek a reform at most, instead of a revolutionary overthrowing of the world.[25] In this sense, the two negative elements of forced labor, that is fear and service, are deemed as necessary and formative activities.[26] Thus, Kojève adds, "the work that frees man is hence necessarily, in the beginning, the forced work of a slave who serves an all-powerful master, the holder of all real power."[27]

The double-sided nature of labor complicates the master-slave relationship even further with Kojève's observation that even after the slave frees himself thanks to the forced labor, "he in fact remains this slave."[28] He fights and gains self-consciousness in order to realize his true consciousness as a slave. Kojève writes, "Thus he frees himself, so to speak, only to be a Slave freely, to be still more a Slave than he was before having formed the *idea* of freedom."[29] However, this deficiency also creates a positive effect, for, as Kojève puts it, "he *is* not actually free, because he has an *idea* of Freedom, an idea that is *not* realized but that can be realized by the conscious work of transformation of given existence, by the active abolition of Slavery."[30] Therefore, the slave's idea of freedom is superior to the master's conception of freedom since the master's vision does not go beyond the given reality.

Hegel's understanding of labor in the master-slave dialectic leaves room for several important questions that arise from the complex position of labor within the contemporary system of capitalist production. More concretely, Hegel is unclear as to *how* the slave gains a critical consciousness and rises up before the powerful master in a situation conditioned by an utmost power asymmetry in which the absolute power has full control of the (labor of the) slave. How exactly does the slave manage to cultivate the creative force out of forced labor and break free from the command of the omnipresent power? The reality of workers under the unjust capitalist system of production, a system of unequal exchange as seen in Negri's Marxist argument, renders Hegel's view of labor far too optimistic. It is along this line that Marx's famous critique of Hegel stands. While Marx praises the Hegelian dialectic for grasping the positive nature of labor, he charges Hegel with seeing only the positive side of labor. The problem, in the young Marx's eyes, is that Hegel conceives nature in abstract terms.[31] Following Feuerbach who accused Hegel of inverting the activity of real human beings into "absolute spirit," Marx contends that Hegel reduces the human being and its activity to self-consciousness and spiritual labor.[32]

A more piercing charge comes, however, from the Martinican thinker and revolutionary Frantz Fanon. Fanon reads Hegel's master-slave dialectic from the standpoint of the colonial context in which the Hegelian logic of mutual recognition is expressed in a conflict between black and white. The colonial context makes the Hegelian trope of mutual recognition a romanticized idealism, since the master finds the slave laughable instead of seeking recognition from him.[33] Rather, the white master simply imposes labor on the black slave. All he expects from the slave is labor and servitude. Meanwhile, unlike the Hegelian slave who finds meaning and self-consciousness in work, Fanon's black slave finds no liberation in work.[34] The black slave does not succeed in objectifying the master, a vital step that leads to subjectivity in Hegelian dialectic, because he wants to be *like* the master. Instead of considering his own subjectivity first, the slave always has in mind the subjectivity of the master.[35] Unlike Hegel's slave who successfully transcends his reality through labor, "labor for Fanon's slave becomes bestial condition."[36] The existential impasse belongs to the black slave—rather than the master—who desires to be recognized as a subject and yet is never granted such recognition by the master. A contemporary voice of resonance comes from Judith Butler who, similarly, identifies the problem of (un)recognition in Hegel by pointing out how the linkage between desire and recognition within the Hegelian tradition misses the crucial problem, namely the failure of recognition or "unrecognition." The central place that recognition occupies in Hegelian thinking and the following assertion that all desire is a desire for recognition, Butler points out, fails to grasp the reality of many lives that are not recognized by the prevailing social norm.[37]

Both Marx's and Fanon's critical insights on labor and the master-slave relation take us to the critical examination of the gap that lies between forced labor and creative labor in Hegel and Negri. As I discussed above, for both Hegel and Negri, labor is the human being's power to create his or her own world. In both of their accounts, rising up against the fearful presence of the master entails that the oppressed take the risk of death and break free from the situation of forced labor. Again, on what basis does the transition from forced labor to creative labor take place in the context of oppression where the slave's "whole being has been seized with dread"[38] and where his whole creative power and body is subject to the lord's fetishistic command?[39] Certainly, Kojève's insight that when the slave repeats his act of labor "he repeats it in different conditions, and his act itself will be different,"[40] is far from satisfying when we remember that it is precisely the repetition of simple labor instigated by both the advancement of technology and the division of labor that intensifies the poor working condition of the workers even further.[41] Nonetheless, Kojève does point out that the process of education and transformation by labor through which the worker surmounts the terror of death and finally opposes the master "is long and painful."[42] It is the description of this long and painful process, I argue, that is largely missing in Hegel's and Negri's narratives. Indeed, Negri is right when he argues that the pain of the ones suffering from injustice is incommensurable and insurmountable. Likewise, Hegel offers a detailed account of the pain and the fear that the slave undergoes before the frightening command of the mighty master.

> For this consciousness has been fearful, not of this or that particular thing or just at odd moments, but its whole being has been seized with dread; for it has experienced the fear of death, the absolute Lord. In that experience it has been quite unmanned, has trembled in every fibre of its being, and everything solid and stable has been shaken to its foundation.[43]

Hegel's existential drama of suffering and painful agony finds resonance in Fanon's phenomenological reflection in *Black Skin, White Masks*: a poignant description of the lived experience of the black body in a white world. It is an experience that Fanon describes as "being an object in the midst of other objects," a crushed subject who is rather reduced to a nonbeing, a sense of nonexistence;[44] a fractured subject who cries for recognition, yet denied, fixed under the white gaze, and "hated, despised, detested, not by the neighbor across the street . . . but by an entire race."[45] It is this experience of insurmountable pain beyond measure that makes Fanon turn away from the romantic idea of recognition, for he finds no signs of alterity lurking in the atrocious dynamic between the master and the slave. Fanon denies, basically, any condition of alterity or exteriority within the given reality. In contrast, both Hegel and Negri find in labor the creative power to create one's own world: The slave all of a sudden breaks from what seemed to be an all-powerful and endless cycle of bondage by rebelling against the master. Despite his accentuated emphasis on the disruptive power of negativity and self-reflection, Hegel, ironically, skips or glosses over the painful process of regressing into the dark depth of the negative, the night of the abyss lurking at the bottom surface of the dialectical self-reflection. As Butler comments, following Kierkegaard, the infinitely self-replenishing subject of the Hegelian dialectic does not seem wholly engulfed by the negative: "No matter how many times his world dissolves, he remains infinitely capable of reassembling another world."[46] She further raises the insightful question as to how often "suffering simply erode[s] whatever ground there is," instead of prompting "the reconstruction of a world on yet firmer ground."[47]

The magical resilience or leap that Hegel's slave takes needs to be somehow situated upon a solid logical base within the system of Hegelian thought.

Where then in Hegel's philosophy can we locate the theoretical base for such a moment of creative movement? That this important theoretical connection remains somewhat obscure in Hegel makes it unsurprising for us to see the same ambiguity in Negri as his revolutionary account is framed by Hegel's dialectic.

## THE LIVING LABOR

The Argentinian Mexican philosopher of liberation Enrique Dussel also reads labor as the creative source of transformation. In his commentary on Marx's *Economic Manuscripts of 1861–1863*, Dussel proposes the notion of "living labor" as the source of alterity that lies before and beyond the totalitarian rule of capital. The initial inspiration for Dussel's creative reading of Marx comes from Schelling, who suggests the notion of a beginning before the beginning. Schelling, who, prior to Hegel, posited the idea of Being as a dynamic and dialectical process of becoming, presents the idea of an a priori of Being, which indicates that which precedes Being. It could also be called "nothing" since it lies before "something." At the same time, the nothing before something is also the creative source preceding Being, since the something, in order to become itself, needs to negate the nothing, the exteriority lying in and before itself.[48] Dussel then moves to the Marxist notion of the production or creation of value. Value, in the philosophical or Hegelian terms, can be translated as the foundation of capital, or, in other words, the Being of capital. From the worker's standpoint, the production of value is also the reproduction of "the value of salary in the necessary time," which also amounts to the notion of measure. This means that the production of value cannot be separated from the notion of measure. The problem arises with surplus value, an innovative discovery of Marx's, which indicates the extra value existing between the price invested in the production of the good and the final exchange value. Simply put, the basis of surplus value is the un(der)compensated human labor force, which, consequently, enables the exploitation of workers and provides the ground for capital accumulation. The capitalist system of production and its (re)creation of value is based on this inequivalence of measure. However, Dussel argues that from a different viewpoint this could also mean that in surplus labor the worker creates value from nothingness or from the outside of capital because the worker is not creating from the value foundation (capital). It is in this vein that Marx defines "creation of value" as the creation of a product without being founded in capital. In Marx's words, this is called "living labor" which means the nonobjectified labor, the "not-capital, not-objectified labour."[49]

From what, then, does value derive? As I have mentioned already, the primary source of value production is human labor. However, Dussel claims, although human labor is the constant object of appropriation and exploitation, at the same time, Marx views it as the living site of alterity, a "living labor." He quotes Marx: "The worker . . . has the possibility of beginning it again from the beginning, because his life is the source in which his own use value constantly confronts capital again in order to begin the same exchange anew."[50] By making reference to Schelling's idea of nothing or otherness prior to Being, Dussel posits living labor as the a priori of capital, as the exteriority coming before the totalizing system of capital. Therefore, Marx claims that in what appears to be the totality of capital and in the exploitative structure of surplus labor, the worker does not reproduce. Rather, the worker's labor is an act of a new creation. Against the traditional reading of Marx, Dussel argues that Marx points to the exteriority of capital, rather than its totality. Likewise, the starting point of Marx is the "outside" of the seemingly all-enclosing totality of capital.

To recapitulate and clarify the logical moves that Dussel makes, Dussel does draw a clear demarcation between forced labor and labor as the source of creative power. The former is objectified labor, a labor possessed, consumed, controlled, and exploited by capital whereas the latter is the creative source, the agent and the creator of value, which points to the exterior or anterior of capital. The line that divides these two is certainly ambiguous, and this blurred division begins to mark signs of reversal or subversion as capital reveals the ontological cracks of its very own ground.

Capital contains its opposite, its otherness, within itself. Its apparent totality unveils its own limitation because its actual reality is achieved only by the exteriority lying in its inner structure, since capital is unable to produce value without living labor. As Dussel has demonstrated, capital can buy "labor capacity" but not labor as living labor, in its corporeality, which exceeds the terms of value and measure.

> The price of the labour capacity in the wages, covers an essential fallacy: it is thought that the value of labour is paid when in reality only the value of the labour capacity is paid. The "labor capacity" has value because the corporeality of the labourer has assumed, consumed and incorporated commodities (means of subsistence) which have value. . . . In a certain way, as the incorporation of wages, the "labor capacity" is now the fruit of objectified labour also—and thus it shall be commensurable, interchangeable, sellable for money: both shall be objectified, past labour. But "living labour" shall never have value; thus, its non-value could not be determined; it shall not have a price nor shall it be able to receive wages . . . because it is the "creating source of value."[51]

The gap between forced labor and creative labor parallels this a priori exteriority or immanent alterity. It reveals that the nonbeing, the opposite, is an integral part of being and reality. Reality is shaped and structured by this disquieting contradiction. Dussel's insight is perhaps a reminder that the Hegelian dialectic is structured by the principle of paradox in which the binaries of subject-object and interiority-exteriority no longer subsist. As I discussed earlier, the foundational edifice of the Hegelian dialectic is structured around the modality of recognition. The Hegelian subject, in its immediate essence, is incomplete and opaque to itself since a part of its essence remains ungraspable and external to itself. The Hegelian subject, therefore, is conditioned by a certain sense of finitude, impossibility, and loss: An inscrutable exteriority structures its ontological edifice.

As a consequence, the reversal of the interior/exterior binary is constantly at play in Hegel's system as the exterior arises from the interior, and the exterior shapes the interior at the same time. Contradiction or opposition is therefore an intrinsic structure of self-consciousness. As Hyppolite comments on the role of "force" in consciousness' dialectical movement, "in order to exist as force driven back on itself, reflected back on itself, an other must approach and call for it to turn in upon itself."[52] What lies in the interior is actualized only when it is evoked by what lies outside. At the same time, it is only in the immanent reality where alterity is found: "The inverted world, therefore, is not to be sought in *another* world. It is present in this world, which is simultaneously itself."[53] The crucial significance of the Hegelian dialectic lies in the fact that it invokes the power of transformation not by resorting to a transcendent synthesis. Rather, dialectical transcendence emerges out of the traces of exteriority immanent in the reality of the subject/consciousness.[54] It indicates the discovery of what was previously unrevealed, "the dramatic moment where the hidden is made manifest."[55] Perhaps Slavoj Žižek provides one of the most lucid explanations regarding this point, as he insists that the movement of synthesis in the Hegelian dialectic, namely the "negation of negation," is, in a sense, a change of perspective or "parallax shift," which turns failure into the condition of possibility.[56]

Therefore, we could go back to the master-slave dialectic and read the slave's self-discovery as the moment of discovering the trace of alterity imprinted in the fabric of his own finite reality, rather than viewing it as the appearance of a (new) reality from nothing. The slave recognizes the emergence of a reality that was previously obscure, implicit, yet not without reality. More important, however, this indicates that despite Marx's and Fanon's admonitions, there is an essential part of reality that eludes the full grasp of the totality of capital (the master) and forced labor: the common good that is shared by all which cannot be fully appropriated or possessed, namely, labor as the source of creative power or, as Dussel calls it, "living labor." The discovery of the implicit reality, however, is not indicative of a serendipitous encounter. Rather, such discovery is the result of what Hegel calls the "negation of negation." Before the denial of mutual recognition by the master, the slave rejects (and therefore negates) the perpetuation of the reality of loss and death. It signifies the rejection of defeat as a permanent state of being by transforming it into a new possibility.

Perhaps we could draw further insights from Fanon on the question of the dialectical self-creation of the slave to strengthen Dussel's critique. If we agree with Nigel Gibson, who contends that Fanon's political thought is essentially dialectical, we could also follow his reflection on the conditions that make possible the break from the cycle of oppression for Fanon's slave. In his reading of Fanon, Gibson also articulates several important questions regarding the failure of recognition in Hegel, a state where, in Gibson's parlance, "the dialectic becomes motionless," in which "there is dread but no beginning through labor."[57] He then raises a similar question to the one I am asking in this essay, that is, regarding the possibility of the black slave's escaping the circle of subjection. The clue, for Gibson, lies in the constructive political ideas that Fanon suggests in his last book, *The Wretched of the Earth*. Whereas the somewhat pessimistic account in *Black Skin, White Masks* does not leave us with an answer or hope regarding the slave's impasse, in his later work, Fanon goes on to advance a program of decolonial resistance deeply rooted in a firmly self-determined black consciousness. From this, Gibson suggests that Fanon turns to a radical self-reflection, a regress into his self-consciousness, which results in the birth of a newly acquired sense of self-determination, namely black consciousness. Since mutual recognition is denied by the other encountered in the external world, Fanon turns to the otherness *within*. It is only the powerful act of retreating to the painful wound of one's own that leads one to a possible reconstruction of the shattered self. As Gibson observes, if the master-slave dialectic ruptures dialectic, thus leading us to a Manichaean worldview, "consciousness is, in fact, forced back into self-certainty and the dialectic reappears in Black consciousness which becomes a basis for a new cognition."[58]

The dialectical journey toward the truth, self-discovery, and self-creation is a self-lacerating process that entails the dissolution of the self, the acceptance of its total loss, and the emergence of a new subject whose reality includes the nonreal, the opposite, *the other*. The labor of truth-finding through radical self-reflection can be perhaps described as an experience of groundlessness. As Jean-Luc Nancy suggests, the whole process of the Hegelian passage into the journey of the subject's becoming itself can be seen as an experience of the abyssal depth, the unfathomable groundlessness. This ground, Nancy writes, "founds only to the extent that it sinks in itself."[59] The abyss, in its original,

Neoplatonic sense, symbolizes the unsearchable indeterminacy at the heart of being. Meanwhile, this indeterminacy also signifies the very act of crossing or "passage" from determinacy to indeterminacy and then to a renewed form of determinacy again: an act of transformation and construction that entails both *de*-construction and *re*-construction. In other words, sinking into the abyssal depth of the self opens the door for the transformation of finitude into the ground of new possibility. In this sense, we can conclude that it is only the retreat to the self that allows Fanon's slave to discover the indestructible source of alterity immanent in his being.

Meanwhile, we can see how Dussel's reading of Hegel as the champion of a totalitarian ontology is, in a way, a misplaced accusation. Dussel's criticism of Hegel is, to a certain extent, legitimate as he bases his critique on Hegel's Eurocentric conception of world history and geopolitical imaginary in which he excludes Africa from the development of Spirit in world history. However, it is important to note that Hegel's highly problematic view of history betrays his own fundamental principle that structures his entire philosophical vision. Indeed, contrary to Dussel's charge, Hegel presents precisely the same point that Dussel is making. Dussel's claim that metaphysics (the affirmation of the reality of nonbeing) transcends ontology (the mere affirmation of being) finds a striking resonance in Hegel: "The ethical consciousness must, on the account of this actuality and on account of its deed, *acknowledge its opposite as its own actuality.*"[60]

Although Dussel's creative insight sheds light on identifying the trace of immanent alterity in Hegel, his following analysis undermines, ironically, his own framework/principle of openness as he presses the notion of transcendence perhaps too hard. In emphasizing the exteriority of living labor, Dussel renders living labor an all-transcending absolute category by naming it a "transcendental critique," thus undermining the link between interiority and exteriority or immanence and transcendence.[61] Therefore, in order to loosen up the absolutist nature of Dusselian transcendence, I suggest that we read Dussel back through the Hegelian lens or the Fanonian mode of radical self-reflection. The dialectic movement at work in both Hegel and Fanon signals the emergence of alterity from *within*.

Meanwhile, Negri's reading of Job is also anchored in a similar structure of immanent exteriority/alterity as Negri bases the exteriority of labor on the exteriority of suffering, which lies beyond the system of measure and equivalence. Nevertheless, Negri's notion of pain and suffering does not amount to a metaphysical abstraction. Rather, it is through the experience of corporeal pain that Job is led to the questions of ethics and thus to the definition of truth.[62] Likewise, Negri argues, Job's resistance was through the body: a bodily struggle.[63] In resonance with Hegel and Dussel, the radical alterity of incommensurable otherness (suffering) in Negri finds its ground, paradoxically, in the most immanent level of material experience. What appears to be an all-encompassing power of oppression (capital) reveals its crack as the imposed pain on the body reveals itself to be the very site of absolute alterity. Therefore, for Job too, pain is the source of radical self-reflection and new beginning: "Being in pain is the thrust toward the resurrection of life; it is the prophecy of the resurrection of bodies."[64]

As I clarified already, what I have attempted to do in this chapter is not to provide the missing answer in both Hegel and Negri's works. Both of their works—and more so Hegel's work—already bear the answer to the critical questions I raised earlier. However, this answer or connection remains somewhat unclear in their works, particularly, in the master-slave dialectic as it leaves the hints to this inquiry obscure. Reading Hegel's and Negri's dialectic of labor through Dussel (and with the help of Fanon) helps clarify the implicit traces of immanent exteriority in their thought and thus makes the envisioning of a dialectic of recognition, confrontation, and creative transformation a viable project. What appeared to be the opposite, "the other" turns out to be a constitutive part of the reality, as an "always already there," thus marking the crack of the ontological edifice. This opening indicates the irreversible gap between both the subject and the object *and* within the subject itself as the other remains outside the grasp of appropriation. At the same time, this signifies that an inscrutable otherness is harbored in the immanent and seemingly coherent structure of the subject. Therefore, it points to the dissolution or failure of totality, failure of subjectivity, and the failure of (the all-transcendent) God. The divine epiphany experienced by Job does not take place simply as an abrupt rupture irrupting from a sheer exteriority. Rather, it is by the *labor* of discovering alterity in the immanent reality, "the revelation of the divinity within history," that Job comes to a new definition of divinity as the creative, transformational power of opposition and resistance.[65]

The death of God proclaimed by the creative labor (living labor), as Negri suggests, does not only hint at the denunciation of the system of absolute injustice or the collapse of metaphysical foundations (ontotheology). Rather, it indicates that the transformation of forced labor into creative labor takes place only through the journey of one's struggle for freedom, that is, through the labor of self-reflection in which he or she comes to discover the sources of exteriority immanent in reality. This process requires what Kojève called the "long and painful" journey of transformation, a crucial bridge leading to the potential answer to my critical questions, which is absent in the master-slave dialectic. Nevertheless, Hegel remarks elsewhere in the *Phenomenology* that the road to the dialectical transformation is a "way of despair" marked with the "loss of its own self" and of its truth.[66] This is why Spirit wins its truth only when it finds itself in *"utter dismemberment."*[67] If recognition and freedom are denied by the master or the capitalist system of production, perhaps we could suggest that there exists another kind of common good for the dispossessed which lies beyond the measures of appropriation: the shared experience of suffering out of which a renewed and self-determined consciousness or subject might emerge. The revolutionary labor of proclaiming the death of the ontotheological deity and the totalitarian system of domination begins with the grief born out of this suffering: grief for the reality of the dispossessed whose lives resemble an incomplete death, grief for the death of God, and for the death of both the self and his or her world. Yet in it, in this dark night of the abyss, in the constant oscillation between grief and hope, we glimpse the alterity within, the possibility of the resurrection of the divine within our flesh and history. Certainly, walking through the abyss of the death of God is a solitary journey; yet we find in it ties of solidarity with the immeasurable suffering and the cries of many nameless others.

## NOTES

1. Karl Marx and Friedrich Engels, "The Communist Manifesto," in *The Marx-Engels Reader*, ed. Robert Tucker (New York: W. W. Norton, 1978), 483.
2. Ibid., 479, 483.
3. In his groundbreaking essay "Coloniality of Power, Eurocentrism, and Latin America," Anibal Quijano demonstrates how race was invented as the tool of domination by the colonial ideology. Quijano argues that race, as a category of social classification, was used in order to justify the colonial relationship in which the system of forced labor was legitimized. See Mabel Moraña, Enrique Dussel, and Carlos A. Jáuregui, "Colonialism and Its Replicants," in *Coloniality at Large: Latin America and the Postcolonial Debate*, ed. Mabel Moraña, Enrique Dussel, and Carlos A. Jáuregui (Durham, N.C.: Duke University Press, 2008), 9; Anibal Quijano, "Colonialidad del Poder y Clasificación Social." *El Giro Decolonial: Reflexiones Para Una Diversidad Epiestémica Más Allá del Capitalismo Global*. Santiago Castro-Gomez and Ramon Grosfoguel, eds. Bogota: Siglo del Hombre Editores, 2007.
4. Antonio Negri, *The Labor of Job: The Biblical Text as a Parable of Human Labor*, trans Matteo Mandarini (Durham, N.C.: Duke University Press, 2009).
5. Karl Marx and Friedrich Engels, *The Communist Manfesto* (London: Penguin Books, 2002), 227.
6. Negri, *Labor of Job*, xi.
7. Ibid.
8. Ibid., 10.
9. Ibid., 43.
10. Ibid., xiv.
11. Ibid.
12. Ibid., 96.

13. Alexandre Kojève, *Introduction to the Reading of Hegel: Lectures on the Phenomenology of Spirit* (Ithaca, N.Y.: Cornell University Press, 1980).
14. G. W. F. Hegel, *Phenomenology of Spirit*, trans. A. V. Miller (Oxford: Clarendon Press, 1977), 111.
15. Kojève, *Introduction to the Reading of Hegel*, 3.
16. According to Kojève's commentary, the desire of recognition, which forms the I, is an emptiness that receives a real positive content only by negating action that satisfies desire in destroying, transforming, and assimilating the desired non-I. See Hegel, *Phenomenology of Spirit*, 113; Kojève, *Introduction to the Reading of Hegel*, 4.
17. Judith Butler, *Subjects of Desire: Hegelian Reflections in Twentieth-Century France* (New York: Columbia University Press, 1987), 48.
18. Jean Hyppolite, *Genesis and Structure of Hegel's Phenomenology of Spirit* (Evanston, Ill.: Northwestern University Press, 1974), 158.
19. Kojève, *Introduction to the Reading of Hegel*, 19, 46.
20. Ibid., 22.
21. Ibid., 25.
22. Georg Lukács, "Hegel's Economics during the Jena Period," in *Hegel's Dialectic of Desire and Recognition: Texts and Commentary*, ed. John O'Neill (Albany: State University of New York Press, 1996), 111–12; Shlomo Avineri, "Labor, Alienation, and Social Classes in Hegel's *Realphilosophie*," in *Hegel's Dialectic of Desire and Recognition*, ed. O'Neill, 195.
23. Avineri, "Labor, Alienation, and Social Classes," 194–201.
24. Hegel, *Phenomenology of Spirit*, 117.
25. Kojève, *Introduction to the Reading of Hegel*, 29.
26. Hegel, *Phenomenology of Spirit*, 119.
27. Kojève, *Introduction to the Reading of Hegel*, 27.
28. Ibid., 49.
29. Ibid.
30. Ibid., 49–50.
31. Karl Marx, "Critique of Hegel," in *Hegel's Dialectic of Desire and Recognition*, ed. O'Neill, 39.
32. Christopher Arthur, *Dialectics of Labour: Marx and his Relation to Hegel* (Oxford: Basil Blackwell, 1986), chap. 4.
33. Frantz Fanon, *Black Skin, White Masks*, trans. Charles Lam Markmann (New York: Grove Press, 1968), 220.
34. Charles Villet, "Hegel and Fanon on the Question of Mutual Recognition: A Comparative Analysis," *Journal of Pan African Studies* 4, no. 7 (2011): 44.
35. Ibid.
36. Lou Turner, "On the Difference between the Hegelian and Fanonian Dialectic of Lordship and Bondage," in *Fanon: A Critical Reader*, ed. Lewis Gordon, T. Denean Sharpley-Whiting, and Renee White (Malden, Mass.: Blackwell, 1996), 147.
37. Judith Butler, *Undoing Gender* (New York: Routledge, 2004), 2–3.
38. Hegel, *Phenomenology of Spirit*, 117.

39. As Butler comments on the bodily dimension lying around the desire between the Lord and the slave, the slave is required "to be the body that he [the Lord] endeavors not to be." See Butler, *Subjects of Desire*, 53.
40. Kojève, *Introduction to the Reading of Hegel*, 51.
41. Lukács, "Hegel's Economics during the Jena Period," 111–12.
42. Kojève, *Introduction to the Reading of Hegel*, 53.
43. Hegel, *Phenomenology of Spirit*, 117.
44. Fanon, *Black Skin, White Masks*, 109.
45. Ibid., 118.
46. Butler, *Subjects of Desire*, 22.
47. Ibid.
48. Enrique Dussel, *Towards an Unknown Marx: A Commentary on the Manuscripts of 1861–63*, trans. Yolanda Angulo (London: Routledge, 2001), xvii. Schelling's idea finds its origin in the seventeenth-century mystic Jakob Böhme, who first suggested the notion of the a priori of Being in which God becomes God by negating the nothing or otherness lying before itself.
49. Marx, *Grundrisse* (New York: Penguin Books, 1973) 277, 288; Dussel, *Towards an Unknown Marx*, 7.
50. Marx, *Grundrisse*, 283.
51. Ibid., 10–11.
52. Hyppolite, *Genesis and Structure*, 124.
53. Ibid., 138. Emphasis mine.
54. Ibid.
55. Robert Williams, *Recognition: Hegel and Fichte on the Other* (Albany: State University of New York Press, 1992), 201.
56. Slavoj Žižek, *The Sublime Object of Ideology* (London: Verso, 1989), 199; Slavoj Žižek, *The Parallax View* (Cambridge, Mass.: MIT Press, 2009), 27.
57. Nigel Gibson, *Fanon: The Postcolonial Imagination* (Cambridge: Polity, 2003), 33, 36.
58. Ibid., 40.
59. Jean-Luc Nancy, *Hegel: The Restlessness of the Negative*, trans. Jason Smith and Steven Miller (Minneapolis: University of Minnesota Press, 2002), 15.
60. Hegel, *Phenomenology of Spirit*, 284.
61. See Dussel, *Towards an Unknown Marx*, 7; Dussel, "Eurocentrism and Modernity (Introduction to the Frankfurt Lectures)," *boundary 2* 20, no 3 (1993):76.
62. Negri, *Labor of Job*, xxi.
63. Ibid., xx.
64. Ibid., 86.
65. Ibid., 97.
66. Hegel, *Phenomenology of Spirit*, 49.
67. Ibid., 19.

# ❧ Thoreau Goes to Ghana: On the Wild and the Tingane

ANATOLI IGNATOV

A pile of stones marks the abode of Thoreau, who sought refuge from a society that dulls, commodifies, and domesticates. Today, the urge to build a hut in the woods and simplify our lives—to front "only the essential facts of life" and the Wild that enchants and lures us into communion with Nature—remains strong.[1] The shrine memorializes a way of living that revealed that there is more to "Economy"—the opening chapter of *Walden*—than markets and humans. The stones have become totems of the various conservationist, back-to-nature, anti-industry, nonconformist, voluntary simplicity, do-it-yourself, and homesteading communities who continue to act on Thoreau's intuitions.

A pile of stones also marks the *tingane*, the abode of the Earth gods of the Gurensi people of Northern Ghana.[2] Gurensiland is mapped out into a network of *tingana* (plural)—sacred groves, rocks, rivers, caves, grasslands—in which the spirits of the ancestors live with the clan or the village. Other trees, rivers, and rocks mark the boundary from tingane to tingane. Seasonal sacrifices are performed to each tingane by indigenous clans presided over by the *tindaana* (earth priest). The tindaana mediates between the Earth gods, the ancestors and the community. He wears animal skins and a black twined cap or a calabash as the insignia of his office of the custodian of the land (*tiŋa*). He allocates land for settlement, building, farming, animal rearing, market- and graveyard-siting, and various development projects. The tingane is propitiated by the tindaana's offerings of millet flour, local beer (*daamolega*), and animals. It is on the pile of stones that the blood of the fowls and animals is poured and the feathers of the fowls placed. The tingane, in turn, assists the community with good harvests, fertility, and procreation, warding off droughts and diseases. Most tingana are both habitats for the community spirits and for the various medicinal plants and trees, birds' nests, bats, larger reptiles and mammals, and reservoirs of water. As the stones demarcate tiŋa as a sacred enclosure, they trouble demarcations between subject and object, nature and culture, living and nonliving. Some stones become deceased humans; others are border-crossing signs. Humans are the extended kin and family of tiŋa, who manifests her presence in stones.

What happens if Thoreau goes to Ghana? What happens if we read *Walden* on nature and economy after talking to a Gurensi earth priest? This essay stages encounters between Thoreau's Wild and the Gurensi tingane. The goal is to explore an ethic of living well within the earth's capacities through a set of experimental tactics that enrich sensation and help recraft anthropocentric sensibilities. Nietzsche describes such tactics of self-artistry as "self-overcoming," Foucault as "arts of existence."[3] I will use these ideas to explore how political responses to the ecological crisis shift once we take seriously the powers of earthly forces to shape our identities. This would expand on recent trends in political theory—such as Bennett's "New Materialism"—which challenge understandings of politics as an exclusively human domain by rethinking political contestation as including influences from nonhuman bodies.[4]

Both Thoreau and the Gurensi earth priest engage in human-nonhuman assemblage-making at the crossroads of market and community economies. Both prompt us to reexperience economy as an assemblage that distributes multiple degrees of agency and creativity along a continuum of human and more-than-human bodies and forces. Such cross-cultural encounters might help us reconnect what we now see as distinct spheres of the "economic," the "ecological," and the "spiritual." They might make visible politico-economic relations as ecological relations; ecological relations as kinship relations, intertwining humans, other species, gods, and the earth (tiŋa). More than asking whether Thoreau's ideas about economy and distributed agency can be transferred to different ethical and geographical contexts, I seek to highlight what productive engagements are possible at the point where such ideas are no longer transferable and the limits of concepts such as agency, economy, and subjectivity become evident.

There is another reason to take political theory to "the field": to explore the contribution of ethnography to political theory and in particular to the recent new materialist explorations. Ethnography reveals the limits of political theory's heavy reliance on textual analysis, a commitment that blocks our ability to explore the ways in which philosophy intersects with everyday life. Political theory and ethnography could strengthen each other: If a fine-tuned ethnography can uncover the subtle workings of everyday life and their entwinement with questions of the earth's agency, political theory can help develop the conceptual specificity of those dynamics. As an ethnographer, I became a participant in a privileged experience that sensitized me to the ways in which Gurensi tindaanas, chiefs, and elders body forth and interact with a lively earth that, in turn, interacts with and nurtures them. As a theorist, I came to appreciate the worth of such lived experiences of "ourselves" in which I was bestowed new lifeworlds and identities, and which as such harbor disquieting newness.[5] Ethnography allows me to show that the ethical practices described by the New Materialist or Thoreau are already approximated and lived elsewhere by large numbers of people.

Such a conversation might not only deepen Western ecopolitical imaginaries but also enrich the practice of theory as such. Thoreau relies on abstract conceptual distinctions such as nature/culture, subject/object, and domesticated/wild to perform an economy of simple living, which intertwines natural processes with social practices of ethical subject formation. The Gurensi people, in contrast, invite us to partake in a multiplicity of lived experiences that continually escape the order imposed by Western philosophical categories on such multiplicities. The earth priest theorizes as he locates spiritual power in stones just as, in *Walden*, Thoreau conducts a radical ethnography of Concord's everyday life. By putting thought and lived experience on a par, the dialogue between Thoreau and the earth priest suggests the outlines of a practice of political theory that is less concept-centric. We can now alternate between theory and ethnography as two overlapping registers or distributions of emphasis within political thinking.

As we "front" together and shift between the registers of the Wild and the tingane, economy itself can be perceived as an ethical practice with an ecological and political cast: a process enacted by various assemblages of earthen bodies and forces. I show how a dialogue between Thoreau and the Gurensi tindaana prompts us to refigure key concepts of the anthropocentric repertoire of mainstream understandings of economy: (1) Production: the earth becomes a coproducer of the material conditions of human life and the common good rather than an economic resource; (2) wealth becomes the capacity to mobilize ancestral assistance and mutually supportive networks of aid and reciprocity between humans and nonhumans rather than an immense accumulation of commodities; (3) property: poetic/spiritual enclosures that reveal ways of apprehending the land without possessing it as enclosed commons; (4) work: practices of negotiated interdependence with other economy-makers rather than monotonous, alienated labor.[6] The life of the marketplace is revealed as one among many contemporary forms of life rather than the terminal stage of social evolution.

The next two sections examine how each set of practices, Thoreau's and the tindaana's practices of economy-making, are woven into the land and into habits of perception, place, and the body. Whereas Thoreau's model in *Walden* focuses on micropractices of the self, the Gurensi earth priest helps us see how such arts of existence apply to groups of people. If it is Thoreau's solitary communing with Walden that extends his body into natural processes and forces, it is the experience of being a part of a farming community bound together by the earth gods that enables the Gurensi to come to terms with nature so that everyday activities can take place. I end by putting Thoreau and the Gurensi into a direct dialogue with the aim of mobilizing a practice of theory as a creative process of concept invention that coarticulates with ethnography.

## FROM POSSESSIONS TO POETIC ENCLOSURES OF THE LAND

Thoreau's cabin at Walden, built from a mix of easily available, reused man-made and Nature-furnished materials, is a living monument to Thoreau's friendship and collaboration with the pine tree.[7] Thoreau compares it to a birdcage in a neighborhood of "those wilder and more thrilling songsters of the forest . . . the wood-thrush, the veery, the scarlet tanager, the field-sparrow, the whippoorwill."[8] Just as the cabin is a "seat" for his flesh and bones, the earth provides an accommodation for Thoreau's house, "*seated* by the shore of Walden pond."[9] Thoreau thus presents a literal *oikos* (household economy) as profoundly dependent on a larger ecosystem, governed by the interplay of permanence and impermanence. The life cycle and rhythm of Thoreau's poetic dwelling interact with his and the earth's life cycles as intertwined rhythms, revealing the fleeting character of private property and the impossibility of "enclosing" the living processes of the earth.

The impossibility of "enclosure" leads Thoreau to translate his own acquisitive tendencies into poetic modes of satisfaction of needs and wants. His imagination is a trustee, not an owner, of other people's possessions, such as orchard woodlots and pastures. The closest Thoreau comes to having his fingers "burned by actual possession" is when he buys the Hollowell farm, which he resells to the owners for what he had paid when they change their minds.[10] Yet the experience enriches Thoreau as he "retains" the landscape and "encloses" the farm in a rhyme:

> I have frequently seen a poet withdraw, having enjoyed the most valuable part of a farm, while the crusty farmer supposed that he had got a few wild apples only. Why, the owner does not know it for many years when a poet has put his farm in rhyme, the most admirable kind of invisible fence, has fairly impounded it, milked it, skimmed it, and got all the cream, and left the farmer only the skimmed milk. The real attractions of the Hollowell farm, to me, were; its complete retirement, being about two miles from the village . . . the gray color and ruinous state of the house and barn, and the dilapidated fences . . . the hollow and lichen-covered apple trees, gnawed by rabbits, showing what kind of neighbors I should have.[11]

Thoreau's alternative mode of land use and appropriation—*poetic enclosure*—provides access to multiple kinds of nonmaterial wealth and limits the earth-destroying tendencies of consumption. Unlike the farmer who "deforms" the landscape, treats the soil as a property, and "knows Nature but as a robber," the poet retains the landscape and rejoices in the sight of "dilapidated fences" and other traces of the loss of human consumption and control.[12] The poet's enclosure of the land enlivens without destroying and uses only renewable energy sources; it lacks utility for a market with winners and losers. Thoreau's poetic enclosure draws on processes of earthly excess and regeneration, childhood recollections, and the enfolded nature of time in order to produce the good life. It allows the influx of experience to make its impact on the sensorium. Need-reduction and contemplation replace consumption, as the quality of relationships between human, rabbit, and bird neighbors increases. This exemplifies a poetic economy of bodily comportment, sensory intensification, and connection.

Thoreau reclaims economy as a site of everyday ethical practices, enacting new "body-economies" at the core of which is the negotiation of interdependence between humans and nonhumans.[13] Such an economy is based on satisfying a small set of modest needs, which are intertwined with the needs of birds, trees, soils, and lakes. Concerns about the exploitative interdependence between producers and nonproducers are linked to a concern for the unaccounted-for exploitation of the nonhuman world. In *Walden* our beds are recognized as our "night-clothes" and more-than-human extended skin, "robbing the nests and breasts of birds to prepare this shelter within shelter."[14] When Thoreau looks at the carloads of pine, spruce, Manilla hemp, and the palm leaf headed to cover "flaxen New England heads," he does not see timber or commodities for sale. He sees "proof-sheets" of nature's contribution to the economy and lists the multiple ecological and anthropological uses these bodies served before they acquired the status of "goods."[15] In Thoreau's economy, goods are never fully uprooted from the productive economy of nature. Production is revealed to be consumption: Consumption occurs all along the commodity chain, as raw-material extraction and manufacturing consume both human and ecological wealth. Rather than a uniquely human capacity, production becomes a conjoint human-nonhuman endeavor that highlights the role of humans as co-producers and converters of primary products from the earth. Thoreau's economy encourages the production of relational goods such as cross-species kinship and neighborliness, the consumption of which does not reduce the available stock.[16]

In *A Winter Walk* Thoreau calls forth from the potentials of his body-economy a series of such affinities with winter's productive economy. During his winter stroll, the poet draws on the "slumbering subterranean fire in nature which never goes out" and which courses through the materiality of all earthly existence, including Thoreau's own breast.[17] Rather than a harsh winter environment, in which an industrial economy would be brought to a halt without an immense waste of energy, the poet discerns vital, thriving natural productivity at work all year round. This intensified perception of the interdependencies between human subjectivity and earthly processes renders economy a more than human domain. Humans are now positioned not as masters but as co-participants in a vibrant earthly economy: "We fancy ourselves in the interior of a larger house. The surface of the pond is our deal table or sanded floor, and the woods rise abruptly from its edge, like the walls of a cottage."[18] Thoreau's winter walk enables the experience of becoming a "piece of forest furniture" and a member of the "natural family of man."[19] Such descriptions register the agency of a powerful and infinitely patient earth in contrast to recent environmentalist representations of the earth as a fragile body perturbed by human interference.

For all his celebration of the powers of Nature, Thoreau's practice of walking also reveals another, ambiguous side of the poet that threatens to reincorporate these powers back into the human. Early in the essay "Walking" Thoreau tells us that he walks at least four hours a day. Walking is not merely an exercise or a stroll but Thoreau's "enterprise of the day," which requires relinquishing all familial and social attachments: "If you are ready to leave father and mother, and brother and sister, and wife and child and friends, and never see them again,—if you have . . . settled all your affairs, and are a free man, then you are ready for a walk."[20] For Thoreau, any space of politics has an outside. To opt out, all one needs to do is to walk away or, better, walk outdoors.[21] Walking runs on one's bodily energy and becomes an expression of self-sufficiency and trust in the body's capacities.

Ironically, in this essay, Thoreau, the proponent of setting one's own route, portrays himself as waiting for an invitation to walk into Nature: "Unto a life which I call natural I would gladly follow . . . but no moon nor fire-fly has shown me the causeway to it."[22] The walker travels a shifting boundary between nature and civilization, without finding home in either domain. Each walk redistributes the balance between domestication and wildness, identity and excess across Thoreau's body.

Thoreau's transcendence is not so much vertical as it is horizontal, spatial, and earthbound.[23] Transcendence is the activity of transcending propelled by the recognition of the excess of perception and incompleteness experienced in Thoreau's encounters with Nature. For all of his attempts to walk over to the Wild, Thoreau remains distanced from Nature's mysteries because of his complicated relationship with the march of Western progress to humanize Nature. The sunset inspires Thoreau "to go to a West as distant and as fair as that into which the sun goes down."²⁴ Walking west horizontalizes encounters between humans and nonhumans. As the companion of the sun whose rays bathe all equally, the saunterer suspends the tendency to rank order the bodies he confederates with. At the same time, the walker is revealed to be a "Great Western Pioneer" who follows in the footsteps of the white settlers and conquistadors, including Columbus, who "felt the westward tendency more strongly than any before. He obeyed it and found a New World for Castile and Leon."²⁵ Thoreau advocates leaving the established society of the "Old World and its institutions" in order to re-create that society in the new "wilder" setting of Oregon. The pioneers tap into wildness to revitalize the Europeans who follow in their wake. He praises the Indian for having closer ties to Nature, yet he also needs the Indian to disappear (or he sees this outcome "natural") for Western progress to unfold: "I think that the farmer displaces the Indian even because he redeems the meadow, and so makes himself stronger and in some respect more natural."²⁶ To "go native" requires the disappearance of the native and, however reluctantly, the conquest and destruction of nature. Thoreau is both a chronicler and a benefactor in a land humanized by conquest. He learns how to farm without sharing the doom of those who had cultivated the earth before him to make way for his poetic trusteeship of the land.²⁷

If Thoreau's walks—with all their contradictions—trouble the default regime of anthropocentric perception, so does his practice of hoeing beans at Walden. While the beans are growing, Thoreau hoes from "five o'clock in the morning till noon," a labor that is repetitive, even monotonous, but still different from the alienated labor of Concord businessmen and farmers.²⁸ Diligent hoeing is a part of an assemblage where the human co-acts with a range of other economy-makers: "My auxiliaries are the dews and rains which water this dry soil, and what fertility is in the soil itself."²⁹ The task of his daily toil is to persuade "the earth to say beans instead of grass" and to "make this portion of the earth's surface, which has yielded cinquefoil, blackberries ... sweet wild fruits and pleasant flowers, produce instead this pulse."³⁰ This experience of work as an orchestrated activity, located in the mutually cooperative relationship between human and nonhuman participants, would bring Thoreau's bean field closer to the seasonal rain-fed ecology of the Gurensi farm. The relation between Thoreau and the earth is characterized by mutuality and intimacy, though not equality.

Of course, one might object to Thoreau on several grounds: How can this model be applied to large groups of people? Can this Thoreauvian ethic of living well with less be sustained and reproduced without its ambiguities? In the next section, I turn to the Gurensi people to address these questions. As Thoreau goes to Ghana, will Nature remain "wild"? We have seen that the traveler can encounter the land both as a frontier of Western progress and as poetic commons that temper such drives toward mastery. Apprehending and degrading the earth can become mixed up with yielding to its lively agencies. It may be that in the contrast with the Gurensi earth priest the poet becomes scrubbed of the pioneer. At the same time, certain things that the Gurensi feel ambivalent about may become apparent too.

## "THE EARTH IS LIKE A SKIN": BLOOD, EXCHANGE, AND SPIRITUAL ENCLOSURES

Unlike Thoreau's Nature, Nature in Gurensiland is experienced as the visible domain of the spiritual world: a heterogeneous assemblage of smaller gods. Some aspects of nature express themselves as spirits and vice versa. This is how the earth gods, wind gods, rain gods, and sky gods, which together express the turbulent materiality of tiŋa, arose. Tiŋa (literally "earth" or "land" in Gurene) is the irreplaceable biophysical foundation of community life.[31] Gurensi earthen compounds rise out of the oikos of tiŋa as assemblages of humans, family gods, and livestock that grow old and wither away together.

The gate of each compound faces west: "You don't leave the gate towards the sun. . . . You are not of the same position as the sun."[32] Such reverence for the sun contrasts with the poet-sun companionship in Thoreau's "Walking". The humility not to compete with god—the sun—finds architectural expression that makes the Gurensi compound impervious to the heavy rainstorms that come from the east during the rainy season. Rivers and streams vanish during the dry season. Amid this grassy and seasonally changing landscape certain majestic baobab trees or clusters of trees and shrubs, streams, rocky ranges, or heaps of stones persevere and exert powerful presences. They are almost inevitably tingana.

A tingane might mark the location of the settlement of the first ancestor—the pioneer settler and key ancestor of a village—or a powerful place identified by a soothsayer. Most of my informants described the *tindaana*—a Gurene shorthand for *tiŋa daana*, that is, "custodian" or "owner of the earth"—as the "original settler" of the land and emphasized the prominent role of his family in community life. The areas identified by the "original" settlers as places of sacrifice to the earth gods became the abodes for the spirits of the whole community. Three different types of earth gods can bear the name tingane: *yaabatia* (ancestral trees); tingane proper; and *tinkugere* (land spirits). The main god that serves the whole community is the *tinkugere*, a circle of stones arranged on the ground.

The tindaana (earth custodian) holds custody of the *tinkugere*. In Bolgatanga, all who approach the land spirits remove their shoes and upper body clothes. The removal zone can range from a radius of as little as ten to as many as forty or fifty barefoot paces from the circle of stones. Some elders trace this prohibition "back to nature": When their ancestors were alive, they were naked. This is why you take your shoes off—it is an "abomination" to keep them on.[33] In this same area, all articles of the tindaana's regalia have to be made of nature-made materials such as sheepskins and goatskins and locally sourced plant fibers. The totality of these articles is vested with special powers; individual articles like bracelets might be where the spirit of a tindaana's father resides.

A body adorned only with animal skins emphasizes the importance of bodily comportment and receptivity to tiŋa, itself conceived as a set of spiritual practices rather than as raw material for conceptualization or land development. The skins generated lively debates during my interviews and discussions with Gurensi elders. The word *tingane* is derived from *tiŋa* (land or earth) and *gan*ɛ(skin), some elders insisted, the latter being a reference to the earth priest's bodily adornment. Others interpreted ganɛ as a reference to "the skin of the earth," the delicate womb of a woman in which we are all buried. Taking your shoes off ensures that you tread gently on tiŋa's delicate skin, signaling a posture of humility and respect for the earth. Such respect is also manifest in the taboo against lighting a fire on the tiŋa. The earth does not belong to humans, but humans belong to the earth. It is to her womb that everyone returns upon death, dissolving lived hierarchies: "You may have an ancestor, I might have an ancestor, he may have his ancestors, they are all contained in the womb of the woman. That is the tiŋa. . . . We are all within the same place. So it is somebody who takes care of our ancestors."[34]

The tingane becomes an image of the earth's productivity, fertility, and regenerative powers. The womb of the earth is where the seeds co-sown by the Earth gods and the Gurensi farmer sprout to life:

> When a man sleeps with a woman . . . the woman didn't just drink water to get pregnant . . . the gods also intervened. If it doesn't rain, the crops would not fruit . . . if he doesn't sleep with her she won't give birth and tiŋa would not go well [tiŋa ka maale]. If it doesn't rain, tiŋa ka maale, if a man doesn't sleep with a woman she wouldn't give birth.[35]

Fertility comes "when a man sleeps with a woman," when the sky god gives rain to the earth, and the earth gives birth to the trees that spring in the tingane. "The woman is a womb. If you bury a human being in the grave it means a child in the woman's womb. It is very important that the womb contains the dead."[36] The intimate intercourse between living, dead, and unborn, the organic and the inorganic, binds together fertility, health, and rainfall in a web that is more than metaphorical. The *tinkugere* assures that the community partakes in the earth's capacities to regenerate life. It reactivates deceased matter into the ecological becoming of the earth: The decomposition of a living body is simultaneously the composition of *a* life, the assembling of the dead body's parts into new vegetal and mineral relations.

"Yes," the elders concur, "the tinkugere is a woman in the Zoko and Sirigu areas."[37] But here the word *tingane* comes from *tiŋa* and *gaɲe* (literally, "exceed" or "surpass, be more than something"). The tingane is a god; it "sends the sacrifice to god because that is the one which is nearer to the supreme, to the creator."[38] The tiŋa surpasses all others.[39] The tingane takes blood because blood is life and that is what the ancestors do not have. You want the ancestors to know that you have sacrificed a whole animal and what color the animal was—that's why you put the feathers on the blood. The community needs fowls of all colors to respond to unanticipated events and seasonal changes. A red fowl is sacrificed to avert a serious problem; a white fowl, to give thanks; a black fowl, to deal with something hidden or gloomy.

The key feature of this community economy is the nonmarket system of exchange. This is sometimes a ritual exchange of animal blood and human life: "The spirits take blood because, for example, when a witch gets someone, they take the person's blood just that we humans do not see it with our eyes but the spirits do. So this is why the spirit too takes blood of the animals in exchange to save the person's soul."[40] Other forms of exchange include daily exchange of greetings, courtesies, entertainment and music; "exchange of seeds, exchange of food, exchange of children, even in marriage . . . strengthening the bond between two families by creating a marriage between their children"; labor-pooling processes that involve setting aside days when people go to work on each others' farms or assist each other with the building of a new compound.[41] It is not only individuals but groups—families, clans, gods, and spirits—that carry on such exchanges, often mediated by the tindaana, the soothsayer (*baga*), the chief of medicine (*bagenabasɔ*), or the chief (*Naba*). The things that are exchanged are not exclusively goods, property, and objects of economic value.[42] Neither is the purpose "mere subsistence," for the act of giving creates social relationships and redistributes the surplus that has been co-produced by gods, spirits, and humans. This is an economy of relationships and sufficiency, in which wealth is measured "in the level of integration of people in their natural and spiritual environment, in the quality of their relationships with the society around them."[43] A farmer's family is rich if it has a large network of mutual aid, ancestral support, reciprocity on which they can count and that can ensure the ongoing flourishing of the community. These economies resonate with Thoreau's poetic economy, in which wealth is derived from the richness of human entanglements with kindred earthly bodies and forces. For Thoreau, wealth lies in the bodily intensification and poetic amplification of the productivity and wealth already present in nature. Wealth is not generated first and foremost through the "goods" of Thoreau's labor in the bean field but through the sensations that such labor elicits and intensifies within the rich mix of the poet's "inner nature."

It is, in contrast, the nonliving—the ancestors and the Earth gods—who are the real sources and owners of wealth in Gurensiland. Whereas Thoreau's poetic custody privileges individuality, earth priests are land trustees in the sense that they are responsible for addressing the spiritual needs of the land and the community spirits. In many parts of Gurensiland earth priests are "nature-chosen": The tindaana is selected by the spirits of the ancestors and not by his age, wisdom, wealth, or status. It is the "skin," the shrine itself that serves as the repository of ownership of the land and not the person of the tindaana. The tinkugere's heap of stones entails a particular form of ordering and enclosing the tiŋa—spiritual or ritual enclosure—bound up with ancestral presences, a cluster of clans and natural forces. Like Thoreau's poem, a spiritual enclosure is relational and nonpossessive in the narrow economic sense. Unlike the poem, which has "fenced," "impounded," and "milked" the land, Gurensi enclosure is a two-way reciprocal street. It is essential to take care of the earth's spiritual needs so that the earth continues to nurture her inhabitants.

For Thoreau, the apprehension of the land amounts to a set of lived strategies that reside most fully within the human domain. For the Gurensi, humans constitute merely one node in a field of apprehension and transformation of landscapes; the ancestors (i.e., the earth) embody this apprehension for reasons that humans can only try to interpret.[44] After all, the landowners themselves are enclosed in the womb of the tiŋa: "Everything comes from the ground. Our crops, the deceased are buried there, everything is contained in the tiŋa."[45] The ancestors have a vested interest in the land, and their consent has to be obtained by the tindaana before land is given to a land seeker or a deceased person is buried. Thoreau, in contrast, does not seek such consent from the escaped slaves, Irish workers, and deceased Native Americans who continue to haunt his cabin at Walden and the local woods. He attempts to live less as his European ancestors and more through "the Indian" example that mediates his relationship to the land.[46] The substitution of one set of ancestors for another loosens up his appropriative tendencies but hardly alters his pioneering sense of entitlement to settle there. In contrast, clearance from the Gurensi tingane is needed for development, even if building a new school or a hospital means that the earth gods themselves have to move to another abode within the tiŋa.

Can political theory enrich our understanding of the changing role of the tindaanas in contemporary governance and politico-economic transformations in Ghana? This essay has sought to transport us from categorical imperatives to the actual use of beliefs in contexts where familiar distinctions such as religious/secular and living/dead become untenable. Is it even appropriate to reduce the rich chronicles of Gurensi lived experience to "beliefs"? What is at stake in the distinction between experiences of the earth as a supernatural being and as ancestors/elders? Should we employ the abstract category of "agents" for the ancestors as if they were autonomous entities "within" nature?[47] The conversation between Thoreau and the earth priest highlights the limits and dangers of an enduring tendency to import Western models of economy, politics, religion, and personhood as ways of comprehending the lifeworlds of others. It makes a difference whether the food given to the tingane is described in terms of "paying tribute" and "respect" to the eldest "elders" or in terms of "ancestor worship." The former description situates the ancestors (i.e., the earth) within politics and within a continuum of intergenerational eldership that forms the foundation of Gurensi political authority. The latter removes them from politics and relocates them within religion and cult because we, Westerners, find these domains more appropriate to accommodate our own dealings with the dead.[48] Honoring the ways in which the Gurensi people "model" their livelihoods requires that we recognize both the authority of the earth in politico-economic life and the role of the tindaanaship as a mechanism of redistribution of political power between the living and the dead. The tindaanaship ensures that development proceeds in accord with the ever-changing spiritual needs and "invisible governances" of the earth. Religion in places like Northern Ghana can be also understood as a bricolage of political experimentation to pursue opportunities in spiritual, economic, and social lifeworlds.[49]

The idea that the "ancestors" must be separated from the living "elders" belongs to a medley of ethnocentric convictions that shape neocolonial representations of indigenous peoples' relationships to the land as mere subsistence or occupancy rather than as competing—albeit different—forms of property and ownership. Because African practices do not approximate those of their Western counterparts in the cornfields of Iowa or the greenhouses of the Netherlands, African farmers are assumed to have no prior "investment" in the land. The absence of physical marking or of signs of transformation of the land through "improvement"—like Thoreau's Indian who was not fully able to "redeem the meadow"—renders such lands "unused" and ready to be grabbed by contemporary pioneers. The dialogue between Thoreau and the Gurensi accentuates familiar Western imaginaries of economy as culturally specific phenomena that enter into processes of contestation and hybridization with competing imaginaries. According to the latter, "land" can be felt as something more than a durable surface over which generation after generation transfer communal rights. Such commons can be experienced as a web of socioecological relationships between humans and the earth—relationships of property, nonetheless. In Thoreau's America, the sphere of "economy," unlike politics, looms so large that the poet cannot walk away from it. In Gurensiland, economy as such hardly exists: A political continuum of eldership continues to draw ecology, economy, and theology together, making it difficult to demarcate clearly one "sphere" from the others.

## THE EARTH PRIEST AND THE POET

These collisions and resonances bring to light the ways in which Gurensi ecotheology and Thoreau's ecopolitical imaginary might enrich each other. Thoreau constructs a carefully modulated relation to the Wild, and the Gurensi to the tingane. Both involve a heightened sense of receptivity to the powers of the earth over processes of ethical will formation. Thoreau seeks experiences that enchant the senses anew, disrupting the habitual order of perception. One begins to experience familiar entities in new ways: "Life consists with wildness. . . . One who pressed forward incessantly and never rested from his labors . . . would always find himself in a new country."[50] Each walk outside, for Thoreau, is also a journey inward through the fecund mix of the wild and the familiar that forms one's personal interior. The Wild is de-placed and more portable than the tingane, which is attached to a specific, multidimensional territory and bound to the nonlinear history of the clan or the village.

In the Gurensi tiŋa, there is hardly room for Thoreau's Wild. Tiŋa refers to (1) land, ground, earth, the physical world, and (2) country, town, settlement.[51] Tiŋa is the whole community, be it trees, stones, humans, or spirits; it is the ground on which we are sitting and "in which we bury."[52] You cannot have "wild" Nature without the settlement or vice versa.

The tingane illustrates the translatability of any mode of existence into any other within the tiŋa, which is to say that humans, bats, stones, and gods perpetually transform. A human turned into a baobab tree and a god who resides in a stone still bear the same name: my grandfather, my ancestor, my *yaaba*. The time someone spent as a tree and the time someone spent as a human belong to the same lineage, a relation that takes a form of identity between what might be considered as two dissimilar species of things. The tingane is a web of lived relationships with the earth, which provides people with good harvests, food, and more people and which is, in turn, given food, protection, and respect. The tingane is not a god before those relationships but through those relationships in a world of multiple gods and becoming that is not separate from humans. Only the sky god (*wine*) is outside tiŋa, but he cannot be worshipped directly; the Creator can be only petitioned through tiŋa's intercourse with the sky, which brings forth rain, fertility, and new tingana.

This web of immanent lived relationships contrasts with Thoreau's *as if* stance of transcendence that prompts him to reexperience himself as if he is "part and parcel of Nature." Through a series of everyday economic practices, Thoreau becomes enchanted by the earthly forces and wild elements that course around and through his body-economy. Rather than taming these elements in the service of consummate human agency, Thoreau valorizes the disruptive effects of such encounters upon the normal, default self: "We need the tonic of wildness. . . . We need to witness our own limits transgressed, and some life pasturing freely where we never wander."[53] The sensuous attractiveness and unruliness of these forces serves as a counterforce to human habits and an impetus to transcend, to go beyond, and to enact "higher laws." Thoreau's transgressive transcendence is about lines of flight, about crossings over to a heteroverse of the Wild: "If the day and the night are such that you greet them with joy, and life emits a fragrance like flowers and sweet-scented herbs, is more elastic, more starry, more immortal—that is your success."[54] This practice of transcending carries with it a certain enchantment and momentum that resonates with Gurensi sacrifice and ritual, which also open access to a different, uncanny state of knowing and encountering nature. Not everyone in Gurensiland has the tindaana's or soothsayer's privileged access to the sacred. Not everyone in Concord shares Thoreau's impetus to recraft a body through metaphors such as the high, immortal, starry, and transcendental.

Besides such shared moments of dwelling in uncanny experiences, Thoreau and the earth priest front the Wild and the tingane differently. Whereas Thoreau *transcends*, the earth priest *petitions*. Each practice of an eco-economy involves shifting back and forth between different registers of passivity and activity. However, it makes a difference whether the locus of redistributing agency between human and earthen economy-makers lies in the soil marked by a circle of stones or in a poem.

The poet is simultaneously cultivated and wild, given and made, and constructs himself as an object, which is then subjected to various tactics of experimentation. By a "conscious effort of the mind" we can become our bodies' "spectator" that allows us to negotiate our capacities for experience and observation, our roles as both subjects and objects.[55] This doubleness "makes us poor neighbors and friends sometimes" as it encourages us to see Thoreau's rabbit, lake, and bird neighbors as potentially instrumentalizable. However, it is this "spectator" quality that enables Thoreau to keep the Wild at bay in order to maintain a proper relation between our instinct for wildness and our "higher" instincts: "I caught a glimpse of a woodchuck stealing across my path, and felt a strange thrill of savage delight, and was strongly tempted to seize and devour him raw. . . . I found in myself, and still find, an instinct toward a higher, or, as it is named, spiritual life, as do most men, and another toward a primitive rank and savage one, and I reverence them both."[56]

The spectator renders Thoreau more agentic so that he loosens up the will to mastery over the earthen forces that his body draws in. Ironically, Thoreau's "higher" instinct is employed in the service of greater cooperation with nonhumans rather than for the purposes of rank ordering. This self-conscious chronicler of data and a heightened degree of human agency constitutes only one dimension of the (inter-)subjectivity through which Thoreau engages the rest of the world. Multiple modes of subjectivity extend from natural and cosmic processes to Thoreau's body and vice versa: "What is man but a mass of thawing clay? . . . Who knows what the human body would expand and flow out to under a more genial heaven?"[57] Self-making (auto-poiesis) is a project of producing a fine-tuned earthbound body from two, interwoven sets of materials: The first are the dull, conventional tendencies that have settled into one's bones and habits, and the second are the more lively processes of nonhuman nature. Both sets are operative within the individual.

In the context of ecological degradation that affects Gurensiland today, can Thoreau's "doubleness" and his use of the nature/culture problematic equip the Gurensi people with new crisis-coping mechanisms? The "spectator" allows the Gurensi to distance themselves from the immediacy of lived experience so that they can register as earth-degrading certain everyday practices whose ecological consequences are deferred in time. This way the sea of black polythene bags that engulf the land or the use of pesticides such as DDT or Aldrin could be perceived as things that puncture the womb of the earth rather than as modern-day enhancements of people's ongoing relationship with the tiŋa. Consumer goods, modernization, and ancestral knowledge could be seen as contradicting or undermining each other rather than as part and parcel of tiŋa's productive economy.

However, as the Gurensi learn from Thoreau what Thoreau felt ambivalent about becomes more conspicuous. For Thoreau, a self-governing body-economy cannot be actualized without establishing a proper relationship to the Wild, a relationship of ability, activity, sauntering. The way the poet harmonizes human existence with nature has, in part, a sense of rendering natural the conquest of nature. This poetic crusade would be productively troubled by a certain passivity, nonpower, and humility at the heart of the experience of tingane's power. The tindaana's role is to register the spiritual needs of the land and make them known to the whole community. He is a key intermediary between the living and the nonliving: "The yaabas or the ancestors are scattered everywhere in the tinga. . . . He will go around, consult the soothsayer to find out their needs. . . . He does not own that land. He takes care of the bush land."[58] The possibility to share with others this nonpower afforded by ritual becomes subjectivity-forming. It locates village residents within the womb of a woman rather than within the wild embrace of Nature or within the domain of higher laws. Gurensi ethical formation involves a series of conversations and exchanges between extended families of humans, gods, earthen bodies, and spirits that affect each other through reciprocal (and asymmetrical) relationships rather than subject/object dynamics. These subjectivities are collective more-than-human assemblages: They transform into animals, plants, natural bodies such as rocks and ponds, and even cultural artifacts such as ancestral horns and rings, which participate alongside us in a community economy.

In poetic enclosures, ownership is vested in a poem. In spiritual enclosures, ownership is vested in a shrine, in a mineral body. Can the tinkugere be like the poem? I suspect not quite. The tinkugere is less a referent to the incorporation of the earth into human ethical order and thinking and more a set of living, negotiated practices that aim to attune human ethical order and thinking to nature: "Our food is gotten from the tiŋa, our water is gotten from the tiŋa, our buildings are gotten from the tiŋa, almost everything that is made to make life comfortable is gotten from the tiŋa. And our ancestors are from the tiŋa. . . . They are from the *tiŋa* because all the earth gods are on the tiŋa. . . . Our life depends on the tiŋa, spiritually, socially, whatsoever."[59] The earth and the human are already felt as nonseparable. The earth simultaneously has a social, legal, economic, political, and spiritual authority that entitles her to rule Gurensiland: "Everything that is done on this earth is done on the tiŋa."[60] Thoreau also wants to say that Nature rules by default. However, his concept-mediated practices of active self-fashioning do not equip him with sufficient resources to relinquish the "human" as one who is never "wholly involved in Nature."[61] The best one can do is to command that human part of the self to register Nature's rule without submitting fully to it. But would a full submission always mean submission to a human idea of nature? This is less clear. Perhaps this difficulty lies in another submission: that of philosophy to the influence of concepts such as agency and property that fail to capture the diversity and complexity of lived encounters between human bodies and a nonappropriable, life-generating earth.

Thoreau privileges solitude above other competing modes of econosociality, but he underplays the role of human community that is indispensable for Gurensi ethical life. The dialogue between the two highlights the radically incomplete nature of the modern image of the human body as a self-enclosed "individual." This image does not exhaust what it means to be human, and its incompleteness prompts one to seek alliances with other bodies, be it ponds, spirits, human neighbors, crocodiles, or extraordinary stones. Thoreau acts as if he can exempt himself from public life, at least as long as such a polity does not include hawks, squirrels, ponds, and so on. In Gurensiland such exemptions are neither feasible nor even grammatically possible. The dialogue between the poet and the earth priest reveals that a body or a person is always more than itself: It is a composite of relations, events, and affections that bind humans and nonhumans into webs of kinship, solidarity, and reciprocity.

Theory and ethnography are two related modes of artistic production of effects on such bodies or persons. The idea is to allow the thick chronicles of lived experience that ethnography makes visible to affect us without recuperating them as Western philosophy. The earth priest's supplicating can scrub Thoreau of his troubled (and troubling) relationship to Western progress. It can transform him into a poet who has given up on the romantic fantasy of the "Wild" and has embraced an ongoing and inescapable relationship to nature. Thoreau's "doubleness" and nature/culture problematic, in turn, might help the Gurensi emerge as a fully complex ethical universe that is not in perfect harmony with nature either.

## NOTES

1. Henry David Thoreau, *Walden* (Princeton, N.J.: Princeton University Press, 2004), 90; John Updike, introduction to *Walden*, ix–x.
2. The Gurensi live in the Bolgatanga Municipal and Bongo districts in the Upper East Region of Ghana. The term *Gurensi* is a common but controversial ethnic identification as some of the Gurensi's neighbors use the term in a derogatory sense. In English-speaking conversations, and in conversations with Ghanaians unfamiliar with the Upper East, one often hears *"Frafra,"* a colonial term derived from a local greeting, which lumps together the Gurensi and the Boosi alongside the Nabnam and the Tallensi. Despite the lack of consensus, most of the elders and knowledge-holders I interacted with insisted on the use of the name "Gurensi." For a study that illuminates the distinctive genealogies and oral histories of the Gurensi and the Boosi see Christopher Azaare, *A History of the Bongo District* (forthcoming).
3. See Michel Foucault, *The Use of Pleasure: The History of Sexuality*, vol. 2, trans. Robert Hurley (New York: Vintage, 1990); Friedrich Nietzsche, *Thus Spoke Zarathustra*, trans. Adrian Del Caro (Cambridge: Cambridge University Press, 2006).
4. See Jane Bennett, *Vibrant Matter: A Political Ecology of Things* (Durham, N.C.: Duke University Press, 2010).
5. I conducted fieldwork in Ghana during two trips in December 2011–January 2012 and July 2012–February 2013. I employed a blend of ethnographic participant observation and in-depth interviews to analyze the ways in which Gurensi earth shrines (*tingana*) may be seen as windows into broader interdependencies between subjectivity and earthly processes. For a compelling discussion of the relationship between philosophy and ethnography see also Michael Jackson, *Lifeworlds: Essays in Existential Anthropology* (Chicago: University of Chicago Press, 2013).

6. For a discussion of the term *economy-makers* and my expansion of the term see Arturo Escobar, *Territories of Difference: Place, Movements, Life, Redes* (Durham, N.C.: Duke University Press, 2008), 100, and J. K. Gibson-Graham and Gerda Roelvink, "An Economic Ethics for the Anthropocene," *Antipode* 41, no. S1 (2010): 320–46.
7. Thoreau, *Walden*, 42.
8. Ibid., 86.
9. Ibid.
10. Ibid., 82.
11. Ibid., 82–83.
12. Ibid., 165–66.
13. Gibson-Graham and Roelvink, "Economic Ethics," 329–30.
14. Thoreau, *Walden*, 13.
15. Ibid., 119–20.
16. Serge Latouche, *Farewell to Growth* (Malden, Mass.: Polity, 2009), 70. See also E. F. Schumacher, *Small Is Beautiful: Economics as if People Mattered* (New York: Harper Perennial, 2010), 50–55; and Thomas Princen, Michael Maniates, and Ken Conca, *Confronting Consumption* (Cambridge, Mass.: MIT Press, 2002).
17. Henry David Thoreau, "A Winter Walk," in *Collected Essays and Poems* (New York: Library of America, 2001), 96.
18. Ibid., 101.
19. Ibid., 101, 105.
20. Henry D. Thoreau, "Walking," in *Excursions* (Seaside, Ore.: Watchmaker Publishing, 2010), 93–94
21. Ibid., 98.
22. Ibid., 117. See also James Martel, *Love Is a Sweet Chain: Desire, Autonomy, and Friendship in Liberal Political Theory* (London: Routledge, 2001), 149–50.
23. Ibid., 154.
24. Thoreau, "Walking," 103.
25. Ibid.; Martel, *Love Is a Sweet Chain*, 158.
26. Thoreau, "Walking," 110; Martel, *Love Is a Sweet Chain*, 150–52.
27. Martel, *Love Is a Sweet Chain*, 186.
28. Ibid., 161.
29. Ibid., 155.
30. Ibid., 155, 157.
31. David Millar, "Improving Farming with Ancestral Support," in *Ancient Roots, New Shoots: Endogenous Development in Practice*, ed. Bertus Haverkort, Katrien van't Hooft, and Wim Hiemstra (London: ZED Books, 2003), 153–68.
32. Interview with Gurensi house builders, by Anatoli Ignatov and Jacqueline Ignatova, January 6, 2013.
33. Gurensi elders, in discussion with Anatoli Ignatov and Jacqueline Ignatova, January 7, 2013.
34. Interview with Chris Azaare, by Jacqueline Ignatova and the author, Gowrie, March 3, 2013. The egalitarian representations of a mother/earth/womb natalism of this kind can hardly conceal the patriarchal nature of gender practices within

the Gurensi patrilineal descent and primogeniture system, in which office and property devolve on the eldest male descendant. The "earth as womb" natalism and the status of ancestresses should not foreclose the experiencing of the spiritual enclosures of the land as patriarchal "commons."

35. Interview with elders, December 14, 2012.
36. Interview with Azaare, March 3, 2013.
37. Discussion with elders, January 7, 2013.
38. Interview with elders, December 14, 2012.
39. Interview with Azaare, March 3, 2013.
40. Interview with informant, by Jacqueline Ignatova and the author, December 16, 2012. Witches can be also a serious signal of some of the questionable gender practices mentioned earlier or, more generally, of scapegoating, even if the latter is not necessarily gender-based.
41. Interview with Bakari Nyari, by Jacqueline Ignatova and the author, Tamale, February 13, 2013.
42. Marcel Mauss, *The Gift: Forms and Functions of Exchange in Archaic Societies* (Mansfield Centre, Conn.: Martino, 2011).
43. Emmanuel Seni N'Dione, et al., "Reinventing the Present: The Chodak Experience in Senegal," in *The Post-Development Reader*, ed. Majid Rahnema and Victoria Bawtree (London: Zed Books, 1997), 369.
44. Elizabeth Povinelli, "Do Rocks Listen? The Cultural Politics of Apprehending Australian Aboriginal Labor," *American Anthropologist* 97, no. 3 (1995): 513.
45. Interview with Azaare, March 3, 2013.
46. Martel, *Love Is a Sweet Chain*, 170–71.
47. See Nurit Bird-David, "Beyond 'The Original Affluent Society': A Culturalist Reformulation," *Current Anthropology* 33, no. 1 (1992): 25–47.
48. See Igor Kopytoff's "Ancestors as Elders in Africa" *Africa: Journal of the International African Institute* 41, no. 2 (1971): 129–42.
49. David Hecht and Maliqalim Simone, *Invisible Governance: The Art of African Micropolitics* (New York: Autonomedia, 1994).
50. Thoreau, "Walking," 108.
51. Kropp Dakubu, Awinkene Arintono, and Avea Nsoh, *Gurenɛ—English Dictionary* (Legon: Linguistics Department, University of Ghana, 2007), 170.
52. Interview with Chris Azaare, by Jacqueline Ignatova and the author, Gowrie, August 15, 2012.
53. Thoreau, *Walden*, 317–18.
54. Ibid., 216–17.
55. Ibid., 134–35.
56. Ibid., 210.
57. Ibid., 307.
58. Interview with Chris Azaare, March 3, 2013.
59. Interview with informants, by Jacqueline Ignatova and the author, March 1, 2013.
60. Ibid.
61. Thoreau, *Walden*, 134–35.

# Climate Debt, White Privilege, and Christian Ethics as Political Theology

CYNTHIA D. MOE-LOBEDA

Climate change may be the most far-reaching manifestation of white privilege and class privilege yet to face humankind. Caused overwhelmingly by the world's high-consuming people, climate change is wreaking death and destruction first and foremost on impoverished people who also are disproportionately people of color.[1] The island nations that will be submerged or rendered unsuitable for human habitation by rising sea levels, subsistence farmers the world over whose crops are easily undermined by climate change, and coastal peoples without resources to protect against and recover from the fury of climate-related weather disaster are not the people largely responsible for greenhouse gas emissions. Nor are they, for the most part, white.

Many voices of the Global South recognize this as climate debt or climate colonialism and situate it as a continuation of the colonialism that enabled the Global North to enrich itself for five centuries at the expense of Africa, Latin America, Indigenous North America, and parts of Asia. Within the United States too, communities of color and low-income communities will continue to suffer most from the extreme storms as well as the respiratory illness, food insecurity, and disease brought on by climate change. Environmental racism and white privilege strike again in climate change and the ocean acidification that stems from it.

Few of Earth's goods are more deeply common goods serving the common good(s) than Earth's atmosphere.[2] We human creatures—as well as Earth's other creatures—hold in common our need for it and its delicate climate-regulating mechanisms. Jeopardizing it puts all other common good(s) in harm's way. What we do not hold in common is our access to those endangered goods such as food and water. As climate change renders them scarcer, corporate- and finance-driven global capitalism assures that some people can access and profit from nature's goods while others cannot.

This essay posits climate change as a moral matter of climate debt, white privilege, and class privilege. It then draws on tools of Christian ethics as political theology to frame a moral response. The third section sketches aspects of that response including a potentially disempowering paradox, an understanding of morally empowering vision, and criteria for climate policy and action that take seriously the climate debt and climate privilege dimensions of climate change.

## CLIMATE CHANGE, CLIMATE DEBT, AND WHITE PRIVILEGE

Why look at climate change as white privilege and as a matter of climate debt? Economically privileged people of the Global North will help generate a livable and just future to the extent that we cultivate what Walter Benjamin called "presence of mind," which includes "precise awareness of the present moment."[3] The defining feature of the present moment is climate change. How clearly we perceive it will shape how we address it, and that will determine the future of life on Earth. Sharp awareness of the present moment for a society whose material wealth is built—through historical processes—on the impoverishment of many people around the globe requires awareness of that legacy and of its ongoing embodiment in the present. The legacy of colonialism and neocolonialism is embodied, of course, in virtually every aspect of our present, but here we consider one. It is the crisis that now threatens life on Earth: climate change and the ways of life that cause it.

Inquiry into climate change and other forms of ecological degradation is often devoid of its historical and social structural (political-economic and ideological) roots. Inadequate analysis leads to inadequate diagnosis and remedies. What constitutes the morally right resolution to a current moral dilemma depends on what the problem is understood to be. To illustrate: When asked in the mid-1940s about the "Negro problem" in America, James Baldwin responded: "There isn't any Negro problem; there is only a white problem." The history of white racism in the United States in housing, health care, law, education, exposure to toxic land use, and more would have been dramatically different had we recognized and addressed race as a "white problem" rather than as a black problem.

Response to the perilous reality of climate change—where the peril actually is acknowledged in the United States—is frequently framed around the principle of sustainability. Climate change as a matter of sustainability calls for reducing carbon emission and thus carbon footprint through technological advances, energy efficiency, energy conservation, and replacing fossil fuels with renewable energy sources. The moves are crucial, to be applauded and supported. Yet from an ethical perspective that recognizes climate change as a matter of climate debt, white privilege, and class privilege, these moves—while vital—are inadequate. To the extent that they parade as adequate, they are dangerously deceptive.

In contrast, if climate change is seen also as a problem of climate debt, then more is required in response. Debt owed by the wealthy to the impoverished calls for compensation. If climate change is seen also as a matter of race and class-based climate privilege, then a moral response includes acknowledging and challenging that privilege.

Climate debt is a term coming from the Global South to describe the imbalance between those who suffer and die from climate change and those contributing most to it. More specifically, "climate debt" refers to the disproportionate per capita use of the atmospheric space for carbon sinks by industrialized countries in the past and present.[4] Climate debt theory posits that the costs of adapting to climate change and of mitigating it are the responsibility of the countries that created the crisis, the industrialized world. Said differently, "The polluter pays." In short, the idea of "climate debt" holds wealthy countries and companies accountable for the impacts of their historical and current overemissions of greenhouse gases (GHG) and thus overconsumption of atmospheric space.

Climate debt is seen to have three interdependent forms of repayment:

> Deep emission cuts in the developed world.
> Payment for the costs of adaptation: payment for the cost of dealing with the damages produced by climate change in countries that did not cause it. Adaptation costs include both damage prevention and response to damage after the fact.
> Payment for the costs of mitigation: Decrease the rate of climate change. This requires reducing emissions. The choices—for economically impoverished nations seeking economic development—are to (1) forgo economic development opportunities because they cause emissions or (2) bypass the heavy use of carbon-emitting fossil fuels in economic development, using instead clean renewable energy technologies, which are more expensive than fossil fuels. Both choices are enormously costly for nations lacking financial and technological resources. Payment from industrialized wealthy nations for the costs of mitigation in the Global South may be seen as compensation for the fair share of atmospheric space that countries of the Global South will not use if they are to reduce carbon emissions.

A complementary proposal is to "exchange" climate debt for the odious and illegitimate debt "owed" by many of the world's poorest nations to the wealthier industrialized nations and their financial institutions.

Many voices from the Global South argue that climate debt must figure centrally in climate negotiations, international trade and investment treaties, and development policy. Indeed, in environmental law, development economics, and environmental science, climate debt is becoming recognized as a critical factor in climate policy.[5]

Here we bring to the table a few relevant tools and perspectives from Christian ethics, as one form of political theology. Christian traditions may be a vital moral resource precisely because—from its birth—Christianity bore at its core a notion of goods held in common. Struggling to understand what that means in each new time and place is inherent in Christian history.

A word of clarification is in order regarding the interdiscipline of Christian ethics and the location of this essay in it. Christian ethical traditions—reflecting Christianity itself—have, from the outset, been multivocal and often contradictory. They have served the ends of oppression and destruction as well as liberation and radical social justice. Christian ethics have undergirded patriarchy, white supremacy, ecological violence, and some of human history's most heinous movements—including slavery and the genocide of peoples in the continents that became known as the Americas. Christian ethical traditions also have been foundational for some of humankind's great justice movements, such as abolitionist and civil rights movements in the United States, liberation movements in Latin America and Africa, and efforts to uproot patriarchy and class-based exploitation. This essay and the tools of ethics it develops are situated in a trajectory of Christian ethics that acknowledges this paradoxical history, and that practices ethics as both a self-critical and a constructive discipline. This trajectory criticizes those Christian beliefs and practices that have served the forces of oppression and destruction; reclaims liberative voices in Christian traditions that have been repressed or ignored by dominant streams of Christianity; and reconstructs the tradition for the sake of faithfulness to God's call to justice and Earth care. Thus, in this essay I draw on Christian ethics to challenge neoliberalism and postcolonialism; in other work I have exposed strands of Christian ethical traditions that supported these movements.

## TOOLS AND PERSPECTIVES FROM CHRISTIAN ETHICS AS A POLITICAL THEOLOGY

Ethics commonly is seen as a normative discipline—responding to the question of "What ought to be?" or "What ought we do and be?" Christian ethics as a political theology, however, brings a fierce commitment to engage also the descriptive task of ethics—to ask "What is?" and to do so from a critical perspective. By this I mean a perspective that brings power dynamics to the center of ethics and seeks an understanding of reality that prioritizes perspectives from the margins of power and privilege.[6] A caveat is necessary: No person situated in privilege can claim to read reality from the margins. However, a critical perspective holds that one can and must make every effort to do so, always acknowledging the limitations of that effort. That is a central challenge and commitment of Christian ethics done from positions of historically accrued privilege.

This challenge bears four implications. They are staunch commitment to (1) disclose where power imbalance and its consequences go unacknowledged, (2) ferret out historical and structural roots of those power asymmetries and the inequity that they breed, (3) acknowledge their cumulative consequences, and (4) accept commensurate moral responsibility. Let us see what happens in an ethical account of climate change shaped by these four commitments.

First, however, a word about "who."[7] This essay grapples with the moral dilemma of a particular people of whom I am one. I speak of this people as "we," referring to U.S. citizens who also are white and are economically privileged.[8] We are material beneficiaries of the colonial and neocolonial history that has shaped life on Earth in the last half millennia. We are descendants of the tribes of Europe who colonized four continents and ravaged their peoples, and we have inherited the material wealth accumulated in that process. Moreover, our material lives are dependent—again through political, economic, and military systems—on the current exploitation of people and natural goods the world over. Finally, as citizens of a "democracy," we have—at least theoretically—the political agency to challenge those systems. (Much of what I say herein may pertain to U.S. citizens who are not white-identified or who are not economically privileged, or to other people of the Global North. However, the "we" here is more specific.)

I recognize that the boundaries of this "we" are ambiguous. In many senses, all U.S. citizens participate in economic and ecological exploitation, yet many also are exploited through inadequate wages, nonexistent or sparse benefits, poor working conditions, wage theft, regressive taxation, conversion of affordable housing, exorbitant health care costs, and more. As a result, many live in poverty that may have life-threatening consequences or maintain a constant struggle to avoid poverty. These people are not my primary audience, but more important, they are not the "we" of whom I speak. This is crucial. Ethical obligations are particular. God's call to love neighbor as self—arguably the basic moral norm of Christian life—takes divergent forms depending on just who that "self" is.

I move now to formulate an ethical account of climate change that takes seriously a theologically rooted commitment to power analysis and to the well-being and perspectives of people of the margins.

*Disclose Power Imbalance and Its Consequences*
White privilege is one axis of asymmetrical power in the United States. A system of privilege exists when one category of people is denied something of value in a society simply because they are considered a part of that category.[9] A central feature of a system of privilege is "dominance."[10] This means that people of the privileged category tend to occupy positions of power. Not all people in the dominant category are powerful, but positions of power are disproportionately filled by the privileged category.[11] In our world today, the people who determine policies that affect climate do not tend to be those who are losing their homes or livelihoods due to climate change. The indigenous residents of Alaskan villages currently being lost to rising seas, the victims of malaria's increase as a result of climate change, and the estimated twenty-five million environmental refugees are not at the tables of power in climate-related policymaking. The environmental justice movement is committed to uncovering and dismantling "the unequal protection against toxic and hazardous waste exposure" experienced by communities of color and impoverished communities. However, at the heart of that movement is the commitment also to expose and undo the systematic exclusion of people of color from environmental decisions affecting their communities. That is, the environmental justice movement addresses power imbalance.

Denial—a second defining feature of privilege systems—allows the sinister dynamics of privilege, including asymmetrical power relations, to continue unrecognized by those who benefit from them. U.S. history is shaped by denial of white privilege. The sociologist George Lipsitz writes that in the United States clear perception of the present "requires an understanding of the existence and the destructive consequences of the possessive investment in whiteness that surreptitiously shapes so much of our public and private lives."[12] Denial means denial of the existence of privilege and of the power imbalances that sustain and flow from it. Ignoring the mounting ecological debt and its deadly consequences is also ignoring the white privilege inherent in it.

Entitlement is a third hallmark of white privilege and other systems of privilege. As a whole, the descendants of Europe in the United States have assumed that we are entitled to use of the ecosphere as a carbon dump site. We tend to assume that if I have earned my money, house, car, yard, and vacation by my hard work, then I have the right to use them, to build my life as I see fit within the norms of my society and the limits of the law.

Dominance—or power imbalance—is a central feature of privilege. Denial and entitlement, two other linchpins of privilege, attempt to justify or legitimate that power imbalance. In light of "our" finely honed ability to maintain power structures that exploit people of color and impoverished people, deny that our material wealth is built on exploitation, and assume our entitlement, *it is likely that the dominance, denial, and sense of entitlement inherent in climate change will continue unless explicitly resisted*. This would mean continuing not to recognize and take moral responsibility for the disproportionate impact that climate change has on people of color and economically impoverished people. More important for our purposes here, it would mean denying the disproportionate responsibility borne by the world's high-consuming minority—largely white.

In this case, we, the high-consuming and economically privileged minority, would continue to:

Respond to climate change in ways that reduce our carbon footprint
  and protect ourselves from the worst of the disastrous impact
Respond primarily with charitable assistance to mitigate the disastrous
  impacts of climate change on vulnerable people of the Global South
Assume that all nations have *equal* obligations to reduce carbon
  emissions
Fail to compensate for climate debt.

The probable consequences are sinister. To illustrate: When yields of the world's staples diminish due to rising temperatures, neoliberal international trade and investment mechanisms ("free" market) would enable corporate agribusiness and the finance industry to raise prices and maximize profit. In the process, those of us with investments in those industries would gain financially, whereas impoverished people would be priced out. That is, once again economic policy would engender starvation.[13] The norms of dominance, denial, and entitlement have been built over the centuries.

*Acknowledge Historical and Structural Roots*
Christian ethics' effort to read reality for the margins of power and privilege entails looking beyond apparent causes to their structural and historical roots. Two historical dynamics—colonialism and neoliberalism—link climate change to white privilege and class privilege.

COLONIALISM
Colonialism established the legal and moral norm: According to the Doctrine of Discovery, Europeans and their descendants had the divinely mandated "moral and legal right . . . to invade and seize indigenous lands and to dominate Indigenous Peoples," regardless of the cost to those lands and peoples. Exploitation and domination were morally mandated. These patterns continue today to shape distribution of power and of the goods necessary for life

with dignity. The World Council of Churches, in repudiating the Doctrine of Discovery, writes:

> Patterns of domination and oppression that continue to afflict Indigenous Peoples [and other communities of color] today throughout the world are found in numerous historical documents such as Papal Bulls, Royal Charters and court rulings. For example, the church documents *Dum Diversas* (1452) and *Romanus Pontifex* (1455) called for non-Christian peoples to be invaded, captured, vanquished, subdued, and reduced to perpetual slavery and to have their possessions and property seized by Christian monarchs. Collectively, these and other concepts form a paradigm or pattern of domination that is still being used against Indigenous peoples.[14]

NEOLIBERALISM

Neoliberalism (or corporate colonialism) deregulated and reregulated finance and trade in order to remove democratic constraints to maximizing wealth accumulation and concentration.[15] Elsewhere I have identified defining features of the neoliberal global economy, its constituative elements, and its impact on economic disparity and ecological degradation.[16] Suffice it here to note that neoliberalism opened floodgates to extractive industries and the exploitation of both labor and Earth's goods. According to a United Nations Human Development Report, by the late twentieth century—after two decades of neoliberal policies and practices—225 people had wealth equal to that of 47 percent of humankind.[17] For many, poverty spells death.

Commonly known as "free trade," neoliberalism reregulated not only trade but also finance. With financialization of the global economy—what I have called the "free investment" agenda—trade in money products far outpaced trade in goods and services. Speculative investment by the few, unaccountable to any bodies politic and not paying commensurate taxes to them, soared. Wealth, and with it power, was further concentrated in few hands, as became evident in the recent (and ongoing) global financial crisis.

Neoliberalism has two broad impacts on climate change and climate debt. The increase in trade and Foreign Direct Investment (FDI)—especially in extractive industries—results in increased GHG emissions, including emissions from the use of extracted oil and coal. Second, the financial benefits of carbon-fat industry and commerce accrue disproportionately to large corporations and finance institutions whose beneficiaries are people of the Global North.

*Acknowledge Cumulative Impacts*

Viewing inequity with an eye to cumulative impacts is a third requirement of Christian ethics' effort to read reality from the undersides of power and privilege. Colonialism and neoliberalism produced vastly unequal access to Earth's natural goods, aggravating poverty and the wealth gap. "[The global poor] and we depend on a single natural resource base, from the benefits of which they are largely and without compensation, excluded. The affluent countries and the elites of the developing world divide these resources . . . without leaving 'enough and as good' for the remaining majority of humankind."[18]

This misdistribution of access to water, land, and mineral wealth was an initial form of ecological debt. To it was added another—the corporate practice of transferring ecologically dangerous production plants to countries of the Global South in order to avoid environmental regulations.[19] "Pollution havens" joined tax havens.[20] If maximizing profit is the primary goal and value of corporate activity, then moving plants to where costs of production are cheaper is "necessary" and "good." The ensuing environmental devastation to workers and to the people whose water and food are poisoned and whose homes and farmlands destroyed does not count. Yet the corporate profits are applauded on Wall Street.

Climate injustice is the most recent form of ecological debt. With greenhouse gas emissions, notes ethicist Michael Northcott, "the rich are using the atmosphere of the poor to absorb their waste carbon."[21] Some activists and theorists of the Global South refer to this as climate colonialism. The National Council of Churches in India declares:

> Climate change and global warming are caused by the colonization of the atmospheric commons. The subaltern communities are denied their right to atmospheric commons and the powerful nations and the powerful within the developing nations continue to extract from the atmospheric common disproportionately. In that process they have emitted and continue to emit greenhouse gases beyond the capacity of the planet to withstand. However, the subaltern communities with almost zero footprint are forced to bear the brunt of the consequences of global warming.[22]

In an eloquent plea to the world community, Mohammed Nasheed, president of the Maldives, implored: "Please ladies and gentlemen, we did not do any of these things [lead high carbon-emission lifestyles], but if business goes on as usual, we will not live. We will die. Our country will not exist."[23] William Rees and Laura Westra make the case that excessive consumption translates into "violence" against those who suffer most from climate change. "Not acting to reduce or prevent eco-injustice," they write, "would convert erstwhile blameless consumer choices into acts of aggression." "Over-consuming nations (and individual over-consumers) must come to terms with the fact that the ancient concept of gluttony-as-deadly-sin has acquired new modern meaning."[24]

*Assume Moral Responsibility*

The fourth and most challenging piece of Christian ethics' commitment to the margins is accepting the moral responsibility produced by the structural power imbalance, historical roots of that power asymmetry and of climate change, and the cumulative impacts of these dynamics. If climate change were not connected, historically and contemporarily, to our overconsumption and to the public and corporate policies, power alignments, and practices that enable it, then dramatically reducing our carbon footprint and giving charitable relief and assistance would be ethically adequate responses to climate-related suffering. We would be called to "greener" living and to generosity in helping the victims. Climate policy and energy policies could aim primarily at emissions reduction.

However, this response is an utterly inadequate and deceptive moral lens if we play a significantly disproportionate causal role in climate change, have benefited from it, and have the resources and political freedom to do something about it. If affluent societies are disproportionately responsible for climate change, and if those societies have accumulated their wealth historically and contemporarily from fossil-fuel-based economies that have generated the climate crisis, then emissions reduction and assistance for climate refugees and for mitigation, while a moral imperative, is not a morally adequate response.

The matter is made worse if those culpable societies have produced economies that impoverish vulnerable peoples, thus rendering them less able to survive the vicissitudes of climate-change-related "nature disasters." These connections hurl our moral world into tormenting tumult. Life lived in ways that cost other people their lives, where alternatives exist or are in the making and where political action toward them is possible, is not a moral life. What would it mean to accept moral responsibility for climate change as a matter of white privilege and climate debt? The remainder of this essay probes that question.

## MORAL RESPONSE

A paradox haunts the urgent quest for moral power in the face of climate change—especially as complexified by the reality of white privilege, class privilege, and climate debt. On the one hand, a large sector of U.S. society does not "get it." They do not realize the magnitude of ecological danger, the brutal consequences for people most devastated by it, and our vast culpability. Not recognizing the dire threat, they do nothing to address it. On the other hand, when denial is overcome, an impending sense of doom and powerlessness may loom, threatening to overpower any sense of moral power to "do something" that will "make a difference." Said differently, we cannot meet the challenge of climate change unless we see what is going on. Yet the more one knows, the more powerless one may feel. The knowledge necessary for moral acting also impedes it. The challenge, then, is not merely unmasking the systemic and historical roots and consequences of climate change but doing so in ways that evoke moral action.

*Morally Empowering Vision*
I am convinced that moral power is enabled by holding steadfastly to three forms of vision:

> Seeing "what is going on."
> Seeing "what could be"—that is, more just and sustainable alternatives to "the way things are" that are emerging in principle, public policy, and practice around the globe.
> Seeing ever more fully the sacred Spirit of life coursing throughout creation and leading it—despite all evidence to the contrary—into abundant life for all.

The third of these acknowledges or hopes for sacred powers at work in the cosmos enabling life and love ultimately to reign over death and destruction. It confirms what the ecotheologian Sallie McFague refers to as "our hope against hope that our efforts on behalf of our planet are not ours alone but that the source and power of life in the universe is working *in and through us* for the well-being of all creation, including our tiny part in it."[25]

Christian ethics, as a form of political theology, has at its heart the crucial task of holding these three in one lens. Vision of this sort is subversive because "it keeps the present provisional and refuses to absolutize it."[26] It reveals a future in the making and breeds hope for moving into it.

*Behavioral, Structural, and Consciousness Change: An Interplay*
The second mode of vision—alternatives to "the way things are"—is in itself an invitation to reductionism. It is often evident in my classrooms. Many of my students argue that structural change in the form of major public policy change, legal mandates, and large-scale institutional change is the only path to a more just and sustainable future. Lifestyle or behavioral change (e.g., riding bikes or buses instead of driving, giving up beef and packaged food, drinking fair trade coffee, boycotting Walmart, shopping at co-ops and farmers markets), they insist, is ineffectual and relatively insignificant.

Other students argue the opposite. Social structural change, they aver, will not occur to the extent that we need. What is needed are individual people and households deciding to live in ways that are ecologically sound and economically nonexploitative and then doing so (behavioral change). Still others focus on major underlying change in consciousness. What is needed, they assert, is a "new story," a vastly recalibrated cosmology and moral anthropology.

Few concepts are more important to moral agency than recognizing the constructive interplay between changes at these three levels: behavioral and structural levels and the level of consciousness. They are woven together on the path toward climate justice. A fuller treatment of climate change as a matter of climate debt and white privilege would explore all three strands and their intertwining. The limitations of a single chapter focus our attention here on what may be the most complex and contested of these three arenas of change: structural change—that is, change in public policy, corporate structure and operations, and other societal institutions. To illustrate, I focus even more specifically on one aspect of structural change: public policy.[27] Public policy is a worthy focus because, while often considered a vehicle of structural change, it also is a potent shaper of human behavior and consciousness.

Public policy related to climate change and energy will increasingly be at the forefront of public debates at both national and international levels. Public policy advocacy is one gateway through which U.S citizens who also are privileged by color and class may address climate change not only as a matter of sustainability but also of climate debt and the undue "privilege" produced by whiteness and class status. Needed are guidelines for that stream of action.

*Four Principles*
Enter here the power of guiding principles as criteria for policy formation and assessment. As noted at the outset, often in climate discussions, the guiding principle is ecological sustainability. Alone, however, this principle fails utterly to address the white privilege, class privilege, and climate debt aspects of climate change. To address these issues calls for ecological sustainability to be joined by three other principles. Climate policy will be guided by the principles of sustainability and principles of:[28]

> Environmental equity: Policy will promote equity in use of environmental space and will seek compensation for ecological debt.
> Economic equity: Policy will prioritize meeting human needs and Earth's needs over maximizing profit and accumulating wealth.
> Economic democracy: Policy will promote distributed and accountable economic power.

*The Four Principles Illustrated: Climate Policy*
How are responsible citizens to enact these four principles in public policy advocacy? What are the public policy implications of taking responsibility for

climate debt and the environmental racism inherent in climate change? How might these four principles inform public policy formation and advocacy? The relevant moral questions here include:

> Who should bear the costs of mitigation (efforts to reduce emissions and increase carbon sinks), and to what extent does that depend on historic responsibility for climate change and the capacity to bear the costs?[29]
>
> Who should bear the cost of adaptation (efforts to minimize the damages that will occur due to climate change—e.g., flood prevention, crop changes, development of medicines to deal with spreading diseases—and dealing with the damages that do occur), and to what extent does that depend on historic responsibility and the capacity to bear the costs?
>
> Climate policy conceptualizes financial responsibility for mitigation and adaptation in terms of nations. However, the "benefits" accrued from processes that emit greenhouse gases are not evenly distributed within nations. (For example, the wealth accrued in the United States through petroleum extraction around the globe has not been equitably distributed within the United States.) Nor are the burdens of climate change equitably distributed within nations. What sectors within the United States have the right to the costly protection mechanisms against climate-related disasters and protection from the rising costs of energy? What sectors of U.S. society ought to bear the costs of financing adaptation and mitigation in impoverished areas?
>
> Enormous profits continue to be made by fossil-fuel extractive industries. Who ought to be substantively involved in making decisions regarding whether U.S.-based extractive industries are allowed to operate, especially on Indigenous lands or lands of other marginalized communities?

Response to these questions is different if guided by the four aforementioned principles than if guided singularly by the principle of ecological sustainability. For example, the principle of democracy would call for participatory and publicly accountable decisions about extractive industries. People most affected by the industries' operations would have a substantive role in decision making.[30] Public policy guided by the principles of economic equity and environmental equity would assume historical responsibility and acknowledge cumulative impacts by applying what the United Nations Framework Convention on Climate Change (UNFCCC) calls "common but differentiated responsibilities and respective capabilities" (art. 3.1). That is, national, local, and state public policy and international negotiations would require wealthy countries that have been major per capita emitters in the past to take the lead in emissions reductions and in assisting developing countries' adaptation and mitigation efforts through finance and technology transfers. The reasons are two: accounting for historic responsibility and greater existing financial and technological resources. The UNFCCC says as much. Wealthy countries, it declares, shall provide financial resources and technological transfers needed by countries of the South for mitigation and adaptation (art. 4.3). This includes funding to "keep petroleum in the ground in fragile environments." Domestic policy would allow need and human rights to determine allocation of resources for adaptation and mitigation in the United States rather than the ability to pay (market). This would enable communities of color and low-income communities to benefit from relief and rescue, protection measures, energy cost subsidies (to mitigate increased energy costs), health care for climate-change-related disease, and so on.

Although actual domestic and global policy mechanisms are beyond the scope of this essay, I illustrate directions that they might take.[31] International and domestic public policy guided by the four aforementioned principles would:

1. Limit and reduce greenhouse gas emissions "in accordance with the levels advocated by the scientific community . . . through mechanisms that are controlled by the public sector, generate revenue, are transparent, are easily understandable by all, can be set up quickly, and have a track record of improving environmental quality."[32]
2. Avoid cap-and-trade policies that allow wealthy and high-polluting companies and industries to buy their way out of reductions; instead, charge for carbon emissions and do so upstream at points of extraction.[33] A carbon charge could "provide a revenue stream to support research and development of the necessary technologies as well as provide financial assistance . . . to mitigate the economic burden on all impacted by increased energy cost."[34]
3. Avoid policy that equalizes environmental or economic burden between impoverished communities (and nations) and wealthier communities (and nations). An example of policy to avoid was the trade-related provision in the American Clean Energy and Security Act passed by the house in 2009 that would have penalized developing countries with additional fees on their exports if they did not adopt reductions commitments equal to those of the United States.

4. Treat "climate financing" not as development aid but rather as "a legal obligation of developed countries which made commitments under the UNFCCC."[35]
5. Support Indigenous peoples' efforts to fight fossil-fuel extraction on their lands and commodification of their natural goods on the global market.
6. Cease locating toxic land use and fossil-fuel development in communities of color and impoverished communities.
7. Honor the "unalienable right of . . . people-of-color, Indigenous Peoples and low-income communities, who are and continue to be disproportionately impacted by climate change . . . to have [their] voices shape what is the most significant policy debate of the twenty-first century."[36]

## IN CLOSING

The two terms—"common" and "good(s)"—can inflect variously as can the theologies that link them. Yet a widespread moral sensibility holds that the good and the goods provided by this fecund Earth are to be shared. Earth's atmospheric ability to maintain a climate amenable to life may be the most fundamental of all goods needed in common by all humans and by otherkind. Climate debt and climate privilege, however, radically transgress the assumption that the atmosphere is to benefit all in common.

Christian ethics offers vital tools to the quest for an ethical approach to climate change—an approach that accepts moral responsibility for climate change as a matter of privilege and climate debt. I considered four: (1) disclosing power imbalance and its consequences; (2) uncovering their historical and structural roots; (3) acknowledging cumulative consequences; and (4) accepting moral responsibility commensurate with these disclosures. Key ingredients of accepting moral responsibility for climate change are a threefold framework for moral vision and the interplay of change at the levels of behavior, social structure, and consciousness or worldview. To illustrate the second of these—structural change—I viewed public policy as one vehicle for structural change, a vehicle that also shapes behavior and consciousness. Finding the principle of sustainability to be necessary but inadequate for climate policy that accounts for climate debt and privilege, I proposed the complementary principles of environmental equity, economic equity, and economic democracy.

Societies and sectors that benefit materially from historic and contemporary processes that "fuel" climate change are called to put brakes on it in ways that honor the fundamental understanding that Earth's atmosphere is for the good of all. If we fail to see the race and class privilege inherent in climate change, we could address it in ways that vastly increase existing gaps in power and privilege, enabling the "privileged" to survive and thrive while others do not.

NOTES

1. For example: The estimated six hundred million environmental refugees whose lands will be lost to rising seas if Antarctica or Greenland melt significantly will be disproportionately people of color, as are the twenty-five million environmental refugees already suffering the consequences of global warming. So too the people who will go hungry if global warming diminishes crop yields of the world's food staples—corn, rice, and wheat. The 40 percent of the world's population whose lives depend on water from the seven rivers fed by rapidly diminishing Himalayan glaciers are largely not white people. As recognized by the UN Conference on Sustainable Development, climate change "represents the gravest of threats to the survival" of some island nations. These nations are composed of people who are predominantly not white. See http://sustainabledevelopment.un.org/futurewewant.html.
2. For an ecotheological treatment of the common good see John Hart, *Sacramental Commons: Christian Ecological Ethics* (Lanham, Md.: Roman and Littlefield, 2006).
3. Walter Benjamin, "Madame Ariane: Second Courtyard on the Left," in *One-Way Street* (London: New Left Books, 1969), 98–99, cited in George Lipsitz, *The Possessive Investment in Whiteness: How White People Profit from Identity Politics* (Philadelphia: Temple University Press, 1998), 2.
4. Some refer to climate debt as "carbon debt." It is seen as one form of "ecological debt." "Climate debt" was introduced to the international discourse by Latin American NGOs at the 1992 UN conference at Rio. For more on "ecological debt," see the websites of Ecuador's Accion Ecologica, European Network for the Recognition of Ecological Debt (ENRED), England's Christian Aid, Friends of the Earth International, and World Council of Churches (WCC). See also Athena L. Peralta, ed., *Ecological Debt* (Quezon City: WCC, 2004); Andrew Simms, *Ecological Debt: The Health of the Planet and the Wealth of Nations* (Pluto Press, 2005); WCC Central Committee, "Statement on Eco-justice and Ecological Debt," 2009. http://www.oikoumene.org/en/resources/documents/central-committee/2009/report-on-public-issues/statement-on-eco-justice-and-ecological-debt.
5. For the three fields respectively, see, for example, Karen Mickelson, "Leading Towards a Level Playing Field, Repaying Ecological Debt, or Making Environmental Space," *Osgoode Hall Law Journal* 43, nos. 1&2 (2005): 137–70; Duncan McLaren, "Environmental Space, Equity and the Ecological Debt," in *Just Sustainabilities: Development in an Unequal World*, ed. Julian Agyeman, Robert D. Bullard, and Bob Evans (Cambridge, Mass.: MIT Press, 2003), 19–37; and T. Buhrs, "Sharing Environmental Space: The Role of Law, Economics and Politics," *Journal of Environmental Planning and Management* 47 (2004): 429–47. See also a long-term study led by University of California scientists published in U. Thara Srinivasan et al., "The Debt of Nations and the Distribution of Ecological Impacts from Human Activities," *Proceedings of the National Academy of Science* 105 (2008): 1763–73.

6. This commitment, while theoretically launched in liberation theologies and the political theologies that preceded from them, is firmly grounded in Scripture and the notion that the God revealed in Jesus and in his faith forbears, the ancient Hebrews, is a God who (1) worked through people and peoples on the underside of power and (2) rejected relations of oppression and exploitation. Theology knows these ideas as the "epistemological privilege of the poor" and "God's preferential option for the poor."
7. This paragraph and the following one are drawn from Cynthia Moe-Lobeda, *Resisting Structural Evil: Love as Ecological-Economic Vocation* (Minneapolis: Fortress Press, 2013).
8. By this I connote people whose economic lives might be described in the following terms: Their income is not totally dependent on wages or salaries. They have backup resources (i.e., family support, possibility of buying a less expensive home, investments, etc.). A severe recession probably would not place them in a position of having no home, inadequate food, or no access to health care, transportation, or other necessities. Perhaps more significant to this project, the economically privileged have enough economic resources that, without jeopardizing the basic ingredients of life for themselves and their dependents, they *could* make economic choices (pertaining to consumption, investment, employment, etc.) that would serve the cause of economic justice and ecological health, *even if those choices were to diminish their own financial bottom line.* They could choose, for example, to buy local, shun Walmart or other companies with exploitative practices, invest in socially and ecologically responsible investment funds, purchase a hybrid car or commuter bike, boycott products even if they are less expensive than the alternative, take time away from income earning work and dedicate that time to efforts for social change. This category of "economically privileged" is porous. "Basic necessities for life," "adequate food," and "poverty," for example, have many meanings. And the people fitting this description of economic privilege occupy widely ranging economic strata. Nevertheless, the intent is to signify the large body of U.S. citizens whose economic status bears these characteristics.
9. An early generative work on systems of privilege is Peggy McIntosh, "White Privilege and Male Privilege: A Personal Account of Coming to See Correspondence through Work in Women's Studies," Working Paper No. 189, *Center for Research on Women*, Wellesley College, Wellesley, Mass., 1088.
10. Allan Johnson, *Power, Privilege, and Difference*, 2nd ed. (2001; New York: McGraw-Hill, 2006), 91–95.
11. Ibid.
12. Lipsitz, *Possessive Investment in Whiteness*, 4.
13. See Mike Davis, *Late Victorian Holocausts: El Niño Famines and the Making of the Third World* (London: Verso, 2001) for an account of famine stemming from economic and other public policy.
14. WCC Executive Committee, "Statement on Doctrine of Discovery and Its Enduring Impact on Indigenous Peoples," February 17, 2012. http://www.oikoumene

.org/en/resources/documents/executive-committee/2012-02/statement-on-the-doctrine-of-discovery-and-its-enduring-impact-on-indigenous-peoples

15. My understanding that neoliberalism has entailed more "reregulation" in favor of financial institutions than "deregulation" is spurred by Tayyab Mahmud, in "Is It Greek or Déjà Vu All Over Again: Neoliberalism and Winners and Losers of International Debt Crisis," *Loyola University Chicago Law Journal* 42 (2011): 629–712.
16. See Moe-Lobeda, *Resisting Structural Evil*, Supplement to chapter 2 at http://resistingstructuralevil.com. For an account of "market myths" undergirding neoliberalism and its impact on democratic processes and trajectories, see Cynthia D. Moe-Lobeda, *Healing a Broken World: Globalization and God* (Minneapolis: Fortress Press, 2002), chaps. 3 and 2, respectively.
17. UNDP, *Human Development Report, 1998* (New York: Oxford University Press, 1999), 29–30. For additional figures on global poverty see "Fast Facts: The Faces of Poverty," at www.unmilleniumproject.org/resources.
18. Thomas Pogge, "Priorities of Global Justice," *Metaphilosophy* 32, nos. 1/2 (2001): 6–24.
19. This complements outsourcing to countries with weak labor regulations, low wages, and corporate tax breaks.
20. "Pollution haven" refers to "any instance involving the relocation of capital induced by cost savings arising from disparate regulations between countries." Matthew Clarke, "The End of Economic Growth? A Contracting Threshold Hypothesis," *Ecological Economics* 69: 11 (2010): 2219.
21. Michael Northcott, *A Moral Climate: The Ethics of Global Warming* (Maryknoll, N.Y.: Orbis Books, 2007), 84.
22. Rev. Christopher Rajkumar, Executive Secretary, Commission on Justice, Peace and Creation, National Council of Churches in India—in conversation with him.
23. At the UN Summit on Climate Change, Copenhagen, September 22, 2009.
24. William Rees and Laura Westra, "When Consumption Does Violence," in *Just Sustainabilities*, ed. Agyeman, Bullard, and Evans, 16.
25. Sallie McFague, *The Body of God: An Ecological Theology* (Minneapolis: Fortress Press, 1993).
26. Walter Brueggemann, *Prophetic Imagination* (Philadelphia: Fortress Press, 1978), 119, 44.
27. Central to moral agency in the face of social structures that appear insurmountable, is the recognition that they were constructed by human beings and therefore can be changed by them. The actions and social structures causing climate change were enabled and encouraged by public policies. They can, therefore, be replaced by other public policies.
28. These four principles are developed and illustrated in Moe-Lobeda, *Resisting Structural Evil: Love as Ecological-Economic Vocation*, chapter 8.
29. The World Bank's *World Development Report 2010* estimates: "In developing countries mitigation could cost $140 to $175 billion a year over the next 20 years (with associated financing needs of $265 to $565 billion)," and the costs to developing

countries "between 2010 and 2050 of adapting to an approximately 2 degree Celsius warmer world by 2050 is in the range of $75 billion to $100 billion a year." Cited by Martin Kohr, "The Equitable Sharing of Atmospheric and Development Space: Some Critical Aspects," *South Centre Research Paper* 33 (November 2010): 28. See also James Martin-Schramm, *Climate Justice: Ethics, Energy, and Public Policy* (Minneapolis: Fortress Press, 2010), 40.

30. Thus, for example, the Wayana in the Amazon jungles of southeast Suriname; the Ogani of the Niger Delta in Nigeria; the Lummi near Bellingham, Washington, in the United States; the Dongria Kondha in India's state of Orissa; and the First Nations peoples near Canada's tar sands would have a voice in determining if and how gold, petroleum, coal, or bauxite was to be taken from or transported through their lands.

31. For extensive treatment of this matter, see Erik Paredis et al., *The Concept of Ecological Debt: Its Meaning and Applicability in International Policy* (Rosemead: Academia Scientific, 2008). See also Maxine Burkett, "Climate Reparations," *Melbourne Journal of International Law* 29, no. 10 (2009): 516–35; Mickelson, "Toward a Level Playing Field"; and Carmen Gonzalez, "Environmental Justice and International Environmental Law" in Alam, S. et al (Eds.) *Routledge Handbook of International Environmental Law*, ed. S. Alam et al. (Abingdon: Routledge, 2009), 77–97.

32. Environmental Justice Leadership Forum on Climate Change, "Principles of Climate Justice," http://www.weact.org/Portals/7/EJ%20Leadership%20Forum%20 Principles.pdf.

33. See the Congressional Budget Office study, "Policy Options for Reducing $CO_2$ Emissions, February 2008," chap. 1. See: http://www.cbo.gov/publication/41663. See also the "People's Agreement" produced by the World People's Conference on Climate Change and the Rights of Mother Earth, Cochabamba, Bolivia, April 19–22, 2010. See http://pwccc.wordpress.com/support.

34. The Environmental Justice Leadership Forum on Climate Change (EJLFCC), "Carbon Charge and Environmental Review Emissions Reduction Strategy Policy Paper," http://www.weact.org/Portals/7/Carbon%20Charge%20Proposal%20 Final.pdf.

35. Kohr, "Equitable Sharing of Atmospheric and Development Space," 28.

36. EJLFCC, "Principles of Climate Justice."

∽ Common Flesh, Common Democracies

## Between a Rock and an Empty Place: Political Theology and Democratic Legitimacy

PAULINA OCHOA ESPEJO

Since the 1990s, political theorists have renewed an old debate about the theological origins of the concept of sovereignty. In particular, they have focused on how these origins affect the legitimacy of contemporary democracy. Mainstream democratic theory stemming from Enlightenment thought holds that state rule is legitimate when the people are the highest authority in the polity. That is, democratic government is legitimate to the extent that the people are sovereign. Popular sovereignty, as found in the social contract tradition, emerges from individual consent and the ideal of general consensus reached by deliberation.[1] Thus popular sovereignty becomes the main pillar of secular political thought because it grounds state legitimacy in reason and individual autonomy. In sum, according to mainstream democratic theory, popular sovereignty gives the state an immanent, secular foundation.[2] However, as many critics of mainstream Enlightenment thought have argued throughout the twentieth century, the concept of sovereignty is not itself secular: It has a long history with deep theological roots.

According to some political theologians, particularly those influenced by Carl Schmitt, the idea of popular sovereignty can never be fully detached from its theological inheritance.[3] In *Political Theology: Four Chapters on the Concept of Sovereignty*, Schmitt famously wrote: "All significant concepts of the modern theory of the state are secularized theological concepts."[4] In particular, he argued that the concept of sovereignty corresponds to the concept of divine will in the theological doctrines that dominated seventeenth- and eighteenth-century Europe. Given that the idea of a sovereign will that is above the law is incompatible with the immanent foundation of the state that the social contract proposes, any attempt to ground the law on immanent foundations ends up in contradictions and logical paradoxes.[5] Schmitt concluded from these claims that the concept of sovereignty necessarily retains its theological underpinnings, and so it necessarily undermines the normative commitments of secular liberal modernity, particularly the idea of unqualified liberal individual rights.[6] Hence, for Schmitt, autonomy and secularization are both chimeras.

However, other scholars have interpreted differently the theological inheritance of modern political thought. Hans Blumenberg and Charles Taylor, for example, agree that modern politics cannot completely shed its theological past. But they believe that modern thinkers have used the state's theological legacy to create new and legitimate institutions that do not depend on religious belief.[7] In this view, modern secular politics remains legitimate and authoritative provided that it is democratic, even if it must acknowledge and confront its theological past.

These two approaches, then, are opposing extremes in the debate about the permanence of political theology. As such, they share a common concern. For both approaches, the main issue is whether the modern state can be legitimate without religious belief unifying a population and thus giving a liberal state a preconstitutional grounding. Most champions of secularism worry that political theology always presupposes shared religious belief and thus engenders an exclusionary community unified around religious dogma. In these secularists' view, the state can and must distance itself from an illiberal religious grounding and thus should abandon political theology.[8] Political theologians in the tradition of Schmitt also believe that the modern state requires a secular grounding to be fully legitimate in its own terms. But they hold that democracy searches for immanence, openness, and pluralism in vain. The modern state always carries with it the cumbersome inheritance of sovereignty, so it cannot do away with some degree of dogmatism and violence.[9]

However, there is a third position in the political theology debate that has quietly arisen in liberal circles and become an obligatory reference in debates about representation, populism, and democratic legitimacy.[10] This position is chiefly associated with Claude Lefort but has many affinities and connections to Hannah Arendt's views on the matter. According to it, political theology has positive connotations.[11] What keeps a democratic order from collapsing into exclusionary authoritarianism is precisely the legacy of divine sovereignty. In this view, the legacy of political theology does not threaten liberal secular modernity, but rather shores it up by allowing the state to draw legitimacy from a source external to itself. According to Lefort, traditional religious sovereignty left "an empty place" in its wake. Thus in secularized modernity, the hope and promise of democracy depend on respecting this negative space and leaving it open. "The permanence of the theologico-political" thus preserves democracy by leaving a negative trace of the divine in the state.[12]

In this essay, I scrutinize this third position and argue that despite its many strengths in explaining twentieth-century totalitarianism, it cannot give democracy the moral guidance it promises. Lefort's idea of the "empty place of power" suffers many of the weaknesses of the early modern concept of sovereignty, particularly the decisionistic conception of divine and earthly power.[13] True, thinking of popular sovereignty as a negative space that demands distance and awe may at first seem to solve the logical problems that emerge from the analogy between God and Sovereign. But closer inspection shows that a negative conception of popular sovereignty undermines many of the values that have traditionally motivated democratic politics. These values include autonomy and equality, but also political participation, care for others, and care for the world we live in. For to the extent that the popular sovereign remains transcendent or "other" to actual people, law and government will continue to usurp the people's legitimate role in the democratic state. Rather than thinking of the people as a radically disembodied and purely symbolic reference standing for ideal justice and right, a positive conception of the people can challenge actual injustices and create alternatives for action that had not been possible before. The people is neither the unified and exclusionary "People-as-One" of totalitarianism nor a radically disembodied purely symbolic "empty place."[14] Between these options there are a myriad of possibilities. Here I concentrate on one of them: the "People as a Process." Conceived in this way, I argue, the people is not unified or complete; hence, it does not seek to become an absolute standard of right. But at the same time, I argue, the people does exist, and it can become the positive source of political morality that animates democracy and constitutes the common good for which we search in this volume. Moreover, asserting the people as process, a positive force that requires creativity and produces change, allows us to incorporate into politics the energy and power of symbolic and religious thinking, while avoiding the legal limbos and contradictions of sovereignty.

Given that the people as process is indeterminate, it cannot be described solely in the abstract. To talk about the people, we need specific accounts of concrete practices of political contestation, as well as other lived practices relating individuals and communities to each other and to the places where they dwell. Thus in the last section of this essay, I illustrate these practices with examples drawn from seeing the American people as a process. The constant creative changes the people undergoes can be best seen at the border of the United States and Mexico, where the "Security Fence" at the border symbolizes sovereignty, and the people as process creatively works around it.

## POLITICAL THEOLOGY IN POLITICAL THEORY: SOVEREIGNTY AS AN "EMPTY PLACE"

In political theory, the term "political theology" is often associated with Schmitt's essay of the same title.[15] The term is at the center of discussions about the secularization of political concepts and, specifically, how their theological origins affect the legitimacy of contemporary democracy. This debate on the causes and consequences of political theology in democracies goes beyond examining the historical legacies of the relation between church and state. Blumenberg, for example, argues that thinkers in the modern era built upon their theological inheritance to create new and legitimate forms of government that do not depend on religious thinking and instead concentrate on the metaphysical and symbolic features of politics shared by both religious and secular orders.[16] However, the debate's main point of contention remains the concept of sovereignty and how it brings with it religious ideas to the modern world.

According to Schmitt and his contemporary followers—of whom Giorgio Agamben is perhaps the best known[17]—all political orders have a common feature: the concept of sovereignty. In all regimes, the sovereign, or "he who decides on the exception,"[18] is a product of the legal order, and to that extent the sovereign belongs to the state. But at the same time, the sovereign stands outside the legal order so as to ground the law and establish the contours of the community that is created and governed by law. Thus sovereignty chiefly functions to link the legal order to an "external" source of legitimacy. Sovereignty structures society, both internally and externally, by providing criteria of exclusion that form society's external boundaries and internally differentiate society within the state. However, in doing so, the sovereign must be itself outside the law, just as the divine sovereign stood outside the world, and in politics this relationship introduces arbitrariness and creates legal limbos that undermine the principles that animate liberal democracy. (The best example of a legal limbo allowed by the sovereign exception is the concentration camp. This, of course, is not a relic of totalitarianism, as the politics of exceptionalism in Guantánamo Bay have shown in the last decades.) In this view, sovereignty is inevitable, and so are the exclusions it brings with it.

According to Lefort, by contrast, the theological legacy of the modern conception of popular sovereignty is not the problem. In fact, this legacy is precisely what saves democracy from drifting into authoritarianism. In particular, it prevents democracy from reaching the legal arbitrariness and exclusionary rage characteristic of totalitarianism. Lefort agrees with Schmitt, and with other scholars of political theology such as Leo Strauss,[19] that all political orders require an external source of legitimacy. But Lefort differs from other recent versions of this argument by believing that sovereignty is not necessarily the substitute for divine sanction. The symbolic function that a religiously authorized monarch fulfilled in premodern societies can be superseded in modern political institutions.

For Lefort, the state requires an "external" source of legitimacy, but this is not only a logical requirement to stabilize its legal order. The reference unifies the community symbolically, and it is a condition for establishing legitimacy. This is true even for states that justify rule on the basis of democratic procedures and liberal principles and therefore claim not to require controversial ethical or metaphysical assumptions to do so. This happens because the stability of any democratic state relies on principles that democratic procedure cannot provide. Liberal democratic theories cannot justify democratic procedures democratically, or internally. For example, the principle of individual autonomy may justify rule democratically through consent or contract. But a contract cannot itself justify contract as a democratic procedure of justification, because one would require a previous contract to justify the first contract, which in turn would require a prior contract, and thus we are off on an infinite regress. Also, a liberal justification of the state espouses the principles of freedom and equal respect for persons but cannot rely on democratic procedures to justify these principles without circularity because any democratic procedure presupposes them. Moreover, if one argued that legitimate democratic principles could emerge from public deliberation in the form of a popular will, one would encounter a similar difficulty. For a deliberative justification requires individuals with the capacity and disposition to deliberate, but deliberation itself cannot determine what precisely this capacity and disposition are because any legitimate deliberation presupposes these terms. In sum, given that a democratic state cannot create its own ground, at least some elements of the state's justification must come from outside of liberal principles or democratic deliberation. This view is best exemplified by the form of government that Hannah Arendt called "authoritarian." In her view, "the source of authority in authoritarian government is always a force *external* and superior to its own power; it is always this source, this *external* force which *transcends* the political realm, from which the authorities derive their authority, that is, their legitimacy, and against which their power can be checked." [20]

For Lefort, a political society needs religion to the extent that "every religion states in its own ways that human society can only open on to itself by being held in an opening it did not create."[21] Premodern societies could "open unto themselves," or assert their identity, and relate to their own future, and to other societies, only when they saw themselves as whole and complete. But according to Lefort, societies could not be complete unless they were grounded on something external ("A different time, a different space"[22]), which is the hallmark of religious thought, but also philosophical self-reflection. The historical and mythical narratives typically associated with religion were something necessary to society, which was thus "held in an opening it did not create." What made possible this opening was that something else created it, that an external grounding gave it limits and internal structure. Thus, premodern religious society was anchored in a fixed view of nature and sustained by an external or suprasensible realm that gave nature its laws and its internal order. In other words, religion unified society from the outside. Yet contemporary democracies cannot accept religious dogma as their ground because it is incompatible with individual autonomy. So they must come up with something that simultaneously explains the relation of human society to the "beyond" that gives society meaning and yet does not jeopardize autonomy and pluralism.

Throughout medieval Christianity, the connection between the suprasensible realm that gives meaning to the world and unity to society was represented by the figure of a ruler that communicated directly with the divine. The king was sovereign, and his person mediated between divine right and mundane politics. Moreover, his physical body gave a concrete locus for the symbolic idea of the body politic.[23] However, after the advent of the modern revolutions,[24] the social distinctions that had structured premodern society vanished. The king and religious narratives ceased to articulate the relations of society with the divine, but the structure of mediation between society and an exterior force that gave it meaning remained necessary to order society. In sum, modern societies inherited the state's power structure but replaced divine right with secular popular sovereignty and the principles of individual freedom and equality that animate modern democratic thought. The main outcome of this revolutionary change was to unhinge traditional sovereignty without completely displacing it.

For Lefort and other political theologians, a risk inheres in preserving the symbolic role of traditional sovereignty. If one understands sovereignty as a way of linking political power to the transcendent ground that gives it meaning, then sovereignty endangers modern politics. When the legal figure of the sovereign is conceived as a dogmatic source of legitimacy standing above the law, it compromises liberal principles of autonomy and equality. This is particularly dangerous when the sovereign becomes an abstract image of the people symbolically unified: either by a totalizing ideology or by the exclusion of ethnic groups perceived as "alien" or "other." Indeed, this is the mechanism that Schmitt saw at work in modern liberal politics. However, according to Lefort, modern politics is not doomed to this outcome. Democracy managed to substitute popular sovereignty for divine right by *not occupying* the place of the king and thinking of the representation of power as an "empty place."

The "empty place" by which democracy represents power refers chiefly to the fact that in a liberal democracy, government is divided, and power periodically redistributed. When a government checks its power through internal division and rulers accept electoral defeats, no individual or group within society can fully embody the state's power. According to Lefort, democratic discourse states that power belongs to no one, that those who exercise power do not possess it; and they do not, indeed, embody it; that the exercise of power requires a periodic and repeated contest; that the authority of those who are vested with power is created and re-created as a result of the manifestation of the will of the people.[25]

At a deeper level, the discourse of an empty place means that legitimacy cannot refer explicitly to an "outside" (assigned to the divine) or an "inside" (a constituted exclusionary community). In democracies all legal and political institutions are designed to contain conflict, and this institutional structure can (actually and symbolically) sustain this "empty space." In democracies, the instituting subject of society, the people, is revealed to be indeterminate. The people is never a substantive unit. So,

> when an empty place emerges, there can be no possible conjunction between power, law and knowledge, and their foundations cannot possibly be enunciated. The being of the social vanishes or, more accurately, presents itself in the shape of an endless series of questions (witness the incessant, shifting debates between ideologies). The ultimate markers of certainty are destroyed, and at the same time is born a new awareness of the unknown element in history.[26]

Thus, for Lefort (as interpreted by a sympathetic critic) "modern politics signals a loss and a gain: it entails a loss of unity and security, but harbors the gain of openness and radical questioning."[27] Democracy gives up the substantive unit of society in exchange for political freedom.

Lefort's idea of an "empty place," then, seems attractive for at least two important reasons. First, it is attractive because it promises a solution to one of the chief problems of modern political theory. It grounds the state's legitimacy and society's cohesion without giving them a specific dogmatic content that could threaten autonomy and the liberal principles of freedom and equality. If "the people" is defined negatively as a space of contestation, where different positions can engage with each other without appropriating power in the name of one particular view or set of principles, then democracy can maintain the idea of a sovereign people without turning that people into a subject with a particular will. The negative definition limits each individual's or group's claim to power. Hence it prevents a majority from capturing the whole state. The negative view of the popular sovereign enables an engagement among different groups who have contrasting (and even contending) points of view without threatening the unity and the stability of the political regime.

Second, the idea of representing the power of the state as an "empty place" is also attractive because it explains why a democracy degenerates into totalitarianism when a group or an individual occupies the seat of power in the name of the unified people. When "the people" ceases to be a negative standard of reference and becomes a concrete subject, the state's legitimacy depends on finding the people's concrete will, and thus it requires making the people homogenous and unified: what Lefort calls "The People-as-One." Thus a totalitarian state will seek to quash dissent or even eliminate parts of the population that would threaten ethnic or cultural unanimity of an idealized concrete people. In totalitarian regimes an idealized concrete people usurps the rightful place of the popular sovereign. But in regimes with an "empty space," the sovereign's place is left intact.

Lefort's view of political theology then is valuable because it shifts the course of the existing debate in political theory. He achieves this goal by retaining an analogy of the divine and the seat of power, but this time as an analogy of negative political theology. Rather than substituting the divine with a concrete body, it substitutes it with an "empty place." Unlike Schmitt and his followers, Lefort does not give us a view of the modern state that requires secularization but cannot achieve it, and a view of modern politics that is always prone to dogmatism and violence. Instead, negative political theology allows Lefort to retain the important features of an order sustained by the suprasensible, and still envision the modern liberal state as a form of political organization that avoids the dangers of totalitarianism and makes space for political pluralism and contestation.

### THE LIMITS OF THE NEGATIVE

Lefort's idea of the "empty place" is an invaluable resource in political theory. It explains the impossibility of popular unification, it helps democrats avoid dogmatism, and it could eventually prevent totalitarian rule by exposing the mechanism by which that rule constructs "The People-as-One." However, despite its strengths, Lefort's negative view of legitimacy cannot provide the positive political morality that democracy requires: When criticizing the notion of "The People-as-One," Lefort also dismisses the possibility that a real people, that is, a civil society or engaged citizenry, could act. In his view, the popular sovereign is an empty space defined by institutional and legal structures; it is only a transcendent standard of justice and legitimacy. That is, rather than "The People-as-One," the citizens become "The People-as-No-One."[28] The idealized people conceived as a regulative ideal becomes "other" to actual individuals in the political arena, and in this manner both representative rule and actual political power within the democratic state will always seem to usurp the power that legitimately belongs to the people.

The negative conception of popular sovereignty can undermine democratic politics because in a democracy "the people" should not be just a symbolic referent that protects society from the tyranny of any one particular point of view; it should also be the standard that guides action and motivates change. When the people is defined only negatively, we avoid dogmatism, but we also lose the guiding standard. The legal and institutional articulation of democracy discussed in the preceding section can make us forget that the people is not only a metaphor or an idealization transformed into a legal referent. Historically, "the people" refers to the risen masses that may disrupt the workings of the economic realm and that may subvert the social order as experienced during the era of revolutions. Without some concreteness, the people becomes solely an abstract criterion of justice that legitimizes democratic rule, and this criterion is as interpreted by the legal and political elites that exercise actual power. Thus "the people" conceived negatively becomes a rhetorical device that lacks the legitimizing force bestowed on it by political philosophers during the era of revolutions.

Moreover, the idea of the empty place of power may perpetuate some of the problems inherent in the concept of sovereignty, namely, the need for a final personal decision. One of the main strengths of popular sovereignty conceived as an "empty place" is that this conception prevents usurpation. If the people is an empty place, nobody can take its rightful place. But this raises the question of what precisely is being usurped. The definition of the negative space already presupposes a positive definition of the people, which defines the realm of authorized political power. Thus, those who have the power to determine the limits of political authority (that is, those who *decide* what precisely are the limits of the place that ought to remain empty) end up appropriating all the power of the state. Those who can legally and institutionally decide on the boundaries of the "empty place" end up usurping power.

It is true that representing democratic power as an empty place can work as the symbolic referent that enables some degree of social cohesion in the legal state. However, this role also can entrench the present contours of the legal order and generate political quietism. According to the negative view, the empty place of power should not be disrupted, both because it is considered unintelligible or ineffable and, more important, because it is considered sacred. This means that dogmatism has been moved back one step: Now the sovereign decision emerges in the prohibition on occupying the empty place or disrupting its existing contours. Hence those who establish the constitutional laws creating the mechanisms of separation of powers and those who pass the original laws that prevent any particular person or group from acting in the name of the unified people are now the ultimate deciders and the holders of power. Thus by claiming to establish an "empty place," there is a risk that an elite usurps the people's rightful place. In politics, these are the limits of the negative.

The resources of negative theology at first seem perfect for dealing with the legacies of the divine. However, there are crucial disanalogies between theology and politics that eventually undermine the ideals of democracy. The analogy of Sovereign and God that is at the center of this negative theology can cause problems because it gives the people particular characteristics that are not required in democratic politics. When articulating a negative conception of God, negative theology cannot assert dogmatically any divine characteristics, but it still asserts God. Similarly, in the negative view of popular sovereignty, no given citizen or group within the polity can fully describe the substance of the people's will without doing violence to democracy. But citizens and representatives can, and in fact should, invoke "the people" as the condition of possibility of democracy and the guarantor of the space of contestation. However, there is a crucial disanalogy between theology and political thought: All negative theologians agree that there is a divine object, but democrats need not believe that the people's will is sacred.

If we espouse the metaphor of the empty place as sacred, we must accept that negative space's very existence and precise contours of the negative space are not up for discussion. But the precise contours of this bounded people are not a fact that we encounter (in the way we encounter the world that we presumed bound by transcendence). A bound people is rather the product of a political decision that somebody had to make. This means that the space of power is not truly empty: Somebody usurps the place of power when that person decides the limits of the empty place by establishing liberal spheres of individual rights and laws entrenching constitutional conventions.

This last conclusion shows why the idea of the empty space can ultimately undermine the ideal of autonomy and equality. Some members of society had the chance to define the scope of contestation, whereas others just received it. Receiving the limits is incompatible with autonomy, and being the subject of a prior decision that did not involve one's point of view undermines equality. But the negative view of power also goes against other cherished political ideals such as political participation, care for others, and care for the world: If the negative ideal protects you from tyrants, it also protects you from changing the very scope and limits of the people; it entrenches the rules that limit participation and the boundaries of citizenship.

A negative political theology is not only a legal fiction. It is also a symbolic ground that draws the contours of society and determines the criteria of inclusion and exclusion. A negative view protects the existing people from tyranny, but it does not provide a way to change the actual people and the existing practices that make it up. If the "empty space" is viewed as the space of contestation, then the metaphor is misleading. The space of contestation is not empty: It is in fact fully occupied. Even if it is not unified, the space of contestation is full of differing views and full of individuals asserting their views; it is full of political changes and encounters; it is full of clashes and relations that are themselves creative and constitute a concrete political process.

## THE PEOPLE AS PROCESS

A "fully occupied place of power" can also be compatible with a view that celebrates political theology. But rather than thinking of the people either as a concrete unified body or as a purely symbolic reference standing for ideal justice and right, this requires that we embrace a positive conception of the people that is compatible with pluralism. Such a conception, I argue, can avoid the problems of sovereignty just as Lefort's formulation did, but it can also make sense of the modern intuition that a concrete people has the right to challenge actual injustices, and it can create alternatives for action and cooperation that had not been possible before popular organizations intervened. Yet such a conception must deal with the logical problems of sovereignty, as well as the challenges of symbolically constructing unity and social cohesion on the basis of political action.

Elsewhere, I proposed the conception of the *people as process*.[29] This conception of the people is not molded directly from theological views, but it takes seriously the challenge of political theology, as it acknowledges the symbolic role of religion, and the inevitable role of metaphysical views in the task of founding and legitimizing a political order. This appreciation of religion differs from Schmitt's or even Lefort's political theology in that it does not seek to reproduce by analogy the structure of divine sovereignty. Nor does it seek to reproduce the political representation of the state's "external" ground.

For this reason, process is useful here. Process philosophy can give a metaphysical ground to the state without opposition or complete transcendence. (This view may sound alien at first, but it is not new. Even within the history of Christian thought there have been influential figures who defined divinity in this manner.)[30] Thus, process presents a contestable metaphysical principle that internalizes the ground of politics and makes sense of the idea of autonomy and democratic self-creation. Following Bergson's and Whitehead's process philosophies, I see creative process as the ground that lends order and coherence to politics even as it introduces change and innovation in the political realm. By so doing, it provides the ontological conditions for self-creation.[31]

Process philosophy is not dualistic, and for this reason it could solve the problem that Schmitt's political theology reproduced in modern politics—the problem that by substituting divine will with a popular sovereign we inevitably reintroduce the problem of an ultimate "external" decider. Like Schmitt's and

Lefort's political theology, process philosophy takes seriously the role of metaphysics in ethics and the philosophy of the state. However, unlike those views, process philosophy does not espouse structural dualism—the opposition of "one" and "other." Instead, it proposes the concepts of "change" and "relation" as the ground of philosophical thought, given that process philosophy holds that time and process are the principal categories of metaphysics. On this view, process—rather than things or substance—is metaphysically ultimate.[32] Thus process philosophy incorporates the perceived indeterminacy of nature and skepticism about the abstractness of reason into a comprehensive metaphysical view. From such a view, there could emerge a political philosophy that takes into account the metaphysical problems that Schmitt and his followers perceive but does not generate the same political structures they think inevitable. Moreover, a processual political philosophy provides a metaphysical ground to account for processes of self-creation and self-legitimization. Hence it could solve the problem inherent in a dogmatic source of political authority external to the democratic process.

On this view, the people as process is a concrete entity capable of acting in the world, but it does not fall into the problems of the "People-as-One," for the people is not taken to be unified and complete at any given time. The people is open to the future and to its own past, and it can be considered a coherent entity because its trajectory is coordinated by aims that it itself sets as it changes. The people is in fact sovereign and can decide, provided that you don't conceive it as a unified subject with a will but rather as a series of events in which individuals partake.

The people, conceived as an indeterminate process, is not unified or complete, but it does exist, and it can become the positive source of the political morality that animates democracy. By asserting the people as a positive force that requires creativity and produces change, we can incorporate into politics the energy and power of symbolic and religious thinking. But we can also avoid getting caught up in the legal limbos and contradictions of sovereignty.

## MIRACLES AT THE WALL

Standing between totalitarianism and the contradictions of liberalism seems to put us between a rock and a hard place. Both positions are inherited from religious thinking, and they can both be seen as usurpations of the divine according to different conceptions of God. On the one hand, totalitarianism usurps divine omnipotence, and on the other hand, liberalism usurps the mystical intuition of the existence of a God of which nothing can be predicated. I believe that eschewing the analogy of God and Sovereignty altogether is the first step toward moving the discussion forward. Yet this does not mean that a secular view can ignore the importance of political philosophy's metaphysical ground and ontological basis. Acknowledging this importance is not just a logical imperative but also the result of admitting the importance of religious sensibility in political action. Too, it is an acknowledgment of the concrete power that religious sensibility can bring to organized individuals, even within secular democracies. Yet all this talk about the concrete people and the actual processes that constitute it does not go very far unless we provide concrete examples of what different political theologies of the people look like, and what practical consequences they have. In this last section, I spend some time giving examples of the three models of political theology that I have discussed in this essay. First, I go back to Schmitt's substitution of divine will by popular sovereignty. Second, I turn to Lefort's analogy of negative theology in the liberal notion of the "empty place" of politics; and finally, I illustrate my proposal of the "People as Process."

An example of the first model of political theology is well known: totalitarianism. The connection between decisionist political theology and totalitarianism was already clear in Schmitt's own lifetime. His view of sovereignty was both a consequence of the changes that were already under way in 1930s Europe and a harbinger of the Holocaust. A people that had previously been unified by religious narratives became secularized and replaced a divine sovereign with a sovereign people. The sovereign people, in turn, were sacralized as a Nation, whose unity was symbolized by ethnic purity embodied in the totalitarian leader. Totalitarianism thus illustrates how the idea that a concrete people can be sovereign may produce exclusionary violence, and it warns us against the overly optimistic conceptions of popular power. This warning is particularly pertinent given that the idea of popular sovereignty comes back periodically in the guise of a populist leader who quashes dissent and tries to make society homogenous in the name of the popular will.

Lefort's representation of popular power as an "empty place" can be best seen in the liberal appropriation of popular sovereignty as a conceptual pivot in the theory of liberal democracy. "The empty place" is defined by specific democratic procedures that enable political contestation and by institutions designed on the basis of separation of powers and checks and balances. In this view, the people is only a regulative idea, or a symbolic reference that defines the conditions for the possibility for electoral democracy, power sharing, and contestation of political positions. "The empty place" signifies the limits of political contest that prevent parties from tearing the state apart. A clear example of this view can be found in the "We the People" of the American Constitution. In the Constitution, "the people" is not a concrete group of individuals or a specific social body; instead, it is the ground of a legislative discussion, and the frame providing the rules and procedures that sustain the legal process. This example illustrates both the success of a negative political theology and the problems that may arise from it. The model sustains contestation and avoids tyranny, but it can seriously undermine the freedom and equality of those who are not already part of the procedure. Holding the constitutional "We the People" as sacred entrenches the procedures and legal rules that already exist, gives undue power to the Supreme Court, and restricts the scope of participation of those who are not already included in the citizenry. Here, the "empty place of power" becomes the sacred scope of the electoral and the legal realm, and it draws sharp boundaries around those forms of political action that are not already included in liberal institutions. This is the limit of the analogy with negative theology: Although we can understand why a negative view of the divine avoids dogmatism while preserving faith, it is unclear why the "sacred" space of already existing institutions should not be desecrated by all those who wish to change the contours of what already exists. Why should we not change institutions? Why should we not include those who wish to participate in American politics but are not already citizens of the state? The "empty place" is not really empty: It is symbolically occupied by those who define the boundaries of political power and the contours of its institutions. Moreover, it is physically defined by the geographical borders of the state. Hence the demand for preserving it as a sacred realm may lead to both philosophical quietism and political conformism.

The third model is less common in the literature but much more familiar to each of us. Rather than representing power in the abstract, it turns to the everyday events that give meaning to our lives and the lives of communities. This model turns to those events that structure meaning within the concrete flow of our everyday lives and political practices. In theory, the people as process is an unfolding series of events coordinated by self-creating practices of constituting, governing, or changing a set of institutions.[33] Thus, a particular example cannot show us a people as a whole; it can only illustrate how a given event can have consequences that change the direction of a democratic process, how individual and seemingly small or irrelevant events can actually change institutions and eventually help change the trajectories of the people as a whole.

Some events that create the people are highly visible and impossible to ignore. These are momentous events that establish a historical narrative: declarations of war, battles, or determinant elections. Nobody could deny the importance of events like the 9/11 attacks, or the 2000 and 2008 elections in recent American history, for example. However, the events that make a people as process and allow it to become the ground of democratic politics are less notable (though no less important). What matters most are the small cumulative changes that alter the self-understanding of a community.

Think, for example, of a type of event that occurs every day not far from San Luis Rio Colorado in the Mexican state of Sonora: A group of Central American immigrants sets off to cross the border without authorization from either the Mexican or American governments. As they cross through gaps in the "Security Fence" at the border, they participate in a settled practice that changes the face of the American people. And by doing so, they partake in the process that constitutes it. This event is both concrete and symbolic—it actually changes the face of the American people, just as one drop in a trickling stream is part of what eventually becomes a current. Here, the current is demographic and cultural change; but the border crossing is also a symbolic act that pits the people against the sovereign might of the state. The wall at the border was designed to physically guard the state's security and to symbolically protect a given idea of the American nation and its political institutions. The wall symbolizes sovereignty conceived as a limit and a boundary. Yet the daily events of crossing slowly change the people's boundaries without destroying the underlying background of meaning and the institutions that protect political freedom. After all, those crossings are also part of a national political conversation: They are the object of bitter disagreement, which over time constitutes new institutions and creates changes even among those who have never been in a border state or never been affected by legal limbos.

When individuals who partake in the process become aware of how these events change the American people, they may consciously bring in their creativity and use it to reconstitute the symbolic background that reproduces meaning in society. Society changes when immigrants cross the border, and "the people" is constituted as a conversation in different voices. In this process, religiosity plays a very important role, even if it does not have the structuring power of a sovereign that connects the political realm to the divine. For example, immigrants bring their faith and their religious practices across the border. Among Mexican immigrants, the image of the Virgin of Guadalupe is particularly important because it represents the Mexican nation and the historical development of that Catholic country, including its conflictual history with a secular state. However, as it crosses the border, the religious image changes too. It now becomes part of a distinctly American conversation about race relations, about ethnic and racial pride. Thus it becomes a character in a new historical narrative. In the traditional model of political theology, the image of the Guadalupe could be interpreted as part of the secularization of the Catholic Mexican people, where the secular Mexican nation takes over the sacralizing function of the divine in politics. But this story would be completely alien to the sovereign American people, itself constituted by a secularized Protestant "constitutional faith." However, if we conceive the people as a process, as a positive force that requires creativity and produces change, we can now incorporate into a common discussion different views of the relation of religious faith and politics. Now we can incorporate the energy and power of symbolic and religious thinking into a plural debate. But by making religious thinking one among many voices, the people as process can curtail the power of sovereign decisionism (and the resulting exclusionary consequences). The people as process participates in politics and prevents the entrenchment of one dominant view surrounded by a sacred religious or secularized legal halo.

Everyday events at the border may seem particularly important because of their symbolic weight within a national political conversation. But the events that make up a people as process are not always this visible. They are part of each individual's life, and they do not require special legal or religious sanction to be part of a political conversation. When people participate in politics through art, communal organization, public service and debate, they transform the sovereign's edges. They change the people both physically and symbolically, and they contest and change the rules from the outside without concern for the sacredness of the now existing legal contours of "the people." Any event, like the border crossings, may threaten the current legal order and the state's existing cultural unity, but it does so by creating something of more value: the internal transformation of the actual people that justifies democracy. The people thus conceived can transcend entrenched legal barriers. Moreover, it can supply the symbolic resources that give meaning to political action by opening the people to others and by caring for the specific relations and physical spaces where its transformation takes place.

## POLITICAL THEOLOGY AND DEMOCRATIC LEGITIMACY

With the idea of the "empty place" of politics, Claude Lefort made an important contribution to the debate on political theology. His insight explains how the legacy of religious thought influenced the development of totalitarianism in the twentieth century, and it clearly exposes the risks of committing to an idea of democracy that is not clearly aware of its own limitations. Those political philosophies that "occupied" the space left behind by religious legitimacy ended up becoming dogmatic ideologies and supporting tyrannical regimes. Lefort's contribution is to turn democratic theory insight out: Rather than affirming the claim of popular sovereignty, it negates those claims that do not recognize their own problems, their indeterminacy, and the margins of uncertainty in their positions. What Lefort's "negative" political theology negates is dogmatism and violence in the name of any one point of view.

Contemporary democratic theory has recognized and celebrated this contribution. However, this negative formulation has its own problems and risks. A merely negative view of popular sovereignty is insufficient for democratic legitimacy because it undermines the positive and productive role of the people in politics. Lefort's theory does not make sufficiently clear that in both politics and theology, negative positions do not merely negate and refute. If we want democracy to legitimize the state, we must also make a positive claim, a crucial affirmation: The people remains a guiding standard for the political common good. Yet to make this claim without going back to the danger of a totalitarian people, or dangerous populism, we need to find a way to both affirm the people as a force of positive change and negate it as an absolute standard of right. We need a way of thinking that allows us to negate dogmatism and assert openness without self-contradiction. This is the main promise of process thought for democratic theory.

My proposal then is an affirmation: *The people is a process*. But it is an affirmation that includes its own limitations. The idea of the people as process allows us to recover the contributions of negative political theology while making them compatible with the people as a source of positive political change. As a process, the people is not unified or complete. This means that the people's voice is not dogmatic; it is not the absolute standard of right. Yet the people does exist. When we assert the people as process, we put forward a positive force that produces change. And only because of these positive characteristics can the people be the guiding source of political morality without which democracy makes no sense. The "People as Process" is open, and for this reason it can sustain the ideals of equality and individual freedom that legitimate democratic government. But the people as process also conveys the thought that equality and political freedom themselves depend on indeterminacy and creativity: the ground and condition for the existence of the common good.

## NOTES

1. J. W. Gough, *The Social Contract: A Critical Study of Its Development* (Westport, Conn.: Greenwood Press, 1978).
2. For contemporary examples of this view see Jürgen Habermas, *Between Facts and Norms: Contributions to a Discourse Theory of Law and Democracy*, trans. William Rehg (Cambridge, Mass.: MIT Press, 1996); John Rawls, *Political Liberalism* (New York: Columbia University Press, 1993); John Rawls, *A Theory of Justice* (Cambridge, Mass.: Harvard University Press, 1999).
3. The seminal text in this debate is Carl Schmitt, *Political Theology: Four Chapters on the Concept of Sovereignty*, trans. George Schwab (Cambridge: MIT Press, 1985). Among the theorists informed by this text are Giorgio Agamben, *Homo Sacer: Sovereign Power and Bare Life* (Stanford: Stanford University Press, 1998); Ernst-Wolfgang Böckenförde, "Politische Theorie und politische Theologie," in *Religionstheorie und politische Theologie*, ed. Jacob Taubes (Munich: Wilhelm Fink, 1983),16–25; Jacques Derrida, "Force of Law: The Mystical Foundations of Authority," in *Deconstruction and the Possibilty of Justice*, ed. Drucilla Cornell, Michael Rosenfeld, and David Carl-

son (New York: Routledge, 1992), 3–67; Ernesto Laclau, "On the Names of God," in *Political Theologies*, ed. Hent de Vries and Lawrence Sullivan (New York: Fordham University Press, 2006), 137–47; Avishai Margalit, "Political Theology: The Authority of God," *Theoria* 106, no. 52 (2005): 37–50; Heinrich Meier, "What Is Political Theology?," in *Leo Strauss and the Theologico-Political Problem*, ed. Heinrich Meier (Cambridge: Cambridge University Press, 2006), 77–87; Hent de Vries, *Religion and Violence: Philosophical Perspectives from Kant to Derrida* (Baltimore: Johns Hopkins University Press, 2002).

4. Schmitt, *Political Theology*, 36.

5. I discuss this problem in detail in Paulina Ochoa Espejo, "Does Political Theology Entail Decisionism?," *Philosophy and Social Criticism* 38, no. 7 (2010): 725–43; Paulina Ochoa Espejo, "On Political Theology and the Possibility of Superseding It," *Critical Review of International Social and Political Philosophy* 13, no. 4 (2010): 475–94.

6. Carl Schmitt, *The Crisis of Parliamentary Democracy*, trans. Ellen Kennedy (Cambridge, Mass.: MIT Press, 1985).

7. Hans Blumenberg, *The Legitimacy of the Modern Age*, trans. R. M. Wallace (Cambridge, Mass.: MIT Press, 1985); Charles Taylor, *A Secular Age* (Cambridge, Mass.: Belknap Press of Harvard University Press, 2007).

8. Robert Audi, *Religious Commitment and Secular Reason* (Cambridge: Cambridge University Press, 2000); Jürgen Habermas, "On the Relationship between the Liberal State and Religion," in *The Frankfurt School on Religion*, ed. Eduardo Mendieta (New York: Routledge, 2005), 339–48.

9. Derrida, "Force of Law"; Laclau, "On the Names of God": Vries, *Religion and Violence*.

10. Claude Lefort, *Democracy and Political Theory*, trans. D. Macey (Minneapolis: University of Minnesota Press, 1988). For interpretations in English, see Bernard Flynn, *The Philosophy of Claude Lefort: Interpreting the Political* (Evanston, Ill.: Northwestern University Press, 2005); Samuel Moyn, "Claude Lefort, Political Anthropology and Symbolic Division," *Constellations* 19, no. 1 (2012): 37–50.

11. Hannah Arendt, *On Revolution* (New York: Penguin, 1990); Hannah Arendt, "What Is Authority?" in *Between Past and Future: Eight Exercises in Political Thought* (New York: Penguin, 1968), 91–142.

12. Claude Lefort, "The Permanence of the Theologico-Political?" in *Democracy and Political Theory* (Cambridge: Polity, 1988).

13. To understand the legal and political consequences of decisionism, see David Dyzenhaus, ed., *Law as Politics: Carl Schmitt's Critique of Liberalism* (Durham, N.C.: Duke University Press, 1998), Andreas Kalyvas, "From the Act to the Decision: Hannah Arendt on the Question of Decisionism," *Political Theology* 32, no. 3 (2004): 320–46; John P. McCormick, "Political Theory and Political Theology: The Second Wave of Carl Schmitt in English," *Political Theory* 26, no. 6 (1998): 830–54; Heinrich Meier, *The Lesson of Carl Schmitt: Four Chapters on the Distinction between Political Theology and Political Philosophy* (Chicago: University of Chicago Press, 1998

14. Lefort, "Permanence of the Theologico-Political."

15. Schmitt, *Political Theology*.

16. Blumenberg, *Legitimacy of the Modern Age*.
17. Agamben, *Homo Sacer*.
18. Schmitt, *Political Theology*, 5.
19. Leo Strauss, *Spinoza's Critique of Religion*, trans. Elsa Sinclair (New York: Schocken, 1965).
20. Arendt, "What Is Authority," 97. My emphasis.
21. Lefort, "Permanence of the Theologico-Political," 222.
22. Ibid., 223.
23. Lefort refers to the notion of the king's "two bodies" (empirical and sacred) by citing Ernst Kantorowicz, *The King's Two Bodies: A Study in Medieval Political Theology* (Princeton: Princeton University Press, 1997).
24. For Lefort, the paradigmatic revolution is the French, of course, but he traces the main changes in modern political thought to Machiavelli. Claude Lefort, *Machiavelli in the Making*, trans. Michael Smith (Evanston, Ill.: Northwestern University Press, 2012).
25. Lefort, "Permanence of the Theologico-Political," 225.
26. Ibid., 228.
27. Fred Dallmayr, review of *The Philosophy of Claude Lefort: Interpreting the Political*, by Bernard Flynn, *Notre Dame Philosophical Reviews* (2006).
28. Ibid.
29. Paulina Ochoa Espejo, *The Time of Popular Sovereignty: Process and the Democratic State* (University Park: Pennsylvania State University Press, 2011).
30. A good example of such a view is the political philosophy of Nicholas of Cusa, also known as Nicholas Cusanus. Cusanus developed in the fifteenth century a conception of God as Non Aliud. According to this conception, God is "not-other," and it mediates between transcendence and immanence. I discuss this view in more detail in Ochoa Espejo, "Does Political Theology Entail Decisionism." See also Jasper Hopkins, Introduction to *Nicholas of Cusa on God as Not-Other, a Translation and an Appraisal*, ed. Jasper Hopkins (Minneapolis: Artur Banning, 1983), 3–26.
31. Henri Bergson, *The Creative Mind*, trans. Mabelle L. Andison (New York: Philosophical Library, 1946); Henri Bergson, *The Two Sources of Morality and Religion*, trans. R. Ashley Audra and Cloudesley Brereton with the assistance of W. Horsfall Carter (New York: Henry Holt, 1937); Alfred North Whitehead, *Process and Reality: An Essay in Cosmology* (1927–28; New York: Free Press, 1978). I discuss their views in Paulina Ochoa Espejo, "Creative Freedom: Henri Bergson and Democratic Theory," in *Bergson, Politics and Religion*, ed. Alexandre Lefebvre and Melanie White (Durham, N.C.: Duke University Press, 2012); Ochoa Espejo, *Time of Popular Sovereignty*, chaps. 6 and 7.
32. Whitehead defines creativity, his "category of the ultimate," in terms of an irreducible pluralism—as "the many become one and are increased by one." Whitehead, *Process and Reality*, 21.
33. Ochoa Espejo, *Time of Popular Sovereignty*, 156.

# ❧ From the Theopaternal to the Theopolitical: On Barack Obama

VINCENT LLOYD

Political theology has come into vogue as a response to the secularist repression of the religious. This repression makes us forget the theological ancestors of our ostensibly secular political vocabulary. To remember the robustness of religion, its inescapable presences, shadows, and echoes, is threatening to the status quo. Religion has become one difference among many in our variegated world—one box to check next to gender, sexuality, disability, race. Each difference is treated as on par with each other, and so properly managed, and so impotent. The depths of difference that might challenge hegemonic ideology are ignored, leaving difference as preference, as taste, as consumer choice.[1] To remember religion is thus to be critical, to summon those forgotten depths of difference, which call into question the necessity of the status quo.

Moreover, to remember religion is to reject an account of the common good as competing preferences to be managed by a neutral arbiter, the nation-state. Religious visions of the common good need not simply be individual beliefs; they are woven into the fabric of a community. The personal can be political, for it was never personal at all. Religious visions of the common good need not be positive, revealed from the heavens. They can be negative, calling into question false visions of the common good advanced by hubristic humans. Our relationship with God and, as this chapter argues, our relationship with our fathers can provide critical leverage for examining how we are to live together. Black experience, the experience of the most marginalized, can be uniquely revelatory, providing access to that critical leverage.

If all significant political concepts today are secularized theological concepts, might it also be that all significant theological concepts are transferred from the domain of the family? The sovereign rules the state as the sovereign God ruled the world—as the sovereign father ruled the family. He imposes law, adjudicates disputes, recognizes who does or does not count as one of his people, and he loves. He deserves respect and reverence. He is not chosen, and his rule is inescapable. But has this familial provenance of the theological, and the political, also been forgotten—or repressed?

God the father sounds quaint, just as quaint as worshipping the king. Today, for those who choose to speak of God, we have gender-neutral language. A generation of feminist critique has exposed how patriarchy, a human ideology, sullied speech about God.[2] To consider God as father is treated as taboo by the liberal norms governing much theological discourse, the same liberal norms transgressed by speaking of political concepts as fundamentally theological (political theology, for Carl Schmitt, was quintessentially an antiliberal project; today perhaps it fancies itself antineoliberal). My hypothesis: The exploration of the theopaternal lags behind exploration of the theopolitical because the fight against patriarchy lags behind the fight against theocracy. It is only after theocracy becomes entirely implausible that the very real, very potent connections between the theological and the political can be examined clearly, that the theological can be seen as a resource to reinvigorate the political. The grip of patriarchy may have been loosened—that it can even be named shows this—but the struggle continues. This does not, however, mean that investigation of the theopaternal is premature. For if secularism is the management of religion by liberalism or neoliberalism, then it is prudent to suspect that the disease affects gender as well. The management of gender and the management of religion may very well go hand in hand, and so political theology as a critical project may need to coordinate with the theopaternal to enhance the critical force of each.[3] In other words, and echoing the Marxian formulation from the "Jewish Question," the fight against theocracy and the fight against patriarchy both are struggles for civil rights, for recognition of group autonomy.[4] To achieve our humanity requires critical theory and praxis that cuts deeper. The theopolitical and theopaternal promise to lead us in such a direction.

Political theology does not claim to reduce political concepts to theological ones. Rather, it calls on us to acknowledge and examine the connections, both historical and conceptual, between political and theological ideas. Seeing those connections can allow us to mobilize them to advance justice, and it can allow us to sniff out political mystifications that rely on implicit theological premises. Similarly, observing that religious ideas have affinities with ideas about the family, or that historical evidence points to transference from one domain to the other, is not in itself a reason to dismiss or degrade religious ideas. (Feuerbach and Freud had additional reasons that led them to their skeptical conclusions.) Even the conclusion that human ideology (patriarchy) contaminated religious ideas does not seem especially helpful, considering that theology is human words about God, and human words always already bare the taint of ideology. It is not the words that are most important—not that God is called "father"—but the network of concepts that go along with fatherhood and that inform the theological. They inform the theological, so, by transitivity, they inform the political. They are articulated together: the theopaternal and the theopolitical.

After Freud, the theopaternal might seem exhausted. What more can be said than that longing for God is longing for a fantasy father? But the theopolitical could be similarly queried: What more can be said than that political rulership is modeled on the lordship of God? In each case, there is much more to be said conceptually, historically, and phenomenologically. The nuances of the theopolitical and the theopaternal can be probed in documents, artifacts, literature, art, and ethnography. Doing so does not reinforce theocracy or patriarchy, but rather explores the continuing relevance of the religious and the paternal: their workings, their continuing presences, their repressions, and their possibilities for transformation.

Thinking about the theopaternal in a narrow sense, the suggestion that God is a substitute for flawed or weak fathers quickly exhausts its initial plausibility. Belief in God while we witness evil seems no different from belief in a strong father when we realize that he is weak. Belief in a God seemingly absent from much of the world seems no different from belief in a father who left during childhood, or who died oversees, or who was never known. Belief in God enfleshed in man seems no different from belief in a son growing up and becoming a father. The father-substitute account of theopaternity seems motivated by a dogmatically atheistic dismissal of God, by a need to explain away belief in God. If we acknowledge that divinity and paternity are both in some sense mythological, yet both are still potent, both still find traction in lived experience, then we open ourselves to richer continuities. In other words, just as an inevitable part of growing up is realizing that one's father makes mistakes and yet still recognizing him as father, an inevitable part of theism is realizing that there are aspects of God that we will never understand and yet still recognizing God as God. God and father mark present absences. To deny this is to deny the reasonableness of a huge number of ordinary people; it is to deny their humanity. To imagine medieval Christians cowering at the threat of hellfire, motivated to act because of the absoluteness of God's power, ignores how ordinary people live their ordinary lives.

Conventional wisdom, or popular psychology, has it that moving beyond an overbearing father involves a dialectic of refusing authority and desiring alternate authority. Once it is clear that saying no to the father is a live option, it may be embraced by saying no interminably, or it may be concealed by finding someone else who does not accept no for an answer. In short, the son may become a hippie or join the military; the daughter may become promiscuous or find an abusive husband. Conventional wisdom further has it that these two options, in the healthy child, are for a time dialectical, and that after a time a healthy middle is established—at which point the child has become an adult, ready to have children of her or his own, with only faint echoes of the father still informing her or his life. In unhealthy individuals, the two options remain polarized, the dialectic blocked, the figure of the father animating all of his child's life. The theopaternal analogues are obvious. Some theists cling to extremes of dogmatic belief or spiritual experience; atheists entirely reject the figure of God, fully immersing themselves in human affairs (or both, for example taking the market as a new God).

But conventional wisdom is always ideological, advancing the interests of the wealthy and powerful. Under the guise of obviousness and reasonableness, conventional wisdom conceals the service it performs to the status quo. So we should be suspicious of a dialectical account of paternity, one that sees youthful indiscretions and strivings as a necessary path out from the shadow of the father, culminating in healthy adulthood. We should be suspicious of accounts of the theopaternal that frame themselves as having overcome dogmatic and antinomian impulses. And we should be suspicious of the theopolitics that results. Moreover, just as the critical leverage attained by political theology is fully exercised not only by exposing religious concepts lurking beneath political concepts but also by pointing to alternative theopolitical concepts, the critical leverage of the theopaternal is fully exercised when the conventional wisdom about the paternal is not only explicated but also relativized by presenting alternatives. Conventional wisdom presents us with just one account of paternity. There are others.

I take Barack Obama's *Dreams from My Father* (1995) and *The Audacity of Hope* (2006) as examples of the coarticulation of the theopaternal and the theopolitical.[5] Obama's first book is an example of the theopaternal: Father and God are effectively interchangeable, and the young Obama is on a dialectical quest for both. Obama's second book is an example of the theopolitical consequences of his underlying account of the theopaternal. The much-praised and much-maligned pragmatism that characterizes Obama's politics is, I claim, the direct consequence of his account of fatherhood/divinity. An alternative account of theopaternity presents itself when the position of fatherhood is put under erasure: when the father is black. Tragically, despite his black father, Obama rejects this theopaternal alternative, instead aligning himself with the interests of the wealthy and the powerful.

According to Obama's account in the introduction, *Dreams from My Father* grew out of interest from publishers generated by his election as president of the *Harvard Law Review*. Originally he had intended to write a book about policy. When he started work on the manuscript, however, "longings leapt up to brush my heart," and "distant voices appeared, and ebbed, and then appeared again" (xiv). A policy book seemed "premature": First, Obama needed to grapple with his past. In other words, Obama self-consciously presents the narrative of his search for a father, a spiritual search, as the background against which his politics should be read. This background is one of remembering and desiring, the affects animating *Dreams from My Father*—and, I claim, animating Obama's theopaternal dialectic.

The book starts with Obama receiving a phone call telling him that his father, whom he barely knew, had died. We learn: "At the time of his death, my father remained a myth to me" (5). It ends with a twenty-eight-page block quotation from a relative in Kenya describing his family history, culminating in an explanation of who Obama's father truly is. In between are three roughly equal parts, the first describing Obama's childhood in Hawaii and Indonesia, with a few pages on his early college years in California. The second part chronicles—better, dramatizes—Obama's community-organizing work in Chicago. The final part describes the trip Obama takes to visit his relatives in Kenya the summer before law school. An epilogue notes that his life has been fairly stable and uneventful in the six years since that trip and before the writing of the book—"a relatively quiet period, less a time of discovery than of consolidation" (437). In other words, *Dreams from My Father* is a coming of age tale, a story about a boy becoming a man. That process is animated by a quest for his father. When he finds his father, his life stabilizes. He becomes a man. Indeed, the final pages of the epilogue demonstrate his manliness: After more than four hundred pages almost devoid of romance, Barack marries Michelle. (In *The Audacity of Hope* we learn that after Michelle's father died, while the couple was still dating, Obama stood at his grave and promised to take care of his daughter.)

Obama's father left when he was a baby. In his childhood, in Indonesia, his mother would invoke "the distant authority of my father" (50). (It is tempting to say something about the New Testament resonances of the pious mother affirming an omnipotent, absent father.) The image of the father as seat of authority was augmented by his mother's descriptions: "He hadn't cut corners." "He was diligent and honest." "He had led his life according to principles" (50). In other words, the little content that Obama was given to fill in the image of his father simply referred to the role of father as seat of authority, doing what is proper. Moreover, Obama's mother makes the father-image eclipse all else: "I would follow his example, my mother decided. I had no choice" (50). This is the quintessential father, or father-fantasy, made ideal through his absence. He was not only idealized, but sacralized. His father's principles might not lead to worldly power, might even lead to worldly hardship, but they "promised a higher form of power" (50). To identify with the seat of authority, with the source of normativity, is always to be in the right, regardless of the world's initial reaction.

His father returned to visit when Obama was in middle school. Obama describes himself and his mother as apprehensive. But not in school: "I explained to a group of boys that my father was a prince . . . like the king of the tribe" (63). With no experience of a concrete father, an ideal authority was substituted. "After a week of my father in the flesh, I had decided that I preferred his more distant image, an image I could alter on a whim—or ignore when convenient" (63). For those whose fathers are nearby, the fantasy of the father is necessarily more malleable, able to incorporate the many potentially discrediting experiences that arise in an ordinary man's life. But for Obama, the fantasy was shattered abruptly, its status as fantasy revealed. The fantasy was not exposed to his classmates, for Obama's father was charming, charismatic, and enigmatic—enigma, after all, is the prerequisite for charm and charisma. Obama describes himself as petrified when his father visits his classroom to talk about Africa, but the students and teachers are wowed by him. Indeed, the narrative of *Dreams* is driven by the mystery of Obama's father's charm. "If my father hadn't exactly disappointed me, he remained something unknown, something volatile and vaguely threatening" (63). Obama's fantasy is undone and yet everyone else is entranced: A mystery remains. It is clear that the father has the power to entrance, has charisma—gifts of the gods—so Obama's quest continues.

Obama describes his encounters with black classmates in his youth, but the only black grown-up he encounters is Frank, a drinking buddy and longtime friend of his white grandfather. Frank and his grandfather both grew up in Kansas. After a career as an avant-garde poet, Frank occupies the dark recesses of Hawaiian life, sporting a gray Afro, frequenting the red light district, and haunting dive bars, reminiscing. One night, after Obama's grandfather accuses his grandmother of racism, the high school–aged Obama seeks Frank out. In a cinematically narrated scene, Obama finds Frank's house: "Inside, the light was on, and I could see Frank sitting in his overstuffed chair, a book of poetry on his lap, his reading glasses slipping down his nose. I sat in the car, watching him for a time, then finally got out and tapped on the door" (89). Frank answers with "Want a drink?" Frank soon reveals that Obama's grandfather, who presents himself as racially enlightened, is from the perspective of a black contemporary like Frank deeply racist. The point is brought home when Frank notes that Obama's grandfather considered his black childhood maid "a regular part of the family," and Frank concludes, "You can't blame Stan for what he is. . . . He's basically a good man. But he doesn't *know* me. . . . He *can't* know me, not the way I know him" (90). Frank goes on to explain that the capacity to know a black man comes from the experience of humiliation and fear. Whereas the grandfather might fall asleep in Frank's house, Frank could never fall asleep in the grandfather's house—because of that fear.

Obama presents this encounter as a literally earth-shattering revelation. As he returned home, "The earth shook under my feet, ready to crack open at any moment. I stopped, trying to steady myself, and knew for the first time that I was utterly alone" (91). Obama had imagined his grandfather serving as a substitute father, not black but attuned to the problems faced by blacks. Frank reminds Obama of the absence not only of his father but of his black father, a father who could understand and communicate the texture of the social world to his son—that is to say, a father who could fulfill the proper role of father. In the absence of this, Obama is alone in the universe, his belief in anything beyond himself gone, a reluctant atheist, as it were.[6]

The result is self-destructive behavior. Obama gets into drink and drugs. Billie Holiday's music in the background represents the possibility of tragic decline. According to the narration, Obama did drugs not to prove his blackness, but to escape it. He wanted "something that could push questions of who I was out of my mind, something that could flatten out the landscape of my heart, blur the edges of my memory" (93–94). From his youthful perspective, all difference was voided in the world of drugs. "Everybody was welcome into the club of disaffection" (94). To illustrate this, Obama adds, "Nobody asked you whether your father was a fat-cat executive who cheated on his wife or some laid-off joe who slapped you around whenever he bothered to come home" (94). Because of his conversation with Frank, Obama realized that his white family didn't succeed in their role of ushering him into the social order. They couldn't do that, because they would never understand the experience of being black in America. With the possibility of entering into the social order closed off, Obama turned to an antinomian world of drink and drugs. In that world, the identity of your father didn't matter because there was no role for the father, no aspiration to be inducted into the adult order, or to become a father oneself. Without father, or God, there was no need to learn the rules.

And yet, inexplicably, Obama did move on; this was only a phase. He offers no explanation. He records his mother's concern that nothing would come of him (he was in high school, apparently uninterested in college). Then, suddenly, things change. "I had graduated without mishap, was accepted into several respected schools" (96). It seems significant that, in a narrative driven by posing and answering questions, a transformation occurs that is not even allowed to present itself as in need of explanation. Even though Obama hedges, saying that at first he was "just going through the motions" at college, the antinomianism he had just described instantly vanishes. The implicit response to the unasked explanatory question seems to be: He found black people. At Occidental College, he found black friends, whom he vividly describes in the narrative, and he was involved in black student life. By the end of his studies, he begins to resemble his father. Obama's mother and sister come to visit him during college, and he precisely reenacts the behavior of his father during his father's only visit to the youthful Obama (although the narrative voice is curiously silent on the resemblance). When Obama's father visited, he tells the youthful Obama to stop watching *How the Grinch Stole Christmas* (!) and "Go in your room and study now" (67)—causing much protest from Obama's mother and grandparents, and the implicit realization that his father's authority was precarious and contested. A decade later, Obama relates that he "scolded Maya [his younger half sister] for spending one evening watching TV instead of reading the novels I'd bought for her" (123). He also told his mother that the NGO she was working for perpetuated neocolonialism. In short, he was struggling to become his father, or to occupy the role of father, to not only be an authority but to represent the normative order.

Yet at that point, in college, Obama was only striving to imitate the human father he vaguely knew; he was still distant from a divine father, from the theopaternal. For that, he had to become an instrument of justice, to make right the whole world, not only his family—and so bring redemption. According to Obama, the "idea of organizing" he held "was a promise of redemption" (135). Through bringing members of a community together to build power that would allow community members themselves to address their collective problems, Obama envisioned making the world right—that is, fulfilling the theopaternal role. Moreover, Obama's college encounters with youthful black nationalists and radicals had left him empty and unfulfilled, still at a distance from the African American community. Obama presents organizing as a means to understand African American identity in a way that rejects crude ancestral or blood ties. "Through organizing, through shared sacrifice, membership had been earned" (135). Sacrifice leads to redemption, and for Obama this means both upholding the normative order (i.e., advancing justice) and claiming his biological father's legacy. As yet, however, this sacrifice leading to redemption goes unnamed; it remains thoroughly secularized, just as Obama's desire for his father remains fully sublimated.

The longest section of *Dreams from My Father* chronicles Obama's experiences as a community organizer in Chicago. The final pages of the preceding section, about Obama's childhood and young adulthood, are taken up with a dream about his father that makes Obama awaken in tears. In the Chicago section of the book, again narrated cinematically, Obama faces obstacles, learns lessons, and has his heart warmed by seeing ordinary people realize that they can wield power to advance the interests of their communities. In particular, he surrounds himself with practical, working-class black women—though he shyly denies any romantic entanglements (in his epilogue, he describes Michelle as similar to these women). The women he meets have common sense and good hearts; the men he meets are powerful but tragically flawed. The women need saving; the men fail to save them. The final chapter in part 2 revolves around two such men, Harold Washington and Jeremiah Wright. In both Obama seems to find potential father substitutes (at this point his biological father had died in Kenya, his story still largely unnarrated). In both, Obama sees flawed paths to redemption, one through electoral politics and one through Afro-Christian religiosity. Both are implicitly contrasted to the redemption Obama is pursuing through community organizing. By the end of the chapter, Obama aligns himself with Wright, and he decides to leave his community organizing work to pursue law school, which he understands to be a stepping-stone to electoral politics. In other words, Obama understands himself to be growing up: He realizes that the men he admires are flawed, but he gains the courage to move away from the good-hearted women of "the community" to become a man himself, to become religious and to become political, knowing that it means embracing his imperfections, knowing that redemption is only possible in a fallen world.

Harold Washington, the first black mayor elected in Chicago, had captured the hearts of Chicago's black community, with fantasy. Or at least that is how Obama depicts him. His image—much like Obama's today—graced the walls of barbershops, a point of unity in a difficult, gloomy black world. Washington's election had offered "these people a new idea of themselves." Obama concludes, "Like my idea of organizing, [Washington] held out an offer of collective redemption" (158). Although Obama does not say much about Washington the man (an opacity reminiscent of the way Obama himself is now depicted), the effects of Washington's ascendancy are mixed. It makes Obama's organizing work harder because some of the individuals whom Obama aspires to gather together to build community now defer to Washington and the black officials he appointed. When Washington visits a project that Obama's ordinary-women leaders had put together, the women are so starstruck by Washington that they forget to ask for his commitment for continuing assistance in their work. When Washington dies, the coalition of ostensibly social justice–minded political leaders that supported him quickly collapses. Obama explicitly relates Washington to his own father: "More than anything, I wanted Harold to succeed; like my real father, the mayor and his achievements seemed to mark out what was possible; his gifts, his power, measured my own hopes" (230). Like Obama's father, Washington is charismatic—"full of grace and good humor." Like a spiritual leader, "Harold's presence consoled, as Will's Jesus consoled, as Rafiq's nationalism consoled." But ultimately, the father figure is charismatic because lacking: "Beneath the radiance of Harold's victory . . . nothing seemed to change. . . . I wondered whether he, too, felt a prisoner of fate" (231).

Who could escape the confines of fate if not a minister of the Lord? Obama's religious conversion marks the finale of part 2 of *Dreams from My Father*. It marks the end of Obama's quest for redemption through community organizing and the transition to his journey to Africa, to finally find his human father. Obama's acknowledging his relationship with his heavenly father is curiously positioned as the prerequisite for establishing a relationship with his deceased human father. The conversion is foreshadowed by the narrative's depiction of Obama realizing that he is faithless; in his words, "I was a heretic" (163). He reflects further, "Or worse—for even a heretic must believe in something, if nothing more than the truth of his own doubt." Surrounding himself with the good-hearted, commonsense women of his community organization was not enough. It was love without risk, affirmation without critique—critique that could only come from a representative of the normative order, from a male minister, who turned out to be Jeremiah Wright. In Wright's church, Obama found a mix of reverence for African heritage, black spiritual sensibility, and progressive, critical reflection on issues affecting blacks in Chicago and beyond. But Obama was still skeptical, even after talking to Wright one on one. It is not until after Harold Washington dies that Obama decides to attend a service at Wright's church, the departure of one substitute father fueling the quest for another. The topic of the sermon was "The Audacity of Hope," and Wright, according to Obama, described various places of suffering and despair, but adds that some (in this case the biblical Hannah) look upward to the heavens—"She dares to hope. . . . She has the audacity . . . to make music . . . and praise God" (293). As Obama narrates it, the congregation begins to shout and clap, performing their hope. "I imagined the stories of ordinary black people merging with the stories of David and Goliath, Moses and Pharaoh, the Christians in the lion's den, Ezekiel's field of dry bones. These stories—of survival, and freedom, and hope—became our story, my story" (294). The chapter concludes with Obama realizing that there are tears on his face. He realizes this after a boy sitting next to him hands him a tissue. Obama has accepted a heavenly father, and he has also accepted his own capacity to be a father.

In Kenya Obama meets his father's family, and he hears stories about his father—or rather, in the narrative construction, he discovers the truth about his father, for the first time gaining solid knowledge about him rather than just fleeting images and dreams. One of his first experiences in Kenya, at the airport, is the pleasure of hearing his family name pronounced correctly and recognized. An airport employee searching for his lost luggage knew his father: Their families were friends. Obama meets various relations and quasi relations. When he learns that the paternity of his half brother Bernard is less than certain, he wonders if his feelings toward him should change. Then he looks at the masses of young black men at a bus stop: "I suddenly imagined Bernard's face on all of them, multiplied across the landscape, across continents. Hungry, striving, desperate men, all of them my brothers" (336). In Africa Obama does not find a living father; he finds a national father, or a racial father, and so a nation, or race, of brothers. He also learns that his father was himself a son, that the only person that Obama's father ("the Old Man") feared was Obama's grandfather. This was the grandfather who had worked for the British and alienated the rest of his family, who had been strong and opinionated—perhaps, like Obama's father, more strong than wise. "What your grandfather respected was strength. Discipline. This is why, even though he learned many of the white man's ways, he always remained strict about Luo traditions. Respect for elders. Respect for authority. Order and custom in all his affairs" (407).

The father of his father, too, was a locus of normativity. This grandfather had converted to Christianity for a time but found that it undermined his sense of order and authority with "such ideas as mercy towards your enemies, or that this man Jesus could wash away a man's sins" (407). The grandfather wanted a purer God, a closer unity of God and father, and this he found in Islam. Father and grandfather Obama embraced the role of the father pathologically and so caused problems for themselves. Each saw the father figure as an unequivocal seat of authority, disregarding social norms that would temper this authority. Obama's father embraced this role to an even greater extreme, abandoning Islam for atheism. As Obama's half sister puts it, the Old Man (their father) never understood the role of Big Man. The Big Man accumulates authority through social networks, favors, relations, and so on; the Old Man imagined that authority could be had with a Harvard degree. His downfall came when he did not respect his bosses while he was working for the government, and the quintessential Big Man, Kenyatta, the ruler of the country, banished him from government employment.

The first chapter of *Dreams* in some ways parallels the last. A family history is told, of personalities and relationships and migrations. But the first chapter is a transparent history, a white history: the story of Obama's mother's family, told in the narrator's voice. In the final chapter we finally learn of Obama's father's family, not from the narrator but in the words of a relative, reconstructed as if from the mouth of a Hollywood African. But one example: "Well, this was a very serious matter, especially when your grandfather refused to return the shaman's potions. The next day, the council of elders gathered beneath a tree to resolve the dispute" (411). Ironically, what Obama attempts to frame as the climax of his story, the moment when the mystery is revealed, his prose performs as American fantasy. A few pages later, in the epilogue, Obama reports a conversation with a Kenyan teacher who says that Americans are always disappointed in Africa because they come seeking a fantasy. The teacher shares that she wants her daughter not to be "authentically African," a fantasy, but to be "authentically herself" (435). However, the performance of Obama's narration suggests that the two are one: the fantasy of the authentically African, with a council of elders resolving disputes under a tree, makes it possible for Obama to be authentically himself, or what he takes to be authentically himself. The whirlwind of the theopaternal dialectic is complete, but its completion is in fantasy.

Obama has solved the riddle of his paternity, or so he thinks, just as the finale of Obama's community-organizing narrative was to solve the riddle of theology. In both cases, Obama traverses the fantasy: acknowledging fantasy as fantasy, impure and adulterated, while acknowledging the continuing force and practical importance of the fantasy. And this theopaternal dialectic has political consequences. *Dreams from My Father* includes scattered references to policy positions anticipating the political future of Obama; more often it contains broader suggestions about the political. In his epilogue he concludes that law is, on the one hand, "glorified accounting that serves to regulate the affairs of those who have power—and that all too often seeks to explain, to those who do not, the ultimate wisdom and justness of their condition" (437). On the other hand, "law is also memory; the law also records a long-running conversation, a nation arguing with its conscience" (437). This precisely encapsulates the theopolitical consequences of the theopaternal for Obama. Law, which is normativity abstracted and institutionalized, is at once disappointingly hollow and warmly robust. The father or God is absent and flawed but also embracing and potent. To fixate on either extreme is a mark of immaturity.

This dialectic animates *The Audacity of Hope*, the book Obama wrote to consolidate the "rising star" status that the media offered him after his keynote address at the 2004 Democratic National Convention—and to further his presidential ambitions. A mix of policy prescriptions and anecdotes, the book presents each issue as eliciting two extreme responses, one that kills the father and the other that re-creates him. Obama, unlike myriad other politicians, has grown up: He has looked for and found his father, and his God, so that theopaternal fantasies no longer skew his political vision—or at least this is what he wants the reader to believe.

In a chapter titled "Values," Obama presents his time living with his white grandparents as a lesson in the proper relationship to authority. His grandfather would impose "an endless series of petty and arbitrary rules," which at first Obama would try to argue against (with his "talent for rhetoric"). The young Obama would have better reasons than his grandfather, and his grandfather would become "flustered" and "angry." But then the high school–aged Obama "started thinking about the struggles and disappointments [his grandfather] had seen in his life" and "started to appreciate his need to feel respected in his own home" (67). He realized that there are times when it is best to defer to authority even when one thinks one has the best reasons; there are times when tradition requires reverence. As Obama notes, such realizations are "what we all must go through if we are to grow up" (67). And they are what we must bring to politics. A few pages later Obama writes of the necessary reverence for the Constitution, exemplified by Senator Byrd. Obama is dismissive of both "the comfort offered by the strict constructionist" and the freedom offered by critical legal theorists, for whom the original text does not serve as an anchor (on his account). The latter entails "the freedom of the relativist, the rule breaker, the teenager who has discovered his parents are imperfect and has learned to play one off of the other—the freedom of the apostate" (92). Here we find the theopaternal coarticulated with the theopolitical: the desires and pathologies elicited by divine and human fatherhood, rejection (the young Obama's rebellion), and substitution (the grandfather's petty rules) are exactly mirrored in the realm of politics (the relativist and the strict constructionist, respectively).

This is also how Obama narrates his loss in the 2000 congressional election, and his ultimate victory in the 2004 Senate race. He had been overconfident, perhaps elevating himself into the role of fantasy father (now he was a father, with two young daughters). Afterward there was "denial, anger, bargaining, despair" and, eventually, "I arrived at acceptance—of my limits, and, in a way, my mortality" (4). Mortality and immortality slip easily between the personal and the political here. Acceptance and mortality lead to growth: "It was this acceptance, I think, that allowed me to come up with the thoroughly cockeyed idea of running for the United States Senate" (5). As a member of the Senate, what Obama particularly admires is the general atmosphere of collegiality among his more senior colleagues—which, it would seem, is premised on the sort of mortal acceptance that Obama himself attained. There were friendships between Democrats and Republicans of this older generation, which Obama reports (from an "old Washington hand") was caused by the shared experience of the Second World War, an experience of mortality and acceptance if ever there was one. Without that shared experience of war, Washington has become bitterly partisan. Obama pauses to note what was elided in the "old days" by this collegiality, such as stalled civil rights legislation, McCarthyism, the absence of women, and income inequality. But as he does so often, Obama notes hesitations and objections only to inoculate his narrative from their force: The tone remains one of nostalgia. Indeed, this is a characteristic rhetorical strategy of the theopaternal dialectic, making explicit its limitations as part of its positive claim. This older generation of politicians functions as a godfather to be revered but also contextualized.

After the World War II generation, according to Obama, U.S. politics became polarized because of what happened during the sixties. The critique of the "Establishment" leveled by youth during that decade was either embraced by politicians or it was rejected by politicians who attempted to create a new Establishment, a new godfather. This is the psychodrama played out by Democrats and Republicans today, in Obama's telling. The future president assures us that he can appreciate both sides because the psychodrama occurred in his life as well. He "sought justification" for his "adolescent rebellion" in the Black Panthers and the Rolling Stones. "If I had no immediate reasons to pursue revolution, I decided nevertheless that in style and attitude I, too, could be a rebel, unconstrained by the received wisdom of the over-thirty crowd" (30). But this was just a phase, Obama assures the reader, and he grew out of it. He writes, "By the time I enrolled in college, I'd begun to see how any challenge to convention harbored within it the possibility of its own excesses and its own orthodoxy" (30). He now considers that rebellious phase one of "self-indulgence and self-destructiveness." He was able to overcome it by returning to "the values my mother and grandparents [i.e., his white relatives] had taught me" (30)—a return to orthodoxy, as it were. In this way Obama was able to understand why Ronald Reagan and his *"Father Knows Best* pose" appealed to many voters. Obama could remember before his rebellion how he had liked the Hawaii military bases "with their tidy streets and well-oiled machinery, the crisp uniforms and crisper salutes" (31). He, too, had been susceptible to the appeal of father substitutes, to the wisdom (fantasy) that father knows best.

In addition to chapters on such topics as the Constitution, economics ("Opportunity"), foreign affairs, values, and family, *The Audacity of Hope* includes a chapter on faith and a chapter on race. In this framing, Obama precisely mirrors the contemporary tendency, which I assert has its origins in neoliberalism, to treat religion and race as two differences among many. Of course, each difference is different, with specific choices available and specific tints to those choices, but each can be assembled in rows of boxes to choose, choices for the contemporary consumer of difference and identity—where identity is composed of a certain pattern of chosen differences. Faith is important to Obama, and is important to the image of Obama. He is a Democrat who is not afraid to speak about religion: This is the image he embraces. Presenting the usual theopaternal dialectic, Obama frames liberals as rejecting God as father, conservatives as uncritically affirming God's authority. In doing so, Obama overlays his own parents' religious convictions: His father was raised Muslim but turned atheist; his mother was a spiritual seeker, taking the young Obama to Christian churches, Buddhist temples, Shinto shrines, "and ancient Hawaiian burial sites" (204). But Obama went to Catholic and then Muslim schools, encountering religiosity with stronger commitment. Obama rejects all of these options, including his mother's "professed secularism." He does, however, find in his mother a spiritual sense that she herself was unable to articulate. Obama writes that "she possessed an abiding sense of wonder, a reverence for life and its precious, transitory nature," and "she worked mightily to instill in me the values that many Americans learn in Sunday school: honesty, empathy, discipline, delayed gratification, and hard work" (205). It was her spiritual nature that "sustained me despite the absence of a father": It was worship for God in everything but name. And it was her spiritual nature, according to Obama, that made him study "political philosophy, looking for both a language and systems of action that could help build community and make justice real" (206). At the same time, Obama affirms, "My fierce ambitions might have been fueled by my father—by my knowledge of his achievements and failures, by my unspoken desire to somehow earn his love, and by my resentments and anger towards him" (205). Here again we have a coarticulation of the theopaternal and the theopolitical, spirituality and fatherhood jointly making a certain politics possible.

The chapter on race in *The Audacity of Hope*, like the rest of the book, contains little that is unexpected or controversial. There are still problems facing racial minorities in America, according to Obama, but those problems need carefully tailored, smart solutions, not solutions that simply continue past practice or are fueled by resentment. In this text, as in a number of speeches, Obama calls for the black community to take responsibility and to embrace certain values—a position that Obama associates with the mainstream of the black community, as found "around kitchen tables, in barbershops, and after church" (254).[7] Neither the position of white liberals nor that of white conservatives, according to Obama, this middle road appreciates the difficulties faced by black Americans but also recognizes the importance of a work ethic, two-parent households, and sexual restraint. Obama's prescription: "Community-based institutions, particularly the historically black church, have to help families reinvigorate in young people a reverence for educational achievement, encourage healthier lifestyles, and reenergize traditional social norms surrounding the joys and obligations of fatherhood" (245). He also writes that deeper than these considerations is the need for a robust American economy, which would benefit people of all races.

At this point the theopaternal dialectic strains so much as to become little more than raw ideology. The account of human-divine fatherhood that seemed natural, that was so engrained in conventional wisdom, loses plausibility when considered against the background of race in the United States.

With more than a million black men in prisons, with many more under the supervision of the criminal justice system in some way, with many more unable to work, vote, or find places to live because of criminal convictions, with many more under the supervision of the court system through child support proceedings, with many more terrorized by police harassment on a daily basis, commending the "middle path" of healthy fatherhood seems absurd. Instead of moderation there should be righteous indignation. Such a temperament does not force a choice of one of two extremes. Such a temperament asks why the issue is framed in a way that presents these two options. Then it clears the table and ponders new ways of framing the conversation.

The institution of fatherhood for black men is systematically undermined by a state apparatus which treats black men as incapable of fatherhood. Black fatherhood is always already under erasure, for it is incapable of fulfilling its paternal function of bringing a child into a world of social norms. If the father himself is but a second-class citizen—if even that, as the Thirteenth Amendment prohibiting slavery makes an exception for prisoners—then the father can never be an authority, can never fulfill his role as representative of the social order for his son. Or, in theopaternal terms, if God is a black father, God is always qualitatively different from a world that can recognize only white fatherhood. To recognize God as black father is to recognize an authority illegible to worldly authorities, to acknowledge the provisionality of all worldly authorities. It is to refuse the comfort offered by the array of options presented with such confidence by the world. As it happens, that is precisely the way that a major strand of the Christian tradition understands God, qualitatively different from humans—we might say: not as a father, but as a black father.

This is what Obama tragically misses in his self-narrations. He is searching for a black father but can accept only a white father, and this contaminates his theopolitical vision. He is looking for a figure who cannot exist, because black fatherhood is continually undermined, illegible. But for his story to have a happy ending, for the quest to be fulfilled, he must find a father. The father he finds gives satisfaction, gives meaning to his existence, simplistically. Believing that fathers can be found, that it just takes persistent searching and cathartic tribulations, Obama's desire and rage become quietude, become cold and critical analysis of the options on the table. Such is the white theopaternal-theopolitical, the God/father whose normative force is in continuity with the authorities of the world, where piety involves practical wisdom toward better justice rather than a leap of faith in the midst of terrible injustice. Here is a stark difference concerning how to envision movement toward the common good.

This is what Frank, Obama's black Hawaiian sage, understood, so unsettling the young Obama. What Frank thinks makes people capable of knowing, of understanding, is that "they've seen their fathers humiliated" (90). That nugget is what makes Obama feel alone, what makes him turn to drink and drugs. An absent father, or a reconstituted father, is not a humiliated father. The white paternal dialectic, of rejection and reembrace, is premised on a father who is flawed, but flawed because the world is flawed, his tragedy mirroring the tragedy of the world. The humiliated father, in contrast, is humiliated not because of his flaws but because of his race, and so offers no straightforward path to redemption (such as acceptance of the world as it is). Obama takes this nugget of wisdom from Frank, but then ignores it, returning to the embrace of his white mother, searching for his father through her eyes. From this white perspective, Obama's father and his father's father can be understood only as pathological in their response to the Americans and the British, respectively. These men's apparent stubbornness, their apparent commitment to their own authority over social norms, appears vicious. From Frank's perspective, in contrast, it appears as the reality of black manhood, of black fatherhood. Obama's father and father's father express, rather than repress, the oxymoronic status of the black father, the way fatherhood is always put under erasure for black men. Here is the result that Obama is unable to see: that the wisdom of the world, from this black theopaternal perspective, is idolatrous, a systematic distortion of what is actually the case—just as the black father and the white world are always out of sync. The humiliated God, crucified on the cross, is always out of sync with the social norms of the day. The idolatry of the theopaternal is the ideology of the theopolitical. Obama's misunderstood theopaternity results in pragmatism; understood rightly, it would result in a critique of ideology.

What does this mean for practical politics, or for the presidency of Barack Obama? Rather than criticizing Obama's advocacy of a certain position, this chapter questions how Obama goes about approaching a policy issue. For example, regarding the health care debate of Obama's first term, some liberals were frustrated that Obama did not pursue a nationalized, "single payer" option. However, the path Obama chose was perfectly reasonable: After much advice, analysis, and political calculation, Obama concluded that it was the most likely path to ensuring universal access to health care. But relying on advice, analysis, and political calculation does not necessarily move toward justice, does not necessarily advance the common good. Many people think that it does. These are comfortable people, well trained at swimming in ideological waters. Polemically, these are *white* people. Obama has resources to approach politics differently, but he has ignored those resources. *Black* experience, religious and paternal, would motivate bracketing even the best reasons in the service of justice. It would motivate stepping back from political questions for a moment to ask moral questions, and using those moral questions to frame a new political debate. Obama has refused such an approach.

## NOTES

1. See Lisa Duggan, *The Twilight of Equality? Neoliberalism, Cultural Politics, and the Attack on Democracy* (Boston: Beacon, 2004), and Jodi Melamed, *Represent and Destroy: Rationalizing Violence in the New Racial Capitalism* (Minneapolis: University of Minnesota Press, 2011), though both neglect religion.
2. Most notably Mary Daly, *Beyond God the Father: Toward a Philosophy of Women's Liberation* (Boston: Beacon, 1973), and Rosemary Radford Reuther, *Sexism and God Talk: Toward a Feminist Theology* (Boston: Beacon, 1983). See also Johannes Baptist Metz and Edward Schillebeeckx, eds., *God as Father?* (Edinburgh: T&T Clark, 1981).
3. Cf. Janet R. Jakobsen, "Sex + Freedom = Regulation," *Social Text* 23, no. 3–4 (2005): 285–308.
4. Karl Marx, "On the Jewish Question," in *The Marx-Engels Reader*, ed. Robert Tucker (New York: Norton, 1978), 26–46.
5. Barack Obama, *Dreams from My Father: A Story of Race and Inheritance* (New York: Three Rivers Press, 2004); Barack Obama, *The Audacity of Hope: Thoughts on Reclaiming the American Dream* (New York: Three Rivers Press, 2006).
6. On this mourning for an absent black father, or absent black past, and on how refusing such mourning can advance ideology critique, see Stephen Best, "On Failing to Make the Past Present," *Modern Language Quarterly* 73, no. 2 (2012): 453–74. See also Vincent Lloyd, "Of Fathers and Sons, Prophets and Messiahs," *Souls: A Critical Journal of Black Politics, Cultures, and Society* 16, no. 3–4 (2014): 209–26.
7. Obama made this point most famously in a Father's Day address to an African American church in Chicago in 2008: "Text of Obama's Fatherhood Speech," *Politico*, June 15, 2008, http://www.politico.com/news/stories/0608/11094.html.

# ❧ Democratic Futures in the Shadow of Mass Incarceration: Toward a Political Theology of Prison Abolition

ELIAS ORTEGA-APONTE

*The study of penal institutions is imperative because they are a microcosm of society.*
—JUANITA COTTO-DÍAZ, "CHICANA(O)/LATINA(O) PRISONERS"

Michelle Alexander's book *The New Jim Crow: Mass Incarceration in the Age of Colorblindness* has forced a nation to face the racist dimension of punishment in the United States. Since its publication in 2010, the national public arena has been discussing various dimensions of mass incarceration and debating the possible avenues for change.[1] *The New Jim Crow* is one more installment in a long list of jeremiads against the nation's racist punishment practices. The nation was once again asked to face how securing the financial success and political dominance of white supremacy precludes people of color from full democratic inclusion. How does mass incarceration operate if not as a tool that continues the flow of benefits to the white population while primarily impoverishing communities of color?[2] As the sociologist Juanita Díaz-Cotto explains, prisons "are themselves a means by which societal elites attempt to control the behavior of groups seen as threatening the status quo."[3] Taking a deep look at the systemic injustices perpetuated through policing and the reality of a burgeoning prison population composed largely of communities of color has reopened the nation's chattel slavery legacy, staining the illusion of the postracial peace heralded in contemporary political speech.

Whether because of the shock of discovering that Jim Crow–like practices are put in effect through our national justice system or because of the awareness of the high price tag of high imprisonment rates linked with increasingly diminished investment returns, the movements for prison reform generally and prison abolition particularly have been gaining vigor. No longer sustained almost exclusively by prison activists, prison educators, and those with incarcerated loved ones, these movements are now gaining a larger constituency of local churches and denominational church bodies involved with legislation and producing small group study guides on Alexander's book.[4] Multiple community organizations, Occupy-style movements such as Occupy4Prisoners, and even state-level initiatives such as New Jersey Steps are mobilizing in numbers that attempt to think a change in and perhaps the abolition of our current penal system.[5] The growing choir sings the long dissonant note in the hymn of American democracy that it had wished to harmonize since the nation's founding. Because of the jarring discord created as a result of structurally embedded white supremacy, democracy remains a dream deferred for people of color and the working poor, increasingly affecting the search for a common good at home and in the larger global society. The question Langston Hughes posed in his historical moment, "What happens to a dream deferred?" continues to be asked in ours, perpetuating the search for an answer:

> Does it dry up
> like a raisin in the sun?
> Or fester like a sore—
> And then run?
> . . . . . . . . . . . .
> Maybe it just sags
> like a heavy load.
> Or *does it explode?*[6]

In our present democracy, where the reality of mass incarceration of communities of color looms large, does the commodification of punishment practices pose a threat to the possibilities of democratic futures? Are our democratic aspirations intertwined with the prison-industrial complex (PIC) in such a way that, if we are to hope for democratic future(s), we need to seriously engage in prison abolition practices? Can a political theology rise to the challenge of confronting the prison-industrial complex? The challenge is clear—if the strand of political theology concerned with radical democracy is to be relevant to the realities and sufferings of communities of color most directly affected by the prison-industrial complex and if it is to radically contribute to the ongoing dismantling of the coloniality of the economics of white supremacy, it needs to focus its critical lenses on the dismantling of PIC.

As a system of oppression that thwarts, limits, and continually impinges on the political power, socioeconomic viability, and flourishing of communities of color, PIC also threatens the future survival of democracy. Because of this, a prison abolition perspective must help shape political theology. Shaped by this perspective, political theology would position itself as a contemporary link in the abolitionist tradition stemming from Frederick Douglass, W. E. B. Du Bois, James Baldwin, and Angela Davis, among others. These thinkers have fiercely engaged the shortcomings of American-style democracy in their search for the achievement of democratic aspirations. It is the ongoing struggle for the democratic futures seeded within these aspirations that ultimately positions prison abolition as a task for political theology.

If, as Juanita Díaz-Cotto asserts, prisons are a microcosm of society, and if radical democracy, as proposed by Jeffrey W. Robbins, is a democracy that "insists upon the immanence of our common life together and the generative power that comes from our modes of cooperation, both already present and still to come,"[7] then the tales that punishment practices tell of the nature and state of the democratic present cannot be ignored. The shape of democratic futures depends on our collective response to our national punishment practices. Does the enfleshment of democratic hopes that a more just common life in the future requires be able to stand against the prison-industrial complex, and, borrowing from David Theo Goldberg, denounce the PIC's "sociality of race" that attempts to preserve the *quasi-messianic* community of whiteness through the violence it inflicts on colored bodies at home and abroad?[8]

My reflections on these questions lead me to believe that a political theology of prison abolition is necessary for a viable radical democracy. In this essay, I argue that our current national practices of mass incarceration, concurrent with their commodifying profit-making capacities after the economic restructuring of the 1970s and '80s, are outflows of America's legacy of slavery.[9] The preservation of a democracy built by white supremacy relies on the transubstantiation of chains into handcuffs. I propose that the radical democratic impulses present in political theology may chart a way forward if it is able to take on the task of prison abolition as central to its framework. My efforts here are not to fully flesh out a political theology of prison abolition, but to lay the groundwork for one.

My argument unfolds in two parts. The first part considers the works of Frederick Douglass, W. E. B. Du Bois, and James Baldwin to theorize what I term the *economics of white supremacy*. The economics of white supremacy produced and continues to enforce social, political, and economic arrangements that aim at ensuring subservience to white supremacy. The subservience to this system operates primarily for economic but also political gain. In the system created by the economics of white supremacy, colored bodies labor to create and preserve a democratic existence from which they are excluded. Before the Reconstruction Era, this was achieved through the institution of slavery. After Reconstruction, it followed the road from segregation to its current mass-incarceration practices.

In the second part of this essay, I present my views on the limits of radical democracy to promote a vision of the democratic future of people of color that live under the constant threat of the prison-industrial complex. I pose the question of whether radical democracy passes the test posed by the collective challenges of Douglass, Du Bois, and Baldwin. Despite my doubts concerning the ultimate viability of radical democracy, I offer a proposal for its reradicalization. A radical democracy able to engage the challenges of Douglass, Du Bois, and Baldwin may be able to challenge mass incarceration and therefore sketch out a more democratic social, political, and economic commons necessary for current times.

## THE ECONOMICS OF WHITE SUPREMACY

*The (no)Condition for Democratic Inclusion*
The dynamics by which white privilege accumulates wealth and power have received sustained attention. These analyses expose how structures of oppression foment social inequalities—the reallocation, positioning, enforcement, and maintenance of resources from one segment of society to secure the advantages and dominance of another through aggressive forms of racialization. Whether through its theorization as a racial project as put forward by Michael Omi and Howard Winant, the historical narration of the rise of whiteness by Nell Irvin Painter, the internal critique of white privilege by Tim Wise, or Eduardo Bonilla-Silva's engagement with racial color blindness as the current dominant racist ideology, much continues to be said about the roles race and racism play in the creation of systemic and personal forms of oppression.[10] I agree with much of what these scholars write about the roles race and racism have played and continued to play in the United States and globally. The line that I pursue veers a slightly different way in order to highlight how practices that were first experimented with during the time of American slavery have found ways to transmute themselves in present times into practices of mass incarceration. In this way, racialized forms of oppression are enforced through punishment, resulting in economic exploitation put in place by practices of social and political disenfranchisement.[11]

Drawing on the works of Frederick Douglass, W. E. B. Du Bois, and James Baldwin, my analysis of mass incarceration reveals it as an extension of slavery connected not only to economics but also to democratic inclusion.[12] Their combined perspectives question whether democratic practices in the United States are inclusive enough to embrace people of color without a prior fight to unmask their enslavement by the coloniality of American-style democracy. If their analyses of American democracy confirm my suspicion that the reconstruction of democratic aspirations requires the unmasking of and battle against the ways in which democracy has been colonized through enslavement practices such as mass incarceration, then I will have succeeded in proposing a political theology of prison abolition.

My engagement with the critiques of American democracy as presented by Douglass, Du Bois, and Baldwin starts with the unpacking of the concepts of coloniality and the decolonial option of resistance. Walter Mignolo, one of the foremost decolonial thinkers, has exposed how empire building depends on coloniality—the control, suppression, and erasure of alternative forms of knowing, being, and sensing in order to secure their exploitation. In the words of Walter Mignolo:

> "Coloniality" offers a needed sense of comfort mainly to people of colour in developing countries, to migrants and . . . to a vast quantitative majority whose life experiences, long- and short-term memories, languages and categories of thoughts are alien to the life experiences, long- and short-term memories, languages and categories of thought that brought about the concept of "biopolitics" to account for mechanisms of control and state regulations.[13]

According to Mignolo, coloniality points out that the development of modernity in its intellectual and sociopolitical extensions would not have been possible without its underlying colonial logic. This colonial logic unveils ruthless habits of thinking, being, and sensing possible only through the domination of any form of thinking, being, and sensing that follow a path different from its own. Colonial logic has an ontological and an epistemological dimension in which the bodies and ways of knowing and being of non-Westerns are cast through the lenses of colonial difference and thus declared invalid. Invalidated in this way, they do not register as subjects; instead they are translated via colonial logic as less than the colonizers. More radically, what this perspective proposes is that subjects and knowledges under the mark of colonial difference do not register in the context put in place by biopolitics' control mechanisms and regulations. In order to be recognized and be marked as *bios*, and therefore be subject to be controlled, a prior status as "subject" in the epistemic and ontological realm of the colonizer was necessary. If a way of being and knowledge did not enjoy the status as granted to official ways of knowing and being first, then it could not be removed from the polity because it did not register as worthy of recognition. However, such a system came to be challenged in practice time and again; the ongoing challenges to the hegemony of modernity exposed the underside of this project.[14]

Mignolo calls for a decolonial approach that delinks certain practices as an antidote to coloniality. In this way, decoloniality operates by delinking the insidious forms of being, sensing, knowing, and embodiment derived from Western/colonial/modern onto-epistemic domination. For Mignolo then, biopolitics, just like modernity, has its own underside—body-politics.

Body-politics in and of itself is not a solution; it also needs to be resisted and overcome.

> Thus, body-politics is the darker side and the missing half of bio-politics: body-politics describes decolonial technologies enacted by bodies who realized that they were considered less human at the moment they realized that the very act of describing them as less human was a radical unhuman consideration. Thus, the lack of humanity is placed in imperial actors, institutions and knowledges that had the arrogance of deciding that certain people they did not like were less human. Body-politics is a fundamental component of decolonial thinking, decolonial doing and the decolonial option.[15]

Body-politics reveals the need to track the ways in which the bodies outside of *bios* expose the limits of biopolitics. For Mignolo the Bandung Conference represented a key moment, and one of high intensity, in the formulation of delinking. In this conference, Mignolo asserts, radical thinkers collaborated to delink their ways of thinking, knowing, and being from the structures of Western coloniality.[16]

I harbor suspicions regarding Mignolo's particular articulation of the decolonial option and in fact, whether such a clean break is possible at all. However, despite my reservations, Mignolo's thought has greatly influenced my own thinking concerning the importance of body-politics for the decolonial option and the need to question Western, modern colonial logics in the attempt to unearth hidden possibilities. At this point I deviate from Mignolo and choose to locate delinking at a moment earlier than the Bandung Conference to a time when democracy began to deeply root itself in the United States. The aim is not to supersede Mignolo's proposal but to attempt to ground the decolonial option in the geopolitical site with which this essay is concerned, the United States.

I turn to Frederick Douglass's speech, "The Meaning of the Fourth of July for the Negro," as an example of the delinking practice necessary for grounding a critique of the prison-industrial complex.[17] In this speech we find an indictment of the limitations of a national democracy (biopolitics) that enslaved part of its population (body-politics). At the occasion of an invitation to address a white audience on a day of national celebration, the gifted orator lifted the veil of American horror to his listeners.

His words thundered as follows:

> Your high independence only reveals the immeasurable distance between us. . . . The rich inheritance of justice, liberty, prosperity and

independence, bequeathed by your fathers, is shared by you, not by me. The sunlight that brought light and healing to you, has brought stripes and death to me. This Fourth of July is yours, not mine. You may rejoice, I must mourn. To drag a man in fetters into the grand illuminated temple of liberty, and call upon him to join you in joyous anthems, were inhuman mockery and sacrilegious irony.[18]

In this way, Douglass can be read as delinking the universal hope for justice, liberty, and prosperity from their tarnished instantiation in the young republic shy of its first centenary. Nation-building watershed events, when delinked from their logic of coloniality, put on display not only the exclusion of nonwhites from the ideal of "the citizen" and from the larger aspirations of the nation but also that such exclusions threaten the nation's democratic possibilities. For Douglass, the underside of one of the foundational events in the American democratic experiment, like the Fourth of July, is the everyday racialized exploitation on which it has been built. Once unmasked as established on the logic of coloniality, where the inheritance of democracy was not equally shared by those living on American soil, such an event ought to be resisted. A democracy idealized as the result of striving for human ideals of justice forged a trail that included the removal of First Nation Peoples,[19] an aggressive geographic expansion westward,[20] and the institution of chattel slavery[21]—all over against the ideals that may have once inspired the struggle against imperial England. Such is the compression of space and time created by coloniality; the colonized and colonizer occupy simultaneously yet disjointedly spaces and times.

Free whites and slaves populated different yet concurrent times, dissimilar yet parallel places. Although whites might not have been aware of places and times other than their own, the slaves were not ignorant of the white spaces and times from which they were barred. Douglass takes his critique further by highlighting the irony of his situation in giving his address: "Do you mean, citizens, to mock me, by asking me to speak today?" Douglass then concludes that without facing the nature of slavery and denouncing it, "America is false to the past, false to the present, and solemnly binds herself to be false to the future."[22] In the closing moments of this speech, Douglass asks and answers for his audience the meaning of the Fourth of July for the Negro. It is a day, Douglass says, "that reveals to him more than all other days of the year, the gross injustice and cruelty to which he is the constant victim"; furthermore, Douglass explains to an audience inebriated by the facade of its greatness, that "your celebration is a sham; your boasted liberty an unholy license; your national greatness, swelling vanity . . . your shouts of liberty and equality, shallow mockery."[23] Douglass's fearless denunciations of the underside of

American democracy, slavery, and the mockery it represented to the American republic, still reverberate today and continue to pose deep questions about the trajectory of American society, questions that need answers if we are to aspire to a shared democratic commons.[24]

In my reading of Douglass, I have shown how one can see in his "Fourth of July Speech" a delinking practice exposing the nexus between the institution of slavery as an engine of economic gain and a vision of democratic citizenship only possible through the creation of a racialized underclass in line with Mignolo's analysis of coloniality. Having set this in place, I move now to W. E. B. Du Bois's critique of the racialization process of democracy, which not only subjugates people of color but also cannibalizes its own children as it betrays their aspirations.

I read W. E. B. Du Bois as cementing the critique initiated by Douglass. His insightful commentary on the process of racialized democracy engages the Reconstruction period and reveals the falsity denounced by Douglass. In this way, Du Bois laid bare how the racialization process of democratic living not only continues to find creative ways to preserve the subjugation of peoples of color (body-politics), but also (and this is often lost), how by default places a limit on mostly immigrant and poor white workers from becoming full citizens (bio-politics).

In *Black Reconstruction in America*, Du Bois ponders, even though the Reconstruction period after the Civil War presented opportunities for new forms of social arrangements and robust democratic practices, why such practices did not come to fruition. Du Bois explains that the "well-paid American laboring class formed, because of its property and ideals, a petty bourgeoisie ready always to join capital in exploiting common labor, white and black, foreign and native." Thus, at the heart of these failures were economic incentives whereby exploiters secured a steady labor force by giving economic incentives to thrifty immigrants who sought to join this socioeconomic class.[25] The hopes of former slaves were consequently betrayed and dissolved in the competition among immigrants, free negroes, former slaves, and the white working class, all who failed to achieve full democratic inclusion in the postslavery nation-rebuilding experiment. A new slavery arose as the nation emerged from the Civil War. "The upward moving of white labor," Du Bois explains, "was betrayed into wars for profit based on color caste." What does this means for democracy? It means that "democracy died save in the hearts of black folk." It would seem, in light of Du Bois's analysis, that economic interests could potentially betray the development and nurturing of shared democratic common goods. Moreover, democracy is potentially shaped by preceding economic considerations. Du Bois's analysis highlights how "the plight of the white working class throughout the world today is directly traceable to Negro slavery in America, on which modern commerce and industry was founded."[26] Du Bois's conclusion is that after 1863, the "resulting color caste founded and retained by capitalism was adopted, forwarded and approved by white labor," and thus harnessed colored labor to white economic interests not only in America but worldwide. According to Du Bois, this subordination "became [the] basis of a system of industry which ruined democracy and showed its perfect fruit in World War and Depression."[27]

With equal measures of irony and sympathy, in the chapter *The Transubstantiation of a Poor White*, Du Bois charges Andrew Johnson with failing to seize a moment that could have rewritten the nature of American democracy. He identifies Johnson as the "Poor White South," which in "deserting its economic class and itself . . . became the instrument by which democracy in the nation was done to death, race provincialism deified, and the world delivered to plutocracy."[28] For Du Bois, Johnson faced two choices: on the one hand, a democracy including poor whites and blacks, and on the other, the autocratic option led by big business and slave barons. Although the first option could have undone the ruling body-politics of the day, the latter prevailed and reinforced the body-politics established by coloniality.

Today, the nation faces a similar choice: either the continued monetization of the punishment of mostly people of color, along with the policies and interest groups that support them, or the reconstruction of our justice system, including the possible abolition of the penal system as currently known. According to Du Bois, Johnson "ended in forcing a hesitant nation to choose between the increased political power of a restored Southern oligarchy and votes for Negroes," and he sided with the former.[29] Unlike with Johnson, in our time the question remains in need of an answer; so far, however, we have followed in Johnson's footsteps.

Following Du Bois, we see that the headwaters of American democracy flow, not from the north of idealists' hopes of a common national beacon of hope to guide those under repressive regimes to freedom, but from the south of slavery and slavery's aftermath, from a world that masquerades as an elegant plantation house. In the words of the historian Peter H. Wood, plantations "were in fact privately owned slave labor camps, sanctioned by the powers of the state, that persisted for generations," and this was a world of "perpetual exploitation and incessant degradations built on racist ideology and overwhelming physical force."[30] Could this description of plantations also be used to describe the nature of prisons? The thought of such a possibility echoes in Du Bois's remark: "Democracy died, *except in the hearts of black folks*, for the preservation of this world." In his time, it was clear to him that democracy could not coexist with the world of the plantation or its mutated variations; what is not clear is whether today, democracy and mass incarceration can coexist. If Du Bois's analysis holds true, it seems that they cannot.

As I have argued so far, in following Douglass's and Du Bois's assessments of the state of democracy in the United States, it becomes increasingly clear how the coloniality of U.S. democracy aims to subjugate forms of knowing, being, and sensing of bodies of color and curtail the democratic aspirations of people of color to fuel its position in the world. Borrowing from Du Bois, I say that today, through the mass imprisonment of communities of color, American democracy remains linked to "the damnation of slavery, the frustration of reconstruction and the lynching of emancipation." Entangled with nightmares of lynching, repression, and imprisonment, the democratic dreams of folks of color remain deferred. In light of this ongoing deferral, we could add Wood's assessment that "we Americans are still unable to grasp the full depth of the huge collective wound that predated the country's founding and that haunted its infant and adolescent years."[31] In Wood's words, one can hear echoes of Douglass's and Du Bois's critiques. However, we should read Wood against the grain of the critic of America's racist ways, James Baldwin. Such a reading will reveal a deeper and necessary truth for the delinking of democracy from coloniality.

Baldwin once said, "How slowly the mills of justice grind if one is black." Not only is justice slow to come for people of color, but Baldwin, in a jeremiad, observed how darker races possess knowledge of the reality of how white dominance shapes social worlds: "Whatever it is that white Americans want, it is not freedom—neither for themselves nor for others."[32] Without a real education of the enslavement of black people and their continued oppression that shapes the national identity and conception of freedom, the affirmation and defense of such a democracy may also signal its undoing. According to Baldwin, "The reality, the depth, and the persistence of the delusion of white supremacy in this country causes any real concept of education to be as remote and as much to be feared, as a change or freedom itself."[33] This fear perpetuates modern forms of enslavement in the name of democracy. Today, the delusion of white supremacy and the democratic failure that it perpetuates in the United States prevents any actual education about mass incarceration that would reveal its racist dimensions. Instead, public demagogues insist that, its proven failure aside, the ongoing policing and burgeoning prison population of people of color is necessary to the securing of democracy and the nation's citizenry.

Bringing together the thought of Douglass, Du Bois, and Baldwin, I hope to have shown how an economics of white supremacy, namely the subjugation of labor in the interest and service of whiteness and currently in the form of mass imprisonment, militates against the realization of real democracy. If democracy fails, it is because it is feared, as was revealed by Du Bois's insights into Jackson's choice—because a true democratic ethos overturns the realities that preserve the privileges of white power while sinking most others into poverty. "Democracy has failed because so many fear it," says Du Bois. "They believe that wealth and happiness are so limited that a world full of intelligent, healthy, and free people is impossible, if not undesirable." Because of this failure of democratic imagination, Du Bois concludes, "[So] the world stews in blood, hunger, and shame. The fear is false, yet naught can face it but Faith."[34]

*Mass Incarceration and the Profitability of Punishment*
During the last forty years, the prison system has grown exponentially as a direct result of changes in legislation that put in place mandatory minimum sentences, and stringent policies regarding certain forms of drug possession and crimes. As it has turned out, prison growth has equaled big business.[35] The epidemiologist Ernest Drucker describes the current dynamics of mass incarceration as a fast-spreading epidemic. In a little more than thirty-five years, the prison population has grown tenfold, from 250,000 in the 1970s to over 2.5 million. This epidemic has affected African American and Latino/a youth the most; although they represent only 3 percent of the total U.S. population, they account for more than 30 percent of the prison population.

In urban communities, nine out of ten families are affected by this plague. In Drucker's analysis, "Individuals who are afflicted are also socially marginalized and often become incapacitated for life—unable to find decent work, get proper housing, participate in the political system, or have a normal family life." Furthermore, "The children of families affected by this new epidemic have lower life expectancy and are six to seven times more likely to acquire it themselves than the children of families not affected."[36] For Drucker, the use of mass incarceration in the U.S. is related to social and political purposes disconnected from law enforcement goals.[37] Such a disconnect reveals the underlying body-politics at work as described in the previous section. Although it has proved to be ineffective in deterring crime, mass incarceration has proven effective in gutting out the human capital of urban communities, disrupting families, and in general jettisoning disadvantaged communities' chances of improving their socioeconomic and political conditions.[38]

The prison boom has meant that the last four decades have seen an increase in prison budgets as in no other time in history and a move toward fund allocation for punishment as a deterrent—that is, longer imprisonment as a way to reduce crime—at the cost of basic social services. According to Drucker, the average annual cost per inmate is $25,000 per incarcerated person, or about

$60 billion annually in addition to several billion dollars invested in building new prison facilities. According to Drucker, "We have created a large privatized 'correctional industry,' which, among other offensive aspects, offers new investment opportunities on Wall Street for operating 'for-profit' prisons." In light of this profitability, and how the private sector has transubstantiated punishment into a lucrative business, "it is no wonder the system has become self-perpetuating."[39] Julia Sudbury expresses similar concerns:

> The mutually profitable relationship between private corporations and public criminal justice systems enables politicians to mask the enormous cost of their tough-on-crime policies by sidestepping the usual process of asking the electorate to vote for "prison bonds" to raise funds to build publicly operated prisons.[40]

This relation of profit between the private sector and the criminal justice system is in sync with Du Bois's assessment of Johnson's sacrificing of democracy at the altar of a profitable plutocracy. Prison buildup has not only been effective in disenfranchising communities of color. Paradoxically, it has also provided a political boost to rural working-poor white communities, siphoning political and economical power from communities of color—a dynamic that Du Bois pointed out also took place during the slavery era. For some rural, working-poor, white communities, the "population growth" achieved by housing prisoners of color has provided additional monetary aid and increased political representation; by the same token, communities losing human capital to incarceration have experienced a decrease of economic assistance and political representation.[41]

According to the Public Policy Institute of California, 55 percent of California's adult population is Latino/a or nonwhite. In terms of correction three in four inmates are Latino/a or nonwhite, 41 percent being Latino/a and 29 percent being African American; African American men and women have the highest probability of being incarcerated, followed by Latinas/os.[42] Foreign-born Latinos/as have a low incidence of incarceration, but this changes with the second generation. Thus it is important to keep an eye on the generational differences among Latino/as; the depressing reality is that Latino young males have a 50/50 change of being in some shape, way, or form in the corrections system.[43] In addition, according to a 2009 Pew Report, 31 percent of Latino/as between the ages of sixteen and twenty-five expressed knowing a friend or relative participating in gang-related activity.[44]

As troubling as the conditions of male prisons are, women experience a far worse fate. These conditions strongly reveal the body-politics operative in current incarceration practices. Robin Levy and Ayelet Waldman point out three reasons why women in prisons are vulnerable to rights violations: (1) women prisons tend to be more geographically isolated contributing to lax oversight; (2) they are likely nonviolent offenders; and (3) women in prison are more likely to have experienced sexual and physical abuse prior to incarceration and thus are less likely to complain of abuses within the prison system and therefore more likely to suffer serious health consequences.[45] As Michelle Alexander points out, "The overwhelming majority—over 90 percent—of women in prison have suffered sexual and/or domestic abuse, and have lived in extreme poverty. They find themselves behind bars primarily for minor drug offenses and crimes of poverty and survival. Sometimes they are locked up for crimes of violence, typically when they dare to fight back against their abuser."[46] The current status of our legal system employs policies that manipulate self-defense policies as an option for accused women.[47]

In summary, I have shown that the burgeoning of prisons in the United States disproportionately affects communities of color. It reduces their human capital while shifting economic and political power to white communities, what I called earlier the economics of white supremacy. And their bodies become vulnerable to physical, sexual, and psychological abuse. It is in this light that I understand the prison-industrial complex as threatening the possibilities of democratic futures.

## POLITICAL THEOLOGY'S RADICAL DEMOCRACY UNDER THE SHADOW OF LOCKDOWN

### Is Radical Democracy Possible?

Amid the current realities of communities of color and the high costs of safeguarding white democracy imposed on people of color through the centuries, it would seem reasonable to be skeptical of the hopes offered by radical democracy. Can radical democracy delink itself from the burdensome legacy of democracy's racist past and present? Despite skepticism, I do consider this possible. As Du Bois put it, *democracy died except in the hearts of black folks.* It may be that a rearticulation of radical democracy through people of color will hold a key for the viability of democratic futures. I consider this below.

Commenting on a paradox inherit in Ernesto Laclau's conception of radical democracy, namely the postulation of inevitable political patterns based on the exclusionary character of identity constitution in the face of an indeterminate social reality, Alexandros Kioupkiolis says that it "shows the non-necessary nature of its foundations by keeping 'always open and ultimately undecided' the entwinement between particular contents and social order itself, which is shorn of pre-fixed elements."[48] Kioupkiolis's critique seeks to point out a peculiar quirk in Laclau's theorizing of hegemony, that, while not prescribing "a particular model of democratic politics or ethics," nonetheless "establishes structural places, elements and processes that can be filled in by different contents and give rise to variable figures of the social"; furthermore, "in its very capacity as the parameter-setting horizon, hegemony circumscribes the bounds of political possibility."[49] My concern is as follows: Are forms of hegemonic struggles excluded from the agonic battlefield of new political possibilities? And if so, what does this mean for radical democracy?

Let's call to mind Douglass's critique of the position of Negroes in celebrations of the Fourth of July. Ideologically, the occasion commemorating the independence of the United States was predicated on the identity that excluded the metropolis, England. This hegemonic moment of identity formation, and the social arrangements it made possible, obscured prior hegemonic moments of the enslavement of black people and the control of poor white labor as documented by Du Bois. Mignolo's critique of coloniality presses us to consider the possibility that because of the body-politics economy of current democratic practices imprinted with the legacy of the economics of white supremacy, any hegemonic struggle on the part of communities of color take place in a different topos.

It is plausible that as a form of identity formation, the concept of identity itself is predicated on the exclusion of other possibilities. This is what I take Kioupkiolis to mean; in fact, Kioupkiolis does not dismiss Laclau's attempt but rather affirms that radical democracy "is very much about keeping alive the struggle among different perceptions of democracy." The lively contestation of competing democratic views are "vital for the expansion of freedom and equality as it can bring into relief the deficiencies and limitations that mar the various constitutions of democracy."[50] In other words, such contestations actually assume the possibility of a community's participation while leaving open the possibility for its exclusion. If democracy requires exclusion, as Laclau suggests, does radical democracy also require exclusion? More to the point, is radical democracy able to overcome the legacy of the economics of white supremacy? Or is the hegemony of communities of color also deferred?

At the heart of this line of questioning lies the query of whether radical democracy can come face to face with its own embedding in Western-style democracy that necessitates dynamics fueled by coloniality. Janet Conway and Jakeet Singh have made this point. In their critique of Laclau and Chantal Mouffe, they conclude that radical democracy, not having fully broken from its heritage in liberal democracy, is "a radicalization, democratization and deepening of the type of political regime already characteristic of the modern West, a project that does not seek to 'create a completely different kind of society.'"[51] Thus, in its continual use of the symbols and the resources of that tradition, as Conway and Singh point out, radical democracy does not problematize the role of European colonialism that produced the European and, I add, American democracy and their subjects with varying degrees of subjections. When the economics of white supremacy and the colonial legacy of democracy are taken into account, it would seem that radical democracy's counterhegemonic strategy to the hegemony of democracy becomes severely compromised.

If this is the case, then as Theodor Adorno said, "Whatever wants nothing to do with the trajectory of history belongs all the more truly to it." For this reason, he concluded that history "promises no salvation and offers the possibility of hope only to the concept whose movement follows history's path to the very extreme."[52] If we follow this line of thought, the survival of democracy in America depends in its being thoroughly historicized. As Douglass pointed out, America has been false to the past, to the present, and bound to be false in the future; thus, without such historicization, it remains unlikely that radical democracy will fare otherwise. The following words of Alexis de Tocqueville come to mind: "Throughout history, the hope of freedom has been at the heart of slavery to soften its harshness."[53] Could the continual longing for democracy, even in its most progressive and or radical forms, turn out to be a way to *soften the harshness* of a continual legacy of oppression without fully overcoming it?

May people of color hope for a democracy yet to come? Or is this a foolish dream? Is the hope for radical democracy today as empty a promise as the Fourth of July was when Douglass wrote? Perhaps. Yet however bruised, deformed, and compromised democracy may be, stony is the road we *trod forward*.[54] With the American South in mind and in order to exhort a group of black youth, Du Bois wrote:

> Here three hundred and twenty-seven years ago, they began to enter what is now the United States of America; here they have made their greatest contribution to American culture; and here they have suffered the damnation of slavery, the frustration of reconstruction and the lynching of emancipation.[55]

Will democracy come if the lynching of mass incarceration comes to an end? With this question in mind, I consider the possibility of radical democracy once again.

*A Democracy to Come?*
It would seem that present conditions of social oppression force the consideration that democracy, even radical democracy, is in dire need of a new articula-

tion. Jacques Rancière, expressing his agreement with Jacques Derrida's conception of democracy, concludes that "the time of a democracy to come is the time of a promise that has to be kept even though—and precisely because—it can never be fulfilled." In this, I agree with Rancière. My agreement with Rancière also argues that in Derrida's conceptualization, democracy to come exists as a transcendental horizon, in contrast to liberal democracy's existence as an institution and form of government, and as a result, democratic praxis disappears in Derrida's vision.[56]

Rancière desires to prevent the disappearance of "the political invention of the Other or the *heteron*; that is the political process of subjectivation." For Rancière, this democratic practice that maintains the necessity of subjectivation is necessary because this process "continually creates 'newcomers,' new subjects that enact the equal power of anyone and everyone and construct new words about community in the given social world."[57] Furthermore, Rancière prefers a political over an ethical interpretation of the "infinite respect for the other" injunction, one that focuses not on waiting for an Event to come, but "instead the democratic shape of an otherness that has a multiplicity of forms of inscription and of forms of alteration or dissensus."[58] However, all this leaves untouched the following question: Have democratic practices ever existed? If so, for whom? Here lies the point where we disagree.

Embracing other forms of alteration and dissensus as Rancière proposes, although offering a hopeful alternative, provides no clear assurance of a break from the grip of coloniality and the economy of white supremacy. Would decolonial practices of crashing into the time and space of the existing democracy move things forward? I imagine Rancière agreeing with this, but I am not convinced, at least yet, that *all* forms of alteration and dissensus will do. To my mind come Baldwin's reflections on black power. Baldwin reminds us:

> When Stokely [Carmichael] talks about black power, he is simply translating into black idiom what the English said hundreds of years ago and have always proclaimed as their guiding principle, black power translated means the self-determination of people. . . . But it is astounding . . . that whereas black power, the conjunction of the word "black" with the word "power," frightens everybody, no one in Christendom appears seriously to be frightened by the operation and the nature of white power.[59]

In this spirit, I raise the following question: Would we recognize a political theology of prison abolition as a democratic option? In this way, I come face to face with the question that started this argument in the first place: Why is it necessary to conceive a political theology of prison abolition?

## A POLITICAL THEOLOGY OF PRISON ABOLITION(?)

In my estimation, any possible reconstruction of political theology's radical democratic home cannot take place without confronting the deep meanings present in the opening stanza of Pamela Mordocai's poem "This is the way." Here, the innocuous task of doing laundry betrays a threat, the same threat haunting democratic futures.

> Monday. This is the way we wash our clothes.
> Whites on this side for they need special care.
> Put the darks yonder in a separate pile.
> Sort coloureds—light, not-so-light, darkish over here,
> each shade in its right place as the hymn says.
> White in the water first as it behooves,
> gentled in Ivory flakes with temperate scrub,
> then set on coral stones to profit from the sun's
> abundant coin. Now and then, on tougher stains, rub
> with brown soap and a tip of Adam's ale
> till blemishes erased, garments gleam clean.
> Coloureds get shift according as they pale.
> Darks last, slapped on the beating stone, hung on the fence.
> To coddle drugging clothes don't make no sense.[60]

To say "Thus reads the story of democracy in America thus far" would not be far from the truth. In fact, democracy in America has operated through what David Theo Goldberg in his development of a political theology of race calls a *sociality of the skin*. This political theology, grounded as it is in the experience of South African apartheid, provides a unique lens for a critique of the prison-industrial complex. What is the prison-industrial complex if not a racial apartheid gaining global dimensions?

Goldberg comments that in "a sociality of the skin, threat, threatening, and being threatened are inextricably intertwined in the psycho-social dynamics of power's racial articulation." Life under the society of the skin means an existence threatened at every moment. This domination is highly volatile since "the domination of the dominant is fueled by the threat they invest in the very existence and expression of the subjugated."[61] Such processes of domination are given a sense of stability through the *sacralization of race*, a dynamic that absolutizes sovereignty and unleashes punishment and cruelty without constraint; furthermore, it "presupposes forgetting, forgoing the memory of past injustice as prelude to living together" in the nation-making project. Restorative justice, based on memory, re-membering and piecing together the past, has no place in the nation-building.[62]

A political theology of prison abolition will be charged with the task of remembering the past and pressing American democracy to live up to Douglass's challenge. Instead of being false to the past, false to the present, and false to the future as a precondition of nation-making, it must be true to its openness to the possibility of democracy or to the hope that is yet to be revealed. For our time, one of the sites in which this struggle presents itself to us most immediately is in the prison-industrial complex.

## NOTES

1. Michelle Alexander, *The New Jim Crow: Mass Incarceration in the Age of Colorblindness* (New York: New Press, 2010).
2. See Todd R. Clear, *Imprisoning Communities: How Mass Incarceration Makes Disadvantaged Neighborhoods Worse* (Oxford: Oxford University Press, 2007).
3. Juanita Díaz-Cotto, "Chicana(o)/Latina(o) Prisoners: Ethical and Methodological Considerations, Collaborative Research Methods and Case Studies," *Latino Studies* 6, no. 1–2 (2008): 5.
4. Denominational bodies like the Unitarian Universalist Association, the United Methodist Church, and the United Church of Christ, among others.
5. Other organizations are National Reentry Resource Center, Reentry Organizations and Resource (ROAR), and Prison Fellowship International among others.
6. Langston Hughes, *Selected Poems of Langston Hughes* (New York: Vintage Books, 1990), 268.
7. Jeffrey W. Robbins, *Radical Democracy and Political Theology* (New York: Columbia University Press, 2011), 191.
8. See David Theo Goldberg, *The Threat of Race: Reflections on Racial Neoliberalism* (Malden, Mass.: Wiley-Blackwell, 2009), 308–9.
9. In this work, I'll be concerned with mass incarceration and will bracket the outgrowth of deportation regimes; I am developing this connection in a manuscript currently titled *Ghostly Bones: An Africana Critique of Political Theology*.
10. Nell I. Painter, *The History of White People* (New York: W. W. Norton, 2011); Tim J. Wise, *Colorblind: The Rise of Post-racial Politics and the Retreat From Racial Equity* (San Francisco: City Lights Books, 2010); Michael Omi and Howard Winant, *Racial Formation in the United States: From the 1960s to the 1990s* (New York: Routledge, 1994); Eduardo Bonilla-Silva, *Racism without Racists Color-blind Racism and the Persistence of Racial Inequality in Contemporary America* (Lanham, Md.: Rowman & Littlefield, 2010).
11. See Khalil Gibran Muhammad, *The Condemnation of Blackness: Race, Crime, and the Making of Modern Urban America* (Cambridge, Mass.: Harvard University Press, 2010).
12. My choices here intend to highlight three particular moments in the crucible for American democracy: pre-emancipation/emancipation Douglass, postreconstruction into the midcentury Du Bois, the 1960s Baldwin.

13. W. D. Mignolo, "Geopolitics of Sensing and Knowing: On (de) Coloniality, Border Thinking and Epistemic Disobedience," *Postcolonial Studies* 14, no. 3 (2011). Also see Janet Conway and Jakeet Singh, "Radical Democracy in Global Perspective: Notes from the Pluriverse," *Third World Quarterly* 32, no. 4 (2011): doi:10.1080/01436597.201 1.570029.
14. Irene Silverblatt, "Colonial Peru and the Inquisition: Race-Thinking, Torture, and the Making of the Modern World," *Transforming Anthropology* 19, no. 2 (2011): 132–38; Linda Martín Alcoff, "An Epistemology for the Next Revolution," *Transmodernity: Journal of Peripheral Cultural Production of the Luso-Hispanic World* 1, no. 2 (2012); Walter Mignolo, *The Darker Side of Western Modernity: Global Futures, Decolonial Options* (Durham, N.C.: Duke University Press, 2011).
15. W. D. Mignolo, "Epistemic Disobedience, Independent Thought and Decolonial Freedom," *Theory, Culture & Society* 26, no. 7–8 (2009): doi:10.1177/02632764093 49275.
16. Mignolo, "Geopolitics of Sensing and Knowing," 275.
17. My choice in turning toward delinking aims at the expansion of the abolitionist line of thought of Angela Davis and her use of Douglass.
18. Frederick Douglass, "The Meaning of July Fourth for the Negro," in *The World's Great Speeches*, ed. Lewis Copeland, Lawrence W. Lamm, and Stephen J. McKenna (Mineola, N.Y.: Dover, 1999), 805.
19. See George E. Tinker, *Missionary Conquest: The Gospel and Native American Cultural Genocide* (Minneapolis: Fortress Press, 1993), and Andrea Smith, *Conquest: Sexual Violence and American Indian Genocide* (Cambridge, Mass.: South End Press, 2005).
20. Reginald Horsman, *Race and Manifest Destiny: The Origins of American Racial Anglosaxonism* (Cambridge, Mass.: Harvard University Press, 1981).
21. Orlando Patterson, *Slavery and Social Death: A Comparative Study* (Cambridge, Mass.: Harvard University Press, 1982).
22. Douglass, "Meaning of July Fourth for the Negro," 805.
23. Ibid., 807.
24. See J. A. Colaiaco, *Frederick Douglass and the Fourth of July* (New York: Palgrave Macmillan, 2006).
25. W. E. B. Du Bois, *Black Reconstruction in America: An Essay toward a History of the Part Which Black Folk Played in the Attempt to Reconstruct Democracy in America, 1860–1880* (New York: Oxford University Press, 2007), 13.
26. Ibid., 30.
27. Ibid., 24.
28. Ibid., 198.
29. Ibid., 195.
30. Peter H. Wood, "Slave Labor Camps in Early America: Overcoming Denial and Discovering the American Gulag," in *Inequality in Early America*, ed. Carla Gardina Pestana and Sharon V. Salinger (Hanover, N.H.: University Press of New England, 1999), 234.
31. Ibid., 222.
32. James Baldwin, *Collected Essays* (New York: Library of America, 1998), 797–98.

33. Ibid., 798.
34. W. E. B. Du Bois, *The World and Africa; and Color and Democracy* (New York: Oxford University Press, 2007), 302.
35. Donna Selman and Paul Leighton, *Punishment for Sale: Private Prisons, Big Business, and the Incarceration Binge* (Lanham, Md.: Rowman & Littlefield Publishers, 2010).
36. Ernest Drucker *A Plague of Prisons: The Epidemiology of Mass Incarceration in America* (New York: New Press, distributed by Perseus, 2011) (Kindle edition, Locations 645–49).
37. Ibid. (Kindle Locations 686–88).
38. See Clear, *Imprisoning Communities*.
39. Drucker (Kindle locations 768–73).
40. Julia Sudbury, "Celling Black Bodies: Black Women in the Global Prison Industrial Complex," *Feminist Review*, no. 80 (2005): 162–79. See also Anne Bonds, "Profit from Punishment? The Politics of Prisons, Poverty and Neoliberal Restructuring in the Rural American Northwest," *Antipode* 38, no. 1 (2006): 174–77; R. M. McLennan, *The Crisis of Imprisonment: Protest, Politics, and the Making of the American Penal State, 1776–1941* (Cambridge: Cambridge University Press, 2008), chap. 3.
41. H. A. Thompson, "Why Mass Incarceration Matters: Rethinking Crisis, Decline, and Transformation in Postwar American History," *Journal of American History* 97, no. 3 (2010): 703.
42. Ryken Grattet and Joseph Hayes, "California's Changing Prison Population," Public Policy Institute of California, http://www.ppic.org/main/publication_show.asp?i=702.
43. Rubén G. Rumbaut, "Turning Points in the Transition to Adulthood: Determinants of Educational Attainment, Incarceration, and Early Childbearing among Children of Immigrants," *Ethnic and Racial Studies* 28, no. 6 (2005): 1041–86.
44. See Pew Research Center ongoing reporting on crime statistics, www.pewresearch.org.
45. Ayelet Waldman and Robin Levi. *Inside This Place, Not of It: Narratives from Women's Prisons* (San Francisco: McSweeney's Books, 2011), 17.
46. Michelle Alexander, "Without Sweet Company," in *Inside This Place, Not of It: Narratives from Women's Prisons*, ed. Ayelet Waldman and Robin Levi (New York: McSweeney's, 2014), Kindle ed., location 109.
47. Michelle L. Meloy and Susan L. Miller. *The Victimization of Women: Law, Policies, and Politics*. Oxford: Oxford University Press, 2011
48. A. Kioupkiolis, "Keeping It Open: Ontology, Ethics, Knowledge, and Radical Democracy," *Philosophy and Social Criticism* 37, no. 6 (2011): 696.
49. Ibid.
50. Ibid., 697.
51. Conway and Singh, "Radical Democracy in Global Perspective," 692.
52. Theodor W. Adorno and Henry W. Pickford, *Critical Models: Interventions and Catchwords* (New York: Columbia University Press, 2005), 17.
53. Alexis de Tocqueville, *Democracy in America: And Two Essays on America*, ed. Gerald E. Bevan and Isaac Kramnick (London: Penguin, 2003), 424.

54. Cain Hope Felder, *Stony the Road We Trod: African American Biblical Interpretation* (Minneapolis: Fortress Press, 1991).
55. W. E. B. Du Bois, "Behold the Land," in *The World's Great Speeches*, ed. Lewis Copeland, Lawrence W. Lamm, and Stephen J McKenna (Mineola, N.Y.: Dover, 1999), 818.
56. Jacques Rancière and Steve Corcoran, *Dissensus: On Politics and Aesthetics* (London: Continuum, 2010), 58–9.
57. Ibid., 59.
58. Ibid., 61.
59. Baldwin, *Collected Essays.*, 752–53.
60. Pamela Mordecai, *Subversive Sonnets: Poems* (Toronto, Ont.: TSAR Publications, 2012), 23
61. Goldberg, *Threat of Race*, 290.
62. Ibid., 308.

# ❧ Rupturing the Concorporeal Commons: On the Psychocultural Symptom of "Disability" as Life Resentment

SHARON BETCHER

*Give me your crutches so I can put them through x-ray. Now walk through the metal detector. You can walk, can't you?* Sir, I say, going eye-to-eye with the transportation safety (TSA) officer at the airport's security checkpoint, I use crutches because I have only one leg. *Right. Okay, give her back her crutches and, you! You will have to be hand-searched.* Complying yet again with some of the most invasive moves legally warranted by our recent innovation on security measures—down the V-neck sweater, under each breast, along the ravaged seam of my left hip, up the thighs to the crotch, and now the crack in the derriere, the request yet again inevitably comes, *Hand over the other shoe.* No offense, I say, but I think we are here actually waiting for the *proverbial* shoe to drop.

Despite difference being everywhere in a postmodern world, "disability" remains like a mote caught in the eye—terribly visible and completely unthinkable. Whereas civil rights movements insisted that woman was not "deformed" man and blacks were not "degenerate" whites so as to claim registry within modern humanism, disability, the signifier of that underlying negative difference, remains "invalid." Although disability has served in the modern period as "the master trope of human disqualification" (again, as the degenerative caustic underlying modern notions of gender as well as race),[1] disability is considered in the Western university and broader public a topic of marginal relevance—the concern of but an insignificant minority, purportedly the last, if failed vestige of identity politics.

The theorist Lennard Davis, analytically considering disability in relation to the civil rights and then poststructuralist banquet of difference, tips this minoritization of disability difference on its head: "Disability isn't just missing from a diversity consciousness . . . , disability is *antithetical* to diversity as it now stands." Although "diversity nicely suits neoliberal capitalism" insomuch as it "conceals financial inequality" and does not challenge "neoliberal belief in the free and autonomous subject," such diversity can be prized "only as long as we discount physical, cognitive, and affective impairments," this "collective *memento mori* of human frailty." And so, Davis concludes, "That peculiar sameness of difference in diversity has as its binary opposite the abject, the abnormal."[2] In other words, "disability," which limned our notions of gender and race, remains the trope by which we "establish differences between human beings not as acceptable or valuable variations but as dangerous deviations."[3] Such a conclusion suggests that, despite civil rights legislation and deconstructive theory, one of the keystones of modernism remains stubbornly intact.

To persons living with disabilities, this situation—that of being constituted as the abject difference that will not resolve, thus holding the sediment of modernism but being greeted with a dismissive public—suggests that we, culturally speaking, appear unwilling to release the belief that certain others are constitutionally inferior. As the disabilities theorist Tobin Siebers puts it, "The continued existence of the practice of interpreting disability as deviance rather than as human variation reveals a shocking conclusion hard to accept in this day and age. . . . Disability represents at this moment in time the final frontier of justifiable human inferiority."[4] Western culture can smartly insist on evolutionary cosmology, which necessarily assumes morphological variation within place and across time, and yet reassure itself of its aristocratic taste by resort to this categorical disqualification—that is, by dissing disability.

This remains equally true in feminist thought where aspirations to "the body" can yield to the goodness of the discarnate *"Poser"* (Claire Dederer),[5] dressed for success by the cycles of capitalist consumer commodification or rigidly self-righteous in her eco-green yoga wear. Feminists recuperated the term "body" and its material terrain from the underside of an earlier dualistic management strategy that valued the masculine spirit or mind more than the feminine body or physicality. Feminist theology contrarily argued appreciatively for human embodiment with and through an immanence of spirit. Yet feminism's recuperation of the undervalued body has not impeded either disability abjection or the ways in which cultural ideologies today capitalize on the body. Given the cultural command performances expected of us today in terms of ability, health, beauty, and productivity, *body* can invite the hallucinatory delusion of wholeness and the temptation to believe in agential mastery and control.[6]

Let me then ask, why are we still waiting for the proverbial shoe to drop? "Why is it that at the beginning of the twenty-first century—with its multiple geo-political insecurities and anxieties, its distinctly ambivalent expectations of the future, and its growing awareness of internal pressures—the western world and its developed counterparts should be so unsettled by anomalous embodiment?"[7] And if, as civil rights legislation and feminist philosophy contended, woman was not deformed man any more than black was degenerate white, then what continues to allow feminism to stand apart from disability studies? In fact, given the expectations publicly established through the scientific valorization of biotechnology and genetics as well as the economic downturn and its pressures on businesses and health care resources, the general public resentment of disability may actually be increasing.

The disabilities theorist Margrit Shildrick surmises that what appears to make disability so threatening to "normates" may be the evident permeability of body boundaries,[8] for disability but "crystallizes the vulnerability of embodiment in general."[9] "Flux and instability are not peculiar to the anomalous body," she reminds us; these are rather "the conditions of all corporeality."[10] But if flux is the condition of all corporeality, the category of disability rather names, it seems to me, a psychocultural symptom, a psychological "fixation" in the eye of the beholder—the one who, like the TSA official, both registers corporeal variation ("She has only one leg!") and yet cannot think it ("There is no 'other' shoe").

If so, "disability" has more to do with normates' roiling unconscious, resenting the terms of life and becoming (a resentment projected in turn on more obviously variable bodies) than with persons living with morphological impairments. Since "disability" names the keystone in the edifice of modern humanism, this would suggest that, despite both civil rights movements and poststructuralist efforts, it will take something more affectively deliberative if the proverbial other shoe is to fall within the Western mind.

"Dissing" disability constitutes a psychoethical judgment against the conditions of a world of becoming, against life then. Disability, I will assert, names the location of existential ressentiment within modern culture, which cuts a chasm, a bioracial divide, within our concorporeal commons. The categorical refusal to resolve this binary of able/disabled legitimates resentment against life that is, in turn, assumed into sociality, biopolitics, theology and the assumptions of practical, even religious, activism. Even in theological circles, we still demand that bodies "hand over the other shoe." Theology, like other aspects of culture, assumes a determined preference for the normate, for wholeness, without critical assessment of this presumed naturalism—whether in terms of cosmology or metaphysics. But if we are today to believe in this world[11]—when even waking anxiety begins to assess "the inheritance of loss," as the novelist Kiran Desai names it[12]—then this judgment against life—that is, "disability"—must be resolved.

Thinking through "disability" lies equally between our liberal Christian theology (frequently judged "nonfunctional" in today's spiritual marketplace) and our capacity to love the world of our postapocalyptic future. What's at stake, as I see it, is a spirituality of resilience or, more precisely, a spiritual practice of forbearance that knows how to negotiate the failure of idealism, capitalist surrealism (its ideology of limitless subjective possibility), and moral melancholy. When this "too much to see or to think" (that is, "disability") resolves into a world of becoming as but one variation thereof, then we might have found the resilience to withstand the inheritance of loss.

## OF DISABILITY AND THE COMIC IMPULSE

Early in my academic career, I was asked to assess several books on disability for the *Religious Studies Review*. Among them was a book by Robert Garland titled *The Eye of the Beholder: Deformity and Disability in the Graeco-Roman World*.[13] Although Garland offers his reader an archaeological collection of Graeco-Roman representations of morphological deformity, he could not resist the temptation to make essentializing comments about disability: "Derision of the disabled is almost certainly a universal phenomenon," he observes. "Odious and despicable though the derision of the disabled may be, it is," he concludes, "fundamental to the comic impulse."[14] I sputtered and fumed through the analysis, trying to be even-keeled. But on finishing the review, I made a production (myself as the only audience) of tearing up Garland's book. Obviously, in Garland's case, the proverbial shoe was never going to fall.

I have recently wondered though if Garland had unconsciously put his finger on not a universal truth, but a broadscale, social agreement: Did he not, in a Freudian vein, point out the affect of pleasurable sadism in the cultural construction of the able over against the disabled? If derision of the disabled has been in some way fundamental to the comic impulse (as Garland claims), does (not?) culture get pleasure from it in the same way as Freud's fabled toddler gets pleasure from his or her first defecatory deposit in the toilet bowl? In that scene, sphincteral muscles are aroused, pleasure arriving with the moment of separation and expulsion. Comparably, while "dissing" disability constitutes a sadistic discharge, this "pleasurable" explusion generates some degree of likable sociality—both in terms of solidarity and as, in terms of cultured taste, a sense of superiority.

Let me illustrate: When a corporeal impairment is present within communities, metaphors unconsciously boil up in speech that serve like telltale flags of psychic discomfort. Wherever I go, I—a left-leg amputee, which is obvious because I do not wear a cosmetic prosthesis—hear how "we must put legs" under our agenda, since obviously "we don't want to be left limping around in such vulnerable economic times." Where a member of the deaf culture resides, all are suddenly worried that they may have turned a deaf ear to student concerns. Where the differently sighted work, anxieties about leadership being a case of "the blind leading the blind" are repetitiously voiced. Disability occasions the retching of the unconscious. For those living with disability, such scenes constitute an environment of microaggression, often rationalized away by the group at large, which refuses to look at its underlying pattern of disgust (hidden as that feeling may be by the unconscious pleasure of expulsion). Yet these episodes, wherein the unconscious retches, are so impairment specific that one cannot excuse these metaphors that ask for social solidarity of the majority over against the other.

Disgust underlies our culture's relationship to disability. In the West this "gatekeeper emotion," culturally habituated and specific, roils and recoils in the presence of those signifying disease, trauma, decay, or anomalous morphology.[15] Thus the propulsive energy of disgust holds normates apart from those marked with "degeneracy." The philosopher Catherine Malabou explains: "When we formulate a negative judgment in logic, . . . when we pronounce the non-attribution of such and such a predicate to such and such a substance"—as the very word "disability" does, I suggest, thus marking some persons as "the disabled"—"we symbolically and intellectually repeat a primitive gesture of excluding or spitting out." Malabou continues:

> Negation thus has a clear *affective* origin. . . . The only possibility of being that such . . . an object has when it is judged harmful . . . by the ego is that of being expelled from being. Not reduced to non-being, but well and truly thrown out of being. Excluded from the register of beings. The . . . denied is ontological spit. A rejection from presence.[16]

Disgust can happen in the blink of an eye or the turn of a street corner. Over time patterns of disgust appear to be the better part of reason, reason sorting the valuable from the "invalid."

In coughing or vomiting out the other, disgust tears through the tissue of social flesh, the tissue of our human commons, for flesh is, I want to presume with Maurice Merleau-Ponty, something we share: "Instead of multiple, but separate and discrete corporealities, there is a tissue of intercorporeality[, inclusive of sensation]"—flesh, in philosophical terms—"in which each body is open to and affected by others."[17] Flesh names the fact that we humans are only ever "concorporeal," the body itself only ever *interpretively* known and lived within a shared affective environment. Flesh names the awareness that "the . . . body, anything but enclosed, is now turned outside in an irreducible heterogeneity."[18] As Merleau-Ponty puts it, "This flesh of my body is shared by the world."[19]

Emotions, the affective or neural wiring of social flesh, "do things," the philosopher Sara Ahmed reminds us. Specifically, "emotions work to secure collectives through the way in which they read the bodies of others."[20] Emotions—and this is important to my reading of flesh as social commons—"are not simply 'within' or 'without,'" Ahmed notes, but form the ambient atmosphere in which we live.[21] A sense of collectivity takes place as an effect of our alignment with certain emotions. In other words, "feelings make 'the collective' appear" in its purported sameness.[22] Whereas Ahmed speaks of "hate" informing racism and thus surfacing "blackness," I would suggest that disgust likewise "works to create the very outline of different figures," especially of "bodies . . . imagined as pure." Disgust works propulsively, like hate, "to stick or to bind" the wholesome with the nation, citizenship, and inalienable human rights. In this sense, disgust produces a pleasurable expulsion, a separation within social flesh, this concorporeal commons. Disgust creates bodies—"the disabled"—who appear then both "terribly visible and too much to think." In one move disgust sets apart those figures it "constitutes as a 'common' threat,"[23] while it brings an emotional sense of security, purity, normalcy, and superiority to the collective. Disgust at "the disabled" constitutes "a containment strategy that suggests modernity's high investment in control, mastery and fantasies of invulnerability," even as, maybe especially as we move into the twenty-first century with its postapocalyptic forebodings.[24]

Culling out "disabled" individuals from the commons of social flesh has been a social management strategy that unloads human interdependence by "in-valid/ating" certain persons' human worth. But if we turn the psychological scene back upon itself, "disability" refers us rather to a deep anxiety inherent in humanism's relation to flesh. Disability, I am suggesting, names not a particular impairment or a certain set of bodies, but rather constitutes a psychocultural symptom of the onlooker, the normate. Variously said, impairment or anomalous morphology produces in the eye of its beholder an affective awareness "of what it means to be human in a world governed by radical contingency."[25] When bodies are labeled "disabled," society makes these expelled others carry our dread of the precarious vulnerability of existence. By creating the set-aside named "the disabled," society with unconscious, if self-satisfied, pleasure shields its eyes from the contingent risks of becoming; it buffers the existential conditions of precariousness by marginalizing certain bodies and excluding them from the pool of aesthetic value.

Disability would then constitute a residual *cultural* symptom—not a somatic problem of a particular set of bodies. "It is," Ahmed insists, "through the intensification of feeling that bodies and worlds materialize and take shape, or that the effect of boundary, fixity and surface is produced."[26] A culture that categorically keeps a set of bodies in reserve and labels them "in/valid" is a culture that not only clings to its normative ideals but also cultivates an entrenched, affective resentment against life. That resentment, in turn, plows a chasm through the human commons, through social flesh. In the age of neoliberal responsibilization, when health itself increasingly becomes a moral, social demand (even if also, simultaneously, a productive pleasure), this bioracial divide becomes all the more morally tempting. But for those of us called to love the world as God has loved it, that undergirding resentment against life constitutes something of a theological problem.

## THE NATURAL IS WHAT DIFFERS

The political theorist William Connolly has suggested that such openness as insinuated in a world of becoming—a world of capacious prodigality and fragility, a world "so complex as to consist of many interpenetrating spheres of reality" and in which there is "no all-form either already there or towards which we are inherently tending"—can occasion ressentiment. Connolly distinguishes *resentment* as "disappointed drives that cross over into the terrain of entrenched dispositions towards revenge"[27] and ressentiment, a kind of refusal to believe in world time. Ressentiment shows itself as a refusal of "the most general terms of human existence, . . . of mortality, suffering, grief and the irreversibility of time."[28] Persons attracted to what Nietzsche called the "winter doctrines" of stasis and essence, "express," Connolly explains, "persistent [ressentiment] against the flesh, pain, limited capacity to know, vulnerability to disorganization and susceptibility to death that mark the human condition. . . . This existential [ressentiment] infiltrates into stingy moral ideals, conceptions of truth, practices of identity, judgments of normality, and systems of punishment."[29]

In summary fashion, Connolly suggests how everyday resentments, such as issues of economic inequality, suffering, sickness, exploitation, and fundamental misfortune, interact with each other, then fold over and form a deep ridge of existential ressentiment that shapes political, economic, and religious ideologies. That is to say, resentments—as disappointed drives in social, economic, and political scenes—can themselves build, burrow, and bunker down into ressentiment. "The existential dimension [of ressentiment] may even be accentuated today," Connolly surmises, "in part because of the minoritization of the world taking place before our eyes at an accelerated pace."[30] And for persons who "unconsciously resent the world for not coming equipped with assurance of salvation," such ressentiment, Connolly astutely observes, can and often will be projected against "those constituencies . . . who have . . . opened a wound in your creed."[31]

If we set Connolly's insight into the ways in which "a world of becoming" can flush up ressentiment and his assessment of projection as a resolve thereto *alongside* the history of disability and disability studies' awareness of the impetus to deal murderously with bodies so rationally categorized,[32] it is not hard to arrive at the conclusion that "disability" names one location where ressentiment comes into sociocultural—political, economic, theological—formation. Disability—when encountered hysterically as too much to think, as "monstrosity"—names but that which rends the creed of the beholder. "The existence of monsters," writes the philosopher and physician George Canguilhem, "calls into question life in its capacity to teach us order. . . . All that is needed is one loss of this confidence, one morphological lapse, one specific appearance of equivocation, and a radical fear seizes us."[33] From the perspective of one considered a morphological lapse, "to be perceived as invalid" or "monstrous" is "to be seen [as] anomalous or contrary to order."[34] But "disability" has in the first instance to do with the psychological disposition of the eye of the normate and his or her belief about the constitution of the world. Disability marks, in the first instance, that event where one's projection of "the law of life," whether in the form of a sovereign God or a presumed law of nature fails (that is, "how the world should work" goes off the rails), and so one ensconces ressentiment. Ressentiment counterproduces the cultural hallucination "ableism"—the belief in wholeness, integrity, efficiency, productivity, the fit and perfect body, and a sense of ontological order. Simply, ressentiment produces normalcy.

In a world of multiple actants and assemblages and evolutionary erring, there will be no assurance of health, security, wholeness. "Disability" thus marks a deeply entrenched, metaphysically instantiated ressentiment against flesh for such pervasive aspects of human life as pain, illness, difficulty, and suffering. Frankly, the resolve to disappear these presumably "in/valid" differences have included such cultural strategies and technologies as infanticide, amniocentesis, rehabilitation, Nazi genocide, and mainstreaming—that is, "tolerant inclusion" under the conditions of the normal. The culturally broad and historically deep resolve to create a category of the disabled and the will to dispense with them, as hinted at in this brief history of tactics, suggests a deeply entrenched human ressentiment against the very vulnerability of existence, a refusal to acknowledge evolutionary erring as primary.[35] Again, I am here assessing "disability" as a psychic dispossession, as ressentiment in the eye of the beholder.

Disability, to repeat my point, names the location of existential ressentiment that has been rationalized and theologized, for categories of disability punitively remark on the mere, if apparently intolerable fact that human becoming remains mutable—that our sociality, policies, urban design, and biological and ecological considerations of technology must take this into account. Comparably, metaphysics that refuse to admit the reality of pain—by, for example, making it a mere aspect of "the Fall"—manifest, as Nietzsche suspected, not love of this world, but nihilism.[36] This ressentiment has in the West taken two primary forms: (1) Christian scales of transcendence, which presume Edenic origins and heavenly horizons without mutation and/or pain, and (2) those evolutionary views of natural order informed by notions of entelechy, which see "beautiful mutants" as "gross, retarded, animalistic, early primate type individuals"[37] to be extinguished in the fight that awards survival to the fittest. Both of these have been ways of judging the world—wherein a presumed order has been asserted by refusing variation.[38] To cull out "disabled bodies" allows for social insistence on natural order, the constructive pleasure of (class) superiority, and the orderliness—as distinct from the vital energetics—of materialism. But such ressentiment against life—as held in the categorical disqualification "disability," which then floats our idealism, our cosmologies—captures and constrains the very resiliency, solidarity, and endurance we will need when facing our postapocalyptic futures.

Christian theology and culture have had, to be sure, a shorthand existential declaration for speaking about being resident in this world of becoming—namely, "brokenness." Christianity sees itself, when making this profession, as accepting the variations, even pain, of nature ever differing with itself. Numbers of persons living with disability have suffered the presumptive whitewashing of our difference in this proposal for world inclusion—the sentiment that "we are all broken anyway." Although evocations of "brokenness" acknowledge fragmenting within world becoming, they also problematize it. Lamenting brokenness, assuming thereby to side with the culturally marginalized, insidiously and inherently reasserts a God's-eye view and thus also a creedal belief in order and integrity from which "the disabled" have presumably deviated. "The multiple constitutive power of the ocular is . . . at its most telling and negative in the annals of the Judeo-Christian religions in which the gaze of God—in testaments Old and New—gives testimony to the monstrosity and sinfulness of impairment," the theorist Bill Hughes writes. "From the moment that the complexity and chaos of the visible are reduced to order," he insightfully concludes, "the bad and the ugly enter the domain of the known."[39] Hughes recognizes that this view infuses disability with sin and guilt, which will not be assuaged by others' vowed companionship, that is, that "we are all broken." Persons disabled, contrarily, neither identify our bodies as "broken" nor do we worry these into such an existential problem as the annals of Christian theology have.

To miss the point of human existence and so to live unskillfully, exacerbating suffering—which is how I would define Christianity's teaching of original sin—cannot fairly be summed up in the confession of "brokenness" rhetorically exchanged in our culture. In fact, cultural pathologization actually contributes to what the ancient and Reformation fathers identified as sin—the tendency to be "curved in upon the self," to make the self the project of a lifetime—even, if here, in the name of health, transformation. Variously said, that rhetorical naming of our self in the world as broken, given our Oprah-philic wound culture of sofa confessionals, can veritably lock us into the egoic project of governance of "the body"—rather than living self, as the philosopher Jean-Luc Nancy put it (and do hear his Catholic cultural background), as "mass extended" or "mass proffered" toward the good of all.[40]

The rhetoric of "brokenness" refuses to accept life as a chaotic stew; it continues to hide from self-consciousness its existential ressentiment by reference to a higher order. A theology replete with classical notions of "The Fall" will, amid the collision of bodies, rest the centrality of the right to power, the right to define, with the powerful, with the eyes of the dominant.[41] And frankly, such a way of naming our residence in the world actually misses the ironic sense of humor among crips, who have already slipped away from that way of seeing the world. That which allows us to self-identify as "dis/abled" or, more aptly, "crip" is the queering snigger that all of humanity always also lives precariously on the virgule.

In a world of becoming, "the natural is what differs. . . . Difference is not an exception . . . , but something that happens in the natural course of things." In a world of becoming there are no grounds for conceiving of disability as an aberration. Categorically establishing "disability" prevents us as humans from honoring and living into a "world of becoming." Simply put, "life and biology have their share of risks."[42] Or variously, "Where things are mobile at bottom, Being, as stable essence, never arrives."[43]

Social systems have, however, been more or less murderous in protecting their notions of order—whether metaphysics, the order of creation, social normalcy, or cultured taste. Even systemic integration and rehabilitation can be felt as efforts at some level for disappearing our crip difference rather than seeing it as integral within a world of becoming. Such practices—assumed to be generators of tolerant inclusion—justify, as the theorist Henri-Jacques Stikers explains, a metaphysics of control and mastery, rather than building solidarity around the inescapable vulnerability of flesh:

> The very primordial function that the disabled fill . . . [has been as] proof of the inadequacy of what we would like to see established as references and norm. They are the tear in our being that reveals its open-endedness, its incompleteness, its precariousness. . . . They are the thorn in the side of the social group that prevents the folly of certainty and of identification with a single model.

No human culture has been to date ready, Stiker insinuates, to accept nature as a generator of differences.[44]

An ontology, theology, and politics developed around "A World of Becoming" and its correlate, flesh as a social commons—these offer us that opportunity for thinking nature as a generator of differences. Flesh makes alterity central. Flesh might also, therefore, allow us to talk about the truth of lives which metaphysics has often hidden from the sociocultural agenda—pain, disease, transience, aging, error, fear, and corporeal limit, if also, as Virginia Woolf insists, the epiphanies and critical insights that come with illness.[45] Flesh, the theologian John Caputo reminds us, "can never achieve . . . absolute invulnerability."[46] Flesh might even be described, now thinking with the philosopher Judith Butler, as presenting us with "a primary vulnerability to others, one that we cannot will away without ceasing to be human."[47] Flesh leaves us always uncomfortably inside out or, simply, "outside ourselves."[48]

One understands, from the locus of flesh, why Butler moves in her work *Giving an Account of Oneself* toward "a relational politics, one in which the exposure and vulnerability of the other makes a primary ethical claim upon me." Not only does the religiophilosophical practice of nonviolence begin at this level of flesh, of concorporeality, where the retching of disgust threatens to tear us flesh from flesh; but, she continues, "our political situation consists in part in learning how best to handle—and to honor—this constant and necessary exposure."[49] In an age of ecological blowback, this is an even more important consideration, given that increasingly disabilities eventuate from what we have dumped into the environment. Contrary to our cultural assumptions about disability affecting "an individual" and therefore being few in number and/or of marginal concern, increasingly physical and intellectual warping of human bodies transpires through how we have failed to tend social flesh. When we marginalize persons living with disabilities, we then commit a second act of human-on-human injustice—setting outside human sociality those we have already asked to carry a body burden of environmental toxins. With that in mind, I turn to the religious task of putting disgust to work so as to regenerate—where there has been disability exclusion—the commons of social flesh.

## PUTTING DISGUST TO WORK

Robert Garland supposed disability to be the "butt" of all humor. In so doing, he naturalized disability abjection by insinuating disgust of morphological anomaly at the base of the comic impulse and therefore unconsciously legitimated, I have argued, ressentiment against life itself. I have suspected that his statements might be socially descriptive, although not "essentially" true. Further, I have proposed that disgust transpires within the affective atmosphere of social flesh. If so, then we will need to find ways—beyond the feminist theology of "the body" and philosophical poststructuralism—to deal with the gatekeeper emotion, which generates this severance within social flesh.

Religions have known ways of training the soul, or, if you prefer, of retraining the gut brain (where, for example, the cultural habituation of disgust takes hold). Such training practices interrupt the relay from the gut to the lightning-quick emotional resolves of the amygdala. Connolly himself subtly insinuates that earlier Christian monastic practices might be deployed in redeveloping a more democratic public: "Ecclesiastical practices of ritual are translated by Nietzsche and Foucault into experimental arts of the self and by Deleuze into an experimental micropolitics of intersubjectivity. Each tries to shift ethical practices that impinge *on the visceral register* from their uses . . . in the Augustinian confessional . . . , but each also strives to make investments in this domain that exceed the scope of secular self-representations." Engaging one's own visceral register is important to the ethos of a pluralist culture, Connolly insists, "because such work on oneself can sometimes untie knots in one's thinking, . . . can pave the way for new movement in the politics of becoming, and . . . can help to install generosity and forbearance in to ethical sensibilities."[50] I want, therefore, to situate this psychoanalytic assessment of disability abjection as a symptom of a broadscale ressentiment against a world of becoming next to the reflections of the twentieth-century French activist Simone Weil.

Amid her aphorisms related to "The Mysticism of Work," Weil insinuates "the use of disgust," as even that connected with manual labor, for spiritual practice. "Why has there never been a mystic, work[er] or peasant, to write on the use to be made of disgust for [spiritual, philosophical] work [on the self]," she simply queries. Then she observes: "Our souls fly from this disgust which is so often there, ever threatening, and try to hide it from themselves by reacting vegetatively." Of it she concludes, "Disgust in all its forms is one of the most precious trials sent to a [person] as a ladder by which to rise."[51] Weil suspected that working through disgust—not engorging it by using it to build sociality, not naturalizing or theologizing our gut reactions—would bring us to the cusp of the sacred. As if meditating on Psalm 22:14, "For [God] did not despise or abhor the affliction of the afflicted," she sees this as the epitome of the holy: to hold even that which has revulsed us, those we find abject, without judgment. Weil echoes insights of Augustine's "revolutionary thought . . . that an observer's shame or embarrassment in the presence of the handicapped is an artifact of disunion with his or her Creator"[52] and the sentiment shared a millennium after Augustine by Martin Luther, who insisted that disability dread was roused by Satan to occasion the sin of avoidance.[53] In some ways, this philosophical practice of "break[ing] open the human perspective" on disgust and "free[ing] it from its history of mediocre moral and religious conditioning" might, retrospectively, be said to be central to Weil's work, even as she wonders why no one precisely has taken up the challenge.[54]

Weil's own phenomenological attention to affliction noted two phenomena that we've incidentally happened upon within culturally sustained disability abjection and that might, in her soulful philosophical practice, be termed "unskillful": (a) the tendency to allow disgust to carry us on its propulsive, even pleasurable (Freud would remind us) waves away from the encounter with what we find aversive, and (b) the inflamed, murderous tendency to want to eradicate the disgusting. "[Humanity] has the same carnal nature as animals," she observes. "If a hen is hurt, the others rush upon it, attacking it with their beaks. . . . Our senses attach all the scorn, all the revulsion, all the hatred that our reason attaches to crime, to affliction."[55] Weil concludes her phenomenological observations with a quick reference to the possibility of having, however, worked spiritually with disgust in relation to this aggressive impulse: "Everybody despises the afflicted to some extent, although practically no one is conscious of it"—everyone, that is, "except for those whose soul is inhabited by Christ." [56] This, in fact, seemed to constitute the epitome of Christology in her philosophical vision: to lovingly span the chasm toward that which has been made accursed by affliction, to break the "law of gravitation" by which humans attack that which revulses us.[57] Affliction, which I have yoked here with the affect of disgust and coincidentally with the psychocultural symptom of "disability," was for Weil a decisive epistemological locus: "Through affliction, the world of necessity 'enters' our bodies and souls: we realize that we humans belong to an impersonal world . . . [, that] we do not create or control the world, not even this intimate perplexing world that we call 'I.'"[58]

"A loving attention to the real," the theologian Alyda Faber writes, summarizing Weil's philosophy, "renounces habitual consolations: that suffering will be redeemed, that ultimately nothing will be lost, that affliction strikes the sinful or careless or weak." Weil's was, Faber concludes, a vision of soulfulness that by "renouncing claims to well being . . . free[d] us to consent to what is, to experience . . . both the shocks of affliction and shocks of beauty" without seeking redemption from or in them.[59] Honestly, persons living with disability would welcome such a nonredemptive presence with a keen eye for beauty. By working through disgust in the region of the affective intellect, we might arrive at forbearance as a width of the heart. The tissue of our shared flesh can be sacramentally reverenced—rather than torn, thus vomiting out "the disabled" in disgust.

I set out with a discussion of the category of disability in relation to Western metaphysics, suggesting how a revision thereof—by way of thinking "a world of becoming"—absolves "disability" and admits the wide swath of becoming flesh. In a "world of becoming," pain, suffering, and even impairment appear to be quite natural. If so, then "disability" rather appears as a psychic disposition within the eye of the beholder, as ressentiment against life's great openness. The spiritual practice of forbearance enjoins us to receive and hold the world, even as its tectonic plates shift, without putting our adrenals on red alert. "Christianity demands that one accept suffering with courage as an element of finitude and affirm finitude in spite of the suffering that accompanies it," the twentieth-century theologian Paul Tillich insisted in regards to the path of faith. "This affirmation is only part of the great love for life as a whole that Christians express with the word 'believe.' To be able to believe means to say yes to life, to this finitude."[60] This surely implies forbearance in our relation to life itself—releasing expectations about the way the world "should be," forgiving life for not being ideal, promising happy endings, or offering us recognition.

Such practiced forbearance, bringing nonjudgment into a cultivated appreciation for a "world of becoming," prepares one for "the studied exposure of our mutual vulnerability"[61]—for love of the flesh. Flesh, I've suggested, names not so much corpuscles and goose bumps at the skinline of a body as a kind of social commons and sacred horizon in respect of this shared, if sentient tissue. The neo-Marxist philosophers Michael Hardt and Antonio Negri write of shrugging off the nostalgia for modern social bodies, privatized and mastered by rationalism into "wholeness," thus coming in touch with "a kind of social flesh, a flesh that is not a body, a flesh that is common, living substance . . . —an elemental power," like the force of wind or sea, from the potential of which we may form a new society.[62] But flesh, as Richard Kearney points out, also names the "kenotic emptying out of transcendence into the heart of the world's becoming"—of God becoming flesh of our flesh, and nothing more (or less!), that is, "The Christian God wants nothing to do with a vertical relation of subordination."[63] Speaking of this not so much as a God "hidden in immanence" as a "sacramental acoustic of natural existence," Kearney—applying the phenenomological suspension of assumptions—simply speaks appreciatively of "the holy *thisness* of our flesh-and-blood existence."[64]

### FORBEARANCE WITH A POSTAPOCALYPTIC WORLD SCENE

Since the middle of the twentieth century, we have become "a world that lives with the reality of . . . 'possible annihilation' everyday."[65] While waiting for the proverbial shoe to drop has been identified with everything from the atomic bomb to climate disaster, from viral pandemic to asteroid, a form of literature has been proliferating not so interested in that event of apocalypse as in what comes after, a genre known as "postapocalyptic."[66] Think, for example, of Lois Lowry's *The Giver* Quartet, Suzanne Collins's *The Hunger Games*, Cormac McCarthy's *The Road*, graphic novels such as *Tank Girl*, the movie *The Book of Eli*, even Disney's *Wall-E*, or, earlier, the cyberpunk author William Gibson's short story "The Winter Market." This narrative genre visits humanity sifting through the ruins, distilling how we will redefine ourselves as societies.[67] Ironically, disability has, within this literary genre, moved from modernity's locus of sick body on a pallet before the divine healer to lead character, from unique and exceptional demand on sympathy to pervasive condition within sociality. The "clean slate" of an apocalyptically washed world starting over yields—within postapocalyptic frames—to bodies cripped and krumped among the ruins, persons working to *detourn* technological debris as prostheses of new sociality.[68] As the disabilities theorist Clare Barker puts it, while speaking of disability in those other "postapocalyptic" or, namely, "postcolonial" zones, "The reconstruction of civil imagining is undertaken . . . not just through mobilizing the trope of disability but through the privileging of disability subjectivities."[69]

Figurations—this "crip" of postapocalyptic narrative as also modernity's "Man of Reason"—carry the possibilities we imagine for human life. So what then shall we make of the figuration of the crip as emergent in these postapocalyptic ruins? What constructive potencies for human life and sociality does postapocalyptic literature hopefully fold, like origami, into this figuration? Intriguing, isn't it, this pivot from disability as aesthetic sore on the eyeball, as "ugly," to the "rune" thrown "to find new ways of looking, new patterns to create meanings in the new world."[70] Contrary to Western modern humanist reason, the crip tells us anew about being human, this figuration assuming all corporeality to be "porous and provisional."[71] In that vein, the figural crip of postapocalypticism may be, like the self-identified crip, a "doing, an . . . onto-epistemological enactment of the world."[72] Crips challenge modern culture to break through the rigid boundaries of "reason" attached to the capitalization of value, including the commodification of the body via labor value, as well as to yield the illusory sense of the security-immunity cordon in modern subjectivity. The crip performatively "questions the givenness of the different categories of 'human,' examining the practices through which these different definitions are stabilized and destabilized"[73]—including the modern subject's reassurance of belonging via normalcy and hierarchical distance from marked bodies, as well as its sense of its own superior value or "mattering" in the world. Comparably, postapocalyptic literature conserves disability and uses it to think creatively about living on with a "cripped" earth, if you will. The crip as icon, I propose, fathoms forth a possible love of life in the handhold of the Anthropocene, this passage when humanity becomes the overwhelming force of nature and planetary evolution.

Rosemarie Garland-Thomson, a disabilities studies scholar, may not use the term "soul-craft" in her apologia titled "The Case for Conserving Disability," but one religious might. "Conserving disability" speaks to an alternative vision of nature wherein the picture of health refers not to bounded self-enclosure or its dream of purity but to living with carnivalesque vigor amid the human and planetary manifold, having learned "to abide the unexpected, to live with dissonance, to rein in the impulse to control."[74] Such insights are strikingly parallel to—yet previously unexamined in light of—theological teachings regarding the spiritual virtues and, further, resonant with ecological ethicists' call to relinquish our quest for the domination of nature.

Even the historian of science Donna Haraway reminds theologians that the postapocalyptic tableau of crip figurations reaches back to include the grotesque Suffering Slave-Servant Jesus, interpolated through Isaiah 53, among others.[75] How distinct that cripped figural of the sacred is from the biblical scholar Adolph von Harnack's "vital, pure and busy" Jesus, the Healer, of modern liberal reconstructionist vision—a vision still informing progressive imaginations today.[76] Thinking with the crip as key figuration, we might live toward that knowledge that "disability names the common underpinning of all human becoming"[77] and so begin to live flesh and finitude with more resilience. There's no guarantee of it, of course: We could see disgust and revulsion choose all more rigorously puritanical modalities in stressed times. Economics and the neoliberalization of health can make the screening out of "life not worthy of life" seem reasonable in dire times. But the crip figurally invites a path of living flesh and finitude nonviolently, without judgment, along the skinline.

The crip or, if you will, disability theology, thus stands (ah-hem, sits, wheels, limps . . . with attitude, of course) between modern theology—with its Jesus as Healer, intent on fixing, rehabilitating into the norms of the upright—and a theology able to love the world "even through this"—that is, life in postapocalyptic register. Disability occasions the suspension of belief in reasonable causality, of karma, and, in this way, of absolutizing metaphysics. As Jean-Luc Nancy—himself a bit crip, given his heart transplant—puts it, "We know that we are bereft of horizons and, with them, justifications for misfortune (maladies, injustices)."[78] When disability speaks, it will "unmoor our collective fantasies in the 'promise' of eradication or cure,"[79] fantasies not indistinct from considering "life as something to be judged and found wanting."[80] Releasing the commodity enabled pursuit of "wholeness," that "comforting return to the organism,"[81] the crip invites us rather to learn to be with the world in its own quirks of becoming. "Disability contributes a narrative of a genuinely open future, one not controlled by the objectives, expectations, and understandings of the present," Garland-Thompson observes. And she concludes, "Rather than dictating a diminished future, disability opens a truly unpredictable, even unimaginable, one and, in doing so, confounds Promethean prognosis."[82] Consequently, disability theology finds itself consonant with theologian Catherine Keller's "tehomic ethic" for postapocalyptic times: "To love is to bear with the chaos . . . , to recognize there the unformed future."[83]

## NOTES

1. Sharon L. Snyder and David T. Mitchell, *Narrative Prosthesis: Disability and the Dependence of Discourse* (Ann Arbor: University of Michigan Press, 2001), 3. Also cited in Tobin Siebers, *Disability Aesthetics* (Ann Arbor: University of Michigan Press, 2010), 24.
2. Lennard J. Davis, "Why Is Disability Missing from the Discourse on Diversity?" *Chronicle of Higher Education*, September 25, 2011.
3. Siebers, *Disability Aesthetics*, 24.
4. Tobin Siebers, "Aesthetics and the Disqualification of Disability" (paper presented and distributed at the Society for Disabilities Studies Annual Conference, San Jose, Calif., June 17, 2011), 12.
5. In *Poser: My Life in Twenty-Three Yoga Poses* (Farrar, Straus and Giroux, 2011), Claire Dederer confesses that she "started going to yoga because I wanted other people to admire my goodness." Obsessed with pushing just the right stroller, choosing the most ecologically conscious diaper, and appropriately performing attachment parenting, Dederer's core values suggest the just intentions of many North American liberal feminists. And yet as yoga poses work their ways through various energy locks on her body, it is just this well intentioned goodness . . . of a "judging mind" . . . that comes into question. "What if the opposite of good . . . was real?" she asks herself one day (271), realizing that the "goodness" she had been cultivating had more to do with hypervigilance (thus with fear, self-consciousness, and insecurity) than honestly engaging, through sweat and struggle, the reality at hand. Despite her "discarnate" or pretentious beginnings, yoga—Dederer concludes—"helped to reverse the goodness-to-reality ratio in my life" (303).
6. See Sharon Betcher, "Becoming Flesh of My Flesh: Feminist and Disability Theologies on the Edge of Posthumanist Discourse," *Journal of Feminist Studies in Religion* 26, no. 2 (2010): 107–39.
7. Margrit Shildrick, *Dangerous Discourses of Disability, Subjectivity, and Sexuality* (London: Palgrave Macmillan, 2012), 1.
8. Ibid., 4.
9. Ibid., 17.
10. Ibid., 14.
11. Gilles Deleuze and Felix Guattari, *What Is Philosophy?* trans. Hugh Tomlinson and Graham Burchell (New York: Columbia University Press, 1994), 75.
12. Kiran Desai, *The Inheritance of Loss* (New York: Atlantic Monthly Press, 2006).
13. Robert Garland, *The Eye of the Beholder: Deformity and Disability in the Graeco-Roman World* (Ithaca, N.Y.: Cornell University Press, 1995).
14. Ibid., 73, 75.
15. Susan B. Miller, *Disgust: The Gatekeeper Emotion* (Hillsdale, N.J.: Analytic Press, 2004).
16. Catherine Malabou, *Ontology of the Accident: An Essay on Destructive Plasticity*, trans. Carolyn Shread (Cambridge: Polity Press, 2012), 81, emphasis added.
17. Shildrick, *Dangerous Discourses*, 26.
18. Roberto Esposito, *Bios: Biopolitics and Philosophy*, trans. Timothy Campbell (Minneapolis: University of Minnesota Press, 2008), 159–160.

19. Ibid., 160.
20. Sara Ahmed, "Collective Feelings: Or, the Impressions Left by Others," *Theory, Culture & Society* 21, no. 2 (2004): 25.
21. Ibid., 25, 28.
22. Ibid., 27.
23. Ibid., 26.
24. Shildrick, *Dangerous Discourses*, 51.
25. Ato Quayson, *Aesthetic Nervousness: Disability and the Crisis of Representation* (New York: Columbia University Press, 2007), 17.
26. Ahmed, "Collective Feelings," 29.
27. William E. Connolly, *A World of Becoming* (Durham, N.C.: Duke University Press, 2011), 6.
28. William E. Connolly, "A World of Becoming," in *Democracy and Pluralism: The Political Thought of William E. Connolly*, ed. Alan Finlayson (London: Routledge, 2010), 228.
29. Ibid., 259–60.
30. Ibid., 229–30.
31. Ibid., 228.
32. Henri-Jacques Stiker, *A History of Disability*, trans. William Sayers (Ann Arbor: University of Michigan Press, 1999), 8–9.
33. Georges Canguilhem, *The Normal and the Pathological* (New York: Zone Books, 1991). Also in Stiker, *History of Disability*, 6, 7.
34. Bill Hughes, "The Constitution of Impairment: Modernity and the Aesthetic of Oppression," *Disability and Society* 14, no. 2 (1999): 157.
35. Scott DeShong, "The Nightmare of Health: Metaphysics and Ethics in the Signification of Disability," *Symploke* 15, nos. 1–2 (2007): 271–72.
36. Tyler T. Roberts, *Contesting Spirit: Nietzsche, Affirmation, Religion* (Princeton: Princeton University Press, 1998), 14
37. Adam Pottle, *Beautiful Mutants* (Halfmoon Bay, B.C.: Caitlin Press, 2011), 23.
38. In a review of Stephen J. Gould's *The Structure of Evolutionary Theory* (2002), the disabilities scholar David Mitchell affirms that "Darwinian theory"—with its appreciation of "randomness and non-directed nature" as well as adaptive "interactions with the environment"—"can be used to destabilize social beliefs in disability as synonymous with organismic insufficiency." Whereas "previous theories of species development hinged upon beliefs in a mechanism of internal determinism that guided species toward increasing perfection" (namely, the notion of "entelechy"), "Darwin overturned these notions by positing that species development occurs through a haphazard process (termed *natural selection*) where some organismic characteristics prove accidentally fortuitous to certain environmental conditions." See "Evolutionary Theory," in *Encyclopedia of Disability*, vol. 2, ed. Gary L. Albrecht (Thousand Oaks, Calif.: Sage, 2006), 642.
39. Hughes, "Constitution of Impairment," 163.
40. Jean-Luc Nancy, *Corpus*, trans. Richard A. Rand (New York: Fordham University Press, 2008).

41. Hughes, "Constitution of Impairment," 163.
42. Stiker, *History of Disability*, 12.
43. Connolly, "Suffering, Justice, and the Politics of Becoming," *Culture, Medicine, and Psychiatry* 20, no. 3 (1996): 264.
44. Stiker, *History of Disability*, 10.
45. Virginia Woolf, *On Being Ill*, introduction by Hermione Lee (Paris: Paris Press, 2002).
46. John D. Caputo, *Against Ethics: Contributions to a Poetics of Obligation with Constant Reference to Deconstruction* (Bloomington: Indiana University Press, 1993), 201.
47. Judith Butler, *Precarious Life: The Powers of Mourning and Violence* (New York: Verso, 2004), xiv.
48. Ibid., 27.
49. Judith Butler, *Giving an Account of Oneself* (New York: Fordham University Press, 2005), 31–32.
50. William E. Connolly, *Why I Am Not a Secularist* (Minneapolis: University of Minnesota Press, 1999), 28.
51. Simone Weil, *Gravity and Grace*, trans. Emma Crawford and Mario von der Ruhr, rev. ed. (1947; London: Routledge, 2002), 179.
52. Brian Brock, "Augustine's Hierarchies of Human Wholeness and Their Healing," in *Disability in the Christian Tradition: A Reader*, ed. Brian Brock and John Swinton (Grand Rapids, Mich.: William B. Eerdmans, 2012), 74.
53. M. Miles, "Martin Luther and Childhood Disability in 16th Century Germany: What Did He Write? What Did He Say?" *Journal of Religion, Disability and Health* 5, no. 4 (2001): 9.
54. Ann Pirruccelloa, "Making the World My Body: Simone Weil and Somatic Practice," *Philosophy East and West* 52, no.4 (2002): 479.
55. Lest we think our world (at the least, our modern Western world) surely beyond such irrational acts as attacking "the afflicted" as chickens attack the wounded, Jack Levin, a professor of sociology and criminology, reminds us that "hate crimes against people with disabilities are widespread and often involve extraordinary levels of sadism." In his article "The Invisible Hate Crime," Levin reminds his readers that the February 2010 torture and murder of a thirty-year-old mentally challenged woman from Greensburg, Pennsylvania, was "anything but unique" and that, even given the serious underreportage of such, "Americans with disabilities experience serious violence at a rate nearly twice that of the general population" and sexual violence at a rate "four times higher than that of people without disabilities." Yet even activists—able to rally in the wake of Matthew Shepard's and James Byrd's deaths, given the virulence of sexual and racial prejudices exhibited in those deaths—seem to have, Levin notes, "emotional 'tunnel vision'" where hate crimes of persons with disabilities are involved. In hate crimes the sadistic pulsion "enjoyed" by a culture that pushes itself away from "the disabled" becomes violently exercised. See Jack Levin, "The Invisible Hate Crime," *Pacific Standard*, Legal Affairs, March 1, 2011. Also published on the web at http://www.psmag.com%2Flegal-affairs%2Fthe-invisible-hate-crime-27984 (accessed September 11, 2012).

56. Simone Weil, *Waiting for God*, trans. Emma Craufurd, rev. ed. (1951; New York: Perennial Classics, 2001), 71.
57. Ibid., 72, 75.
58. Alyda Faber, *"Dancer in the Dark*: Affliction and the Aesthetic of Attention," *Studies in Religion* 35, no. 1 (2006): 87.
59. Ibid., 88.
60. Dorothee Soelle, *Suffering*, trans. Everett R. Kalin (Minneapolis: Fortress Press, 1975), 107. Soelle quotes Paul Tillich, *Systematic Theology*, vol. 2, trans. Arthur Wills (Chicago: University of Chicago Press, 1957), 70.
61. Alyda Faber, "The Post-Secular Poetics and Ethics of Exposure in J. M. Coetzee's 'Disgrace,'" *Literature and Theology* 23, no. 3 (2009): 309.
62. Michael Hardt and Antonio Negri, *Multitude: War and Democracy in the Age of Empire* (New York: Penguin, 2004), 192–93.
63. Richard Kearney, *Anatheism: Returning to God after God* (New York: Columbia University Press, 2010), 94, 91.
64. Ibid., 95.
65. Christina J. Smith, "What Disappears and What Remains," master's thesis, North Carolina State University, 2007.
66. Postapocalyptic literature has been dated back to the middle of the twentieth century, beginning with Walter M. Miller Jr., *A Canticle for Leibowitz* (Philadelphia: J. B. Lippincott, 1960).
67. Smith, "What Disappears," 54.
68. Postapocalyptic literature assumes no apocalypse—no defeat of a corrupt world, no telling revelation or exposure such that "truth" or meaning is known with certitude.
69. Clare Barker, *Postcolonial Fiction and Disability: Exceptional Children, Metaphor and Materiality* (London: Palgrave Macmillan, 2011), 30. Intriguingly, James Berger, recognized as a key theorist of the postapocalyptic (see his *After the End: Representations of Post-Apocalypse* [Minneapolis: University of Minnesota Press, 1999]), starts his theoretical undertaking by writing of his experience of growing up with a disabled sister, although he never explicitly explains how he thinks these scenes of the postapocalyptic and that family scene are related. Lois Lowry, author of *The Giver* quartet, likewise acknowledges that one experiential condition of her own writing has been living with a daughter who became disabled owing to a neurospinal virus.
70. Chandra Phelan, "Research Reveals That Apocalyptic Stories Changed Dramatically 20 Years Ago," *io9*, October 29, 2009. http://io9.com/5392430/research-reveals-that-apocalyptic-stories-changed-dramatically-20-years-ago (accessed February 25, 2013).
71. Shildrick, *Dangerous Discourses*, 26.
72. Kelly Fritsch, "Crip Cuts: On the Boundary Work of Enacting Disability" (paper presented at the Society for Disability Studies, Denver, June 2012), 7.
73. Karen Barad, *Meeting the Universe Halfway: Quantum Physics and the Entanglement of Matter and Meaning* (Durham, N.C.: Duke University Press, 2007), 808.

74. Rosemarie Garland-Thomson, "The Case for Conserving Disability," *Bioethical Inquiry* 9, no. 3 (2012): 339–55.
75. Donna Haraway, "Ecce Homo, Ain't (Ar'n't) I a Woman, and Inappropriate/d Others: The Human in a Post-Humanist Landscape," in *Feminists Theorize the Political*, ed. Judith Butler and Joan W. Scott (London: Routledge, 1992), 86–100.
76. Adolph von Harnack, *The Mission and Expansion of Christianity in the First Three Centuries*, vol. 1, trans. James Moffatt (New York: G. P. Putnam's Sons, 1908). The biblical scholars John Dominic Crossan and Marcus Borg work significantly with the reconstruction of late modern (twenty-first-century) Western Christianity around the image of Jesus as healer.
77. Shildrick, *Dangerous Discourses*, 10.
78. Jean-Luc Nancy, *Adoration: The Deconstruction of Christianity*, vol. 2, trans. John McKeane (New York: Fordham University Press, 2013), 73.
79. David Mitchell, Introduction to Stiker, *A History of Disability*, ix.
80. Clare Colebrook, *Deleuze and the Meaning of Life* (London: Continuum, 2010), 25.
81. Ibid., 113.
82. Garland-Thomson, "Case for Conserving," 352.
83. Catherine Keller, *The Face of the Deep: A Theology of Becoming* (New York: Routledge, 2003), 29.

## ⁕ The Common Good of the Flesh: An Indecent Invitation to William E. Connolly, Joerg Rieger, and Political Theology

KAREN BRAY

*And those bursts of laughter, bouts of sensual heat, workers' movements, consumption habits, hurricanes, geological formations, climate patterns, contending gods, electrical fields, spiritual upheavals, civilizational times, species changes, and planetary rotations—they, too, participate in this veritable monster of energies, making a difference before melting down to be drawn again into new currents, and again.*
—WILLIAM E. CONNOLLY, POSTLUDE TO *A World of Becoming*

### SEX OFF THE BRAIN

If we were to have listened to nervous fathers of girls, to advertisements for fast cars, to reality shows, and teen comedies, we would have learned that men have too much sex on the brain. Yet as I began to delve deeper into the work of political theology, the problem seemed to me to be quite the opposite: Sex was too much off the brain; or if on the brain, then sexual thoughts were sanitized and made decent by the time they reached the page. Sex in contemporary political theology felt less like a name for an embodied act, a forceful mode of desire in the world, and more exclusively like an identity marker within a play of political allegiances. If sex was discussed in terms of the political, it was done so as a nod toward the formation and control of gendered identities and not as the potent force of political life I suggest it can be. And so although sexual identities may have been marked, sexual desire remained largely undertheorized. It was this lack of theorization that I sought to diagnose at the conference from which this volume comes. The problem was not prudishness. The thinkers I engage are not meek men. They are in fact quite promisingly, and in the sense I will offer here, obscene.

The obscene is that which reveals flesh to be flesh.[1] Marcella Althaus-Reid turns this definition proposed originally by Jean-Paul Sartre—and not affirmingly so—into a productive theological method. Her foundational book, *Indecent Theology: Theological Perversions in Sex, Gender and Politics*, seeks to correct a profoundly problematic omission by liberation theology: sexual honesty.[2] She develops an "indecent theology," which uncovers and engages the potency of sexuality for the formation of metaphors of God. This theological method explicated by Althaus-Reid forms the foundation of what I am calling a methodology of the obscene. This methodology of the obscene is the process of uncovering the sexual implications inherent in our theologies. For Althaus-Reid every theology implies a decision or condition of right sexual belief and action. Right "sex" is a marker of right family relation, right economic relation, and right bodily relation to God. This essay builds on the work of Althaus-Reid; "sex" marks the way our desires, as well as those for God, are regulated by social and historical modes of control.

This expansive definition helps undergird the assertion that theology is a sexual act. Whether they acknowledge it or not, theologians find metaphors for the holy from within our experiences of sexuality. Problematically too often, theologians either eschew their own sexuality and desire for the sake of keeping theology decent or affirm their own sense of sexuality at the expense of others. Althaus-Reid, in criticizing such a theology, is not proposing that ethical decisions about right sexual behavior cannot or should not be taken. Rather, she seeks to expose the ways theology too often condemns or depoliticizes sexual pleasures: "Theology is a sexual divinized orthodoxy (right sexual dogma) and orthopraxy (right sexual behaviour); theology is a sexual action. Theologians, therefore, are nothing else but sexual performers who need to take many ethical and sometimes partisan sexual decisions when reflecting on God and humanity, because theology is never innocuous or sexually innocent or neutral."[3] This need not mean that theologians should not take ethical stances regarding sex. Rather, this is the call for a theological uncovering, for a methodology of the obscene.

Right sexual orthopraxy and orthodoxy are constructed both from overt sexual prescriptions and from the silences created when the multiplicity of desire remains unnamed. Althaus-Reid argues that liberation theology, in divorcing sexuality from poverty, loses the richness of divine metaphors formed at the intersection of the erotic and the economic. To explicate this point she turns to female lemon vendors in Argentina who do not wear underwear. Althaus-Reid asks what might it mean that the smell of their sex mingles with that of their economic trade, the sweet and sourness of lemons. She then moves to how these smells might infect zones of worship and faith. What difference it might make if one were to pray or write theology without underwear. What smells might mingle in acts of communion with God? Here, Althaus-Reid is affirming a broader definition of sex to include the ways in which we accept or reject our bodies and how we engage them in various political, theological, and economic endeavors. Do we view our desire as dirty and unworthy of God or as part of the beauty of creation—a beauty found even in its most pungent or "indecent" scents and sense? Sex and indecency can become markers for an embrace of the entirety of who we are, the holiness of our messiness. This embrace intimately affects which economic and political rights we deem ourselves worthy of holding. Therefore, if theology is never sexually innocent, it must be practiced as obscenity in action—revealing flesh to be flesh—disrobing oppressive dogmas clothed in the garments of neutrality.

Many postsecular thinkers practice a similar methodology of the obscene. Taking a cue from Carl Schmitt's proposition that all modern concepts of the state are secular theological concepts, Joerg Rieger and William Connolly reveal the flesh of capitalism to be flesh, uncovering its theology to be theology—never innocent or neutral. Yet simultaneously they oppose Schmitt's dogmatic Christian counter to a dogmatic secularism. Here the revealed "flesh" not only symbolizes the acts of indecency that show that when one undresses secular capitalism, one sees its theological undergarments, but also asks us to see the obscene maneuver such an undressing entails. Just as Althaus-Reid's revelation that all theology is sexual theology challenges the oppressive sanitizing of a purportedly innocent Christianity, Rieger's and Connolly's exposing gesture challenges the neutrality of capitalism.

In *No Rising Tide: Theology, Economics and the Future*, Rieger details the ways in which the neoliberal economic proposal, "A rising tide will lift all boats," is in fact a theological assertion. This rising-tide theology carries with it bold faith claims: that economic deregulations promote growth, that tax cuts for powerful corporations and the wealthy spur the economy, and that wealth gathered at the top eventually trickles down.[4] These claims rely on the partisan belief in a providential market. Like the followers of an omnipotent God, disciples of market fundamentalism obey the market without question. Althaus-Reid similarly problematizes this kind of fundamentalist dogmatism, including dogmatic sexual propositions. For Althaus-Reid, the mainstream theology taught in churches often proposes an "acceptable" Christian history in which women and dissidents are subjected to violence and sexual torture: "We may see this as a second-rate porno film where Eve gives birth in pain forever; Tamar is raped interminably by her brother in his bedroom; Jesus hangs naked from a cross, hands nailed, blood coming from a crown of thorns on his head; Mary says yes to the first angel in her life who appears in her room."[5] Teaching these stories of sexual violence as though they were unproblematic hides the hard-core nature of this theology underneath soft-core veils.

The theology of the market, as described by Rieger, similarly claims a soft-core erotic, proposing notions of liberty through consumerism as though they were decent. After 9/11 Americans were told to prove our liberty by shopping. Consumerism was hailed not only as decent as in innocent, but further as in *the* decent way to live in the wake of tragedy: consumerism as salvation. When presidential candidates win elections by promising not to raise taxes, the rationale given is that our economy, and through it we, will be saved when Americans have as much capital to spend as possible. There is no need to worry about how the lack of tax revenue contributes to the slashing of social services, often the last threads of a salvific safety net, because we will be saved through our ritual exchanges at the cash register. This theology is hard-core, as it binds consumers into a state of servitude to a market in which we are told we will find freedom.

Most of our boats will not be rising. The more we pursue and play this rigged aspirational game, the more we are actually tightening the straps of our bondage, clasping the handcuffs tighter on our wrists, pushing the gags further into our mouths, and giving ourselves over to our chains. These acts of submission do not represent the erotic play of power and powerlessness, of submission as subversion found in much of the BDSM culture. Rather, we unknowingly, if willingly, submit through manipulation and so lack or refuse the safe-word needed to set ourselves free. In this way, the theology of market fundamentalism dresses itself up not merely as soft-core, but more so as life-giving, when in actuality the more unveilings we perform, the more its hard-core reality is revealed. As Lauren Berlant has noted, aspirational politics often create a state of "cruel optimism": "A relation of cruel optimism exists when something you desire is actually an obstacle to your flourishing."[6] Market fundamentalism is cruelly optimistic; it promises freedom and human flourishing, while placing ever more impediments on our paths. Rieger uncovers this cruelty in the mimetic desire encouraged by capitalism.[7] Revealing how our faith that a rising tide will lift all boats hinders our flourishing, Rieger practices a methodology of the obscene and strips away any sense of neutrality within capitalistic desire.

Key to the problematic faith claims of American capitalism, Rieger argues, is the belief that desires arise naturally. Although conventional wisdom might hold that it's natural to desire a larger home or that we inherently are drawn toward a certain body type, these desires are nurtured by an entire class of managers—advertisers included—who know very well that their livelihoods depend on the production of desire. As Rieger notes, "This produced desire produces our gods, as Luther realized: the god of prosperity, whose existence is proved by economic gain; the god of the market, who claims to lift all boats; and the god of charity, who seeks to shape economically disadvantaged people in the image of their benefactors—as fellow consumers."[8] In producing our gods, desire similarly produces our view of humanity. Advertising works as catechism, teaching women that if we were to just lose weight, put on the right makeup, and cook with the right brand of chicken, we could have what we "naturally" desire: to be loved by a handsome, able-bodied, white, rich man. And if he were to just buy the right diamond, drive the right car, and smell like the right deodorant, he could get what he must naturally desire, a thin, young, busty, shaved, and docile woman. Not only by what we consume but more so by consumption's end goal, what we are promised to achieve through our purchases, is humanity defined. Therefore, our very ability to be properly human depends on this mimetic desire that longs after the lifestyles and identities of those whose boats keep rising, as the rest of us are left to the undertow.

A similarly alluring methodology of the obscene may be found in William Connolly's *Capitalism and Christianity, American Style*. His obscenity comes primarily in his stripping down of what he terms the Evangelical-Capitalist-Resonance-Machine. This resonance machine is bounded together by shared fundamentalist faiths: The belief in an omnipotent God resonates with that of an omnipotent market. As this relation is amplified, the machine becomes increasingly invested in the stabilizing force of the Christian-family-erotic assemblage, in which, as Connolly writes:

> The radical Christian right *compensates for* a series of class resentments and injustices produced by the collision between cowboy capitalism and critical social movements by promising solace in the church and the family; it then cements (male) capitalist creativity to the creativity of God himself, fomenting an *aspirational politics* of identification by workers with men of prowess and privilege; these self-identifications and compensatory entitlements then encourage those sweltering in the pressure cooker to demonize selected minorities as nomadic enemies of capitalism, God, morality, and civilizational discipline.[9]

This demonization stabilizes capitalism along with evangelical Christianity, in that class resentment, which might resonate with leftist social movements, is subdued by the promise of superiority over many involved in those movements, whether they be African Americans, women, homosexuals, transgendered people, the disabled, or the global poor. Here, Connolly has done away with capitalism's neutrality and has revealed much of what is at stake for sexual and gendered minorities, and yet from him there is more to be desired.

Although both Connolly and Rieger aptly employ a methodology of the obscene in the above acts of theological uncovering, they stop short of truly enfleshing an alternate theology: one of the common good of the flesh, which might arouse in us the spirit to counter the commodification of the flesh and the production of both mimetic desires and those for revenge. It is the invitation for each to move deeper into the boudoir, to undress not only theologies undergirding capitalism but also their own philosophies, that is offered by this essay.

## DESIRE WITHOUT ORGANS

Perhaps most striking about the lack of any overt discussion of sexuality (not as identity but as an enfleshed potency) is the prominent place that discourses of desire play in theological critiques of capitalism. Yet for all this talk of desire, there is little talk of sex. Economic desire as detailed by most political theologians seems to be a desire without organs, not one without body, but one lacking in the pelvic thrusts that propel and animate our world. Connolly and Rieger are no exceptions; their fine explorations of the role of desire in economic spheres remain incomplete; there is more to undress.

According to Rieger, desire gives value to societal order.[10] Yet, he asks, what gives value to desire? Rieger examines the importance of perpetual desire for capitalism and uncovers its problematic teleology: "The subordination of evaluation to desire at personal, institutional and systemic levels is the fundamental corruption of democratic capitalism."[11] Desire-without-ends traps consumers in a perpetual need for more, more stuff in order to become who we are supposed to be. The theology of desire implied in market fundamentalism is one in which the ultimate telos is not up for assessment of value for human flourishing. In keeping an eye toward future consumption, while ignoring what consumption has to do with how we live in the present (a catastrophic omission for the climate) this theology mirrors the eschatalogies of Christian fundamentalism. Both fundamentalisms, market and Christian, ask us to live for the future, where we will be saved by either spiritual riches or material wealth; and both often do so while disregarding the evaluation of life as such.

Radical Orthodox theologians raise similar questions in terms of the teleological promises of capitalistic desire. According to John Milbank, the problem of the subordination of evaluation to desire has arisen because we have lost sight of the true telos, the value of all values reflected in Christ. In a soteriological gesture he argues for a return to a monarchic Christian understanding of absolute good: "Where there is no public recognition of the primacy of the absolute good as grounded in the super-human, then democracy becomes impossible."[12] Taking a more democratic approach, Rieger proposes a greater sense of materialism in conjunction with spirituality.

For Rieger capitalistic desire is about fulfilling who we wish to be through the objects we *pursue*.[13] We will never *be* enough, for we will never *have* enough. This is where mimetic desire for the lives lived by those at the top works to shape our ontologies. If our very sense of being is defined by whether we have succeeded at mimicking those merrily floating along on the surface of the tide, then the fact that we are continually dragged under by their wake is catastrophic. This impossibility of becoming what we are told we must become results in resentment. This resentment, in search of comfort, manifests itself in the ECRM as faith in a false salvation, one promised by an unwavering belief that a rising tide *will* lift all boats, and/or that a fundamentalist God *will* redeem *his* followers. Therefore, unlike Milbank, Rieger resists replacing an ever more impossible to reach capitalistic telos with a transcendent Christian one, and instead proposes a return to a different materialism coupled with a different spirituality.[14] Rieger seeks a Christian spirituality found in acts that improve the material conditions of the marginalized. This Christianity is the Christianity of the servant and not of the king. This Christianity takes the material conditions of life as its utmost value, such that evaluation would no longer be subordinated to perpetual desire.

In the acts of undressing detailed above, Rieger has proven himself obscene: proposing other ways of walking with God, other practices of evaluation, and other visions of materialism. Yet in terms of the method requested by this essay, in terms of theological indecency, he has fallen short of full consummation. Indeed, Rieger acknowledges the ways in which marginalized people, including those suffering under patriarchal and homophobic hierarchies, are most cruelly oppressed by market fundamentalism. In doing so, he fruitfully engages capitalistic desire's problematic implications for the politics of identity. However, Rieger remains in the realm of political identities—those that can be classed as stable groups of people and not interacting planes of flesh. Hence, in a world that needs more indecency, Rieger's work may, if only as it stands now, be just too decent.

To be sure, Rieger does acknowledge the political power inherent in embodied experience. He calls for a common good based on productive participation in life and the creative possibility of all beings. This creative possibility comes from the tragedies that befall and the acts of resistance undertaken by those whose boats do not rise. He proposes the possibilities in what Sally McFague has termed the "wild spaces":

> A wild space is whatever does not fit the stereotypical human being in each of us—what some think is our "nature," which is really that which we have become as people produced by the demands of the free market. A wild space is created in rifts with the status quo, for instance in traumatic moments such as when a child dies, when having to deal with substance abuse, or when confronting clinical depression. Such a wild space might also be created when the last of our economic safety nets crumble.[15]

These spaces reflect queer sensibilities. For instance, we might find a wild space in a rejection of an inherent gendered "nature." Further, there are resonances here with queer theories that find political potential in moments of depression, failure, and negativity.[16] These spaces of loss and lament, the spaces of vulnerability to the world, *can* also make the world vulnerable to political changes needed in the face of such trauma. And yet are these melancholic moments the only wild spaces vibrating with theological and political potential? What of the wild spaces of the erotic and the ecstatic? The spaces opened up in penetration by another? The spaces found in a lover's stroke of our cheek? The spaces created by a first kiss? The spaces exposed when one finally grants herself permission to love whomever she loves? The spaces of orgasm? Surely these wild spaces have just as much creative energy as those of the traumatic, the melancholic, and the catastrophic. These spaces have just as much potency to resist what the market has demanded of us. And in not naming them as such, Rieger risks not only a problematic theodicy that might glorify the power of suffering, but also a continued closeting, a covering up of supposedly deviant desires in favor of keeping the struggle decent. To better counter capitalistic desire we can invite, beg for, more indecency.

Connolly expresses a greater appreciation for the creative potential of the erotic when he acknowledges that when we glimpse both a sense of divine grace and our implication in nature, our "awareness of the human body as a medium through which resonances pass is enhanced."[17] In this embrace of the affective power of the flesh, of resonance—which for Connolly is not mere metaphor but the actual rhythm that vibrates between bodies—he begins to expose an alternate sexual theology. Nonetheless, explicit discussions of the erotic effects of a resonance machine remain in the negative: the negative effects of the Christian-family-erotic assemblage and its oppression of certain identities and desires. Connolly risks wearing the garbs of the tragic while shrouding the power of the tantalizing; he has not yet enfleshed an erotic other-way.

Here it is important to turn toward the title of this section. To name political theology's engagement with desire as a desire-without-organs is meant both to point to our sexual organs, and their conspicuous absence from this discourse, and to propose an alternative view of affect, one in concert with and influenced by Gilles Deleuze and Félix Guattari's conception of a body-without-organs (BwO). Taken from the schizophrenic writings of Antonin Artaud, for Deleuze and Guattari, a BwO is that which has not congealed into an organism or coded synthesis but rather remains a limit plane, containing flows of energy and intensities.[18] Every actual body has a virtual dimension, which represents the space of potentiality and becoming. The BwO behaves like the vectors of potentiality of an egg before it has developed into an organism containing an organization of organs.[19] Here, Deleuze and Guattari do not mean to denigrate any fleshly organs, but rather to propose the BwO as an alternate state of potentiality to that of the fixed organization of the organs known as the organism. This space of undifferentiated organs, one of potentialities, might also be a space of *desire without organs*, yet one found quite often in the stimulation of our sexual organs (the largest of which is indeed the skin, that porous casing that ironically breaks down our sense of self-enclosure). Desire, to be sure, is already an integral part of Deleuze and Guattari's conception of the BwO and the animation of potentiality implied in its inability to ever become a full organism. Yet to formulate desire as I have in this essay—in which I both name the necessity for political theology to recognize its failure to acknowledge sexual organs and call for it to embody a desire-without-organs—is to gesture toward how "desire" in these discourses has become already coded, an organism too clearly defined and incased in zones economic and not erogenous. More directly put, desire, as currently discussed in political theology, seems too static, defined simplistically as unregulated desire for material wealth, desire as manipulated consumerism and not as enlivening communal force. We might see a similarly static concept of desire in traditional theology, in which discourses of the erotic code desire as a signifier of the sinful and not a force of the salvific. Desire-without-organs as named here is that erotic pelvic thrust which helps us break down any fixed desire statically coded in the body politic and the body of the church.

This desire-without-organs, tied to our sexual organs, might be the very desire that courses through a space of becoming (and perhaps even *cuming*) together. Hence it is when Connolly delves deeper into theologies of becoming that one sees a sexual theology reflected, yet unnamed as such, in *A World of Becoming*: "When desire contains abundance it is reducible to neither the pole of selfishness nor that of altruism, rather, spirals of presumptive generosity become coded into relations between desiring agents as such."[20] Might these spirals of relation come to life not merely in spheres already acknowledged by Connolly—political campaigns, cyberspace, military organizations, churches, the courts[21]—but profoundly also in the bedroom, on the kitchen counter, or the living room floor? If sexual relations are nurtured, respected, and honored for the potential they inherently contain, then scenes where sexuality is animated become the zones of political and ethical formation in which an abundance of desire can engender presumptive generosity.

It is here, in Connolly's embrace of the theologies and a/theologies of becoming proposed by Catherine Keller, John Thatamanil, and Friedrich Nietzsche, that this abundance of desire reveals its potential:

> If you embrace a world of becoming in which the shape of desire is important to the quality of collective life, one critical task (among others) is to instill networks of desire with a greater degree of positivity. You

do so in part by pursuing tactics of the self in which individuals draw upon tools and small assemblages to affect themselves; you do so more robustly through strategic action on larger networks of desire, and most importantly through resonances back and forth between these levels.[22]

Here, Connolly's thought grants us flashes of its potential for greater indecency. Connolly extrapolates on some of these tactics in which one might better engage networks of desire: priming your dream life before bed, meditating, praying, watching particular films over others, reading provocative texts, joining this church rather than that, participating in certain patterns of consumption and investment and avoiding others, voting in one way or another, and joining or refuting certain political movements.[23] But of course this list could continue. To it we might add: choosing this or that lover, embracing or rejecting your own sexuality, learning to love or hate your body, finding shame or beauty in the commonness of your flesh, and embracing or denigrating the common good of the flesh. Connolly does not go there, and so he touches on the indecent, without becoming truly obscene. And we can press him to be more obscene, for if you have been shown generosity by your lover; if you have chosen to be a generous lover; if you have learned to value consent over coercion, consummation over consumption; if you have come to understand that not only does no mean no, but also yes means yes; if you have experienced the pleasure of every cell in your body being animated by the caress of another; if you have perhaps even more so learned to find pleasure in the pleasuring; and if you have found this on that most personal of levels, that space of the ec-static in which you are brought beyond yourself into commune with a lover—then how much more will you have internalized through the local the global need for generosity; the right to pleasure; and the equality of your being with all beings? Conversely, if you have been subjected to the horrors of violent sex or even to mediocre sex, *bad* sex, sex in which your cuming had nothing to do with that of your lover; sex in which consent was murky at best, in which "no," "maybe," and "I'm not sure," meant "yes"; sex in which your fantasies, your desires, and your inclinations were designated as perverse, silly, or inconsequential, then how much more would resentment and not responsiveness define your orientation toward the world beyond the bedroom?

The process of unearthing the sexual ideologies within our theologies invites us not only back into the bedroom, onto the kitchen counter, but also asks us to heed that of which Connolly reminds us: We find productivity of desire most importantly in the resonance between the individual tactics of the self and the more conscious networks of public action. The importance of this resonance is found both in the necessity to embrace the power of sexual desire for our political work and in the fact that while sex can be oh so good, it can also hurt oh so bad. Sex and violence are all too often intermingled. Rape is used as a tool for war; in the United States in 2007 63 percent of all homicides committed by men against women were attributed to intimate relations.[24] Globally, as the fight for sexual and gender liberation has expanded, so too has feminicide,[25] reaching epidemic levels.[26] Furthermore, beyond the global tragedies tied to oppressive sexual theologies, the multitude of quotidian interactions experienced in the econopolitical sphere—including those listed above by Connolly and seemingly unrelated to the exploits of the boudoir—could be seen as sexual acts, a proposition explored further below.

## PAYING YOUR TAXES: A SEXUAL PERFORMANCE

Yes, choosing which church, political movement, investment practice, film, and dream to engage in are sexual acts; they are deeply entangled in how we tap into more positive desires and in how we view our own humanity, including our sexuality. But so too is paying your taxes a sexual act, a point Lauren Berlant and Michael Warner persuasively argue in their own obscene essay, "Sex in Public":

> The sex act shielded by the zone of privacy is the affectional nimbus that heterosexual culture protects and from which it abstracts its model of ethics, but this utopia of social belonging is also supported and extended by acts less commonly recognized as part of sexual culture: paying taxes, being disgusted, philandering, bequeathing, celebrating a holiday, investing for the future, teaching, disposing of a corpse, carrying wallet photos, buying economy size, being nepotistic, running for president, divorcing, or owning anything "His" and "Hers."[27]

Paying taxes as sexual performance? Is this one perversion too far, a move away from our traditional definitions of sex that seems to stretch the limits of the very word and so perhaps robs it of its power? I think not. We can view sexual acts as any acts that project a sanctioned way of being gendered and sexual in the world. Each of these above acts implies and promotes familial relations often built around heterosexual conventions, time, and space; they contain a proposal for sexual orthodoxy and orthopraxy.

Tax and inheritance practices carry such a sexual force that their reach has extended into the chambers of the Supreme Court. In the 2013 decision that struck down the Defense of Marriage Act (DOMA), one can see the importance of tax law to the definition of legal marriage. In this case, the court agreed with the argument made by the plaintiff Edie Windsor, the widow of Thea Spyer, her partner of forty-four years, whom she had married in Canada in 2007. The argument charged that DOMA violated her right to equal protection under the law due to the fact that the federal government refused to recognize their marriage and taxed Windsor's inheritance from Spyer as though they were strangers. How we are taxed contains deeply sexual issues, all the more so when the government has designated certain forms of kinship to be worthier than others, an issue of equality that will not disappear even as the freedom to marry for homosexual couples becomes federal law. Indeed, that the fight for equality is a fight to participate in monogamous dyadic marriage continues a sexual theology based around domestic family time, no matter what combination of genders exist within the partnership. To carry wallet photos, buy economy size, and own anything "His" and "Hers" is to participate in what J. Halberstam has called "reproductive temporality," which upholds conceptions of normalcy tied to the heteronormative nuclear family.[28] Everyday acts of participation in or rejection of "repro-time" can be called sexual acts.[29] The production of products labeled "His" and "Hers" assumes not only heterosexuality but also monogamous coupling and traditional gender roles. Buying in bulk assumes a large family and the economic realities this entails. These are sexual acts of family planning and lovemaking.

This is not to say that in order to construct an indecent theology we must demonize having children and getting married. Rather practicing indecency is about revealing the flesh of these quotidian acts to be flesh, showing their theologies to be sexual theologies. And these are theological questions, as theology is concerned with that to which "your heart clings."[30] Theology is concerned with sexual orthodoxy and orthopraxy.[31] And ultimately theology is concerned with who we believe participates in the holiness of life.

To be sure, Connolly recognizes the role of desire in each of these quotidian moments, both in diagnosing the affectual resonance of political, governmental, and economic actions and in promoting the microtactics of the self that must be undertaken in order to resist dangerous narratives. For instance, he explores how perception is dependent on a matrix of affect, movement, and sensory receptions that structures everyday life and is open "to subliminal influence by mystics, priests, lovers, politicians, parents, military leaders, filmmakers, teachers, talk show hosts, and TV advertisers."[32] Perception then plays a role in shaping sexual orthodoxy and orthopraxy. Perception, which often feels inherently individual and private, is actually, like desire, socially mediated.

One such example of this constructed perception, which Connolly explores in greater depth, is that manipulated within the environment created by our post-9/11 surveillance state. It is worth quoting Connolly, who here draws on Merleau-Ponty, at length:

Let's return to Merleau-Ponty's finding that to perceive depth is implicitly to feel yourself as an object of vision. In a disciplinary society this implicit sense morphs into a more intensive experience of being an actual or potential object of *surveillance* in a national security state . . . the indubitable experience of self-visibility now swells into that of being an object of surveillance. Everyday awareness of that possibility recoils back upon the shape and emotional tone of experience. Traffic cameras, airport screening devices, Social Security numbers, credit profiles, medical records, electric identification bracelets, telephone caller ID, product surveys, NSA sweeps, telephone records, license plates, Internet use profiles, IRS audits, drivers' licenses, police phone calls for "contributions," credit card numbers, DNA records, fingerprints, smell-prints, eyeprints, promotion and hiring profiles, drug tests, street and building surveillance cameras, voter solicitation, school records, job interviews, police scrutiny, prison observation, political paybacks, racial profiling, email solicitations, church judgments, divorce proceedings, and the publication of sexual proclivities. As surveillance devices proliferate, the experience of *potential* observability becomes an increasingly active element in everyday life. . . . The cumulative message? Watch out. Are you a war dissenter? Gay? Interested in drugs? An atheist who talks about it? A critic of the war on terrorism, drug policies, or government corruption? Sexually active? Be careful.[33]

Although the two are approached from different registers (not inconsequential given that Warner and Berlant were writing three years prior to 9/11 and Connolly a decade after), the confluence of the above list with that of the actions that Berlant and Warner define as part of sexual culture is undeniable. Although not explicitly named so by Connolly, each of these acts of surveillance can be seen as sexual acts. Connolly does acknowledge that sexual activity and sexual orientation are entangled in the spaces of threat caused by the surveillance state and further recognizes that there are those in the urban underclass who experience heightened levels of threat from this state,[34] yet there is more in the apparatus to be revealed. For instance, surveillance itself can be understood as a sexual act. To be gazed upon and to be threatened by that gaze is the everyday experience of women, homosexuals, people of color, and the differently abled. Further, this gaze often comes with sexual and ontological implications, particularly for women, and even more so for women of color, objectified by such a gaze—turned into objects either to be sexually desired or discarded.

As a woman's worth is too often tied to whether or not she is desired sexually, the reach of surveillance in our lives takes on an ever more complicated and threatening role. For instance, Karla F. C. Holloway argues that in our national script, the bodies of women and blacks have always been, and are already, public.[35] From clinical trials to genomics and reproductive capacities, the bodies of women and blacks in America have been subjected to public manipulation, definition, and control. Even within discourses on equality we make certain bodies essentially public: "It is as if the fourteenth amendment's assurance of equal protection has come to mean that women and blacks would be noticeable first through the legal identity they constitutionally occupy, and only later, and only perhaps, as private persons."[36] Bodies perpetually subjected to the legal, medical, and social gaze are historically more vulnerable to the surveillance state and its theological implications for how we might engender approved sexual orthodoxy and orthopraxy. For instance, in the United States, the bodies of women, homosexuals, and black people have often been the territories on which wars over state policy are fought and which have been most closely scrutinized and manipulated into appeasing the surveillance state and its orthodox assertions that we should get married, practice a certain family planning, and be clearly marked as one gender or another for the sake of documents of identification.

This does not mean that the gaze as such should be considered merely destructive. There are welcomed gazes: the adoring gaze from a lover, a child, a proud parent, or friend may make us feel truly seen. There may even be a productive power in the negative gaze, in the look of disgust, as it produces needed rebellion and community formation. Of course, there is a difference between a gaze that lends itself to greater recognition and a gaze, often found in the security state, which leads to practices of misrecognition. In order to see better into just which of these gazes we are partaking of, we need to be able to name the gaze as such, to name acts of surveillance and misrecognition as theological and sexual acts—acts that define our relation to God, authority, self, and one another. Revealing the sexual ideology nurtured by the surveillance state, showing its flesh to be flesh, allows us to imagine other ways to go about gazing on and with one another.

It is essential at this point to recognize that even this essay may be problematically engaged in the rhetoric of perverting, stripping down, and unveiling. Perhaps in upholding the necessity of these acts of exposure my gaze risks exploiting the very bodies already gazed upon without consent, called and misrecognized as indecent, and exposed against their will, including but not limited to those of women of color. Yet my goal in calling for a methodology of the obscene has been just the opposite. I have sought not to expose those already objectified but rather to reveal the gears behind the machinery of objectification and, in this uncovering, to resist the privatization of sex, which has served to grease the wheels—served to keep certain desires and bodies from speaking.

Connolly has endeavored to pull back the curtain, revealing the gears at work within the machineries of the state. He reveals the ways in which the econopolitical infects all spheres of life, helping form a sense of being human and the human predicament through a set of cultural orientations expressed in zones as diverse as church sermons, TV dramas, and professional sports.[37] However, in leaving the bedroom out of this cultural equation his work unintentionally fortifies this sense that sex is merely personal, when in fact it courses through political, economic, and ethical decisions.

Additionally, these same everyday tactics theorized by Connolly, Berlant, and Warner reflect Rieger's exploration of capitalistic desire. Investment and consumption practices, the rituals of heteronormative family time—elaborate weddings, engagement parties, and baby showers; the purchasing of accessories marked "His" and "Hers"; the stigma of economy-size shopping, obesity, and food stamps; life insurance policies; and inheritance tax laws—all play into the theology of capitalistic desire in which human ontology is entangled with an aspirational politics. These entanglements make necessary the microtactics of positive desire: the creation of alternate resonance machines and of sexual acts of resistance to the very game of success that keeps most of us in a perpetual state of drowning.

The vitality of the microtactics of the self, those that might cultivate alternate desires to those produced by capitalism, leads me once again to invite political theology into the bedroom. I might even *beg* political theologians to recognize the potency of the erotic and further reveal flesh to be flesh. For in maintaining merely a whisper around sexual desire, these theologians risk contributing to the silencing of the very constituencies they seek to serve. Further, the microtactics behind how we consume and consummate, all the everyday ways we tap into our desires, those that engender presumptive generosity and those that engender repression, intermingle with macrotactics of recognition and maybe even revolution. Therefore, we might begin with our own tactics of the self—those practiced as theologians, and so as sexual actors.

## REFUSING TO MAKE LOVE TO SOMEONE WHOSE PLURIPOTENTIALITY HAS CONGEALED

To practice my own methodology I will attempt to make explicit the erotic implications in Connolly's work. We might uncover a certain sexual potency in his appreciation for an open theism whose "risking, learning, and loving god might learn to expand its care for the diversity of being."[38] In welcoming this God, we embrace not only a divine caretaker but also a divine lover. This understanding of God is reflective of the process philosopher Alfred North Whitehead's conception of the "primordial nature of God" as "the Eros of the Universe."[39] According to Whitehead, Divine Eros is the active force entertaining all ideal possibilities and thus that part of God's very nature that engenders the desire for their realization.[40] The open and loving God may be that spark of deep desire within us and that enlivening spirit between us, luring us toward greater communion. Therefore, this risking, loving, and *lover* God might find its own ecstasy in the sexual possibilities inherent in the multiplicity of our becomings.

Connolly becomes more explicitly sexually active when in the conclusion to *A World of Becoming* he writes of Jerry Lewis—an unlikely sexual icon. Riffing on Deleuze's own assertion that Lewis's characters teach us about what is involved in refined sensitivity to the world, Connolly explicates *The Nutty Professor*. He argues that the female lead, a cheerleader named Stella Purdy, yearns for a combination of Lewis's two personae in the film: the socially awkward, yet sensitively attuned to the world, Professor Kelp, and the smooth-talking, Dean Martinesque Buddy Love. Stella Purdy is attracted to Buddy but recognizes that without the sensitivity embedded in Professor Kelp, Buddy could become unbearable.[41] Hence, Connolly provocatively, if geekily, asks, "Who wants to make love to someone whose pluripotentiality has congealed?"[42] In this moment of indecent sexual pondering, Connolly recognizes how we may become bodies-without-organs and yet remain utterly infused with our sexuality. Through this recognition, he reveals how we might affect our possibilities for becoming together in sexual encounters mediated by our pluripotentiality. And so our sexual desire might too be seen as desire-without-organs, such that we refuse to let our pluripotentiality and that of the ~~objects~~ subjects of our desire ever congeal.

The tactic of the self that honors one's pluripotentiality by refusing to sleep with one whose own has congealed or with one who makes of her lover a misrecognized object instead of a fellow traveler in the world of becoming is a political act. Simply put, when we tap into the potency of the democratic in our bedrooms, we lust for it in our boardrooms, classrooms, and courtrooms. Indeed, we might extend this political act toward our becoming with God. We theologians might better recognize that our desire for God is in part a sexual desire. If we refuse to make love to someone whose pluripotentiality has congealed, then how much more so must we refuse to love, to desire, to worship, a God whose pluripotentiality we have chosen to congeal?

If God, our divine lover—one who engenders a yearning for ever greater communion—is not yet done becoming what God will become, then, in our moments of erotic encounter with such an open God, we can be lured to resist resentment toward this divine mutability, embracing instead the holiness of God's potential with grace, generosity, and gratitude. This God of our desire, this God who becomes and truly cums with us, this God who is open to the riskiness involved in potentiality, this obscene God, comes from the underside, as Rieger might say. Yet this underside God comes not just as a God in solidarity with the marginalized but further as a divinity that resonates and vibrates with and within us—and perhaps even more so in the rhythms found between us in our erotic encounters. And yet while we embrace the divinity pulsing in our sexual rhythms, we must not forget the ways in which God moves with equal vitality in all zones of our becoming. For it was never the intention of this essay nor of our saint of indecency Marcella Althaus-Reid to subordinate the economic to the erotic, but rather to reveal how the two are inseparable. Hence, this lover God is not just on the side of the sexually and economically oppressed; this God *is* oppressed by any theology that seeks to congeal God's pluripotentiality. This God is a God of the flesh, of the ever porous, messy, and regenerative flesh. A congealed flesh is dead flesh, flesh ready for the taking. Flesh that is divinely alive—flesh that is encouraged to flourish, to let that which has died fall away making room for new cellular formations—is flesh that opens us up to the common good, to our need for one another, to our refusal to let our movements, our revolutions, our churches, our philosophies, our beliefs, and our classrooms ever congeal. Therefore, we sexual actors need to perform a theology that honors the common good of the flesh so that we may counter demands for pounds of flesh packaged up as goods for exchange and exclusion.

By practicing a methodology of the obscene, we can disrobe repression but also perform sexual expression. For we face sexual theological challenges not only from capitalism but also from conservative theologies dressed up as radical critiques of the market. For instance, Stephen Long has argued that a necessary return to "a disciplined economic life will also require a reaffirmation of disciplined sexual activity." Long is right: Sex and economics are utterly entangled. But it is the very risk of moving from this acknowledgment to a renewed policing of sex that begs for a countertheology. The work of Rieger and Connolly provide this opportunity, one that can come to fruition if we push them to be ever more obscene.

We can invite political theologians into the bedroom, persuading them to embrace the flesh of those theories left untouched or merely grazed. Indispensable in this project may be the queer theories that have refused to disentangle that which can never be so: the embodied, the economic, and the erotic. For as one oracular typo in an earlier draft of another essay in this volume fortuitously noted, "Today one of our political parties wants to bust pubic unions." Of course, "public unions" was intended, but it is no coincidence that both labor *and* labia, when empowered, threaten those in the Evangelical-capitalist-resonance-machine.

It is these barely tapped queer theories that help return us to the wild spaces noted in Rieger, both those of the tragic and those of the tantalizing. This work is animated by the intensities produced by the remainders of the system, the overflow of energy pulsing through our resonance machines that allows them to burst open. They amplify dissonances that ask us to rethink our resonances:

> What are the dissonances? A past replete with religious ritual clashes with an alternative representation of God in a film, church, or school; an emergent practice of heterodox sexuality encourages you to question established habits in other domains; the interruption of a heretofore smooth career path disrupts previously submerged habits of anticipation.[43]

We may indeed find these dissonances in queer subcultural arenas: in the punk-rock drag show detailed by José Esteban Muñoz in *Cruising Utopia* or the archives of lesbian zines unearthed by Halberstam in *In a Queer Time and Place*. We might find them in Althaus-Reid's queer God. Or we might find productive dissonance in the work of Honduran women who struggle daily against the plague of feminicide. These are women such as the theologian Carmen Manuel del Cid, who leads retreats in which women begin to redefine sin not as disobedience to a Father God but as the denial of their own right to pleasure.[44] Or we might find productive dissonance in rethinking our tax codes and inheritance laws and in challenging even our liberal concepts of "gay adoption" by asking why we don't consider the runaway transgender youth forced to live on the streets as part of our familial obligations. This would be family in the profound sense touted by Sister Sledge in the great queer anthem "We Are Family" *and* by Jesus Christ, who welcomed into the family of God brothers and sisters not of his blood. These dissonances, provided by lives lived and dreams dreamed from the underside, are theologies of the most indecent and holy kind.

Indeed, we sexual actors can begin in the microtactics of our own desire, lovemaking, and even fucking; but we must let this resonate on a global scale, tapping into the ways in which countercapitalist sexual and theological performances might expand the pluripotentiality of creation and of God. In a theology of becoming, as Connolly notes, quoting Catherine Keller, "The action of God is its *relation—by feeling and so being felt*, the divine invites the *becoming* of the other, by feeling the becoming of the other the divine itself becomes."[45] To become with God, to desire God, to feel God, and to be desired and felt by God, is to grant to God God's full pluripotentiality and to request of God that God feel ours. If this macrotactic of desire for God can inhabit the microtactic of choosing one's lover, and vice versa, how much stronger might we be in our conviction that theology must be plastic, potent, and porous? How much more might we find faith in the holiness of surprise and not stasis? How much more might we be able to say that a wavering faith, one open to dissonance, to challenge, to revolutions of thought and being, is actually the truest faith of all? And as such, how much more might we no longer hold fast to the cruelty inherent in the optimism of unwavering fundamentalist faith, in all its various incarnations?

So let's have sex on the brain, have it pulsing in our organs, tingling in our cells, and on the tip of our tongues. Let's ask of ourselves and others a question posed by the cultural theorist Robert Reid-Pharr in his collection *Black, Gay, Man*, "What do we think when we fuck?"[46] But let us also ask: Whom do we fuck when we think, write, and teach? Whom do we penetrate positively, and whom violently and without consent? Whom do we welcome into the conversation of political theology, whose presence do we desire as part of our common good? And whom do we screw in our lack of desire, recognition, and naming?

I have chosen to be a theologian, and so I shall be a sexual actor. I shall perform the microtactic of sexual invitation. Hence, fellow lovers in this world of becoming, I invite you to join me in the boudoir. And I accept my own invitation to come together with you to practice obscenity, to be faithfully indecent, to never make love to a God whose pluripotentiality I have let congeal. I will strive to perpetually participate in a veritable monster of energies, making a difference before melting (in your theological arms perhaps) down once again, allowing for new currents to move between us. I will try to always be-cuming with you: writing in dialogue and not monologue; taking pleasure in the pleasuring (all the worldly and divine pleasurings in and out of the bedroom) and not only in the being pleased. Will you make a difference, melt, and come now with me, again and again?

## NOTES

1. Marcella Althaus-Reid, *Indecent Theology: Theological Perversions in Sex, Gender, and Politics* (New York: Routledge, 2000), 110.
2. Ibid., 7.
3. Ibid., 87.
4. Joerg Rieger, *No Rising Tide: Theology, Economics, and the Future* (Minneapolis: Fortress Press, 2009), viii.
5. Althaus-Reid, *Indecent Theology*, 93.
6. Lauren Berlant, *Cruel Optimism* (Durham, N.C.: Duke University Press, 2011), 1.
7. Rieger, *No Rising Tide*, 104.
8. Ibid.
9. William E. Connolly, *Capitalism and Christianity, American Style* (Durham, N.C.: Duke University Press, 2008), 34.
10. Rieger, *No Rising Tide*, 194.

11. Ibid., 197.
12. Ibid., 259.
13. Ibid., 94.
14. Ibid., 101.
15. Ibid., 115.
16. See, for instance, Judith Halberstam, *The Queer Art of Failure* (Durham, N.C.: Duke University Press, 2011); Ann Cvetkovich, *Depression: A Public Feeling* (Durham, N.C.: Duke University Press, 2012); and Sara Ahmed, *The Promise of Happiness* (Durham, N.C.: Duke University Press, 2010).
17. Connolly, *Capitalism and Christianity*, 66.
18. Gilles Deleuze and Félix Guattari, *A Thousand Plateaus: Capitalism and Schizophrenia*, trans. Brian Massumi (Minneapolis: University of Minnesota Press, 1987), 153. See also Deleuze and Guattari's original formulation of a BwO (body-without-organs) in *Anti-Oedipus: Capitalism and Schizophrenia*, trans. Robert Hurley, Mark Seem, and Helen R. Lane (Minneapolis: University of Minnesota Press, 1983).
19. Deleuze and Guattari, *Thousand Plateaus*, 153.
20. William E. Connolly, *A World of Becoming* (Durham, N.C.: Duke University Press, 2011), 115.
21. Ibid., 60.
22. Ibid., 115.
23. Ibid., 117.
24. New York State Office for the Prevention of Domestic Violence, "National Data on Intimate Partner Violence," http://opdv.ny.gov/statistics/nationaldvdata/intparthom.html, accessed on June 14, 2013 at 6:08 P.M.
25. According to the Christian ethicist Monica Maher, feminicide is defined as "the Pandemic of women-killing," which, "is made possible by political, cultural and legal structures which support the violence and assure the impunity of perpetrators within a 'social and ideological environment of machismo and misogyny, of normalized violence against women.'" Monica A. Maher, "Daring to Dream: Faith and Feminicide in Latin America," in *Weep Not for Your Children: Essays on Religion and Violence*, ed. Lisa Isherwood and Rosemary Radford Ruether (London: Equinox, 2008), 187–88.
26. According to Victoria Sanford, the Pan-American Health Organization classifies more than 10 homicides per 100,000 inhabitants as an epidemic and public heath concern. According to research conducted by Sanford and Maher, the rate of feminicide in Guatemala and Honduras is well beyond this ratio. Victoria Sanford, "From Genocide to Feminicide: Impunity and Human Rights in Twenty-First Century Guatemala," *Journal of Human Rights* 7, no. 2 (2008): 104–22.
27. Lauren Berlant and Michael Warner, "Sex in Public," *Critical Inquiry* 24, no. 2 (1998): 555.
28. Judith Halberstam, *In a Queer Time and Place: Transgender bodies, Subcultural Lives* (New York: New York University Press, 2005), 3–5.
29. Ibid., 5.
30. Rieger, *No Rising Tide*, 89.

31. Althaus-Reid, *Indecent Theology*, 87.
32. Connolly, *World of Becoming*, 49.
33. Ibid., 53. These observations by Connolly's have taken on even greater weight in the weeks of early June 2013 when Edward Snowden, a former information technology employee of the NSA, leaked information proving that web and social media companies, including Google, Apple, Facebook, and Microsoft, have been providing user data to the NSA.
34. Ibid.
35. Karla F. C. Holloway, *Private Bodies, Public Texts: Race, Gender, and a Cultural Bioethics* (Durham, N.C.: Duke University Press, 2011), 15.
36. Ibid., 10.
37. Connolly, *World of Becoming*, 97.
38. Connolly, *Capitalism and Christianity*, 61.
39. Alfred North Whitehead, *Adventures of Ideas* (New York: Free Press, 1967), 253.
40. Ibid., 277.
41. Connolly, *World of Becoming*, 163.
42. Ibid.
43. Ibid., 56.
44. Maher, "Daring to Dream," 186–213.
45. Connolly, *World of Becoming*, 107.
46. Robert F. Reid-Pharr, *Black Gay Man: Essays* (New York: NewYork University Press, 2001), 88.

# A Socioeconomic Hermeneutics of *Chayim*: The Theo-Ethical Implications of Reading (with) Wisdom

A. PAIGE RAWSON

*It is Wisdom crying out, Understanding raising her voice.*
*She takes her stand at the topmost heights, by the wayside, at the crossroads,*
*Near the gates at the city entrance; at the entryways, she shouts.*
*I call to you, wo/men; my cry is to all people.*
—PROVERBS 8:1–4

Although the Wisdom literature of the Hebrew Bible is relatively ambiguous about socioeconomic wealth—who can access "wealth" and how to do so practically—within these texts there is a shrewd multifaceted agent who rises up to speak out, activating and advocating for the unrestricted access to the resource necessary for the survival of all life: Wisdom. The so-called Wisdom literature in the Hebrew Bible, traditionally limited to the books of Job, Ecclesiastes, and Proverbs, is preoccupied with questions about sociopolitical and economic survival, and in each book Wisdom plays a critical role in gaining access to the resources necessary for the maintenance of life. I understand Wisdom's presence and performance in Genesis 1–3 to be a key to understanding Wisdom in the larger genre (in the Hebrew text and beyond). Wisdom, in my estimation, constitutes the reconfiguration of wealth *as* wealth, the Tree of Life—which is the well of human experience from which such resources are drawn—and the way, strategically speaking, in which to access the resources of experience in order to survive and thrive through the enactment of justice. In socioeconomic systems structured implicitly to sustain the division of labor through the privileging of certain "legitimately" productive, normative, "successful," and, therefore, "recognizable" bodies over others, wealth is monopolized by the former at the expense of the latter.[1] In the book of Proverbs, however, through the (re)appropriation (8:18), reconfiguration (8:10–11), and redefinition (8:19) of wealth and creation-production as wo/man, the fe/male personification of Wisdom embodies both feminine and masculine energy.

Betraying and exploiting the constructedness of gender as binary, Wisdom is standing at the crossroads and raising he/r voice at the intersections of life.

Since mine is a queer postcolonial reading of Wisdom from a socioeconomic perspective, I am attempting to disrupt hierarchical binary taxonomies that include the gender binary. This challenges the reader to "think twice," even three times, about the significance and signification of categorical qualifiers (including pronouns), how wo/men's bodies were abused vis-à-vis phallogocentrism in and through the text (i.e., *whose* voice is hiding behind wo/men, such as Wisdom personified, in the text?) and how these texts might be read for diverse and multiplying meaning rather than either/or.[2] Wisdom does not limit herself to a chosen, elite few but instead contends in Proverbs 8:17b that s/he is always already accessible to any and *every* body in search of he/r.[3] And so, in honor of the bodies marked by the violence of the collusion of capitalism and colonialism parading as a distinctively Christian democracy and in light of the unfettered availability of the wo/man Wisdom and her both fluid and fractured representation as wealth in Proverbs, in this essay I propose that reading wealth with Wisdom invites its reinterpretation, alongside the very concepts of creation-production, in and through a hermeneutic of life (Heb., *chayim*). Such a reading of Wisdom *with* Wisdom renders Wisdom and her wealth as the very marked and multiple, seditious, and oh-so-queer other(ed) bodies categorically denied access to wealth . . . always already rising up at the crossroads.[4]

Only a week after the Twelfth Transdisciplinary Theological Colloquium commenced, on February 14, 2013, over one billion people around the world rose up and took to the streets. The One Billion Rising movement involved demonstrations by goodly folk around the globe, who danced, marched, and spoke out in cities and at various crossroads where violence against women and children occurs most often. Like the Occupy Movement, One Billion Rising was a people's movement birthed out of a common struggle for survival with the intention of forging solidarity among the socially and economically oppressed majority who, by protesting the collusion of democracy and capitalism, were seeking a platform to incite the transformation of an insidious socioeconomic system that can only ever benefit a very small minority. Though it was a specific response to the various forms of violence perpetrated against more than one billion women and girls, like Occupy it also forged a global community of people of all genders, races, ethnicities, classes, and abilities, creating and strengthening both social and economic alliances around the world.[5] The synchronicity of these multifarious bodies rising at manifold crossroads only a week after this colloquium on "Common Good(s)" is fortuitous, as a particular materialization of the movement has inspired both my socioeconomic hermeneutic of Wisdom in Proverbs and my own advocacy for an actualization of justice for every-body in the world.

More than five years ago during a solidarity immersion to the Philippines, I encountered two Filipino/a NGOs whose passion for justice and commitment to the people's movement in the Philippines transformed my politics: Gabriela Philippines and Karapatan ("right/s" in Tagalog).[6] During my time there in 2008 (and again in 2013) our team worked alongside, learned from, and listened to these (primarily) women, who shared their struggle for survival in the face of Western imperialism and globalized capitalism—the imported socioeconomic systems whose enforcement has resulted in the violation of the Filipino people's human rights and has resulted specifically in violence against women and their commodification. The impact Gabriela and Karapatan have had on me is due to myriad ways in which they are the manifold body of Wisdom rising up, "taking a stand at the topmost heights, by the wayside, at the crossroads, crying out" to and for the justice of all people.[7] Through its Filipino and U.S. contingents, Gabriela continues to speak and act out against issues of access, government negligence, and rape.[8]

Wisdom is struggling for survival, and the ways in which s/he is working in and through the political bodies of Gabriela in the Philippines is visceral. S/he speaks for and as "women" but represents the struggle of all nonnormative bodies for survival against systems of domination and dehumanization. I focus on Gabriela's body politic in order to, in the words of Elisabeth Schüssler Fiorenza, "prevent biblical knowledge from continuing to be produced in the interest of domination and injustice" and to remind us that Wisdom is always already embodied practice.[9] Ultimately, it is my contention that Gabriela's strategic affront to the coconstitutive systems of imperialism and capitalism can and should be interpreted as but one modern manifestation of Wisdom and he/r manifesto, which is always already calling us to rise up as Wisdom and cry out at the crossroads for the common good(s) of all.

Like our current global situation for certain communities of "marked" or othered bodies, it has been argued that the Persian Period—the time in which the book of Proverbs and the creation narratives of Genesis were most likely penned—was a time of economic and existential crisis for the postexilic community of Yehud. It was a situation marked by precarity.[10] As such, survival under the Persian Empire would have required shrewdness, sagacity, and creativity—in short, Wisdom.[11] It is for this reason and the numerous intertextual allusions in Proverbs 8–9 to Genesis 1–3 that Wisdom invites us to read these pericopes side by side and face to face. Such a strategy does not merely interpret the textual body responsibly within its so-called original context(s), however; it is also employed out of responsibility to the innumerable othered bodies in various contexts who have suffered the repercussions of the uncritical appropriation of these and other biblical texts. I, therefore, read Proverbs 8:10–9:6 alongside Genesis 1–3 as midrash through what I understand to be a socioeconomic *hermeneutics* of *chayim* (the Hebrew word translated "life" or "survival"), foregrounding Wisdom in/and real wo/men's bodies according to their complex association with life (and, as such, survival tactics) but also with the threat of death.[12]

I also do so queerly. I read Wisdom in the text as *wo/man*, not in order to invert (and thereby reinstate) the hierarchical gender binary, but to disrupt it, since Wisdom herself deconstructs this dichotomy through her fluid gender-play.[13] Before even engaging in exegesis, then, I invite the reader to understand Wisdom queerly as *khoric* womb—both a place and a process of be(com)ing— and as wo/man who perpetually troubles the motif of "female" as always already other than, and juxtaposed in diametric opposition to, "male" (as is often the case in biblical narrative).[14] Wisdom is then both a genre—the body-space of its own articulation—and the very embodiment (and process) of Wisdom. In this way, s/he inhabits the various ways in which we each work Wisdom out in our own skin and in our various communities. As khoric womb of creation, Wisdom is always already induced to and inducing labor, s/he is inhabited by and within the (re)production of each creation event throughout space-time (Prov. 8:22ff.). Reading *with* Wisdom can only ever be a destabilizing, radically embodied endeavor, as s/he reflects the ways in which all bodies (textual or otherwise) just don't "stay put." The reader initiates and is induced, infringed upon, put off, lured by, and drawn into Wisdom's textual body as a contextualized body, one whose wily ways obstinately evade, and even break open, the boundaries of the text as well as the boundaries of a deity who presumably owns the wealth of the world.[15]

"Wealth" includes Wisdom as the tree of Genesis 2:17ff. The deity YHWH Elohim allocates wealth to those who most effectively bear *his* image, a far cry from Elohim's reflections in Genesis 1:27 (what a difference the title "Lord" can make). While these bearers in the Hebrew tradition are often God's virtuous male subjects, Genesis 1:27 reflects otherwise, and Proverbs 31 is another exception. Wisdom in Proverbs might be read as the feminine other to the divine male regent, as in the good wife of chapter 31. However, I propose that Wisdom cannot be limited by or to this interpretation. S/he is not merely (m)other in opposition to the divine patriarch, nor merely as his multiple, but (like *khora*) as imbalanced, multiplying cosmic event. I read Wisdom, therefore, as an urge or energy, intentionally, even strategically, in excess and beyond the control of the One (masculine) God and his binary gender system.

The influence of poststructuralist feminism on my reading of Wisdom bears remarking. Luce Irigaray, in particular, who writes, *"Never being simply one*, [woman is] a sort of expanding universe to which no limits could be fixed and which would not be incoherence nonetheless. . . . Woman always remains several, but she is kept from dispersion because the other is already within her and is autoerotically familiar to her."[16] Because Wisdom is always already a (con)textualized body, then, s/he must be read with or through the Wisdom of "real live" bodies. Therefore, my exegesis is not merely supplemented by but saturated with Wisdom's ways made manifest in both human and nonhuman othered bodies. The purpose of my hermeneutical endeavor is ethical, following my commitment to justice as the negotiation and fleshing out (quite literally) of the "common good(s)" among us all, locally and globally.

Although Wisdom disturbs in and through "real live" bodies, her disruptive presence emerges even before bodies do at creation. Present "in the beginning" of Genesis 1 (Prov. 8:22–30), Wisdom's wealth does not materialize explicitly until Genesis 2:9 with the introduction of the tree of life. Wisdom's association with the tree of life would have most likely been implicit in her ancient interpretive community; however, modern (i.e., foreign) readers must rely on Wisdom's self-disclosure as tree of life in Proverbs 3:18. In fact, when one considers Wisdom's explicit identification with the tree of life in light of her reconstitution of wealth *as* wealth (in Prov. 8:18–19, 21), it seems almost superfluous to argue that reading with Wisdom necessitates a socioeconomic critique of any text where Wisdom is implicated. Therefore, we cannot avoid acknowledging Wisdom's reconfiguration of wealth in our interpretation of Genesis 2:9–3:24 (or any text). Even as Genesis 2:9–3:24—positioned as it is "in the beginning" of the Torah—functions as a root myth for the so-called Abrahamic faith traditions, I understand it to be the primary narrative of socioeconomic conflict in the Hebrew Bible. This origin story is as much about the denial of access to resources necessary for survival as it is about the beginning or formation of a people and a communal identity.[17] For the tree of life (*etz chayim*), "which is the tree of the knowledge of good and evil" (Gen. 2:9), is denied to the farming and/or working class (signified by Adam and Eve) by the landholding political elite, represented by the king, YHWH Elohim.[18] It follows, then, that each of the narratives of the Hebrew Bible that appear after the event in the Garden reflect the complex relationships of wealth, power, and poverty to labor, loss, and accretion found in the Garden, relations that betray a web of economic interactions that necessarily involve the acquisition, embodiment, or disruption of Wisdom and the people's struggle for survival qua Wisdom.[19] Therefore, reading with Wisdom's rhizomatic root system becomes integral if one is to interpret the bodies in the Bible and the ways in which the Bible is in and influencing the interpretation of bodies.

The representations of Wisdom, its interpretation, and its implications for women have understandably held great significance for feminist biblical scholars in light of the struggle for rights, representation, and humanization—especially for Elisabeth Schüssler Fiorenza and Claudia V. Camp.[20] Both scholars have written volumes on Wisdom as the feminine aspect of the divine. In *Wisdom Ways*, Schüssler Fiorenza argues for a "feminist biblical Wisdom interpretation" as spiritual practice and the emancipatory hermeneutical remedy for the transformation of an otherwise kyriarchal field.[21] According to Schüssler Fiorenza, it is not enough "just to understand and appropriate biblical texts and traditions. Rather, feminist biblical hermeneutics has the task of changing biblical interpretation and its Western idealist hermeneutical frameworks, individualist practices, and socio-political relations of domination."[22] That is, the goal is not merely the centering of wo/men as subjects within the biblical text but also the privileging of wo/men's subjectivity in the process of translation. In order to instantiate change, we must begin not with the biblical text but with the lived realities of wo/men within diverse experiences and contexts.[23] In this way, Wisdom becomes a way of reading and upending patriarchy and its modes of making meaning and marking bodies. However, in distinction from Schüssler Fiorenza's interpretation, I read (with) Wisdom as more than anti-imperial feminist hermeneutic, which interprets in order to "abolish relations of domination" and "struggle for autonomy."[24] Though s/he should be interpreted through the experiences of wo/men, Wisdom is only ever a woman. Wisdom for Schüssler Fiorenza, then, is a unidirectional practice and hermeneutic, not a rhizomatic body. In my view, it is not autonomy for which Wisdom struggles, but interdependence: Wisdom's way is not to invert but to undermine and ruin hierarchal binaries.

Although Schüssler Fiorenza reflects on the ways in which we might read Wisdom in contemporary women's movements, she and other feminist scholars have taken great care to reconstruct the "original" context of the text, attempting to reimagine the world in which the woman Wisdom was written.[25] For her part, Claudia Camp has written extensively on what Wisdom's representation reveals about the context in which it was penned. In her book *Wisdom and the Feminine in the Book of Proverbs*, Camp asserts, "Wisdom personified as a woman appears to have had the potential for profound symbolic impact in the post-exilic period."[26] She proceeds to highlight the multiple female figures in Proverbs, including the "household manager" of chapter 31, and concludes that although there is no explicit correlation drawn between Wisdom and these women, there are "many points of contact."[27] Ultimately, for Camp, the "interweaving of the various female images" in Proverbs reflects the importance of both women and wisdom in the building of house, family, and, therefore, society and communal identity in a kingless postexilic era.[28]

Camp later ventures beyond Proverbs (yet still within the feminine) in *Wise, Strange, and Holy*, as she builds on her previous exploration of female representation in the Hebrew Bible. The primary focus of Camp's research is the construction (or coconstitution) of the Strange Woman and the formation of identity within the priestly rhetoric of purity as she sought to expose "an ideological cover for persistent tensions [of identity, theodicy, politics, authority, and purity]" within the postexilic community of Yehud.[29] Camp interrogates the rhetorical function of gendered strangeness in the priestly class's preservation of purity (particularity and priority) through the annihilation of the Other.[30]

The slippages that emerge in any gendered "process of stranger-making" are for Camp particularly acute in the hyperbolic, imposed opposition of the Strange Woman (*ishah zarah*) of Proverbs 7 and the woman Wisdom (*chokmah*) of chapters 8 and 9.[31] Performing a "deconstructive reading of the text," Camp reads their relationship through the trickster motif, "undercutting its most obvious message of absolute opposition between good and evil . . . and highlighting their paradoxical but experientially validated unity."[32] Although the biblical scholar is not working out of an explicitly poststructuralist theoretical frame, the intersections with queer and postcolonial critiques of identity and gender are undeniable: exposing the very apparatus by which the notion of the other/difference is constructed and calcified in opposition and subordination to the One/Same.[33] Camp, however, takes this disruption no further in either her reflections on the context in which this bifurcation was constructed or its implications for the Yehudim or contemporary wo/men. Camp's critique of one-dimensional feminist readings is incisive but does not attend to the ways Wisdom as the Strange Woman troubles the gender norms out of which s/he was constructed.

Drawing from both Camp and Homi Bhabha, Mayra Rivera moves in this very direction in "God at the Crossroads," her postcolonial, feminist Sophialogical intervention. Rivera reads Sophia as a disruptive force whose "undecidable ontological position . . . will not be resolved. Her identity remains indefinable and, for that matter, open."[34] Bhabha's hybridity is integral to Rivera's identification of Sophia at the crossroads—a textual allusion to her liminality.[35] The text's unambiguous emphasis on ascension in Proverbs 8:1–2a, where Wisdom is "raising" her voice, "crying out," and taking her stand at the highest place in the city, are for Rivera depictions of "divine transcendence," functioning as acts of Sophia's resistance to the economy of the Same.[36] I consider such a reading of *Chokmah* through Rivera's lens of relational transcendence to be a necessary liberative intervention—particularly for persons repeatedly oppressed by the economic expansionist projects of neocolonial capitalism (i.e., globalization)—and integral to my own, yet I cannot help but read *Chokmah's* positionality even more queerly.

As much as it resists bifurcation, a postcolonial rendering of the feminine hybrid Sophia such as Rivera's, still comes uncomfortably close to simply inverting hierarchical dualisms, thereby reinstating the very binaries it seeks to disrupt.[37] While attending to the cultural complexities Wisdom's representation reflects, other than a reference to the fluidity of Sophia's identity for ancient readers of Logos—who "did not construe the gender difference between Sophia and Logos as an insurmountable boundary"—Rivera does not consider how Wisdom's transcendence troubles the binary gender system.[38] In fact, even as Rivera elucidates the ontological indeterminacy of Wisdom and God in their gender performance, she unintentionally reinforces the notion of desire as heteronormative: the provocation of a hybrid Sophia, both wise and strange, is that she "could excite not only Israel's men but Israel's God!"[39] Rivera articulates Sophia's hybridity in terms of her gender (re)presentation, for she identifies Sophia's self-description as explicitly destabilizing the dualism of the "male God's presence" and "female 'form.'"[40] However, in Rivera's prioritizing of the "fluid communion—rather than absolute opposition" of God and creation, she also neglects to interrogate the binary between the ontological categories "male" and "female" and between God (as He) and Wisdom (as She).[41] As a postcolonial interpretation of Wisdom, Rivera's work attends to the appropriation of feminine Sophia by masculine Logos, but she does not identify Wisdom's own strategic (re)appropriations as a part of her critical resistance to domination.[42]

The resistance Rivera detects is in Sophia's transcendence. It is Wisdom's transpositions—at the uppermost heights, on the byways, and at the city gates—which are for Rivera, as for me, reflective of her transcendence as well as her audacious occupation of civic spaces. Wisdom occupies the places where text and tradition locate honorable men and "loose women" (7:12) and in so doing s/he both resists any tidy opposition to the Strange Woman (whom I understand to represent Folly) and refuses conformity to normative gender roles. What Rivera (as Silvia Schroer before her) deems Sophia's transcendence of categorical classification, I consider *Chokmah*'s strategic undermining; further, Rivera's Sophialogical hybridity I interpret as multiplicity.[43] For that which Kathryn Tanner has asserted of transcendence—that it is "the model for resistance to the Same"—may be true of Wisdom in he/r transcendence as well as her descents.[44] Wisdom rises *up*-on the wayside, representing the depths of human experience because her home is the earth (Prov. 9:1) *and* the way to *sheol* (7:27).

The wealth of Wisdom may very well transcend understanding, but it is her understanding in the struggles at the crossroads that releases the well of Wisdom running deep, indiscriminately desiring bodies, and incessantly erupting from below. Wisdom dissents in her indecent, transcending descent.[45] Wisdom is not one (nor in one place), however, and could never be only two—as the notion of hybridity implies.⁴⁶ Wisdom, like female sexuality for Luce Irigaray, is

> always at least double, goes even further: it is plural. She finds pleasure almost anywhere . . . the geography of her pleasure is far more diversified, more multiple in its differences, more complex, more subtle, than is commonly imagined—in an imaginary rather too narrowly focused on sameness. "She" is indefinitely other in herself. This is doubtless why she is said to be whimsical, incomprehensible, agitated, capricious.⁴⁷

Irigaray continues making an assertion that has been spoken of Wisdom in the Hebrew Bible: that he/r words are contradictory and "her language, in which 'she' sets off in all directions [leaves] 'him' unable to discern the coherence of any meaning."⁴⁸ What Irigaray once posited of the economy of female sexuality and pleasure is also true of the social and sexual economy of Wisdom as wo/man: S/he transcends not only the binary gender system but also her own bifurcation.

One moment Wisdom, the next Folly (as the Strange Woman), the diverse voices and descriptions of Wisdom within Proverbs testify to Wisdom's incoherence and elusivity. Wise and strange, top and bottom, left and right, inside and out collide with every body in between and beyond the bifurcated boundaries of intelligibility and normativity, continually emerging and diverging. Disrupting already all-too-fragile body borders from the first acts at creation—when the s/word of Elohim cut (*bara*) the heavens and the earth and separated dark from light—to this day, Wisdom exists to trouble not only this dichotomy but any and every hierarchical dualism (i.e., male/female, owner/object, proprietor/property, master/slave).⁴⁹ Wisdom is not simply in the transcending, the rising up, and the descending or undermining: Indeed, Wisdom is in the occupying of bodies with/in the boundaries and beyond borders.

Always already occupying the places and processes of the struggle for survival, Wisdom is embodied in the experiences of those reading with he/r as they seek understanding at the illimitable crossroads of life. The Hebrew Bible itself bears witness to the wounds of he/r textual ab/uses by the s/word of a phallocratic economy that casts woman and Wisdom as commodity, goods exchanged for capital. Wisdom becomes Folly (and Folly, Wisdom) as s/he persistently foils the tireless attempts to bifurcate, cut up, and contain he/r in the text and its interpretation in various capitalistic and gender "normative" contexts. Wisdom responds, as/in queer bodies, in the deconstruction of binaries and through reappropriation.⁵⁰ Chokmah/Sophia not only disturbs the boundary between Wisdom and Folly, instead of resisting her commodification, s/he claims or owns it.[51] Having been affiliated with king YHWH Elohim, yet subjected to the king's commodification of Wisdom as woman, s/he has acquired wealth through its very reconfiguration. In Proverbs 8:10–11, Wisdom argues her case and attempts to persuade her audience by comparing herself to, and even exceeding the value of, silver, gold, rubies: "goods." Slowly shifting, Wisdom then claims ownership: "Riches and honor belong to me, enduring wealth and success" (8:18). And by verse 19 s/he has fully transitioned, stating that the fruit s/he produces (as wo/man, womb, and tree of life) is even better than fine gold or choice silver.[52]

Wisdom has built a house, yet s/he refuses to remain behind closed doors; s/he prefers a more public persona than the privacy of her own home allows.[53] Standing in *Sheol*, rising up on the heights, crying out at the crossroads, Wisdom is anything but a lady and not intelligible as (gentle)man. YHWH's fellow craftsman and confidant (*amon*) at creation (Prov. 8:30), in Proverbs 3:18–19, Wisdom is revealed to be the Tree of Life (*etz chayim*), the one resource in the garden YHWH Elohim withholds and to which He [*sic*] attempts to prevent access. In the TNKH verse 18 reads, "She is a tree of life to those who grasp her, and whoever holds on to her is happy." The word translated "happy" here could also be translated "fortunate," "striding" or "led," implying that one guided by Wisdom likewise leads a fruitful, productive, and even—I contend—provocative, defiant, deviant life.[54]

Wisdom's backlash in response to her confinement by the deity is her transcendence of (con)textual boundaries, her (re)appropriation of wealth, and her resistance to bifurcation, even as s/he reveals her own activity to be commensurate with that of the masculine deity. Wisdom speaks strangely, foolishly, and quite queerly, from a space of slashed subjectivity, which s/he transforms through the back(s)lash of he/r own creative subjectivity—*extremis malis extrema remedia* ("desperate times call for desperate measures").[55] Wisdom is queer because s/he is one that is never only *one* as always already manifest in the experiences of the many othered bodies struggling to be seen. Wisdom speaks from he/r lived experience, and this is precisely why Wisdom's hermeneutic—the very way s/he understands and is understood—is a hermeneutic of life.

And Wisdom, bearing the scars of sedition, offers he/r wealth indiscriminately, even indecently, to any body who wants it: "Those who love me I love, and those who seek me will find me" (Prov. 8:17, TNKH). As the Tree of Life, Wisdom extends her branches and calls out, "Come . . . Swing . . . Eat . . . Play."[56] As the Strange Wo/man, Folly, Wisdom is persuasive, seductive, loose, and loud.[57] Yet as the very vehicle of sagacity he/rself, *Chokmah* will not force he/rself on those who do not yearn for he/r (see Prov. 7:5, 21; 9:13). Though Wisdom extends herself to all, she knows her own worth as wealth. To the ones who reject he/r urgency and advising, who in their preference for simplicity refuse to see the fecundity of Wisdom's complex multiplicity, Wisdom merely mocks, mimics, and keeps moving (Prov. 1:22–32).

A veritable assemblage of contradictions that cradles and contends the unity of opposites s/he represents and explodes, Wisdom is a queer body of queer bodies refusing to remain in one place, both but never either and perpetually transgressing binary divisions. Cut by the divine s/word into infinite bodies at creation, like the wandering womb of Plato's cosmology *Timaeus*, Wisdom is khora, the Sophia-Logos, who hurls he/rself into the cosmos in and through any body embracing and embodying he/r through innumerable creative events. Wisdom, then, is multiple and multiplying, s/he is in all ways always already in all and all in, except when s/he isn't. *Zarah* and *Chokmah*, Strange and Wise—so very Wise because so Strange—Wisdom is found in the manifold materializations of bodies marked as illegitimate and unintelligible by Western capitalism's colonizing codification. It is, then, precisely their appropriation of the strange and wily ways of Wisdom as wo/man, wealth, and a tree of life that the body politic of Gabriela unintentionally embodies Wisdom's ways.

"Mine are counsel and resourcefulness; I am understanding; courage is mine" (Prov. 8:14, TNKH). Wisdom possesses the very skills and courage for survival in the face of injustices that legitimate tyranny, trafficking, and the commodification of certain bodies by others. Desperate times call for desperate, and disparate, measures; and this is Wisdom's call in and through the work of Gabriela.[58] I know no more apposite exemplar of Wisdom than Gabriela—a modern-day movement and manifestation of Wisdom's *under*-standing, her undermining back(s)lash, and the embodiment of a *he/r*meneutics of *chayim*. My biblical interpretation accompanies activism—the appropriation of and aspiration toward the "common good(s)"—in glocal contexts that, like the Philippines, have been hacked by the nationalism of a U.S. militarism compelling the colonial capitalistic conquest onward as "Christian soldiers."[59]

Having spent time in the Philippines with Gabriela and serving for many years on the United Methodist Church's Task Force to the Philippines, I have become quite familiar with the ways in which these wo/men strategically deploy their bodies as Wisdom to subvert governmental tactics (U.S. and Filipino) that deny access, devastate communities, and destroy life.[60] Gabriela fights in order to procure justice and secure resources, and s/he does so by unconventional, "strange," even foolish, means, which command the attention of government officials and demand a response. Always already in he/r ascending—her rising up and uprising—from the "grassroots," s/he is in-de(s)cent, diving deeper into the struggle that is the human experience. S/he rises up and cries out from the *bukid* (farm) and the *lungsod* (city), from the *palasyo* and the *baran-*

*gay* (barrio), from *lapag* (below) or *sheol* of the *inang-bayan* (motherland). In the rice fields, amid the wilderness, from the plantation to the village, on the underground level and in the "high" courts, at various commercial intersections, on the battlefront and in the picket line s/he understands in a space where heaven is indistinguishable from hell. Embracing the dead in he/r arms, haunted by the disappeared, and having been subjected to extreme forms of violence, s/he holds he/r place in the uppermost heights of the government assembly, he/r anger erupting and disrupting bourgeois complacency. Experience makes Gabriela wise as s/he occupies the crossroads. There is no distinction, yet he/r difference abounds; and in this is Wisdom. S/he is the body of Wisdom universal in the particularity of every body. S/he is the be(com)ing of Wisdom's conduct unbecoming in our world today, and her hermeneutic of *chayim* extends to us an embodied model of the affective awareness of the ecstatic interdependence of all life—but only if and when we take hold of Wisdom.

Wisdom is not merely understanding: S/he is queerly *under*-standing at the crossroads. Standing under structures of dehumanization as s/he does, not to support but to subvert the hegemonic order of empiricism (that is, empire-racism), heteronormativity, and homonationalism, oligarchic opiates that lull bodies to sleep and keep them comatose and docile (Foucault), unknowingly acquiescing to the commodification of culture (hooks), and complicit in the deaths of tens of thousands of unnamed others living worlds away, who are in fact none other than ourselves.[61] Wisdom's belligerent back(s)lash, then, is he/r commitment to undermining theophallocracies, systems that permit limited access—if any at all—to not only resources but also recognizability.[62] Wisdom rises up and transcends even as she undermines through her seditious occupation of the very apparatus upon which such systems are founded.[63] Wisdom's back(s)lash has, in fact, been discernible from "the beginning" (Gen. 1.1; Prov. 8.22–31) as the *he/r*meneutic of *chayim*: Wisdom's effervescent urge to arm us with he/rself as a tool for survival, life in the midst of death in the midst of life. S/he is the ecstatic interdependence that honors the sanctity and creative subjectivity of *all* life.

To read with Wisdom and to *under*-stand Wisdom queerly is to engage the semiotic slippages and the liminal spaces produced and inhabited by wo/men's bodies both inside and outside the text in an effort to honor all life as prec(ar)ious.[64] The by-product, then, of this way of reading is the radical theo-ethical and therefore political effects and affects of a hermeneutics of *chayim* within contemporary contexts—as the relationship of the political and hermeneutical is always already reciprocal. Simultaneously host and guest, Wisdom enters even as s/he receives and thereby disturbs the very conventions by which Proverbs is interpreted and distributed.[65] Disrupting hierarchy and the difference between text/context, transmission/reception, female/male, wealth/

wisdom, transcendence/descent, guest/host, the way of Wisdom blurs not only the boundaries between Wisdom and God and Wisdom and Folly, but between Wisdom's Folly/Chaos and YHWH/Elohim's order(ing).[66] For when the wealth of Wisdom in he/r undermining transcendent multiplicity and precariously excessive fecundity emerges as the/a locus for life (as text), s/he becomes the wandering womb always already creating infinite possibilities for boundless incarnations of a be(com)ing Wisdom accessible to *all* life.[67]

## NOTES

I acknowledge the influence of my adviser-mentors, Kenneth Ngwa and Melanie Johnson-DeBaufre, whose Wisdom work, in the Hebrew Bible and New Testament respectively, has inspired my own theopoetic pursuits.

Unless otherwise noted, all translations are my own.

1. Judith Butler, *Frames of War: When Is Life Grievable?* (New York: Verso, 2009), 50–52. See also Judith Butler, *Precarious Life: The Powers of Mourning and Violence* (New York: Verso, 2004). Here Butler and Elisabeth Schüssler Fiorenza intersect. The biblical scholar contends, "The fundamental need to be recognized as human is constitutive of what it means to be human." Elisabeth Schüssler Fiorenza, *Wisdom Ways: Introducing Feminist Biblical Interpretation* (Maryknoll, N.Y.: Orbis Books, 2001), 88.
2. See Schüssler Fiorenza, *Wisdom Ways*, 57–58.
3. I employ "marked" to signify all "nonnormative" bodies, arguably always already gendered (i.e., feminine) bodies.
4. The use of gender-inclusive pronouns is one effort to foreground Wisdom's queerness and gender fluidity. Noting its various manifestations (knowledge, shrewdness, cunning, trickery, beguilement, etc.), I honor wisdom's demystification—resisting the bifurcation of *Wisdom* and *wisdom*. As "that mediating female personification/hypostasy found in Proverbs and elsewhere," Wisdom is a "proper" noun *and* a "common" noun because potentially present in any-body. Carole Fontaine, *Smooth Words: Women, Proverbs, and Performance in Biblical Wisdom* (London: Sheffield Academic, 2002), 2.
5. See "One Billion Rising Live" (2014), http://www.onebillionrising.org.
6. A delegate of the Cal-Nev UMC Philippines Solidarity Task Force, I traveled with the team to Manila (2009) to escort Melissa Roxas to her trial and learn from and stand with/in support of the people's struggle—encounters made possible by the National Council of Churches in the Philippines, Pastors Ruth Cortez, Jeanelle Ablola, and Michael Yoshii.
7. Derived from the stem of the preposition *al* is the verb *alah*: "to rise up," the preposition often translated "by the wayside," *ale-derek*, may also mean *"up-*on the way." L. Koehler, W. Baumgartner, and J. J. Stamm, *The Hebrew and Aramaic Lexicon of the Old Testament* (HALOT), trans. and ed. M. E. J. Richardson (Leiden: Brill, 1994), 824–27.
8. Gabriela's response to the Aquino administration's ineffective response to the devastation left in the wake of Typhoon Haiyan (Yolanda) is but one example. See "On

Rape Incidents in Areas Ravaged by Typoon Yolanda (Haiyan)," (November 14, 2013), http://www.gabrielaph.com/2013/11/14/on-rape-incidents-in-areas-ravaged-by-typhoon-yolanda-haiyan/.

9. Schüssler Fiorenza, *Wisdom Ways*, 77, 89.

10. See Herbert R. Marbury, "The Strange Woman in Persian Yehud: A Reading of Proverbs 7," in *Approaching Yehud: New Approaches to the Study of the Persian Period* ed. Jon L. Berquist (Atlanta: Society of Biblical Literature, 2007). According to Butler, "Precariousness and precarity are intersecting concepts. Lives are by definition precarious: they can be expunged at will or by accident; their persistence is in no sense guaranteed. . . . Precarity designates that politically induced condition in which certain populations suffer from failing social and economic networks of support and become differentially exposed to injury, violence, and death" (*Frames of War*), 25–26. Although precarity characterized life for "Israel" long before Persian Imperial rule, the emergence of Wisdom literature as a genre bespeaks an important development—particularly concerning (what can be inferred about) Yehud's precarity—not unrelated to the biblical treatment of the mother goddess qua *asherah*, *chavah*, *ishah zarah*, and *chokmah*.

11. Steven Weitzman's analysis of Jews in the Second Temple period, particularly his observations about the "early Jewish struggle for cultural survival," is apt. Of Jews' "survival tactics" Weitzman writes, "They used the imagination's powers to expand the parameters of reality, to overcome the limits of space, time, even death" (*Surviving Sacrilege: Cultural Persistence in Jewish Antiquity* [Cambridge, Mass.: Harvard University Press, 2005], 160). The "*art* of cultural persistence" enabled them to "maneuver between the real and the imagined, to respond to and operate within the constraints of reality but also to transcend them" (160–61). Wisdom is not only transcendence but also strategic (subterranean) subversion.

12. See Hélène Cixous, "The Laugh of the Medusa," trans. Keith Cohen and Paula Cohen, *Signs* 1, no. 4 (1976): 875–93.

13. My use of "fe/male" is a queer thing, political not essentialist. (And I read the feminine beyond the binary.) I employ "fe/male" and "wo/man" here (1) consciously queering (blurring) conceptualizations of female as feminine *in opposition to* the masculine male—applying the term to those marginal characters, who are not overtly "male," and (2) like Schüssler Fiorenza, to "lift into consciousness the linguistic violence of so-called generic male-centered language." Utilizing such terms demands that the reader consider who/what is included in its referent. I conjure both models for their (overstated?) tension(s) (i.e., Schüssler Fiorenza and the "French poststructuralist feminists" [particularly Irigaray]). In *différance*, there is no difference between language's theoretical and political employment (especially *in the feminine*). See Elisabeth Schüssler Fiorenza, *The Power of the Word: Scripture and the Rhetoric of Empire* (Minneapolis: Fortress Press, 2007), 6n21. For an exposition on Hebrew masculinity, see Howard Eilberg-Schwartz, *God's Phallus and Other Problems for Men and Monotheism* (Boston: Beacon Press, 1994).

14. Wisdom is, for me, *khora* and an affective bloomspace (Seigworth and Gregg). Plato introduces his third *genos*—the errant cause and wandering womb of the

cosmos—in *Timaeus*, where χώρα functions as the singular space that is no-place at all whereby and wherein the philosopher is able to conceptualize and conceive the cosmos. Disappointed in the *Timaeus*'s first attempt at a cosmology, Socrates queries his representation of form's materialization. And so he begins again, only now χώρα, the recondite place (beyond νους), becomes the *third space* wherein and whereby the sensible and intelligible touch (of necessity)—an encounter resulting in the conception of all material be(com)ings. In and through her perpetual becoming(s), χώρα becomes the very vehicle that enables Plato to articulate the enigma of genesis—the cosmic space in which form materializes. Without the liminal space χώρα inhabits and expresses, Plato would have been inhibited by Reason in his first account to an illegitimate (because illogical) cosmological event. See John Sallis's incisive exposition in *Chorology: On Beginning in Plato's* Timaeus (Bloomington: Indiana University Press, 1999); also see Patricia Cox Miller's choric reading of Origen's abodes (*De Principiis*) as place and process, which has inspired mine of Wisdom. Cox Miller, *The Poetry of Thought in Late Antiquity: Essays in Imagination and Religion* (Burlington: Ashgate, 2001), 181–82.

15. Luce Irigaray, *This Sex Which Is Not One*, trans. Catherine Porter (Ithaca, N.Y.: Cornell University Press, 1985), 31. Two points of interest: (1) Irigaray appears to be inadvertently gesturing *khora* in her depiction of the feminine (as self-structuring, sustaining); (2) Irigaray's early work, like that of Kristeva and Cixous, has been misinterpreted and inaccurately labeled "essentialist" for her political appropriation of "female" and "feminine" in an effort to disrupt the gender binary and the phallogocentric discourse through which it is constructed and maintained.

16. Ibid.

17. The questions driving my work differ from those of Michael S. Moore and James Kennedy. However, like Moore I employ a lens of socioeconomic conflict—in addition to postcolonial and queer theory. And with Kennedy, I interpret Genesis 2–3 not 4 (as Moore contends) to be the primary socioeconomic conflict. I imagine it as a root system from which the narrative and prose of Genesis (and the Proverbs) developed, framing the interpretation of the entire Bible. See Michael S. Moore, *Wealthwatch: A Study of Socioeconomic Conflict in the Bible* (Eugene, Ore.: Pickwick, 2011); James Kennedy, "Peasants in Revolt: Political Allegory in Genesis 2–3," *Journal for the Study of the Old Testament* 15, no. 47 (1990): 3–14.

18. Within my larger project, the tree of life is the central imagery of wisdom/knowledge in Genesis 1–3, also serving an integral function in the personification of Wisdom beyond Genesis. I understand the *etz da'at tov varah* as merismus and its *vav* as pleonastic or explicative, indicating that it is, in fact, the *etz chayim*. In other words, the "tree of the knowledge of all things" (good *and* bad or [from] good *to* evil) is the "tree of life." Although this association is instrumental to my reading of the *ishah/hava* (the woman Eve), it also indicates the *coincidencia oppositorum* that characterizes Wisdom (in Genesis, Proverbs, and throughout Wisdom literature).

19. I read knowledge (*da'at*) and wisdom (*chokmah*) together (Prov. 2:10). Though they signify differently, their slippages interest me. Knowledge, like discernment (*th'vunah*), is arguably an aspect (metonym, synecdoche) of wisdom (Prov. 2:1).

20. Influential upon my own work is that of Carole Fontaine and Linda Day, feminist biblical scholars who have contributed richly to Wisdom studies. See Fontaine, *Smooth Words*; Linda Day, "Wisdom and the Feminine in the Hebrew Bible," in *Engaging the Bible in a Gendered World*, ed. Linda Day and Carolyn Pressler (Louisville: Westminster John Knox, 2006), 114–27.
21. Schüssler Fiorenza, *Wisdom Ways*, 77, 186–87. Kyriarchy is one of the many neologisms for which Schüssler Fiorenza has become known: it is "a socio-political system of domination in which elite educated propertied men hold power over wo/men and other men." Laura Beth Bugg, "Explanation of Terms (Glossary)," in Schussler Fiorenza, *Wisdom Ways*, 211.
22. Schüssler Fiorenza, *Wisdom Ways*, 89.
23. Ibid., 89–91.
24. Ibid., 88.
25. The editors of and contributors to *Walk in the Ways of Wisdom* appeal to Schüssler Fiorenza's emancipatory criterion in *Rhetoric and Ethic*, rethinking biblical (con)texts to center women. My project resonates more with her exhortation in *Wisdom Ways*: to foreground contemporary women's experience in biblical studies toward increased public awareness and research "in the interest of wo/men." The task of feminist interpreters, then, is not merely translating the Bible for wo/men but learning from/with wo/men "struggling for survival and change in order to be able to 'translate' wo/men's quest for self-esteem and justice into the language of the academy." Schüssler Fiorenza, *Wisdom Ways*, 89. See also Shelly Matthews, Cynthia Briggs Kittredge, and Melanie Johnson-DeBaufre, eds., *Walk in the Ways of Wisdom: Essays in Honor of Elisabeth Schüssler Fiorenza* (Harrisburg, Penn.: Trinity, 2003); Elisabeth Schüssler Fiorenza, *Rhetoric and Ethic: The Politics of Biblical Studies* (Minneapolis: Fortress Press, 1999).
26. Claudia V. Camp, *Wisdom and the Feminine* (Sheffield: Almond, 1985), 291.
27. Ibid., 285–86.
28. Ibid., 290.
29. Claudia V. Camp, *Wise, Strange, Holy* (Sheffield: Sheffield Academic, 2000), 70–71.
30. Ibid., 343. Camp is motioning toward something quite similar to what Sara Ahmed deems "stranger danger," in which the notion of a pure, unified, and whole communal "I" is constituted with and through the representation and intensification of the dangerous impurity of the other. Sara Ahmed, *Strange Encounters: Embodied Others in Post-Coloniality* (New York: Routledge, 2000), 26–35.
31. Camp, *Wise, Strange, Holy*, 70–71.
32. Ibid., 88. Though Camp never explicitly articulates this subversion as a "unity of opposites," the implications are readily apparent.
33. Nietzsche, Foucault, Derrida, Butler, and Bhabha are the primary specters haunting my hermeneutics.
34. Mayra Rivera, "God at the Crossroads," in *The Postcolonial Biblical Reader*, ed. R. S. Sugirtharajah (Malden, Mass.: Blackwell, 2006), 248.
35. Of the stairwell (an adaptation of the African American artist Renée Green's exhibit *Sites of Genealogy*) Bhabha writes, "The stairwell as liminal space, in-between

the designations of identity, becomes the process of symbolic interaction, the connective tissue that constructs the difference between upper and lower . . . [preventing] identities at either end of it from settling into primordial polarities." Homi Bhabha, *The Location of Culture* (New York: Routledge, 1994), 5.

36. Rivera, "God at the Crossroads," 238, 246–47, 249.
37. Stephen D. Moore addresses this very conundrum when he writes, "To deconstruct a hierarchical opposition is not simply to argue that the term ordinarily repressed is in reality the superior term. Rather than stand the opposition on its head in front of a mirror, thereby inverting it but leaving it intact nonetheless, deconstruction attempts to show how each term in the opposition is joined to its companion by an intricate network of arteries. In consequence, the line ordinarily drawn between the two terms is shown to be a political and not a natural reality." Stephen D. Moore, *Poststructuralism and the New Testament: Derrida and Foucault at the Foot of the Cross* (Minneapolis: Fortress Press, 1994), 30.
38. Rivera, "God at the Crossroads," 199.
39. Ibid., 196. While God and Sophia potentially desire to be gendered *as* other, Rivera's depiction of this desire is *for* the other as ontologically gendered male and female respectively. See Judith Butler, *The Psychic Life of Power: Theories in Subjection* (Stanford: Stanford University Press, 1997), 25.
40. Ibid., 195, 200.
41. Ibid., 195–97, 200.
42. Ibid: 198–99.
43. Rivera, "God at the Crossroads," 241, 243, 249; Silvia Schroer, "Wise and Counselling Woman in Ancient Israel: Literary and Historical Ideals of the Personified *hokmâ*," in *A Feminist Companion to Wisdom Literature*, ed. Athalya Brenner (Sheffield: Sheffield Academic, 1995), 67–84. Rivera, like Schroer, has a feminist theological investment in reading Wisdom as transcendent. Schroer writes, "Transcendence and heaven are combined with the feminine. Biblical Sophia meets the requirement of feminist theology to integrate human experience instead of separating or demonizing parts of it, to search for correspondence and interconnections instead of settling for separation and differentiation. She offers help because she is interactive and open: she contains without imposing limits" (83).
44. Quoting Tanner in her appeal to a transcendence "constantly calling into question the certainty of the system" that "becomes a model" for resistance (249). Kathryn Tanner, "Creation as Mixed Metaphor," presented at Drew University's First Transdisciplinary Theological Colloquium (September 30–October 1, 2001).
45. Wisdom's conduct is "unladylike," akin to the panty-less lemon vendors of Marcella Althaus-Reid's Buenos Aires barrio in her queer reimagination of liberation theology. See Althaus-Reid, *Indecent Theology: Theological Perversions in Sex, Gender, and Politics* (New York: Routledge, 2000), especially 1–46.
46. Ironically, even the notion of hybridity (so integral to Bhabha's work and postcolonial studies at large) insinuates a dyad.
47. Irigaray, *This Sex Which Is Not One*, 28–29.
48. Ibid., 29.

49. The axial blur I perceive is not just between *zarah* and *chokmah* or Wisdom and God, but Wisdom and Folly and even God and Folly. For more on the woman of "folly" see Kenneth Ngwa, "Did Job Suffer for Nothing? The Ethics of Piety, Presumption, and the Reception of Disaster in the Prologue of Job," *Journal for the Study of the Old Testament* 33 no. 3 (2009): 359–80; Bernhard Lang, *Wisdom and the Book of Proverbs: An Israelite Goddess Redefined* (New York: Pilgrim, 1986).

50. The threat of Wisdom/Stranger's textual bodily excess and diluvian sexual appetites has contributed to woman's regulation via relegation to the home, and as long as s/he is governed—subjugated and exploited for (re)production—within this economy to ensure its stability, its structures remain intact (see Prov. 31). However, as *ishah* (*chava*/Eve) took hold of the fruit necessary for the Wisdom of discernment (Gen. 2–3) and as *chokmah* obtained knowledge (Prov. 8.12), various (feminist) interpretations reveal that Wisdom in (the hands of) wo/men is *armed and dangerous—refusing* to be refuse, quelled, or quietly resigned to bifurcation. As male and female, good and bad, wise and strange, s/he is always already both/and, *occupying the crack* and the spectrum.

51. The Wise and Strange are indistinguishable in Rivera and Camp's readings of Wisdom *and* in a hermeneutics of *chayim*; Wisdom demands the strange, foolish, and queer to survive—the 'wisdom way' of categorization and observation is inadequate (Fontaine, *Smooth Words*, 4).

52. Noteworthy is Wisdom's utterance of these words soon after a detailed description of the Strange Woman's sexual appetites and (commercial?) activities.

53. The verb for "build" here, *banah*, is used to refer to both the material construction of homes and the building of a family.

54. See also HALOT, 97, for the semantic range of *ashar*. I am providing my own interpretation of the root meaning, which is "to stride" or "to lead."

55. Reading Wisdom transcending hegemonic control and claiming power through identification with the transcendent may be an integral liberative political tactic in the struggle against oppressive structures of power/knowledge. Understanding her *otherwise*, however, I read her as simultaneously frustrating *from below*: rising up to incite others to join, occupy, and be occupied by her but never entirely vacating *sheol*.

56. Like Silverstein's *Giving Tree*, Wisdom is excessively generous. However, unlike the maternal motif, as the Tree of Life Wisdom knows when/how to say "no." Shel Silverstein, *The Giving Tree* (New York: Harper and Row, 1964)

57. As Fontaine asserts, "fools [are] notorious for their inability to do anything properly" (Fontaine, *Smooth Words*, 166–67). The irony of Wisdom *as* Folly is her enactment and embodiment of Folly—often for the sake of survival—offering and requiring much more from the audience than platitudes and passive reception (266).

58. Anthony Appiah writes, "It takes a sense of honor to feel implicated by the acts of others. And it takes a sense of your own dignity to insist, against the odds, upon your right to justice in a society that rarely offers it to women like you; and a sense of the dignity of all women to respond to your own brutal rape not just with indignation and a desire for revenge but with the determination to remake your country,

so that its women are treated with the respect you know they deserve. To make such choices is to live a life of difficulty, even, sometimes, of danger. It is also, and not incidentally, to live a life of honor." Kwame Anthony Appiah, *The Honor Code: How Moral Revolutions Happen* (New York: W. W. Norton, 2010), 204.

59. (Often into otherwise amicable, thriving two-third's world countries.) For a more incisive exploration see William E. Connolly, "The Evangelical-Capitalist Resonance Machine," *Political Theory* 33, no. 6 (2005): 869–86.

60. Gabriela is named after the Ilocano freedom fighter Maria Josefa Gabriela Silang, whose name is an acronym for the group's political commitments: General Assembly Binding Women for Reforms, Integrity, Equality, Leadership, and Action. (I use singular and plural pronouns to refer to Gabriela, since they are many fighting as one.) These wo/men repeatedly place themselves in life-threatening situations—no strangers to precarity—preferring to struggle for survival rather than surrender in silence to unjust political machinations.

61. Michel Foucault, *Discipline and Punish: The Birth of the Prison*, trans. Alan Sheridan (New York: Random House, 1977, repr. 1995); Bell Hooks, *Black Looks: Race and Representation* (Boston: South End Press, 1992), 21–39. Of course, Foucault, Butler, and Jasbir Puar, *Terrorist Assemblages* (Durham, N.C.: Duke University Press, 2007), among others, have claimed similar things much more incisively. I proffer a way to read the Bible with critical sociopolitical theory so that neither is deprived of a mutually beneficial dialogue and in an effort to promote global awareness and/of human rights (violations). Moved by hooks's warning (not unlike Spivak's critique of poststructurlist discourse) about the "commodification of Otherness" and "eating the other," I engage the Filipina NGO Gabriela acknowledging the potential for cultural appropriation and in hopes that I will honor and not erase these wo/men's voices.

62. Butler, *Frames of War*, 51–55.

63. See Michel Foucault, *The History of Sexuality*, vol. 1: *An Introduction*, trans. Robert Hurley (New York: Vintage Books, 1978). Foucault also used the term *dispositif* to signify the discursive mechanisms (of power) that produce and regulate knowledge and bodies within society vis-à-vis political, religious, and educational institutions.

64. A queer reading of Wisdom such as this is indebted to deconstruction and queer theory—neither do I presume that this hermeneutic reflects the text's interpretation in its "original" context nor is it entirely out of the realm of possibility.

65. Wisdom blurs the host/guest binary: "The stranger, here the awaited guest, is not only someone to whom you say 'come,' but 'enter,' enter without waiting, make a pause in our home without waiting, hurry up and come in, 'come inside,' 'come within me,' not only toward me, but within me: occupy me, take place in me, which means, by the same token, also take my place, don't content yourself with coming to meet me or 'into my home.' . . . It is *as if* the stranger or foreigner held the keys." Jacques Derrida and Anne Dufourmantelle, *Of Hospitality: Anne Dufourmantelle Invites Jacques Derrida to Respond*, trans. Rachel Bowlby (Stanford: Stanford University Press, 2000), 123.

66. Chaos à la Derrida might also signify anarchy—a fear of which (as nature), Sara Ahmed asserts, is "an imperative for the formation of government." See Ahmed, *The Cultural Politics of Emotion* (New York: Routledge, 2004), 71. Although Catherine Keller does not read chaos into the God of creation in Genesis, her neologism for Elohim, "manyone," holds such potentiality. Keller, *Face of the Deep: A Theology of Becoming* (New York: Routledge, 2003).
67. *The/a* serves multiple functions here, namely, to emphasize Wisdom as simultaneously particular (definite) and indefinite (common) as well as Wisdom's profane masculine/feminine-divinity.

ACKNOWLEDGMENTS

This volume emerged from a robust and convivial gathering of tenacious scholars for the Twelfth Transdisciplinary Theological Colloquium held at Drew Theological School on February 8–10, 2012. The title was "Common Good/s: Economy, Ecology, and Political Theology," which then became the title of this book. Tenacious we were, but also arbitrarily lucky, because we managed to overcome the record-breaking snow and ice that kept others from attending. William E. Connolly generously shared his time, work, and insights in a keynote lecture and throughout the conference. We are indebted to his characteristic generosity and democratic militancy, which parallels and patterns much of the thinking of the philosophers, theologians, and scholars of religion of this collection. We are also grateful to Mayra Rivera Rivera, Kathryn Tanner, Dan Miller, and Cynthia Moe-Lobeda, who sent on their work electronically so that we could hear from them if not show them Drew's hospitality. Enormous gratitude goes to Drew's student volunteers, especially Natalie Williams and Elijah Prewitt-Davis, who did tremendous work in organizing the event.

Several colleagues gave presentations, and feedback or served as respondents to the papers collected in this volume. For this important collaboration, we thank Shelley Dennis, Elizabeth Freese, P. Joshua Griffin, Peter Heltzel, Jacqueline Hidalgo, Hannah Hofheinz, W. Anne Joh, Hyo-Dong Lee, Beatrice Marovich, Johannes Morsink, Michael Oliver, Jeffrey Robbins, Sara Rosenau, and Santiago Slabodsky.

Our beloved colleague Otto Maduro, although scheduled to participate, was already battling the illness that took him from us in May 2013. We miss him dearly. To honor his incalculable contributions to our community of learning, we say: "Otto Maduro, *presente!*" This was also the last colloquy at which our dedicated and wise Fordham editor, Helen Tartar, graced Craig Chapel with her quiet, intense, and creative presence. She too is dearly missed. There was knitting to commemorate Helen at the 2013 colloquium.

Fondly known as TTC, Drew's annual colloquy aims to foster a fresh style of theological discourse that is both pluralist and constructive. Committed to the long-range transformation of theological and religious imagery and ideas, this series continues Drew's deep history of engaging historical, biblical, and cultural hermeneutics, contemporary philosophy, movements of social justice, and experiments in theopoetics. In this spirit, TTC XII expanded its program with a day and a half of events for undergraduates, master's students, and community members called "Living the Common Good/s: The Promise and Challenge of Activisms Today." We were thrilled to have the writer-activist Nathan Schneider give a keynote address on Occupy Wall Street and a workshop on ways in which scholars of religion might engage more deeply in the wider public square, both through publication and nonacademic employment.

In the days before the colloquium, there were workshops on homelessness, climate change, food justice, race, religion and queer sexualities, and both parish and interfaith organizing. We thank Rev. Harper Fletcher from GreenFaith; Debi Hall-Dean of Partners in ACTS in Newark; Stevi Lischin from the Monmouth Center for World Religions and Ethical Thought; Darnell L. Moore; George Schmidt; Michael Sniffen from St. Matthew and Luke in New York, a hub for Occupy Sandy; and Leena Waite from America's Grow-a-Row. Both Jonathan Golden from Drew's Center for Religion, Culture, and Conflict and Amy Koritz from the Center for Civic Engagement were of great support in planning the public events of this part of the conference.

We are proud that the gatherings and publications of Drew's Transdisciplinary Theological Colloquium cultivate the verdant edges of scholarship in religion and theology. This would not be possible without the considerable support of the Deans of the Theological School, then Jeffrey Kuan and now Javier Viera. TTC XII faced uncommon weather but could not be cowed. Given the urgency of the climatic times, our vibrant, if partial, assemblage still managed to think the common divergently together, and therein lay the hope that this volume makes space for readers to imagine and materialize some common good/s.

CONTRIBUTORS

AN YOUNTAE is a visiting assistant professor in the Department of Religion and Philosophy at Lebanon Valley College. His research explores the boundary between Western religious thought, continental philosophy of religion, and postcolonial theory. He is currently finishing up his first book manuscript titled *The (De)Colonial Abyss: Negativity and the Cosmopolitical Future.*

SHARON BETCHER is a freelance academic, living on Whidbey Island, Washington, and an affiliate professor of theology and a research and teaching fellow at Vancouver School of Theology, Vancouver, B.C. She is the author of *Spirit and the Politics of Disablement* (Fortress, 2007) and *Spirit and the Obligation of Social Flesh: A Secular Theology for the Global City* (Fordham, 2013) as well as essays on ecological, postcolonial, and disabilities theologies within multiple anthologies.

KAREN BRAY is a PhD candidate in theological and philosophical studies in religion at Drew University. She is an adjunct professor of religious studies at Eugene Lang College of the New School University in New York City. Karen teaches classes in queer and postcolonial theologies, world Christianities, sexual ethics, and affect theory. Her current research employs feminist theories of affect, temporality, and work in order to construct countercapitalist soteriologies.

WILLIAM E. CONNOLLY is the Krieger-Eisenhower Professor at Johns Hopkins University where he teaches political theory. His recent books are *Pluralism* (2005), *Capitalism and Christianity, American Style* (2008), *A World of Becoming* (2011), and *The Fragility of Things: Self-Organizing Processes, Neoliberal Fantasies, and Democratic Activism* (2013). In a recent poll of political theorists in America he was ranked fourth in influence over the last twenty years, after Rawls, Habermas, and Foucault.

CLAYTON CROCKETT is professor and director of religious studies at the University of Central Arkansas. He is the co-author, with Jeffrey W. Robbins, of *Religion, Politics and the Earth: The New Materialism* (2012), and the author of *Radical Political Theology: Religion and Politics after Liberalism* (2011) and *Deleuze beyond Badiou: Ontology, Multiplicity and Event* (2013).

GARY DORRIEN is the Reinhold Niebuhr Professor of Social Ethics at Union Theological Seminary and Professor of Religion at Columbia University. He is the author of seventeen books and approximately 250 articles that range across the fields of ethics, social theory, theology, philosophy, politics, and history. His book *Kantian Reason and Hegelian Spirit* won the Association of American Publishers Award for the best book in Theology and Religious Studies in 2012.

PAULINA OCHOA ESPEJO is an associate professor of political science at Haverford College. She specializes in contemporary political theory and the history of political thought. She is the author of *The Time of Popular Sovereignty: Process and the Democratic State* (Penn State University Press, 2011). Her articles have appeared in the *Journal of Politics, Critical Review of International Social and Political Philosophy, Philosophy and Social Criticism, Scandinavian Journal of Social Theory, Metapolitica,* and *Nexos*.

CHARON HRIBAR is a co-coordinator of the Partnership for Religion and Education in Prisons Program at Drew University and serves as the Poor People's Campaign Program Coordinator for the Kairos Center for Religions, Rights, and Social Justice at Union Theological Seminary in the City of New York while finishing her PhD in religion and society at Drew. Her recent research examines the structural violence of poverty and explores the capacity of Christian social ethics to reimagine a radical response to the growing disparity of wealth and poverty in the midst of a twenty-first-century global economic crisis.

ANATOLI IGNATOV is an assistant professor of sustainable development at Appalachian State University. His research reworks Euro-American political theory through ethnographic encounters with African ecological practices and knowledges. Anatoli's work has appeared in *Theory & Event, borderlands,* and *Law, Culture and the Humanities*.

MELANIE JOHNSON-DeBAUFRE is an associate professor of New Testament and early Christianity at Drew Theological School. She specializes in the politics, ethics, and materiality of ancient Christianity and its interpretation in the present. She is the author of *Jesus among Her Children: Q, Eschatology, and the Construction of Christian Origins* (Harvard University Press, 2006), and co-author, with Jane Schaberg, of *Mary Magdalene Understood* (Continuum, 2006). She is currently working on a book using spatial theory to reimagine the Pauline assemblies as politically productive and contested spaces.

CATHERINE KELLER is the George T. Cobb Professor of Christian Theology at the Theological School of Drew University. In her teaching, lecturing, and writing, she develops the relational potential of a theology of becoming. Her books reconfigure ancient symbols of divinity for the sake of a planetary conviviality—a life together, across vast webs of difference. Thriving in the interplay of ecological and gender politics, of process cosmology, poststructuralist philosophy and religious pluralism, her work is both deconstructive and constructive in strategy.

VINCENT LLOYD is an assistant professor of religion at Syracuse. His research focuses on the intersection of religion, race, and political theory. Among his publications are *The Problem with Grace: Reconfiguring Political Theology* (Stanford University Press, 2011) and an edited collection, *Race and Political Theology* (Stanford University Press, 2012). Lloyd coedits the journal *Political Theology*.

CYNTHIA D. MOE-LOBEDA is Professor of Christian Ethics at Pacific Lutheran Theological Seminary, a member school of the Graduate Theological Union in Berkeley. She is on the faculty of the Department of Theology and Religious Studies, Environmental Studies Program, and Graduate School of Theology and Ministry. Dr. Cynthia Moe-Lobeda has lectured or consulted in Africa, Asia, Europe, and many parts of North America in theology and ethics. She is the author of *Healing a Broken World: Globalization and God* (Fortress, 2002), *Public Church: For the Life of the World* (Fortress, 2004), *Resisting Structural Evil: Love as Ecological-Economic Vocation* (Fortress, 2013), and numerous articles and chapters. She is co-author of *St. Francis and the Foolishness of God* (Orbis, 1993 and 2015), *Say to This Mountain: Mark's Story of Discipleship* (Orbis, 1996), and *The Bible and Ethics: A New Conversation* (Fortress, forthcoming).

DHAWN B. MARTIN is Visiting Assistant Professor in Theological Studies at Hanover College. Her interests and field of study concentrate on the intersections of faith, politics, and social activism.

ELIAS ORTEGA-APONTE is an assistant professor of Afro-Latina/o religions and cultural studies at Drew Theological School. His research focuses on the intersections between race, gender, punishment, and economics. Currently, he is working on a book-length project mobilizing insights from black and brown power movements to proposed a religious abolitionist ethics of the prison-industrial complex.

ELIJAH PREWITT-DAVIS teaches theology at Xavier University as he finishes his PhD in theological and philosophical studies at Drew University. His current research attempts to figure out what Gilles Deleuze meant when he wrote that "only belief in the world can reconnect man [sic] to what he sees and hears." He was the student co-organizer for the conference that produced this book.

A. PAIGE RAWSON is a PhD candidate in biblical studies and women and gender studies at Drew University. Her research interests include Wisdom literatures, poststructuralist theories, orality theory, and Africana studies. Her dissertation project is an oral-literate reinterpretation of the Samson folktale found in the book of Judges through Rastafari hermeneutics at the intersection of queer and affect theory and orality studies.

JOERG RIEGER is the Wendland-Cook Professor of Constructive Theology at Perkins School of Theology, Southern Methodist University. For more than two decades he has worked to bring together theology and the struggles for justice and liberation that mark our age. His work addresses the relation of theology to public life, using tools from cultural studies, critical theory, and religious studies, and reflecting on the misuse of power in politics and economics. He is internationally recognized for his prolific and visionary writing. A selection of his books includes *Occupy Religion: Theology of the Multitude* (2012, with Kwok Pui Lan), *Traveling* (2011), *Grace under Pressure* (2011), *Globalization and Theology* (2010), and *No Rising Tide: Theology, Economics, and the Future* (2009).

KATHRYN TANNER is the Frederick Marquand Professor of Systematic Theology at Yale Divinity School. Her research relates the history of Christian thought to contemporary issues of theological concern using social, cultural, and feminist theory. She is the author of many articles and books, including *Jesus, Humanity and the Trinity: A Brief Systematic Theology* (Fortress, 2001), *Economy of Grace* (Fortress, 2005), and *Christ the Key* (Cambridge, 2010).

JOHN THATAMANIL is an associate professor of theology and world religions at Union Theological Seminary. He has taught a wide variety of courses in the areas of comparative theology, theologies of religious pluralism, Hindu-Christian dialogue, Buddhist-Christian dialogue, the theology of Paul Tillich, and process theology. Tying together these diverse interests is a basic commitment to a deeply metaphysical form of philosophical theology that he takes to be essential for any Christian theology that seeks to be in conversation with non-Christian religious traditions.

NIMI WARIBOKO is Walter G. Muelder Professor of Social Ethics at Boston University. His work focuses on economic ethics, economic theory, philosophy of religion, pentecostal studies, and African social traditions.

## INDEX

Abrahamic religious traditions, power differentials and, 154–55
Adorno, Theodor, 248
aesthetic element, 33
Agamben, Giorgio, 74, 310; potentiality, 211
agape, 68
agency: common good and, 159–60; theo-political trilemma, 125; Thoreau, 268; unencumbered, 137–48; valuing work and, 163
agnostic respect, 132–33
Alexander, Michelle, *The New Jim Crow: Mass Incarceration in the Age of Colorblindness*, 344
Althaus-Reid, Marcella: desire, 387–90; *Indecent Theology: Theological Perversions in Sex, Gender and Politics*, 386–88
American assumption (DuBois), 192
American exceptionalism, American assumption, 192
apophatic accounts of divine transcendence, 95–96
Arendt, Hannah, 308
artist's pessimism, 45
arts of existence, 268
Asad, Talal, 56–57; *Formations of the Secular*, 74
aspirational politics, 390
atheism, ethically pluralist, 10
attraction: creativity and, 33; Nietzsche, 38
*The Audacity of Hope* (Obama), 329, 330, 337–40
austerity, 200
authority, fathers and, 328

Bakunin, Mikhail, 7
Baldwin, James, 346
Bandung Conference, 349

banking. *See* finance industry
Barth, Karl, socialism and, 170
basileia of God, 103–16. *See also* kin-dom of God
basileus, Greek use, 122n51
becoming: cosmic innocence and, 26–27; desire without organs and, 394–95; philosophers on, 26–27; transcendence and, 98–100
being: energy transformation, 79–80; ontological wonder and, 67
beliefs, personal, transcendence and, 94–95
Benjamin, Walter, "The Concept of History," 210–11
Benne, Robert, 172–73
Bergson, Henri, 31
Berlant, Lauren, "Sex in Public," 396
Bhabha, Homi, 413
binaries, basileia of God and, 104–5
biopower, 130–31, 229–30; Foucault, 230
*Black Reconstruction in America* (Du Bois), 192–93, 351–52
*Black Skin, White Masks* (Fanon), 257
Block, Ernst, utopian impulse, 108
body: Christian theology and, 373–74; feminist theology and, 366; public gaze, 398–99
body-politics, 348–49
Bohr, Niels, 28, 50n5
Bonino, José Míguez, 172
border crossings, sovereignty and, 321–22
Brunner, Emil, *The Divine Imperative*, 170
Brzezinski, Zbigniew, 193
Buddhism: Mahayana, 68; Protestant Buddhism, 72n24
bureaucratization of the economy, 172
BwO (body-without-organs), 393–94
Byrd, James, 383n55

Camp, Claudia V.: *Wisdom and the Feminine in the Book of Proverbs*, 412; *Wise, Strange, and Holy*, 412–13
capital, living labor and, 259–60
capitalism: Christian-capitalist resonance machine, 91–92; as Christian democracy, 408; climate change and, 43–45; commodification and, 174; the common, 3–4; common good and, 149–50; common good complexified, 156–57; corporate, 83; democracy and, 5–6; democratic, 173; desire and, 391–96; divine transcendence and, 100–1; as economic practice, 77; financial derivatives, 100–1; forced labor and, 251–52; gendered minorities, 390; God's providence and, 99; invisible hand of the market, 150–51; Lacan, 84–85; love of self, 160; natural order and, 171; politics and, 77; post 1968, 81–87; production of gods, 389–90; self-made man, 160; Žižek, Slavoj, 84
*Capitalism and Christianity, American Style* (Connolly), 390–91
Caputo, John, hospitality, 132
carbon debt, 301n4
Casanova, José, *Public Religions in the Modern World*, 7
Catholic social theology, 170
Catholic substance, 209; monetary system and, 213
Catholicism: liberation theology, 7; Solidarnisc movement, 7
CDO (Collateralized Debt Obligations), 176
center-periphery divides, 128–33
change, creative in nonhuman processes, 31–32
Cheah, Pheng, 124, 125; colonialism, 135; freedom, 136
Cherbury, Lord Herbert, 60
Chick-fil-A, 230–31, 242–43
children, romanticizing in religion, 158–59
Christian-capitalist resonance machine, 91–92
Christian ethics and climate change: cumulative impact, 293–95; historical roots, 292–93; moral response, 295–300; moral responsibility, 295; power imbalance, 291–92; privilege and, 290
Christian ethics, history and, 289
Christian traditions: children in, 158–59; common sense/common good, 196–99; democratic capitalism, 173; labor, 163; sexual violence, 388; status quo and, 198

Christianity: Catholic substance, 212–13; disability and, 373–74; environment and, 89n14; materialism and, 392; medieval, sovereignty in, 312; as movement, 198–99; Pentecostal principle, 212–13; Protestant principle, 212–13; servant versus king, 392
*Christianity and the Social Order* (Temple), 171
christo-eccentric practices, 139–40
chronotime, 44–45
*The Church against the World* (Niebuhr), 199
citizens of the world, 6
civic community, 236–37
civil rights, disability and, 365–66
class: conflicts, religion and, 197–98; resentment, aspirational politics, 390
class-war, Smith, Adam, 171
climate change: capitalism and, 43–45; carbon debt, 301n4; colonialism and, 292–93; cumulative impact acknowledgment, 293–95; moral response, 295–300; moral responsibility and, 295; neoliberalism and, 293; power imbalance, 291–92; sustainability, 287–88; UNFCCC, 298–99; white privilege and, 286–89
climate colonialism, 16, 286–87, 294
climate debt, 286; climate negotiations and, 289; repayment, 288; white privilege and, 287–89
Club of Rome, *The Limits to Growth*, 82
Cobb, John: *For the Common Good: Redirecting the Economy toward Community, the Environment, and a Sustainable Future*, 4–5; "Commonwealth and Empire," 108–9; *Is It Too Late? A Theology of Ecology*, 82; paradox in, 109–10; *Process Theology as Political Theology*, 9
coexistent potentia, 28
Colbert, Stephen, the utopian and, 118
colonial logic, 348
colonialism: as Christian democracy, 408; climate change and, 292–93; climate colonialism, 16, 286–87, 294; corporate (neoliberalism), 293; race and, 264n3
coloniality, 348; Fourth of July speech (Douglass), 350–51, 357
*Come Home, America: The Rise and Fall (and Redeeming Promise) of Our Country* (Greider), 192–93
the common, 1; capitalism and, 3–4; the corporate, 3–4; language, 3–4; suspicion, 4

INDEX | 437

common good: agency's position, 159–60; alternative conceptions, 153–54; capitalism and, 149–50; challenges to, 3–5; complexified, 154–57; conceptions that don't work, 150–53; corporate, 236–41; distortions, 157–59; distribution and, 157, 161–62; humanity and, 154–55; individualism and, 151–53; material world and, 126–27; Paul's letters to Corinthians, 155; power differentials and, 153; power in capitalism, 154; production and, 157, 161–62; redefining, 199–205; religious visions, 326; self-interest and, 151–53, 160–61; special interests and, 152; structural greed, 151; suffering and, 155–56; wealthy persons and, 152–53, 157–58
common good/s, 5–7
common sense, 194–96; Christian traditions, 196–99; religion and, 198–99
*Commonwealth* (Hardt and Negri), 243
Communism, socialism and, 172
community, 236–37
compassion, 68–69
the complex, 35
concentric enclosures, 125–33
"The Concept of History" (Benjamin), 210–11
concorporeal commons, 3
concrescence, 32–33
conflict and social/economic inequality, 193–94
Connolly, William, 1, 6, 12; *Capitalism and Christianity, American Style*, 390–91; Evangelical-Capitalist-Resonance-Machine, 390; methodology of the obscene, 390; refusal of secularism, 55; resentment, 371–72; *Why I Am Not a Secularist*, 7, 74; *A World of Becoming*, 401
consciousness, self-consciousness, 253
consumerism, liberty and, 388–89
consumption, production, 271
contemplative practices, 70n6
contingent being, ontological wonder and, 67
conventional wisdom, theopaternity and, 328–29
the corporate, 3–4
corporate capitalism, 83
corporate colonialism (neoliberalism), 293
corporate common good, 236–41
corporate sovereignty, 239–40
corporate universality, 238
corporations, 230; civic community and, 237; as derivative of the state, 237–38;

Hegel, 237; identities, 240–41; police and, 238–39; subjectivities and, 230–31
cosmological, Whitehead, 51n12
cosmopolitan rights, 129
cosmopolitanism, 124–25, 129–33
cosmopolitical dimension, 43–50
cosmopolitical eccentricities, 128–33
cosmopolitical theology, 124, 141–42
creative change, nonhuman processes, 31–32
creative condensations, Nietzsche, 38
creative labor, 261; death of God and, 263–64; *versus* forced, 256–57, 260. See also living labor
creative possibility, 392; the erotic and, 393
creativity, 30–37, 40
credit-default swaps, 177
creedalization, 55, 60–61
Crockett, Clayton, 2, 12–13, 58; *Radical Political Theology*, 2; sovereignty, 236
cruel optimism in politics, 389
currency swaps, 177

Daly, Herman, *For the Common Good: Redirecting the Economy toward Community, the Environment, and a Sustainable Future*, 4–5
Davis, Lennard, 365–66
DCF (discounted cash flow), 214
Deacon, Terence, *Incomplete Nature*, 51n14
death of God, 10, 73–74, 243; Deleuze and, 232–33, 244–45; factors in, 234; Goodchild, 234–35; immanence, 243; liberation theology and, 231; living/creative labor, 263–64; Nietzsche, 233–34; post-secular theology, 231–34
decolonialism, Douglass, 349–50
"The Deconstruction of God" (Raschke), 74
Dederer, Claire, *Poser: My Life in Twenty-Three Yoga Poses*, 366
deep solidarity, 158
Deists, 60
Deleuze, Gilles: BwO (body-without-organs), 393–94; death of God, 232–33, 244–45; *Difference and Repetition*, 78; nonequilibrium thermodynamics, 81; thermodynamics, 78; *A Thousand Plateaus*, 88; transcendence, 232
deliteralization, 63–64
democracy: capitalism and, 5–6; Du Bois on, 356; economic democracy, 174–86; racialization, 351–52
democratic capitalism, 173
democratic legitimacy, 307–23

democratic militancy, 11
democratic socialism, 171–72
democratization, 5–6
depoliticization of religions, 55
dereligionization, 55; of traditions, 62–65
derivatives, banking and, 176–77
Derrida, Jacques, ethics, 132
desire: BwO (body-without-organs), 393–94; capitalism and, 389–90, 391–96; economic, 391; evaluation, subordination of, 391; indecency and, 395; production, 389–90; productivity, 395–96; social order and, 391; social/historical modes of control, 387–88; without organs, 393–95
detextualization, 63
devotion, religion as object, 59–60, 62
dialectical theology, 170
difference, 78–9, 373–74
*Difference and Repetition* (Deleuze), 78
differential creativity, 34–35
disability, 365–66; Christian theology and, 373–74; civil rights and, 365–66; comic impulse and, 368–71; crips, 379–80; as cultural symptom, 370–71; derision, 368–69; disgust and, 368–70, 375–78; diversity and, 365–66; Garland-Thomson, Rosemarie, 379–80; hate crimes and, 383n55; in/valid, 370–72; metaphors in language, 368–71; postapocalyptic narrative and, 378–80; resentment, 367, 371–73; as threat, 367
disgust: disability and, 368–70, 375–78; Weil, Simone, 376–77
dissipative systems, 79–80
dissonances, queer subculture, 402–3
distribution, 161–62
diversity: disability and, 365–66; neoliberalism and, 365–66
*The Divine Imperative* (Brunner), 170
divine sovereignty, 104
divine transcendence: apophatic accounts, 95–96; authoritarian deployment, 95; becoming and, 98–100; capitalism and, 100–1; divine agency and, 98; *versus* immanence, 91–92; personal beliefs and, 94–95; resonance machine and, 94. *See also* transcendence
Dodd-Frank bill, 176
dogmatism, countering, 97
DOMA (Defense of Marriage Act), 396–97
dominant self-interest, 160–61
Douglass, Frederick, 346; "The Meaning of the Fourth of July for the Negro," 349–51, 357
*Dreams from My Father* (Obama), 329–37

Dressler, Markus, religion-making, 57–58
Du Bois, W. E. B.: American assumption, 192; *Black Reconstruction in America*, 192–93, 351–52; on democracy, 356; on Andrew Johnson, 352; racialization of democracy, 351–52
duality, unilateral, 76
Dussel, Enrique, living labor, 250, 258–64
dystopia, 121n41

earth democracy, 2
eccentric, 128
eccentricities, cosmopolitical, 128–33
economic democracy, 174–86, 181; human nature and, 183–84; social theorists and, 185
economic desire, 391
economic growth, hope and, 193–94
economic human rights, 191–92
economic independence, middle class and, 193
economic inequality, 191; normalization, 195; social conflict and, 193–94
economic rationality, faith and, 235
economics: Catholic social theology, 170; dialectical theology, 170; ecumenical theology, 170; liberation theology, 170; religion, resemblance, 150; study of money, 179–80
economics of white supremacy, mass incarceration and, 346–78
economy: bureaucratization of, 172; democratic capitalism, 173; Gurensi people, 269–70, 276–77; limitations to growth, 185–86; physicality, 185–86; Thoreau, 268–74
ecotheology, 77
ecumenical theology, 170
emergence: creativity and, 32–33; the political as, 124–27
emerging church movement, basileia of God and, 104
empty place of power, 309, 312–14, 319–20; limitations, 314–17
energy, 78; being as energy transformation, 79–80; Deleuze, 78; intensity, 78–79; non-theology, 79; repetition, 78
the engaged, 137
enlightened self-interest, 161
The Enlightenment: critique of Christian tradition, 61; valuing work, 198
entanglement, 29–30, 50n9; vibrations theme, 31
entities, 51n10; attraction and repulsion, 33; vibrations and, 31

entropy: difference and, 78; gradient reduction, 80; heat death, 79
eros, 68
eternal objects, 25, 35–37, 52n22
eternal return, Nietzsche, 25
ethics: as hospitality, 132; social ethics, 169–70. See also Christian ethics and climate change; Christian ethics, history and
ethnography, 268–69
evaluation, subordination to desire, 391
Evangelical-Capitalist-Resonance-Machine, 390
exceptionalism, sovereignty and, 7–8
exclusion in discourses, 125
*The Eye of the Beholder: Deformity and Disability in the Graeco-Roman World* (Garland), 368–69

*Facing Gaia* (Latour), 10–11
faith, economic rationality and, 235
family, basileia, 114–15
Fanon, Franz, 250; *Black Skin, White Masks*, 257; master-slave dialectic, 256–58; *The Wretched of the Earth*, 261
fatherhood, black men and, 341–42
fathers: God and, 327–28; God as father, 326–27; sovereignty and, 326–27. See also theopaternity
Federal Council of Churches of the USA, 170
Federal Reserve, 215; establishment, 180; populist Right and, 180–81
fe/male, 420n13
feminicide, 405n25, 405n26
feminist biblical hermeneutics, Wisdom and, 411–12
feminist theology: basileia of God and, 104; body and, 366; disability studies and, 366–67
fetishization, 55, 60, 62, 64
Filipino women and Western imperialism and, 409
finance industry, 176–80
financial derivatives, 100–1
Folly (Wisdom), 415–16
*For the Common Good: Redirecting the Economy toward Community, the Environment, and a Sustainable Future* (Cobb & Daly), 4–5
forced labor *versus* creative, 256–57, 260
*Formations of the Secular* (Asad), 74
Foucault, Michel: biopower, 230; governmentality, 230
FRB (Federal Reserve Board), 215
free speech, secular/sacred divide, 126

freedom: Cheah, 136; market miracles and, 224–26
fundamentalism: market fundamentalism, 388–87, 392; political enfranchisement, 7; resonance machine, 390; return of religion and, 231
*Future Christ: A Lesson in Heresy* (Laruelle), 75

Galbraith, John Kenneth, *Money: Whence It Came, Where It Went*, 179
Garland, Robert, *The Eye of the Beholder: Deformity and Disability in the Graeco-Roman World*, 368–69
Garland-Thomson, Rosemarie, 379–80
gaze, bodies as public, 399
gender: basileia movement, 107–12; gendered minorities, 390–91; gender-inclusive pronouns, 419n4, 420n13; liberation theology and, 386–87; in speaking of God, 327; Wisdom literature and, 408
genealogy of religion, 57–59
*General Theory of Victims* (Laruelle), 87–88
Gibson, Nigel, 261
the given, 136
Gladden, Washington, 184
global capitalism: austerity and, 200; commodification and, 174; great error (Nietzsche), 235–36
globalization, 4–5; contingency, 241
God, 10, 231–34; as black father, 341–42; eternal objects and, 35–37; as father, 326–27; fathers and, 327–28; gender-neutral pronouns, 327; from God *versus* of God, 76; kin-dom, 2; language used, 327; murder of, 234–36; sovereignty and, 7–8. See also death of God
gods, production of, 389–90
Goldberg, David Theo, 360–61
Goodchild, Philip, death of God, 234–35
goods, 5. See also common good/s
governmentality, 230
gradient reduction, 80–81
Gramsci, Antonio: Catholic Church, 207n20, 207n25; middle class and, 192; *Prison Notebooks*, 194–95; ruling-class hegemony, 196
Green Revolution, 82
Greider, William, *Come Home, America: The Rise and Fall (and Redeeming Promise) of Our Country*, 192–93
Guattari, Felix: BwO (body-without-organs), 393–94; *A Thousand Plateaus*, 88
guild socialist movements, 175

Gurensi traditions, 267–68; earth priest, 279–83; economy, 276–77; land use, 277–79, 281–82; Nature, 274–76
Gutiérrez, Gustavo, 171–72

Habermas, Jürgen, postsecularism, 7
Hamilton Project, 195
Hardt, Michael, 229–30; *Commonwealth*, 243
Harman, Graham, *Prince of Networks: Bruno Latour and Metaphysics*, 51n10
hate crimes, disability and, 383n55
heat death (entropy), 79
Hegel, Georg Wilhelm Friedrich: civic community, 236–37; death of God, 232–33, 243; *Korporationon*, 231, 237; Left Hegelians, 238; "Lordship and Bondage," 249–50, 252–58; master-slave dialectic, 83, 249–50, 252–58; *Phenomenology of Spirit*, 83, 232–33, 249–50; *Philosophy of Religion*, 231, 233; *Philosophy of Right*, 231; *The Philosophy of World History*, 240–41; police and, 238–39; *Realphilosophie*, 254–55; unhappy consciousness, 232–33; unhappy self-consciousness, 232–33
hegemony: global capitalism and, 200, 203; political possibility and, 357; power and, 194–96; religion and, 197–99
Heisenberg, Werner, 28, 50n5; coexistent potentia, 28
Heraclitus, Nietzsche inspiration, 25–27
Hesiod, Nietzsche inspiration, 25–27
Hobbes, Thomas, sovereignty, 236
*homo economicus*, 4
hope, 107; economic growth and, 193–94
hospitality, 129, 132
human rights: economic human rights, 191–92; incarnation and, 126–27
humanist onto-theologies, 135–36
humanity, common good and, 154–55

identity: corporations, 240–41; religious, 55–56, 59–60
idols, state as, 235–36
IMF (International Monetary Fund), 178
immanence: death of God and, 243; *versus* transcendence, 91–92
immortality, Whitehead, 36
incarnation: the agnostic and, 132–33; cosmopolitanism and, 124–25; human rights and, 126–27; power and, 140–41; Schneider, Laurel, 138–39
incarnational politics, 124–25
incarnational relationality, 125
incarnational theology, 138–41

income, gaps, 4
*Incomplete Nature* (Deacon), 51n14
indecency: desire and, 395; sexual theologies, 397
*Indecent Theology: Theological Perversions in Sex, Gender and Politics* (Althaus-Reid), 386–88
individualism, common good and, 151–53
ingression: aesthetic element and, 33; self-organization and, 32
inheritance, sex and, 396–97
innocence, becoming and, 26–27
insurrection, 87–89
intensity, 78–79
interest-based monetary system, 215–16
interpretive schemes, 65
intersubjectivity, 40
*Into the Cool* (Schneider and Sagan), 80–81
intuition, ontological wonder and, 67–68
in/valid (disability), 370–72
invention of religion, 56–60; modernity and, 57–58
*The Invention of Religion in Japan* (Josephson), 58–59
invisible hand of the market, 150–51
Irigaray, Luce, 415
*Is It Too Late? A Theology of Ecology* (Cobb), 82

Jacobinism, 207n30
Japanese, religion and, 58–59, 71n14
Jewish traditions: children in, 158–59; labor, 163
Job, labor and, 249, 250–51
Johnson, Simon, *Thirteen Bankers*, 178
Josephson, Jason Ananda, *The Invention of Religion in Japan*, 58–59
jouissance, 84–86

Kant, Immanuel: *cosmopolis*, 135; cosmopolitan right, 129; cosmopolitanism, 129–30; self-organization and, 33–34; transcendence, 232
Keller, Catherine, 53n30
khoric womb, 420n14; Wisdom and, 410
Kierkegaard, Søren, 8
kin-dom of God, 2, 103–4; overconnection, 110. *See also* basileia of God
King, Martin Luther, Jr., 199–200, 201
kingdom of God: *versus* basileia, 108–9; children in, 158–59; Cobb, John, 108–9; utopian social thought and, 13
Klare, Michael T., *The Race for What's Left: The Global Scramble for the World's Last Resources*, 83

Kojève, Alexandre, master-slave dialectic, 253–55, 256–57
Kwak, James, *Thirteen Bankers*, 178

labor: forced, capitalism and, 251–52; forced *versus* creative, 256–57; Job and, 249; living labor, 250, 258–64; "Lordship and Bondage" (Hegel), 252–58; Marxist theory, 251; master-slave dialectic, 249–50, 252–58; meanings, 248; Negri, 250–51; religious traditions, 163; value and, 251; valuing, 162–63
*The Labor of Job* (Negri), 249, 250–52
Labriola, Antonio, philosophy of praxis, 195–96
Lacan, Jacques, 83–86
Lange, Oscar, *On the Economic Theory of Socialism*, 175
language: the common, 3–4; gender-inclusive pronouns, 419n4, 420n13; God, 327; metaphors on disability, 368–71
Laruelle, François: *Future Christ: A Lesson in Heresy*, 75; *General Theory of Victims*, 87–88; non-philosophy, 75; the One, 76; philosophy, 75; unilateral duality, 76
Latour, Bruno, *Facing Gaia*, 10–11
Lefort, Claude, 308; empty place of power, 309, 312–17, 319–20; The People-as-One, 314–17; sovereignty's theological legacy, 310–11
Left Hegelians, 238
legitimacy, sovereignty and, 309–23
Lewis, Jerry, 404
liberalism, religious thinking and, 318–22
liberation theology, 170; basileia of God and, 104; Catholicism of, 7; death of God and, 231; kingdom of God, 109; radical theology and, 232; sexual honesty, 387
liberty through consumerism, 388–89
life, emergence and, 32–33
*The Limits to Growth* (Club of Rome), 82
literalization, 55, 60, 61, 72n23; deliteralization, 63–64; literal truth, 61
*Living in the End Times* (Žižek), 84
living labor, 250, 258–64; death of God and, 263–64
logic, 37
loving one's neighbor, 160

Mahayana Buddhism. *See* Buddhism: Mahayana
Mandair, Arvind-Pal, religion-making, 57–58

market fundamentalism, 388–89, 392; marginalized people and, 392; theology of desire, 391
market miracles, 210; force of, 221–24; human freedom and, 224–26; political theology, 220–24
Marxist theory: labor, 248, 251; utopian social dreaming and, 113, 115; value, 251
mass incarceration: economics of white supremacy and, 344–46; as epidemic, 354–56. *See also* prisons
master-slave dialectic, 83, 249–50, 252–58; creative labor and, 260–61; Fanon, 256–58; Kojève, 253–55, 256–57; self-consciousness, 253–55
material world, common good and, 126–27
materialism, Christianity and, 392
McCann, Dennis, 172–73
mechanosphere, 88
medieval Christianity, sovereignty and, 312, 70n6
meditation, 70n6
Meidner Plan (Sweden), 182–83
Merleau-Ponty, Maurice, 397–98
metaphysical, Whitehead, 51n12
methodology of the obscene: Althaus-Reid, 387; Connolly, 390; cruel optimism in politics, 389; desire, 389–90; repression and, 402–3
Metz, Johannes Baptist: middle class religion, 192; religion's dual function, 197–98
microaggression, 368–71
middle class, 191; economic independence and, 193; fluidity, 206n15; Gramsci, 192; ideology, 195; Metz, Johannes Baptist, 192; myth of, 199–205
Mignolo, Walter: body-politics, 348–49; decolonialism, 348–49
miracle, 209; definition, 211–21; market miracles, 210; PPF, 221–24; predictability and, 223; Rosenzweig, 220–21
misplaced concreteness, 29
modernity: globalization of contingency, 241; invention of religion, 57–58; literal truth, 61; religion and, 54
Moltmann, Jürgen, 171–72
Mondragon network (Spain), 181–82; capitalist society, 186
monetary system: Catholic substance and, 213; Pentecostal principle and, 216–17; PPF and, 217–18; Protestant principle and, 213–16; tripartite structures, 210
monetization of punishment, mass incarceration and, 354–56

*Money: Whence It Came, Where It Went* (Galbraith), 179
Monsanto, 135
Mordocai, Pamela, "This is the way," 360
More, Thomas, *Utopia*, 106, 111, 112
murder of God, 234–36

nation-state sovereignty, 239–40
natural as difference, 373–74
Negri, Antonio, 229–30; *Commonwealth*, 243; *The Labor of Job*, 249, 250–52
neoconservativism, Christian social ethics and, 172–73
neoliberal globalization, problems, 4–5
neoliberalism: climate change and Christian ethics, 293; corporate colonialism, 293; diversity and, 365–66; global capitalism and, 174
*The New Jim Crow: Mass Incarceration in the Age of Colorblindness* (Alexander), 344
New Materialism, 268
Newtonian concepts, Whitehead and, 27–28
Niebuhr, Reinhold, 169; capitalism and the church, 198–99; Christianity as movement, 198–99; *The Church against the World*, 199; religion's dual function, 197–98; social gospel and, 170; socialism and, 170
Nietzsche, Friedrich: attraction and repulsion, 38; creative condensations, 38; death of God, 233–34; eternal return, 25; global capitalism as great error, 235–36; Heraclitus, 25–27; Hesiod and, 25–27; ressentiment, 45–48; State as idol, 235–36; theodicy, 45–47; thinking, 38; *Thus Spoke Zarathustra*, 41–42; transcendence, 40; *Twilight of the Idols*, 26–27; Whitehead comparison, 41–43; *Will to Power*, 37–39; writing style compared to Whitehead, 30
*No Rising Tide: Theology, Economics and the Future* (Reiger), 4, 388–89
nonequilibrium thermodynamics, 80–81
non-philosophy, 75
non-theology, 76–77; energy, 79; theology and, 76–77
Northcott, Michael, *Political Theology of Climate Change*, 10
Novak, Michael, 173

Obama, Barack: *The Audacity of Hope*, 329, 337–40; *Dreams from My Father*, 329–37
objet a, 85, 86
the obscene, 386–87. *See also* methodology of the obscene
Occupy Wall Street, 158, 163; Left Hegelians, 238; police and, 238–39
*oikonomia*, 104
Oliver, Harold, 61
*On the Economic Theory of Socialism* (Lange), 175
the One, vision-in-One, 75–76
One Billion Rising movement, 408–9
ontological wonder, 67–69
orientation, 65–66
the other: the big Other, Lacan, 84; consciousness and, 253; political invention, 359

panexperientialism, 32–33
patriarchy, speech about God, 327
patterns, eternal objects, 52n22
Paul (Saint): common good, Corinthians, 155; political theology, 8–9; *The Political Theology of Paul* (Taubes), 8; radicalization, 9
Pentecostal principle, 209, 210; monetary system and, 216–17
people as process, 17, 309, 317–18
The People-as-One, 314–17
perception: Merleau-Ponty, 397–98; sexual orthodoxy/orthopraxy and, 397–98
Persian Period, 409–10
*Phenomenology of Spirit* (Hegel), 83, 232–33, 249–50; "Lordship and Bondage," 249–50, 252–58
philosophers: on becoming, 26–27; process philosophers, 51n10
philosophy: Laruelle, François, 75; sufficient philosophy, 76. *See also* non-philosophy
philosophy of praxis, 195–96; Catholic Church and, 197
*Philosophy of Religion* (Hegel), 231, 233
*Philosophy of Right* (Hegel), 231
*The Philosophy of World History* (Hegel), 240–41
PIC (prison-industrial complex), 345–46
pincer movement, in Whitehead, 34–35
planetary subjects, 4
pluralism, 69, 136–37
pluralist secularization, 9
pluripotentiality, 400–4
the plurovocal, 127
police, corporations and, 238–39
the political, 125; as antithetical, 127; concentric enclosures and, 126; defining, 125–26; as incarnational field of emergence, 124–27; Ward, Graham, 127–28
political power as social operation, 128

INDEX | 443

political theology, 74, 229–30; Christian ethics as, 289–95; democratic legitimacy and, 307–23; of the earth, 2; liberation theology and, 8–9; market miracles, 220–24; Paul's, 8; postsecularism and, 74; repression of religious, 326; return to religion and, 10, 74; Schmitt's terminology, 309–10; theology and, 7
*Political Theology: Four Chapters on the Concept of Sovereignty* (Schmitt), 307–8
*Political Theology of Climate Change* (Northcott), 10
*The Political Theology of Paul* (Taubes), 8
politicization of religion, 63
*The Politics of God* (Tanner), 92, 96
polydoxy, 20n4
*Poser: My Life in Twenty-Three Yoga Poses* (Dederer), 366
possessions, Thoreau, 270–74
postapocalyptic narrative, disability and, 378–80
post-secular theology, death of God, 231–34
postsecularism, 7; political theology and, 74; shift, 58
power: common good and, 150–53; Hardt, 229–30; hegemony and, 194–96; incarnation and, 140–41; Negri, 229–30; political power as social operation, 128; Ward, Graham, 128. See also biopower; empty place of power
power differentials: Abrahamic religious traditions, 154–55; common good and, 153
power imbalance: Christian ethics and climate change, 291–92; denial and, 291; dominance and, 291–92; entitlement and, 291
PPF (production possibilities frontier), 209, 216–24
PPF (Put People First) strategy, 199–205
preadaptations, 37
precarity, 420n10
predatory lending, 176
predestination, 92–93
prehension, aesthetic element and, 33
presumptive generosity, 11
priestcraft, 60
Prigogine, Ilya, 79–80
*Prince of Networks: Bruno Latour and Metaphysics* (Harman), 51n10
prison abolition, 346, 360–61
prison-industrial complex: Douglass' Fourth of July speech, 349–50; monetization of punishment, 352, 354–56
*Prison Notebooks* (Gramsci), 194–95

prisons: plantations and, 352–53; women in, 355–56
private banks, 179–80
process philosophy, 317–18
process theology, basileia of God and, 104
*Process Theology as Political Theology* (Cobb), 9
production, 161–62; as consumption, 271; of gods, 389–90; marginal value of product, 222; PPF and, 216
productivity of desire, 395–96
Protestant principle, 209; monetary system and, 213–16
Protestant Reformation, 60
*Public Religions in the Modern World* (Casanova), 7
publicly controlled companies, 185

qualitative orientation, 65–66
quantum theory, 25–28
queer subculture, dissonances, 402–3
queer theories, wild spaces and, 392–93

race: racialization of democracy, 351–52; sacralization, 360–61; social classification and, 264n3; sociality of the skin, 360–61. See also prisons
*The Race for What's Left: The Global Scramble for the World's Last Resources* (Klare), 83
radical democracy, 356–59
Radical Political Theology, 73–74
*Radical Political Theology* (Crockett), 2
radical theology, 73; Laruelle and, 75; liberation theology and, 232; religion without religion, 75
Rancière, Jacques, 359
Raschke, Carl, "The Deconstruction of God," 74
reading practices, 63–64
the Real, 76
real creativity, 32
*Realphilosophie* (Hegel), 254–55
realists, speculative realists, 51n10
Reformation. See Protestant Reformation
reification, 55, 60, 61–62, 64
Reiger, Joerg, *No Rising Tide: Theology, Economics and the Future*, 4, 388–89
relationality, ontological wonder and, 67–68
religion: alternative conceptions, 153–54; Catholic substance, 212–13; class conflicts and, 197–98; colonial encounter and, 60; common sense and, 198–99; conceptions that don't work, 150–53;

religion *(continued)*
  depoliticization, 9, 55; deprivatization, 7; dereligionization, 9, 55; dual function, 197–98; economics' resemblance, 150; establishment, basileia and, 109; hegemony formation and, 197–99; invention, 55–60; liberation and, 197; as object of devotion, 59–60, 62; Pentecostal principle, 212–13; political society's need, 311; politicization, 63; protest and, 197; Protestant principle, 212–13; *versus* religious impulse, 72n29; repression and political theology, 326; resurgent, 54; return of, 54–56, 74; social consciousness shaping, 197–99; status quo and, 197; tradition becoming, 55; transhistorical reality, 58; without religion, 75
religionization, 55, 60–62
religion-making, 56–60
religious identities, 55–56, 59–60; ontological wonder and, 67; textualization and, 60
religious impulse, 72n29
religious liberty: concentric enclosures, 126; secular/sacred divide, 126; traditional view and, 126
repetition, 78; difference and, 78; objet a, 85
representational thinking, 39
repulsion: creativity and, 33; Nietzsche, 38
resentment, 241–43; aspirational politics, 390; disability and, 371–73
resonance machine, 91–92; Evangelical-Capitalist-Resonance-Machine, 390
ressentiment, 45–48
resurgent religion, 54
resurrection *versus* insurrection, 87–89
Reuther, Rosemary Radford, 172
rising-tide theology, 388–89
rituals, therapeutic regimes and, 66
Rivera, Mayra, 413–14
Robbins, Jeffrey, 58, 231–32
Rosenzweig, Franz: miracle, 220–21; predictability, miracle and, 223
rule of the banks, 180–81
ruling class, ideology, 194–95

sacralization of race, 360–61
Sagan, Dorion, *Into the Cool*, 80–81
SBNR (spiritual but not religious), 56
Schmitt, Carl, 7–8, 74; miracle, 221–24; *Political Theology: Four Chapters on the Concept of Sovereignty*, 307–8; political theology terminology, 309–10; sovereignty, 134, 310; too-big-to-fail, 239–40
Schneider, Eric D., *Into the Cool*, 80–81
Schneider, Laurel, 138–39
Schüssler Fiorenza, Elisabeth, 412–13
scripture, textualization and, 60
secular: learned distinction, 57–58; post-secular shift, 58
*A Secular Age* (Taylor), 6–7
secularism: Connolly, 55; legitimacy of democracy, 308; *versus* secularization, 9; separation of public and private, 74
secularization: modernity and, 54; pluralist, 9; *versus* secularism, 9
secular/sacred, non-discrimination issues, 126
self-consciousness, 253
self-cultivation: contemplative practices, 70n6; orientation, 65–66; traditions and, 56
self-interest: common good and, 151–53; dominant, 160–61; enlightened, 161; loving one's neighbor, 160
self-made man, 160
self-organization, 32; Kant and, 33–34
self-overcoming, 268
sex, paying taxes as performance, 396–400
"Sex in Public" (Berlant and Warner), 396
sexual honesty, 387; dogmatic sexual propositions, 388
sexual ideologies, 395–96
sexual minorities, 390–91
sexuality, metaphors of God, 387
Shepard, Matthew, 383n55
Shildrick, Margrit, 367
Siebers, Tobin, 366
singularity, ontological wonder and, 67
Smith, Adam: class-war, 171; common good, 149–50
Smith, Wilfred Cantwell, 56–57; fetishization of religion, 62; religion as object of devotion, 59–60
social conflict, economic inequality and, 193–94
social ethics, 169–70
social gospel, 169–70; kingdom of God, 109; rule of the banks and, 180–81
social mobility, 191
socialism: Communism and, 172; democratic socialism, 171–72; Lange, Oscar, 175; state socialism, 175–76
socialist criticism, 171–72
sociality of the skin, 360–61
solidarity, deep solidarity, 158
Solidarnosc movement, 7
Sophia, Wisdom and, 413–14, 417
sovereignty: border crossing and, 321–22; challenging traditional models, 133–38; corporate, 239–40; Crockett, 236; demo-

cratic politics undermining, 315; divine, 104; as empty place, 309–14, 312–17; fathers and, 326–27; God and, 7–8, 326–27; Hobbes, 236; medieval Christianity, 312; nation-state, 239–40; theological origins, 307–8; theopolitical trilemma, 125; as unlimited authority, 127
special interests, common good and, 152
speculative dimensions, 29
spiritual disciplines, therapeutic regimes and, 66
spirituality, Whitehead, 47
Stackhouse, Max, 172–73
the state: corporations as derivative, 237–38; as idol, 235–36; subjectivity, 231
state socialism, economic democracy and, 175–76
Stengers, Isabelle, 79–80
Strange Woman (Wisdom), 413
structural greed, 151
subjectivity, 40; corporations and, 230–31; the state, 231
suffering, common good and, 155–57
sufficient philosophy, 76
surveillance: as sexual act, 398; women's worth, 398–99
sustainability, climate change and, 287–88

Tanner, Kathryn, *The Politics of God*, 92, 96
Taubes, Jacob, *The Political Theology of Paul*, 8
taxes as sexual performance, 396–400
Taylor, Charles, *A Secular Age*, 6–7
Taylor, Mark C., 73–74
teleosearching, 33
Temple, William, *Christianity and the Social Order*, 171
textualization, 55, 60; detextualization, 63
theodicy, 45–47
theology: cosmopolitical, 141–42; ethically pluralist, 10; incarnational, 138–41; of the market, 388–89; of multiplicity, 125; non-theology and, 2, 76–77; participation in holiness of life, 397; political theology of the earth, 2; practiced, 6; as sexual act, 387–88
theopaternity, 327–28; conventional wisdom and, 328–29
theopolitical trilemma, 125, 127–28
therapeutic regimes, 66, 68–69
thermodynamics, 78–81
thinking: Nietzsche, 38; representational, 38
*Thirteen Bankers* (Johnson and Kwak), 178
Thoreau, Henry David: agency, 268; economy, 267–74; land use, 271–74; possessions, 270–74; stones, 267; transcendence and, 280; *Walden*, 267–71; Wild, 279–83; *A Winter Walk*, 271–72
*A Thousand Plateaus* (Gilles and Guattari), 88
*Thus Spoke Zarathustra* (Nietzsche), 41–42
Tillich, Paul, 73; Catholic substance, 209; socialism and, 170
too-big-to-fail, Schmitt, 239–40
torsion, 131
totalitarianism, religious thinking and, 318–22
tradition: becoming religion, 55; definition, 212; dereligionizing, 62–65; self-cultivation and, 56
traditional view, concentric enclosures and, 126
transcendence, 130; Deleuze, 232; Kant and, 232; Keller, Catherine, 53n30; Nietzsche, 40; Sophia, 414–15; Thoreau, 272–73, 280; Wisdom, 414–16. *See also* divine transcendence
transcendental illusion, thermodynamics, 79
transcorporeality, 125, 139
truth, 72n23; literal truth, 61
*Twilight of the Idols* (Nietzsche), 26–27

unencumbered agency, 137–38
UNFCCC (United Nations Framework Convention on Climate Change), 298–99
unhappy consciousness, 232–33
unilateral duality, 76
unpredictability, creativity and, 31
utopia: archaeological mode, 116; architectural mode, 116; Block, Ernst, on, 108; contestation, 109; disconnection, 108; dystopias, 121n41; foreign students, 119n13; as method, 108; paradox, 109–10; term usage, 106; twentieth-century, 106–7
utopian social dreaming, 104–7; basiliea and, 111–16; Colbert, Stephen, 118; Marxist theory and, 113, 115; paradox, 113–14; pedagogy, 114–15
Utopian Studies, 105–7

value, Marxist theory, 251
valuing work, 162–63; the Enlightenment, 198
VaR (Value at Risk), 177
vibrations, entities and, 31
vision-in-One, 75–76
Volcker Rule, 176
voucher programs for schools, 191

*Walden* (Thoreau), 267–71
Wallich, Henry, hope and economic growth, 193–94
Ward, Graham: political as power, 127–28; transcorporeality, 139
Warner, Michael, "Sex in Public," 396
weak messianic power, 210–11
wealth, Wisdom's, 410–11
wealthy persons, common good and, 152–53, 157–58
Weil, Simone, disgust, 376–77
West, Cornel, 172
white privilege: climate change and, 286–301; climate debt and, 287–89; power imbalance and, 291–92
white supremacy: Christian ethics and, 289; democratic inclusion of people of color, 344–45. *See also* economics of white supremacy, mass incarceration and
Whitehead, Alfred North, 5; coexistent potentia, 28; cosmological, 51n12; creativity, 30–33; Divine Eros, 400–1; entanglement, 29–30, 31; entities, 33, 51n10; eternal objects, 25, 35–37, 52n22; Greek thought, 27; immortality, 36; metaphysical, 51n12; misplaced concreteness, 29; Newtonian concepts and, 27–28; Nietzsche comparison, 41–43; pincer movement, 34–35; as process philosopher, 51n10; quantum theory and, 25, 27–28;

space, 29; speculative dimensions, 29; as speculative realist, 51n10; spirituality, 47; writing style compared to Nietzsche, 30
*Why I Am Not a Secularist* (Connolly), 7, 74
wild spaces, 392–93
*Will to Power* (Nietzsche), 37–39
Winquist, Charles, 73–74
*A World of Becoming* (Connolly), 401
*Wisdom and the Feminine in the Book of Proverbs* (Camp), 412
Wisdom literature, 407–8; crossroads, 408–9, 413–16, 418; feminist biblical hermeneutics, 411–12; Folly, 415–16; Gabriela, 409, 417–18, 425n60; gender and, 408; gender in, 410; as khoric womb, 410, 420n14; Sophia, 413–15, 417; *under*-standing, 418; Strange Woman, 413; survival and, 409; transcendence, 414–16; wealth and, 410–11; wo/man and, 410; YHWH and, 416
*Wise, Strange, and Holy* (Camp), 412–13
women: Filipino, Western imperialism and, 409; worth, surveillance and, 398–99
workers: labor, valuing, 162–63; mutual funds and, 184
*A World of Becoming* (Connolly), 401
*The Wretched of the Earth* (Fanon), 261

Žižek, Slavoj, *Living in the End Times*, 84

## TRANSDISCIPLINARY THEOLOGICAL COLLOQUIA

Laurel Kearns and Catherine Keller, eds., *Ecospirit: Religions and Philosophies for the Earth.*

Virginia Burrus and Catherine Keller, eds., *Toward a Theology of Eros: Transfiguring Passion at the Limits of Discipline.*

Ada María Isasi-Díaz and Eduardo Mendieta, eds., *Decolonizing Epistemologies: Latina/o Theology and Philosophy.*

Stephen D. Moore and Mayra Rivera, eds., *Planetary Loves: Spivak, Postcoloniality, and Theology.*

Chris Boesel and Catherine Keller, eds., *Apophatic Bodies: Negative Theology, Incarnation, and Relationality.*

Chris Boesel and S. Wesley Ariarajah, eds., *Divine Multiplicity: Trinities, Diversities, and the Nature of Relation.*

Stephen D. Moore, ed., *Divinanimality: Animal Theory, Creaturely Theology.* Foreword by Laurel Kearns.

Melanie Johnson-DeBaufre, Catherine Keller, and Elias Ortega-Aponte, eds., *Common Goods: Economy, Ecology, and Political Theology.*

www.ingramcontent.com/pod-product-compliance
Lightning Source LLC
Chambersburg PA
CBHW020634300426
44112CB00007B/115